THE TRAIL WEST

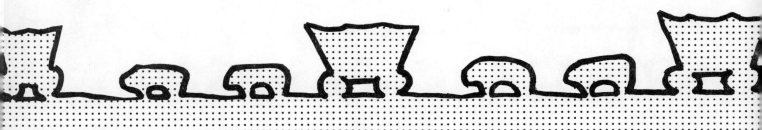

THE TRAIL WEST

A Bibliography – Index to Western American Trails, 1841–1869

John M. Townley

Copyright 1988 by John M. Townley. All rights reserved.
Published 1988.
Printed in the United States of America

Jamison Station Press
A Division of Great Basin Studies Center
7115 Pembroke Drive, Reno, NV, 89502

LIBRARY OF CONGRESS CATALOGING IN PUBLICATION DATA

Townley, John M.
  THE TRAIL WEST: A BIBLIOGRAPHY-INDEX TO WESTERN AMERICAN
TRAILS, 1841-1869.

Library of Congress Catalog Number 88-082101
ISBN 0-913381-05-5

For ERIN....
A 'trail widow' these past three years.

Contents

PREFACE

In 1980, while preparing a history of Truckee Meadows and Reno (Nevada), the compiler of this volume planned a chapter on California Trail remnants and sites within the Meadows. The obvious primary source of data for the 1840's and 1850's in Truckee Meadows was emigrant literature, either diaries or recollections, since there was no permanent settlement in the valley during most of those years. While searching for trail accounts in library card catalogs two general cataloging rules were noted, first, that all trail journals were listed under a single Library of Congress subject category, 'Overland Journeys to the Pacific,' and second, that catalogs failed to point out which particular routes within the western trail network were used to reach the Pacific coast, or the year of travel. It proved impossible from either card catalogs or existing bibliographies to isolate those primary accounts or secondary works related to travel through the Reno area. Eventually, over a thousand manuscripts, books and articles had to be reviewed in order to find seventy-plus Truckee Meadows items. After that project, it was clear that a comprehensively indexed guide to all trail literature was needed.

Much the same situation had been noted at the Nevada Historical Society during the period that the compiler served as director. Total numbers of reference questions fielded by the staff were grouped annually by subject and the consistent leader each year was western American trails. Patrons frequently asked for data on lesser-known routes not described in standard reference guides. Frank O'Bryan, a Society volunteer trail consultant, designed a detailed guide to trail items in western Nevada libraries that was the precursor to this volume.

The motivating question was how to organize a bibliography so that readers interested in major or minor trails, years, or trail-related subjects could survey appropriate sources with a minimum of effort. Prior bibliographic compilations had commonly limited sources to manuscripts only, books or journal articles alone, or particular geographic areas. They failed to either gather all appropriate items for western North America or to adequately index trail segments, individual years of travel, or peripheral subjects. There was no single reference tool that surveyed the entire field of western North American trails.

The final format included diaries, recollections, books, articles, theses/dissertations, graphics and maps. Although originally intended as parts of the planned volume, newspaper articles and letters were later deleted - to keep the book within designed page limits - except when such items appeared uniquely valuable to potential readers. Not all items, either manuscript or print, have been included. If quality was marginal to none, many were deleted. The time frame extended from 1841's initial California-bound settlers (Bidwell-Bartleson, et al.,) to the completion of the transcontinental railroad in 1869. Another choice was to extend the trail theme to include staging, freight lines and the telegraph. Additionally, sources important to subjects related to the trail experience were collected and indexed in detail. A final decision was to include a chronological list of sources which would include primary and secondary sources by year.

Readers will find sources organized somewhat more elaborately than in earlier trail reference volumes. The major overland routes have been divided into forty-two separate components. Each of these trail segments has been indexed by year and major subject area (bibliographies, maps, or graphics). By referring to the appropriate trail segment index, the reader can quickly find sources for specified portions of a major trail network and avoid those items not pertinent to a given locality. This emphasis on means for identifying data by trail segment derives from the compiler's frustration in amassing data for a particular region.

A recent phenomenon in trail work is scholarly specialization among trail-related subjects. Effort was made to locate and include peripheral items that might contain trail information. Ultimately, over twenty subject categories were identified and indexed.

Multiple spellings of an author's name among various libraries confounded all efforts to be clarified. Often, two or more archives held copies of similar diaries or recollections. The originator of the manuscript would be identified by a last name or initials in one repository and by his/her full name in another. Occasionally, a family or given name was spelled in slightly different form between libraries. Further, diaries appeared in differing editions, since family members often hand-transcribed the original into copies which varied in accuracy and content. This fluctuation in spelling was compounded in women's manuscript material since the later addition of a married name resulted in more variations between like items. In all above instances, notations were made in the author list pointing out known items that might be copies. However, in order not to miss diaries that might be useful, all forms of a name were shown in the author list.

This project was designed as an experiment in compilation and publication, as well as format. As most bibliographers point out, a finding aid is obsolete from the date its manuscript is completed. Therefore, the time required for editing and printing should be kept to a minimum. Likewise, bibliographies are often careers rather than finite projects, leaving potential readers without quidance for decades. In planning this volume, the compiler limited himself to two years of research and travel, followed by six months of editing and printwork, hopefully resulting in a timely compendium. This time frame was possible only through modern desktop publishing techniques. The critical question was whether a non-specialist could approach a major historical field, survey its literature and publish a useful reference tool. Readers can judge if the premise worked.

Some five thousand manuscript and print items were listed. Time limitations required a scan of contents rather than careful reading, and there may be errors in routes described within journals either incomplete or inexact. A surprising number of sources recorded multiple trips and contained passages which were indexed in subject categories as well. These aberrations meant that total numbers of diaries, general studies and subject works exceeded the number of sources listed by author. Possible duplications were listed individually, in order to reduce the risk of omitting a useful source. The following three statistical summaries show how these sources were arranged in the text:

Chronological List

Year	Manuscripts	Books	Articles	All Diaries/ Recollections	General Sources	Total
1841	6	17	12	35	29	64
1842	2	13	6	21	–	21
1843	11	16	18	45	21	66
1844	9	4	10	23	13	36
1845	25	27	25	77	11	88
1846	41	36	42	119	79	198
1847	63	31	27	121	28	149
1848	27	21	17	65	8	73
1849	245	142	149	536	103	639
1850	203	76	64	343	13	356
1851	46	22	30	98	4	102
1852	53	76	73	202	5	207
1853	90	64	55	209	13	222
1854	49	23	25	97	6	103
1855	15	9	13	37	3	40
1856	29	15	11	55	7	62
1857	19	15	19	53	–	53
1858	18	23	22	63	16	79

1859	67	43	36	146	14	160
1860	35	27	29	91	3	94
1861	24	8	15	47	5	52
1862	52	29	27	108	6	114
1863	46	14	25	85	4	89
1864	77	28	28	133	5	138
1865	47	23	32	102	10	112
1866	35	13	28	76	5	81
1867	7	9	7	23	-	23
1868	9	5	5	19	1	20
1869	8	1	11	20	1	21
TOTALS	1358	830	861	3049	413	3462

Subjects

Bibliographies	85	Mail	165
Biographies	216	Maps	167
Equipment and Teams	105	Medical Aspects	23
Flora and Fauna	19	Military	115
Freight Lines	290	Pony Express	173
Geography	547	Social	142
General Overland Items	197	Stage and Express	719
Government	163	Telegraph	49
Graphics	106	Trail Preservation	271
Guidebooks	172	Train Government	58
Indians	205	Utah & the Mormons	79
Livestock Trails	103	TOTALS	4169

Trail Segments

	Diaries	General		Diaries	General
Applegate	46	21	Mexico	85	24
Barlow	110	11	Military	-	115
Beale	43	40	Montana	159	60
Beckwourth	28	6	Mormon Trail	290	88
Bozeman	53	26	Mullan	17	26
Bradshaw	3	23	Noble's	18	10
Bridger	457	3	Oklahoma	24	15
California	1732	226	Old Spanish Trail	24	30
Canada	44	59	Oregon	654	143
Cherokee	127	14	Oregon to California	20	11
Dakotas	51	44	Pikes Peak	195	85
Fort Hall	162	-	Pony Express	-	173
Freight	57	232	Rio Grande	90	16
Gila	199	79	Salt Lake Corridor	121	63
Hastings	55	22	Salt Lake Cutoff	279	8
Indians	-	205	Santa Fe	149	67
Lander	51	7	Simpson	91	14
Lassen	149	14	Stage and Express	29	690
Livestock Trails	26	77	Texas	119	8
Marcy	43	13	Truckee	231	14
Meek	36	7	Washington	27	20

Travel plans were so stringent that second visits to institutions for verifying manuscript or print sources could not be scheduled. In three cases, The Society of California Pioneers, Historical Department of the Church of Jesus Christ of Latter Day Saints, and the University of Washington - Special Collections Department, those institutions were closed or access-limited at the time the compiler arrived. Therefore, sole items in the custody of those repositories could be missing from this bibliography. Other bibliographies were stringently reviewed to locate sources held by the above three libraries.

Following is a list of periodicals reviewed for trail items. National historical journals were searched via bibliographies to free time for searching local and state publications which had escaped earlier compilations. Southern periodicals, disappointingly, held far fewer trail items than other regional quarterlies.

ADOBE TRAILS (Hayward [California] Historical Society). Vols 1 - 22.
ALABAMA REVIEW. Vol. 1 - 1987.
AMERICAN HERITAGE. To 1964.
AMERICAN HISTORY ILLUSTRATED. Vol. 1 - 1986.
AMERICAN WEST. Vol. 1 - 1988.
ANNALS OF WYOMING. Vol. 1 - 1988.
ARIZONA AND THE WEST. Vol. 1 - 1988.
ARIZONA HIGHWAYS. Vol. 1 - 1988.
ARIZONA HISTORICAL REVIEW. Vol. 1 - 1936.
ARKANSAS HISTORICAL QUARTERLY. Vol. 1 - 8.
BEAVER. Vol. 1 - 1986.
BYU STUDIES. Vol. 1 - 12.
BRITISH COLUMBIA HISTORICAL QUARTERLY. Vol. 1 - 21.
BRITISH COLUMBIA STUDIES. Vol. 1 - 1984.
BUTTE COUNTY DIGGIN'S. Vol. 1 - 1985
CALIFORNIA HISTORICAL SOCIETY QUARTERLY. Vol. 1 - 1985.
CALIFORNIAN ILLUSTRATED MAGAZINE. 1880 - 1882, 1891 - 1894.
CAMP PERIODICAL. Vol. 1 - 1986.
CHICAGO WESTERNERS CORRAL. Vol. 1 - 1983.
CHRONICLES OF OKLAHOMA. Vol. 32 - 1984.
COLLECTORS CLUB PHILATELIST. 1922 - 1939.
COLORADO MAGAZINE. Vol. 1 - 1981.
CONTRIBUTIONS MONTANA HISTORICAL SOCIETY. Vol. 1 - 1940.
CORRAL DUST. Vol. 1 - 1967.
COVERED WAGON. 1941 - 1984.
COWLITZ HISTORICAL QUARTERLY. Vol. 19 - 28.
DELAWARE HISTORICAL QUARTERLY. Vol. 1 - 1984.
DENVER WESTERNERS BRAND BOOK. Vol. 1 - 1977.
DESERT MAGAZINE. Vol. 1 - 1982.
DIALOGUE. Vol. 1 - 1984.
EDINBURGH REVIEW. 1841 - 1851.
EL PALACIO. Vol. 1 - 1984.
AN ENDURING LEGACY. Vol. 1 - 1986.
ENGLISH WESTERNERS BRAND BOOK. Vol. 1 - 1985.
FAR-WESTERNER. Vol. 1 - 1985.
FLORIDA HISTORICAL JOURNAL. Vol. 1 - 1972.
FRESNO - PAST & PRESENT. Vol. 1 - 1986.
FRONTIER AND MIDLAND. Vol. 1 - 1939.
FRONTIER TIMES. Vol. 1 - 1988.
GATEWAY HERITAGE. Vol. 1 - 1985.
GEORGIA HISTORICAL QUARTERLY. Vol. 1 - 1973.
GLEANINGS (Napa County Historical Society). Vol. 1 - 1986.
GOLDEN ERA. 1885 - 1891.
GREAT PLAINS JOURNAL. Vol. 1 - 1985
GREAT PLAINS QUARTERLY. Vol. 1 - 1985.
GRIZZLY BEAR. 1907 - 1920.
HALCYON. Vol. 1 - 1988.
HEART THROBS OF THE WEST. Vol. 1 - 1952.
HESPERIAN. 1858 - 1863.
HIGH COUNTRY. Vol. 1 - 1984.
HISTORIC KERN. Vol. 1 - 1959.
HISTORICAL SOCIETY OF SOUTHERN CALIFORNIA QUARTERLY. Vol. 1 - 1984.
HUMBOLDT HISTORIAN. Vol. 1 - 1988.
HUNTINGTON LIBRARY QUARTERLY. Vol. 1 - 1986.
HUTCHINGS MAGAZINE. 1856 - 1861.
IDAHO YESTERDAYS. Vol. 1 - 1986.
ILLINOIS HISTORICAL SOCIETY JOURNAL. Vol. 1 - 1985.
INDIAN HISTORIAN. Vol. 1 - 13.
INDIANA MAGAZINE OF HISTORY. Vol. 1 - 1973.
JOHN WHITMER HISTORICAL ASSN. JOURNAL. Vol. 1 - 1985.
JOURNAL OF ARIZONA HISTORY. Vol. 1 - 1985.
JOURNAL OF MORMON HISTORY. Vol. - 1984.
JOURNAL OF SOUTHERN HISTORY. Vol. 1 - 1986.
JOURNAL OF THE WEST. Vol. 1 - 1986.
KANSAS CITY CORRAL TRAIL GUIDE. Vol. 1 - 1979.
KANSAS HISTORICAL QUARTERLY. Vol. 1 - 43.
KANSAS HISTORY. Vol. 1 - 1985.
KIVA. Vol. 1 - 1983.
LA PENINSULA. Vol. 1 - 1987.
LA POSTA. Vol. 1 - 1986.

LA VISTA. Vol. 1 - 1975.
LAKE TAHOE HISTORICAL SOCIETY NEWSLETTER. Vol. 1 - 1987.
LAND OF SUNSHINE. 1894 - 1901.
LANE COUNTY HISTORIAN. Vol. 1 - 1987.
LAS CALAVERAS. Vol. 1 - 1986.
LOS ANGELES CORRAL BRAND BOOK. Vol. 1 - 1983.
LOS TULARES. Vol. 1 - 1986.
LOUISIANA HISTORICAL QUARTERLY. Vol. 1 - 1951.
LUCKY LAND OF LASSEN. 1959 - 1964.
MADERA COUNTY HISTORIAN. Vol. 1 - 1984.
MARIN COUNTY HISTORICAL SOCIETY BULLETIN. Vol. 1 - 1980.
MARION COUNTY HISTORY. Vol. 1 - 1979.
MARIPOSA SENTINEL. Vol. 1 - 1985.
MASON COUNTY HISTORY. Vol. 3 - 5.
MASTERKEY. Vol. 1 - 1985.
MENDOCINO HISTORICAL REVIEW. Vol. 1 - 1986.
MICHIGAN HISTORY. Vol. 1 - 1972.
MILITARY HISTORY OF TEXAS AND THE SOUTHWEST. Vol. 1 - 1983.
MISSISSIPPI HISTORICAL QUARTERLY. Vol. 1 - 1986.
MISSOURI HISTORICAL REVIEW. Vol. 1 - 1984.
MISSOURI HISTORICAL SOCIETY BULLETIN. Vol. 1 - 1980.
MONTANA: MAGAZINE OF WESTERN HISTORY. Vol. 1 - 1988.
NATIONAL GEOGRAPHIC. Vol. 1 - 1988.
NEBRASKA HISTORY. Vol. 1 - 1987.
NEVADA COUNTY BULLETIN. 1948 - 1986.
NEVADA HISTORICAL SOCIETY QUARTERLY. Vol. 1 - 1988.
NEVADA MAGAZINE. Vol. 1 - 1988.
NEW MEXICO HISTORICAL REVIEW. Vol. 1 - 1988.
NEW MEXICO MAGAZINE. Vol. 1 - 1988.
NEW YORK POSSE BRAND BOOK. Vol. 1 - 1972.
NORTH AMERICAN REVIEW. 1841 - 1869.
NORTH CAROLINA HISTORICAL REVIEW. Vol. 1 - 1972.
NORTH DAKOTA HISTORICAL QUARTERLY. Vol. 1 - 1986.
NORTHEASTERN NEVADA HISTORICAL QUARTERLY. Vol. 1 - 1988.
NOTICIAS. Vol. 1 - 1986.
OHIO HISTORY. Vol. 1 - 1985.
OKANOGAN COUNTY HERITAGE. Vol. 1 - 1987.
OLD NORTHWEST. Vol. 1 - 1985.
OLD SANTA FE MAGAZINE. Vol. 1 - 1916.
OLD WEST. Vol. 1 - 1988.
OREGON HISTORICAL QUARTERLY. Vol. 1 - 1988.
OREGON PIONEER ASSN. TRANSACTIONS. Vol. 1 - 1928.
OUR PIONEER HERITAGE. Vol. 1 - 1978.
OUT WEST. 1902 - 1914.
OVERLAND JOURNAL. Vol. 1 - 1988.
OVERLAND MONTHLY. 1875 - 1923.
PACIFIC HISTORIAN. Vol. 1 - 1987.
PACIFIC HISTORICAL REVIEW. Vol. 1 - 1986.
PACIFIC MONTHLY. 1863-1864.
PACIFIC NORTHWEST QUARTERLY. Vol. 1 - 1983.
PACIFIC NORTHWESTERNER. Vol. 1 - 1986.
PALIMPSEST. 1970 - 1986.
PANHANDLE PLAINS HISTORICAL REVIEW. Vol. 1 - 1961.
PASSWORD. Vol. 1 - 1987.
PIONEER MAGAZINE. 1854 - 1855.
PLAINS ANTHROPOLOGIST. Vol. 1 - 1985.
PLUMAS COUNTY PUBLICATIONS. Vol. 1 - 1975.
POMONA COUNTY HISTORIAN. Vol. 1 - 1981.
PRAIRIE SCOUT. Vol. 1 - 1982.
READERS GUIDE TO PERIODICAL LITERATURE. 1905 - 1985.
RED RIVER HISTORICAL REVIEW. Vol. 1 - 1982.
RENDEZVOUS. Vol. 1 - 1985.
SAN DIEGO CORRAL BRAND BOOK. Vol. 1 - 1978.
SAN DIEGO HISTORICAL JOURNAL/QUARTERLY. Vol. 1 - 1986.
SISKIYOU PIONEER. Vol. 1 - 1986.
SMOKE SIGNAL. 1960 - 1978.
SNAKE RIVER ECHOES. Vol. 1 - 1986.
SOCIETY OF CALIFORNIA PIONEERS QUARTERLY. Vol. 1 - 10.
SOUTH CAROLINA HISTORICAL MAGAZINE. Vol. 73 to 1986.
SOUTHWEST HERITAGE. Vol. 1 - 1975.
SOUTHWESTERN HISTORICAL QUARTERLY. Vol. 1 - 1986.
SOUTHWESTERN STUDIES. Vol. 1 - 1981.
STANISLAUS STEPPING STONES. Vol. 7 - 1986.
SUNSET. 1898 - 1914.
TEXANA. Vol. 1 - 1974.
TOURING TOPICS (WESTWAYS). 1915 - 1984.
TRAIL GUIDE. Vol. 1 - 1978.
TREASURES OF PIONEER HISTORY. Vols. 1 - 1957.
TRUE WEST. Vol. 1 - 1985.
TUVA. 1974 - 1984.
UMPQUA TRAPPER. Vol. 1 - 1985.
UTAH HISTORICAL AND GENEALOGICAL MAGAZINE. 1910 - 1940.
UTAH HISTORICAL QUARTERLY. Vol. 1 - 1985.
VENTURA COUNTY HISTORICAL QUARTERLY. Vol. 1 - 1986.
WAGON WHEELS. Vol. 1 - 1986.
WASHOE RAMBLER. Vol. 1 - 1983.
WEST COAST. 1910 - 1913.
WEST TEXAS HISTORICAL ASSN. YEAR BOOK. Vol. 1 - 1985.
WESTERN EXPRESS. Vol. 1 - 1987.
WESTERN HISTORICAL QUARTERLY. Vol. 1 - 1988.

WILLIAM AND MARY QUARTERLY. Vol. 1 - 1987.
WISCONSIN MAGAZINE OF HISTORY. Vol. 1 - 1987.

It is customary, and certainly merited, to acknowledge the help given authors by the library profession. Without assistance from these knowledgeable, hard-working and amazingly helpful practitioners of their craft, this book would never have passed beyond the concept phase. Fully as valuable have been the prior efforts of trail scholars Louise Barry, Robert H. Becker, Charles L. Camp, J. S. Holliday, Merrill J. Mattes, Dale L. Morgan, John D. Unruh, Henry R. Wagner, and O. O. Winther. Their names are not on the title page, but should be. Also, a considerable debt is owed Codega & Fricke-Consulting Engineers for access to their computer system.

Finally, my thanks to The L. J. Skaggs and Mary C. Skaggs Foundation, and its secretary, Philip M. Jelley, for financial support.

Fraser River Route

Vancouver

C A N A D A

Mullan Road

Ft. Benton

Dakotas

Portland

Oregon to

Oregon Trail

Bozeman

Platte River Road

"Jumping

California

Lassen

Applegate

Ft. Hall

Salt Lake

Ft. Laramie

Nobles'

Ft. Bridger

Hastings

Salt Lake City

Cherokee

Sacramento

Carson Pass

Santa Fe

Off

Salt Lake Corridor

Old Spanish Trail

Places"

Los Angeles

Salt

Beale

Santa Fe

Marcy

Bradshaw

Rio Grande

Gila

M E X I C O

T R A I L S   O F   T H E   A M E R I C A N   W E S T

San Antonio

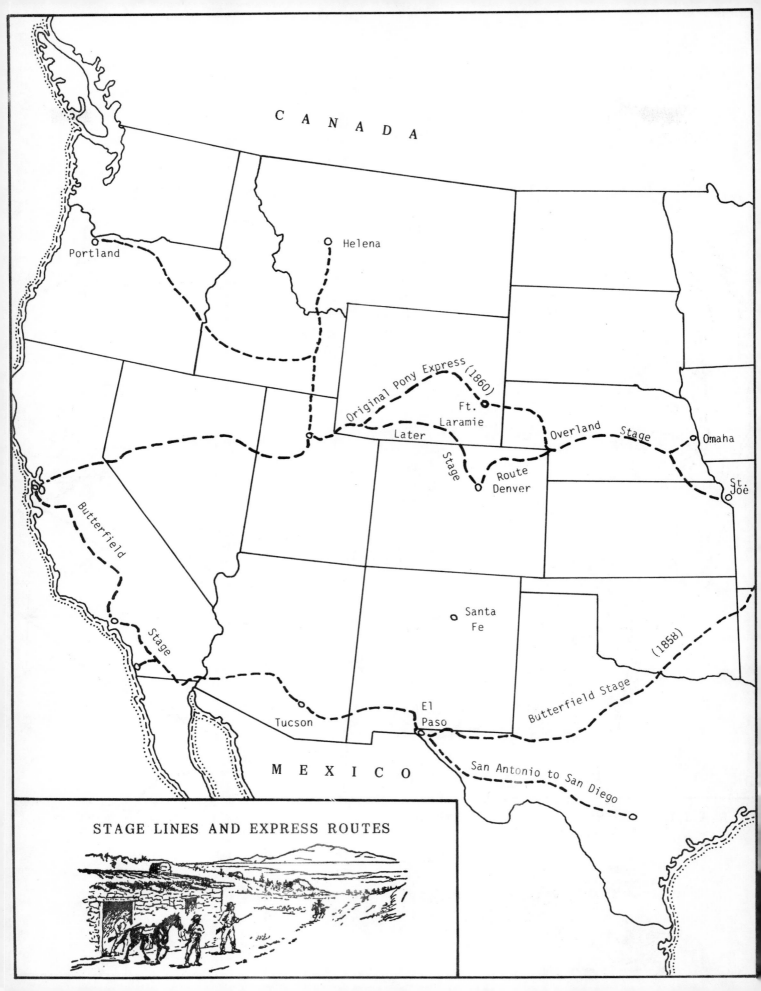

Portland

Helena

CANADA

Original Pony Express (1860)

Ft. Laramie

Later

Stage

Route Denver

Overland Stage

Omaha

St. Joe

Butterfield

Stage

Santa Fe

(1858)

Butterfield Stage

Tucson

El Paso

San Antonio to San Diego

MEXICO

STAGE LINES AND EXPRESS ROUTES

PART I

INTRODUCTION

This section of THE TRAIL WEST is an alphabetical listing by author of print and non-print materials within the general subject category of western American trails. Many non-print or manuscript items have been published later in book or article format. This list does not include both an original manuscript and its subsequent print form. If the item exists in print, only that reference is shown. A manuscript entry indicates that no print version was found.

Author's names are often provided in full, rather than as shown on a title page. This format will hopefully provide maximum information for readers seeking particular individuals for research or genealogical purposes. Another variation from usual bibliographic cataloging is that the author of a diary or reminiscence is always considered as author of the listed item, rather than a subsequent editor. Editors are cross-referenced so that readers seeking an item by editor may find the appropriate listing. Readers should always check both an author's full first, middle name and initials. Often, initials shown on title pages have been later supplemented by full names in library card catalogs.

Titles for print and non-print items are often shortened. Many 19th century titles ran to considerable length and have been subsequently reduced by ellipsis points or standard secondary reference format. The same restrictions have been applied to periodical titles. Also, many of the common historical journals have altered their titles with time. An example is the OREGON HISTORICAL QUARTERLY, which has been the QUARTERLY OF THE OREGON HISTORICAL SOCIETY among other revisions. In those cases, a single title format has been used to reduce confusion.

Facts of publication are usually shown as suggested by THE CHICAGO MANUAL OF STYLE, 13th edition.

Quality among diaries and reminiscences varies widely. To rank such materials for readers, a grading system in five (5) categories has been adopted. Roman numerals reflect qualitative differences: I = 's excellent, II = 's good, III = 's average, IV = 's poor, and V = 's marginal. A distinction is made between diaries and reminiscences, since readers often seek one or the other. The code term "Rem" denotes all reminiscences and is found immediately after the quality code numeral.

Many important trail sources appear in several editions. Listings shown hereafter reflect that version first found during research, not necessarily the first edition.

Newspaper articles, letters, or "trail" fiction are not generally cited. Some items in those categories will be found, when content merited inclusion. Limitations on length required deleting the above items from the bibliography.

Abbreviations employed in this list for major repositories are shown below:

AZHIST...Arizona Historical Society, Tucson
BANCROFT...Bancroft Library, Univ. of CA-Berkeley
BARKER...Barker Texas History Center, Austin
BEINECKE...Beinecke Library, Yale University
BYU...Brigham Young University, Provo
CAHIST...California Historical Society, San Francisco
CSL...California State Library, Sacramento COHIST...Colorado Historical Society, Denver
DENVERPUB...Denver Public Library
HUNTL...Huntington Library, San Marino
KSHIST...Kansas State Historical Society, Topeka
LA...Los Angeles
LDS...LDS Church History Department, Salt Lake City
LILLEY...Lilley Library, Indiana University
MNHIST...Minnesota Historical Society, St. Paul
MONHIST...Montana Historical Society, Helena
MO-WHMC...Western Historical Manuscripts Collection, Univ. of Missouri-Columbia
NBHIST...Nebraska State Historical Society, Lincoln
NEWBERRY...Newberry Library, Chicago
NVHIST...Nevada Historical Society, Reno
ORHIST...Oregon Historical Society, Portland
ORU...University of Oregon, Eugene
SF...San Francisco
SDHIST...San Diego Historical Society
SLC...Salt Lake City
UPAC...Univ. of the Pacific, Stockton
UTHIST...Utah State Historical Society, SLC
UWY...Univ. of Wyoming, Laramie
WA...Washington, DC
WESTX...West Texas Historical Assn. Yearbook
WIHIST...State Historical Society of Wisconsin, Madison

All other repositories, locations or publications are cited in full.

The entire western American trail network has been subdivided into forty-two (42) geographic segments, each with its individual name and geographic description. Following is a trail segment list, description and abbreviation code. Trail identification codes appear only for those works, such as diaries and reminiscences, which recount an actual trip over the subject trail segment. Works pertinent to subject areas, such as stage lines, freighting, specific geographical sites or trail preservation, are annotated solely by their appropriate subject description in a separate subject index.

1. APPLEGATE TRAIL. Lassen Meadows(Mill City, NV)-Black Rock Desert-Tule Lake-Willamette Valley. APPLE.

2. BARLOW CUTOFF. The Dalles(OR)-Barlow Pass-Oregon City. BARLOW.

3. BEALE ROAD. Albuquerque-San Francisco Peaks(Flagstaff, AZ)-Fort Mohave-Government Road-San Bernardino. BEALE.

4. BECKWOURTH CUTOFF. Reno-Beckwourth Pass-Marysville, CA. BECK.

5. BOZEMAN TRAIL. Douglas, WY-Billings, MT-Virginia City, MT. Also includes references to the Bridger Cutoff. BOZE.

6. BRADSHAW TRAIL. Los Angeles-San Gorgonio Pass-La Paz placers(Ehrenberg, AZ). BRAD.

7. BRIDGER CUTOFF. Ft. Bridger, WY-Salt Lake City. BRIDGER.

8. CALIFORNIA ROUTE. Begins at identified starting point on the Missouri River or more southern "jumping-off places" in Arkansas or Texas and ends in California. For trips beginning on Missouri River, the "CAL" code implies that the diarist followed the Platte River to South Pass, avoided Salt Lake City by using the Sublette and Hudspeth cutoffs - or variations thereof - to reach the Humboldt River. The Sierra was crossed via the Carson Pass route. California-bound emigrants who varied from this common pathway have codes for trail segments followed shown within the annotation for their diary or reminiscence. For instance, an emigrant beginning from Independence and exiting at Sacramento after visiting Fort Bridger and Fort Hall before crossing the Sierra via the Truckee River would have the following trail segment code shown in his annotation: CAL(Independence)-BRIDGER-HALL-TRUCKEE. A California-bound emigrant starting overland from Ft. Smith, Arkansas and proceeding via Santa Fe, Tucson and Yuma would show CAL(Ft. Smith)-MARCY-RIO GRANDE-GILA. Each of the secondary codes representing trails taken by the diarist will appear in this list. CAL.

9. CANADA. All Canadian routes are shown in this category. CANADA.

10. CHEROKEE. Fort Smith, Arkansas-Pueblo, CO-Laramie, WY-Fort Bridger-Salt Lake City. CHEROKEE.

11. DAKOTAS. All trails across North or South Dakota, including those following the Red River of the North appear here. DAKOTAS.

12. FORT HALL. Includes trails diverting from the more popular Sublette-Hudspeth corridor north to Fort Hall. Many emigrants detoured to Fort Hall before continuing to California via City of Rocks or Oregon by the Snake River. HALL.

13. FREIGHT. Freighters who recorded trips are identified for readers seeking data on the freighting industry. Such records are annotated as FREIGHT and their routes indexed by year and trail segment codes in the freight subject index. FREIGHT.

14. GILA. Begins on Rio Grande River at points from El Paso to Truth or Consequences, NM and proceeds west by a number of routes to Tucson, then to Yuma via the Gila River. In California, emigrants followed the trail to Cooke's Wells and Warner's Ranch before reaching San Diego or Los Angeles. GILA.

15. HASTINGS. Fort Bridger-Salt Lake City-Pilot Peak-Ruby Marshes-Humboldt River. HASTINGS.

16. INDIANS. Trails associated with aboriginal routes are included here. See the INDIAN subject area index. INDS.

17. LANDER. Begins at Burnt Ranch, Sweetwater River(WY) then north of the Sublette-Hudspeth cutoff corridor to Fort Hall. LANDER.

18. LASSEN. Lassen Meadows(Mill City, NV)-Black Rock Desert-Goose Lake-Yreka, CA. LASSEN.

19. LIVESTOCK. Some readers may seek data pertaining to livestock drives west. Such sources are listed under this code and can be further surveyed under the LIVESTOCK subject index. STOCK.

20. MARCY ROAD. Fort Smith, Arkansas-Canadian River-Santa Fe. MARCY.

21. MEEK CUTOFF. Fort Boise-west by several routes to the Willamette Valley. Includes the Elliott Cutoff. MEEK.

22. MEXICO. This category includes all pathways used to cross Mexico. Annotations will show major communities passed by individual emigrants. MEX.

23. MILITARY. Although purely military travel items are not included in this list, those which either establish major emigrant routes or those of escorts to emigrant parties appear. Consult the MILITARY subject category for items on specific trails. MILITARY.

24. MONTANA. Emigrant records for trails into Montana appear here. Excluded are the Mullan Road and Bridger Cutoff items which have their own codes. Generally this category includes records of emigrants reaching Montana from Dakota Territory or north from Salt Lake City and Fort Hall. MONTANA.

25. MORMON TRAIL. This category could have been shown as a California item, however the large number of LDS diaries with a common route from Council Bluffs to Salt Lake City argued for a separate heading. Readers seeking largely Mormon travel items from Council Bluffs to Fort Bridger and ending in Salt Lake Valley should first review this trail category and then continue to the CAL entries with a BRIDGER subheading. MORMON.

26. MULLAN ROAD. Fort Benton, MT-Missoula-Spokane-Walla Walla. MULLAN.

27. NOBLE'S CUTOFF. Lassen Meadows(Mill City, NV)-Black Rock Desert-Smoke Creek Desert-Susanville-Red Bluff, CA. NOBLE.

28. OKLAHOMA. Fort Smith, Arkansas-southwest across Oklahoma by several routes to Gainesville, TX. Some few other trails also represented. OKLAHOMA.

29. OLD SPANISH TRAIL. Santa Fe-northwest across Colorado and Utah to Green River, then southwest to southern California via St. George-Las Vegas-Barstow. References to Gunnison route from Pueblo, CO to central Utah included. SPANISH.

30. OREGON TRAIL. This category represents a popular pathway from the Missouri River starting points, up the Platte River to South Pass, then west by Fort Hall and Fort Boise before ending at The Dalles. Some Oregon-bound parties used the BRIDGER, LANDER or other cutoffs so those codes should be consulted for Oregon emigrant searches. Any deviations from the common OREGON pathway will show appropriate subheadings in the trail category codes, i.e., OR(Council)-BRIDGER. OR.

31. OREGON-CALIFORNIA TRAILS. After discovery of gold in 1848, growing numbers of routes linked Oregon and California. This category shows records of such trips. OR-CAL.

32. PIKES PEAK. All records of trips to the Colorado area, the bulk of which followed the Pikes Peak excitement of 1859, are shown here. They generally began at the Missouri River and took a variety of trails to central Colorado. See also CHEROKEE and SANTA FE subcategories for possible items. PIKES.

33. PONY EXPRESS. St. Joseph, MO-Salt Lake City-San Francisco. PONY.

34. RIO GRANDE. Taos, NM-Chihuahua, Mexico. RIO GRANDE.

35. SALT LAKE CORRIDOR. Salt Lake City-St. George-Las Vegas-San Bernardino. See also OLD SPANISH TRAIL. SLCOR.

36. SALT LAKE CUTOFF. Salt Lake City-City of Rocks. SLCUT.

37. SANTA FE TRAIL. Independence, MO-Santa Fe, NM. SANTA FE.

38. SIMPSON ROUTE. Salt Lake City-Fish Springs-Ruby Valley-Carson City. SIMPSON.

39. STAGE LINES. See subject index under Stage Lines for data on individual companies and routes. Diaries or other records of stage trips are annotated STAGE and such records are detailed by year and route in the STAGE subject index. Entries in this list are coded as STAGE.

40. TEXAS. Many overland parties traveled to Texas by ship or wagon before heading west. All such entries are coded TEXAS. Since many emigrants beginning their trip in Texas crossed portions of Mexico, readers should consult the MEX code. TEX.

41. TRUCKEE CUTOFF. Lovelock, NV-Wadsworth-Reno-Donner Lake and Pass-Sacramento. TRUCKEE.

42. WASHINGTON TRAILS. All emigrant records reflecting travel in Washington are coded for reader access. WASH.

Trail segment codes offer important information to readers. The codes are compiled in the direction of travel by the individual emigrant. This is almost always east to west. Once understood, the reader can determine the general route of travel for each diary or reminiscence at a glance. First, the high majority of emigrants intended to reach either California or Oregon, although the list does include entries for those seeking intermediary points, i.e., Montana or Utah. For that reason, most trail segment codes begin with either CAL or OR. Both these final destinations have a distinct trail net represented by the CAL or OR code. Deviations make up the remainder of the trail code. For instance, a code CAL(Indep)-Bridger-Simpson shows that the route followed by that particular diarist began his journey to California at Independence, MO, followed the predetermined California trail net until chosing to use the Bridger Cutoff into Salt Lake Valley where he opted to reach California by the Simpson Route. An Oregon-bound traveler's code might be OR(Council)-LANDER-MEEK, indicating a trip beginning at Council Bluffs, using the Lander Road back to Fort Hall, where the party continued along the Oregon trail net to Fort Boise and finishing the trip via the Meek Cutoff - probably to their regret. Canadian travel accounts would begin with the code CANADA, followed by specific trail data for that particular trip. Emigrants to Montana would have a Montana code heading (MONTANA) only if they chose to use the Dakota or Canadian routes and avoided the California or Oregon trail nets. Otherwise, those codes would appear first in the code chain, i.e., CAL or OR.

In some instances, an entry was noted in other bibliographies or card catalogs and proved unavailable for review. In those cases, the code "Not Seen" is added to the annotation.

The year(s) of the trip(s) is the final element of diary or reminiscence annotation.

LIST OF ENTRIES -- ALPHABETICAL BY AUTHOR

ABAJIAN, James D. BLACKS AND THEIR CONTRIBUTIONS TO THE AMERICAN WEST: A BIBLIOGRAPHY AND UNION LIST OF LIBRARY HOLDINGS THROUGH 1970. Boston: Hall, 1974. Bibliography.

ABBEY, James. CALIFORNIA: A TRIP ACROSS THE PLAINS. New Albany, IN: Kent & Norman, Nunemacher, 1850. CAL(St. Jo)-BRIDGER. II. 1850.

ABBOTT, Carlisle S. RECOLLECTIONS OF A CALIFORNIA PIONEER. NY: Neale, 1917. CAL(Council)-BRIDGER-SLCUT. III. Rem. 1850.

ABBOTT, Carolyn. Reminiscences. MONHIST. MONTANA-DAKOTAS. III. Rem. 1862.

ABBOTT, George H. Recollections. ORHIST. OR(Ft. Leav). V. Rem. 1849.

ABBOTT, John G. "To Oregon by Ox Team 59 Years Ago." LANE COUNTY HISTORIAN 27(Sum 1982): 41-44. OR(Westport). IV. 1852.

ABEL, James F. "Hill Beachey and the Railroad Stage Line." NVHIST. Stage.

ABELL, James S. Papers. MNHIST. CAL(Indep)-TRUCKEE. I.

1849.

ABERT, James W. THROUGH THE COUNTRY OF THE COMANCHE INDIANS...1845. Ed. John Galvin. Reprint. SF: Howell, 1970. MARCY(Bent's Fort-Ft. Gibson). I. 1845.

_____. WESTERN AMERICA IN 1846-47. Reprint. SF: Howell, 1966. SANTA FE(Ft. Leav-Santa Fe & return)-RIO GRANDE. I. 1846.

ABLES, T. J. Letter. NEWBERRY. CAL(Indep?)-NOBLE. IV. 1857.

ABRAM, Cynthia. Mount Holyoke Alumnae Records. Mount Holyoke College Library, South Hadley, MA. OR. Not Seen. 1859.

THE ABRIDGED MORMON GUIDE SHOWING THE DISTANCES AND BEST CAMPING PLACES OVER THE NORTH PLATTE ROUTE FROM OMAHA TO SALT LAKE CITY, U., THENCE ON TO THE SALMON RIVER, BANNACK AND VIRGINIA GOLD FIELDS. SLC: Farmer's Oracle, 1864. Guide.

"Abstract of Journals Kept by Lt. Turner...and Lt. Franklin...." In REPORT OF A SUMMER CAMPAIGN TO THE ROCKY MOUNTAINS...IN 1845. 29th Cong., 1st sess., Sen. Doc. 1, pp. 214-17. (1845). CAL(Ft. Leav.-Ft. Laramie)-CHEROKEE(Ft. Laramie-Pueblo)-SANTA FE. V-. 1845.

Account of a Journey to California via Texas and Mexico. HUNTL. CAL-TEX(Brownsville)-MEX(Saltillo-Durango-Mazatlan). III-. Rem. 1849.

"Account of the Building of Mullen's Military Road." Historical Society of Montana CONTRIBUTIONS 8(1917): 162-69. MULLAN-Genl.

ACKLEY, Mary E. CROSSING THE PLAINS.... SF: Author, 1928. CAL(Council). IV. Rem. 1852.

ACKLEY, Richard T. "Across the Plains in 1858." UTAH HISTORICAL QUARTERLY 9(Jul-Oct 1941): 190-228. CAL(Neb. City)-BRIDGER-Ends at SLC. III. 1858.

ADAIR, Sarah D. "Sarah Damron Adair, Pioneer of 1843." TRANSACTIONS Oregon Pioneer Association (1900): 65-82. OR(Indep). Rem. 1843. Not Seen.

ADAMS, B. H. Autobiography. WIHIST. CAL-Genl. Social.

ADAMS, Benjamin F. Correspondence. BEINECKE. CAL-Genl.

ADAMS, Cecelia E. M. "Crossing the Plains in 1852." TRANSACTIONS Oregon Pioneer Association for 1904 (1905): 288-329. OR(Council). II. 1852.

ADAMS, David M. "Biographical Sketch." In AMERICAN BIOGRAPHY AND GENEALOGY, CALIFORNIA EDITION. Ed. Robert J. Burdette. N.p.: Lewis, 1912. CAL(Ft. Smith?)-OKLAHOMA-TEX-GILA. V. 1852.

ADAMS, Elias. ANCESTORS AND DESCENDANTS.... Ed. Frank D. Adams. Kaysville, UT: Private, 1929. MORMON. 1850. Not Seen.

ADAMS, Ellen Tompkins. Manuscript Diary, 1863. BANCROFT. CAL(Council)-Ends Ft. Bridger. II. 1863.

ADAMS, Franklin E. "Overland Trail Diary...Upward Bound in 1865." Ed. Walter Edens. OVERLAND JOURNAL 5(Fall 1987): 8-23. CAL(Atchison)-BRIDGER-SIMPSON. III. 1865.

ADAMS, Mary Vowell. SEE: Bliss, Beatrice L. MARY V. ADAMS.

ADAMS, Ramon F. "Horses on the Stage Lines." WESTERN HORSEMAN 15(Aug 1950): 6-7, 30-31. Stage.

_____. THE RAMPAGING HERD: A BIBLIOGRAPHY...OF THE CATTLE INDUSTRY. Norman: Univ. of Oklahoma Press, 1959. Bibliography.

_____. SIX-GUNS AND SADDLE LEATHER: A BIBLIOGRAPHY OF...OUTLAWS AND GUNMEN. Norman: Univ. of Oklahoma Press, 1954. Bibliography.

ADAMS, Samuel H. THE PONY EXPRESS. NY: Random House, 1950. Pony.

ADAMS, W. L. LECTURE ON THE OREGON AND THE PACIFIC COAST. Boston: N.p., 1869. OR. 1848. Not Seen.

ADAMS, William. Recollections. Princeton Univ. Library-Western America. MORMON. Rem. 1849. Not Seen.

ADAMS, William H. Short History. UTHIST. MORMON. V. 1848.

ADKINS, H. Frank. Reminiscence. MONHIST. CAL(Neb. City)-BRIDGER-MONTANA(SLC-Helena). IV. Rem. 1865. Freight.

ADKINSON, Norman B. INDIAN BRAVES AND BATTLES.... Grangeville, ID: County Free Press, 1967. 1862 Indian attack, Salmon Falls, ID.

ADLER, Pat, and Walt Wheelock. WALKER'S RAILROAD ROUTES. Glendale: La Siesta, 1965. Geog-Walker Pass.

"Adventures of Captain Florence and Party." HUTCHINGS' 4 May 1860, 517-20. 1859 Indian attack, Sweetwater Valley.

"Adventures on the Prairies." NORTH AMERICAN REVIEW 144(Jul 1849): 175-95. Overland-Genl.

"Advice to Prospective Emigrants to Oregon." OREGON HISTORICAL QUARTERLY 15(Dec 1914): 295-99. OR-1843-Genl.

AGATZ, Cora W. "A Journey Across the Plains in 1866." PACIFIC NORTHWEST QUARTERLY 27(Apr 1936): 170-74. CAL(Council?)-HALL-MONTANA. V. Rem. 1866.

AGNEW, Brad. "Military Roads in Indian Territory." RED RIVER VALLEY HISTORICAL REVIEW 6(Sum 1981): 31-47. OKLAHOMA-Genl.

AGNEW, Mrs. James D. "Idaho Pioneer of 1864." WASHINGTON HISTORICAL QUARTERLY 15(Jan 1924): 44-48. GEOG-Boise.

AHMANSON, John. PRESENT DAY MOHAMED. Omaha: N.p., 1876. MORMON. Rem. 1856. Not Seen. Utah.

AHNERT, Gerald T. RETRACING THE BUTTERFIELD OVERLAND TRAIL THROUGH ARIZONA: A GUIDE TO THE ROUTE OF 1857-1861. LA: Westernlore, 1973. Stage. Fine Maps.

AINSWORTH, E. M. "Old Austin and Round Rock Road to Fort Concho." FRONTIER TIMES, 6 Jul 1929, 403-09. TEXAS-Genl.

AITCHISON, Clyde B. "The Mormon Settlements in the Missouri Valley." OREGON HISTORICAL QUARTERLY 8(Sept 1907): 276-89. MORMON-Genl.

AJAX, William and Emma. Diary. UTHIST. MORMON. I. 1862.

AKIN, James, Jr. "The Journal of James Akin." UNIVERSITY OF OKLAHOMA BULLETIN. 1919. Reprint. Fairfield, WA: Ye Galleon,

1971. OR(Council). III. 1852.

AKRIGG, G. P. and Helen B. BRITISH COLUMBIA CHRONICLE, 1847-1871. Vancouver: Discovery, 1977. CANADA-Genl.

ALBRIGHT, George L. OFFICIAL EXPLORATIONS FOR PACIFIC RAILROADS. Berkeley: Univ. of California Press, 1921. Govt.

ALBRIGHT, Lorraine H. Ed. Harbert, Joseph W. DIARY.

ALCOCK, Frederick J. "Past and Present Routes to the Canadian Northwest." GEOGRAPHICAL REVIEW 10(Aug 1920): 57-83. CANADA-Genl.

ALCORN, Israel P. Journal. BANCROFT. CAL(West Point). III. 1856.

ALCORN, Rowena L. and Gordon D. PAUL KANE, FRONTIER ARTIST.... Wenatchee, WA: World Press, 1971. Graphics. WASH-Genl.

ALDEN, Wyllis. THE ANCESTORS AND DESCENDANTS OF ISAAC AND IRENE SMITH.... Ed. Harriet C. Fielding. N.p.: Author, 1903. OR(Council)-BARLOW. IV. Rem. 1851.

ALDERSON, William W. Across to Montana. Montana State University Library, Bozeman, MT. BOZE. 1864. Not Seen.

ALDRICH, Lorenzo D. A JOURNAL OF THE OVERLAND ROUTE TO CALIFORNIA! Lansingburgh, NY: Kirkpatrick, 1851. CAL(Ft. Smith)-SANTA FE-RIO GRANDE-GILA. III. 1849.

ALDRICH, Nathan. Letters Written on the Overland Trail in 1852. Held by Mrs. G. O. Fraser, Clarksburg, CA. Not Seen. 1852.

ALDRIDGE, Sarnigan. Diary. CSL. CAL-TEX(Brazos-Van Horn-El Paso)-GILA. III. 1857. Cattle drive.

ALEXANDER, David W. SEE: Barrows, H. D. "Don David W. Alexander."

ALEXANDER, Philip K., Jr. Ed. Kassler, George W. "George W. Kassler."

ALEXANDER, Richard H. THE DIARY AND NARRATIVE OF RICHARD HENRY ALEXANDER.... Ed. Neil Brearley. Richmond, B.C.: Alcuin, 1973. CANADA(Winnipeg-New Westminster). II. 1862.

ALEXANDER, Sara. Little Story. UTHIST. MORMON. IV. 1859.

ALEXANDER, Thomas G., and Leonard J. Arrington. "Camp in the Sagebrush: Camp Floyd, Utah, 1858-1861." UTAH HISTORICAL QUARTERLY 34(Win 1966): 3-21. Geog.

ALEXANDER, William. Diary. BANCROFT. CAL(St. Jo). III. 1859.

ALLEN, Miss A. J. TEN YEARS IN OREGON.... Ithaca, NY: Mack, Andrus, 1848. OR(Indep). II. 1842. OR(Walla Walla-Indep). III. 1845.

ALLEN, Alice Mayhew. EARLY ROADS IN CALIFORNIA. SF: National Society of Colonial Dames of America, 1942. Overland-Genl.

ALLEN, Edward. Letters From the Oregon Trail. BEINECKE. OR(Council). I. 1852.

ALLEN, Edward J. "Edward J. Allen, Pioneer and Roadbuilder." PACIFIC NORTHWEST QUARTERLY 44(Oct 1953): 157-60. OR(Council). 1852. Rem. V. WASH-1863-Genl.

ALLEN, Edward V. "Transportation in the Marysville Area during the 1850's." Senior thesis, Univ. of Santa Clara, 1955. Geog-Marysville. CAL-Genl.

ALLEN, Eleanor. Ed. Hanna, Esther. CANVAS CARAVANS.

ALLEN, Franklin. Journal. LDS. SANTA FE. IV. 1846. CHEROKEE(Pueblo?-SLC). IV. 1847.

ALLEN, George T. "Journal of a Voyage from Fort Vancouver...to...Hudson's Bay." TRANSACTIONS Oregon Pioneer Association 1881 (1882): 38-55. CANADA(Vancouver-Ft. Colville-Jasper House-Ft. Garry-York Factory). II. 1841.

ALLEN, Isaac. Biography. LDS. CAL(Indep)-BRIDGER-HASTINGS-TRUCKEE. V. 1846.

ALLEN, James B., and Ted J. Warner. "The Gosiute Indians in Pioneer Utah." UTAH HISTORICAL QUARTERLY 39(Spr 1971): 162-77. Indians.

ALLEN, Martha Mitten. TRAVELING WEST: 19TH CENTURY WOMEN ON THE OVERLAND ROUTES. El Paso: Texas Western Press/Univ. of Texas, 1987. Social.

_____. "Women in the West: A Study of Book-Length Travel Accounts by Women Who Traveled in the Plains...." PhD diss., Univ. of Texas-Austin, 1972. Social.

ALLEN, Obridge. ALLEN'S GUIDE BOOK AND MAP TO THE GOLD FIELDS OF KANSAS AND NEBRASKA. WA: Waters, 1859. Guide.

ALLEN, Robert A. Collection. NVHIST. Extensive trail collection. OVERLAND-Genl.

ALLEN, Sallie Fox. Account. AZHIST. CAL-SANTA FE-BEALE. III. 1858. Details of Mohave attack at Colorado River.

ALLEN, Sylvester. Diary. COHIST. Freight.

ALLIN, Lawrence. " 'A Mile Wide and an Inch Deep': Attempts to Navigate the Platte River." NEBRASKA HISTORY 63(Spr 1982): 1-15. Geog.

ALLRED, B. W. THE LIFE OF A HORSE AND BUGGY STAGE LINE OPERATOR. WA: Potomac Corral of Westerners, 1972. Stage.

ALLRED, Reddick. "Journal." In TREASURES OF PIONEER HISTORY, vol. 5. Ed. Kate B. Carter. SLC: Daughters Utah Pioneers, n.d. MORMON. Rem. 1847. SLCOR. III. Rem. 1852. SLCOR. III. Rem. 1855.

ALLSOP, I. P. C. Recollections. BANCROFT. CAL(Indep)-BRIDGER. Rem. 1848. Not Seen.

ALLTON, Hiram. Diary. DENVERPUB. CAL(Leav)-CHEROKEE(Julesburg-SLC)-SLCUT-TRUCKEE. III. 1864.

ALLYN, Henry. "Diary." TRANSACTIONS Oregon Pioneer Association 49(1924): 372-435. OR(Council). II. 1853.

ALLYN, Joseph Pratt. THE ARIZONA OF JOSEPH PRATT ALLYN. Tucson: Univ. of Arizona Press, 1974. GILA-Genl.
_____. WEST BY SOUTHWEST...SANTA FE TRAIL, 1863. Dodge City: Kansas Heritage Center, 1984. SANTA FE-BEALE(Ends Prescott). II+. 1863.

ALTER, J. Cecil. JIM BRIDGER. Norman: Univ. of Oklahoma Press,

1962. Biog.

ALTON, Hiram. Journal. BEINECKE. CAL(Leav)-BRIDGER-SLCUT-TRUCKEE. II+. 1864. SEE ALSO: Henry Alton.

ALTROCCHI, Julia C. THE OLD CALIFORNIA TRAIL. Caldwell, ID: Caxton, 1945. Overland-Genl.

ALTSCHULER, Constance W., ed. LATEST FROM ARIZONA! Tucson: Arizona Pioneers' Historical Society, 1969. Stage.

AMARAL, Anthony A. "Wagons by Studebaker." OLD WEST 4(Sum 1968): 56-59. Eqpt.

AMBLER, C. H. SEE: Hoffman, Benjamin. "Diary."

AMES, George Walcott, Jr. Ed. Griffin, John S. A DOCTOR COMES TO CALIFORNIA.

AMES, Peramus G. Diary. HUNTL. CAL(St. Jo). IV. 1850.

AMESBURY, Robert. NOBLES' EMIGRANT TRAIL. Susanville, CA: Lassen Litho, 1967. NOBLE-Genl. Maps.

AMUNDSON, Carroll J. "History of the Willamette Valley and Cascade Road Company." MA thesis, Univ. of Oregon, 1928. Freight.

ANABLE, Henry S. Journals. BANCROFT. CAL(St. Jo)-BRIDGER. II+. 1852.

ANDERSON, Abraham C. TRAILS OF EARLY IDAHO. Caldwell, ID: Caxton, 1940. Geog.

ANDERSON, Alexander C. HAND-BOOK AND MAP...FRASER'S AND THOMPSON'S RIVERS. SF: Le Count, 1858. Guide.

ANDERSON, Charles L. Letters. BANCROFT. CAL(Council)-BRIDGER-SIMPSON. II. 1862. Stage.

ANDERSON, David. THE NET IN THE BAY.... 1854. Reprint. NY: Johnson Reprint, 1967. CANADA(Moose Fort-Ft. Garry). II+. 1852.

_____. "Recollections." COLLECTIONS Nebraska State Historical Society 16(1911): 193-204. PIKES. Rem. 1859. Not Seen.

ANDERSON, Edna Mae. TAMSEN: A STORY OF THE DONNER PARTY. Fort Washington, PA: Chipmunk, 1973. CAL-1846-Genl. Biog.

ANDERSON, George L. "Atchison, 1865-1886, Divided and Uncertain." KANSAS HISTORICAL QUARTERLY 35(Spr 1969): 30-45. Geog.

ANDERSON, H. Allen. "Mountain Pass: A Texas Frontier Landmark." WESTX 53(1977): 57-72. Stage. Geog.

ANDERSON, Harry H. Ed. Dunlop, John W. "From Milwaukee."

ANDERSON, Hattie M. Ed. Smith, Hank. "Mining and Indian Fighting."

ANDERSON, John C. MACKINAWS DOWN THE MISSOURI. Ed. Glen Barrett. Logan, UT: Western Text Society, 1973. Stage(Leav-SLC-Virginia City, MT). 1866.

ANDERSON, Kirk. "Kirk Anderson's Trip to Utah, 1858." Ed. Eugene T. Wells. MISSOURI HISTORICAL SOCIETY BULLETIN 18(Oct 1961): 3-15. CAL(St. Jo)-BRIDGER(Ends SLC). III. 1858.

ANDERSON, Mardi. "Freighting in Buffalo County." BUFFALO

TALES 8(Mar, Apr 1985): 1-4, 14. Freight.

ANDERSON, Maybelle H. Ed. Harmon, Appleton M. HARMON GOES WEST.

ANDERSON, Niles. "Grandfather Was a Forty-Niner." WESTERN PENNSYLVANIA HISTORICAL MAGAZINE 50(Jan 1967): 33-50. CAL(St. Jo)-HALL. IV. 1849.

ANDERSON, William Wright. Diary. LILLEY. OR(St. Jo)-BARLOW. III. 1848.

_____. "The Diary and Memoirs of William Wright Anderson, Oregon Pioneer and Forty-Niner." Ed. Michael F. Williams. PhD diss., Ball State University, 1984.

ANDREE, E. W. TRAVELING IN THE SUNSET TRAIL WITH AN OX TEAM.... Milwaukee: Trade Press, n.d. PIKES(Plattsmouth). IV. Rem. 1860.

ANDREWS, D. B. Journal. BEINECKE. CAL(St. Jo)-TRUCKEE-BECK. II+. 1852.

ANDREWS, Ralph W. INDIANS AS THE WESTERNERS SAW THEM. Seattle: Superior, 1963. Indians.

ANDREWS, Thomas F. "The Controversial Career of Lansford W. Hastings." PhD diss., Univ. of Southern California, 1970. OR-1842-Genl. Biog. Guide.

_____. "The Controversial Hastings Overland Guide." PACIFIC HISTORICAL REVIEW 37(Feb 1968): 21-34. Guide.

_____. "'Ho! For Oregon and California!' An Annotated Bibliography of Published Advice to the Emigrant, 1841-47." PRINCETON UNIVERSITY LIBRARY CHRONICLE 33(Aut 1971): 41-64. Guide. Bibliography.

_____. "Lansford W. Hastings and the Promotion of the Salt Lake Desert Cutoff: A Reappraisal." WESTERN HISTORICAL QUARTERLY 4(Apr 1973): 133-50. Biog. CAL-1846-Genl. HASTINGS-1846-Genl.

_____. "Satire and the Overland Guide: John B. Hall's Fanciful Advice to Gold Rush Emigrants." CALIFORNIA HISTORICAL QUARTERLY 48(Jun 1969): 99-111. Guide.

ANDRUS, Manomus L. Statement. In Charles Kelly Collection. UTHIST. CHEROKEE(?-Pueblo). V. 1846.

ANGELL, Susan P. "Sketch of a Pioneer." TRANSACTIONS Oregon Pioneer Association 1928 (1929): 55-56. OR(?)-BARLOW. V. Rem. 1852.

ANGUS, Ina M. "Toll Roads of Western Nevada." NVHIST. Stage.

ANKENY, Levi. "The Salmon Falls Massacre." FRONTIER TIMES 35(Spr 1961): 6-8, 58-59. 1860 Snake River attack.

ANKENY, Nesmith. THE WEST AS I KNEW IT. Lewiston, ID: Author, 1953. OR(Indep). III. 1843.

ANONYMOUS. "Crossing the Plains in 1852." THE ARGONAUT, 25 April and 2 May 1925, n.p. CAL(Council). 1852. Not Seen.

_____. Diary. Univ. of Arkansas Library, Fayetteville, Ark. CAL(begins Bitter Creek, WY). 1850. Not Seen.

_____. Diary. Indiana Historical Society Archives, Indianapolis, IN. CAL(Weston). II. 1850.

_____. Diary. Mojave Chapter, Daughters of the American Revolution, Fullerton, CA. CAL. 1869. Not Seen.

_____. Diary. BANCROFT. CAL(Ft. Smith)-CHEROKEE-SLCUT(ends City of Rocks). III+. 1854.

_____. SEE: Diary of an Unknown Scout.

ANSCHUTZ, M. W. Letters. KSHIST. Stock.

ANSTED, D. E. GOLD SEEKER'S MANUAL. NY: Appleton, 1849. Guide.

ANTHONY, Erasmus L. Reminiscence. MONHIST. MONTANA(SLC-Helena). Rem. V-. 1865.

ANTHONY, Ross O. "A History of Fort Laramie." MA thesis, Univ. of Southern California, 1930. Geog.

ANTHONY, Webster D. "Journal of a Trip from Denver to Oro City in 1860." COLORADO MAGAZINE 11(Nov 1934): 228-37. PIKES. III. 1860. Freight.

APOSTOL, Jane. "Gold Rush Widow." PACIFIC HISTORIAN 28(Sum 1984): 49-55. Social.

APPLEGATE Family Papers. ORU. Biog.

APPLEGATE, Jesse. SEE: Frear, Samuel T. JESSE APPLEGATE.
_____. "A Day with the Cow Column in 1843." OREGON HISTORICAL QUARTERLY 1(Dec 1900): 371-83. OR(Elm Grove). II. Rem. 1843. Train Orgn.

_____. RECOLLECTIONS OF MY BOYHOOD. Roseburg, OR: Author, 1914. OR(Indep). II. Rem. 1843.

APPLEGATE, Lindsay. "Notes and Reminiscences of Laying Out and Establishing the Old Emigrant Road into Southern Oregon in the Year 1846." OREGON HISTORICAL QUARTERLY 22(Mar 1921): 12-45. OR-APPLE(Willamette Valley-Ft. Hall & return). II. 1846.

APPLEGATE, Mary E. ON TO OREGON! Eds. Adrietta A. Hixon and Waldo Taylor. Weiser, ID: Bess F. Smith, 1947. OR(Indep)-BARLOW. III. Rem. 1852.

APPLEGATE, Virginia W. Recollections. ORHIST. OR(St. Jo)-BARLOW. V-. Rem. 1849.

ARAM, Joseph. "Across the Continent in a Caravan." Ed. James T. Watson. JOURNAL OF AMERICAN HISTORY 1, no. 4(1907): 617-32. CAL(St. Jo)-HALL-TRUCKEE. V. Rem. 1846.

ARBUCKLE, Clyde. "He Marked the Donner Trail." WESTWAYS 56(Jul 1964): 10-11. Pres. Biog-Peter M. Weddell.

ARCHAMBAULT, Amanda A. "Historic Document Tells Early Day Drama of the West." ANNALS OF WYOMING 15(Jul 1943): 229-33. Indians.

ARCHAMBEAU, Ernest R. "The Fort Smith-Santa Fe Trail along the Canadian River in Texas." PANHANDLE-PLAINS HISTORICAL REVIEW 27(1954): 1-26. MARCY-Genl. Maps. Pres.

ARCHER, Patience L. Diary. BYU. MORMON. II. Rem. 1856. MORMON. III. Rem. 1861. MORMON. IV. Rem. 1863.

ARCHIBALD, J. Annie. "A Journey to Pike's Peak and New Mexico." THE SIBYL, 15 Mar, 1 Apr 1859, 529-38. SANTA FE(Lawrence)-

PIKES. IV. 1859.

ARDOLF, Genevieve M. "The Development of Death Valley with Special Reference to Transportation." MA thesis, Univ. of Southern California, 1930. Missing. Geog.

ARGYLE, Archie. CUPID'S ALBUM. NY: M. Doolady, 1866. CAL(Neb. City)-BRIDGER-SLCUT-SIMPSON. V. 1865? Fiction based on previous trip.

ARKSEY, Laura, Nancy Pries, and Marcia Reed. AMERICAN DIARIES: AN ANNOTATED BIBLIOGRAPHY OF PUBLISHED AMERICAN DIARIES AND JOURNALS. 2 vols. Detroit: Gale, 1987. Excellent bibliography.

ARMITAGE, Susan. "Relectant Pioneers." In WOMEN AND WESTERN LITERATURE. Eds. Helen Stauffer and Susan J. Rosowski. Troy, NY: Whitson, 1982. Social.

ARMS, Cephas, and Adonijah S. Welch. THE LONG ROAD TO CALIFORNIA. Ed. John Cumming. Mount Pleasant, MI: Editor, 1985. CAL(Council)-MORMON-SLCOR. II. 1849.

ARMS, George. "The Story of Henry Wells, Expressman and College Founder." AMERICANA 35(Apr 1941): 249-64. Biog. Stage.

ARMSTRONG, J. E. Diary. BANCROFT. CAL(St. Jo)-TRUCKEE. III. 1849.

ARMSTRONG, J. Elza. "Diary." In THE BUCKEYE ROVERS IN THE GOLD RUSH. Ed. Howard L. Scamehorn. Athens, OH: Ohio Univ. Press, 1965. CAL(St. Jo)-TRUCKEE. II. 1849.

ARMSTRONG, J. Ezra. Diary. Ohio Historical Society Library, Columbus, OH. CAL(St. Jo)-TRUCKEE. III. 1849. Same as two preceding items?

ARMSTRONG, John. Journal. BANCROFT. CAL. 1849. Not Seen.

ARMSTRONG, John Christopher. Diary. LDS. SLCOR. V. 1849.

ARMSTRONG, Ruth. "Ranch Home on the Santa Fe Trail." NEW MEXICO 56(Jan 1978): 30-32. SANTA FE-Genl.

ARMSTRONG, William. '49 Experiences. BANCROFT. CAL(St. Jo)-LANDER. III. Rem. 1859.

ARMYTAGE, W. H. G. "H. J. Coke on the Oregon Trail." MID-AMERICAN 31(1949): 258-69. OR(Council). IV. 1850.

ARNOLD, James. FARM WAGONS AND CARTS. North Pomfret, VT: David & Charles, 1977. Eqpt.

ARNOLD, Joseph Warren. "Joseph Warren Arnold's Journal of his Trip to and from Montana, 1864-1866." Ed. Charles W. Martin. NEBRASKA HISTORY 55(Win 1974): 463-552. CAL(Council)-LANDER-MONTANA. III+. 1864.

ARNOLD, Lowell J. "With the Butterfield Stages in Arizona." PROGRESSIVE ARIZONA 4(May 1927): 6-8, 31. Stage.

ARNOLD, Oren. "Slave Girl of the Mojaves." DESERT 3(Mar 1940): 3-8. Graphics. 1852 Gila Bend attack.

ARNOLD, R. Ross. INDIAN WARS OF IDAHO. Caldwell, ID: Caxton, 1932. Indians.

ARRINGTON, James M. Diary. In Arrington Family Collection. UPAC. CAL(Indep?)-Ends on Sweetwater. III. 1851.

ARRINGTON, Joseph Earl. "Skirving's Moving Panorama: Colonel Fremont's Western Expeditions Pictorialized." OREGON HISTORICAL QUARTERLY 65(Spr 1964): 133-72. Biog.

ARRINGTON, Leonard J. SEE: With Alexander, Thomas G. "Camp in the Sagebrush." With Cornwall, Rebecca. RESCUE.

_____. "Brigham Young and the Transcontinental Telegraph Line." IMPROVEMENT ERA 54(Jul 1951): 510-11, 29. Telegraph.

_____. "The Deseret Telegraph - A Church-Owned Public Utility." JOURNAL OF ECONOMIC HISTORY 11(Spr 1951): 117-39. Telegraph.

_____. "Mississippi Mormons." ENSIGN 7(Jun 1977): 46-51. CAL(Indep-Ft. Laramie)-CHEROKEE(Ft. Laramie-Pueblo). IV. 1846. CHEROKEE(Pueblo-SLC). IV. 1847.

ARTHUR, John. "Pioneer of 1843." TRANSACTIONS Oregon Pioneer Association (1887): 96-104. OR-1843-Genl.

"Arthur M. Menefee's Travels across the Plains, 1857." NEVADA HISTORICAL SOCIETY QUARTERLY 9(Spr 1966): 3-28. CAL(St. Jo)-TRUCKEE(ends in Carson Valley). III. 1857.

"Article VI." EDINBURGH REVIEW 78(Jul 1843): 157-92. Overland-Genl.

"Articles of Agreement for an Expedition to California for Gold, 1849." MISSOURI HISTORICAL SOCIETY BULLETIN 20(Oct 1963): 51-55. Train Govt.

ASHLEY, Angeline J. Crossing the Plains. HUNTL. MORMON. II. 1852.

ASHLEY, Delos R. Diary. BANCROFT. CAL-TRUCKEE? III. 1849.

ASHTON, John. "A History of Jack Stock and Mules." MA thesis, Univ. of Missouri, 1924. Teams.

ASK, Mrs. SEE: Knight, Amelia S. "Diary of Mrs. Ask."

ATCHISON, William E. Diary. MONHIST. CAL(Council)-BOZE(Lower Platte Bridge-Virginia City, MT). III. 1864.

"Atchison's Pony Express Riders." Atchison County Historical Society BULLETIN, 15 Aug 1979, 1-2. Pony.

ATHEARN, Lovelia. Ed. Athearn, P. A. "Diary."

ATHEARN, P. A. "Diary." PACIFIC HISTORIAN 2(May, Aug, Nov 1958), 6-7, 13-16, 9-12; 3(Feb, May 1959): 21-23, 39-42. CAL(St. Jo)-TRUCKEE. III+. 1849.

ATHEARN, Robert G. Ed. Burgess, Perry A. "From Illinois to Montana." Ed. Winne, Peter. "Across the Plains in 1863."

_____. "The Fifty-Niners." AMERICAN WEST 13(Sept-Oct 1976): 22-25, 60-61. PIKES-1859-Genl.

ATHEY, James. Narrative. BANCROFT. OR(Westport?). V. Rem. 1843.

ATKIN, (Atkins?) William. Handcart Reminiscence. UTHIST. MORMON. II+. Rem. 1859.

ATKINSON. David E. SEE: Peterson, Charles. MORMON BATTALION TRAIL GUIDE.

ATKINSON. G. H. "Occasional Address." TRANSACTIONS Oregon Pioneer Association for 1880 (1881): 28-38. OR-1848-Genl.

ATKINSON, J. H. "Cattle Drives from Arkansas to California in the Decade before the Civil War." PULASKI COUNTY HISTORICAL REVIEW 16(Mar 1968): 53-56. Stock.

ATMORE, Charles. Diary. COHIST. CAL(St. Jo). V-. Rem. 1843.

ATWOOD, Harriet T. "The Mormon Migration and Adaption to Geographic Environment." VASSAR JOURNAL OF UNDERGRADUATE STUDIES 4(1929): 137-58. MORMON-Genl.

AUBREY, Francois Xavier. "Diaries of Francois X. Aubrey." In EXPLORING SOUTHWESTERN TRAILS, 1846-1854. Ed. Ralph P. Bieber. Glendale: Clark, 1938. BEALE(Tejon Pass-New Mexico by variant route). II. 1853. BEALE(same route as 1853). II. 1854.

AUDUBON, John W. AUDUBON'S WESTERN JOURNAL: 1849-1850. Ed. Frank H. Hodder. Cleveland: Clark, 1906. CAL(Brownsville)-TEX-MEX(Monterey-Parral-Altar)-GILA. I. 1849.

_____. "Illustrated Notes of an Expedition through Mexico and California, 1849-50." MAGAZINE OF HISTORY, Extra No. 41(1936). CAL(Brownsville)-TEX-MEX(Monterey-Parral-Altar)-GILA. I. 1849.

AUERBACH, Herbert E. "Old Trails, Old Forts, Old Trappers and Traders." UTAH HISTORICAL QUARTERLY 9(Jan-Apr 1941): 13-63. SPANISH-Genl.

AULBACH, Adam. A Voice Out of the Past. Idaho Historical Society Library, Boise, ID. CAL(St. Jo)-HALL-MONTANA(Ft. Hall to Bannack). V. Rem. 1863.

AULT, Phil. WIRES WEST. NY: Dodd, Mead, 1974. Telegraph.

AUSTERMAN, Wayne R. "Arms of the El Paso Mail." GUN REPORT 25(Jan 1980): 48-52. Eqpt.

_____. "'Colorado' Burnham and the Jackass Mail." OLD WEST 22(Sum 1986): 22-24. Stage.

_____. "Identifying a 'Lost' Stage Station in Jeff Davis County." PASSWORD 27(Spr 1982): 3-11. Stage. Pres. Geog(La Limpia).

_____. "Parker Burnham, An Expressman of Old El Paso." PASSWORD 27(Spr 1982): 5-14. Biog. Stage.

_____. "Return to the Jornada." PASSWORD 28(Win 1983): 165-71. RIO GRANDE-Genl. Geog(Jornada del Muerto).

_____. "The San Antonio-El Paso Mail, C.S.A." WESTX 58(1982): 77-102. Stage.

_____. SHARPS RIFLES AND SPANISH MULES: THE SAN ANTONIO-EL PASO MAIL, 1851-1881. College Station: Texas A&M Univ. Press, 1985. Extensive bibliography. Stage.

_____. "Van Horn's Wells: Roadside History in Culbertson County." PASSWORD 31(Fall 1986): 161-67. Geog.

AUSTIN, H. B. Trip to Denver. DENVERPUB. PIKES(Beatrice, NB). IV. 1863.

AUSTIN, Henry. Diary. BANCROFT. CAL(St. Jo)-Ends on Raft River. II+. 1849.

AUSTIN, Judith, and Gary Bettis. "A Preliminary Checklist of Guides to Sources in Idaho History." IDAHO YESTERDAYS 21(Fall 1977): 19-26. Bibs.

AVERETT, George W. Autobiography. UTHIST. CAL(St. Jo)-HALL-TRUCKEE. IV. Rem. 1849.

AVERILL, Martha Grace. Ed. Keaton, Charles H. "Crossing the Plains."

AVERY, R. B. Ed. With Allen, W. W. CALIFORNIA GOLD BOOK.

AVESON, Robert. "Leaving Home." In EVENTFULL NARRA-TIVES, No. 13. SLC: Juvenile Instructor, 1887. MORMON. V. 1866.

AVILLO, Philip J., Jr. "Fort Mojave (Arizona) Territory: 1859-1865." MA thesis, Univ. of San Diego, 1969. Geog. Military.

_____. "Fort Mojave: Outpost on the Upper Colorado." JOURNAL OF ARIZONA HISTORY 11(Sum 1970): 77-100. Geog.

AYER, Edward E. Early Reminiscences. CSL. CAL(Council)-BRIDGER-SIMPSON. IV. Rem. 1860.

AYRES, Irvin and Romeyn. Recollections. BANCROFT. CAL(St. Jo)-BRIDGER. V-. Rem. 1853.

AYRES, Samuel M. Letters. MO-WHMC. CAL(Kansas)-BRIDGER-HASTINGS. IV. 1850.

BABB, Mrs. E. S. Papers. Whitman College Library-Eels Northwest Collection, Walla Walla, WA. Not Seen.

BABBITT, Charles H. EARLY DAYS IN COUNCIL BLUFFS. WA: Adams, 1916. Geog.

BABBITT, James E. "Surveyors along the 35th Parallel: Alexander Gardner's Photographs of Northern Arizona, 1867-1868." JOUR-NAL OF ARIZONA HISTORY 22(Aut 1981): 325-48. BEALE-Genl-Graphics.

BABCOCK, Leonard. Recollections. BANCROFT. CAL(Indep)-BRIDGER-SLCOR. II. Rem. 1849.

BABCOCK, William H. Journal. Whitman College-Eels Northwest Collection, Walla Walla, WA. OR(Council)-LANDER. 1859. Not Seen.

BABCOCK, Willoughby M. "Gateway to the Northwest: St. Paul and the Nobles Expedition of 1859." MINNESOTA HISTORY 35(Jun 1957): 249-65. DAKOTAS(St. Paul)-CANADA(Ft. Ellice). II. 1859.

BACHMAN, Jacob H. "Audubon's Ill-Fated Western Journey: Recalled by the Diary of Jacob H. Bachman." Ed. Jeanne S. Van Nostrand. CALIFORNIA HISTORICAL QUARTERLY 21(Dec 1942): 289-310. CAL-TEX-MEX-GILA. III. 1849.

BACHMAN, Lucy. "Roles Played by the Gila Bend Area...." MA thesis, Arizona State Univ., 1941. Geog.

BACHMANN, Frederick W. Ed. With Wm. S. Wallas. Schiel, Jacob. LAND BETWEEN.

BACKUS, Gurdon. Diary. BEINECKE. CAL(St. Jo)-TRUCKEE. II+. 1849.

BACON, Daniel. Letters. National Park Service Library, Omaha. OR(St. Jo). 1851. Missing.

BACON, John M. Narrative. BANCROFT. OR(Indep)-BARLOW.

V. Rem. 1845.

BADMAN, Philip. Diary. BEINECKE. CAL(begins on Sweetwater)-LASSEN. III. 1849. Badly faded.

BAGLEY, Clarence B. THE ACQUISITION AND PIONEERING OF OLD OREGON. Seattle: Argus, 1924. OR(Council). IV. Rem. 1852.

BAGLEY, Daniel. SEE: Bagley, Clarence. AQUISITION.

BAGLEY, William L. Maps of Emigrant Trail through Wyoming. LDS. Maps.

BAILEY, David J. Diary. MONHIST. CAL(Leav)-LANDER-MON-TANA(Ft. Hall-Alder Gulch). II+. Rem. 1865.

BAILEY, G. GREAT OVERLAND MAIL REPORT, OCTOBER 18, 1858. In U.S. Postmaster General's Report. Serial 977, pp. 739-41. Stage.

BAILEY, J. Milton. Letters. BANCROFT. CAL(St. Jo?). IV. 1850.

BAILEY, James G. "Journal." In BAILEY HISTORY, ed. Anita Mar-gie Wallace. Tulsa: Author, 1973. CAL(Leav)-ends Green River. II+. 1862.

BAILEY, James L. Diary. ORHIST. OR(Council)-LANDER(?)-BARLOW. III-. 1863.

BAILEY, Lynn R. Ed. Mowry, Sylvester. "Lt. S. Mowry's Report, 1855." Ed. Gray, A. B. SURVEY OF A ROUTE.

BAILEY, Mary S. "Journal." In HO FOR CALIFORNIA, ed. Sandra L. Myres. San Marino: Huntington, 1980. CAL(St. Jo)-SLCUT. III. 1852.

BAILEY, P. A. "Southwestern Adventure and Exploration." SDHIST. CAL-Genl.

BAILEY, Theodore A. Personal Narrative. UTHIST. CAL(Council)-BOZE. 1866. Not Seen.

BAILEY, Thomas A. Ed. Hubbard, Cal. "The Devil's Highway." Ed. Standage, Henry. MARCH OF THE MORMON BATTALION.

BAILEY, Tom. "Mystery of the Vanishing Wagons." OLD WEST 16(Fall 1979): 26-28, 38-40. OR-Genl.

BAILEY, W. F. "Overland by Butterfield Stage." SUNSET, March 1907, 446-52. Stage.

_____. "The Pony Express." CENTURY, Oct 1898, 882-92. Pony.

BAILEY, Walter. "The Barlow Road." OREGON HISTORICAL QUARTERLY 13(Sept 1912): 287-96. BARLOW-Genl.

BAILEY, Washington. A TRIP TO CALIFORNIA IN 1853. Le Roy, IL: Le Roy General, 1915. CAL(Council). IV. Rem. 1853. Stock.

BAILHACHE, John. "Overland Diary, 1850." Napa [CA] JOURNAL, 20 April 1952. Not Seen.

BAILY, Joe. "The Magruder Murder." PACIFIC NORTHWESTERNER 7(Spr 1963): 17-31. Biog-Hill Beachey.

_____. "Mullan's Axe and Shovel Passage." PACIFIC NORTHWESTERNER 2(Win 1958): 1-8. MULLAN-Genl.

BAIRD, Mabel. "Pony Bob and his Comrades." OVERLAND

MONTHLY, December 1914, 598-605. Pony.

BAIRD, William J. Diary. Colorado College Library-Sp Col, Colorado Springs, CO. PIKES(Atchison-Little Blue River). III+. 1859.

BAKER, Abner S., III. "Experience, Personality and Memory: Jesse Applegate and John Minto Recall Pioneer Days." OREGON HISTORICAL QUARTERLY 81(Fall 1980): 229-60. Social.

BAKER, Charles W. Westward Ho! in 1864. MONHIST. CAL(Council)-BOZE. III. 1864.

BAKER, E. M? "Journal of a March of Company A, 1st Regiment of Cavalry Commanded by 1st Lt. E. M. Baker from Fort Churchill to Ruby Valley...." N.p.,n.d. SIMPSON. III. 1861.

BAKER, George H. "Records of a California Journey." QUARTERLY Society of CA Pioneers 7(1930): 217-43. MEX(Vera Cruz-Mexico City-San Blas). III. 1849.

BAKER, George Holbrook. CROSSING THE PLAINS.... Sacramento: Barber & Barber, 1853? Graphics only.

BAKER, Glen, et al. "Barlow Road Unusual Interest Area...Mount Hood National Forest." Oregon State Library, Salem, OR. BARLOW-Genl.

BAKER, Hozial H. OVERLAND JOURNEY TO CARSON VALLEY AND CALIFORNIA. SF: Book Club of California, 1973. CAL(St. Jo)-BRIDGER-SLCUT. III. Rem. 1859.

BAKER, J. H. "A Trail Driver Who Kept a Diary." WICHITA [KS] EAGLE, 21 Aug 1932, p. 15. TEX(Palo Pinto)-OKLAHOMA. III. 1869. Stock.

BAKER, Jean Rio. "By Windjammer and Prairie Schooner London to Salt Lake City." In COVERED WAGON WOMEN, vol. 3, ed. Kenneth L. Holmes. Glendale: Clark, 1983. MORMON. III. 1851.

BAKER, John F. Personal Experiences. Filson Club Library, Louisville, KY. CAL(Leav)-BRIDGER-to SLC then return to origin. Rem. 1854. Not Seen.

BAKER, Lois I. "Joel C. Inman to Oregon in 1852." LANE COUNTY HISTORIAN 8(Nov 1963): 43-52. OR(St. Jo). V. 1852.

BAKER, Richard. THE OVERLAND STAGE IN COLORADO, 1861-1864. Fort Collins, CO: Historical Research Company, 1942. Stage.

BAKER, Sarah A. Papers. Whitman College Library-Eels Northwest Collection, Walla Walla, WA. OR. 1868. Not Seen.

BAKER, William. Diary. CSL. CAL(Council)-BRIDGER-SLCUT-TRUCKEE(Good description). III. 1852.

BALDRIDGE, Michael. A REMINISCENCE OF THE PARKER H. FRENCH EXPEDITION THROUGH TEXAS & MEXICO TO CALIFORNIA IN THE SPRING OF 1850. LA: Private, 1959. CAL-TEX(Galveston)-MEX-GILA. II. Rem. 1850.

BALDRIDGE, William. Days of 1846. BANCROFT. CAL(Chiles-Walker Party). V. Rem. 1843.

BALDWIN, Alfred. Recollections. BANCROFT. OR(Indep)-MEEK. V-. Rem. 1845.

BALDWIN, Elias J. "Lucky." SEE: Glasscock, C. B. LUCKY BALDWIN.

BALDWIN, J. F. DIARY KEPT BY J. F. BALDWIN...1850. SF: California Patron & Agriculturist, 1887. CAL(St. Jo)-SLCUT. III. 1850.

BALDWIN, Lewis. Diary. Held by Fred A. Rosenstock, Denver, CO. OR. 1849. Not Seen.

BALDWIN, Orval F., II. Ed. Otto, Olive H. "A Mormon Bride."

BALDWIN, W. W. Ed. Duffield, George C. "Driving Cattle."

BALDY, Henry T. Diary. DENVERPUB. CAL(Council)-TRUCKEE-BECK. II+. 1852.

BALF, Mary. THE OVERLANDERS AND OTHER NORTH THOMPSON TRAVELERS. Kamloops?: Kamloops Museum, 1973. CANADA-Genl.

BALL, Larry D. "Federal Justice on the Santa Fe Trail...." MISSOURI HISTORICAL REVIEW 81(Oct 1986). Not Seen.

BALL, Thomas S. and Harriet. Eds. Cook, Peter. LIFE.

BALLANTYNE, Robert M. HANDBOOK TO THE NEW GOLD FIELDS...OF THE FRASER AND THOMPSON RIVER GOLD MINES. Edinburgh: Strahan, 1858. Guide.

_____. HUDSON'S BAY. Edinburgh: Blackwood, 1868. CANADA(York Factory-Norway House-Stone Fort-Ft. Garry). II. 1842. Graphics.

BALLANTYRE, Richard. Memorandum. MORMON(Ends Belle Fourche River, WY). III-. 1848.

BALLARD, Henry. Private Journal. UTHIST. MORMON. III. 1864.

BALLEW, Horace M. Letters. BANCROFT. CAL(St. Jo). V. 1850.

BALLING, E. E. "The Mexico Trails of '49." MA thesis, Univ. of Southern California, 1933. MEX-1849-Genl. Missing.

BALTIMORE, J. M. "In the Prime of the Buffalo." OVERLAND MONTHLY, October 1889, 515-20. Fauna.

BANCROFT'S GUIDE FOR TRAVELERS BY RAILWAY, STAGE AND STEAM NAVIGATION IN THE PACIFIC STATES. SF: Bancroft, 1869. Guide.

"Bancroft's Guide to the Colorado Mines, 1863." CALIFORNIA HISTORICAL QUARTERLY 12(Mar 1933): 3-10. BRADSHAW-Genl.

BANDEL, Eugene. FRONTIER LIFE IN THE ARMY, 1854-1861. Trans. Olga Bandel and Richard Jente. The Southwest Historical Series, No. 11, ed. Ralph P. Bieber. Glendale: Clark, 1932. CAL(Leav.). III. 1858. BEALE(LA-Ft. Mohave). III. 1859.

BANDY, William R. "Mysterious Parsons Bridge." MONTANA 13(Sept 1963): 77-80. Geog.

BANKS, Henry P. Diary. MO-WHMC. CAL(St. Jo)-SLCUT. III. 1852.

BANKS, John E. "Diary, 1849." In THE BUCKEYE ROVERS IN THE GOLD RUSH. Ed. Howard E. Scamehorn. Athens, OH: Ohio Univ. Press, 1965. CAL(St. Jo)-TRUCKEE. II. 1849.

Banning Company. Collection, 1830-1885. HUNTL. Stage-CA.

BANNING, George H. "Stage Wheels over the Padre's Trail." WESTWAYS 26(Jul 1934): 16-17, 33. Stage-CA.

BANNING, William and George H. "Dust of the Swift-Wagon; a

Glimpse of John Butterfield and...Great Southern Overland Mail." TOURING TOPICS 22(Feb 1930): 14-19. Stage.

_____. "Pony Express and the Man Who Paid for It." SUNSET 61(Sept 1928): 13-15, 66. Pony.

_____. "Six-Horse California." TOURING TOPICS 21(Jul 1929): 26-30, 48-49. Stage.

_____. SIX HORSES. NY: Century, 1928. Stage.

_____. "Wheel Tracks of the 'Jackass Mail.'" TOURING TOPICS 21(Nov 1929): 21-25, 84. Stage. Graphics.

BARBER, James V. "The History of Highways in Utah from 1847-1869." MS thesis, Univ. of Utah, 1949. Utah.

BARBER, T. M. Diary. NBHIST. MORMON-Ends North Platte. 1851. Not Seen.

BARCLAY, Alexander. THE ADVENTURES OF ALEXANDER BARCLAY.... Denver: Old West, 1976. SANTA FE-Genl.

BARDIN, James. Diary. BANCROFT. CAL(Indep)-LASSEN. II+. 1855.

BARI, Valeska, ed. THE COURSE OF EMPIRE. NY: Coward-Mc-Cann, 1931. CAL-1849-Genl.

BARKER, Amselm H. DIARY OF 1858 FROM PLATTSMOUTH TO CHERRY CREEK. Ed. Nolie Mumey. Denver: Golden Bell, 1959. PIKES(Plattsmouth). III+. 1858.

BARKER, Emerson N. EARLY COLORADO MAILS. Denver: Nelson, n.d. Mail.

BARKER, Joel. "Colorado Mail Service, 1859-1885." COLORADO MAGAZINE 49(Sum 1972): 219-37. Mail.

BARKER, Watson. "Wading to California: The Influence of the Forty-Niners on the Notion of a Great American Desert." GREAT PLAINS JOURNAL 3(Spr 1964): 35-43. CAL-1849-Genl.

BARLOW ROAD. Portland: Wasco and Clackamas Counties Historical Societies, 1976. BARLOW-Genl.

BARLOW, Samuel Kimbrough. SEE: Wilkins, Mary B. "Pioneer Road Builder."

BARLOW, William. "Reminiscences of Seventy Years." OREGON HISTORICAL QUARTERLY 13(Sept 1912): 240-86. OR(Indep). IV. Rem. 1845.

BARNARD, Helen M. THE CHORPENNING CLAIM. N.p.: M'Intosh, 187? Mail. Stage.

BARNES, Cass C. THE SOD HOUSE. Lincoln: Univ. of Nebraska Press, 1970. Freight.

BARNES, Charles M. "Memoirs of Col. George H. Giddings." SAN ANTONIO EXPRESS, 4-11-18-25 May, 1 June 1902. Biog. Stage.

BARNES, Demas. FROM THE ATLANTIC TO THE PACIFIC, OVERLAND: A SERIES OF LETTERS. NY: Van Nostrand, 1866. CAL(By stage-Atchison-Denver-SLC-SF). IV. 1866. Stage.

BARNES, Joseph W. Ed. Evershed, Thomas. "Journal."

BARNES, Mary S. Pacific Slope Mss, 1769-1895. Stanford Univ. Library-Sp Col, Palo Alto, CA. Extensive holding. Overland-Genl.

BARNES, Sarah J. A Journal. HUNTL. CAL(St. Jo). III-. 1856.

BARNES, Thomas L. Biography. BANCROFT. CAL. V-. Rem. 1854.

BARNETT, Elias. SEE: Scalf, Henry P. THE OVERLAND LETTER.

BARNETT, Joel. A LONG TRIP IN A PRAIRIE SCHOONER. Whittier, CA: Author, 1928. OR(Council)-LANDER. III. Rem. 1859.

BARNEY, James. "Maricopa Wells, A Famous Stage Station of Pioneer Days." SHERIFF 9(Aug-Sept 1955): 57, 59, 61, 63, 65, 67, 69. Geog.

_____. "The Oatman Massacre." SHERIFF 7(Oct-Nov, Dec 1948): 11-13, 24-25, 13, 24-25; 8(Jan 1949): 6, 18-19. Indians.

BARNEY, Lewis. History. UTHIST. MORMON. III-. 1847.

BARNEY, Libeus. LETTERS OF THE PIKE'S PEAK GOLD RUSH. 1907? Reprint. San Jose, CA: Talisman, 1959. PIKES(By stage to Denver). 1859. Stage.

BARNHILL, J. Herschel. "The Way West: The California Trail." RED RIVER VALLEY HISTORICAL REVIEW 6(Sum 1981): 68-76. MARCY(Oklahoma portion).

BARRAS, Judy. THE LONG ROAD TO TEHACHAPI.... Tehachapi, CA: Author, 1976. CAL-Genl.

BARRETT, Glen. Ed. Anderson, John C. MACKINAWS DOWN.

BARRETT, J. William. Ed. Joscelyn, Amos. P. OVERLAND JOURNAL.

BARRETT, James T. "Cholera in Missouri." MISSOURI HISTORICAL REVIEW 55(Jul 1961): 344-54. Medical.

BARRETT, Lenora. "Transportation, Supplies, and Quarters for the West Texas Frontier...1848-1861." WESTX 5(Jun 1929): 87-99. Military. TEXAS-Genl.

BARRETT-LENNARD, C. E. TRAVELS IN BRITISH COLUMBIA. 8 vols. London: N.p., 1862. Not Seen.

BARROWS, H. D. "Don David W. Alexander." ANNUAL PUBLICATION Historical Society of Southern California 4(1897): 43-45. SPANISH. V-. 1841.

_____. "A Two Thousand Mile Stage Ride." PUBLICATION Historical Society of Southern California 3(1896): 40-50. Stage(SF--St. Louis via Butterfield). V. 1860.

BARROWS, William. THE GENERAL: OR TWELVE NIGHTS IN A HUNTER'S CAMP. Boston: Lee & Shepard, 1869. CAL(Council). IV. Rem. 1850.

BARRY, J. Neilson. Ed. Rector, W. H. "Biography."

_____. "The Discovery of the Oregon Trail." PACIFIC NORTHWEST QUARTERLY 28(Oct 1937): 410-12. Geog: South Pass.

_____. "Fort Reed and Fort Boise." OREGON HISTORICAL QUARTERLY 34(Mar 1933): 60-67. Geog.

_____. "The Murals in the State Capitol." OREGON HISTORICAL QUARTERLY 40(June 1939): 149-60. Graphics.

_____. "On the Plains in 1852." OREGON HISTORICAL QUARTERLY 29(Jun 1928): 209-10. OR(Fragment). V. 1852.

BARRY, Louise. Ed. Clark, John H. "Overland to the Gold Fields." Ed. Richardson, Albert D. "Letters." Ed. Robinson, Charles. "Yankee '49er."

_____. THE BEGINNING OF THE WEST: ANNALS OF THE KANSAS GATEWAY TO THE AMERICAN WEST, 1540-1854. Topeka: Kansas State Historical Society, 1972. Bib.

_____. "Fort Aubrey." KANSAS HISTORICAL QUARTERLY 39(Sum 1973): 188-99. Geog.

_____. "The Fort Leavenworth - Fort Gibson Military Road and the Founding of Fort Scott." KANSAS HISTORICAL QUARTERLY 11(Spr 1942): 115-29. Military. Maps.

_____. "The Ranch at Cimarron Crossing." KANSAS HISTORICAL QUARTERLY 39(Aut 1973): 345-66. Geog.

_____. "The Ranch at Cow Creek Crossing (Beach Valley P.O.)." KANSAS HISTORICAL QUARTERLY 38(Win 1972): 416-44. Geog.

_____. "The Ranch at Little Arkansas Crossing." KANSAS HISTORICAL QUARTERLY 38(Aut 1972): 287-94. Geog.

_____. "Ranch at the Great Bend." KANSAS HISTORICAL QUARTERLY 39(Spr 1973): 96-100. Geog.

_____. "The Ranch at Walnut Creek Crossing." KANSAS HISTORICAL QUARTERLY 37(Sum 1971): 121-47. Geog.

BARSNESS, Richard W. "Los Angeles' Quest for Improved Transportation, 1846-1861." CALIFORNIA HISTORICAL QUARTERLY 46(Dec 1967): 291-306. Stage.

BARTHOLOMEW, Jacob. Diary. LILLEY. CAL(St. Jo)-Ends near Beowawe, NV. III. 1850.

BARTLETT, John Russell. Papers. Brown University Library, Providence, RI. Not Seen.

_____. PERSONAL NARRATIVE OF EXPLORATIONS AND INCIDENTS.... NY: Appleton, 1854. CAL-TEX-MEX-GILA. I. 1850-53. Govt.

BARTLETT, Lanier. SEE: Bell, Horace. ON THE OLD WEST COAST.

BARTLETT, Richard A. GREAT SURVEYS OF THE AMERICAN WEST. Norman: Univ. of Oklahoma Press, 1962. Govt.

BARTON, H. D. Diary. CSL. CAL(Council)-MORMON-SIMPSON(Crossed Sierra via Ione-Wellington-Walker River). III-. 1865.

BARTON, William K. COPY OF DIARY.... SLC: N.p., 1966. MORMON. 1852. Not Seen.

BASHORE, Melvin A. "Index to Art Works in LDS Church Periodicals." LDS Church Library, SLC. 1979. Graphics.

BASKERVILLE, William. Diary. DENVERPUB. CAL(Santa Fe)-RIO GRANDE-GILA. II+. 1852. BEALE(Tejon Pass-Santa Fe). II+. 1853.

BATCHELDER, Amos. Journal. BANCROFT. CAL(Indep)-LASSEN. I. 1849.

BATES, Alice L. "The History of the Telegraph in California." PUBLICATION Historical Society of Southern California 9(1914): 181-87. Telegraph.

BATTEY, Marion W. SCENES AND ADVENTURES OF AN OVERLAND JOURNEY TO CALIFORNIA. San Jose, CA: Historical Landmarks Comm., n.d. Not Seen.

BATTY, Donald M. "History of Early Roads and Freighting in the Eastern Uintah Basin, 1672-1920." MA thesis, Utah State Univ., 1970. Utah.

BATTY, Joseph. OVER THE WILDS TO CALIFORNIA.... Leeds, England: J. Parrott, 1867. CAL. V. 1859?

BAUDLE, James A. Diary. BYU. CAL(Savannah)-LASSEN. II. 1849.

BAUER, John E. "The Health Factor in the Gold Rush Era." PACIFIC HISTORICAL REVIEW 18(Feb 1949): 97-108. Medical.

_____. "The Health Seeker in the Westward Movement, 1830-1900." MISSISSIPPI VALLEY HISTORICAL REVIEW 46(Jun 1959): 91-110. Medical.

BAXTER, Don J. GATEWAYS TO CALIFORNIA. N.p.: Pacific Gas & Electric, 1968. Geog-Sierra Passes.

BAXTER, John O. "Las Carneradas: New Mexico's Sheep Trade to Chihuahua and Durango before 1846." MA thesis, Univ. of New Mexico, 1982. Stock. RIO GRANDE-Genl.

BAYARD, William. MEMORIAL OF WILLIAM BAYARD, PROPOSING TO CONVEY THE MAIL FROM ST. LOUIS TO THE PACIFIC ONCE A WEEK.... 31st Cong., 1st sess., n.d. S. Misc. Doc. 2. Mail.

BAYDO, Gerald R. "Cattle Ranching in Territorial New Mexico." PhD diss., Univ. of New Mexico, 1970. Stock.

_____. "Overland from Missouri to Washington Territory in 1854." NEBRASKA HISTORY 52(Spr 1971): 65-87. OR(Council)-WASH. III. 1854.

BAYLESS, Ralph W. "The Pony Express Rider and His Bible." BIBLE SOCIETY RECORD 83(Feb 1938): 31-33. Pony.

BAYLESS, (Bayliss) William H. Diary. DENVERPUB. PIKES(Council?). III. 1860.

BAYLEY, Betsey. "Letter." In COVERED WAGON WOMEN, vol 1, ed. Kenneth L. Holmes. Glendale: Clark, 1983. OR-MEEK. V. 1845.

BAYLEY, Thomas S. "The First Overland Mail Bag for California." DENVERPUB. CAL(Indep)-HALL. IV. Rem. 1848. Mail.

BAYLOR, George W. "Scout to Quitman Canyon." TEXAS MILITARY HISTORY 6(Sum 1967): 149-59. TEX-Genl.

_____. "Tragedies of the Old Overland Stage Route." FRONTIER TIMES 26(Mar 1949): 125-29. Indians.

BEADLE, Elisha. "Letter, June 26, 1853." ORACLE [Pottsville, PA], ? January 1854. CSL. MORMON(Ft. Laramie-SLC). IV. 1853.

BEADLE, J. H. THE UNDEVELOPED WEST; OR, FIVE YEARS IN THE TERRITORIES. Philadelphia: National, 1873. Freight. Fine graphics.

BEAL, Josiah. A Trip. ORHIST. OR(St. Jo). V-. Rem. 1847.

BEALE, Edward Fitzgerald. SEE: Bonsal, Stephen. EDWARD FITZGERALD BEALE.

_____. Collection. HUNTL. Biog.

_____. Diary. BANCROFT. CAL(Ft. Smith)-SANTA FE-BEALE. II. 1858-59.

_____. REPORT...WAGON ROAD FROM FORT DEFIANCE TO THE COLORADO RIVER, 1857-8. 35th Cong., 1st sess., H. Ex. Doc. 124. BEALE. II+. 1857.

BEALL, Frank E. A Dream of an Empire. MONHIST. CAL(Neb. City)-HALL-MONTANA(Ft. Hall-Alder Gulch). III. Rem. 1864.

BEALS, David T., III. "The Leavenworth and Pikes Peak Express Companies." WESTERN EXPRESS 25(Oct 1975): 3-14. Mail-Graphics.

BEAN, George W. SEE: Dees, Harry C. "George Washington Bean."

_____. "The Journal of George W. Bean." Ed. Harry C. Dees. NEVADA HISTORICAL SOCIETY QUARTERLY 15(Fall 1972): 3-30. SLCOR. IV. 1855.

_____. Report. LDS. SIMPSON(SLC-Egan Canyon?). V. 1855. Map.

BEARD, Doris. Ed. Tolles, James S. TRAILS AND TRIALS OF '49.

BEARD, Franklin. Ed. Hopper, Charles. PILGRIMS OF THE PACIFIC.

BEARD, John W. SADDLES EAST: HORSEBACK OVER THE OLD OREGON TRAIL. Portland: Binfords & Mort, 1949. OR-Genl.

BEARSS, Ed., and Arrell M. Gibson. FORT SMITH. Norman: Univ. of Oklahoma Press, 1969. Geog.

BEASLEY, Delilah L. THE NEGRO TRAIL BLAZERS OF CALIFORNIA. NY: Negro Universities Press, 1919. Social.

BEATTIE, George William. Ed. Brown, John. "Diary, 1862." Ed. Jaeger, L. J. F. "Diary of a Ferryman."

_____. "Development of Travel between Southern Arizona and Los Angeles as It Related to the San Bernardino Valley." PUBLICATIONS Historical Society of Southern California 13(1925): 228-57. BRADSHAW-Genl. Map.

_____. "Historic Crossing Places in the San Bernardino Mountains." In George William and Helen P. Beatty Collection. HUNTL. Geog.

_____. "San Bernardino Valley before the Americans Came. CALIFORNIA HISTORICAL SOCIETY 12(Jun 1933): 111-24. Geog.

BEATTY, Willard W. Ed. Lockett, H. C. ALONG THE BEALE TRAIL.

BECHDOLT, Frederich R. "Story of the Overland Mail." SATURDAY EVENING POST, 17 January 1920, 48-54. Stage.

BECK, Morris H. Letters. BANCROFT. CAL(Council). V. 1850.

BECKER, Robert H. Ed. Christy, Thomas. THOMAS CHRISTY'S ROAD. Ed. Wagner, Henry R., and Charles L. Camp. THE PLAINS AND THE ROCKIES.

BECKHAM, Nellie. "Thenea's Bean." ORHIST. OR(Indep). IV.

Rem. 1867.

BECKHAM, Stephen D. "The Barlow Road." OVERLAND JOURNAL 2(Sum 1984): 4-29. BARLOW-Genl.

_____. "The Oregon Trail in Oregon." Salem?: Oregon State Parks System, 1974. OR-Genl. Pres.

BECKLER, Marion. "When Stage Coaches Came to Vallecito...." DESERT 13(Jan 1950): 11-14. Geog. Stage.

BECKMAN, Peter. "The Overland Trade and Atchison's Beginnings." In TERRITORIAL KANSAS. Lawrence, KS: Univ. of Kansas Publications, 1954. Geog.

BECKWITH, E. G. REPORT OF EXPLORATION OF A ROUTE FOR THE PACIFIC RAILROAD, NEAR THE 38TH AND 39TH PARALLELS. 33rd Cong., 2nd sess., S. Ex. Doc. 78. SANTA FE(Leav)-SPANISH(Ends SLC). II+. 1853. Govt. Gunnison's Survey.

BECKWITH, Frank. "Shameful Friday - A Critical Study of the Mountain Meadows Massacre." HUNTL. SLCOR-1857-Genl. Geog. Carefully researched revisionist and anti-LDS study.

BECKWITH, Ruth. "Stage House toward the Hills." DENVER WESTERNERS BRAND BOOK 10(1954): 65-94. Geog.

BEEBE, Beatrice B. "Hunting for the Blue Bucket Diggings." OVERLAND MONTHLY, August 1929, 252, 255. OR(Eugene?-Burnt River). V-. Rem. 1861.

BEEBE, Lucius. "King of the Stagecoach Drivers." HOLIDAY, September 1953, 10-14. Biog-Hank Monk.
_____, and Charles Clegg. U.S. WEST: THE SAGA OF WELLS FARGO. NY: E. P. Dutton, 1949. Stage-graphics.

BEECHER, Maureen U. "Women at Winter Quarters." SUNSTONE 8(Jul-Aug 1983): 11-19. MORMON-1847-Genl.

BEECHING, Robert. Diary. HUNTL. CAL-TEX(Galveston)-GILA. II. 1849.

BEEHRER, George W. "Freighting across the Plains." Ed. Julie B. Colyer. MONTANA 12(Oct 1962): 2-17. CAL(Neb. City)-BRIDGER(Ends SLC). V. Rem. 1858. Freight.

BEERS, Henry P. "The Army and the Oregon Trail to 1848." PACIFIC NORTHWEST QUARTERLY 28(Oct 1937): 339-62. Military.

_____. "A History of the U.S. Topographical Engineers, 1816-1863." MILITARY ENGINEER (June, July 1942): 287-91, 348-52. Military.

BEERS, Lewis (Louis). Across the Continent. UPAC. CAL(St. Jo). I. 1852.

BEESLEY, Clarissa A. "The Mormon Pioneer Caravan of 1931." IMPROVEMENT ERA 34(Aug 1931): 573-75. Pres.

BEESLEY, E. Maurice. Diary. NVHIST. CAL(Indep)-HALL-TRUCKEE. III. 1849.

BEESON, John. A PLEA FOR THE INDIANS.... NY: Author, 1857. OR(Council?)-APPLE. IV. 1853.

BEESON, Welborn. WELBORN BEESON ON THE OREGON TRAIL IN 1853. Ed. Bert Webber. Medford, OR: N.p., 1986. OR(Council)-APPLE. II+. 1853.

BEETON, Barbara. "James Hervey Simpson in the Great Basin." MON-

TANA 28(Jan 1978): 28-44. Biog. SIMPSON-Genl.

BEGBIE, Matthew B. "Journey into the Interior of British Columbia." JOURNAL OF THE ROYAL GEOGRAPHICAL SOCIETY 31(1861): 237-48. CANADA-Genl.

BEGGES, James G. Diary. BARKER. Stage-1860-Overland.

BEIDLEMAN, Richard G. Ed. Suckley, George. "The 1859 Overland Journal."

_____. "Nathaniel Wyeth's Fort Hall." OREGON HISTORICAL QUARTERLY 58(Sept 1957): 197-250. Geog.

BEITLEMAN, John L. "An Attack on the Stage Stations." TRAIL 2(Jun 1909): 5-9. Stage-1864.

BEK, William G. Ed. Keil, William. "From Bethel."

BEKEART, Philip B. Ed. Reading, Pierson B. "Journal."

BELANGER, Art J. THE CALGARY-EDMONTON, EDMONTON-CALGARY TRAIL. Calgary: Frontier, 1973. CANADA-Genl.

BELDE, Walter W. "Red River Trails A, B, C, and BC." MNHIST. DAKOTAS-Maps-Genl.

BELDEN, Josiah. "The First Overland Emigrant Trail to New California." TOURING TOPICS, June 1930, 14-18, 56. CAL(Indep)-HALL. IV. Rem. 1841.

_____. JOSIAH BELDEN 1841 CALIFORNIA OVERLAND PIONEER. Ed. Doyce B. Nunis, Jr. Georgetown, CA: Talisman, 1962. CAL(Indep)-HALL. III. Rem. 1841.

BELDON, L. Burr. "Camp Cady, Army Post on the Mojave, Guards Southland." San Bernardino SUN-TELEGRAM, 23 December 1951, n.p. Geog.

_____. DEATH VALLEY HEROINE. San Bernardino: Inland, 1954. SLCOR-1849-Death Valley.

_____. "Forgotten Army Forts of the Mojave." LOS ANGELES WESTERNERS BRAND BOOK 11(1964): 93-102. BEALE-Genl.

_____. GOODBYE, DEATH VALLEY. Death Valley '49ers Pub. No. 4. San Bernardino: '49ers, 1956. SLCOR-Death Valley-Genl.

_____. "Hostile Indian Attacks...." San Bernardino EVENING TELEGRAM, 4 September 1960, 8-10. BEALE-Genl.

_____. "Indian Attacks Beset Mailmen, Mojave Stages." San Bernardino SUN-TELEGRAM, 20 January 1952, n.p. BEALE-Genl.

BELKNAP, Kitturah P. "Commentaries." (In) COVERED WAGON WOMEN, Vol. 1., ed. Kenneth L. Holmes. Glendale: Clark, 1983. OR(Council)-HALL(Ends Ft. Hall). IV. Rem. 1848.

BELL, Eli. A History. LDS. SLCOR. II. 1854.

BELL, James C., Jr. OPENING A HIGHWAY TO THE PACIFIC: 1838-1846. Vol. 96, No. 1 of Columbia University Studies in History, Economics and Public Law. NY: Columbia, 1921. OR-Genl.

BELL, James G. "A Log of the Texas-California Cattle Trail, 1854." SOUTHWESTERN HISTORICAL QUARTERLY 35(Jan-Apr 1932): 208-37. CAL-TEX(San Antonio)-GILA. II+. 1854. Stock.

BELL, Josias F. Sketches. NEWBERRY. CAL(Indep)-SANTA FE-RIO GRANDE(Ends El Paso). II. 1841. RIO GRANDE-MEX(Bavispe-Guaymas). II. 1842.

BELL, Lizzie. Papers. San Francisco Public Library-California Collection. CAL. 1865. Not Seen.

BELL, Stella J. Ed. Jaques, John. LIFE HISTORY.

BELL, William A. NEW TRACKS IN NORTH AMERICA. 2 vols. London: Chapman & Hall, 1870. CAL(Salina)-SANTA FE- RIO GRANDE-GILA. II. 1867. Stage(SF-SLC-Denver-Salina). II. 1868.

BELSHAW, George. "Belshaw Journey, Oregon Trail, 1853." Ed. Gwen Castle. OREGON HISTORICAL QUARTERLY 32(Sept 1931): 217-39. OR(Council). IV. 1853.

BELSHAW, Maria P. "Diary of a Bride Written on the Trail in 1853." Ed. J. W. Ellison. OREGON HISTORICAL QUARTERLY 33(Dec 1932): 318-33. OR(Grand Ronde-Portland). III. 1853.

BEMIS, Edwin A. "Wagon Master." DENVER WESTERNERS BRAND BOOK (1952): 141-56. Freight.

BEMIS, Samuel F. "Captain John Mullan and the Engineers' Frontier." WASHINGTON HISTORICAL QUARTERLY 14(July 1923): 201-5. MULLAN-Genl.

BEMIS, Stephen A. RECOLLECTIONS.... St. Louis: Private, 1932. CAL. 1860. Not Seen.

BENDER, Averam B. SEE: With Ralph P. Bieber. EXPLORING SOUTHWESTERN TRAILS.

_____. "Government Explorations in the Territory of New Mexico, 1846-1859." NEW MEXICO HISTORICAL REVIEW 9(1934): 1-32. Govt.

_____. "Military Transportation in the Southwest, 1848-1860." NEW MEXICO HISTORICAL REVIEW 32(Apr 1957): 123-50. Military. Freight.

_____. "Opening Routes across West Texas, 1848-1850." SOUTH-WESTERN HISTORICAL QUARTERLY 37(Oct 1933): 116-35. TEX-Genl.

_____. "The Texas Frontier, 1848-1861; II, Government Explorations in Texas, 1851-1860." SOUTHWESTERN HISTORICAL QUARTERLY 38(Oct 1934): 135-48. TEX-Genl.

BENDER, Flora I. "Notes By the Way...1863." NEVADA HISTORI-CAL SOCIETY QUARTERLY 1(Sum 1958): 145-73. CAL(Elkhorn City)-BRIDGER-SIMPSON. III. 1863.

BENEDICT, Gilbert. Reminiscence. MONHIST. DAKOTAS(St. Paul)-MONTANA. III. Rem. 1864.

BENJAMIN, Israel J. THREE YEARS IN AMERICA, 1859-1862. 2 vols. Philadelphia: Jewish Pub. Society, 1952. Stage(SF-Atchison). II. 1861.

BENJAMIN, Theodosia. "The Audubon Party - New York to California, 1849." PACIFIC HISTORIAN 12(Fall 1968): 7-27. CAL-1849-Genl.

BENNETT, Betty. "Colorado's Smoky Hill Trail." SOUTHWEST HERITAGE 3(Jun 1969): 35-37. PIKES-Genl.

BENNETT, Debra Sue. "Dress of the Mormons Who Traveled through Scotts Bluff, Nebraska between 1840 and 1860." MS thesis, Iowa State University, 1976. Social. Graphics.

BENNETT, Elmer F. "Pioneer Women in the Rush to the Rockies."

CORRAL DUST 4(Jun 1959): 9-10. Social.

BENNETT, James. OVERLAND JOURNEY.... Ed. Edward Eberstadt. New Harmony, IN: New Harmony Times, 1906. CAL(St. Jo). II. 1850.

BENNETT, Lucy J. Reminiscence. HUNTL. OR-MEEK. V-. Rem. 1845.

BENNETT, Richard E. "Mormons at the Missouri: A History of the Latter-Day Saints at Winter Quarters and at Kanesville, 1846-52...." PhD diss., Wayne State Univ., 1984. MORMON-Genl. Geog.

BENNETT, Robert A. A SMALL WORLD OF OUR OWN. Walla Walla, WA: Pioneer, 1985. OR-Genl.

_____, comp. WE'LL ALL GO HOME IN THE SPRING.... Walla Walla, WA: Pioneer, 1984. Overland-Genl.

BENNETT, William P. THE FIRST BABY IN CAMP. SLC: Rancher, 1893. Stage.

BENNETT, Winston. "A Pioneer of 1843." San Jose PIONEER, 26 May, 2 June 1877, p. 1. OR(Indep). V. 1842. OR-CAL. V. 1843.

BENNION, Israel. "Before the Arrowhead Trail." IMPROVEMENT ERA 29(Apr 1926): 542-44. SLCOR-Genl.

BENNION, Kenneth S. "On the Trail of the Overland Stage." IMPROVEMENT ERA 34(Sept 1931): 658-61. Stage.

BENNION, Owen C. "Good Indian Spring." UTAH HISTORICAL QUARTERLY 52(Sum 1984): 256-63. SIMPSON-Genl. Geog.

BENSELL, Dr. Reminiscence. Ed. Margaret Bensell Rich. Oregon State Library, Salem, OR. CAL(St Jo). V-. Rem. 1854.

BENSON, Gwen P. Ed. Pack, John. "Biography."

BENSON, John E. Forty-Niner. BANCROFT. CAL(St. Jo)-BRIDGER-SLCUT-LASSEN. II+. 1849.

BENSON, John H. From St. Joseph.... BANCROFT. CAL(St. Jo)-BRIDGER-SLCUT-LASSEN. III+. 1849.

BENSON, Mr. & Mrs. Robert R. "Trinchera Plaza, CO, on Charles Goodnight's Trail to Iliff Ranch." COHIST. Stock. Geog.

BENTON, Delford. Diary. BANCROFT. CAL(Old Ft. Kearny). 1850. Not Seen.

BEOUGHER, Edward M. "Early Day Tranportation in Western Kansas." KSHIST. Stage-Kansas. Pres.

BEPLER, Doris W. "Descriptive Catalog of Western Historical Materials in California Periodicals, 1854-1890." MA thesis, Univ. of California-Berkeley, 1920. Bib.

BERESFORD, J. H. Diary. Ohio Historical Society Library, Columbus, OH. CAL(Indep)-Ends near Elko. II. 1852.

BERGE, Dale L. "The Gila Bend Stage Station." KIVA 33(Apr 1968): 169-243. Stage. Geog.

BERKELEY, George C. THE ENGLISH SPORTSMAN IN THE WESTERN PRAIRIES. London: Hurst & Blackwell, 1861. CAL(Kansas City-Ft. Riley-St. Jo). II. 1859.

BERKIN, William. Reminiscence. MONHIST. MONTANA-1860-Freight.

BERMINGHAM, Twiss. "To Utah by Hand." AMERICAN LEGION MAGAZINE 23(Jul 1937): 24-28, 58-61. MORMON. II. 1856.

BERNARD, Sam. "Recollections." (In) Alf Dixon. "Across the Plains in '40." SAN FRANCISCO CALL, 11 November 1892, n.p. CAL(SLC). Exact route unknown. Rem. 1841. Not Seen.

BERRIEN, Joseph W. "Overland from St. Louis to the California Gold Field in 1849...." Eds. Ted and Caryl Hinckley. INDIANA MAGAZINE OF HISTORY 56(Dec 1960): 237-352. CAL(St. Jo)-HALL. I. 1849.

BERRY, Gerald L. THE WHOOP-UP TRAIL. Edmonton, Alberta: Applied Art, 1953. CANADA-Genl.

BERRY, Swift. CENTRAL OVERLAND PONY EXPRESS ROUTE AND STATIONS IN CALIFORNIA. Placerville, CA: Central Overland Pony Express Trail Assn., 1956. PONY.

BERRY, William & Thomas. Contract. MO-WHMC. Train Govt.

BERTHOLD, Victor M. SEE: With Henry C. Needham, "Hand-Stamped Franks."

_____. "Franks of the Western Express Companies." COLLECTORS CLUB PHILATELIST 5(July, Oct 1926): 129-39, 203-14. Mail.

_____. "Gregory's Expresses." COLLECTORS CLUB PHILATELIST, Oct 1932. Not Seen. Mail.

_____. HANDBOOK OF WELLS FARGO & COMPANY'S HANDSTAMPS. NY: Scott Stamp & Coin, 1926. Stage. Mail.

_____. "Notes for a Biography of Ben Holladay." Location unknown. Not Seen.

_____. "Todd's Express Companies." COLLECTORS CLUB PHILATELIST, Apr, 1932. Mail. Not Seen.

_____. "William H. Russell, Origin and Development of the Famous Pony Express." COLLECTORS CLUB PHILATELIST 8(Jan, Apr 1929): 1-19, n.p. Biog. PONY.

BERTHOUD, E. L. SEE: With S. W. Burt. THE ROCKY MOUNTAIN GOLD REGIONS.

BERTHRONG, Donald J. Ed. Conner, D. E. A CONFEDERATE IN THE COLORADO GOLD FIELDS.

BETTELYOUN, Susan B. Interviews. NBHIST. Indians.

BETTIS, Gary. Comp. With Judith Austin. "Preliminary Checklist."

BETTS, William J. Ed. Flett, John. "From Red River."

BEUMAN, Edna L. "The Story of Fort Churchill and Samuel Buckland, Pioneer." NVHIST. Geog.

BEVRIDGE, Leroy, and Company. Records. MONHIST. Stage.

"Bibliography of Indexes to LDS Sources and Utah Periodicals." UTHIST. Bib.

BICENTENNIAL Pony Express Coordinators. "Nevada Pony Express Route: Historic Digest and Interim Recreation Management Plan." Reno: USBLM, 1975. Pony.

BICENTENNIAL WAGON TRAIN PILGRIMAGE. Kenosha, WI:

Jem, 1977. Pres.

BICKFORD, William H. Diary. BANCROFT. CAL(Indep?)-LAS-SEN. III. 1849.

BIDDLE, B. R. "Diary." Springfield ILLINOIS JOURNAL, May 13, 20, 24; June 6, 8, 17; December 6, 7, 10-15, 17-20, 1849. CAL. 1849. Not Seen.

BIDLACK, Russell E., ed. LETTERS HOME: THE STORY OF ANN ARBOR'S FORTY-NINERS. Ann Arbor: Ann Arbor Publications, 1960. CAL-1849-Genl.

BIDWELL, John. ECHOES OF THE PAST ABOUT CALIFORNIA. Ed. Milo M. Quaife. Lakeside Classics No. 26. Chicago: Donnelley & Sons, 1928. CAL(Indep). II. Rem. 1841.

_____. "The First Emigrant Train to California." CENTURY, Nov 1890, 105-30, 151. CAL(Indep). III. Rem. 1841.

_____. JOHN BIDWELL'S TRIP TO CALIFORNIA, 1841 - THE FIRST EMIGRANT PARTY TO CALIFORNIA BY WAGON TRAIN.... Ed. Francis P. Farquhar. Berkeley: Friends of the Bancroft Library, 1964. CAL(Indep). II. Rem. 1841. Map.

_____. Papers. CSL. CAL-1841-Genl.

_____. "Route Travelled from Cairo, Illinois to Reach Missouri in 1839...and California in 1841." HUNTL. CAL-1841-Genl-Map.

_____, Hubert Howe Bancroft, and James Longmire. FIRST THREE WAGON TRAINS: TO CALIFORNIA, 1841; TO OREGON, 1842; TO WASHINGTON, 1853. Portland: Binfords & Mort, n.d. Overland-Genl.

BIEBER, Ralph P. Ed. Bandel, Eugene. FRONTIER LIFE IN THE ARMY. Ed. Clark, Bennett C. DIARY. Ed. McCoy, Joseph G. HISTORIC SKETCHES. Ed. Webb, James. "Papers." Ed. Willing, George M. "Diary of a Journey."

_____, ed. SOUTHERN TRAILS TO CALIFORNIA IN 1849. Vol. 5 of the Southwest Historical Series. Glendale: Clark, 1937. CAL-1849-Genl.

_____. "The Southwestern Trails to California in 1849." MISSISSIPPI VALLEY HISTORICAL REVIEW 12(Dec 1925): 342-75. CAL-1849-Genl.

_____, and A. B. Bender, eds. EXPLORING SOUTHWESTERN TRAILS, 1846-1854. Vol. 6 of the Southwest Historical Series. Glendale: Clark, 1938. BEALE-Genl. GILA-Genl.

BIEBER, Susie A. "Captured by the Indians." NVHIST. Geog. Indians.

BIERTU, F. Journal. HUNTL. GILA(LA-Tucson). IV. 1860.

BIGELOW, Daniel R. Diary. Washington Historical Society Library, Tacoma, WA. OR(Council?). V. 1851.

BIGFORD, Clare O. "Early History of Nebraska City." MA thesis, Univ. of Nebraska, 1931. Geog.

BIGGS, Donald C. THE PONY EXPRESS. SF: Private, 1956. Pony.

BIGLER, Henry William. BIGLER'S CHRONICLE OF THE WEST. Ed. Erwin G. Gudde. Berkeley: Univ. of California Press, 1962. CAL(Leav)-SANTA FE-RIO GRANDE-GILA. II. 1846. CAL(Sutter's)-SLCUT-Ends SLC. II. 1848.

_____. "Bigler's Journal in 1849." OVERLAND MONTHLY 12(Oct 1888): 381-85. SLCOR. II. 1849.

_____. "Diary...in 1847 and 1848 with Notes." OVERLAND MONTHLY 10(Sept 1887): 233-45. GILA(Yuma-San Diego). III. 1847. TRUCKEE(Sutter's-Donner Lake). III. 1848.

_____. "Extracts from the Journal of Henry W. Bigler." UTAH HISTORICAL QUARTERLY 5(Apr, Jul, Oct 1932): 35-64, 87-112, 134-60. GILA. II. 1846. CAL(Sutter's)-SLCUT-Ends SLC. V. 1848. SLCOR. III. 1849.

BILL, Joseph H. "Notes on Arrow Wounds." AM. JOURNAL OF MEDICAL SCIENCES 44(1862): 365-87. Medical.

BILLINGSLEY, Amos S. Diary. Norlin Library-Western Historical, Univ. of Colorado, Boulder, CO. PIKES(Omaha)-Stage. V. 1861.

BILLINGTON, Ray A. "Books that Won the West: The Guidebooks of the Forty-Niners and Fifty-Niners." AMERICAN WEST 4(Aug 1967): 25-32, 72-75. Guide.

_____. "The Overland Ordeal." WESTWAYS 59(May 1967): 12-15, 58. CAL-1849-Genl.

BINGHAM, Erastus. SKETCH OF THE LIFE.... Comps. Norman F. Bingham, Lilliam B. Belnap, and Lester Scoville. Ogden, UT: N.p., 1953. MORMON. 1847. Not Seen.

BINGHAM, Thomas. History. UTHIST. CAL(Leav)-SANTA FE. V. 1846. CHEROKEE(Pueblo-SLC). V. 1847.

BIRCH, Brian P. "Crossing Wyoming With the Forty-Niners: Cornish Impressions of the Trek West." ANNALS OF WYIMING 59(Fall 1987). CAL-1849-Genl.

BIRD, Annie Laurie. OLD FORT BOISE. Caldwell, ID: Caxton, 1971. Geog.

BIRD, Edwin R. Journal. NEWBERRY. CAL(Indep)-Ends Bear River. II. 1854.

BIRGE, Julius C. THE AWAKENING OF THE DESERT. Boston: Gorham, 1912. MORMON. III. Rem. 1866. By Stage. Indians. Utah.

BIRNEY, Fletcher W., Jr. Ed. Forsdick, Stephen. "On the Oregon Trail to Zion."

BIRNEY, Hoffman. ROADS TO ROAM. NY: Burt, 1930. Pres.

BISHOP, Francis A. Itinerary of Route. In Paul & Helen Henderson Collection, UWY. CAL(Placerville)-NOBLE-SLCUT. II+. 1857.

BITTON, Davis. GUIDE TO MORMON DIARIES AND AUTOBIOGRAPHIES. Provo, UT: Brigham Young Univ. Press, 1977. Bib.

BIXBY-SMITH, Sarah. ADOBE DAYS. Cedar Rapids, IA: Torch, 1925. CAL(Council)-MORMON-SLCOR. IV. 1852.

BJORING, Bob, and Susan Cunningham. EXPLORER'S AND TRAVELLERS' JOURNALS DOCUMENTING EARLY CONTACTS WITH NATIVE AMERICANS IN THE PACIFIC NORTHWEST, 1741-1900. Univ. of Washington Libraries Bibliography Series No. 3. Seattle: Univ. of Washington Libraries, 1982. Indians.

BJORK, Kenneth O. WEST OF THE DIVIDE: NORWEGIAN MIGRATION TO THE PACIFIC COAST, 1847-1893. Northfield, MN: Norwegian-American Historical Assn., 1958. Overland-Genl.

BLACK, Mary Louisa. DIARY OF OVERLAND TRIP...1865. Medford, OR: Black, 1973. OR(Council)-BARLOW. III. 1865.

BLACK, Robert C. Ed. Shutterly, Lewis. DIARY.

BLACK, Wilfred W. "Historians and the Tradition of Pioneer Hardships." PhD diss., State Univ. of Iowa, 1942. OVERLAND-Genl.

BLACKBURN, Abner. Reminiscences. NVHIST. Frequent trips between California and Utah, 1846-1851. See Index. IV. Rem. Also published in edited form by PONY EXPRESS COURIER, July 1948, 3-6, 14; Aug 1948, 8-11; Sept 1948, 7-10; Oct 1948, 7-9; Nov 1948, 8, 13; Mar 1949, 8-9. SEE ALSO: Herb Hamlin.

BLACKTON, Jim. "Forgotten Fort Piute." TRUE WEST 5(Nov-Dec 1957): 14-16. Geog.

BLACKWOOD, Jane. Diary. Clarke Library, Central Michigan Library, Mt. Pleasant, MI. CAL(Council)-TRUCKEE. 1853. Not Seen.

BLAIR, Austin. THE CHORPENNING FRAUD. WA: National Democratic Executing Resident Committee, 1872? Mail.

BLAIR, Roger P. "Saving Our Powder." OVERLAND JOURNAL 1(Fall 1983): 4-11. Pres: Big Sandy, WY.

BLAKE, Anson S., ed. "Working for Wells Fargo - 1860-1863." CALIFORNIA HISTORICAL QUARTERLY 16(Mar, Jun 1937): 30-43, 172-81. Stage.

BLAKE, Charlotte. "Jesse Applegate, His Attitude toward the Oregon Indians." REED COLLEGE BULLETIN 21(Nov 1942): 17-27. Biog.

BLAKE, George A. "Journal of a March of U.S. Recruits...Fort Benton to Fort Vancouver, W.T." N.p., 1860. OR(Fort Benton)-MULLAN-Ends at The Dalles. I. 1860.

BLAKE, Winslow. Diary. WIHIST. CAL(Council)-BRIDGER-SLCUT-TRUCKEE. II. 1852.

BLAKELEY, Russell. "Opening of the Red River of the North to Commerce and Civilization." MINNESOTA HISTORICAL COLLECTIONS 8(1898): 45-66. DAKOTAS-Genl.

BLAKISTON, Thomas. REPORT ON THE EXPLORATION OF THE KOOTANIE AND BOUNDARY PASSES. Woolwich: Author, 1859. Geog.

BLANCHARD, James L. Letter. In Paul & Helen Henderson Collection, UWY. CAL(Council). V. 1852.

BLANCHARD, Jonathan. "The 1864 Overland Trail...." Ed. Robert H. Keller, Jr. NEBRASKA HISTORY 63(Spr 1982): 145-67. CAL(Council)-BOZE. IV. 1864.

BLANCHET, A. M. A. JOURNAL OF A CATHOLIC BISHOP ON THE OREGON TRAIL. Ed. Edward J. Kowrach. Reprint. Fairfield, WA: Ye Galleon, 1978. OR(Westport). II. 1847.

BLEAK, James G. "Handcart Travelog." BANCROFT. MORMON. III-. 1856.

BLEICH, Pamela. "A Study of Graduate Research in California History in California Colleges and Universities." CALIFORNIA HISTORICAL QUARTERLY 43(Sept, Dec 1964): 231-46, 331-43; 44(Mar, Jun, Sept, Dec 1965): 35-49, 139-63, 237-50, 333-48; 45(Jun 1966): 149-61. Bib.

BLESS, Bertha. WESTON. Weston, MO: Chronicle, 1969. Geog.

BLINN, Richard F. Diary. KSHIST. SANTA FE(Kansas City)-Ends Cimarron Crossing. V. 1868.

BLISS, Beatrice L. MARY VOWELL ADAMS. Myrtle Creek, OR: Author, 1972. OR(Council). II. 1852.

BLISS, Edward. A BRIEF HISTORY OF THE NEW GOLD REGIONS OF COLORADO TERRITORY.... NY: American, 1864. Guide.

_____. "Denver to Salt Lake by Overland Stage in 1862." COLORADO MAGAZINE 8(Sept 1931): 190-97. CHEROKEE. II. 1862. Stage.

BLISS, Robert S. "The Journal of Robert S. Bliss with the Mormon Battalion." UTAH HISTORICAL QUARTERLY 4(Jul, Oct 1931): 67-96, 110-28; 27(Oct 1959): 381-404. CAL(Leav)-SANTA FE-RIO GRANDE-GILA. III. 1846. MORMON. III. 1848.

BLOCH, Louis M., Jr. OVERLAND TO CALIFORNIA IN 1859: A GUIDE FOR WAGON TRAIN TRAVELERS. Cleveland: Bloch, 1983. Guide.

BLOCK, Eugene. GREAT STAGECOACH ROBBERS OF THE WEST. Garden City, NY: Doubleday, 1962. Stage.

BLONDEAU, Bernard S. Account Books. NBHIST. CAL-Genl. Road ranches on Platte River.

BLOOD, James A. Diary. CSL. CAL(Indep?)-BRIDGER-SLCUT. III. 1850.

BLOOD, Jane W. JANE WILKIE HOOPER BLOOD. Ed. Ivy Hooper Hill. Logan, UT: J. P. Smith, 1966. MORMON? 1854. Not Seen.

BLOOD, Katie E. Ed. Brown, John E. MEMOIRS.

BLOOM, Henry S. Diary. CSL. CAL(Council)-BRIDGER-HASTINGS. II. 1850.

BLOOM, Lansing. Ed. Chamberlin, William H. "From Lewisburg to CA."

BLOSS, Roy S. PONY EXPRESS, THE GREAT GAMBLE. Berkeley: Howell-North, 1959. Pony.

BLOSSOM, Frederick A. Ed. TOLD AT THE EXPLORERS CLUB.

BLOUET, B. W. "Meteorological Experiences of the Forty-Niners Crossing the Great American Desert." WEATHERWISE 28(Dec 1975): 250-53. CAL-1849-Genl. Not Seen.

BLOYD, Levi. "Grave of California Gold Rush Days of 1849." JEFFERSON COUNTY HISTORY 2(1955): 23-30. Grave of George Winslow. Pres.

_____. "Inscription Rock." JEFFERSON COUNTY HISTORY 3(1955): n.p. Geog.

BLUE, Daniel. THRILLING NARRATIVE...OF PIKE'S PEAK GOLD SEEKERS.... 1860. Reprint. Fairfield, WA: Ye Galleon, 1968. PIKES(Kansas City-Denver via Smoky Hill). III. 1859. Cannibalism.

BLUMENSCHEIN, Helen G. "Historic Roads and Trails to Taos." EL PALACIO 75(Spr 1968): 9-19. RIO GRANDE-Genl.

BLUMENTHAL, Walter H. "Sailwagons: Navigating the Grassy Sea of the Plains." NEW YORK WESTERNERS BRAND BOOK 12(1965): 32-33. Eqpt.

BLUNT, Phineas U. Notes of Travel. BANCROFT. CAL(Ft. Smith)-MARCY-RIO GRANDE-GILA. I. 1849.

BLUTH, John F. "Confrontation with an Arid Land: The Incursion of Gosiutes and Whites into Utah's Central West Desert, 1800-1978." PhD diss., BYU, 1978. SIMPSON-Genl. Pony. Overland-Genl. Telegraph.

BLYTHE, Samuel F. Diary. ORHIST. CAL(St. Jo)-BOZE?-MONTANA. III. 1866. CAL(Council)-MORMON(Stage)-MONTANA(SLC-Helena). IV. 1868.

BOARDMAN, John. "Journal of John Boardman...." UTAH HISTORICAL QUARTERLY 2(Oct 1929): 99-121. OR(Westport?). II. 1843.

BOATMAN, Mary L. Reminiscence. MONHIST. CAL-MONTANA. V-. Rem. 1865.

BOATMAN, Mary R. Biography. Washington State Historical Society Library, Tacoma, WA. OR(Council). III. Rem. 1852.

BOATMAN, Willis. Story of My Life. Washington State Historical Society, Tacoma, WA. OR(Council). V. Rem. 1852.

BOBBITT, Theodore N. Reminiscences. NBHIST. Freight.

BODE, Edward. Ed. Kleinsorge, Chas. "MO to CA, 1854."

BODER, Bartlett. "Eastern Mail for the Pony Express." MUSEUM GRAPHIC 10(Sum 1958): 12-13. Pony.

_____. "The Pony Express." MUSEUM GRAPHIC 11(Win 1959): 4-31. Pony.

_____. THE PONY EXPRESS. St. Joseph, MO: St. Joseph Museum, 1959. Pony.

BOGART, Nancy M. Reminiscences. HUNTL. OR. V. Rem. 1843.

BOGGS, John. Diary. BANCROFT. CAL(Council). III. 1849.

BOGGS, W. S. SEE: With Mel C. Nathan. THE PONY EXPRESS.

BOGGS, William M. Reminiscences. CSL. CAL(Indep)-BRIDGER-HASTINGS-TRUCKEE. IV. Rem. 1846.

BOLLER, Henry A. "Across the Sierra Nevada." LIPPINCOTT'S 1(Jun 1868): 615-21. Stage-Virginia City, NV-Colfax, CA. II. 1866.

BOLLING, Dwayne. Ed. Foster, William C. "Gold Rush Journey."

BOLTON, Curtis E. Diary. BYU. MORMON. 1849. Not Seen.

BOMBER, Elizabeth A. "A History of Oregon City from 1829 to 1849." MA thesis, Reed College, 1939. Geog.

BOND, ? FOOT TRAVELS ACROSS THE PLAINS. Richmond, IN: Friends, 1868. CAL(Leav?)-SIMPSON. V. Rem. 1865.

BOND, George. JOURNAL. N.p., 1938. OR(Council). III. 1853.

BOND, J. Harman. "A Journey to the Forks of the Red River of the North." Ed. Arthur H. Moehlman. NORTH DAKOTA HISTORICAL QUARTERLY 6(Apr 1932): 231-38. DAKOTAS(St. Paul-Ft. Garry by stage). II. 1860.

BOND, Robert. Diary. BEINECKE. CAL(Indep)-BRIDGER-Ends SLC. IV. 1849.

BOND, Samuel R. Journal of Expedition Sent by Government to protect emigrants to Gold Regions on Washington and Oregon frontiers by the Northern Overland Route. Ed. Helen M. White. MNHIST. OR-DAKOTAS(St. Paul)-MULLAN. I. 1862.

BONESTELL, Louis H. "Autobiography." QUARTERLY Society of California Pioneers 4(Jul 1927): 117-35. CAL-MEX(Vera Cruz-Mexico City-Mazatlan-Baja CA to San Diego). II. 1849.

BONINE, Dr. Diary. Fort St. Joseph Museum, Niles, MI. CAL(Indep)-HALL-TRUCKEE. 1849. Not Seen.

BONNER, John H. Daily Journal. BANCROFT. CAL(Council)-NOBLE. II. 1861.

BONNER, Thomas D. THE LIFE AND ADVENTURES OF JAMES P. BECKWOURTH. 1856. Reprint. Lincoln: Univ. of Nebraska Press, 1972. Biog. BECK-Genl.

BONNER, Thomas N. Ed. Schiel, Jacob. JOURNEY.

BONNEY, Benjamin F. "Recollections of...." Ed. Fred Lockley. OREGON HISTORICAL QUARTERLY 24(Mar 1923): 36-55. CAL(Indep)-TRUCKEE. IV. Rem. 1845.

BONSAL, Stephen. EDWARD FITZGERALD BEALE...1822-1903. NY: Putnam's, 1912. Biog. BEALE-Genl.

BOOCOCK, Dana G. "Military and Civilian Management of the Plains Indians along the Oregon Trail, 1846-1855." Senior thesis, Princeton University, 1983. Military. Indians.

BOOK Club of California. MOUNTAIN PASSES AND TRAILS OF CALIFORNIA. SF: Club, 1979. Geog.

BOONE, George L. Recollections. ORHIST. OR(Indep). Rem. 1848. Not Seen.

BOOSINGER, George. SEE: Craig, John. "Letter."

BOOTH, Caleb. Diary. BEINECKE. CAL(Council)-SLCUT-Ends Lassen Meadow. III. 1850.

BOOTH, Edmund. EDMUND BOOTH, FORTY-NINER. Pub. No. 3. Stockton: San Joaquin Pioneer and Historical Society, 1953. CAL(Council). III+. Rem. 1849.

BOOTH, John. IN MEMORIAL. Austin, NV: Reveille, 1884. CAL. 1853. Not Seen.

BOOTH, Margaret. Ed. Dinwiddie, David. OVERLAND FROM INDIANA.

BOOTH, William. "Diary." In EARLY UTAH PIONEERS, LEVI HAMMON AND POLLY CHAPMAN BYBEE, comp. Betsy R. Greenwell. Kaysville, UT: Inland, 196? MORMON. 1851. Not Seen.

BOQUIST, Laura B. CROSSING THE PLAINS...1862. N.p.: Tritt, 1930. CAL(Council)-BRIDGER-SIMPSON. III. Rem. 1862.

BORDEN, Stanley T. "Some Stage Coach Robberies in Butte County." Butte County Historical Society DIGGIN'S 12(Sum 1968): 3-7. Stage.

BOREIN, Edward. STAGECOACHES OF THE OLD WEST. Comp. Nicholas Woloshuk, Jr. Santa Fe: Institute of Fine Art, 1968. Stage-Graphics.

BOREN, Kerry R. "Jack Slade's Grave Located." FRONTIER TIMES 50(Apr-May 1976): 24-26, 56. Biog.

BORING, Claude T. "Mountain Meadows Massacre: A Revaluation." MA thesis, Univ. of Southern California, 1961. Geog. SLCOR-1857-Genl.

BORTHWICK, Alexander E. "The Westering Journal of Alexander Elijah Borthwick, 1867-1869." Ed. James G. Engiles. MA thesis, Univ. of Oregon, 1977. OR-1869-Genl.

BOSTWICK, Norris. "Camping on the Butterfield Trail." QUARTERLY Historical Society of Southern California 43(Dec 1961): 426-39. Pres(LA - El Centro).

BOTT, Emily A. "Joseph Murphy's Contribution to the Development of the West." MISSOURI HISTORICAL REVIEW 47(Oct 1952): 18-28. Eqpt.

BOULDIN, James E. Diary. Stanford Univ. Library-SpCol, Palo Alto, CA. GILA(Mimbres River-LA). II+. 1849. Flora/Fauna.

BOURNE, Ezra. Diary. BANCROFT. CAL(Indep). III+. 1850.

BOUTON, Helen, and Natalie White. "How the Pioneers Moved Westward (Curriculum Units for Elementary Schools, No. 2)." California Dept. of Education BULLETIN, no. 1(Apr 1938): N.p. Excellent teacher's guide, 5th grade level.

BOWDEN, Martyn J. "The Great American Desert and the American Frontier, 1800-1882: Popular Images of the Plains." In ANONYMOUS AMERICANS: EXPLORATIONS IN NINETEENTH-CENTURY SOCIAL HISTORY. Ed. Tamara K. Hareven. Englewood Cliffs, NJ: N.p., 1971. Overland-Genl.

BOWEN, E. A. "Pikes Peak Fifty-Niner: The Diary of E. A. Bowen." Ed. Duane A. Smith. COLORADO MAGAZINE 47(Fall 1970): 269-311. PIKES(St. Jo). III. 1859.

BOWEN, James E. Diary. BANCROFT. OR(Council)-APPLE. III. 1851.

BOWEN, William A. "Migration and Settlement on a Far Western Frontier: Oregon to 1850." PhD diss., Univ. of Southern California, 1972. OR-Genl.

_____. THE WILLAMETTE VALLEY: MIGRATION AND SETTLEMENT ON THE OREGON FRONTIER. Seattle: Univ. of Washington Press, 1978.
OR-Genl.

BOWER, Donald E. FRED ROSENSTOCK: A LEGEND IN BOOKS AND ART. Flagstaff, AZ: Northland, 1976. Biog. Not Seen.

BOWERING, George. Journal. HUNTL. MORMON. I. 1852.

BOWERS, John H. Letters. In Bowers-Flag Family Papers. American Antiquarian Society, Worcester, Mass. CAL(Council)-BRIDGER-SIMPSON. IV. 1864.

BOWERS, Lemuel. Diary. In Leland F. Smith and Family Collection. MNHIST. CAL(Council)-Ends North Platte Ferry. V. 1850.

BOWLES, J. Frank. "Overland Trip to California in 1850." FRONTIER TIMES 4(Feb 1927): 12-15. CAL-TEX(San Antonio)-GILA. IV. 1850.

BOWLES, Samuel. ACROSS THE CONTINENT.... Springfield, Mass.: Author, 1866. Stage(Atchison-Denver-SLC-SF-Vancouver). II. 1865. Utah.

BOWMAN, E. L. (I?). "Diary." In WAGONS WEST, ed. Elizabeth Page. NY: Farrar & Rinehart, 1930. CAL(St. Jo)-Ends on Little Blue River. V-. 1849.

BOWMAN, Eldon G. "Beale's Road." ARIZONA HIGHWAYS 60(Jul 1984): 2-11. BEALE-Genl.

_____. A GUIDE TO THE GENERAL CROOK TRAIL. Flagstaff?: Museum of Northern Arizona & Boy Scouts, 1978. GILA-Genl. Maps.

_____, and Jack Smith. BEALE'S ROAD THROUGH ARIZONA. Flagstaff?: Westerners, 1979. BEALE-Genl.

BOWMAN, Frank. Diary. ORHIST. CAL(Council?)-HALL. IV. 1850.

BOX, James. ADVENTURES AND EXPLORATIONS IN NEW AND OLD MEXICO. NY: Miller, 1869. MEX-Genl. GILA-Genl.

BOYACK, Mrs. A. R., comp. "Oregon Trail Trek No. Eight: Lander Road." ANNALS OF WYOMING 31(Apr 1959): 77-93. LANDER-Genl. Maps.

_____. (Hazel Noble Boyack). "Historic Fort Laramie, The Hub of Early Western History, 1834-1849." ANNALS OF WYOMING 21(July-Oct 1949): 170-80. Geog.

BOYD, William H. STAGECOACH HEYDAY IN THE SAN JOAQUIN VALLEY, 1853-1876. Bakersfield, CA: Kern County Historical Society, 1983. Stage.

_____. "The Stagecoach in the Southern San Joaquin Valley, 1854-1876." PACIFIC HISTORICAL REVIEW 26(Nov 1957): 365-72. Stage.

BOYLE, Charles E. "Diary - 1849." Columbus, Ohio DISPATCH, October 2 - November 11, 1849. Not Seen.

BOYLES, J. C. "He Witnessed the Death Valley Tragedy of '49." DESERT 3(Feb 1940): 3-6. SLCOR-1849-Genl.

BOYLES, John R. "None Dream But of Success...." TENNESSEE HISTORICAL QUARTERLY 36(Win 1977): 512-23. CAL(Ft. Smith)-MARCY-RIO GRANDE-GILA. V-. 1849.

BOYLES, John S. Letters. BANCROFT. Not Seen.

"Boy's Funeral Followed Oregon Trail." MISSOURI HISTORICAL REVIEW 25(Oct 1930): 194-95. Social.

BOZEMAN, John M. Estate Papers. Montana State University, Missoula, MT. BOZE-Genl. Not Seen.

Bozeman Trail Manuscripts. LILLEY. BOZE-Genl.

BOZORTH, (Bozarth?) Mrs. L. A. Narrative. ORHIST. OR(Council). V. Rem. 1852.

BRAATZ, Ned E. "An Historical Geography of Major Transportation Routes across the Laramie Plains." MA thesis, Univ. of Wyoming, 1972. Geog. CHEROKEE-Genl.

BRACKENRIDGE, William D. "Journal...1841." CALIFORNIA HISTORICAL QUARTERLY 24(Dec 1945): 326-36. OR-CA. IV. 1841.

BRACKETT, A. G. "A Trip through the Rocky Mountains." CONTRIBUTIONS Montana Historical Society 8(1917): 329-44. MONTANA(Ft. Bridger-Virginia City, MT-Ft. Ellis). II. 1869.

BRADBURY, Anson. Journal. MO-WHMC. CAL(St. Jo). II. 1859.

BRADFORD, James O. Papers. Stanford Univ. Library-SpCol, Palo Alto, CA. Pony. Stage.

BRADLEY, A. M. (B?). Diary. BANCROFT. CAL(St. Jo). III+. 1850.

BRADLEY, Doris R. "For Services Rendered." NEVADA HISTORICAL SOCIETY QUARTERLY 20(Fall 1977): 184-91. Stage.

BRADLEY, Glenn D. THE STORY OF THE PONY EXPRESS. Chicago: McClurg, 1914. Pony.

BRADLEY, Henry and Nancy J. Journal. BEINECKE. CAL(Council)-BRIDGER-SLCUT-Ends Wells. II. 1852.

BRADLEY, James H. "The Oregon Trail: Capture of an Emigrant Train by the Piegan Chief, Little Dog." CONTRIBUTIONS Montana Historical Society 9(1923): 288-99. Indians.

_____. Papers. MONHIST. MONTANA-Genl. Freight.

BRADLEY, Lenore, and William Crowley. TREKKIN' WEST: AN EMIGRANTS GUIDE TO OREGON. N.p.: Kansas City Museum, N.d. Not Seen.

BRADLEY, N. J., and H. Journal. BEINECKE. CAL(Council)-BRIDGER-SLCUT. 1852. Not Seen.

BRADLEY, Theodore X. "The Cariboo Trail to Barkerville." PACIFIC NORTHWESTERNER 8(Spr, Sum 1964): 17-28, 46-48. CANADA-Cariboo Route.

BRADWAY, J. C. Journal. Princeton Univ. Library-Western America, Princeton, NJ. PIKES(Council). I. 1859.

BRADWAY, Joseph R. Diary. CSL. CAL(St. Jo)-BRIDGER-SLCUT-NOBLE. II. 1853. Flora.

BRADY, Charles C. "From Hannibal to the Gold Fields...." Ed. Glenn Price. PACIFIC HISTORIAN 4(Nov 1960): 142-52; 5(Feb 1961): 5-14, 77-83. CAL(St. Jo)-TRUCKEE. IV. Rem. 1849.

BRADY, Peter R. Biography. Arizona State Library, Phoenix, AZ. CAL-TEX(San Antonio)-MEX-GILA. II. Rem. 1854.

BRAINARD, David. Diary. BANCROFT. CAL(Leav)-SANTA FE-RIO GRANDE-GILA. II+. 1849.

BRALY, John H. MEMORY PICTURES. LA: Private, 1912. OR(Indep). III+. Rem. 1847.

BRANCH, E. Douglas. "Frederick West Lander, Road-Builder." MISSISSIPPI VALLEY HISTORICAL REVIEW 16(Sept 1929): 172-87. Biog.

BRAND, Donald D. THE HISTORY OF SCOTTS BLUFF, NEBRASKA. Berkeley: National Park Service, 1934. Geog.

BRANDT, Charles A. TO OREGON WITH OX TEAMS.... N.p.,n.d. OR(Neb. City)-BARLOW. II. 1851.

BRANSTETTER, Peter L. LIFE AND TRAVELS.... St. Joseph, MO: Messenger, 1913. CAL(St. Jo)-TRUCKEE. II+. 1850.

BRATT, John. TRAILS OF YESTERDAY. Chicago: University Publishing, 1921. CAL(Neb. City)-Ends Fort Kearny. Rem. 1866. Freight.

BRATZ, J. P. "Some Aspects of Postal Extension into the West." AM. HISTORICAL ASSN. REPORT (1909): 143-67. Mail.

BRAY, Edmund. Letter. BANCROFT. CAL(Council)-BRIDGER-HALL-TRUCKEE. V. Rem. 1844.

BRAYER, Herbert O. Ed. Shelley, Edward. "Western Journal."

_____. "Insurance Against the Hazards of Western Life." MISSISSIPPI VALLEY HISTORICAL REVIEW 34(Sept 1947): 221-36. Train Govt.

_____, and Garnet M. Brayer. AMERICAN CATTLE TRAILS, 1546-1900. Bayside, NY: Western Range Cattle Industry, 1952. Stock.

BREARLEY, Neil. Ed. Alexander, Richard H. DIARY.

BRECKENRIDGE, William C. "Gold Hunters of Forty-Nine." MO-WHMC. CAL-1849-Genl.

BREDLOW, Thomas G. "Stagecoach!" FRONTIER TIMES 34(Sum 1960): 16-17, 52.

BREEN, Harry J. "A Short Sketch of the Lives of Patrick and Margaret Breen and their Family. Members of the Ill-Fated Donner Party of 1846." In Herbert Brame Papers, UPAC. Biog.

BREEN, John. Dictation. BANCROFT. CAL(Indep?)-BRIDGER-HASTINGS-TRUCKEE. II. Rem. 1846.

BREEN, Patrick. "Diary." Ed. Frederick J. Taggart. Academy Pacific Coast Historical Society PUBLICATIONS 1(Jul 1910): 271-84. TRUCKEE. III. 1846.

BRENCHLEY, Julius. SEE: With Jules Remy. A JOURNEY.

BRERETON, George. "Overland to California in 1841." MA thesis, Univ. of California-Berkeley, 1926. CAL-1841-Genl.

BRESEE, Floyd E. "Overland Freighting in the Platte Valley, 1850-1870." MA thesis, Univ. of Nebraska, 1937. Freight.

BRETON, Thor. "The Old Mariposa Road." FAR-WESTERNER 7(Apr 1960): 1-8. Freight. CAL-Genl.

BREWER, William H. ROCKY MOUNTAIN LETTERS, 1869.... Ed. Edmund B. Rogers. Denver: Colorado Mountain Club, 1930. Stage(Cheyenne-Denver). IV. 1869.

BREWERTON, George D. OVERLAND WITH KIT CARSON, A NARRATIVE OF THE OLD SPANISH TRAIL IN '48. Ed. Stallo Vinton. NY: Coward-McCann, 1930. SPANISH. II. 1848.

BREWSTER, Orville D. "The History of the Ute Pass Trail." Colorado College Library-SpCol, Colorado Springs, CO. Geog.

BREYFOGLE, Joshua D., Sr. Diary. BANCROFT. CAL(St. Jo)-BRIDGER-SLCUT. II. 1849.

BRICE, James. REMINISCENCES OF TEN YEARS EXPERIENCE ON THE WESTERN PLAINS: HOW THE UNITED STATES MAILS WERE CARRIED BEFORE THE RAILROADS REACHED THE SANTA FE TRAIL.... Kansas City, MO: Author, 1905? Mail. Graphics.

BRIER, John Wells. "The Argonauts of Death Valley." GRIZZLY BEAR 9(Jun 1911): 1-4, 7. SLCOR-1849-Genl.

_____. "The Death Valley Party of 1849." OUT WEST 18(Mar, Apr 1903): 326-35, 456-65. SLCOR-1849-Genl.

BRIER, Juliet Wells. SEE: Leadingham, Grace. "Juliet Wells Brier."

BRIGGS, Albert. Narrative. BANCROFT. OR(St. Jo). IV. Rem.

1847.

BRIGGS, Carl, and Clyde Francis Trudell. QUARTERDECK & SAD-DLEHORN: THE STORY OF EDWARD F. BEALE, 1822-1893. Glendale: Clark, 1983. Biog. BEALE-Genl.

BRIGGS, Catherine C. "Beale's Road across Northern Arizona." MA thesis, Univ. of Southern California, 1930. BEALE-Genl.

BRIGGS, Harold E. "Early Freight and Stage Lines in Dakota." NORTH DAKOTA HISTORICAL QUARTERLY 3(Jul 1929): 229-61. Freight. Stage.

BRIGGS, Joshua E., and Ruth Flowerree. A PIONEER MISSOURIAN. Boston: Christopher, 1939. CAL(Council)-BRIDGER-SIMPSON. V. Rem. 1863. CAL(Council)-SLCUT-LASSEN. V. Rem. 1864.

BRIGHAM, Lillian. HISTORICAL GUIDE TO COLORADO.... Denver: Daughters of the American Revolution, 1931. Pres.

BRIGHT, Verne. "The Folklore and History of the 'Oregon Fever'." OREGON HISTORICAL QUARTERLY 52(Dec 1951): 240-53. OR-1843-Genl.

BRINCKERHOFF, Sidney R. SEE: With Rosalie Crowe. EARLY YUMA.

_____. "Passport to Mexico." JOURNAL OF ARIZONA HIS-TORY 8(Spr 1966): 54-59. Train Govt.

BRININSTOOL, E. A. SEE: With Grace Hebard. BOZEMAN TRAIL.

BRINKERHUFF, Dick. LIFE AND ADVENTURES.... Custar, OH: Custar News, 1915. CAL. 1850. CAL. 1857. Not Seen.

BRISBANE, William. Journal. HUNTL. CAL(Leav)-SANTA FE-RIO GRANDE-GILA. I. 1849.

BRISTOL, C. C. BRISTOL'S TRAVELLER'S GUIDE, THROUGH THE UNITED STATES AND CANADAS.... Buffalo, NY: Jewett, Thomas, 1850. Guide.

BRISTOL, D. Sherlock. THE PIONEER PREACHER. Chicago: Revell, 1887. OR(Council)-LANDER. V. Rem. 1862. Indians.

BRISTOW, Elijah, Sr. LETTERS. Eugene, OR: Lane County Pioneer-Historical Society, 1961. CAL(Indep). V. 1845.

BRISTOW, John T. THE OVERLAND TRAIL: OLD MILITARY ROAD AND PONY EXPRESS ROUTE. Horton, KS: Headlight, 1937. CAL-Genl. Stage.

BRITISH Columbia. Lands and Works Dept. OVERLAND COACH ROAD. New Westminster, BC: GPO, 1868. CANADA-Genl.

BROADSIDES. Readers should consider reviewing the large collection of such items at the BEINECKE.

BROADWELL, J. W. "Crossing the Plains with the McMurphy Train, 1864." LUCKY LAND OF LASSEN 2(Oct 1960): 17-37. CAL(Council)-SLCUT-NOBLE. IV. Rem. 1864.

BROCKWAY, H. S. ACROSS THE SOUTHERN TRAIL TO CALIFORNIA. Mt. Pleasant, MI: N.p., 1982. CAL-TEX(La Grange)-GILA. IV. 1849.

BRODE, H. S. Ed. Thibodo, Augustus. "Diary."

BRODIE, Fawn M. Ed. Burton, Richard F. CITY OF THE SAINTS.

Ed. Piercy, Frederick. ROUTE FROM LIVERPOOL.

BROMBERG, Erik. "A Bibliography of Theses and Dissertations concerning the Pacific Northwest and Alaska." PACIFIC NORTHWEST QUARTERLY 40(Jul 1949): 203-52. Bib.

_____. "A Bibliography of Theses and Dissertations concerning the Pacific Northwest and Alaska: A Supplement, 1949-1957." OREGON HISTORICAL QUARTERLY 59(Mar 1958): 27-84. Bib.

_____. "Bibliography of Theses and Dissertations concerning the Pacific Northwest and Alaska: A Supplement, 1958-1963." OREGON HISTORICAL QUARTERLY 65(Dec 1964): 362-91. Bib.

_____. "Bibliography of Theses and Dissertations, Pacific Northwest and Alaska: Supplement, 1964-70." OREGON HISTORICAL QUARTERLY 72(Sept 1971): 225-79. Bib.

_____. "A Further Bibliography of Theses concerning the Pacific Northwest and Alaska." PACIFIC NORTHWEST QUARTERLY 42(Apr 1951): 147-66. Bib.

BROOKS, Alden F. Diary. Princeton Univ. Library-Western America, Princeton, NJ. CAL(Council)-BRIDGER-SLCUT-TRUCKEE-Ends Wadsworth, NV. II. 1859.

BROOKS, E. W. THE JOURNAL OF A FORTY-NINER. London: Brooks, 1967. CAL(St. Jo)-BRIDGER-SLCUT-LASSEN. III. 1849.

BROOKS, Elisha. A PIONEER MOTHER OF CALIFORNIA. SF: Harr Wagner, 1922. CAL(Council)-TRUCKEE-BECKWOURTH. IV. Rem. 1852.

BROOKS, Juanita. Ed. Heywood, Martha S. NOT BY BREAD ALONE. Ed. Lee, John D. "Diary of the Mormon Battalion." Ed. Stout, Hosea. ON THE MORMON FRONTIER.

_____. "The Mountain Meadows: Historic Stopping Place on the Spanish Trail." UTAH HISTORICAL QUARTERLY 35(Spr 1967): 137-43. Geog.

_____. THE MOUNTAIN MEADOWS MASSACRE. Norman: Univ. of Oklahoma Press, 1962. SLCOR-1857-Genl.

_____. "A Place of Refuge." NEVADA HISTORICAL SOCIETY QUARTERLY 14(Spr 1971): 13-24. SLCOR-1858-Genl.

_____, and Robert Glass Cleland. A MORMON CHRONICLE: THE DIARIES OF JOHN. D. LEE, 1848-1876. San Marino: Huntington, 1955. Biog.

BROOKS, Noah. "The Plains Across." CENTURY 63(Apr 1902): 803-20. CAL-Genl.

BROOKS, Quincy Adams. "Letter...1851." OREGON HISTORICAL QUARTERLY 15(Sept 1914): 210-15. OR(Indep?). V. 1851.

BROOKSHIER, Frank. THE BURRO. Norman: Univ. of Oklahoma Press, 1972. Teams.

BROTHERTON, I. N. Ed. Fulkerth, Abbey E. "Aunt Abby's Diary."

BROUSTER, George W. Letters. MO-WHMC. CAL(St. Jo)-TRUCKEE. IV. 1850.

BROWDER, William. Diary. BANCROFT. CAL. V. 1853.

BROWER, Steve, and Damon Oklerking. A CORRIDOR TRAIL NET-WORK FOR IOWA'S LANDSCAPE. Des Moines: Iowa Conservation Comm., 1973. Pres.

BROWN, A. Theodore. FRONTIER COMMUNITY: KANSAS CITY TO 1870. Columbia: Univ. of Missouri Press, 1963. Geog.

BROWN, Adam. "Over Barren Plains and Rock-Bound Mountains...." Ed. David M. Kiefer. MONTANA 22(Oct 1972): 17-29. CAL(St. Jo)-BRIDGER-SLCUT. III. 1850.

BROWN, Adam M. THE GOLD REGION. Allegheny, PA: Purviance, 1851. CAL(St. Jo)-BRIDGER-SLCUT. Not Seen. Complete version of above item.

BROWN, Alonzo F. AUTOBIOGRAPHY.... Pasadena, CA: N.p., 1922. OR(Council)-LANDER-APPLE. IV. Rem. 1859.

BROWN, Ann Bruning, Gilberta Bruning Hughes, and Louise Bruning Erb. WAGON TRAILS AND FOLK TALES. Laramie, WY: Authors, 1980. Freight-WY.

BROWN, Arthur J. "The Promotion of Emigration to Washington, 1854-1909." PACIFIC NORTHWEST QUARTERLY 36(Jan 1945): 3-18. WASH-Genl.

BROWN, Benjamin. Diary. ORU. OR(Council). III. 1860.

BROWN, Charles. Diary. Iowa State Historical Society Archives, Iowa City, IA. CAL(Council). III. 1850.

BROWN, Charles R. "My Experiences on the Plains in 1861 in Assisting in the Construction of the first Telegraph Line across the Continent." Western Union Company Library, New York City. Telegraph.

BROWN, "Aunt" Clara. SEE: Bruyn, Kathleen. "AUNT" CLARA BROWN.

BROWN, D. Alexander. "A Girl with the Donner Pass Party." AM. HISTORY ILLUSTRATED 1(Oct 1966): 43-49. CAL-1846-Genl.

BROWN, Dee. SEE: With Martin Schmidtt. FIGHTING INDIANS.

_____. "Along the Santa Fe Trail." AM. HISTORY ILLUSTRATED 15(Oct 1980): 8-13, 42-44. SANTA FE-Genl.

_____. "The Day of the Buffalo." AM. HISTORY ILLUSTRATED. 11(Jul 1976): 4-7, 42-49. Fauna.

_____. FORT PHIL KEARNY, AN AMERICAN SAGA. NY: Putnam's, 1962. Geog. BOZE-Genl.

_____. THE GALVANIZED YANKEES. Urbana: Univ. of Illinois Press, 1963. Military.

_____. "The Pony Express." AM. HISTORY ILLUSTRATED 11(Nov 1976): 4-7, 44-50.

BROWN, Elam. BIOGRAPHY OF ELAM BROWN. Martinez, CA: Contra Costa Press, 1879. CAL(St. Jo)-BRIDGER-HALL-TRUCKEE. IV. Rem. 1846.

BROWN, Harvey S. Statement. BANCROFT. CAL(Indep)-CHEROKEE-SLCOR. IV. Rem. 1849.

BROWN, J. Robert. A JOURNAL OF A TRIP ACROSS THE PLAINS, 1856. Columbus, OH: Author, 1860. CAL(St. Jo)-BRIDGER-SLCUT. I. 1856.

BROWN, James Berry. JOURNAL OF A JOURNEY...1859. Ed. George R. Stewart. SF: Book Club of California, 1970. CAL(Neb. City)-LANDER-LASSEN. III. 1859.

BROWN, James S. LIFE OF A PIONEER. SLC: Cannon & Sons, 1900. CAL(Sutter's to east)-SLCUT-Ends SLC. II. 1848. SLCOR. II. 1849.

BROWN, James W. Reminiscence. MONHIST. Freight.

BROWN, Jean M. "(Wind)Wagons Ho!" HERITAGE OF THE GREAT PLAINS 14(Fall 1981): 14-24. Eqpt.

BROWN, Jennie B. FORT HALL ON THE OREGON TRAIL. Caldwell, ID: Caxton, 1932. Compiled from author's PhD diss., University of California-Berkeley, 1930. Geog.

BROWN, Jesse. "The Freighter in Early Days." ANNALS OF WYOMING 19(Jul 1947): 112-16. Freight.

BROWN, John. SEE: McFarland, G. "A Legacy Left Behind."

BROWN, John. Diary. ORHIST. OR(St. Jo)-Ends Fremont's Ford. V. 1852.

BROWN, John. Diary. ORHIST. OR(Council). II. 1852.

BROWN, John. "The Diary of John Brown, 1862." Ed. George W. Beattie. PUBLICATIONS Historical Society of Southern California 13(1927): 360-64. BEALE(LA-Ft. Mohave). III. 1862.

BROWN, John. PIONEER JOURNEYS FROM NAUVOO, ILLINOIS, TO PUEBLO, COLORADO, IN 1846, AND OVER THE PLAINS IN 1847. N.p., n.d. CAL(Indep-Ft. Laramie)-CHEROKEE(Ft. Laramie-Pueblo-Indep). V. Rem. 1846.

BROWN, John Evans. "Memoirs of a Forty-Niner." Ed. Katie E. Blood. JOURNAL OF AMERICAN HISTORY 2(Jan 1908): 129-54. CAL(Indep)-LASSEN. II. 1849.

BROWN, John G. JOHN M. JACOBS AND THE BOZEMAN TRAIL. Billings, MT: Gazette, n.d. BOZE-1863-Genl.

BROWN, John Henry. "The Chihuahua-El Paso Expedition in 1848." FRONTIER TIMES 15(Nov 1937): 57-59. TEX(San Antonio-Horsehead Crossing). IV. Rem. 1848.

_____. REMINISCENCES AND INCIDENTS OF 'THE EARLY DAYS' OF SAN FRANCISCO. 1886. Reprint. SF: Grabhorn, 1973. CAL-CHEROKEE-HALL-TRUCKEE. V. 1843. CAL(To Midwest)-TRUCKEE-HALL-CHEROKEE. V. 1844. CAL. V. 1845.

BROWN, John Lowery. "The Journal of John Lowery Brown of the Cherokee Nation...1850." Ed. Muriel H. Wright. CHRONICLES OF OKLAHOMA 12(Jun 1934): 177-213. CAL(Stillwell, OK)-CHEROKEE-HASTINGS. III+. 1850.

BROWN, John Mason. "Diary." FILSON CLUB HISTORICAL QUARTERLY 24(Apr, Jul 1950): 103-36, 246-75. OR-DAKOTAS(Fort Union)-MULLAN. Stage(Portland-Sacramento-SLC-St. Jo). II+. 1861.

BROWN, John Z. AUTOBIOGRAPHY OF PIONEER JOHN BROWN. SLC: Private, 1941. CHEROKEE. IV. Rem. 1846. MORMON. IV. Rem. 1847. MORMON. IV. Rem. 1848. SLCOR. IV. Rem. 1849. MORMON. IV. Rem. 1860. MORMON. IV. Rem. 1862.

BROWN, Joseph. CROSSING THE PLAINS IN 1849. Marysville, CA: n.p., 1916. CAL-LASSEN. V. Rem. 1849.

BROWN, Joseph E. THE MORMON TREK WEST. Garden City, NY: Doubleday, 1980. MORMON-1847-Genl. Maps.

BROWN, Joseph H. Trip...in Winter. In Oregon Misc., BANCROFT.

OR(Oregon City)-Ends St. Jo. III. 1848.

BROWN, Joseph Henry. Autobiography. ORU. OR(St. Jo)-BAR-LOW. III. Rem. 1847. Good description of Barlow crossing.

BROWN, Kenneth. "California Roads and Trails, 1825 to 1848; as Revealed by some Contemporary and Near-Contemporary Observers." MA thesis, Stanford University, 1936. CAL-Genl.

BROWN, Mary. SEE: Rosenburg, Daniel. MARY BARLOW.

BROWN, Milton. Diary. ORHIST. OR(Oregon City east to Utilla Valley). V. 1847.

BROWN, Orlando. Diary. CAHIST. OR(Council). 1852. Not Seen.

BROWN, Randy. "Attack on the Kelly-Larimer Wagon Train." OVERLAND JOURNAL 5(Win 1987): 16-39. Indians. Geog(Douglas, WY).

BROWN, Robert L. THE GREAT PIKES PEAK GOLD RUSH. Caldwell, ID: Caxton, 1985. PIKES-Genl. Not Seen.

BROWN, Sharon. "What the Covered Wagon Covered." OVERLAND JOURNAL 4(Sum 1986): 32-39. Social.

_____. "Women on the Overland Trails - A Historical Perspective." OVERLAND JOURNAL 2(Win 1984): 35-39. Social.

BROWN, Tabitha. "A Brimfield Heroine." OREGON HISTORICAL QUARTERLY 5(Jun 1904): 199-205. OR-APPLE? IV. 1846.

BROWN, Terry. "An Emigrants' Guide for Women...." AMERICAN WEST 7(Sept-Oct 1970): 12-17, 63. Social. Guide.

BROWN, Vernon H. "American Airlines along the Butterfield Overland Mail Route." CHRONICLES OF OKLAHOMA 33(Spr 1955): 2-13. Stage.

BROWN, Wilfred H. THIS WAS A MAN. North Hollywood, CA: Author, 1971. Biog: Jesse Applegate.

BROWN, William E. THE SANTA FE TRAIL. Santa Fe: U.S. National Park Service, 1963. SANTA FE-Genl. Fine maps. Pres.

BROWN, William Richard. AN AUTHENTIC WAGON TRAIN JOURNAL.... Mokelumne Hill, CA: Horseshoe, 1985. CAL(Council)-BRIDGER-SLCUT. II. 1853.

BROWNE, J. M. "Out on the Plains." OVERLAND MONTHLY 16(Nov 1890): 495-508. Pecos River Crossings.

BROWNE, J. Ross. ADVENTURES IN THE APACHE COUNTRY.... Reprint. Tucson: Univ. of Arizona Press, 1974. GILA-1864-Genl. MEX. II. 1864.

_____. "A Dangerous Journey." HARPER'S 24(May, Jun 1862): 741-56, 6-19. CAL(SF-San Luis Obispo). III. 1849.

BROWNE, Lina F. Ed. Huning, Franz. TRADER ON THE SANTA FE TRAIL.

BROWNLEE, Robert. AN AMERICAN ODYSSEY.... Ed. Patrick A. Etter. Fayetteville: Univ. of Arkansas Press, 1986. CAL(Ft. Smith)-MARCY-RIO GRANDE-GILA. II. 1849. Comprehensive bibliography.

BRUBAKER, Albert. A Trip. MONHIST. CAL(Council)-HALL-MONTANA(Snake River to Virginia City). IV. Rem. 1864.

BRUCE, Henrietta S. "A History of the Oregon Central Military Wagon Road Company...." MA thesis, Univ. of Oregon, 1936. Freight.

BRUCE, Robert. THREE OLD PLAINSMEN. NY: Author, 1923? Freight.

BRUFF, Joseph Goldsborough. GOLD RUSH: THE JOURNALS, DRAWINGS AND OTHER PAPERS OF J[oseph]. GOLDSBOROUGH BRUFF. Eds. Georgia W. Read and R. Gaines. NY: Columbia Univ. Press, 1949. CAL(Ft. Kearney)-LASSEN. I+. 1849. The standard against which other edited diaries are compared.

BRUFFEY, George A. EIGHTY-ONE YEARS IN THE WEST. Butte, MT: Butte Miner, 1925. CAL(Council)-HALL-MONTANA. V. Rem. 1863.

BRUMGARDT, John R. Ed. Johnston, Francis J. THE BRADSHAW TRAIL.

BRUNDAGE, T. J. Diary. MONHIST. CAL(Council)-BOZE. IV. 1864.

BRUYN, Kathleen. "AUNT" CLARA BROWN. Boulder, CO: Pruett, 1971. PIKES(Leav). V. 1859. A black woman's trip.

BRYAN, Charles W., Jr. "From Marthasville to Marysville in 1850." MISSOURI HISTORICAL BULLETIN 19(Jan 1963): 115-26. CAL(Leav). V. 1850.

BRYAN, Erin. Diary. BARKER. TEX-1853-Genl.

BRYAN, F. T. "Report...on a..Road between Fort Riley and Bridger's Pass." ANNALS OF WYOMING 17(Jan 1945): 24-55. CHEROKEE. III. 1856.

BRYANT, Edwin. WHAT I SAW IN CALIFORNIA...1847. 1849. Reprint. Palo Alto, CA: Lewis Osborne, 1967. CAL(Indep)-BRIDGER-HASTINGS-TRUCKEE. I. 1846.

BRYANT, Isaiah W. Diary. U.S. National Park Service Library, Omaha, NB. CAL(Council). 1853. Missing.

BRYANT, Luvina C. "Recollections." PORTLAND OREGONIAN, Summer, 1936, n.p. NBHIST. OR(Council). 1862. Not Seen.

BRYANT, William Cullen. THE PLAINS AND THE SIERRAS. Camp Nevada Monograph No. 5. Reprint. Reno: Camp Nevada, 1979. Good graphics.

BRYARLY, Wakeman. SEE: Potter, David M. TRAIL TO CALIFORNIA.

BUCHANAN, George W. "Oregon and California." OREGON HISTORICAL QUARTERLY 11(1910): 307-12. Guide.

BUCHANAN, James. MESSAGE OF THE PRESIDENT.... 36th Cong., 1st sess., S. Doc. 42. Serial 1033. Indians-Snake River. Mountain Meadows Massacre.

BUCHNER, John S. Overland Trip. In J. K. Meidenbaur Letters. WIHIST. CAL(Council). III. 1852.

BUCKINGHAM, Harriet T. "Crossing the Plains in 1851." In COVERED WAGON WOMEN, vol. 3, ed. Kenneth L. Holmes. Glendale: Clark, 1983. OR(Council)-BRIDGER-SLCUT. III. 1851.

BUCKINGHAM, Henry. Journey. BYU. OR(Council)-BRIDGER-SLCUT. III. Rem. 1850.

BUCKLAND, Samuel. SEE: Beuman, Edna L. "Story of Fort Churchill."

BUCKNER, Simon B. Letters. Filson Club Library, Louisville, KY. SANTA FE. 1851. Not Seen.

BUDD, Daniel H. Diary. Widener Library, Harvard Univ., Cambridge, MA. CAL. 1852. Not Seen.

BUFFUM, Joseph C. Diary. CAL(Indep)-HALL-TRUCKEE. II. 1849.

BUFKIN, Don. "Geographic Changes at Yuma Crossing, 1849-1966." ARIZONA & THE WEST 28(Sum 1986): n.p. Geog. Not Seen.

BULLOCK, Thomas. Diary. UTHIST. MORMON(Route over Wasatch into SLC). III. 1847.

BUNCH, E. J. and Thomas. Journal. Indiana State Library-Archives, Indianapolis, IN. CAL(St. Jo)-Ends on Humboldt River. II +. 1852.

BUNDSCHU, Henry A. "Francis Xavier Aubry." PACIFIC HISTORIAN 5(Aug 1961): 111-23. Biog.

BUNDY, R. A. Reminiscence. ORHIST. OR(Council). V-. Rem. 1865.

BUNYARD, Harriet. "Diary...1868." Ed. Percival J. Cooney. PUBLICATIONS Historical Society of Southern California 13(1924): 92-124. CAL-TEX-GILA. II. 1868.

BURBANK, Augustus R. Journals & Diaries. BANCROFT. CAL(St. Jo)-TRUCKEE. I. 1849.

BURCH, John C. Missouri to California. Princeton Univ. Library-Western History, Princeton, NJ. CAL(St. Jo?). IV. Rem. 1850.

BURCHAM, Mildred B. "Scott's and Applegate's Old South Road." OREGON HISTORICAL QUARTERLY 41(Dec 1940): 405-23. APPLE-1846-Genl.

BURGERT, Daniel, and Manilus S. Rudy. "The Rough Road West." COLUMBUS DISPATCH MAGAZINE, 8 June 1969, 46-53. CAL(Indep)-Ends on Bear River. III. 1849.

BURGESS, Jackson. PILLAR OF CLOUD. NY: Putnam's, 1957. SANTA FE(Bent's Fort via Smoky Hill River). II +. 1858.

BURGESS, Joseph H. "Grandfather Burgess Was a Forty-Niner." ILLINOIS HISTORICAL JOURNAL 53(Win 1960): 404-9. CAL(St. Jo). V. Rem. 1849.

BURGESS, Perry A. "From Illinois to Montana in 1866: The Diary of Perry A. Burgess." Ed. Robert G. Athearn. PACIFIC NORTHWEST QUARTERLY 41(1950): 43-65. CAL(Neb. City)-BOZE. II. 1866.

BURGUM, Edwin G. "The Concord Coach." COLORADO MAGAZINE 16(Sept 1939): 173-80. Stage.

BURGUNDER, Ben. "The Recollections of...." Ed. J. Orin Oliphant. WASHINGTON HISTORICAL QUARTERLY 17(Jul 1926): 190-210. OR(Council)-LANDER. V. Rem. 1862.

BURKE, Marguerette R. Ed. Hudson, Henry J. "Henry James Hudson and the Genoa [Nebraska] Settlement."

BURKE, W. S. DIRECTORY OF THE CITY OF COUNCIL BLUFFS AND EMIGRANTS' GUIDE. Council Bluffs, IA: Nonpareil, 1866. Guide.

BURKEY, Elmer R. Collection. COHIST. PIKES-1859-Genl.

BURKLEY, Frank J. THE FADED FRONTIER. Omaha: Author, 1935. PIKES. V-. Rem. 1859.

BURKLEY, Vincent. SEE: Burkley, Frank J. THE FADED FRONTIER.

BURLINGAME, Mr. & Mrs. "Journals." In ADVENTURES IN THE FAR WEST. Ed. Mrs. C. V. Waite. Chicago: Private, 1882. CAL(St. Jo)-BRIDGER-Ends SLC. II. Rem. 1862.

BURLINGAME, Merrill C. "The Influence of the Military in the Building of Montana." PACIFIC NORTHWEST QUARTERLY 29(Apr 1938): 135-50. MONTANA-Genl. Military.

_____. "John M. Bozeman, Montana Trailmaker." MISSISSIPPI VALLEY HISTORICAL REVIEW 27(Mar 1941): 541-68. Biog.

_____. JOHN M. BOZEMAN. N.p.: Private, 1941. BOZE-Genl. Biog.

BURNAP, Willard A. WHAT HAPPENED DURING ONE MAN'S LIFETIME, 1840-1920. Fergus Falls, MN: Burnap Estate, 1923. PIKES. IV. Rem. 1859.

BURNETT, Betty. "Goodale's Cutoff." OVERLAND JOURNAL 3(Win 1985): 30-34. OR-Ft. Hall to Ft. Boise-Genl.

_____. "Oregon City During the Emigration." OVERLAND JOURNAL 2(Spr 1984): 4-8. Geog.

BURNETT, Finn. SEE: David, Robert B. FINN BURNETT.

BURNETT, Hugh B. "Wagons in the Southwest: Some Were Monsters on Wheels." SAN DIEGO WESTERNERS BRAND BOOK 5(1978): 55-66. Freight. Graphics.

BURNETT, Peter Hardeman. AN OLD CALIFORNIA PIONEER. 1880. Reprint. Oakland: Biobooks, 1946. OR(Indep). IV. Rem. 1843.

_____. "Letters of Peter H. Burnett." Ed. Joseph Schafer. OREGON HISTORICAL QUARTERLY 3(Dec 1902): 398-404. Guide.

BURNHAM, Martin. Reminiscences. ORHIST. CAL(Indep). V. Rem. 1850.

BURNS, James F. "James Franklin Burns, Pioneer." Historical Society of Southern California QUARTERLY 32(Mar 1950): 61-66. CAL-MORMON-SLCOR. V-. 1853.

BURNS, Louis F. "Old Trails across Northern Osage County." CHRONICLES OF OKLAHOMA 59(Win 1981-2): 422-29. Stock.

BURR, Eugene P. "A Detailed Study of the Aubry Cutoff of the Santa Fe Trail and Fort Aubry." EMPORIA STATE RESEARCH STUDIES 23(Sum 1974): 5-72. Biog-Aubry. Geog. Maps.

BURRAL, George P. A Trip. BANCROFT. CAL(St. Jo)-Ends South Pass. II. 1849.

BURREL, Mary. Diary & Letter. BEINECKE. CAL(Council)-BRIDGER-SLCUT. II. 1854.

BURRELL, Louisa. Ed. Wade, Almira. "Across the Plains in 1849."

BURRES, John L. Memoirs. ORHIST. CAL(Council). II. Rem. 1854.

BURRIS, David. Narrative. BANCROFT. CAL-LASSEN. IV. Rem. 1849.

BURROUGHS, J. N. Recollections. CAHIST. CAL(Missouri). Rem. 1856. Not Seen.

BURROWS, Rufus G. Anecdotes. CSL. CAL(Indep)-HALL-TRUCKEE. IV. Rem. 1848.

_____, and Cyrus Hull. A LONG ROAD TO STONY CREEK. Ashland, OR: Lewis Osborne, 1971. CAL(Indep)-TRUCKEE. V. Rem. 1848.

BURT, S. W., and E. L. Berthoud. THE ROCKY MOUNTAIN GOLD REGIONS. 1861. Reprint. Denver: Old West, 1961. Guide. Maps.

BURTON, Alma P. THE MORMON TRAIL FROM VERMONT TO UTAH. SLC: Deseret, 1966. MORMON-Genl. Pres.

BURTON, Henry W. Diary. UWY. CAL(St. Jo)-HALL-TRUCKEE-Ends Truckee Meadows. II. 1849.

BURTON, Mary. In Stenhouse, Mrs. T. B. TELL IT ALL.... Hartford, CN: Worthington, 1874. MORMON. 1856. Not Seen.

BURTON, Richard F. THE CITY OF THE SAINTS.... Ed. Fawn M. Brodie. 1860. Reprint. NY: Knopf, 1963. Stage: St. Jo-Benicia. I. 1860.

BURTON, Robert T. Account. UTHIST. MORMON(SLC-Green River). III. 1862.

BURWELL, Lewis. Statement. BANCROFT. CAL-SANTA FE-SPANISH-SLCOR. V. Rem. 1853.

BUSH, Charles W. Five Letters. BANCROFT. CAL(St. Jo)-SLCUT-LASSEN. V. 1849.

BUSHNELL, Daniel E. Diary. Society of California Pioneers Library, SF. CAL(Council)-LANDER-HALL. 1862. Not Seen.

BUSHNELL, David I., Jr. DRAWINGS BY GEORGE GIBBS IN THE FAR NORTHWEST, 1849-1851. Smithsonian Misc. Collections Vol. 97, No. 8. WA: Smithsonian, 1938. Graphics.

BUSHNELL, George E. Diary. Held by Gregory Franzwa, St. Louis, MO. CAL(Neb. City)-CHEROKEE(Ft. Collins-SLC)-SIMPSON. 1864. Not Seen.

BUSHNELL, James A. THE AUTOBIOGRAPHY OF.... Eugene, OR: Lane County Pioneer-Historical Society, 1959. OR(Savannah Landing). V. Rem. 1852.

BUSHNELL, John C. NARRATIVE, 1833-1912. Eugene, OR: Lane County Pioneer-Historical Society, 1959. OR(Savannah Landing)-MEEK. V. Rem. 1853.

BUSS, Mrs. Geo. E. AUNT AMELIA'S DIARY. Ed. Sara Ovenholt. Mattituck, NY: Ovenholt, 1965. PIKES. III. 1866.

BUTLER, J. A. Journal. BANCROFT. CAL(West Point)-Ends Carson Valley. III+. 1856.

BUTLER, Peter. Letters. BANCROFT. OR(Council). V. 1853.

BUTSCHER, Louis C. Ed. Wurttemberg, Paul W. "Brief Biography."

BUTTERFIELD, Ella A. "Butterfield Overland Despatch." TRAIL 18(Dec 1925): 3-9. Stage-Smoky Hill Route, 1865.

BUTTERFIELD, Ira H., Jr. "Michigan to California in 1861." MICHIGAN HISTORY 2(Jul 1927): 392-423. CAL(Neb. City)-LAS-

SEN. III. Rem. 1861.

BUTTERFIELD, James T. "Interesting Account of a Trip across the Plains in 1853." Ed. Mrs. F. O. Tompkins. GRIZZLY BEAR 2(Jan 1908): 42-45. CAL(Council). V-. Rem. 1853.

_____. Journeys. CSL. CAL(Council)-SLCUT-TRUCKEE. IV. Rem. 1853. Unedited version of above item.

"Butterfield Overland Mail, 1958 in Oklahoma." CHRONICLES OF OKLAHOMA 36(Win 1958-59): 478-81. Pres.

Butterfield Overland Mail Centennial. Scrapbook. MO-WHMC. Pres.

Butterfield Overland Mail Company. THROUGH TIME SCHEDULE BETWEEN ST. LOUIS...AND...CALIFORNIA. N.p., 1858.

"Butterfield Stage Route." LOS TULARES 16(Sept 1953): 1, 3-4. Pres.

"Butterfield Stage Route, Tulare County, CA. [Map]." LOS TULARES 37(Sept 1958): 3-6. Maps.

"The Butterfield Stages." LA PENINSULA 9(Feb 1958): 3-6. Stage-San Mateo County, CA.

Butterfield's Overland Despatch. PROSPECTUS OF BUTTERFIELD'S OVERLAND...1865. NY: Harrison, 1865. Stage.

BYARS, William H. "Carrying the Mail in Southern Oregon, 1856-1858." Ed. David A. Ramsted. LA POSTA 11(Dec 1980): 2-15. Mail.

BYERS, Frank S. "From the West to East in '65." TRAIL 18(Jan 1926): 5. Stage(Denver-Atchison via Smoky Hill route). IV. 1865.

BYERS, William N. A HAND BOOK OF THE GOLD FIELDS OF NEBRASKA AND KANSAS.... NY: Derby & Jackson, 1859. Guide.

_____. "The Oregon Odyssey of William N. Byers." Ed. Merrill J. Mattes. OVERLAND JOURNAL 1(Jul, Fall 1983): 14-23, 12-21; 2(Win, Spr 1984): 14-23, 23-28. Also in TRAIL, July-Aug-Sept, 1926. OR(Council)-BARLOW. II. Rem. 1852.

BYNUM, J. M. Ed. Ormsby, Waterman. BUTTERFIELD OVERLAND.

BYNUM, Lindley, ed. THE RECORD BOOK, RANCHO SANTA ANA DEL CHINO. LA: Fremont High School, 1935. GILA-Genl.

Byrne Family Papers. BANCROFT. CAL(Kansas City)-LANDER. V. 1859.

CADY, Samuel. Recollections. Indiana State Library, Indianapolis, IN. CAL(St. Jo). Rem. 1850. Not Seen.

CAGE, R. A. "The Lowden Empire: A Case Study of Wagon Roads in Northern California." PACIFIC HISTORIAN 28(Sum 1984): 32-48. Freight.

CAGWIN, Hamden A. THE TRAVEL DIARY OF.... Ed. Louisa Dorsey Cagwin. N.p.: Editor, 1974. CAL(St. Jo)-Ends Bear River. II. 1850.

CAGWIN, Louisa D. Ed. Cagwin, Hamden A. TRAVEL DIARY.

CAINE, John T. "Journal of...." HEART THROBS OF THE WEST 5(1944): 217-80. SLCOR. III+. 1854.

CALDEMEYER, Richard H. "The Overland Mail and Stage to Salt Lake City, 1847-1961." MA thesis, Washington Univ., 1931. Mail. Stage.

CALDWELL, George L. "The Pony Express." CAVALRY JOURNAL 33(Apr 1924): 173-79. Pony.

CALDWELL, Martha B., comp. ANNALS OF SHAWNEE METHODIST MISSION. Topeka: Kansas State Historical Society, 1939. Geog.

_____. "When Horace Greeley Visited Kansas in 1859." KANSAS HISTORICAL QUARTERLY 9(Spr 1940): 115-40. Stage.

CALDWELL, T. G. "Notes of a Journey, 1849." In GOLD RUSH...OF J. GOLDSBOROUGH BRUFF, eds. Georgia W. Read and R. Gaines. NY: Columbia Univ. Press, 1949. CAL(Little Blue)-HALL-LASSEN. III. 1849.

California Division of Beaches and Parks. REPORT OF INVESTIGATION ON LOCATION, COST AND ACQUISITION AND DEVELOPMENT OF OVERLAND EMIGRANT TRAIL. Sacramento: State Parks Comm., 1949. CAL-Genl.

"The California Dog Express." HUTCHINGS' 5(Feb 1861): 321-23. Stage.

California Interstate Telephone Company. ROMANTIC HERITAGE OF THE MOJAVE RIVER VALLEY. Barstow?: Author, N.d. Geog.

"California Landmarks. GRIZZLY BEAR 2(Apr 1908): 12-13, 31. Pres(Donner Lake Monument).

"California Overland Express." LEISURE HOUR 14(n.d.): 11-60. Not Seen.

California Volunteer Infantry, Co. "C," 4th Infantry. CALIFORNIA CIVIL WAR DIARY, 1862. Iowa City: Univ. of Iowa, n.d. GILA(San Pedro, CA-Yuma). III. 1862.

"The California Wagon Route." DE BOW'S REVIEW 21(Jul 1856): 58-63. Govt-Petition for Wagon Road.

CALL, Asa C. Diary. CAHIST. CAL(Ft. Kearny). Rem. 1850. Not Seen.

CALL, Oscar. Diary. BARKER. TEX-1858-Genl.

CALL, W. W. Reminiscence. BANCROFT. CAL(Indep)-SLCUT. IV. Rem. 1849.

CALLAWAY, Lew L. "Joseph Alfred Slade; Killer or Victim." MONTANA 3(Jan 1953): 5-34. Biog. Stage. Freight.

CALLISON, John J. DIARY OF...1852. Eugene, OR: Lane County Pioneer-Historical Society, 1959. OR(Neb. City)-Ends Independence Rock. III. 1852.

CALVIN, Ross. Ed. Emory, W. H. LT. EMORY REPORTS.

CAMDEN, Charles. SEE: Eaton, Edna B. "Charles Camden."

CAMERON, J. B. Journal. Stanford Univ. Library-SpCol, Palo Alto, CA. CAL-TEX(Pecos River)-GILA. II+. 1849.

CAMERON, Janet S. "Early Transportation in Southeastern Ventura County." VENTURA COUNTY HISTORICAL SOCIETY QUARTERLY 10(Nov 1964): 1-16. Geog.

CAMP, Charles L. Ed. Clyman, James. JAMES CLYMAN. Ed. Wagner, Henry R. THE PLAINS AND THE ROCKIES. Ed. White, Philo. NARRATIVE. SEE: With Reva Stanley. "A Mormon Mission."

_____. "Colonel Philip Leget Edwards and his Influence upon Early Immigration to the Far West." CALIFORNIA HISTORICAL QUARTERLY 3(1924): 78-83. Guide.

_____, ed. JAMES CLYMAN, FRONTIERSMAN. Portland: Champoeg, 1960. OR(Indep). I. 1844. CAL(Sutter's)-TRUCKEE-HASTINGS-BRIDGER. 1846. Biog.

_____. "Kit Carson in California." CALIFORNIA HISTORICAL QUARTERLY 1(Oct 1922): 115-51. Biog.

_____, ed. "William Alexander Trubody and the Overland Pioneers of 1847." CALIFORNIA HISTORICAL QUARTERLY 16(Jun 1937): 122-43. CAL-1847-Genl. Rem.

CAMPBELL, Albert H. REPORT UPON THE PACIFIC WAGON ROADS.... 35th Cong, 2nd sess., S. Ex. Doc. 36. Govt.

_____. The Clarno Era. ORHIST. Stage.

CAMPBELL, David. Pioneer of 1846. BANCROFT. CAL(Indep)-HALL-TRUCKEE. V. Rem. 1846.

CAMPBELL, Emma L. Ed. Campbell, Remembrance. "Carry On."

CAMPBELL, Eugene E. SEE: With Fred R. Gowans. FORT BRIDGER.

CAMPBELL, J. A. A Trip. MONHIST. DAKOTAS-MONTANA. V. 1866.

CAMPBELL, James. Diary. BANCROFT. CAL(St. Jo)-TRUCKEE. III-. 1850.

CAMPBELL, John L. IDAHO: SIX MONTHS IN THE NEW GOLD DIGGINGS.... NY: Tribune, 1964. Guide.

CAMPBELL, John V. "The Sinclair Party - An Emigration Overland along the Old Hudson Bay Company Route from Manitoba to the Spokane Country in 1854." WASHINGTON HISTORICAL QUARTERLY 7(Jul 1916): 187-201. CANADA-WASH. III. 1854.

CAMPBELL, Margaret. WAGONS WESTWARD. El Monte, CA: Latin American Village, 1949. Graphics.

CAMPBELL, Murray. "The Postal History of Red River, British North America." Historical and Scientific Society of Manitoba PAPERS 3(1951): 7-19. CANADA-Genl. Mail.

CAMPBELL, Newton G. Memories of Travel. BANCROFT? Not Seen.

CAMPBELL, Mrs. Paul. "Benoni Morgan Hudspeth." IDAHO YESTERDAYS 12(Fall 1968): 9-13. CAL-Genl. Hudspeth Cutoff.

CAMPBELL, Remembrance H. "Carry On." Ed. Emma L. Campbell. N.p., 1930? CAL(Council)-SLCUT. IV. Rem. 1853.

CAMPBELL, Robert. Letter. NBHIST. MORMON. 1850. Not Seen.

CAMPBELL, Robert L. Journal. LDS. MORMON-SLCOR(to southern Utah). II. Rem. 1849.

CAMPBELL, Ruth J. "St. Joseph, MO: Gateway to the West." MA thesis, Univ. of Southern California, 1946. Geog.

CAMPBELL, T. N., and William T. Field. "Identification of Comanche Raiding Trails in Trans-Pecos Texas." WESTX 44(Oct 1968): 128-44.

Indians. TEX-Genl.

CAMPBELL, William. SEE: Courtney, W. B. "Pony Boy."

CAMPER, Henry W. "Why I Crossed the Plains to California in 1850." Ed. Gertrude E. Merryman. DIGGINS 26(Fall 1982): 57-64. CAL(Council)-SLCUT. IV. Rem. 1850.

Canada and British Columbia. CORRESPONDENCE...RELATIVE TO A ROAD AND TELEGRAPH FROM CANADA TO BRITISH COLUMBIA. Parliamentary Papers No. 438 and 402. London: N.p., 1863 and 1864. Telegraph. CANADA-Genl.

CANADY, Nicholas, Jr. "Letters from the West: A Survey of Reports by Travelers in the NEW ORLEANS PICAYUNE, 1837-60." In TRAVELERS ON THE WESTERN FRONTIER, ed. John F. McDermott. Urbana: Univ. of Illinois Press, 1970. Bib.

CANDEE, J. G. Letter. CSL. CAL(Ft. Smith)-MARCY-RIO GRANDE-GILA. IV. 1849.

CANDLER, G. M. THE WAY WEST. London: American Museum, N.d. OVERLAND-Genl.

CANN, T. H. "From the Mississippi to the Valley of the Sacramento." OVERLAND MONTHLY 45(Jun 1905): 526-28. CAL(St. Jo). V. Rem. 1854.

CANNON, James D., ed. CENTENNIAL CARAVAN: STORY OF THE 1947 CENTENNIAL REENACTMENT OF THE ORIGINAL MORMON TREK. SLC?: Sons of the Utah Pioneers, 1948. Pres.

CANNON, George Q. A TRIP TO CALIFORNIA. SLC: Juvenile Instructor, 1869. SLCOR. III. Rem. 1849.

CANNON, John Q. Ed. Layton, Christopher. AUTOBIOGRAPHY.

CANNON, Miles. "Fort Hall on the Saptin River." WASHINGTON HISTORICAL QUARTERLY 7(Jul 1916): 217-32. Geog.

CANTWELL, James C. and Catherine. Jessie Cantwell Hilburger Papers. Washington State Library-Northwest Collection, Seattle, WA. OR-WASH. 1844. Not Seen.

CANTWELL, James S. Journal. Ed. Blair R. Holmes. UTHIST. MORMON. V. 1856.

CAPERTON, John. Letter. Filson Club Library, Louisville, KY. GILA(El Paso-San Diego). 1849. Not Seen.

CAPLES, Mrs. James. Overland Journey. CSL. CAL(St. Jo)-TRUCKEE. Rem. 1849. CAL(Council). IV. Rem. 1863.

CAPLES, Margaret S. Reminiscences. Washington State Univ. Library-SpCol, Pullman, WA. OR(Plattsmouth). IV. Rem. 1852.

"Captain Townsend's Battle on the Powder River." MONHIST. BOZE. II. 1864. Indians.

CARD, Cicero. Diary. Clarke Library, Central Michigan Univ. Mt. Pleasant, MI. CAL(Neb. City)-BOZE-LANDER-MONT. 1863. Not Seen.

CARDINELL, Charles. "Adventures on the Plains." CALIFORNIA HISTORICAL QUARTERLY 1(Jul 1922): 57-71. CAL-TEX(Port Lavaca)-GILA. III. Rem. 1849.

CARDON, A. F. "Mountain Meadows Burial Detachment, 1859: Tommy Gordon's Diary." UTAH HISTORICAL QUARTERLY 35(Spr 1967): 143-46.

Geog.

CAREY, Charles H. Ed. Talbot, Theodore. JOURNALS.

CAREY, Thomas G. Papers. DENVERPUB. Telegraph.

CARLETON, J. Henry. "The Overland Route to California: Major Carleton's Tables of Distances." AMERICAN REGISTER AND MAGAZINE 4(Jul 1850): 246-52. Guide.

_____. THE PRAIRIE LOGBOOKS. Reprint. Chicago: Caxton, 1943. CAL(Ft. Leav-South Pass). I. 1845. Military. Indians.

CARLETON, James H., and William C. Mitchell. SPECIAL REPORT OF THE MASSACRE AT THE MOUNTAIN MEADOWS.... 57th Cong., 1st sess., H. Doc. 605. Little Rock: True Democrat, 1860. Govt. Geog.

CARLEY, Maurine. SEE: Trenholm, Virginia. THE SHOSHONIS.

_____. "Bozeman Trail Trek: Trek No. 14 of the Emigrant Trail Treks." ANNALS OF WYOMING 36(Apr 1964): 43-77. Pres.

_____. "Bridger Trail Trek: Trek No. 17 of the Historic Trail Series." ANNALS OF WYOMING 37(Apr 1967): 108-28. Pres.

_____. "Cheyenne-Deadwood Trail Trek: Trek No. 15 of the Emigrant Trail Treks." ANNALS OF WYOMING 37(Apr 1965): 75-109. Pres.

_____. "Cheyenne-Deadwood Trail Trek No. 2: Trek No. 16 of the Historic Trail Treks." ANNALS OF WYOMING 38(Apr 1966): 84-103.

_____. "Emigrant Trail Trek No. Nine." ANNALS OF WYOMING 31(Oct 1959): 213-26. Pres.

_____. "Emigrant Trail Trek No. Ten." ANNALS OF WYOMING 32(Apr, Oct 1960): 103-23, 219-38. Pres.

_____. "Fifth Segment of the Oregon Trail: Green River to Cokeville." ANNALS OF WYOMING 45(Fall 1973): 249-63. Pres.

_____. "The First Fifty Miles of the Oregon Trail in Wyoming. Wyoming's Eastern Border to Warm Springs." ANNALS OF WYOMING 42(Apr 1970): 77-103. Pres.

_____. "Fourth Segment of the Oregon Trail in Wyoming: Tom Sun Ranch to South Pass." ANNALS OF WYOMING 42(Fall 1972): 268-86. Pres.

_____. "Oregon Trail and California-Mormon Trails: Fort Bridger to Wyoming's Western Border." ANNALS OF WYOMING 41(Apr 1969): 113-30. Pres.

_____. "Oregon Trail Trek No. One." ANNALS OF WYOMING 27(Oct 1955): 163-94. Pres.

_____. "Oregon Trail Trek No. Two." ANNALS OF WYOMING 27(Apr 1956): 41-67. Pres.

_____. "Oregon Trail Trek No. Three." ANNALS OF WYOMING 28(Oct 1956): 167-92. Pres.

_____. "Oregon Trail Trek No. Four." ANNALS OF WYOMING 29(Apr 1957): 67-85. Pres.

_____. "Oregon Trail Trek No. Five." ANNALS OF WYOMING 29(Oct 1957): 177-94. Pres.

_____. "Oregon Trail Trek No. Six." ANNALS OF WYOMING 30(Apr 1958): 37-52. Pres.

_____. "Oregon Trail Trek No. Seven." ANNALS OF WYOMING 30(Oct 1958): 193-213. Pres.

_____. "Overland Stage Trail - Trek No. 1." ANNALS OF WYOMING 33(Apr 1961): 73-101. Pres.

_____. "Overland Stage Trail - Trek No. 2." ANNALS OF WYOMING 33(Oct 1961): 195-214. Pres.

_____. "Overland Stage Trail - Trek No. 3." ANNALS OF WYOMING 34(Oct 1962): 235-49. Pres.

_____. "Point of Rocks - South Pass City Freight Road Trek: Trek No. 18 of the Historic Trail Treks." ANNALS OF WYOMING 40(Apr 1968): 107-27. Pres.

_____. "Second Segment of the Oregon Trail in Wyoming: Cold Spring to Fort Fetterman." ANNALS OF WYOMING 42(Oct 1970): 252-74. Pres.

_____. "Third Segment of the Oregon Trail, Douglas to Independence Rock: Trek No. 22 of the Historic Trail Treks." ANNALS OF WYOMING 43(Fall 1971): 270-95. Pres.

CARLISLE, Norman. "Exploring the West's Pioneer Trails." CORONET 49(Mar 1961): 102-9. Pres.

CARLSON, Edward. "The Martial Experiences of the California Volunteers." OVERLAND MONTHLY 7(May 1886): 480-96. BEALE(Wilmington, CA - Ft. Mojave). IV. Rem. 1863.

CARMER, Carl. "Here is my Home at Last. AMERICAN HERITAGE 14(Feb 1963): 26-33, 98-102. CAL-Genl.

CARNES, David. Journal. BANCROFT. CAL(St. Jo)-TRUCKEE. II+. 1849.

CARPENTER, Augustine D. Diary. Society of California Pioneers Library, SF. Not Seen.

CARPENTER, Dan. Journal. Kansas City Public Library, Kansas City, Mo. CAL(Iowa Point). 1850. Not Seen.

CARPENTER, Edwin H. Ed. Wilson, Benjamin D. "Benito Wilson."

CARPENTER, Helen M. "Across the Plains in 1858." In HO FOR CALIFORNIA, ed. Sandra L. Myres. San Marino: Huntington, 1980. CAL(Westport?)-TRUCKEE. II. 1857.

CARPENTER, James C. I Crossed the Plains in the 50's. KSHIST. CAL(Council)-BRIDGER-SLCUT. III. Rem. 1852.

CARR, John. A VULCAN AMONG THE ARGONAUTS. Ed. Robin Lampson. SF: Geo. Fields, 1936. CAL(Leav)-BRIDGER-SLCUT. IV. Rem. 1850.

CARR, William. "Depredations by the Yumas." PUBLICATIONS Historical Society of Southern California 6(1903): 52-56. Geog. Indians.

CARRIGER, Nicholas. "Diary." In OVERLAND IN 1846, ed. Dale L. Morgan. Georgetown, CA: Talisman, 1963. CAL(Neb. City)-BRIDGER-TRUCKEE. III-. Rem. 1846.

CARRIKER, Robert C. FORT SUPPLY.... Norman: Univ. of Oklahoma Press, 1970. Geog.

CARRINGTON, Albert. "Diary of Albert Carrington." HEART THROBS OF THE WEST 8(1947): 77-146. MORMON. II+. 1850. MORMON. II+. 1851.

CARRINGTON, Francis C. MY ARMY LIFE.... Philadelphia: Lippincott, 1910. Military.

CARRINGTON, Henry. "Map of the Platte River Ford." PUBLICATIONS Nebraska State Historical Society 21(1930): N.p. Geog.

CARRINGTON, Henry B. "History of Indian Operations on the Plain, 1866." BEINECKE. BOZE-1866-Genl.

CARRINGTON, Margaret I. AB-SA-RA-KA, HOME OF THE CROWS. Philadelphia: Lippincott, 1868. Military.

CARSON, Kit. SEE: Camp, Charles L.

CARSON, Sandra M. "Music: A Softer Pleasure along the Oregon-California Trail." OVERLAND JOURNAL 4(Spr 1986): 36-39. Social.

CARSTARPHEN, James E., and Clayton Keith. MY TRIP TO CALIFORNIA IN '49. Louisiana, MO: Authors, 1914. CAL(St. Jo)-HALL. V. Rem. 1849.

CARSTENSON, Vernon. Ed. Crockett, Samuel B. "Diary."

CARTER, B. F. OVERLAND TO SANTA FE. Winterset, IA: Madisonian, 1913. SANTA FE. IV. Rem. 1851.

CARTER, E. S. THE LIFE AND ADVENTURES OF E. S. CARTER. St. Joseph, MO: Combe, 1896. OR(Leav). V-. Rem. 1852.

CARTER, Henry W. Narrative. BANCROFT. CAL(Leav)-SANTA FE-RIO GRANDE-GILA. III+. Rem. 1857.

CARTER, Kate B. Ed. Allred, Reddick. "Journal."

_____. "Communications of Early Utah." HEART THROBS OF THE WEST. SLC: Daughters of the Utah Pioneers, 1947. UTAH.

_____. "Development of Transportation." HEART THROBS OF THE WEST, Vol. 2. SLC: Daughters of the Utah Pioneers, 1940. UTAH.

_____. "Graves along the Trail." OUR PIONEER HERITAGE 16(1973): 421-76. Social.

_____. "March of the Mormon Battalion." HEART THROBS OF THE WEST, Vol. 7. SLC: Daughters of the Utah Pioneers, 1947. GILA-1846-Genl.

_____. "Mississippi Saints." OUR PIONEER HERITAGE 2(1959): 421-76. Biog.

_____. THE MORMON BATTALION. SLC: Daughters of the Utah Pioneers, 1956. GILA-1846-Genl.

_____. THE NEGRO PIONEER. SLC: Daughters of the Utah Pioneers, 1956. Social.

_____. A PIONEER JOURNAL, FORSGREN COMPANY.... SLC: Daughters of the Utah Pioneers, 1944. MORMON. III. 1853.

_____. "Pioneer Mail Routes, Carriers and Contractors." In HEART THROBS OF THE WEST 12(1951): 53-92. Mail. Stage.

_____. RIDERS OF THE PONY EXPRESS. SLC: Daughters of the Utah Pioneers, 1947. Pony.

_____. "Roads of Early Utah." HEART THROBS OF THE WEST, Vol. 1. SLC: Daughters of the Utah Pioneers, 1947. Utah.

_____. "The Spirit of Emigration." HEART THROBS OF THE WEST, Vol 4. SLC: Daughters of the Utah Pioneers, 1943. MORMON-Genl.

_____. "The Story of Telegraphy." OUR PIONEER HERITAGE 4(1961): 509-72. Telegraph.

_____. "They Came in 1847." HEART THROBS OF THE WEST, Vol. 8. SLC: Daughters of the Utah Pioneers, 1947. MORMON-1847-Genl.

_____. "They Came in '48." HEART THROBS OF THE WEST 9(1948): 453-524. MORMON-1848-Genl.

_____. "They Came in '50." HEART THROBS OF THE WEST, Vol. 11. SLC: Daughters of the Utah Pioneers, 1950. MORMON-1850-Genl.

_____. "Toll Gates, Bridges and Ferries of the West." HEART THROBS OF THE WEST." 10(1949): 104-16. Overland-Genl.

_____. "Trails and Pioneer Freighters Who Followed Them." HEART THROBS OF THE WEST 10(1949): 53-103. Freight.

_____. UTAH AND THE PONY EXPRESS. SLC: Utah Printing, 1960. Pony.

_____. "Women of the Mormon Battalion and the Mississippi Saints." HEART THROBS OF THE WEST, Vol. 2. SLC: Daughters of the Utah Pioneers, 1940. Social.

_____, and Clara B. Steele. THE MORMON BATTALION. SLC: Utah Printing, 1956. GILA-Genl. Utah.

CARTER, Kathryn T. STAGECOACH INNS OF TEXAS. Waco, TX: Texian, 1972. Stage. Graphics.

CARTER, Tolbert. "Pioneer Days." TRANSACTIONS Oregon Pioneer Association 1906(1907): 65-103. APPLE(Lost River-Eugene). III. 1846.

CARTER, William A. "Diary of Judge William A. Carter." ANNALS OF WYOMING 11(Apr 1939): 75-110. CAL(Atchison)-Ends Ft. Bridger. II. 1857.

CARTER, William Alexander. Papers, 1858-1884. DENVERPUB. Stage.

CARTWRIGHT, David W. "A Tramp to California." In NATURAL HISTORY OF WESTERN WILD ANIMALS. Toledo, OH: Blade, 1875. CAL(St. Jo)-LASSEN. III. Rem. 1852.

CARVALHO, Solomon N. INCIDENTS OF TRAVEL AND ADVENTURE IN THE FAR WEST.... Ed. Bertram Wallace Korn. 1857. Reprint. NY:
Kraus, 1971. CAL(Westport)-SANTA FE-SPANISH. II. 1853.

CASE, Chester. "The Development of Roads between Oregon and California." MA thesis, Univ. of California-Berkeley, 1955. OR-CAL-Genl. Stage. Mail.

CASE, Frank. "Experiences on the Platte River Route in the Sixties." COLORADO MAGAZINE 5(Aug 1928): 146-51. MORMON. IV. 1865. Freight.

CASE, Hamet H. Diary. BANCROFT. OR(Laramie)-LANDER. III+. 1859.

CASE, William M. "Reminiscences of William M. Case." Ed. H. S. Lyman. OREGON HISTORICAL QUARTERLY 1(Sept 1900): 269-77. OR(Council)-Ends Ft. Laramie. V. Rem. 1844.

CASEBIER, Dennis G. SEE: With Chester King. BACKGROUND TO HISTORIC RESOURCES.

_____. THE BATTLE AT CAMP CADY. Tales of the Mojave Road No. 2. Norco, CA: Author, 1972. Geog.

_____. CAMP ROCK SPRING, CALIFORNIA. Tales of the Mojave Road No. 3. Norco, CA: Author, 1972. Geog. BEALE-Genl.

_____. CARLETON'S PAH-UTE CAMPAIGN; FORT PAH-UTE, CALIFORNIA; THE MOJAVE ROAD. Tales of the Mojave Road No. 1. Norco, CA: Tales, 1972-75. BEALE-Genl. Military.

_____. FORT PAH-UTE, CALIFORNIA. Tales of the Mojave Road No. 4. Norco, CA: Tales, 1974. Military. Geog. Graphics.

_____. THE MOJAVE ROAD. Tales of the Mojave Road No. 5. Norco, CA: Tales, 1975. Fine account of events and geography along the Beale Road. Superior graphics. BEALE-Genl.

_____. MOJAVE ROAD GUIDE. Norco, CA: Tales, 1986. Not Seen.

_____. THE MOJAVE ROAD IN NEWSPAPERS. Tales of the Mojave Road No. 6. Norco, CA: Tales, 1976. BEALE-Genl. Graphics.

CASLER, Melyer. A JOURNAL GIVING THE INCIDENTS...1859---OVERLAND ROUTE. 1863. Reprint. Fairfield, WA: Ye Galleon, 1969. CAL(Council)-BRIDGER-SLCUT. III+. 1859.

CASSELL'S EMIGRANT'S GUIDE TO CALIFORNIA. London: Cassell, Petter & Galpin, 1855. Guide.

CASSERLY, Eugene. SOME CONSIDERATIONS IN FAVOR OF THE PASSAGE OF SENATE BILL NO. 47. N.P.: Author, 1866. Telegraph.

CASSIN, Francis. Statement. BANCROFT. CAL(Indep). V-. Rem. 1849.

CASTLE, Gwen. Ed. Belshaw, Geo. "Belshaw Journey."

CASTLEBERRY, Lillie C. "Transplains Expeditions, 1850-1860." MA thesis, Univ. of Texas-Austin, 1933. Overland-Genl.

CASTLEMAN, P. F. Diary. BANCROFT. CAL(St. Jo)-LASSEN. II+. 1849.

A CATALOGUE OF THESES AND DISSERTATIONS CONCERNING THE CHURCH OF JESUS CHRIST OF LATTER-DAY SAINTS, MORMONISM AND UTAH, COMPLETE TO JANUARY, 1970. Provo, UT: BYU Printing Service, 1971. Not Seen. Bib.

CATHEY, Andrew. "The Cathey Wagon Train." Comp. J. L. Pritchard. CSL. CAL(Ft. Smith)-OKLAHOMA-TEX-GILA. V-. 1852.

CATLIN, George. CATLIN'S NOTES FOR THE EMIGRANT TO AMERICA. London: Author, 1848. Guide.

CATTELL, Hester. Ed. Estabrook, Joseph H. "Crossing the Plains."

CAUGHEY, John Walton. Ed. Stover, Jacob. "Narrative." Ed. Ware, Joseph. EMIGRANTS' GUIDE.

_____. RUSHING FOR GOLD. Berkeley: Univ. of California Press, 1949. CAL-1849-Genl.

_____. "Southwest from Salt Lake in 1849." PACIFIC HISTORICAL REVIEW 6(Jun 1937): 143-64. SLCOR. II. 1849.

_____. "The Transit of the Forty-Niners." In ESSAYS IN WESTERN HISTORY IN HONOR OF PROFESSOR T. A. LARSON, ed. Roger Daniels. University of Wyoming Publications 37. Laramie: Univ. of Wyoming, 1971. CAL-1849-Genl.

CAUTHORN, Benjamin R. Trip to Montana. BYU. OR(Neb. City)-CHEROKEE(Ft. Collins-Ft. Bridger)-MONTANA(Snake River-Helena-Boise)-BARLOW. I. 1865.

CAUTHORN, James D. Diary. ORU. OR(Neb City)-Ends Ft. Bridger. III. 1865. Same as prior item.

CEDARHOLM, Caroline. A NARRATIVE.... N.p. n.d. Trip to Arizona. Not Seen.

"Centennial of the Pony Express." Chicago Westerners BRAND BOOK 17(Apr 1960): 9-12, 13-16. Pony.

Central Overland California and Pike's Peak Express Company. Binding Articles, 1861. NBHIST. Stage.

_____. VIGNETTE OF EXPRESS RIDER. PONY EXPRESS TO SAN FRANCISCO IN TEN DAYS. PASSENGER EXPRESS TO DENVER CITY AND PIKE'S PEAK GOLD REGIONS IN FIVE DAYS.... NY: Root, Anthony, 1860? Broadside.

CENTRAL OVERLAND ROUTE AND TRANSCONTINENTAL TELEGRAPH THROUGH NEVADA, 1858-1868. Oakland: Trash, 1985. SIMPSON-Genl. Telegraph.

CHABOT, Frederick C., comp. "Texas Mail Service and the San Antonio Post Office." U.S. Postal Service Library, Washington, DC. Not Seen.

CHADWICK, Samuel. Diary. WIHIST. CAL(Council)-TRUCKEE-BECKWOURTH. II. 1852.

CHAFFEE, Eugene B. "Early History of the Boise Region, 1811-1864." MA thesis, Univ. of California-Berkeley, 1931. Geog.

CHAFFIN, Thomas A. Traveling.... MONHIST. CAL(Ft. Scott)-MONTANA(Snake River-Bannack). IV. Rem. 1864.

CHALFANT, W. A. DEATH VALLEY: THE FACTS. Palo Alto: Stanford Univ. Press, 1930. Geog. SLCOR-1849-Genl.

_____. OUTPOST OF CIVILZATION. Boston: Christopher, 1924. Stage.

CHALMERS, Robert. "The Journal of Robert Chalmers." Ed. Charles Kelly. UTAH HISTORICAL QUARTERLY 20(Jan 1952): 31-55. CAL(Indep)-BRIDGER-HASTINGS. II. 1850.

CHALONER, Henry. "Western Express Companies." BANCROFT. Stage.

CHAMBERLAIN, Samuel E. MY CONFESSION. NY: Harper, 1956. CAL-MEX(Parras)-GILA. IV. Rem. 1848.

CHAMBERLAIN, William E. Diary. BANCROFT. CAL(St. Jo)-HALL-TRUCKEE. II. 1849.

CHAMBERLAIN, William Edwin. Diary. CSL. CAL(Indep)-BRIDGER-HASTINGS. II. 1849.

CHAMBERLAIN, William H. "From Lewisburg to California." Ed. Lansing Bloom. NEW MEXICO HISTORICAL REVIEW 20(Jan,

Apr, Jul, Oct 1945): 14-57, 104-80, 239-68, 336-57. CAL(Ft. Smith)-MARCY-RIO GRANDE-GILA. I. 1849.

CHAMBERS, Andrew Jackson. RECOLLECTIONS. Reprint. Fairfield, WA: Ye Galleon, 1975. OR(St. Jo). V. Rem. 1845.

CHAMBERS, Elizabeth H. INCIDENTS IN THE LIFE.... N.p.: Author, 1910? OR(Indep). IV. 1845.

CHAMBERS, J. Mae. Ed. Chambers. JUDGE THOMAS M. CHAMBERS.

CHAMBERS, Margaret W. "Reminiscences." In RECOLLECTIONS, comp. Andrew Jackson Chambers. Fairfield, WA: Ye Galleon, 1975. OR(St. Jo). V. Rem. 1851.

CHAMBERS, Thomas McCutcheon. JUDGE THOMAS M. CHAMBERS, eds. Retta Chambers Hultgren and J. Mae. Chambers. Shelton, WA: Editors, 1945. OR. V. 1845.

CHAMBERS, William and Robert. "Journey from New Orleans to California." CHAMBERS' JOURNAL, 1 Dec 1855, 337-41, 364-68, 371-75. CAL(Westport). IV. 1849.

CHAMPNESS, W. TO CARIBOO AND BACK IN 1862. 1865. Reprint. Fairfield, WA: Ye Galleon, 1972. CANADA(New Westminster-Fraser River). I. 1862.

CHANDLER, Knowlton H. Journal. Illinois State Historical Library, Springfield, IL. CAL(St. Jo)-TRUCKEE-BECKWOURTH. III. 1852.

CHANDLER, Robert J. "The California News-Telegraph Monopoly, 1860-1870." Historical Society of Southern California QUARTERLY 53(Win 1976): 459-84. Telegraph.

CHANDLESS, William. A VISIT TO SALT LAKE.... London: Smith, Elder, 1859. CAL(Atchison)-BRIDGER-SLCOR. II. 1855.

CHANEY, Raymond D., Jr. "San Diego and the Overland Mail." SDHIST. Stage.

CHAPEL, Charles E. GUNS OF THE OLD WEST. NY: Coward-McCann, 1961. Fine analysis and graphics. Eqpt.

CHAPMAN, A. H. Diary. MNHIST. CAL(St. Jo)-Ends Bear River. III. 1850.

CHAPMAN, Arthur. THE PONY EXPRESS. NY: Putnam, 1932. Pony.

CHAPMAN, Darius H. Diary. NBHIST. PIKES(Neb-City-Plattsmouth area only). II. 1859.

CHAPMAN, Gerald. "Exploring for the Telegraph in British Columbia, 1865-1866." BEAVER 66(May 1986). Not Seen.

CHAPMAN, William W. Diary. In Paul and Helen Collection. UWY. CAL(St. Jo)-Ends Raft River. III. 1849.

CHAPPELL, Gordon S. "The Fortifications of Old Fort Laramie." ANNALS OF WYOMING 34(Oct 1962): 145-62. Geog.

CHAPUT, Donald. FRANCOIS X. AUBREY - TRADER, TRAILMAKER AND VOYAGEUR...1846-1854. Western Frontiersman Series No. 16. Glendale: Clark, 1975. CAL(San Jose)-BEALE-Ends Santa Fe. III. 1853. Freight.

CHARLTON, Joseph J. Autobiography. Washington State Historical Society Library, Tacoma, WA. OR(Council). IV. Rem. 1850.

CHASE, Don M. PACK SADDLES AND ROLLING WHEELS...TRANSPORTATION IN SOUTHERN OREGON AND NORTHWESTERN CALIFORNIA FROM 1852. Crescent City, CA: Author, 1959. Stage. Freight.

CHASE, Doris Harter. Ed. Harter, George. CROSSING THE PLAINS.

CHATHAM, J. W. Diary. BARKER. CAL(Indep)-SANTA FE-Ends near Albuquerque. I. 1849.

CHEADLE, Walter B. CHEADLE'S JOURNAL OF TRIP ACROSS CANADA, 1862-1863. Edmonton: Hurtig, 1971. CANADA(St. Anthony-Ft. Garry-Ft. Edmonton-Yellowhead Pass-Victoria). I. 1862-63. Graphics.

CHEEK, Larry. "Bushwhacked on the Trail." OLD WEST 8(Sum 1972): 20-21, 64-65. 1851 ambush at Cajon Pass.

CHEESMAN, David W. "By Ox Team from Salt Lake to Los Angeles, 1850." Ed. Mary E. Foy. PUBLICATIONS Historical Society of Southern California 14(1930): 271-338. SLCOR. III. 1850.

CHEMIDLIN, Nicholas. Reminiscences. MONHIST. MONTANA(Ft. Ridgeley-Helena). IV. 1864.

CHENEY, J. W. "The Story of an Immigrant Train." ANNALS OF IOWA 12(Jul 1915): 81-97. CAL(Kansas City)-SANTA FE-BEALE-Ends at Colorado River. III. 1858. Detailed account of attack at Mohave Villages.

_____. FROM A SOLDIER'S PEN. Keosauqua, IND?: Author, 1918? CAL(Kansas City)-SANTA FE-BEALE-Ends at Colorado River. V-. 1858.

CHENOWETH, F. A. "Occasional Address." TRANSACTIONS Oregon Pioneer Association (1882): 28-34. OR(Leav). Rem. IV. 1849.

CHICK, Washington H. Reminiscences. KSHIST. CAL(Kansas City). V-. Rem. 1849.

CHILD, A. L. "Gold at Pike's Peak - Rush for - Stampede." TRANSACTIONS Nebraska State Historical Society 1(1885). PIKES-Genl.

CHILD, Andrew. OVERLAND ROUTE TO CALIFORNIA. 1852. Reprint. LA: Kovach, 1946. Guide.

THE CHILDREN ON THE PLAINS, A STORY OF TRAVEL AND ADVENTURE FROM THE MISSOURI TO THE ROCKY MOUNTAINS. London: T. Nelson, 1872. Children's fiction based on actual trip. CAL(Leav)-BRIDGER. Graphics. No date.

CHILES, Henrietta M. Diary. BARKER. CAL(Indep?)-Ends near Ft. Laramie. III. 1850.

CHILES, Joseph Ballinger. SEE: Giffen, Helen S. TRAIL-BLAZING PIONEER.

_____. Visit to California in 1841. BANCROFT. CAL(Indep). V. Rem. 1841. Bidwell-Bartleson Party.

CHILLSON, Lorenzo D. Diary. HUNTL. CAL(Plattsmouth)-HALL. III. 1859. SIMPSON(Austin)-CHEROKEE(SLC-Ft. Halleck). III. 1865. Stage-1865.

CHIMNEY ROCK. N.p.: U.S. National Park Service, n.d. Geog.

CHISLETT, Mr. "Narrative." In Stenhouse, Thomas B. THE ROCKY

MOUNTAIN SAINTS.... London: Ward, Lock, and Tyler, 1874. MORMON. Rem. 1856. Not Seen.

CHITTENDEN, Hiram M., and A. T. Richardson, eds. LIFE, LETTERS, AND TRAVELS OF FATHER PIERRE-JEAN DE SMET, S.J., 1801-1873. 4 vols. NY: Harper, 1905. Biog.

CHORPENNING, George. A BRIEF HISTORY OF THE MAIL SERVICE.... WA: N.p., 187? Mail.

_____. THE CASE OF GEORGE CHORPENNING.... WA: M'Gill & Witherow, 1874. Mail.

_____. STATEMENT AND APPENDIX.... WA: N.p., 1889? Excellent summary of Chorpenning's claim. Mail. Stage.

_____, and Elizabeth Woodward. [To Accompany H. Res. No. 157] REPORT [of] THE COMMITTEE ON INDIAN AFFAIRS. 37th Cong, 3d sess., 1863. H. Rep. No. 61. Mail.

"Chorpenning's First Overland Pony Express." PONY EXPRESS 27(Feb 1961): 3-5. Mail.

CHOTEAU, B. "Choteau's Log and Description of the Trail." In OLD SPANISH TRAIL, eds. LeRoy R. and Ann W. Hafen. Glendale: Clark, 1954. SPANISH-Genl.

CHRISMAN, Harry. LOST TRAILS OF THE CIMARRON. Denver: Sage, 1961. Stock. Freight. Stage.

CHRISTENSEN, C. C. A. "By Handcart to Utah...." Trans. Richard L. Jensen. NEBRASKA HISTORY 66(Win 1985): 333-48. MORMON. V. Rem. 1857.

CHRISTIAN, Lewis C. "A Study of the Mormon Westward Migration...and Evaluation of the Factors that led to the Mormons' Choice of Salt Lake Valley as the Site of their initial Colony." PhD diss., BYU, 1976. MORMON-1847-Genl. Geog.

CHRISTIANSEN, John R. "Traveling the Old Pony Express Trail." MOUNTAINWEST 2(Apr 1976): 29-32, 36. Pres.

CHRISTIANSEN, Larry D. "The Mormon Battalion in Cochise County." COCHISE QUARTERLY 13(Aut-Win, 1983): 1-42. GILA-1846-Genl.

CHRISTIE, Blanche. "Phineas Banning, with Special Reference to the Development of Transportation in Southern California." MA thesis, Univ. of Southern California, 1932. Biog. Freight.

CHRISTY, Thomas. THOMAS CHRISTY'S ROAD.... Ed. Robert H. Becker. Denver: Old West, 1969. CAL(Council). II. 1850. Maps.

CHURCHILL, Claire Warner. Ed. Stewart, Agnew. "The Journey to Oregon."

CHURCHILL, Stillman. Diary. MNHIST. CAL(Indep?)-LASSEN. II+. 1849.

CHURCHILL, Willoughby. MEMORIES OF OWEN HUMPHREY CHURCHILL AND HIS FAMILY. Ed. Marion Churchill Raulston. N.p.: Editor, 1950. OR(Council). IV. 1851.

CIPRIANI, Count Leonetto. CALIFORNIA AND OVERLAND DIARIES.... Ed. Ernest Falbo. Portland: Champoeg, 1962. CAL(Westport)-BRIDGER-SLCUT. III. 1853.

"Circular of the Overland Mail Company." TRAIL 2(May 1909): 10-11. Stage.

CISNE, Jonah G. "Across the Plains and in Nevada City...."

COLORADO MAGAZINE 27(Jan 1950): 49-57. PIKES(Atchison). III. 1860.

CLAMPITT, John W. ECHOES FROM THE ROCKY MOUNTAINS. Chicago: Belford, Clarke, 1889. Overland-Genl. Superb line drawings.

CLANDENING, William H. "Across the Plains in 1863-65." NORTH DAKOTA HISTORICAL QUARTERLY 2(Jul 1928): 247-72. DAKOTAS(St Paul)-MONTANA. III. 1863. CAL(Montana-Council)-MONTANA(Virginia City-Snake River)-Ends Council Bluffs. III. 1864.

CLAPP, John T. A JOURNAL OF TRAVELS.... 1851. Reprint. Kalamazoo, MI: Museum, 1977. CAL(Council). III+. 1850.

CLARK, ? Diary. NVHIST. CAL(Humboldt River-Carson Pass). III. 1852.

CLARK, Alvah. "Diary." (In) ACROSS THE PLAINS AND BEYOND, ed. Ruth Conard. WA: N.p., n.d. OR(Council)-BARLOW. 1852. Not Seen.

CLARK, Anna Nolan. "He Blazed the Trail." NEW MEXICO 19(Feb 1941): 21-23, 38-40. Biog-Richard L. Wooton.

CLARK, Anson. Overland in 1850. CSL. CAL(St. Jo)-BRIDGER-SLCUT. III. Rem. 1850.

CLARK, Benjamin S. Diary. Society of California Pioneers, SF. Not Seen.

CLARK, Bennett C. "Diary of a Journey from Missouri to California in 1849." Ed. Ralph P. Bieber. MISSOURI HISTORICAL REVIEW 23(Oct 1928): 3-43. CAL(Westport)-HALL-TRUCKEE. II. 1849.

CLARK, Calvin P., and Helen E. TWO DIARIES. Denver: Denver Public Library, 1962. PIKES(Leav)-SANTA FE-CHEROKEE. IV. 1859. PIKES(Council). IV. 1860.

CLARK, Carter B., comp. "Research Tools, Guides and Bibliographies on Arizona History: A Selected List." ARIZONA & THE WEST 24(Spr 1982): 39-56. Bib.

CLARK, Charles M. A TRIP TO PIKES PEAK.... Chicago: S. P. Rounds, 1861. PIKES(St. Jo). I. 1860. Good lithographs.

CLARK, Costmor H. Journal. NVHIST. CAL(South Pass)-BRIDGER-HASTINGS. II. 1850. Virtually illegible.

CLARK, Dan E. "The Movement to the Far West during the Decade of the Sixties." WASHINGTON HISTORICAL QUARTERLY 17(Apr 1926): 105-13. Overland-Genl.

CLARK, Donald H. "Remember the Winter of....? Weather and Pioneers." OREGON HISTORICAL QUARTERLY 54(Jun 1953): 140-48. Social.

CLARK, Eva T. Ed. Gill, William. CALIFORNIA LETTERS.

CLARK, George T. "Across the Plains and in Denver, 1860." COLORADO MAGAZINE 6(Jul 1929): 131-40. PIKES(Council). III+. 1860.

CLARK, Harrison C. "The Organization of the Oregon Emigration Company." OREGON HISTORICAL QUARTERLY 16(Sept 1915): 205-27. Train Govt.

CLARK, Helen E. SEE: With Calvin P. Clark. TWO DIARIES.

CLARK, Jessie L. "Boyd's Ferry on the Cache La Poudre."

COLORADO MAGAZINE 26(Oct 1949): 287-90. Geog.

CLARK, John. "California Guide, 1852-56." BEINECKE. CAL. Virtually Illegible. 1852?

CLARK, John Hawkins. "Overland to the Gold Fields of California in 1852...." Ed. Louise Barry. KANSAS HISTORICAL QUARTERLY 11(Aug 1942): 227-98. CAL(St. Jo)-BRIDGER-SLCUT. II+. 1852.

CLARK, John R. Diary. BYU. MORMON. 1864. Not Seen.

CLARK, Jonathan. "The Diary of Dr. Jonathan Clark." ARGONAUT, 1-8-15-22 August 1925, p. 3. each issue. CAL(Council)-LASSEN. IV. 1849.

CLARK, Keith, and Lowell Tiller. TERRIBLE TRAIL: THE MEEK CUTOFF, 1845. Caldwell, ID: Caxton, 1966. MEEK-1845-Genl.

CLARK, Mabell S. "The First Loup River Ferry." NATIONAL HISTORICAL MAGAZINE of the Daughters of the American Revolution 74(Feb 1940): 16-17. Geog-Loup River Ferry.

CLARK, Pal. Ed. Mullan, John. "Journal."

CLARK, Robert M. "Robert M. Clark's Journey." In Paul and Helen Henderson Collection. UWY. CAL(St. Jo). III. Rem. 1850.

CLARK, Roger W. "Annotated and Critical Study of THE LIFE OF THE EMIGRANT, GREAT SALT LAKE CITY, AND MORMONISM AT HOME by a Georgian." MA thesis, Yale Univ., 1931. MORMON. IV. 1850.

CLARK, Sterling B. HOW MANY MILES FROM SAINT JO? Ed. Ella Sterling Mighels. SF: Taylor & Taylor, 1929. CAL(St. Jo): BRIDGER-SLCUT-TRUCKEE. IV. 1849.

CLARK, Thomas D. Ed. Perkins, Elisha D. GOLD RUSH DIARY. Ed. Gray, Charles. OFF AT SUNRISE.

——. "Edwin Bryant and the Opening of the Road to California." In ESSAYS IN WESTERN HISTORY IN HONOR OF PROFESSOR T. A. LARSON. Ed. Roger Daniels. Univ. of Wyoming Pub. 37. Laramie: Univ. of Wyoming, 1971. CAL(Indep)-BRIDGER-TRUCKEE. III. 1846.

CLARK, Wanda. "History of Nirom Hawley." LANE COUNTY HISTORIAN 14(Fall 1969): 51. OR(Council)-BARLOW. IV. 1852.

CLARK, William. "A Trip across the Plains in 1857." IOWA JOURNAL OF HISTORY AND POLITICS 20(Apr 1922): 163-223. CAL(Leav)-BRIDGER-SLCOR. II. Rem. 1857. Freight.

CLARK, William S. Biographical Sketch. BANCROFT. CAL(Indep)-BRIDGER-HASTINGS-TRUCKEE. V. Rem. 1846.

CLARKE, Asa. B. TRAVELS IN MEXICO AND CALIFORNIA. Boston: Wright & Hasty, 1852. CAL-MEX(Monterey-Chihuahua-Santa Cruz)-GILA. II+. 1849.

CLARKE, Charles G. Ed. Millington, Ada. "Journal."

CLARKE, Dwight L. Ed. Turner, Henry S. THE ORIGINAL JOURNAL.

——. STEPHEN WATTS KEARNEY: SOLDIER OF THE WEST. Norman: Univ. of Oklahoma, 1961. Biog.

CLARKE, H. T. "Freighting - Denver and the Black Hills." PROCEEDINGS AND COLLECTIONS Nebraska State Historical Society 5(1902): 299-312. Freight.

CLARKE, Harriet T. SEE: Buckingham, Harriet C. "Crossing the Plains."

CLARKE, Helen P. "Sketch of Malcolm Clarke." CONTRIBUTIONS Historical Society of Montana 2(1896): 255-68. MULLAN-Genl. Indians.

CLARKE, Isaac. Journal. LDS. MORMON. II. 1849.

CLARKE, S. A. PIONEER DAYS OF OREGON HISTORY. 2 vols. Portland: J. K. Gill, 1905. OR-Genl.

CLAWSON, Calvin. Writings. MONHIST. Freight.

CLAWSON, Linn E. "Early Freighting in Northeastern Nevada: A Look at the Equipment, the Teams and One Local Route." NEVADA HISTORICAL SOCIETY QUARTERLY 28(Sum 1985): 122-38. Freight. Eqpt.

CLAYCOMB, William B. "John S. Jones: Farmer, Freighter, Frontier Promoter." MISSOURI HISTORICAL REVIEW 73(Jul 1979): 434-50. Biog. Freight. Stage.

CLAYTON, Dick. "The Old Weber Stage and Pony Express Station." HOBBIES 44(Apr 1939): 71-73. Pony. Geog.-Echo Canyon, UT.

CLAYTON, William. THE LATTER-DAY SAINTS' EMIGRANTS' GUIDE. St. Louis: Missouri Republican, 1848. MORMON. III. 1847.

_____. WILLIAM CLAYTON'S JOURNAL. SLC: Deseret, 1921. MORMON. I. 1847.

CLEAVER, Benjamin. Diary. ORHIST. OR(Begins Burnt River)-BARLOW. II. 1848.

CLEGG, Charles. SEE: With Lucius Beebe. U.S. WEST.

CLEGHORN, Daniel B. Diary. In W. W. Morrison Collection. UWY. PIKES(Council). V. 1861.

CLELAND, Robert G. Ed. Pownall, Joseph. "From Los Angeles to Mariposa." SEE: With Juanita Brooks. A MORMON CHRONICLE.

_____. "An Exile on the Colorado." Los Angeles Westerners BRAND BOOK 6(1956): 17-30. Biog(Thomas W. Sweeney). Geog(Yuma).

_____. "John Bidwell's Arrival in California." PUBLICATIONS Historical Society of Southern California 10(1915-1916): 110-13. CAL-1841-Genl(Sierra crest to Marsh's Ranch).

_____. PATHFINDERS. One of the California Series, John R. McCarthy, General Editor. LA: Powell, 1929. Overland-Genl.

_____. "Transportation in California before the Railroads, with especial Reference to Los Angeles." PUBLICATIONS Historical Society of Southern California 11(1920): 60-67. CAL-Genl.

CLEMENS, Samuel L. SEE: Twain, Mark.

CLEMINSON, John. Diary. CSL. CAL(Indep?)-SANTA FE-RIO GRANDE-GILA. II. 1851.

CLEMMER, Richard O. "The Tail of the Elephant: Indians in Emigrant Diaries, 1844-1862." NEVADA HISTORICAL SOCIETY QUARTERLY 30(Win 1987): 269-90. Indians.

CLIFFORD, Henry H. SEE: With Edgar B. Jessup and M. C. Nathan. EARLY CALIFORNIA MAIL BAG.

_____. "California Gold Rush Express Covers and Western Express Companies, 1849-1895." HUNTL. Stage.

_____. "Western Express: A Study in Gold Rush Communications." Los Angeles Westerners BRAND BOOK, 1950 (1951): 33-44. Stage.

CLIFFORD, Josephine. "Crossing the Arizona Deserts." OVERLAND MONTHLY 4(Jun 1870): 537-44. Stage(LA-Tucson). 1869.

CLIFTON, John. "Diary." In MORE THAN GOLD IN CALIFORNIA. Ed. Mary B. Ritter. Berkeley: Ritter, 1933. CAL(St. Jo)-TRUCKEE. III. 1849.

CLINE, Gloria G. EXPLORING THE GREAT BASIN. Norman: Univ. of Oklahoma Press, 1963. Overland-Genl.

CLINKINBEARD, Anna Dell. Ed. Clinkinbeard, Philura V. ACROSS THE PLAINS.

CLINKINBEARD, Philura V. ACROSS THE PLAINS IN '64. Ed. Anna D. Clinkinbeard. NY: Exposition, 1953. OR(Council). III. Rem. 1864.

CLOUD, Roy W. ON THE TRAILS OF YESTERDAY. SF: Harr Wagner, 1931. CAL(St Jo)-BRIDGER. IV. 1853.

CLOUGH, L. W. "Sheep Follow Advancing Golden Frontier, and Murder of Shepherds of Men Speeds Entry of Colonizers' Flocks." COLORADO WOOL GROWER 3(Sept 1937): N.p. Not Seen.

CLOUGH, Wilson O. Trans. Simonin, Louis. ROCKY MOUNTAIN WEST.

CLOVER, M. "Holidays that make History; Retracing the Oregon Trail" PARENTS 50(Jul 1975): 42-43. Pres.

CLUFF, Harvey H. Journal. BYU. MORMON. V. 1850. MORMON. V. 1856. MORMON. V. 1865.

CLYMAN, James. SEE: Camp, Charles L. "James Clyman." Camp, Charles L. "Tracking the Spoor."

THE COACH-MAKERS' ILLUSTRATED HAND-BOOK. Philadelphia: I. D. Ware, 1872. Stage-Eqpt.

COATS, Felix G. On the Golden Trail. CSL. CAL(Indep)-HALL-TRUCKEE. V. Rem. 1849.

COBB, Frank M. "The Lawrence Party of Pike's Peakers (1858) and the Founding of St. Charles." COLORADO MAGAZINE 10(Sept 1933): 194-97. PIKES. IV. 1858.

COBBEY, John F. Journal. BYU. CAL(St. Jo). I. 1850.

COBURN, Catherine A. "Narrative." In HISTORY OF THE OREGON COUNTRY, vol. 3, ed. Harvey W. Scott. Vol. 3. Cambridge: Riverside, 1924. OR(St. Jo?)-BARLOW. IV. Rem. 1852.

COBURN, Jesse L. LETTERS OF GOLD: CALIFORNIA POSTAL HISTORY THROUGH 1869. Canton, OH: U.S. Philatelic Classics Society, 1984. Mail. Comprehensive bibliography. Stage. Graphics.

COCHRAN, Kathryn. "The Bascom Affair Revisited." DESERT 41(Dec 1978): 12-15. Stage.

COCKHILL, Brian, and Dale L. Johnson, eds. GUIDE TO

MANUSCRIPTS IN MONTANA REPOSITORIES. Missoula: Univ. of Montana Library, 1973. Bib.

CODY, Cora. "John Bidwell: His Early Career in California." MA thesis, Univ. of California-Berkeley, 1927. CAL-1841-Genl. Biog.

CODY, William F. "Buffalo Bill." SEE: With Henry Inman. GREAT SALT LAKE TRAIL.

COFFEY, Alvin A. "A Black Pioneer's Trip to California." PACIFIC HISTORIAN 13(Jan 1969): 58-62. CAL(St. Jo)-HALL-LASSEN. V. Rem. 1849.

COIT, Daniel W. SEE: Gilman, William C. A MEMOIR.

_____. DIGGING FOR GOLD - WITHOUT A SHOVEL: THE LETTERS OF DANIEL WADSWORTH COIT FROM MEXICO CITY TO SAN FRANCISCO, 1848-1851. Ed. George P. Hammond. Denver: Old West, 1967. CAL-MEX(Mexico City to San Blas). V. 1849. Graphics.

_____. THE DRAWINGS AND LETTERS OF DANIEL WADSWORTH COIT. Ed. Edith M. Coulter. SF: Book Club, 1937. CAL-MEX. V. 1849. Graphics.

COKE, Henry J. SEE: Armytage, W. H. "H. J. Coke on the Oregon Trail."

_____. A RIDE OVER THE ROCKY MOUNTAINS TO OREGON AND CALIFORNIA. London: Richard Bentley, 1852. OR(Council). I. 1850.

COLBY, W. Howard. A CENTURY OF TRANSPORTATION IN SHASTA COUNTY, 1821-1920. Association for Northern California Records and Research Occasional Pub. No. 7. N.p., 1982. LASSEN-Genl. Stage.

COLE, Cornelius. MEMOIRS.... NY: McLoughlin, 1908. CAL(Indep)-BRIDGER-SLCUT. V. Rem. 1849.

COLE, David N. ASSESSING AND MONITORING BACK-COUNTRY TRAIL CONDITIONS. Ogden, UT: U.S. Dept. of Agriculture, 1983. Pres.

COLE, Frank L. "The Establishment and Administration of Mail Communications in Oregon." MA thesis, Univ. of Oregon, 1958. Mail.

COLE, Garold. AMERICAN TRAVELERS TO MEXICO, 1821-1972; A DESCRIPTIVE BIBLIOGRAPHY. Troy, NY: Whitson, 1978. Bib.

_____. TRAVELS IN AMERICA...AN ANNOTATED BIBLIOGRAPHY OF TRAVEL ARTICLES IN PERIODICALS, 1955-1980. Kansas City: Hudson, 1905. Bib.

COLE, Gilbert L. IN THE EARLY DAYS ALONG THE OVERLAND TRAIL IN NEBRASKA TERRITORY IN 1852. Kansas City: Hudson, 1905. CAL(St. Jo). IV. Rem. 1852.

COLE, James H. "James Harvey Cole's Story." FARWESTERNER 9(Oct 1968): 5-9. CAL(Leav). V. 1853. Cattle Drive.

COLE, Lucy W. Story. UTHIST. MORMON. IV. Rem. 1856.

COLEGROVE, George L. Life Story. BANCROFT. Stage(Council-SIMPSON-SF). V. Rem. 1863.

COLEMAN, Louis, Leo Rieman and B. C. Payette, comps. CAPTAIN JOHN MULLAN.... Montreal: Payette Radio, 1968. Biog. MULLAN-Genl.

COLEMAN, William T. Sketch. BANCROFT. CAL(St. Jo). V. Rem. 1849.

COLFAX, Schuyler. "Honorable Schuyler Colfax's Journey from the Missouri River to California in 1865." WESTERN GALAXY 1(1888): 320-57. CAL(Atchison)-PIKES-CHEROKEE(Denver-SLC)-SIMPSON. II. 1865.

COLLEY, Charles C. SEE: With Dennis Reinhartz. MAPPING.

COLLIER, David C. Letters. Univ. of Colorado Norlin Library-Western Historical Collections, Boulder, CO. PIKES-Genl.

COLLIER, James. SEE: Goreman, Grant. ADVENTURES OF JAMES COLLIER.

COLLINS, Catherine W. "An Army Wife Comes West...." Ed. Agnes Wright Spring. COLORADO MAGAZINE 31(Oct 1954): 241-73. Stage: Ft. Laramie to Omaha. IV. 1864.

COLLINS, Dabney O. "Escalante's Trail, Or Plunder Road of the West." Denver Westerners BRAND BOOK 21(1966): 357-74. SPANISH-Genl.

_____. "The First Stagecoach into Denver." COLORADO OUT-DOORS 27(Jul-Aug 1978): 22-26. PIKES-1859-Genl-Stage.

COLLINS' EMIGRANT GUIDE TO THE GOLD MINES OF THE ROCKY MOUNTAINS. Charles W. Martin Collection. Omaha, NB. Guide.

COLLINS, Mrs. Frank. "Reminiscences...." Ed. Frank Lockley. OREGON HISTORICAL QUARTERLY 17(Dec 1916): 358-72. OR(Caples Landing, MO). V-. Rem. 1844.

COLLINS, Ivan L. HORSE POWER DAYS: POPULAR VEHICLES OF NINETEENTH CENTURY AMERICA. Stanford: Stanford Univ. Press, 1953. Eqpt.

COLLINS, John S. ACROSS THE PLAINS IN '64. Omaha: Author, 1904. CAL(Council)-MONTANA. III. Rem. 1864.

COLLINS, Karen L. "Guide to Diaries in the University of Texas Archives Produced before 1900." MA thesis, Univ. of Texas-Austin, 1967. Bib.

COLLINS, Lowell D. Ed. Collins, Smith. SMITH COLLINS.

COLLINS, Martha A. "Memories of Two Young Girls." CAHIST. CAL(Council). V. Rem. 1852.

COLLINS, Smith. SMITH COLLINS, PIONEER. Ed. Lowell D. Collins. Klamath Falls, OR: Editor, 1965. OR(Kansas)-APPLE. III. 1846.

COLLINS, William. "Overland Journeys in Oregon and California of the U.S. Navy Exploring Expedition." PhD diss., Univ. of New Mexico, 1966. OR-CAL-1841-Genl.

COLLISTER, Oscar. "Life of [a] Wyoming Pioneer...." ANNALS OF WYOMING 7(Jul, Oct 1930): 343-61, 370-78. Telegraph.

COLTER, John R. "Bret Harte as a Wells Fargo Express Gun Guard." OVERLAND MONTHLY 68(Dec 1916): 535-36. Stage.

Columbus, Ohio Citizens. REPORT ON THE TERRITORY OF OREGON.... Columbus, OH: Ohio Statesman, 1843. OR-1843-Genl.

COLVIG, William M. "Indian Wars of Southern Oregon." OREGON HISTORICAL QUARTERLY 4(Sept 1903): 227-40. Military.

COLYER, Julie B. Ed. Beehrer, George W. FREIGHTING.

"Comanche Springs Improved." FRONTIER TIMES 11(Jun 1934): 393-95. Geog.

"The Comanches and the Comanche War Trail." FRONTIER TIMES 16(Apr 1949): 160-63. TEX-Genl.

COMMITTEE ON POST OFFICES AND POST ROADS...THE MEMORIAL OF THE CALIFORNIA STAGE COMPANY.... 36th Cong., 1st sess., 1860. S. Rpt. No. 275. Mail.

COMMITTEE ON POST OFFICES AND POST ROADS...THE PETITION OF GEORGE CHORPENNING, JR.... 34th Cong., 1st sess., 1856. H. Rpt. No. 323. Mail. Govt.

"Committee Report Butterfield Overland Mail." CHRONICLES OF OKLAHOMA 36(Win 1958-1959): 446-72. Pres. Map.

A COMPLETE 1859 GUIDE TO THE GOLD MINES IN KANSAS AND NEBRASKA, WITH A DESCRIPTION OF THE SHORTEST AND ONLY ALL RAILROAD ROUTE TO KANSAS.... Boston: Rand & Avery, 1859. Guide.

COMPTON, Henria P. MARY MURDOCK COMPTON. N.p.: Author, 1953. CAL(Indep)-BRIDGER-SLCUT-TRUCKEE. IV. Rem. 1853.

COMPTON, James H. Diary. BANCROFT. CAL(Council)-BRIDGER-SLCUT. III+. 1853.

COMPTON, Mary Murdock. SEE: Compton, Henria P. MARY MURDOCK COMPTON.

COMSTOCK, David A. GOLD DIGGERS AND CAMP FOLLOWERS: THE NEVADA COUNTY CHRONICLES, 1845-1851. Grass Valley, CA: Comstock Bonanza Press, 1982. CAL-1849-Genl.

COMSTOCK, Loring S. A JOURNAL OF TRAVELS ACROSS THE PLAINS...1855. Oskaloosa, IA: Clarkcraft, 1971? CAL(Council)-TRUCKEE. III+. Rem. 1855.

COMSTOCK, Noah D. "Diary." In Elizabeth Comstock Papers. WIHIST. CAL(Ash Hollow)-TRUCKEE. II. 1853.

CONARD, Howard L. UNCLE DICK WOOTON. One of the Lakeside Classics, ed. Milo Milton Quaife. Chicago: Donnelley, 1957. CAL(Taos)-SPANISH-SLCUT. IV. 1852. Sheep drive. Freight. Geog: Raton. Stage.

CONARD, Ruth. Ed. Clark, Alvah. "Diary."

CONDIT, Philip. Diary. ORU. OR(Council). IV. 1854.

CONDIT, Sylvanus. Diary. ORU. OR(Council)-BARLOW. III. 1854.

CONDON, Phoebe. "Ezra Meeker: His Mansion, Monuments and Mission." AMERICAN WEST 10(Mar 1973): 10-11. Pres.

CONDRON, Harry D. "The History of the Knapheide Wagon Company." MA thesis, Univ. of Missouri-Columbia, 1941. Eqpt.

_____. "Knapheide Wagon Company, 1848-1943." JOURNAL OF ECONOMIC HISTORY 3(May 1943): 32-41. Eqpt.

CONE, Anson S. "Reminiscences." Ed. H. S. Lyman. OREGON HISTORICAL QUARTERLY 4(Sept 1903): 251-66. OR(St. Jo). V. Rem. 1846.

CONE, G. C. Diary. Fred Rosenstock Collection, Denver, CO. CAL(St. Jo)-BRIDGER-SLCUT. 1849. Not Seen.

CONGER, Sarah M. "Journal of a Journey across the Plains from St. Joseph, Michigan, to California, in 1849-50." MS thesis, Univ. of California-Los Angeles, N.d. Missing.

CONKLING, Margaret B. SEE: With Roscoe P. Conkling. BUTTERFIELD OVERLAND MAIL.

CONKLING, Roscoe P. "The Butterfield Overland Mail in California." Los Angeles Westerners BRAND BOOK (1948): 17-26. Stage.

_____. WATERMAN LILY ORMSBY, II. Los Angeles Corral of Westerners Keepsake No. 46. LA: Westerners, 1958. Stage(Butterfield, 1858).

_____, and Margaret B. Conkling. THE BUTTERFIELD OVERLAND MAIL, 1857-1869. 2 vols. Glendale: Clark, 1947. Mail. Stage.

CONLEY, Washington. Diary. Indiana State Library, Indianapolis, IN. PIKES. 1860. Not Seen.

CONLIN, Joseph R. "Eating on the Rush: Organizing Meals on the Overland Trail." CALIFORNIA HISTORY 64(Sum 1985): 218-25, 244. Social.

CONMY, Peter T. THE STEVENS-MURPHY-MILLER PARTY OF 1844. SF: Native Sons of the Golden West, 1942. CAL-1844-Genl.

CONNELLY, Thomas L. "The American Camel Experiment: A Reappraisal." SOUTHWESTERN HISTORICAL QUARTERLY 69(Apr 1966): 442-62. Teams.

CONNELLEY, William E. SEE: With Frank Root. OVERLAND STAGE.

CONNER, Daniel E. A CONFEDERATE IN THE COLORADO GOLD FIELDS. Eds. Donald J. Berthrong and Odessa Davenport. Norman: Univ. of Oklahoma Press, 1970. PIKES. I. Rem. 1859.

CONNOR, Ben A. SEE: Crawford, Lewis F. REKINDLING OLD CAMPFIRES.

CONNOR, Seymour V., and Jimmy M. Skaggs. BROADCLOTH AND BRITCHES: THE SANTA FE TRADE. College Station, TX: Texas A&M Press, 1977. SANTA FE-Genl.

CONNOR, T. J. Diary. ORHIST. OR(Council). III. 1853.

CONRAD, David E. "Explorations and Railway Survey of the Whipple Expedition, 1853-1854." MA thesis, Univ. of Oklahoma, 1955. CAL-1853-Genl. Govt.

_____. "The Whipple Expedition in Arizona, 1853-1854." ARIZONA & THE WEST 11(Sum 1963): 147-78. CAL(Ft. Smith)-MARCY-BEALE. II. 1853.

_____. "The Whipple Expedition on the Great Plains." GREAT PLAINS JOURNAL 2(Spr 1963): 42-66. CAL(Ft. Smith)-MARCY-BEALE. II. 1853. Govt. Biog.

CONSIDINE, J. L. "Eleven Days to Saint Joe!" SUNSET, October 1923, 36. Pony.

CONSTANT, Isaac. "A Brief Review." Ed. Lavinia Jane Robinson. In "Amos Merriman and his Descendants," comp. W. W. Merriman. Illinois State Historical Library, Springfield, IL. OR(Indep)-APPLE. III. 1852.

CONTRACT-OVERLAND PACIFIC MAILS. 40th Cong., 3d sess.,

1869. H. Rpt. 37. 1868 Wells Fargo Mail Contract.

CONWAY, Alan, ed. THE WELSH IN AMERICA: LETTERS FROM THE IMMIGRANTS. Minneapolis: Univ. of Minnesota Press, 1961. Overland-Genl.

CONWAY, Cornelius. THE UTAH EXPEDITION.... Cincinatti: Safety Fund Reporter Office, 1858. Utah.

CONWAY, Mary. "Little Rock Girl Rides on Horseback to California in Gold Rush Days." PULASKI COUNTY HISTORICAL REVIEW 12(Mar 1964): 6-9. CAL(Ft. Smith)-MARCY-RIO GRANDE-GILA. IV. 1849.

CONYERS, E. W. "Diary...1852." TRANSACTIONS Oregon Pioneer Association, 1905. (1906): 423-512. OR(Council)-BARLOW. II+. 1852.

COOK, Clarice. "To California by Prairie Schooner, 1841-1860." UPAC. Overland-Genl.

COOK, F. S. "Captured by Indians." UTHIST. 1865 Rock Creek, WY indian attack.

COOK, Gertrude F. Family Papers. Univ. of Arkansas Library-SpCol, Fayetteville, Arkansas. OR(Indep). 1852. Not Seen.

COOK, Mary E. Diary. MONHIST. Stage(Ft. Benton-Helena). 1868.

COOK, Peter. LIFE OF PETER COOK. Eds. Thomas S. and Harriet Ball. Portland: Metropolitan, 1959. CAL(Council)-BRIDGER. IV. Rem. 1850. CAL(Council). IV. Rem. 1861.

COOK, Phineas W. LIFE AND HISTORY.... N.p, n.d. MORMON? 1848. Not Seen.

COOK, William J. "Diary." Unionville [Missouri] REPUBLICAN, July-December, 1935. CAL(St. Jo). II+. 1850.

COOKE, Lucy R. CROSSING THE PLAINS IN 1852. Modesto: N.p., 1923. CAL(Council)-BRIDGER-Ends SLC. II. 1852. CAL(SLC)-SLCUT. II. 1853. Utah.

COOKE, Philip St. George. THE CONQUEST OF NEW MEXICO AND CALIFORNIA.... NY: Putnam's, 1878. CAL(Leav)-SANTA FE-RIO GRANDE-GILA. I. Rem. 1846.

_____. JOURNAL. 31st Cong., Spec. Sess., No. 1. Serial 547. CAL(Santa Fe)-RIO GRANDE-GILA. I. 1846.

_____. "March of the Second Dragoons...Fort Leavenworth to Fort Bridger in 1857." Ed. Hamilton Gardner. ANNALS OF WYOMING 27(Apr 1955): 43-61. Ft. Leav. - Ft. Bridger. II. 1857.

_____. SCENES AND ADVENTURES IN THE ARMY. Philadelphia: Lindsay & Blakiston, 1857. Ft. Leav - Ft. Bridger. II. 1857.

COOMBS, Susan B. "San Gorgonio Pass, Early History to 1880." Banning [California] Library. BRADSHAW-Genl. Not Seen.

COON, Polly. "Journal." In COVERED WAGON WOMEN, vol. 5, eds. Kenneth Holmes and David C. Duniway. Glendale: Clark, 1986. OR(Council)-Ends near Salmon Falls, ID. III. 1852.

COONEY, Percival J. Ed. Bunyard, Harriet. "Diary."

COONS, Frederica B. THE TRAIL TO OREGON. Portland: Binfords & Mort, 1954. OR-Genl.

COOPER, Arvazena A. "Pioneer across the Plains." In GROWING UP

FEMALE IN AMERICA, ed. Eve Merriam. NY: Dell, 1971. OR(Kansas)-LANDER-BARLOW. IV. Rem. 1863.

COOPER, Frederick A. Biography. UTHIST. MORMON. IV. 1859.

COOPER, Joseph W. Statement. BANCROFT. CAL(St. Jo). V-. Rem. 1849. CAL(Leav). V. Rem. 1851. CAL-TEX?-GILA. V-. Rem. 1858.

COOPER, Rose L. Ed. Loomis, Orrin S. "Life Story."

COOPER, Thomas. Reminiscences. MONHIST. DAKOTAS-MONTANA. V. Rem. 1864.

COOPER, Thomas C. "Arizona History in ARIZONA HIGHWAYS: An Annotated Bibliography." ARIZONA & THE WEST 16(Spr, Sum 1974): 33-64, 157-88. Bib.

COPELY, Jesse S. Ed. Sinclair, James. CAREER.

COPLEY, Josiah. KANSAS AND THE COUNTRY BEYOND. Philadelphia: Lippincott, 1867. Guide.

COQUILLARD, Alexis. Diary. Indiana State Library Archives, Indianapolis, IN. CAL(Indep)-Ends Sweetwater River. III+. 1849.

CORBETT, Henry W. Letter Books. CSL. Stage-Oregon.

CORBETT, Pearson H. JACOB HAMBLIN, THE PEACEMAKER. SLC: Deseret, 1952. Biog. SLCOR-Genl.

_____. "Jacob Hamblin, Western Frontiersman...." MS thesis, BYU, 1944.

CORBETT, William P. "Oklahoma's Highways: Indian Trails to Urban Expressways." PhD diss., Oklahoma State Univ., 1982. Not Seen.

_____. "Rifles and Ruts: Army Road Builders in Indian Territory." CHRONICLES OF OKLAHOMA 60(Fall 1982): 294-309. OKLAHOMA-Genl. Maps.

CORDRY, Mrs. T. A. THE STORY OF THE MARKING OF THE SANTA FE TRAIL. Topeka: Kansas DAR, 1915. Pres.

CORLE, Edwin. THE GILA RIVER OF THE SOUTHWEST. Lincoln: Univ. of Nebraska Press, 1967. Geog.

CORNABY, Hannah. AUTOBIOGRAPHY AND POEMS. SLC: Graham, 1881. MORMON. Rem. 1853. Not Seen.

CORNELL, William. "William Cornell's 1852 Journal, with his Overland Guide to Oregon." Eds. Karen M. Offen and David C. Duniway. OREGON HISTORICAL QUARTERLY 79(Win 1978): 359-93; 80(Spr 1979): 66-101. OR(St. Jo). III. 1852.

CORNING, Leavitt, Jr. BARONIAL FORTS OF THE BIG BEND. San Antonio: Trinity Univ. Press, 1967. TEX-Genl.

CORNWALL, Bruce. LIFE SKETCH OF PIERRE BARLOW CORNWALL. SF: Robertson, 1906. CAL(Council)-BRIDGER-HALL. IV. Rem. 1848.

CORNWALL, Joseph. Crossing the Plains. ORU. APPLE(Ft. Hall-Eugene). V. Rem. 1846.

CORNWALL, Josephus A. "The Cornwall Trek of 1846." Ed. Marion S. Craig. INDEPENDENCE COUNTRY CHRONICLE 14(Jul 1973): 21-44. OR-CHEROKEE(Jamestown, AK-Indep)-APPLE. IV. Rem. 1846.

CORNWALL, Pierre B. SEE: Cornwall, Bruce. LIFE SKETCH.

CORNWALL, Rebecca, and Leonard J. Arrington. RESCUE OF THE 1856 HANDCART COMPANIES. Charles Redd Monographs in Western History No. 11. Provo, UT: BYU Press, 1981. MORMON-1856-Genl.

CORRELL, Harris A. "A Unique Return Trip over the Famous Oregon Trail." OVERLAND MONTHLY 55(Jun 1910): 633-68. Pres.

CORY, Benjamin. Crossing the Plains. UWY. OR(St. Jo)-BARLOW. II. 1847.

COSAD, David. Journal. BANCROFT. CAL(Kansas City)-HALL. III+. 1849.

COSGROVE, Hugh. "Reminiscences...1847." Ed. H. S. Lyman. OREGON HISTORICAL QUARTERLY 1(Sept 1900): 253-68. OR. V. Rem. 1847.

COTTER, Frank E. "Information regarding Fort Piute." BANCROFT. Geog.

COTTON, A. R. Constitution Adopted by a Pioneer Train of 1849. In Pacific Coast Manuscripts. Stanford University Library-SpCol, Palo Alto, CA. Train Govt.

COTTON, Aylett R. "Across the Plains to California in 1849." In TRAILS DIVIDED, ed. Theo. C. Ressler. Williamsburg, IA: Editor, 1964. CAL(Council)-LASSEN. V. Rem. 1849.

COULTER, Edith M. Ed. Coit, Daniel W. "The Drawings and Letters."

Council Point Emigration Company Journal. UTHIST. MORMON. I. 1852.

COUNTRYMAN, Ardell J. A PIONEER'S TRIP ACROSS THE PLAINS. N.p., 1915. CAL(Council)-TRUCKEE. IV. Rem. 1861.

COUNTS, George. Journal. AZHIST. CAL(Ft. Smith)-MARCY-RIO GRANDE-GILA. III-. 1849.

COUPER, J. C. Diary. ORHIST. CAL(St. Jo)-BRIDGER-SLCUT. III+. 1852.

COURTNEY, W. B. "Pony Boy; Interview with William Campbell." COLLIERS, 9 Aug 1930, 24, 34, 37-38. Pony.

COUTANT, Frank R. CARIBOO HIGHWAY. Monroe, CN: Author, 196? CANADA-Genl.

COUTS, Cave J. "Emigrants and Indians: Selections from C. J. Couts' Military Correspondence, 1849." JOURNAL OF SOUTH DAKOTA HISTORY 29(Sum 1983): 165-84. Geog-Yuma.

_____. FROM SAN DIEGO TO THE COLORADO IN 1849: THE JOURNAL AND MAPS OF CAVE J. COUTS, 1821-1874. Ed. William McPherson. LA: Zamorano Club, 1932. GILA(San Diego-Yuma). II+. 1849.

_____. HEPAH, CALIFORNIA! THE JOURNAL OF CAVE JOHNSON COUTS FROM MONTEREY, NUEVO LEON, MEXICO, TO LOS ANGELES, CALIFORNIA, DURING THE YEARS 1848-1849. Ed. Henry F. Dobyns. Tucson: Arizona Pioneers' Historical Society, 1961. CAL-MEX(Monterey-Chihuahua-Santa Cruz)-GILA. I. 1848.

"Covered Wagon Adventure." MODERN MATURITY, Aug-Sept 1974, n.p. Pres.

COWAN, Dora. "Saint Joseph, Missouri, as a Starting Point for Western Emigration, Freight and Mail." MA thesis, Univ. of Missouri, 1939. Geog.

COWAN, John L. "The Oregon Trail." SUNSET 30(Feb 1913): 189-95. OR-Genl.

COWDEN, Henry. Diary. MONHIST. LASSEN(Chico, CA-Humboldt River)-HALL-MONTANA(Ft. Hall-Virginia City). III. 1865.

COWDEN, James. Diary. BANCROFT. CAL(Council)-LASSEN. II. 1853.

COX, C. C. "From Texas to California in 1849...." Ed. Mabelle E. Martin. SOUTHWESTERN HISTORICAL QUARTERLY 29(July, Oct 1925; Jan 1926): 36-50, 128-46, 210-23. CAL-TEX(La Grange)-GILA. II. 1849.

COX, Douglas M. "America's Greatest Infantry March." MA thesis, Western Colorado Univ., 1974. GILA-Genl.

COX, Evelyn. "The Northern Trail to California in 1849." MA thesis, Washington Univ.-St. Louis, 1936. LASSEN-Genl.

COX, George W. Reminiscences. CSL. CAL(Indep)-SLCUT-TRUCKEE. IV. Rem. 1852.

COX, John T. Reminiscences. ORHIST. OR-BARLOW. V. Rem. 1846.

COY, Mrs. John G. "Crossing the Plains in 1862." TRAIL 3(Nov 1910): 5-7. PIKES. V. 1862.

COY, Owen C. THE GREAT TREK. One of the California Series. Ed. John R. McCarthy. LA: Powell, 1931. Overland-Genl.

_____. "The 'Pony Express' Ante-Dated." GRIZZLY BEAR 20(Feb 1917): 4, 24. Pony.

COY, Roy E. "More about the Pony Express." MUSEUM GRAPHIC 13(Win 1961): 3-5. Pony.

COZAD, Justin L. Life and Times. NBHIST. PIKES. III. 1860.
Cragin Collection. Pioneer Museum. Colorado Springs, CO. Freight.

CRAIG, James. "Letters of 1862 Reveal Indian Troubles along the Overland Mail-Route." ANNALS OF WYOMING 15(1943): 150-52. Stage. Mail.

CRAIG, John. "Letter." In OVERLAND IN 1846, ed. Dale L. Morgan. Georgetown, CA: Talisman, 1963. CAL-HALL. V. 1846. CAL-HASTINGS(Return trip to Midwest). V. 1847.

CRAIG, Marion S. Ed. Cornwall, Josephus A. "Cornwall Trek."

CRAMER, Howard R. "California-Oregon Trail, Fort Hall to Goose Creek, Idaho." Preliminary Report for USBLM, Burley, ID. 1973. OR-Genl. Maps.

_____. "The California-Oregon Trail, Thomas Fork to Fort Hall, Idaho - A Preliminary Report." USBLM, Burley, ID. 1972. OR-Genl. Maps.

_____. "The California Trail in Idaho - The Salt Lake Cutoff." Preliminary Report for USBLM, Burley, ID. 1974. SLCUT-Genl.

_____. EMIGRANT TRAILS OF SOUTHEASTERN IDAHO. WA: Dept. of Interior-USBLM, 1976. OR-GENL. Maps.

_____. "Geology and Hudspeth's Cutoff." IDAHO YESTERDAYS 19(Fall 1975): 14-24. OR-GENL.

_____. "Hudspeth's Cutoff - Southeastern Idaho, A Map and Composite Diary." Preliminary Report for USBLM, Burley, ID. 1974. Maps.

_____. "The Oregon Trail, Raft River to Salmon Falls Creek, Idaho." Preliminary Report for USBLM, Burley, ID. 1974. Maps. OR-Genl.

CRAMER, Joseph L. "Manco Burro Pass: New Mexico or Colorado." NEW MEXICO HISTORICAL QUARTERLY 43(Apr 1968): 153-56. Geog.

CRAMER, Ora M. Pioneer Experiences of the Froman Family. Idaho Historical Society Library, Boise, Id. OR-Council)-Ends Boise. III. 1864.

CRAMER, Thomas J. B. Diary. BEINECKE. CAL(Indep?)-BRIDGER-SLCUT. II. 1859.

CRAMER, William E. "The March of our Republic: Is It Unfavorable to Progress and Improvements?" MERCHANT'S MAGAZINE 13(Dec 1845): 546-50. Overland-Genl.

CRAMPTON, C. Gregory. "Utah's Spanish Trail." UTAH HISTORICAL QUARTERLY 47(Fall 1979): 361-83. SPANISH-Genl. Maps.

CRAMPTON, John F. Collection. AZHIST. Stage.

CRANDALL, Eliphalet. Diary. NBHIST. CAL(Plattsmouth). III+. 1859.

CRANDALL, Ethan. Diary. McLeod County Historical Society, Hutchinson, MN. Not Seen.

CRANE, Addison M. Journal. HUNTL. CAL(Savannah)-BRIDGER-SLCUT. I. 1852.

CRANE, Ellery B. "An Overland Trip to California in the Year 1860." PROCEEDINGS Worcester Society of Antiquity 17(1901): 367-87. CAL(Council)-SIMPSON. IV. Rem. 1860.

CRANE, R. C. "Stage-coaching in the Concho Country." WESTX 10(Oct 1934): 58-67. Stage.

CRANFILL, Isom. Diary. ORU. OR(Council?). V. 1847. Train Govt.

CRANMER, Tom C. RULES AND REGULATION, BY WHICH TO CONDUCT WAGON TRAINS.... Kansas City, MO: Commercial Advertiser, 1866. Guide.

CRANSTON, E. "Letters from Pioneer Oregonians." Oregon State Library, Salem, OR. OR(Neb. City). V. 1851.

CRANSTON, Susan A. "An Ohio Lady crosses the Plains." In COVERED WAGON WOMEN, vol 3, ed. Kenneth Holmes. Glendale: Clark, 1983. OR(Neb City?). III. 1851.

CRANSTONE, Sarah M. Diary. ORHIST. OR. III. 1851.

CRAUSBY, Raleigh W. SEE: With Richard Jackson. "Delimitation of the Pony Express Trail."

CRAWFORD, Charles H. SCENES OF EARLIER DAYS.... 1898. Reprint. Chicago: Quadrangle, 1962. OR(Council)-BARLOW. III. Rem. 1851.

CRAWFORD, Ivan C. "The Leadville Muleskinner." COLORADO MAGAZINE 35(Jul 1958): 178-86. Teams.

CRAWFORD, Jeanne R., comp. & ed. WHEELS LED THE WAY: HORSE-DRAWN VEHICLES PLAIN AND FANCY, 1820-1920.

Yakima, WA: Yakima Valley Museum, 1973. Eqpt.

CRAWFORD, Leroy. Diary. ORHIST. OR(Council)-Ends Sweetwater River. II. 1861.

CRAWFORD, Lewis F. REKINDLING CAMP FIRES: THE EXPLOITS OF BEN ARNOLD (CONNOR). Bismarck, ND: Author, 1926. Military. Freight.

CRAWFORD, Medorem. SEE: Fendall, Lon W. "Medorem Crawford."

_____. JOURNAL OF MEDOREM CRAWFORD. Sources of the History of Oregon, vol. 1., No. 1. Eugene: Star, 1897. OR(Indep)-LANDER. II. 1842.

CRAWFORD, P. V. "Journal of a Trip across the Plains, 1851." OREGON HISTORICAL QUARTERLY 25(Jun 1924): 136-69. OR(St. Jo)-BARLOW. III. 1851.

CRAWFORD, Peter W. Narrative. ORU. OR. Rem. 1847. Illegible.

_____. "Peter Crawford's Cowlitz Journal." Longview WA DAILY NEWS, 18 Aug - 16 Oct 1952, N.p. OR(Elizabethton, NB). III. 1847.

CRAWFORD, Thelma. "Transportation across the Great Plains, 1849-1865." MA thesis, Univ. of Oklahoma, 1921. Overland-Genl.

CRAWSHAW, Stuart J. "Where a Sparrow Fell." FRONTIER TIMES 39(Oct-Nov 1965): 51, 66. Geog-Glenrock, WY.

CREECH, E. P. "Similkameen Trails, 1846-1861." BRITISH COLUMBIA HISTORICAL QUARTERLY, 1941, no. 4: 255-67. CANADA-Genl.

CREEL, Virginia F. Diary. MO-WHMC. CAL(St. Jo)-CHEROKEE-Ends SLC. II. 1864.

CREER, Leland H. "The Explorations of Gunnison and Beckwith in Colorado and Utah in 1853." COLORADO MAGAZINE 6(Sept 1929): 184-92. CAL(Leav)-SANTA FE-SPANISH. IV. 1853.

_____. THE FOUNDING OF AN EMPIRE: THE EXPLORATION AND COLONIZATION OF UTAH, 1776-1856. SLC: Bookcraft, 1947. Overland-Genl.

_____. "Lansford W. Hastings and the Discovery of the Old Mormon Trail." WESTERN HUMANITIES REVIEW 3(Jul 1949): 175-86. Jul 1949): 175-86. HASTINGS-1846-Genl. Biog.

CREIGH, Thomas A. "From Nebraska City to Montana, 1866...." Ed. James C. Olson. NEBRASKA HISTORY 29(Sept 1948): 208-37. Freight(Nebraska City)-BOZE. III. 1866.

CREIGHTON, Mary E. Reminiscences. BANCROFT. CAL(Ft. Smith)-MARCY-RIO GRANDE-GILA. V. Rem. 1849.

CREMONY, John C. LIFE AMONG THE APACHES. SF: A. Roman, 1868. GILA-Genl.

CRESWELL, John A. THE CHORPENNING CASE. WA: Union Republican Congressional Committee, 1872. Mail. Stage.

CREUZBAUR, Robert. ROUTE FROM THE GULF OF MEXICO...PACIFIC OCEAN. NY: Long & Brother, 1849. Hoax. Guide.

CRIMMONS, M. L. "The Southern Overland Mail in Texas." FRONTIER TIMES 24(Jul 1947): 483-86. Stage.

CRITTENDEN, P. "Stagecoach Inns of Texas." TRAVEL 118(Sept 1962): 37-38. Stage.

CROCKETT, Edwin. Crossing the Plains in 1853 and Prospecting for Placer Gold in the Great Northwest. Ed. Dan W. Greenburg. Univ. of Idaho Library-SpCol, Moscow, ID. CAL(Council)-LASSEN. IV. Rem. 1853.

CROCKETT, Samuel B. "Diary...." Ed. Vernon Carstenson. BUILDING A STATE, Washington State Historical Society Publications 3(1940): 594-607. OR(St. Jo?)-Ends on Big Sandy River. III. 1849.

CROOK, John. "John Crook's Journal." UTAH HISTORICAL QUARTERLY 6(Apr 1933): 51-62, 110-112. MORMON. V. 1856.

CROOKS, George. Diary. CSL. MORMON. V-. 1851.

CROPPER, Thomas W. FAMILY HISTORY.... Ed. Robert L. Ashley. N.p., 1957. MORMON? 1856.

CROSBY, Jesse W. "History and Journal...." ANNALS OF WYOMING 11(Jul 1939): 145-219. MORMON. III. 1847.

CROSS, Jack L. "Army Road-Building in New Mexico Territory: 1854-1861." PASSWORD 10(Spr 1965): 5-18. Military.

_____. "El Paso - Fort Yuma Wagon Road: 1857-1860." PASSWORD 4(Jan, Apr 1959): 4-18, 58-70. GILA-Genl.

_____. "Federal Wagon Road Construction in New Mexico Territory, 1846-1860." MA thesis, Univ. of Chicago, 1949. Govt. Freight.

_____. "The Pre-Road Building Period in New Mexico Territory." PASSWORD 4(Oct 1959): 141-54. GILA-Genl.

_____. "Wagon Roads across New Mexico: 1846-1860." PASSWORD 7(Win 1962): 16-34. Freight.

CROSS, Osborne. MARCH OF THE REGIMENT OF MOUNTED RIFLEMEN TO OREGON IN 1849. 1851. Reprint. Fairfield, WA: Ye Galleon, 1967. OR(Leav)-BARLOW. I. 1849.

CROSS, Ralph Herbert. THE EARLY INNS OF CALIFORNIA, 1844-1869. SF: Author, 1954. CAL-Genl.

"Crossing the Great American Desert in the '60's." TRAIL 1(Oct 1908): 6-11. PIKES-Stage(Omaha-Denver). IV. 1861.

"Crossing the North Fork of the American River." HUTCHINGS' 4(Aug 1859): 52-55. Geog.

CROUCH, Carrie. "The Old Butterfield Stage." NATIONAL REPUBLIC 17(Mar 1930): 20-21, 27. Stage.

CROW, Norma Lee. "A Comparison of Stereotypes of Pioneer Travel on the Oregon Trail with Pioneer Diaries and Reminiscences." MA thesis, Washington State Univ., 1967. OR-Genl.

CROWDER, David L. "Nineteenth-Century Indian-White Conflict in Southern Idaho." IDAHO YESTERDAYS 23(Sum 1979): 13-18. Indians.

CROWDERS, Vincent. Ed. Eastin, Thomas N. "Kentucky Gold Rusher."

CROWE, Earl. MEN OF EL TEJON: EMPIRE IN THE TEHACHAPIS. LA: Ward Ritchie, 1957. Geog.

CROWE, Rosalie, and Sidney R. Brinckerhoff, eds. EARLY YUMA: A GRAPHIC HISTORY OF LIFE ON THE AMERICAN NILE.

Flagstaff, AZ: Northland, 1976. Geog.

CROWLEY, William. SEE: With Lenore Bradley. TREKKIN' WEST.

CROY, Homer. Papers. MO-WHMC. Overland-Genl.

_____. WHEELS WEST. NY: Hastings, 1955. CAL(Indep)-BRIDGER-HASTINGS-TRUCKEE. III. 1846. Fictionalized Donner Party Account.

CRUMB, Lawrence N. HISTORIC PRESERVATION IN THE PACIFIC NORTHWEST: A BIBLIOGRAPHY OF SOURCES 1947-1978. CPL Bibliographies, Jean S. Gottlieb, ed. Chicago: CPL Bibliographies, 1979. Bib.

CRUMPTON, H. J. and W. B. THE ADVENTURES.... Montgomery, AL: N.p., 1912. CAL(Ft. Smith)-MARCY-RIO GRANDE-GILA. IV. Rem. 1849.

CULBERT, Virginia P. Ed. Perry, Samuel M. "Diary."

CULLEN, John W. Letter. LILLEY. OR(St. Jo). IV. Rem. 1847.

CULLIMORE, Clarence. OLD ADOBES OF FORGOTTEN FORT TEJON. Bakersfield, CA: Kern County Historical Society, 1941. Geog.

CULVER, E. S. "Crossing the Plains in 1869." NATIONAL MAGAZINE 28(Apr 1908): 53-55. CAL(Kansas City)-SANTA FE(Smoky Hill)-RIO GRANDE. V. 1869.

CUMMING, Elizabeth. Letters. UTHIST. MORMON. II+. 1857.

CUMMING, John. Ed. Arms, Cephas, and Adonijah S. Welch. LONG ROAD.

CUMMINGS, Charles J. Diary. BEINECKE. OR(Council)-LANDER-APPLE. II+. 1859.

CUMMINGS, Mariett F. "Diary." In COVERED WAGON WOMEN, vol. 4, ed. Kenneth L. Holmes. Glendale: Clark, 1985. CAL(Ft. Kearny)-BRIDGER-TRUCKEE-BECKWOURTH. II. 1852.

CUMMINS, D. H. "Toll Roads in Southwestern Colorado." COLORADO MAGAZINE 29(Apr 1952): 98-103. PIKES-Genl.

CUMMINS, Sarah J. AUTOBIOGRAPHY AND REMINISCENCES. La Grande, OR: Author, 1914. OR(St. Jo)-BARLOW. IV. Rem. 1845.

CUNNINGHAM, Bob, and A. Tracy Row. "The Journal of Arizona History: A Bibliography of Articles Published during the First Twenty-Five Years." JOURNAL OF ARIZONA HISTORY 27(Sum 1986): n.p. Bib.

CUNNINGHAM, Robert D. "Under the Lash of the Jehu." AMERICAN HISTORY ILLUSTRATED 20(May 1985): 16-21. Stage.

CUNNINGHAM, Susan. SEE: With Bob Bjoring. EXPLORERS' AND TRAVELLLERS'.

CURETON, Gilbert. "The Cattle Trail to California: 1840-1860." Historical Society of Southern California QUARTERLY 35(Jun 1953): 99-109. Stock.

CURETON, William H. Trekking to California. BANCROFT. CAL-CHEROKEE-SLCUT. II. Rem. 1857.

CURRAN, Harold. FEARFUL CROSSING: THE CENTRAL OVER-

LAND ROUTE THROUGH NEVADA. Reno: Great Basin Press, 1982. Overland-Genl.

CURREY, Thomas L. THE SMOKY HILL TRAIL. Western Plains Heritage Pub. 3. Colby, KA: Colby Community College, 1976. PIKES-Smoky Hill-Genl. Graphics.

CURRIER, Cyrus. Journal. Wyoming Historical Society Library, Cheyenne, WY. CAL(St. Jo)-BRIDGER. II. 1849.

CURRY, George B. "Occasional Address." TRANSACTIONS Oregon Pioneer Association (1887):32-47. OR(Council). Rem. 1853. Not Seen.

CURTIS, Mabel R. THE COACHMAN WAS A LADY: THE STORY OF CHARLEY PARKHURST. Watsonville, CA: Pajaro Valley Historical Association, 1959. Stage. Biog.

_____. "The Rowe Family in Pajaro Valley, CA." BANCROFT. CAL(Indep)-TRUCKEE. III. 1850.

CURTIS, Mary. "Amelia Bloomer's Curious Costume." AMERICAN HISTORY ILLUSTRATED 13(Jun 1978): 10-15. Social.

CUSHMAN, Dan. THE GREAT NORTH TRAIL. NY: McGraw-Hill, 1966. Overland-Genl.

CUTHBERT, W. Diary. MONHIST. DAKOTAS(St. Paul)-MONTANA. V. 1862.

CUTTER, Donald C. "Prelude to a Pageant in the Wilderness." WESTERN HISTORICAL QUARTERLY 8(Jan 1977): 5-14. SPANISH-Genl.

CUTTING, A. Howard. Journal. HUNTL. CAL(Council)-CHEROKEE(Julesburg-Bridger Pass-SLC)-SIMPSON-TRUCKEE. II+. 1863.

CUTLER, LaVern. Trans. Hagelstein, Geo. M. "The Hagelstein Diary."

DAGGY, Elias. Diary. MNHIST. CAL(Indep)-HALL. II+. 1850.

DAHLE, Onun B. Reminiscence. WIHIST. CAL(Indep). IV. Rem. 1850.

DAIGH, James M. NUGGETS FROM '49. Ed. Owen Hannant. Reprint. Fairfield, WA: Ye Galleon, 1985. CAL(St. Jo)-HALL. IV. Rem. 1849.

DAIGLE, R. D. "Rediscovering the Trail of the Pioneers." AMERICAN FORESTS 48(Apr 1941): 174-76. Pres.

DAILEY, Benjamin. Diary. Montana State Univ. Library, Missoula, MT. BOZE. 1866. Not Seen.

DAILEY, John L. Diary. DENVERPUB. PIKES. III. 1859.

DAILY, Moses. Journal. UTHIST. Freight.

DAILY, Robert S. DIARY. N.p.: White, 1975? CAL(Council). III. 1850.

DALE, Edward E. Ed. Akin, James, Jr. "Journal."

DALE, Harrison C. Ed. Sublette, William L. "A Fragmentary Journal."

_____. THE ASHLEY-SMITH EXPLORATIONS AND THE DISCOVERY OF A CENTRAL ROUTE TO THE PACIFIC, 1822-1829. Cleveland: Clark, 1941. Overland-Genl.

_____. "The Organization of the Oregon Emigrating Companies." OREGON HISTORICAL QUARTERLY 16(Sept 1915): 205-27. Train Govt.

DALEY, W. H. MANUAL OF PACK TRANSPORTATION. WA: GPO, 1910. Teams.

DALLAM, Richard. Diary and Journal. BEINECKE. CAL-TEX(San Antonio)-GILA. II. 1853. OR-CAL. IV. 1853. Stock.

DALRYMPLE, Ward. Reminiscence. MONHIST. CAL(Kansas)-HALL-MONTANA. V. Rem. 1864.

DALTON, John E. Diary. WIHIST. CAL(Kansas City)-TRUCKEE-BECKWOURTH. II+. 1852.

DAM, Frances L. Account. CAHIST. CAL(Council)-SIMPSON. V-. Rem. 1865.

DAMERON, J. P. AUTOBIOGRAPHY AND WRITINGS.... SF: Author, 1877. CAL(St. Jo). V. 1849.

DAMON, John F. Trip Up Fraser River. HUNTL. CANADA(Victoria-Fraser Mines). II. 1859.

DANA, Joseph. Papers. CAHIST. Train Govt.

DANA, Julian. SUTTER OF CALIFORNIA. NY: Pioneers, 1934. Biog.

DANGBERG, Grace. CARSON VALLEY.... Reno: Carson Valley Historical Society, 1972. Geog.

DANIEL, Janice P. "Dust on their Petticoats." AMERICAN SCENE 13, no. 1(1972): 1-22. Social. Graphics.

DANIELS, Flavius J. Autobiography. CSL. CAL. Rem. 1859. Missing.

DANIELS, Sherrill F. "An Index to and Bibliography of Reminiscences in the Nebraska State Historical Library." PhD diss., Univ. of Nebraska, 1986. Bib.

DANKER, Donald F. "The Influence of Transportation upon Nebraska Territory." NEBRASKA HISTORY 47(Jun 1966): 187-208. Overland-Genl.

_____. "Nebraska Winter Quarters Company and Florence." NEBRASKA HISTORY 36(Mar 1956): 27-50. Geog.

DARBY & MILLER. HISTORY OF CALIFORNIA. Auburn, NY: N.p., 1850. Guide.

D'ARCY, Marianne H. Reminiscences. Ed. Daisy Sanford. ORU. OR(Council). V. Rem. 1846.

DARLING, Lucia. Diary. MONHIST. CAL(Council)-HALL-MONTANA. I. 1863.

DARNEILLE, Dorothy. SEE: With Elizabeth Hiller. FOOD FOR THE EMIGRANT.

DARST, Paul. Diary. ORU. OR(Fort Laramie). IV. 1847.

DARWIN, Charles. Diary. UWY. CAL(Council)-Ends Scott's Bluff. II. 1849.

DARWIN, Charles B. Diaries. HUNTL. CAL(Council?)-BRIDGER-SLCUT-TRUCKEE. I. 1849.

DARY, David A. THE BUFFALO BOOK. Chicago: Sage, 1974. Fauna.

_____. "Marc Simmons' Santa Fe Trail: A Review Essay." NEW MEXICO HISTORICAL REVIEW 63(Jan 1988): 63-70. SANTA FE-Genl.

DAUCHY, Jerome H. Papers. NBHIST. Freight.

DAUGHTERS, J. M. Journal. CSL. CAL(St. Jo)-TRUCKEE-Ends near Wadsworth, NV. III. 1852.

Daughters of the American Revolution, Missouri Society. THE OLD TRAILS ROAD: THE NATIONAL HIGHWAY AS A MONUMENT TO THE PIONEER MEN AND WOMEN. N.p.: DAR, 1911? Pres.

DAULTON, Henry D. SEE: Desmond, Lucille H. "Henry Daulton, I."

DAVENPORT, O. F. Letters. DENVERPUB. CAL(St. Jo)-BRIDGER-HASTINGS-TRUCKEE. 1850. Not Seen.

DAVENPORT, Odessa. Ed. Conner, D. E. A CONFEDERATE IN THE GOLD FIELDS.

DAVENPORT, Timothy W. Dividing the Train. ORU. OR. III. Rem. 1851.

DAVID, James C. "Diary." In "1852 on the Oregon Trail." Ed. Mae Urbanek. ANNALS OF WYOMING 34(Apr 1962): 52-59. CAL(Council)-Ends Ft. Laramie. IV. Not Seen.

DAVID, Robert B. FINN BURNETT, FRONTIERSMAN. Glendale: Clark, 1937. Indians. Military. Rem. Freight.

DAVIDSON, A. F. Maps. BEINECKE. CAL-1846-Platte River to St. Jo.

DAVIDSON, J. W. SEE: Wilke, Philip J., and Harry W. Lawton. EXPEDITION.

DAVIDSON, T. L. "By the Southern Route into Oregon." BANCROFT. OR(St. Jo)-APPLE. IV. Rem. 1847.

DAVIDSON, Winifred. "The Overland Mail: Scrapbook." SDHIST. Stage.

DAVIES, J. Kenneth. MORMON GOLD: THE STORY OF CALIFORNIA'S MORMON ARGONAUTS. SLC: Author, 1984. Utah. CAL-Genl.

_____. "Thomas Rhoads, Forgotten Mormon Pioneer of 1846." NEBRASKA HISTORY 64(Spr 1983): 81-95. MORMON-Genl.

DAVIES, John J. "The Journey of a Mormon from Liverpool to Salt Lake City." Ed. Austil L. Venable. ARKANSAS HISTORICAL QUARTERLY 2(1943): 346-52. MORMON. V. Rem. 1854.

DAVIS, A. S. Diary. Idaho Historical Society Library, Boise, ID. CAL(Council)-BRIDGER-HASTINGS-TRUCKEE. III. 1850. CAL(Nevada City)-TRUCKEE-SLCUT-BRIDGER. III. 1853.

DAVIS, Alonzo E. Pioneer Days.... Arizona State Univ. Library-AZ Collection, Tempe, AZ. BEALE-AZ-Genl.

DAVIS, Alvah I. "Diary of Mr. Davis." TRANSACTIONS Oregon Pioneer Association, 1909 (1910): 355-81. OR(Council). V. 1852.

DAVIS, Daniel. Journal. LDS. MORMON. III. 1855.

DAVIS, Francis W. HORSE PACKING IN PICTURES. NY; Scribner, 1975. Eqpt. Graphics.

DAVIS, Henry T. SOLITARY PLACES MADE GLAD. Cincinnati: Author, 1890. CAL(Neb. City). IV. Rem. 1850.

DAVIS, Hiram. "Journal - 1849." In "Arkansas Golden Army of '49," ed. Francile B. Oakley. ARKANSAS HISTORICAL QUARTERLY 6(Spr 1947): 1-85. CAL-CHEROKEE(Grand Saline)-SLCUT. III. 1849.

DAVIS, Horace. THE OREGON TRAIL. Boston: Wilson, 1910. OR-Genl.

DAVIS, James. "The Mule as a 'Movie' of the Western Trails." OVERLAND MONTHLY 62(Aug 1913): 109-18. Teams.

DAVIS, John E. MORMONISM UNVEILED. Bristol: Jeffries, 1856. MORMON. V. 1853.

DAVIS, Leonard M. "The Historic Sacramento-Auburn Road: From Miners' Trail to Interstate Freeway." BANCROFT. Stage. CAL-Genl.

DAVIS, Leslie B. TRAILS, TRAILS AND MORE TRAILS: ANOTHER HISTORIC PRESERVATION CHALLENGE. N.p., n.d. Not Seen.

DAVIS, Philander C. Account. ORHIST. OR. V-. Rem. 1846.

DAVIS, Sarah. "Diary." In COVERED WAGON WOMEN, vol. 2, ed. Kenneth L. Holmes. Glendale: Clark, 1984. CAL(St. Jo)-BRIDGER-SLCUT-TRUCKEE. III. 1850.

DAVIS, Sylvester. "Diary...." Ed. P. A. F. Walter. NEW MEXICO HISTORICAL REVIEW 6(Oct 1931): 383-416. PIKES-SANTA FE. III+. 1859.

DAVIS, Theodore R. "A Stage Ride to Colorado." HARPER'S 35(Jul 1867): 206-11. PIKES(Smoky Hill Route). 1866. Indians. Stage. Graphics.

DAVIS, W. N., Jr. "The Sutler at Fort Bridger." WESTERN HISTORICAL QUARTERLY 2(Jan 1971): 37-54. Geog.

DAVIS, William C. Ed. With Gladys M. Wilson. "Independence."

DAVIS, William F. "Hitting the Oregon Trail." OREGON GENEALOGICAL SOCIETY BULLETIN 19(Fall 1980): 12-16. OR(St. Jo?)-Wintered in SLC. IV. 1864. OR(SLC-Dalles). IV. 1865.

DAVISON, Paul R. OLD ROLLING WHEELS. N.p., 1969. Geog-Ft. Leav.

DAWSON, Charles. PIONEER TALES OF THE OREGON TRAIL AND JEFFERSON COUNTY. Topeka: Crane, 1912. Overland-Genl.

DAWSON, Glen. "Only Known Copies of Emigrant Guides." Los Angeles Westerners BRAND BOOK 7(1964): 164-71. Guide.

DAWSON, Nicholas "Cheyenne." NARRATIVE OF NICHOLAS 'CHEYENNE' DAWSON.... No. 7 of the Rare Americana Series. SF: Grabhorn, 1933. CAL(Indep)-HALL. III. Rem. 1841. CAL-TEX(Sherman)-MEX-GILA. IV. Rem. 1849.

DAY, Alphonso B. Diary. BYU. CAL(Neb. City)-CHEROKEE(Denver-SLC)-SLCUT. III+. 1859.

DAY, Gershom and Elizabeth. Diary. Ed. Mary E. Trowbridge. UWY.

CAL(Ft. Kearny-Caspar,WY). II. 1849.

DAY, Sherman. REPORT ON THE IMMIGRANT WAGON ROAD EXPLORATIONS. In APPENDIX TO [California] SURVEYOR-GENERAL'S REPORT 2(1855): 77-87. CAL-Genl.

_____. REPORT...ROAD ACROSS THE SIERRA NEVADA. California Legislative Session, 1855. Sen. Doc. 22. CAL-1855-Genl.

DAYNES, Winnifred W. Ed. Woodruff, Emma Smith. "Sketch."

DAYTON, Thaddeus S. "Marking the Paths that Led to Empire." HARPER'S, 14 May 1910, 16-17. Pres.

DEGROOT, Henry. "Crossing the California Sahara." OVERLAND MONTHLY 8(Jul 1886): 52-57. BRADSHAW(San Bernardino-Chucawalla). IV. 1862.

_____. "The Donner Party." OVERLAND MONTHLY 5(Jul 1870): 38-43. CAL-1846-Genl.

DE LAY, Leigh G. "A New Map of the Principal Routes to the Gold Region, Colorado Territory (Drawn by Aug. F. Harvey)." OVERLAND JOURNAL 2(Spr 1984): 29-36. PIKES-Map.

DEQUILLE, Dan. SNOW-SHOE THOMPSON. LA: Glen Dawson, 1954. Mail.

DE SMET, Pierre Jean. LETTERS AND SKETCHES.... Philadelphia: Fithian, 1843. OR(Westport)-MONTANA(Snake River-Deer Lodge-St. Mary's). II. 1841. OR(Return)-MONTANA(St. Mary's-Fort Union)-DAKOTAS. II. 1842. Indians. Flora/Fauna.

_____. NEW INDIAN SKETCHES. NY: Sadlier, 1963. OR(Leav)-Ends South Pass. IV. 1858.

_____. OREGON MISSIONS AND TRAVELS OVER THE ROCKY MOUNTAINS, IN 1845-46. NY: Dunigan, 1847. CANADA(St. Mary's-Edmonton)-MULLAN(St. Mary's-Vancouver). IV. 1846. OR-1846-Genl. CANADA-1846-Genl. Indians.

DEADERICK, David A. Diary. Univ. of Tennessee Library-SpCol. Knoxville, TN. CAL(St. Jo)-SANTA FE-RIO GRANDE-GILA. V. 1849.

DEADY, Lucy A. "Crossing the Plains." TRANSACTIONS Oregon Pioneer Association, 1928 (1929): 57-64. OR-APPLE. IV. Rem. 1845.

DEAN, Thaddeus. A JOURNEY TO CALIFORNIA.... Ed. K. D. Wheeler. Tampa, FL: American Studies, 1979. CAL(Council)-BRIDGER. V. 1852.

DEAVILLE, A. S. THE COLONIAL POSTAL SYSTEMS AND POSTAGE STAMPS OF VANCOUVER ISLAND AND BRITISH COLUMBIA, 1849-1871. Archives of British Columbia Memoir No. 8. Victoria: Provincial Archives, 1928. Mail.

DEBLOIS, Diane. SEE: With Robert D. Harris. CONGRESS...TELEGRAPH.

DECKER, Dean. "Variants of the Slate Creek Cutoff." OVERLAND JOURNAL 2(Sum 1984): 30-35. CAL-Genl.

DECKER, Peter. THE DIARIES OF PETER DECKER.... Ed. Helen S. Giffen. Georgetown, CA: Talisman, 1966. CAL(St. Jo). II. 1849.

DEE, Minnie R. FROM OXCART TO AIRPLANE: A BIOGRAPHY OF GEORGE H. HIMES. Portland: Binfords & Mort, 1939. OR-WASH. IV. 1853.

DEES, Harry C. Ed. Bean, George W. "Journal."

_____. "George W. Bean, Early Mormon Explorer." BRIGHAM YOUNG UNIVERSITY STUDIES 12(Win 1972): 147-62. Biog.

DELAMETER, Guysbert B. Memoranda. BANCROFT. CAL(Old Ft. Kearny). IV. Rem. 1850.

DELANO, Alonzo. SEE: McKee, Irving. ALONZO DELANO'S CALIFORNIA CORRESPONDENCE.

_____. LIFE ON THE PLAINS AND AMONG THE DIGGINGS. 1854. Reprint. NY: Wilson - Erickson, 1936. CAL(St. Jo)-LASSEN. I. 1849.

DELANY, John O. "Up the Missouri to the Montana Mines...1862. Ed. John E. Sunder. MISSOURI HISTORICAL BULLETIN 1(Oct 1962): 3-22; 2(Jan 1963): 127-49. MONTANA-MULLAN. III +. 1862.

DELLENBAUGH, Frederick S. FREMONT AND '49. NY: Putnam's Sons, 1914. Biog.

DELMAR, Josephine. "Perils of a Down-Trip Teamster." FRONTIER TIMES 53(Apr-Mar 1979): 32-34, 53-54. Freight.

DEMAREST, David D. Diary. BANCROFT. CAL-TEX(Galveston)-GILA. II +. 1849.

DEMILT, Alonzo P. THE LIFE, TRAVELS AND ADVENTURES OF AN AMERICAN WANDERER.... Ed. Franklin Y. Fitch. NY: Lovell, 1883. CAL(Kansas City)-TRUCKEE. V. Rem. 1849.

DEMKE, Siegfried. THE CATTLE DRIVES OF EARLY CALIFORNIA. San Gabriel, CA: Author, 1985. Stock.

DEMPSEY, Hugh A. "Howell Harris and the Whiskey Trade." MONTANA 3(Spr 1953): 1-8. Freight.

DENHARDT, Robert M. "Driving Livestock East from California Prior to 1850." CALIFORNIA HISTORICAL QUARTERLY 20(Dec 1941): 341-48. SPANISH-Genl.

DENISON, Bill. Letters of a '49r. Library of Congress, Washington, DC. Not Catalogued.

DENNEY, A. A. SEE: Watt, Roberta F. FOUR WAGONS WEST.

DENNIS, Bryan. Diary. U.S. National Park Service Library, Omaha, NB. CAL(Council)-Ends Black Fork. 1850. Not Found.

DENNY, Arthur A. Journal. Washington State Historical Society Library, Tacoma, WA. OR(Council). III. 1851.

DENNY, Arthur J. "The Pony Express Trail...." NEBRASKA HISTORY 21(Jan-Mar 1940): 13-18. Pony. Map.

DENVER, A. St. Clair. "Letter - Journal." Wilmington, Ohio CLINTON REPUBLICAN, 19 Apr 1850, p. 3; 24 May 1850, p. 3; 31 May 1850, p. 3; 4 Oct 1850, p. 2; 11 Oct 1850, pp. 1-2; 1 Nov 1850, p. 2. CAL(Leav)-HALL. IV. 1849.

DENVER, James W. "The [James] Denver Diary Overland to California in 1850." Ed. Richard E. Meyers. ARIZONA & THE WEST 17(Spr 1975): 35-62. CAL(Leav)-HASTINGS-Ends Lovelock, NV. II. 1850.

DEPREDATIONS AND MASSACRES BY THE SNAKE RIVER INDIANS. 36th Cong., 2nd sess., 1860. Ex. Doc. 46. Serial 1099. 1860

Attack near Salmon Falls, Id.

DERBY, George H. Three Reports. ORHIST. OR-1855-Genl.

DERR, Peter. "Account of Experiences...." In JOURNALS OF THE FORTY-NINERS, eds. LeRoy R. and Ann W. Hafen. The Far West and the Rockies Historical Series, 1820-1875, No. 2. Glendale: Clark, 1954. SLCOR. V. Rem. 1849.

DERRICKSON, Frankie M. Reminiscence. UTHIST. MORMON. V. Rem. 1849.

DESMOND, Lucille H. "Henry Clay Daulton, I." MADERA COUNTY HISTORIAN 9(Jul 1969): 1-5. CAL-BRIDGER-SLCOR. V-. 1853.

DESMOND, M. Benilda. "History of the City of Marysville, CA, 1852-1859." MA thesis, Catholic Univ. of America, 1962. Geog. Stage. Freight.

DESPATCHES FROM UNITED STATES CONSULS IN ACAPULCO, 1823-1906. National Archives, Washington, D.C. MEX-Genl. Not Seen.

DESPATCHES FROM UNITED STATES CONSULS IN CIUDAD JUAREZ [El Paso del Norte]. National Archives, Washington, D.C. MEX-Genl. Not Seen.

DESPATCHES FROM UNITED STATES CONSULS IN MONTEREY, MEXICO, 1849-1906. National Archives, Washington, D.C. MEX-Genl. Not Seen.

DESPATCHES FROM UNITED STATES CONSULS IN VERA CRUZ, 1822-1906. National Archives, Washington, D.C. MEX-Genl. Not Seen.

DETZLER, Jack J. Ed. Stanfield, Howard S. DIARY.

DEVOTO, Bernard. ACROSS THE WIDE MISSOURI. Boston: Little, Brown, 1947. Overland-Genl.

_____. "The Great Medicine Road." AMERICAN MERCURY 11(May 1927): 104-12. OR-Genl.

_____. THE YEAR OF DECISION, 1846. Boston: Little, Brown, 1943. CAL-1846-Genl. OR-1846-Genl.

_____. "Year of Decision: 1846." ATLANTIC 170(Sept 1942): 111-26. CAL-1846-Genl.

DEWEES, Francis P. THE CASE OF GEORGE CHORPENNING.... WA: N.p., 1870. Mail.

DEWITT, Florence S. Ed. Ward, Frances. FRANKIE'S JOURNAL. Ed. Ward, Harriet. PRAIRIE SCHOONER LADY.

DEWITT, Ward G. Ed. Ward, Harriet. PRAIRIE SCHOONER LADY.

DEWOLF, David. "Diary of the Overland Trail, 1849...." TRANSACTIONS Illinois Historical Society 1925 (1926?): 183-222. CAL(Westport)-BRIDGER-SLCUT. II. 1849.

DEXTER, Wheeler O. Reminiscences. MONHIST. DAKOTAS(St. Cloud)-MONTANA. V. Rem. 1866.

DIAMOND, James R. Papers. Univ. of Georgia Library, Athens, GA. Stage-TEX. Not Seen.

Diary of an Unknown Scout. CAHIST. CAL(St. Jo). III. 1854.

DIAZ, Albert J. "A Bibliography of Bibliographies Relating to the History and Literature of Arizona and New Mexico." ARIZONA QUARTERLY 14(1958): 197-218. Bib.

DIBB, William D. Diary. MONHIST. DAKOTAS(St. Cloud)-MONTANA-MULLAN. II. 1862.

DICK, Everett. "The Long Drive." MA thesis, Univ. of Nebraska, 1925. Stock.

_____. VANGUARDS OF THE FRONTIER. NY: Appleton-Century, 1941. Overland-Genl.

DICKASON, David H. "Clarence King's First Western Journey." HUNTINGTON LIBRARY QUARTERLY 7(Nov 1943): 71-88. CAL(St. Jo)-BRIDGER-SIMPSON. IV. 1863.

DICKEN, Samuel N. PIONEER TRAILS OF THE OREGON COAST. Portland: Oregon Historical Society, 1971. Maps.

DICKENSON, Luella. REMINISCENCES OF A TRIP.... SF: Whitaker & Ray, 1904. CAL(Indep)-HALL-TRUCKEE. IV. Rem. 1846.

DICKINSON, D. C. Journal. BANCROFT. CAL(Council). II+. 1852.

DICKSON, Albert J. COVERED WAGON DAYS.... Cleveland: Clark, 1929. CAL(Council)-LANDER-MONTANA. II. Rem. 1864.

DICTIONARY CATALOG OF THE EDWARD E. AYER COLLECTIONS OF AMERICANA AND AMERICAN INDIANS IN THE NEWBERRY LIBRARY. 16 vols. Boston: Hall, 1961. Includes 1st Sup., 1970.

DIEKER, Leo E. A BRIEF HISTORICAL SKETCH: HOLLENBERG RANCH PONY EXPRESS STATION, HANOVER, KANSAS. Hanover, KS: Hanover News, 1959. Geog. Pony.

DIETRICH, F. J., Jr. "Early California in a Mail Bag." WEEKLY PHILATELIC GOSSIP 11(15 Jan 1927): 1045-52. Mail. Graphics.

DILKE, Charles W. SEE: Shepperson, Wilbur S. "Sir Charles W. Dilke."

DILLON, Charles. "The Arrival of the Telegraph in Texas." SOUTHWESTERN HISTORICAL QUARTERLY 64(Oct 1960): 200-12. Telegraph.

DILLON, Richard. Ed. Harris, Benj. B. THE GILA TRAIL. Ed. Hecox, Margaret M. CALIFORNIA CARAVAN. Ed. Loveland, Cyrus C. CALIFORNIA TRAIL HERD. Ed. Rice, Josiah. CANNONEER IN NAVAJO COUNTRY.

_____. SISKIYOU TRAIL: THE HUDSON'S BAY COMPANY ROUTE TO CALIFORNIA. NY: McGraw-Hill, 1975. OR-CAL-Genl.

_____. "Tragedy at Oatman Flat: Massacre, Captivity, Mystery." AMERICAN WEST 18(Mar-Apr 1981): 46-54, 59. Indians.

_____. "When the Siskiyou Trail Came to San Carlos." LA PENINSULA 17(Spr 1974): 23-35. OR-CAL-1841-Genl.

DINES, Glen. BULL WAGON. NY: Macmillan, 1963. Freight-Graphics.

_____. OVERLAND STAGE. NY: Macmillan, 1961. Stage-Graphics.

DINWIDDIE, David or John. OVERLAND FROM INDIANA TO OREGON.... Ed. Margaret Booth. Sources of Northwest History, No. 2. Missoula: State Univ. of Montana, 1928. OR(Council). III.

1853.

DINWIDDIE, W. "Staging through Mountain and Desert." OUTING 34(n.d.): 48. Not Seen.

DIPLOMATIC INSTRUCTIONS OF THE DEPARTMENT OF STATE, MEXICO, 1801-1906. National Archives, Washington, D.C. Not Seen.

"Directions for Trains Crossing the Plains. Maj. General Hancock's General Order No. 29, Dated 25 February 1867." ARMY & NAVY JOURNAL 4(16 Mar 1867): 473. Military.

"Distances on Road between Fort Kearny, Nebraska Territory, and Junction Station, Colorado Territory." National Archives, Washington, D.C. CAL-Genl. Not Seen.

DISTURNELL, J. THE EMIGRANTS GUIDE TO NEW MEXICO, CALIFORNIA AND OREGON.... NY: Author, 1849. A fake.

DIVETT, Robert T. "His Chastening Rod: Cholera Epidemics and the Mormons." DIALOGUE 12(Aut 1979): 6-15. Medical.

DIX, John. Ed. Jones, John W. "Amusing and Thrilling Adventures."

DIXON, Benjamin F. BROCHURE NO. 1 - OVERLAND TO THE PACIFIC, CALIFORNIA COMMITTEE, OVERLAND MAIL CENTENNIALS, 1957-1958. San Diego: Akers, 1965. Stage.

_____. THE OVERLAND MAIL CENTENNIAL. San Diego: San Diego Historical Society, 1958. Stage.

DIXON, Joseph. TOPOGRAPHICAL MEMOIR...AGAINST THE SNAKE INDIANS. 37th Cong., 2d sess., 1861. S. Doc. 1. Serial 1118. 528-40. OR(Fort Dalles-Lake Harney). II. 1860.

DIXON, Olive K. LIFE OF 'BILLY' DIXON. Dallas: Southwest, 1927. Freight.

DIXON, William H. NEW AMERICA. 2 vols. London: Hurst & Blackett, 1867. Stage(Atchison-SLC)-1866. II+. 1866.

DIXON & KASSON'S NEW MAP OF ALL OVERLAND AND OCEAN MAIL ROUTES, 1859. SF: Hutchings & Rosenfield, 1859. Guide.

DOBYNS, Henry F. Ed. Couts, Cave J. HEPAH! CALIFORNIA.

DOCKSTADER, Frederick and Alice. THE AMERICAN INDIAN IN GRADUATE STUDIES: A BIBLIOGRAPHY OF THESES AND DISSERTATIONS. 2 vols. NY: Heye Foundation, 1973-4. Bib.

"Documentary - Excerpts from the New Orleans PICAYUNE between Issues of January 3, 1843, and April 27, 1844, Inclusive." OREGON HISTORICAL QUARTERLY 2(Jun 1901): 187-203. OR-1843-Genl.

"Documents." OREGON HISTORICAL QUARTERLY 3(Dec 1902): 390-426. OR-1843-Genl.

_____. OREGON HISTORICAL QUARTERLY 4(Jun 1903): 168-84. OR-1843-Genl.

_____. OREGON HISTORICAL QUARTERLY 4(Sept 1903): 270-86. OR-1844-Genl.

DODGE, Bertha S. THE ROAD WEST: SAGA OF THE 35TH PARALLEL. Albuquerque: Univ. of New Mexico, 1980. BEALE-Genl.

_____. THE STORY OF INSCRIPTION ROCK. Canaan, NH: Author, 1975. Geog. BEALE-Genl.

DODGE, Elvira. Diary. UPAC. CAL(Council)-BRIDGER-Ends Ogden, UT. II. 1860.

DODGE, Grenville M. "Diary." (In) R. Perkins. TRAILS, RAILS, AND WAR. Indianapolis: N.p., 1929. PIKES(Omaha-Denver-Leavenworth). By Stage. 1865.

DODGE, James H. ACROSS THE PLAINS WITH THE NINTH WISCONSIN BATTERY IN 1862. Military Order of the Loyal Legion..., War Papers 23. WA: Private, 1896. PIKES. V. Rem. 1862.

DODGE, Nathan P. Diary. DENVERPUB. PIKES(Omaha-Denver-Leavenworth). By Stage. 1865.

_____. "Early Emigration through and to Council Bluffs." ANNALS OF IOWA 18(Jan 1932): 162-79. Geog.

DODSON, John F. "Dodson's Death...Journey from Illinois to his Death at Fort Owen in 1852." Ed. George F. Weisel. MONTANA 3(Spr 1953): 24-35. CAL(Council)-HALL-MONTANA. III. 1852.

DOEDERLEIN, Paul. "The Doederlein Diary. Ed. Roger Moldenhauer. CONCORDIA HISTORICAL INSTITUTE QUARTERLY 51(1978): 99-136. CAL(Council)-To Ft. Laramie. 1859. Not Seen.

DOETSCH, Raymond N. JOURNEY TO THE GREEN AND GOLDEN LANDS. NY: Kennikat Press, 1976. Medical.

DOMENECH, Emmanuel H. SEVEN YEARS' RESIDENCE IN THE GREAT DESERTS OF NORTH AMERICA.... 2 vols. London: Longman, Green, Longman, & Roberts, 1860. Indians.

DONAT, Pat. Ed. Quesenbury, William. "William Quesenbury's Journal." Ed. Ridge, John R. "John Rollin Ridge Goes to California."

_____. "Bill Cush's Trek to Texas." FLASHBACK 32(Feb, May, Aug, Nov 1982): 1-14, 5-19, 39-48, 37-48. OKLAHOMA(Ft. Smith)-TEX-To Austin area. I. 1845.

DONNELL, Camilla T. "Early Days at White Salmon and The Dalles." WASHINGTON HISTORICAL QUARTERLY 4(Apr 1913): 105-15. Geog.

DONNER, George and Tamsen. Letters. SEE: Dale L. Morgan. OVERLAND IN 1846.

DORNIN, May. "The Emigrant Trails into California." MA thesis, Univ. of California-Berkeley, 1922. CAL-Genl.

DORR, Francis. Diary. BANCROFT. CAL(Indep)-BRIDGER. V. 1850.

DORRIS, Jonathan T. "Federal Aid to Oregon Trail Prior to 1850." OREGON HISTORICAL QUARTERLY 30(Dec 1919): 305-25. OR-Genl.

_____. "The Oregon Trail." Illinois State Historical Society JOURNAL 10(Jan 1918): 473-547. Copy of author's thesis. Or-Genl.

DOTT, Robert H. "Lt. Simpson's California Road across Oklahoma." CHRONICLES OF OKLAHOMA 38(Sum 1960): 154-79. CHEROKEE-Genl. Biog. Map.

DOUGHERTY, Lewis B. "Experiences of Lewis Bissell Dougherty on the Oregon Trail." MISSOURI HISTORICAL REVIEW 24(1929-30): 371-78, 552-56. OR: Ft. Kearny to Old Ft. Kearny. Rem. 1849. 1854-Freight. Grattan Massacre. Not Seen.

DOUGLAS, Charles D. Narrative. BANCROFT. SIMPSON(Camp Floyd). II+. 1859.

DOUGLAS, James A. Letter. MISSOURI STATESMAN, n.d. U.S. National Park Service Library, Omaha. Missing.

DOUGLAS, Jesse S. "Origins of the Population of Oregon in 1850." PACIFIC NORTHWEST QUARTERLY 41(Apr 1950): 95-108. Social.

DOUGLAS, Sara L. Memories of the Trip. In Paul & Helen Henderson Collection, UWY. OR(Council). V. Rem. 1853.

DOUTHIT, Mary O., ed. A SOUVENIR OF WESTERN WOMEN. Portland: Anderson & Duniway, 1905. Social.

DOWDLE, John C. Journal. UTHIST. MORMON. IV. Rem. 1847. SLCOR. III+. Rem. 1864.

DOWELL, B. F. Diary. Washington State Historical Society, Tacoma, WA. Freight-1856.

_____. Crossing the Plains. BANCROFT. CAL(St. Jo)-HALL-TRUCKEE. III+. 1850.

DOWLING, E. "California - or BUST." SENIOR SCHOLASTIC 111(30 Nov 1978): 10-13. Middle school-level account of the general trail experience. Not Seen.

DOWNES, Clara E. Journal. BANCROFT. CAL(Plattsmouth)-BRIDGER-SIMPSON. I. 1860. Fine descriptive account.

DOWNEY, Fairfax. "Epic of Endurance." READERS DIGEST 35(Oct 1939): 47-53. CAL-1846-Genl.

DOWNING, Finis E. Recollections. LILLEY. PIKES(St. Jo). Rem. 1863. Not Seen.

DOWNS, H. D. "Letter." [In] Byers, William N., and John H. Kellom. HANDBOOK. PIKES. 1858. Not Seen.

DOYLE, Simon. Diary. BEINECKE. CAL(Ft. Kearny)-BRIDGER-SLCUT-LASSEN. II+. 1849. CAL(Plattsburg)-TRUCKEE-BECKWOURTH. III. 1854. Stock drive.

DRAGO, Harry S. Ed. Edwards, Edward H. "The Edwards Letters."

_____. GREAT AMERICAN CATTLE TRAILS. NY: Dodd, Mead, 1965. Stock.

_____. ROAD AGENTS AND TRAIN ROBBERS. NY: Mead, 1973. Stage.

_____. ROADS TO EMPIRE: THE DRAMATIC CONQUEST OF THE AMERICAN WEST. NY: Dodd, Mead, 1968. Overland-Genl.

DRAKE, Francis M. THE EMIGRANT'S GUIDE TO CALIFORNIA. Fort Madison, IA: Evangelist, 1853. Guide.

DRAKE, J. Raman. "Howard Egan, Frontiersman, Pioneer and Pony Express Rider." MA thesis, BYU, 1956. Biog. Pony. Stage. Mail.

DRAKE, Joshua. Diary. HUNTL. CAL(Indep)-HALL. II. 1849.

DRAKE, Samuel A. HINTS AND INFORMATION FOR THE USE OF EMIGRANTS TO PIKE'S PEAK.... Leavenworth, KS: Author, 1860. Guide.

DRANNAN, W. F. PILOTING EMIGRANT TRAINS ACROSS THE PLAINS OF FIFTY YEARS AGO. Chicago: Rhodes & McClure, 1910. SANTA FE-Genl. Indians. Military.

DRAPER, D. M. The Santa Fe Trail. DENVERPUB. SANTA FE(Kansas City)-Ends Las Animas, CO, by freight wagon. IV. 1861.

DRAPER, Elias J. AUTOBIOGRAPHY OF A PIONEER OF CALIFORNIA. Fresno: Evening Democrat, 1904. CAL(Council)-BRIDGER-SLCUT. IV. Rem. 1852.

DRAPER, Ira A. Biographical Sketch. NBHIST. Pony.

DRAPER, Mabel H. THOUGH LONG THE TRAIL. NY: Rinehart, 1946. MORMON. IV. 1865.

DRAPER, W. N. "Early Trails and Roads in the Lower Fraser Valley." BRITISH COLUMBIA HISTORICAL QUARTERLY 7(Jan 1943): 25-35. CANADA-Genl.

_____. "Some Early Roads and Trails in New Westminster District." BRITISH COLUMBIA HISTORICAL QUARTERLY 9(Jan 1945): 25-35. CANADA-Genl.

THE DRAWINGS OF JOHN WOODHOUSE AUDUBON IL-LUSTRATING HIS ADVENTURES THROUGH MEXICO AND CALIFORNIA, 1849-1850. SF: Book Club of California, 1957. Graphics.

DREIBELBIS, John A. "Description of the Country...." In "A Jaunt to Honey Lake Valley and Noble's Pass." HUTCHINGS' 1(Jun 1857): 529-41. NOBLES-Genl.

DRESSER, William. Dresser Papers. BANCROFT. CAL(Council). V. 1850.

DREW, Charles S. OFFICIAL REPORT OF THE OWYHEE RECONNAISSANCE. Jacksonville, OR: Sentinel, 1865. OR(Ft. Klamath-Boise). II. 1864.

DREW, Susan I. Crossing the Plains. ORHIST. OR(Indep)-MEEK? V. Rem. 1853.

DRIGGS, Howard R. SEE: With Ezra Meeker. COVERED WAGON CENTENNIAL. SEE: With Ezra Meeker. OX-TEAM DAYS.

_____. "Anniversary of the Pony Express." NATIONAL EDUCA-TION ASSOCIATION JOURNAL 24(Apr 1935): 122-23. Pony.

_____. "Early Trails as a National Heritage." NEBRASKA HIS-TORICAL MAGAZINE 20(Oct-Dec 1939): 230-41. Pres.

_____. MORMON TRAIL: PATHWAY OF PIONEERS WHO MADE THE DESERTS BLOOM. NY: American Pioneer Trails Assn., 1947. MORMON-Genl.

_____. THE OLD WEST SPEAKS. Englewood Cliffs, NJ: Bonan-za Books, 1956. Overland-Genl. Graphics.

_____. THE PONY EXPRESS GOES THROUGH. NY: Frederick A. Stokes, 1935. Pony. Readable, detailed narrative.

_____. WESTWARD AMERICA. NY: Putnam's, 1942. Overland-Genl.

_____, Arthur W. Proctor, and Ezra Meeker. COVERED-WAGON CENTENNIAL AND OX-TEAM DAYS. NY: World, 1931. Pres.

DRIVER, William. "London to Salt Lake City in 1867...." Ed. Frank D. Reeve. NEW MEXICO HISTORICAL REVIEW 17(Jan 1942): 37-63. MORMON. III-. 1866.

DRUMHELLER, "Uncle Dan." UNCLE DAN DRUMHELLER....
Spokane: Inland-American, 1925. CAL(Kansas City)-TRUCKEE.
IV. Rem. 1854. Pony.

DRURY, Aubrey. "Forty-Niners: As Easterners Saw Them."
AMERICAN HERITAGE 1(Spr 1950): 40-43. Graphics.

_____. "The Livermore Family." BANCROFT. CAL(St. Jo). V.
Rem. 1850.

DRURY, Clifford M. Ed. Peale, Titian. DIARY, OREGON TO
CALIFORNIA...1841.

DRYDEN, C. P. GIVE ALL TO OREGON. NY: Hastings, 1968. OR-
Genl.

DUBOFF, Richard B. "Business Demand and the Development of the
Telegraph in the United States." BUSINESS HISTORY REVIEW
54(Win 1980): 459-79. Telegraph.

DUDLEY, N. A. M. "Battle of Ash Hollow: The 1909-1910 Recollections of General N. A. M. Dudley." Ed. R. Eli Paul. NEBRASKA
HISTORY 62(Fall 1981): 373-99. Military. Indians. Geog.

DUDLEY, Sarah F. "Trip Across the Plains." SEE: McAlister,
Nehemiah. Identical diary.

DUEHLMEIER, Fred D. "The 1847 Mormon Migration." MA thesis,
Univ. of Utah, 1977. MORMON-1847-Genl.

DUFFIELD, George C. "Driving Cattle from Texas to Iowa, 1866." Ed.
W. W. Baldwin. ANNALS OF IOWA 14(Apr 1924): 241-62.
TEX(San Saba)-OKLAHOMA-Ends Burlington, IA. III. 1866.
Stock drive.

DUFFIN, Reg. P. "Here Lies Nancy Hill?" OVERLAND JOURNAL
1(Jul 1983): 4-13. Geog-Kemmerer, WY.

_____. "The Grave of Joel Hembree." OVERLAND JOURNAL
3(Spr 1985): 6-10. Geog-Douglas, WY.

_____. "Mary Fulkerson - A Destroyed Grave." OVERLAND
JOURNAL 2(Fall 1984): 20-22. Geog-Names Hill.

_____. "The Miller-Tate Murder and the John F. Miller Grave."
OVERLAND JOURNAL 5(Fall 1987): 24-31. Train Govt.

_____. "The Nancy Hill Story: The Final Chaper." OVERLAND
JOURNAL 4(Fall 1986): 56-63. Geog-Kemmerer, WY.

DUFFIN, William A. Ed. Way, Phocion. "Overland via 'Jackass Mail'"

DUFFUS, R. L. THE SANTA FE TRAIL. London: Longmans, Green,
1931. Solid, attractive survey.

DUGGLEBY, Donald R. "Hoosiers Travel the Oregon Trail, 1841 to
1853." MA thesis, Indiana Univ., 1948. OR-Genl.

DUKE, Escal F. Ed. Evans, George W. MEXICAN GOLD TRAIL.

DULANY, William H. Letters. Missouri Historical Society, St. Louis.
CAL(St. Jo). 1850. Not Seen.

DUMKE, Glenn S. "Across Mexico in '49." PACIFIC HISTORICAL
REVIEW 18(Feb 1949): 33-44. MEX-1849-Genl.

DUNBAR, Seymour. Ed. Owen, John. LETTERS AND JOURNALS.

_____. A HISTORY OF TRAVEL IN AMERICA. 4 vols. In-
dianapolis: Bobbs - Merrill, 1915. Overland-Genl.

DUNCAN, Charles T. Ed. Greeley, Horace. OVERLAND JOURNEY.

DUNCAN, Edith M. Ed. Hosmer, J. Allen. TRIP TO THE STATES.

DUNCAN, Elizabeth. Diary. Spencer Library, Univ. of Kansas,
Lawrence, KS. CAL(Lawrence)-CHEROKEE-SIMPSON. II. 1867.
Story of a woman's involuntary move west.

DUNCAN, S. Blackwell. "The Legendary Concords." AMERICAN
WEST 8(Jan 1971): 16-17, 61-62. Stage.

DUNDASS, Samuel R. JOURNAL OF SAMUEL RUTHERFORD
DUNDASS, 1849. Steubenville, OH: Conn's, 1857. CAL(Indep)-
BRIDGER-SLCUT. II. 1849.

DUNHAM, E. Allene. FROM IOWA TO CALIFORNIA IN A
COVERED WAGON. Milton, IA: Author, 192? CAL(Council)-
SIMPSON. IV. Rem. 1864.

DUNIWAY, Abigail S. "Journal." (In) COVERED WAGON WOMEN,
Vol. 5. eds. Kenneth L. Holmes and David C. Duniway. Glendale:
Clark, 1986. OR(St. Jo)-BARLOW. II. 1852.

DUNIWAY, David C. Ed. Cornell, William. "William Cornell's 1852
Journal."

DUNLAP, Caroline C. "Ancotty." ORHIST. OR(Council). II. Rem.
1853.

DUNLAP, Catherine C. THE MONTANA GOLD RUSH DIARY OF
KATE [Catherine Cruickshank] DUNLAP. Ed. S. Lyman Tyler.
SLC: Old West and Univ. of Utah Press, 1969. CAL(Council)-
LANDER-MONTANA. II. 1864. Fine maps and printwork.

DUNLAP, James P. Reminiscences. NBHIST. Freight.

DUNLOP, John W. "From Milwaukee to the California Gold Fields."
Ed. Harry H. Anderson. CHICAGO WESTERNERS BRAND
BOOK 26(Oct 1969): 57-59. CAL(Council)-SLCUT. V. 1852.

DUNLOP, Richard. DOCTORS OF THE AMERICAN FRONTIER.
NY: Doubleday, 1965. Medical.

_____. GREAT TRAILS OF THE WEST. NY: Abingdon, 1971.
Overland-Genl. Pres. Maps.

_____. "History Comes Alive along the Road to Oregon." TODAY'S
HEALTH 48(Sept 1970): 44-49. Pres. Not Seen.

_____. "Retracing the Oregon Trail." TRAVEL 130(Sept 1968): 26-
32. Pres.

_____. WHEELS WEST: 1590-1900. Chicago: Rand McNally, 1977.
Overland-Genl-Graphics.

DUNN, J. W. Diary. BARKER. CAL(Dover, Ark)-CHEROKEE-
SLCUT. II+. 1857.

DUNN, Mary B. "The Jackass Mail Line from San Antonio to San
Diego." SDHIST. Stage.

DUNN, Mary M. Comp. Hill, Elizabeth F. UNDAUNTED
PIONEERS.

DUNN, Ruby D. Into the Sunset. Lane County Historical Society,
Eugene, OR. OR(Indep). III. Rem. 1853.

DUNN, Ruth. THE BURNING OF JULESBURG. Julesburg, CO:

Author, 1973. 1865 Indian attack.

DUNN, Thomas. Private Journal. UTHIST. Not Seen.

DUNN, William. "Diary of...Freighter." NEBRASKA HISTORY AND RECORD OF PIONEER DAYS 4(Apr-Jun 1921): 31-32. Freight.

DUNNING, Harold M. THE OVERLAND TRAIL NORTH. Boulder, CO: Author, 1969. CHEROKEE(Berthoud, CO - Virginia Dale Station). Map. Pres.

DUNNING, Ira S. Journal. Wyoming Historical Society Library, Cheyenne, WY. OR(Council)-BARLOW. III. 1853.

DUNPHY, William. Statement. BANCROFT. CAL-TEX(Brownsville)-MEX(Monterey-Durango-Mazatlan). V. Rem. 1848.

DUNSTAN, Edwin. AUTOBIOGRAPHY. Winona, Miss: N.p., 1928. PIKES. II. Rem. 1859.

DURFEE, Joseph A. Diaries. MONHIST. CAL(St. Jo)-LANDER-MONTANA. 1864. Not Seen.

DURHAM, Reed C., Jr. "The Iowa Experience: A Blessing in Disguise." BRIGHAM YOUNG UNIVERSITY STUDIES 21(Fall 1981): 463-74. MORMON-1846-Iowa-Genl.

DURIVAGE, John E. "Through Mexico to California...." In SOUTHERN TRAILS TO CALIFORNIA, ed. Ralph P. Bieber. Glendale: Clark, 1937. CAL-TEX(Brownsville)-MEX(Monterey-Chihuahua)-GILA. I. 1849.

DURLEY, Jeff. Diary. DENVERPUB. CHEROKEE(Denver-Ft. Bridger)-HALL-MONTANA. II+. 1862. Mail.

DURRELL, Edward. SEE: Shumway, George, et al. CONESTOGA WAGON.

DUTTON, Jerome. "Across the Plains in 1850." ANNALS OF IOWA, 3d Series, 9(1900): 447-483. CAL(Council). II. 1850. Not Seen.

DUVAL, Isaac H. "Overland to California." Ed. Gary C. Stein. AMERICAN HISTORY ILLUSTRATED 12(May 1977): 26-36. CAL-TEX(Waco)-GILA. III. Rem. 1849.

DYCK, Cornelius J. "In the California Gold Rush." MENNONITE LIFE 11(Jan 1956): 25-28. CAL(Council)-BRIDGER. V-. 1850.

DYER, Ellen. Journal. BARKER. CAL(Council)-BRIDGER-SLCUT. III. 1860.

DYKE, Dorothy. "Transportation in the Sacramento Valley, 1849-1860." MA thesis, Univ. of California-Berkeley, 1932. Stage. Freight.

DYKES, Jeff. FIFTY GREAT WESTERN ILLUSTRATORS: A BIBLIOGRAPHIC CHECKLIST. Flagstaff, AZ: Northland, 1975. Bib-Graphics.

EADS, Rachel. "Following the Sun in the '50's." FRONTIER TIMES 54(Jun-Jul 1980): 29-33. CAL-TEX(Denton)-GILA. IV. 1857.

EAKIN, Stewart B. A SHORT SKETCH OF A TRIP ACROSS THE PLAINS. Eugene, OR: Lane County Historical Society, 1970. OR(Council)-BARLOW. III. 1866.

EARL, Guy C. "The Enchanted Valley and other Stories." BANCROFT. CAL-TEX-MEX-GILA. V. 1849.

EARL, Robert. Reminiscences. ORHIST. OR(St. Jo). V-. Rem. 1845.

EARLE, George. AN ARGUMENT...IN THE CHORPENNING CASE. N.p., n.d. Mail.

EARNSHAW, William. "Across the Plains." WATERFORD [Wisconsin] POST, 5 Jun - 4 Sept 1897, n.p. NEWBERRY. OR(Council)-LANDER-NOBLE(to Susanville)-OR-CAL(to Jacksonville, OR). Rem. 1860. Not Seen.

East Tennessee and California Gold Mining Company Records. Tennessee State Library and Archives, Nashville, TN. CAL. 1849. Not Seen.

EASTIC, Eleanor A. Ed. Wade, Mark S. THE CARIBOO ROAD.

EASTIN, Lucian J. EMIGRANTS' GUIDE TO PIKE'S PEAK. Leavenworth, KS: Kansas Herald, 1859. Guide.

EASTIN, Thomas D. Collected Data. BANCROFT. CAL(Indep?)-SANTA FE-CHEROKEE-HASTINGS?-TRUCKEE. IV. 1849.

EASTIN, Thomas N. "Kentucky Gold Rusher." Ed. Vincent Crowders. LOUISVILLE COURRIER JOURNAL MAGAZINE, 25 Jan 1948, 34-36. Also BANCROFT. CAL(Indep)-BRIDGER-SLCUT-Ends Humboldt Sink. II+. 1849.

EASTLAND, Joseph G. Letters. CAHIST. CAL-TEX(San Antonio)-MEX. III. 1849.

EASTLAND, Thomas B., and Joseph G. "To California through Texas and Mexico...." Ed. Dorothy H. Huggins. CALIFORNIA HISTORICAL QUARTERLY 18(Jun, Sept 1939): 99-135, 229-50. CAL-TEX(Port Lavaca)-MEX(El Paso-Chihuahua-Mazatlan). II. 1849.

EASTMAN, Stephen W., and Nelson G. Gill. Journal. Iowa State Historical Society Archives, Iowa City, IA. CAL(St. Jo)-LASSEN. III. 1849.

EASTON, L. C. "Captain L. C. Easton's Report: Fort Laramie to Fort Leavenworth via Republican River in 1849." Ed. Merrill J. Mattes. KANSAS HISTORICAL QUARTERLY 20(May 1953): 392-416. CAL(Ft. Laramie-Ft. Leavenworth). II. 1849. Govt. Pikes.

EASTON, Susan W. "Suffering and Death on the Plains of Iowa." BRIGHAM YOUNG UNIVERSITY STUDIES 21(Fall 1981): 431-39. MORMON-Iowa-Genl.

EATON, Edna B. "Charles Camden and the Camden Toll Road." COVERED WAGON (1960): 8-13. CAL-Genl.

EATON, Herbert. THE OVERLAND TRAIL TO CALIFORNIA IN 1852. NY: Putnam's, 1974. CAL-1852-Genl.

EBBERT, George W. "George Wood Ebbert." OREGON HISTORICAL QUARTERLY 19(Sept 1918): 263-67. OR(East from Oregon to St. Jo). V. Rem. 1848.

EBERSTADT, Charles. "On Colorado Guidebooks of '59." In BOOKMEN'S HOLIDAY. NY: New York Public Library, 1943. Guide.

EBERSTAT, Edward. Ed. Sawyer, Lorenzo. WAY SKETCHES. Ed. Root, Riley. "Journal of Riley Root." Ed. Bennett, James. OVERLAND JOURNEY.

EBEY, Winfield S. Papers. Univ. of Washington Library-Manuscripts, Seattle, WA. OR(Council). I. 1854.

ECCLESTON, Robert. OVERLAND TO CALIFORNIA ON THE SOUTHWESTERN TRAIL, 1849.... Eds. George P. Hammond and Edward H. Howes. Bancroft Library Publications No. 2. Berkeley:

Univ. of California Press, 1950. CAL-TEX(Port Lavaca)-GILA. I. 1849. Govt.

EDENS, Walter. Ed. Adams, Franklin E. "Overland Diary."

EDGAR, William F. "One Wagon Train Boss of Texas." OUTING 39(Jan 1902): 381-83. 1866 Indian attack near Fort Davis.

_____. "Historical Notes of Old Land Marks on the Western Slope of the Rocky Mountains - Cantonment Loring." PUBLICATIONS Historical Society of Southern California 3 (1891): 17-19. Geog.

EDGERTON, Mary. A GOVERNOR'S WIFE ON THE MINING FRONTIER. Ed. James L. Thane, Jr. SLC: Tanner Trust, 1976.

Editorial Committee. "The Pony Express." WESTERN EXPRESS 10(Apr, July, Oct 1960): 2-17, 2-12, 3-14; 11(Jan, Apr, July, Oct 1961): 6-16, 3-17, 4-18, 2-8. Pony. Graphics.

EDMONSON, Vera F. "James E. Birch and the California Stage Company." SDHIST. Biog. Stage.

"Edmund Ellsworth Handcart Company." UTHIST. MORMON-1856-Genl.

EDMUNDSON, William. "Overland Diary of William Edmundsen." ANNALS OF IOWA 8(Oct 1908): 516-35. CAL(Council)-BRIDGER-HASTINGS. II. 1850.

EDRINGTON, L. Kay. "A Study of Early Utah - Montana Trade, Transportation and Communication." MA thesis, BYU, 1959. Freight. MONTANA-Genl.

EDWARDS, E. S. TRAILING THE CAMPFIRES. N.p., n. p. BOZE. Not Seen.

EDWARDS, Edward H. "The Edwards Letters and the Wagon Road to Virginia City." Eds. Harry S. Drago and Phyllis Mott. NEW YORK WESTERNERS BRAND BOOK 9, no. 1(1962): 16-19. V. DAKOTAS(Niobrara River Route)-MONTANA. V. 1865.

EDWARDS, Elza Ivan. "Death Valley's Neglected Hero." LOS ANGELES WESTERNERS BRAND BOOK 12(1966): 59-74. Geog.

_____. DESERT VOICES: A DESCRIPTIVE BIBLIOGRAPHY. LA: Westernlore, 1958. Bib.

_____. FREEMAN'S: A STAGE STOP ON THE MOJAVE. Glendale: La Siesta, 1964. Geog.

_____. "INTO AN ALKALI VALLEY:" THE FIRST WRITTEN ACCOUNT OF DEATH VALLEY. LA: Edwards & Williams, 1948. SLCOR-1849-Genl.

_____. LOST OASES ALONG THE CARRIZO. LA: Westernlore, 1961. GILA(Yuma-Warner's). Bib.

_____. "The Mystery of Death Valley's Lost Wagon Train." In LOS ANGELES WESTERNERS BRAND BOOK 11(1964): 181-240. Geog.

_____. THE VALLEY WHOSE NAME IS DEATH. Pasadena: San Pasquale Press, 1940. SLCOR-Death Valley. II. 1849.

EDWARDS, Glenn Thomas, Jr. "Oregon Regiment in the Civil War Years: Duty on the Indian Frontier." MA thesis, Univ. of Oregon, 1960.. Military.

EDWARDS, Philip L. SEE: Camp, Charles L. "Colonel Philip Leget Edwards."

_____. SKETCH OF THE OREGON TERRITORY OR, EMIGRANT'S GUIDE. 1842. Reprint. N.p., 1952. Guide.

EDWARDS, Solomon. Diary. MO-WHMC. PIKES. III. 1864.

EDWARDS, William W. "Old Fort Laramie." JOURNAL MILITARY SERVICE INSTITUTE 52(1913): 121-36. Geog.

EDWARDSON, Tom. "Journey from New Orleans to California." CHAMBERS JOURNAL OF POPULAR LITERATURE, December, 1855, 337-41, 364-8, 371-5. CAL(Kansas City). IV. 1849. Fiction?

EGAN, Ferol. Ed. Martin, Thomas S. WITH FREMONT TO CALIFORNIA.

_____. THE EL DORADO TRAIL: THE STORY OF THE GOLD RUSH ROUTES ACROSS MEXICO. One of the American Trails Series. NY: McGraw-Hill, 1970. MEX-Genl. TEX-Genl. GILA-Genl.

_____. "Incident at Tragedy Springs: An Unsolved Mystery of the California Trail." AMERICAN WEST 8, no. 1(1963): 36-39. Geog. 1848 killing in Carson Pass.

_____. "Journada del Muerto." AMERICAN WEST 6, no. 4(1962): 12-19, 61-63. Geog. RIO GRANDE-Genl.

EGAN, Howard. PIONEERING THE WEST, 1846-1878.... Ed. Howard R. Egan. Richmond, UT: Editor, 1917. Stage. Pony. SIMPSON-Genl.
MORMON-Genl.

EGAN, William M. Journal. UTHIST. SIMPSON. IV. 1863.

EGBERT, Eliza Ann McAuley. "Across the Plains in 1852." POMONA VALLEY HISTORIAN 2(Jan, Apr 1966): 9-24, 65-72. CAL(Council)-TRUCKEE. II. 1852.

EGGENHOFER, Nick. WAGONS, MULES AND MEN. NY: Hastings House, 1961. Eqpt-Graphics.

EIDE, Ingvard H. OREGON TRAIL. Chicago: Rand McNalley, 1973. OR-Genl. Exceptional printwork and graphics.

ELDER, Joseph B. Diary. UTHIST. MORMON. IV. 1856.

ELDRIDGE, Ira. Journal. LDS. MORMON. III. 1861.

ELIOT, Robert. "Off to the Gold Fields with Robert Eliot." WISCONSIN MAGAZINE OF HISTORY 33(Mar 1950): 327-40. CAL-CHEROKEE(Ft. Smith)-MARCY-RIO GRANDE-GILA. IV. 1849.

"Eliza and Margaret Prentice's Trip Across the Plains." NVHIST. CAL(Council)-BRIDGER-SIMPSON. IV. 1860.

ELKINS, Mrs. Mae. The Trials and Tribulations of the Powells' and Centers' in 1845." ORU. OR-1845-Genl.

ELLENBECKER, John G. "Graves along the Oregon Trail." PONY EXPRESS COURIER 3(Nov 1936): 9. OR-Genl.

_____. THE JAYHAWKERS OF DEATH VALLEY. Marysville, KS: Author, 1938. CAL(Council)-BRIDGER-SLCOR. III. Rem. 1849.

_____. THE PONY EXPRESS. Marysville, KS: Author, 1936? Pony.

ELLINGSEN, John D. Ed. Ransdell, Shelton. "Wagon Train Journal."

ELLIOTT, Blanche B. "Stagecoach Days in Douglas County [Oregon]." UMPQUA TRAPPER 3(Sum, Fall 1967): 19-24, 3-4. Stage.

ELLIOTT, Claude. "A Check List of Theses and Dissertations in Texas History, 1907-1952." SOUTHWESTERN HISTORICAL QUARTERLY 58(July, Oct 1954; Jan, Apr 1955): 98-142, 249-87, 372-404, 488-522. Bib.

"Elliott Expeditionary Cutoff." EUGENE [Oregon] REGISTER-GUARD, 16 Jul 1950, n.p. OR(Malheur River - Willamette Valley). III. 1853.

ELLIOTT, Gordon R. BARKERVILLE, QUESNEL AND THE CARIBOO GOLD RUSH. Vancouver: Douglas & McIntyre, 1958. CANADA-Genl.

ELLIOTT, M. "Trail into Timelessness." AMERICANA 13(Nov-Dec 1985): 52-57. SANTA FE-Genl.

ELLIOTT, Russell R. "Nevada's First Trading Post: A Study in Historiography." NEVADA HISTORICAL SOCIETY QUARTERLY 13(Win 1970): 3-11. Geog-Carson Valley.

ELLIOTT, T. C. "Camels in Inland Empire." OREGON HISTORICAL QUARTERLY 30(Jun 1929): 125-28. Freight.

_____. "The Mullan Road: Its Local History and Significance." WASHINGTON HISTORICAL QUARTERLY 14(Jul 1923): 206-9. MULLAN-Genl.

ELLIS, Henrietta C. DIARY. Ed. Beryl Leebrick. Honolulu: Leebrick, 1961. CAL(Council)-CHEROKEE(Ft. Collins-SLC)-SIMPSON. II. 1865.

ELLIS, James A. "Diary." In DIARY, ed. Beryl Leebrick. Honolulu: Leebrick, 1961. CAL(Stage:Julesburg-SLC-SIMPSON). III. 1865.

ELLIS, John M. Ed. Scott, Charles. "The Nevada Indian Uprisings of 1860."

ELLIS, John W. Diary. CSL. CAL(Council). II. 1850.

ELLLISON, J. W. Ed. Belshaw, Maria P. "Diary of a Bride."

ELLISON, Joseph. "The Covered Wagon Centennial...." WASHINGTON HISTORICAL QUARTERLY 21(1930): 163-78. Pres.

ELLISON, Robert S. FORT BRIDGER, WYOMING. Caspar: Author, 1931. Geog.

_____. "Independence Rock and the Oregon Trail." MIDWEST REVIEW 8(Feb 1927): 1-11. Geog.

_____. INDEPENDENCE ROCK, THE GREAT RECORD OF THE DESERT. Caspar, WY: Natrona County Historical Society, 1930. Geog.

ELLMAKER, Enos. "Autobiography." In ELLMAKER NARRATIVE.... Eugene, OR: Lane County Pioneer-Historical Society, 1962. OR(Council?). V. Rem. 1853.

ELLSWORTH, Edmund. SEE: Harlan, Edgar B. "First Mormon Handcart."

_____. "The First Hand-Cart Companies...." Salt Lake City DESERET NEWS, October, 1856, n.p.

ELMER, Elijah. Journal. SDHIST. CAL(Council)-SANTA FE-RIO GRANDE-GILA. III +. 1846.

ELWELL, R. F. "Story of the Overland Mail." OUTING 48(N.d.). Not Seen.

EMERSON, James C. Reminiscence. MONHIST. Freight.

EMERSON, William H. Diary. CSL. CAL(TEX-Brownsville)-MEX(Monterey-Durango-Mazatlan). II. 1849.

EMERY, Joseph A. Omaha to Virginia City. MONHIST. CAL(Council)-BOZE. 1863. Not Seen.

"The Emigrant Trail in Watercolor." NEVADA HIGHWAYS AND PARKS 32(Win 1972): 36-38. Graphics.

EMIGRANT TRAILS OF SOUTHEASTERN IDAHO. SEE: Cramer, Howard R.

EMIGRANT'S GUIDE, BEING A TABLE OF DISTANCES...FROM GREAT SALT LAKE CITY TO SAN FRANCISCO. N.p., n.d. (1850?). BEINECKE. Guide.

THE EMIGRANT'S GUIDE TO CALIFORNIA DESCRIBING ITS GEOGRAPHY, AGRICULTURAL AND COMMERCIAL RESOURCES. London: Pelham Richardson, 1848? Guide.

THE EMIGRANT'S GUIDE TO THE GOLDEN LAND. London: Printed for the Booksellers, 1850. Guide.

"Emigration from Iowa to Oregon in 1843 from THE IOWA JOURNAL OF HISTORY AND POLITICS, 1912, with Reprints of Various Iowa News Accounts of 1843." OREGON HISTORICAL QUARTERLY 15(1914): 285-99. OR-1843-Genl.

EMMETT, Chris. FORT UNION AND THE WINNING OF THE SOUTHWEST. Norman: Univ. of Oklahoma Press, 1965. Military. Geog.

EMORY, William H. SEE: With John Fremont. NOTES OF TRAVEL.

_____. LIEUTENANT EMORY REPORTS. Ed. Ross Calvin. Albuquerque: Univ. of New Mexico Press, 1951. CAL(Leav)-SANTA FE-RIO GRANDE-GILA. II +. 1846.

_____. NOTES OF A MILITARY RECONNAISSANCE FROM FORT LEAVENWORTH TO SAN DIEGO, 1846 - 1847. 30th Cong., 1st sess. H. Ex. Doc. 41. Serial 517. Govt.

_____. REPORT ON THE U.S. AND MEXICAN BOUNDARY SURVEY. 34th Cong., 1st sess. S. Ex. Doc. 135. CAL-1853-Genl. CAL-1854-Genl.

EMPEY, William A. Diary. UTHIST. MORMON. II-. 1852.

_____. "The Mormon Ferry on the North Platte; the Journal of William A. Empey, May 7 - August 4, 1847." Ed. Dale L. Morgan. ANNALS OF WYOMING 21(Jul-Oct 1949): 111-67. Geog. MORMON. II. 1847.

ENGELS, William H. "Diary of a Cattle Drive." FLASHBACK 27(Feb 1977): 31-47. CAL-CHEROKEE(Ft Smith)-SLCUT. III. 1854. Stock Drive.

ENGILES, James G. Ed. Borthwick, Alexander E. "Westering Journal."

ENGLE, Paul M. "Sketches and Surveys Made during the Exploratory Tour of 1857 to Nebraska and Dakota under Lt. G. W. Warren." BEINECKE. DAKOTAS(Sioux City-Ft. Laramie-Niobrara River &

return). 127 colored maps.

ENLOE, Rachel. Papers. CAHIST. CAL(Missouri). 1853. Not Seen.

ENOS, A. A. ACROSS THE PLAINS IN 1850. Stanton?: N.p., 1905. CAL(Council)-BRIDGER-SLCUT. IV. Rem. 1850.

ENOS, James E. Recollections. CSL. CAL(Council). V. Rem. 1855.

EPNER, Gustavus. MAP OF THE GOLD REGIONS IN BRITISH COLUMBIA. Victoria: Epner, 1862. Guide.

EPPARD, Mabelle. "The Southern Emigrant Trails to California." MA thesis, Univ. of California-Berkeley, 1914. CAL-Genl.

EPPERSON, Mrs. B. C. "Diary." (In) HISTORY OF COLUSA COUNTY, CA. SF: N.p., 1880. CALCouncil)-BRIDGER-SIMPSON-TRUCKEE. 1864. Not Seen.

EPSTEIN, Daniel M. "The California Gold Rush as Reported by the Marshall [Michigan] STATESMAN." MICHIGAN HISTORY 34(Mar 1950): 19-28. CAL-Genl.

ERB, Louise Bruning. SEE: Brown, Ann B. et al. WAGON TRAILS.

ERICKSON, Harvey. "Mullan's 1862 Interstate Road." PACIFIC NORTHWESTERNER 18(Fall 1974): 53-66. MULLAN-Genl.

ERKSON, Alexander C. "Statement." In DEATH VALLEY IN '49. Ed. William L. Manly. San Jose, CA: Pacific Tree and Vine, 1894. SLCOR. IV. Rem. 1849.

ERNEST, Clement S. "History in a Mail Pouch: Washington Centennial Stamps and Territorial Covers." PACIFIC NORTHWEST QUARTERLY 44(Oct 1953): 185-89. Mail.

ERSKINE, Gladys S. Ed. Miller, Broncho C. BRONCHO CHARLIE.

ERSKINE, Ignatius. Journals. Texas State Library-Archives, Austin, TX. CAL-TEX(Sequin)-GILA. II. 1854. Stock drive.

ERSKINE, M. H. "A Cattle Drive from Texas to California...." Ed. Walter S. Sanderlin. SOUTHWESTERN HISTORICAL QUARTERLY 67(Jan 1964): 397-412. CAL-TEX(San Antonio)-GILA. III. 1854. Stock drive.

ESCHER, Louise. Ed. Paup, Harrison. ACROSS THE PLAINS IN 1861.

ESPENSCHIED, Lloyd. "Louis Espenschied and his Family." MISSOURI HISTORICAL BULLETIN 18(Jan 1962): 87-103. Eqpt.

ESSIN, Emmett M. "Mules, Packs, and Pack Trains." SOUTHWESTERN HISTORICAL QUARTERLY 74(Jul 1970): 52-80. Teams-graphics.

ESTABROOK, Joseph H. "Crossing the Plains in 1864." Ed. Hester Cattell. TRAIL 2, no. 1(N.d.): 11-13. PIKES. V. 1864.

ESTES, George. THE STAGECOACH. Troutdale, OR: Author, 1925. Stage-OR-Genl.

ETTER, Patrick A. Ed. Brownlee, Robert. AN AMERICAN ODYSSEY.

ETULAIN, Richard W. "Archer B. Gilfillan: Scholarly Sheepherder of South Dakota." SOUTH DAKOTA HISTORY 16(Win 1986). Biog. Stock.

_____., and Merwin Swanson. IDAHO HISTORY: A BIBLIOG-

RAPHY. Rev. 1979. Pocatello, ID: Idaho Univ. Press, 1979. Bib.

EUBANK, Victor. "Log of an Auto Prairie Schooner." SUNSET 28(Feb 1912): 188-95. Pres.

EVANS, Burrell Whalen. Diary. BANCROFT. CAL(Indep?)-BRIDGER-SLCUT-LASSEN. III. 1849.

EVANS, C. B. ANOTHER MONTANA PIONEER. Pasadena: Private, 1960? CAL(Council?)-HALL-MONTANA. V. Rem. 1867.

EVANS, Cleo F. "Transportation in Early Texas." MA thesis, St. Mary's Univ., 1940. Not Seen.

EVANS, Elwood. "The Fraser River Excitement, 1858." BEINECKE. CANADA-1858-Genl.

EVANS, George W. MEXICAN GOLD TRAIL. Ed. Glenn S. Dumke. San Marino, CA: Huntington, 1945. CAL-TEX(Port Lavaca-Eagle Pass)-MEX(Presidio-Chihuahua-Santa Cruz)-GILA. I. 1849.

EVANS, Henry H. WESTERN BIBLIOGRAPHIES. SF: Peregrine, 1951. Bib.

EVANS, James A. Journal. Iowa State Historical Society, Iowa City, IA. CAL(Council)-LANDER-NOBLE. III. 1860.

_____. "Report: Camp Walbach to Green River." KSHIST. CAL(Council)-CHEROKEE(Laramie Plains-Green River)-Ends. III. 1864.

EVANS, James B. Ed. Evans, James W. "A Missouri Forty-Niner's Trip."

EVANS, James W. Journal. BANCROFT. CAL(Indep?)-TRUCKEE. II+. 1850.

_____. "A Missouri Forty-Niner's Trip...." MISSOURI HISTORICAL REVIEW 43(Oct 1948): 38-47. CAL(Weston?)-TRUCKEE. V. 1849.

EVANS, R. M. EVAN'S OFFICIAL MAP OF WASHOE AND THE CARSON VALLEY.... SF: Evans, 1860. Guide.

EVANS, Robley D. A SAILOR'S LOG. NY: Appleton, 1902. CAL(St Jo)-BRIDGER-Ends SLC. Returns to St. Jo by stage. IV. Rem. 1859.

EVANS, Mrs. S. D. A Trip from Washoe, Nevada to Douglas County, Oregon in 1863. ORU. OR-CAL. III. 1863.

EVERSHED, Thomas. "The Gold Rush Journal of Thomas Evershed." Ed. Joseph W. Barnes. ROCHESTER HISTORY 39(Jan-Apr 1977): 1-44. CAL(Indep?)-SLCUT. II. 1849.

EVERSOLE, Mildred. Ed. Oglesby, Richard J. "Richard J. Oglesby."

EVERTS, F. D. Diary. BEINECKE. CAL(St Jo)-Ends Sweetwater River. II+. 1849.

EWING, Floyd F. "James H. Baker: Cattleman and Trail Driver." WESTX 43(Oct 1967): 3-17. Stock.

_____. "The Mule as a Factor in the Development of the Southwest." ARIZONA & THE WEST 5(Win 1963): 315-26. Teams.

EXPEDITION OF CAPTAIN FISK TO THE ROCKY MOUNTAINS. 36th Cong., 1st sess., H. Ex. Doc. 45. DAKOTAS-MONTANA(Bannack to SLC)-Stage(SLC-Atchison). II+. 1863.

"Expeditions of Captain James L. Fisk to the Gold Mines of Idaho and

Montana, 1864-1866." COLLECTIONS State Historical Society of North Dakota 2(1908): 421-61. DAKOTAS-Genl. MONTANA-Genl.

"Extracts from WABASH COURIER (1848-1850) Citing Gold Rush Letters." Indiana State Library-Ms, Indianapolis, IN. CAL-Genl.

"The Fabulous and Mysterious James E. Birch." HARVESTER, 25 Sept 1954, N.p. Biog. Stage. Not Seen.

FAIRBANKS, Ernest E. "Forty-Niners Starved in the Midst of Plenty." SCIENTIFIC AMERICAN, June 1932, 348-9. Social.

FAIRCHILD, Frances. "The Pony Express Service and Harry Roff." PONY EXPRESS COURIER 2(Apr 1936): 6-7. Pony.

FAIRCHILD, Lucius. "California Letters...." Ed. Joseph Schafer. WISCONSIN STATE HISTORICAL SOCIETY COLLECTIONS 31(1931): Entire volume. CAL(St. Jo)-TRUCKEE. IV. 1849.

FAIRCHILD, Mahlon D. "A Trip to the Colorado Mines in 1862." CALIFORNIA HISTORICAL QUARTERLY 12(Mar 1933): 11-17. BRADSHAW. III. 1862.

FALBO, Ernest. Ed. Cipriano, Leonetto. DIARIES.

FALCONER, Arthur R. "A Historical Geography of the Transportation Routes in Baja California from 1533 to 1920." MA thesis, Univ. of California-LA, 1971. MEX-Genl.

FALLON, William. "Extracts from a Journal...." San Francisco CALIFORNIA STAR, 5 Jun 1847, 2-3. TRUCKEE. II. 1847.

FANCHER, J. Diary. Tennessee State Library and Archives, Nashville, TN. Military. Train Govt.

FARAGHER, John M. "Men and Women's Work on the Overland Trail." PACIFIC HISTORIAN 23(Spr 1979): 4-23. Social.

———. "Midwestern Families in Motion: Women and Men on the Overland Trail to Oregon and California, 1843-1870." PhD diss., Yale Univ., 1977. Social.

———. WOMEN AND MEN ON THE OVERLAND TRAIL. New Haven: Yale Univ. Press, 1977. Social.

FARAHER, Johnny, and Christine Stansell. "Women and their Families on the Overland Trail...1842-1867." FEMINIST STUDIES 2(1975): 150-66. Social.

FARMER, J. E. MY LIFE WITH THE ARMY IN THE WEST. Ed. Dale F. Giese. Santa Fe: Stagecoach, 1967. CAL(Leav)-BRIDGER-Ends SLC. IV. Rem. 1858.

FARMER, James. Journal. UTHIST. MORMON-Ends Sweetwater River. II+. 1853.

FARNHAM, Elijah B. "From Ohio to California in 1849...." Eds. Merrill J. Mattes and Esley J. Kirk. INDIANA MAGAZINE OF HISTORY 46(Sept, Dec 1950): 297-318, 403-20. CAL(Indep)-LASSEN. II+. 1849.

FARNHAM, Thomas J. MEXICO: ITS GEOGRAPHY - ITS PEOPLE - AND ITS INSTITUTIONS. NY: Long & Brother, 1846? MEX-Genl.

FARQUHAR, Francis P. Ed. Bidwell, John. JOHN BIDWELL'S TRIP.

———. "Camels in the Sketches of Edward Vischer." CALIFORNIA HISTORICAL QUARTERLY 9(Dec 1930): 332-35. Freight.

FARRAR, John C. Diary. MO-WHMC. CAL(West Point). II+. 1852.

FARRAR, Josia H. "Farrar - Caldwell Family Papers." MO-WHMC. CAL. V. 1853.

FARRELL, Art V. "Staging to the Gold Fields of Southern Idaho Territory." AMERICAN PHILATELIST 63(Jul 1950): 787-92. Stage. Mail.

FARRELL, Dennis. "Adventures on the Plains, 1865-67." COLLECTIONS Nebraska State Historical Society 17(1913): 247-58. Geog-Julesburg.

FARRER, Deerin. Narrative. Paul & Helen Henderson Collection, UWY. OR(Council). V. 1868.

FARRER, William. "Diary." In JOURNALS OF THE FORTY-NINERS, eds. LeRoy and Ann W. Hafen. Glendale: Clark, 1954. SLCOR. II. 1849.

FARRIS, William M. THE 1847 CROSSING OF IMPERIAL COUNTY, CA AND BAJA CA, MEXICO BY THE U.S. MORMON BATTALION. Imperial Valley College Museum Occasional Paper No. 2. El Centro, CA: Imperial College Museum Society, 1976. GILA. III. 1847. Maps.

FAULK, Oddie B. DESTINY ROAD: THE GILA TRAIL AND THE OPENING OF THE SOUTHWEST. NY: Oxford Univ. Press, 1973. GILA-Genl. Mail. Freight.

———. TOO FAR NORTH...TOO FAR SOUTH. Great West and Indian Series, 35. LA: Westernlore, 1967. GILA-Genl.

———. THE U.S. CAMEL CORPS: AN ARMY EXPERIMENT. NY: Oxford Univ. Press, 1976. Teams.

———. "William H. Emory and the Mexican Survey." PACIFIC HISTORIAN 13(Fall 1969): 47-62. Biog.

FAULKNER, Harry. Diary. DENVERPUB. PIKES. III. 1859.

FAULKNER, Hazel P. "Ladies on the Overland Trail." CSL. Social.

FAULKNER, Mont E. "Emigrant - Indian Confrontation in Southeastern Idaho, 1841-1863." RENDEZVOUS 2(Win 1967): 43-58. Indians.

FAUNTLEROY, J. D. "Old Stage Routes of Texas." FRONTIER TIMES 6(Jul 1929): 420-23. Stage-TEX-Genl.

FAUST, Elsie A. Ed. Faust, Henry J. "Synopsis."

FAUST, Henry J. "Synopsis." Ed. Elsie A. Faust. UTHIST. Pony. Biog.

FAVOUR, Alpheus H. OLD BILL WILLIAMS: MOUNTAIN MAN. Chapel Hill: Univ. of North Carolina Press, 1936. Biog.

FAVOUR, John. Diary. BANCROFT. CAL(Council)-BRIDGER-SLCUT-NOBLE-BECKWOURTH. III+. 1859.

FAWKES, Ulla S. Ed. Pigman, Walter G. JOURNAL.

FEBES, J. H. Story of his Trip. MONHIST. MULLAN-1862-Genl.
Federal Writers Project, WPA. DEATH VALLEY: A GUIDE. Boston: Houghton Mifflin, 1939. Geog.

———. THE OREGON TRAIL. NY: Hastings House, 1939. Overland-Genl.

FEE, Art. "The Most Unique Crossing on the Oregon Trail." CAS-CADES EAST 8(Sum 1983): 14-15, 45. Social.

FELLOWS, Fred. "Illustrated Study of Western Saddles." MONTANA 16(Jan 1966): 57-83. Eqpt-Graphics.

FELLOWS, Robert. "The Brigham Young Express and Carrying Company." STAMPS, 29 April 1972, 262-70. Mail.

FELTER, William C. SEE: Griffenhagen, George B. OREGON TRAIL OF PHARMACY.

FENDALL. Lon W. "Medorem Crawford and the Protective Corps." OREGON HISTORICAL QUARTERLY 72(Mar 1971): 55-77. Military. Indians.

FENDER, Stephen. PLOTTING THE GOLDEN WEST: AMERICAN LITERATURE AND THE RHETORIC OF THE CALIFORNIA TRAIL. Cambridge: Cambridge Univ. Press, 1981. Overland-Genl.

FENNER, Lawrence A. Reminiscences. MONHIST. Freight.

FERGUS, James. Papers. MONHIST. DAKOTAS-MONTANA. V. 1860.

FERGUSON, Charles D. THE EXPERIENCES OF A FORTY-NINER IN CALIFORNIA. Ed. Frederick T. Wallace. One of the Far Western Frontier Series. 1888. Reprint. NY: Arno, 1973. CAL(St. Jo)-BRIDGER-SLCUT-NOBLE. III. Rem. 1849.

FERGUSON, Henry O. A Trip to California. CAHIST. CAL(Council)-LASSEN. IV. Rem. 1849.

FERGUSSON, David. REPORT OF MAJOR D. FERGUSSON ON THE COUNTRY, ITS RESOURCES AND THE ROUTE BETWEEN TUCSON AND LOBOS BAY.... 37th Cong, Sp. Sess. S. Ex. Doc. 1. Serial 1174. GILA(Tucson)-MEX(Altar-Libertad). I. 1862. Govt. Maps.

FERRIN, John R. "The Pony Express." UTHIST. Pony.

FERRIS, A. C. "Arrival of Overland Trains in California in '49." CENTURY 42(Jul 1891): 477-78. CAL-1849-Genl.

_____. "To California in 1849 through Mexico." CAL-MEX(Vera Cruz-Mexico City-Guadalajara-San Blas). III. Rem. 1849.

FERRIS, Benjamin G. UTAH AND THE MORMONS. NY: Dix & Edwards, 1854. CAL(Westport)-BRIDGER. II+. 1852. CAL(SLC)-SLCUT. II+. 1853.

FERRIS, Mrs. Benj. G. THE MORMONS AT HOME.... NY: Dix & Edwards, 1856. CAL(Westport)-BRIDGER. II. 1852. CAL(SLC)-SLCUT. II. 1853.

FERRIS, Norman B. Ed. Snedaker, Morris J. "Diary."

FERSTER, James S. Sketch. MONHIST. CHEROKEE-MONTANA. V. 1863.

FERY, Jules H. MAP AND GUIDE TO THE CARIBOO GOLD MINES OF BRITISH COLUMBIA. SF: Truette, 1862. Guide.

FICKLIN, Benjamin F. "Ficklin's Expedition to the Flathead Country in 1858." Ed. Clyde McLemore. FRONTIER AND MIDLAND 16(Aut 1935): 66-69. BRIDGER(Ft. Bridger)-HALL-MONTANA. IV. 1858.

FIELD, James. Diary. ORHIST. OR(St. Jo)-MEEK. II. 1845.

FIELD, Matthew C. PRAIRIE AND MOUNTAIN SKETCHES. Eds. Kate L. Gregg and John F. McDermott. One of the American Exploration and Travel Series. Norman: Univ. of Oklahoma Press, 1957. CAL(Westport)-Ends Green River. I. 1843.

FIELD, William T. With T. N. Campbell. "Identification of Comanche."

FIELDING, Harriet C. Ed. Alden, Wyllis. ANCESTORS AND DESCENDANTS.

FIELDING, Lavinia. "Attitudes toward Experience in Western Travel Narratives." PhD diss., Univ. of Washington, 1975. Not Seen.

FIERMAN, Floyd S. GUTS AND RUTS: THE JEWISH PIONEER ON THE TRAIL IN THE AMERICAN SOUTHWEST. NY: KTAV Pub., 1985. SANTA FE-Genl.

FIFIELD, Allan. "The First Two-Way Road across the Sierra." Stockton Westerners VALLEY TRAILS 2(1968): 76-90. CAL-1848-Genl.

_____. "Wagons East across the Sierra." QUARTERLY Historical Society of Southern California 43(Sept 1961): 276-97. CAL-1848-Genl.

_____. "Why William B. Ide Came to California." FAR-WESTERNER 9(Jul 1968): 2-9. CAL-1844-Genl.

FIKE, Richard E., and John W. Headley. THE PONY EXPRESS STATIONS OF UTAH IN HISTORICAL PERSPECTIVE. WA: GPO, 1979. Pony.

FILCHER, J. A. UNTOLD TRALES OF CALIFORNIA. N.p., 1903. Freight.

FILMORE, J. S. ROUTES TO THE PIKES PEAK GOLD REGIONS. Denver?: Author, N.d. Map.

FINCH, Hampden G. Letters. Indiana State Library-MS, Indianapolis, IN. CAL(Weston). IV. 1850.

FINDLA, James. "Statement." In CHARLES HOPPER AND THE PILGRIMS OF THE PACIFIC, ed. Franklin Beard. La Grange, CA: Southern Mines Press, 1981. CAL(Ind)-HALL-LASSEN. V. Rem. 1847.

FINDLAY Diary. SEE: Clark, John. "The California Guide."

FINDLEY, Rowe. "The Pony Express." NATIONAL GEOGRAPHIC 158(Jul 1986): 45-71. Pony.

FINDLEY, William C. Diary. ORHIST. OR(St. Jo)-BRIDGER. III. 1845.

FINE, Harry L. "Fort Laramie and the Historic Postal Markings of the West." MONTANA 11(Jul 1961): 53-55. Mail.

_____. "Fort Laramie: Post Office in the Old West." LA POSTA 8(Nov 1977): N.p. Mail.

_____. "The Montano Postal Mark." MONTANA 19(Oct 1969): 96-97. Mail.

FINLEY, Newton G. Memories of Travel. BANCROFT. CAL(Indep). IV. Rem. 1852.

FIREMAN, Bert M. Ed. Theobald, John and Lillian. WELLS FARGO.

FIRMAN, Sidney G. Ed. Miller, Joaquin. OVERLAND.

FISCHER, Christiane, ed. LET THEM SPEAK FOR THEMSELVES: WOMEN IN THE AMERICAN WEST. NY: Dutton, 1978. Social.

FISCHER, LeRoy H. "The Historic Preservation Movement in Oklahoma." CHRONICLES OF OKLAHOMA 57(Spr 1979): 3-25. Pres.

FISH, Herbert C. "The Early Development of the Northern Route from the Dakota Land to the Pacific." MA thesis, Washington Univ., 1920. DAKOTAS-Genl. MONTANA-Genl. MULLAN-Genl.

FISH, Joseph. THE PIONEERS OF THE SOUTHWEST AND ROCKY MOUNTAIN REGIONS. 7 vols. Ed. Seymour P. Fish. N.p.: Editor, 1972. Overland-Genl.

FISH, Juliette. Across the Plains. BANCROFT. CAL(Council)-LASSEN. IV. Rem. 1862.

FISH, Lafayette. Across the Plains. BANCROFT. CAL(Council)-BRIDGER-SLCUT-Ends Deep Creek, Ut. II. 1860.

FISH, Mary C. Diary. BANCROFT. CAL(Council)-BRIDGER-SLCUT-NOBLE. II +. 1860.

FISH, Seymour P. Ed. Fish, Joseph. PIONEERS OF THE SOUTHWEST.

FISHBURN, Jesse. Ed. Fryberger, Wilson. "To California."

FISHER, Ezra. "Correspondence...." OREGON HISTORICAL QUARTERLY 16(Dec 1915): 379-412. OR(St. Jo). V. 1845.

FISHER, James S. Diary. Bentley Historical Library, Univ. of Michigan, Ann Arbor, MI. CAL(Council)-BRIDGER-SLCUT. III. 1852.

FISHER, Marcius C. "Recollections of the Experiences of a Boy on the Bozeman Trail." MIDWEST REVIEW 6(Nov 1925): N.p. BOZE. III. Rem. 1866. Freight.

FISHER, Orr. "Exploring the Unknown." PONY EXPRESS 17(Mar 1951): 7-8. Pony.

FISHER, Rachel. "Letters." In COVERED WAGON WOMEN, vol. 1, ed. Kenneth L. Holmes. Glendale: Clark, 1983.

FISHER, Ray. "Letter from Pony Express Rider." PONY EXPRESS, July 1984, p. 11.

_____. "The Pony Express." IMPROVEMENT ERA 52(Feb 1949): 78-79, 124. Pony.

_____. "Sketch of a Pony Express Rider - William F. Fisher." PONY EXPRESS 16(Sept 1949): 3-5. Pony.

FISHER, Samuel. Diary. CAL(Council)-BRIDGER-SLCUT. 1852. Not Seen.

FISHER, William F. "Battle of Egan Canyon Station." PONY EXPRESS NEWSLETTER, July 1948, 7. Pony. Military. SIMPSON-Genl.

_____. "The Dry Creek Massacre." PONY EXPRESS 16(Jan 1950): 3-5. Pony. Geog.

_____. "Narrative." NVHIST. Pony.

_____. "The Schell Creek Murder." PONY EXPRESS COURIER, January 1936, 8, 14. Geog. Stage.

FISK Family Papers. Diary. In A. J. Fisk Subgroup. MONHIST.

DAKOTAS(St. Paul)-MONTANA. II +. 1866.

FISK, James L. SEE: "Expeditions of Captain James L. Fisk."

_____. EXPEDITION FROM FORT ABERCROMBIE TO FORT BENTON. 37th Cong., 3d sess. H. Ex. Doc. 80. OR-DAKOTAS(St. Paul)-MONTANA-MULLAN. II. 1862.

_____. IDAHO: HER GOLD FIELDS AND THE ROUTES TO THEM. NY: Gray, 1863. Guide.

_____. NORTH OVERLAND EXPEDITION, FOR PROTECTION OF EMIGRANTS, FROM ST. CLOUD, MN, VIA FORTS ABERCROMBIE AND BENTON, TO THE ROCKY MOUNTAINS, IDAHO, ETC. 38th Cong., 1st sess. H. Ex. Doc. 45. Serial 1189. DAKOTAS(St. Cloud)-MONTANA-Return by stage, Bannack-SLC-Atchison. II +. 1863.

FISK, Mrs. Van. Reminiscence. MONHIST. CAL(Missouri)-LANDER-MONTANA. V. Rem. 1864.

FISK, Van H. Lost on the Plains. MONHIST. DAKOTAS(St. Paul)-MONTANA. III. 1864.

FITCH, Franklin. Ed. De Milt, Alonzo. LIFE, TRAVELS AND ADVENTURES.

FITCH, J. R. "Report on the Smoky Hill Route to D. A. Butterfield." In "Fort Wallace and its Relation to the Frontier," Mrs. Frank Montgomery. KANSAS HISTORICAL COLLECTIONS 17(1926-1928): 189-283. PIKES-Smoky Hill-1865-Genl.

FITZGERALD, Maurice. "The Lost Immigrants and the Blue Bucket Mine." ORHIST. MEEK. III. 1845.

FJELD, Carl J. BRIEF HISTORY.... Springville, UT: Art City, 1946. MORMON? Rem. 1860. Not Seen.

FLAKE, Chad. SEE: Jones, Ruth M., et al. "Utah, the Mormons and the West."

_____. A MORMON BIBLIOGRAPHY: 1830-1930. SLC: Univ. of Utah Press, 1978. Bib.

FLAKE, Lucy H. TO THE LAST FRONTIER. Mesa, AZ: N.p., n.d. 1850. Not Seen.

FLANAGAN, Sue. TRAILING THE LONGHORNS: A CENTURY LATER. Austin: Madrona, 1974. Stock. Graphics.

FLANDRAU, Grace C. RED RIVER TRAILS. St. Paul?: Great Northern Railway, 1926. DAKOTAS-Genl.

FLEHARTY, William H. Across the Plains. WIHIST. CAL(Council). V-. 1850.

FLEMING, Alice. HIGHWAYS INTO HISTORY. NY: St. Martin's, 1971. Overland-Genl.

FLEMING, L. A., and A. R. Standing. "The Road to 'Fortune': The Salt Lake Cutoff." UTAH HISTORICAL QUARTERLY 33(Sum 1965): 248-71. SLCUT-Genl. Map.

FLETCHER, B. F. Diary. ORHIST. OR-BARLOW. V-. 1864.

FLETCHER, Daniel C. REMINISCENCES OF CALIFORNIA.... Ayer, Mass.: Turner, 1894. CAL. 1853. Not Seen.

FLETCHER, Ellen G. A BRIDE ON THE BOZEMAN TRAIL. Ed. Francis D. Haines, Jr. Medford, OR: Gandee, 1970. CAL(Council)-

BOZE. II. 1866.

FLETCHER, F. N. EARLY NEVADA: THE PERIOD OF EX-
PLORATION, 1776 -1848. Reno: A. Carlisle, 1929. Overland-Genl.

FLETT, John. "From Red River to the Columbia." Ed. William J. Betts.
BEAVER (Spr 1971): 50-55. CANADA(Red River)-Ft. Edmonton-
Ft. McLeod-Walla Walla. V. 1841.

FLINT, Marjorie C. "Coast Line State Company." WESTERN EX-
PRESS 12(Oct 1962): 3-11. Stage.

FLINT, Thomas. "Diary of Dr. Thomas Flint." PUBLICATIONS Historical Society of Southern California 12(1923): 53-127. CAL(Coun-
cil-BRIDGER-SLCOR. III. 1853.

FLORIN, Lambert. WESTERN WAGON WHEELS. Seattle: Superior, 1970. Stage. Freight. Eqpt. Graphics.

FLORY, A. P. Life and Memoirs. Washington State Historical Society
Library, Tacoma, WA. CAL(Council-BOZE. III. 1864. OR(Virginia City, Montana)-HALL-Dalles. III. 1865.

FLOWEREE, Ruth. SEE: Briggs, Joshua E. A PIONEER MIS-
SOURIAN.

FLOYD, Jennie W. "Annotated Bibliography on Texas Found in
American Periodicals before 1900." MA thesis, Southern Methodist
Univ., 1933. Not Seen.

FLOYD, William H., III. PHANTOM RIDERS OF THE PONY EX-
PRESS. Philadelphia: Dorrance & Co., 1958. Pony.

FLOYD, William P. Journal. HUNTL. CAL(Ft. Smith)-MARCY-
BEALE. II +. 1858.

FOERSTER, Bernd. INDEPENDENCE, MISSOURI. Independence,
MO: Heritage Comm., 1978. Pres. Geog.

FOLLMER, George D. Correspondence. NBHIST. OR-Nebraska-
Genl. Pres.

FOLSOM, B. R. Memorandum Book. NBHIST. CAL(Council Bluffs
area only). V. 1854.

FONDA, Charles I. Diary. Bentley Library, Univ. of Michigan, Ann
Arbor, MI. CAL(Council)-SLCUT. IV. Rem. 1850.

FONSECA, W. G. "On the St. Paul Trail in the Sixties." TRANSAC-
TIONS AND PROCEEDINGS Historical and Scientific Society of
Manitoba, no. 56(1900). DAKOTAS-Genl.

FOOTE, H. S. PEN PICTURES..... Chicago: Lewis, 1888.
CAL(Stevens-Murphy Party). 1844. Not Seen.

"For 300 Miles, New Exhibits Mark the Oregon Trail." SUNSET 158(Mar
1977): 54. Pres.

FORBES, ? A TRIP TO MEXICO.... London: Smith, Elder, 1851.
MEX(Vera Cruz-San Blas). III. 1850.

FORBES, Mrs. A. S. "El Camino Real." GRIZZLY BEAR 2(Jan 1908):
36. Pres.

FORBES, Jack D. "The Development of the Yuma Route before 1846."
CALIFORNIA HISTORICAL QUARTERLY 43(Jun 1964): 99-118.
GILA-Genl.

_____. WARRIORS OF THE COLORADO. Norman: Univ. of Ok-
lahoma Press, 1965. Indians. Geog-Yuma.

FORBES, Solomon. Diary. Bentley Library, Univ. of Michigan, Ann
Arbor, MI. CAL(Council)-BRIDGER-SLCUT. II. 1853.

FORBIS, Jonathan F. Reminiscence. MONHIST. CAL-HALL-MON-
TANA. V. Rem. 1864.

FORD, A. T. Life and History. MONHIST. CAL(Council)-LANDER-
MONTANA. V. Rem. 1862.

FORD, Gary D. "Riding the Covered Wagons." AMERICANA 13(Jul-
Aug 1985): 46-49. Pres.

FORD, James. JUST BETWEEN OURSELVES. Ed. Harriet F. Torrey. N.p., 1947? CAL(Indep)-TRUCKEE-BECKWOURTH. IV.
Rem. 1852.

FORD, Nineveh. Pioneer Road Makers. BANCROFT. OR(Westport).
IV. Rem. 1843.

"Ford of History." INCREDIBLE IDAHO 4(Fall 1972): 11-12. Geog-
Three Island Crossing, ID.

FOREMAN, Grant. ADVENTURE ON RED RIVER. Norman: Univ.
of Oklahoma Press, 1937. MARCY. II +. 1852.

_____. THE ADVENTURES OF JAMES COLLIER: FIRST
COLLECTOR OF THE PORT OF SAN FRANCISCO. Chicago:
Black Cat, 1937. CAL(Leav)-SANTA FE-RIO GRANDE-GILA.
IV. 1849.

_____. "The California Overland Mail Route through Oklahoma."
CHRONICLES OF OKLAHOMA 9(Sept 1931): 300-17. Stage.

_____. "Early Trails through Oklahoma." CHRONICLES OF OK-
LAHOMA 3(Jun 1925): 99-119. OKLAHOMA-Genl.

_____. MARCY AND THE GOLD SEEKERS. Norman: Univ. of
Oklahoma Press, 1939. MARCY. II +. 1849. CHEROKEE-Genl.

_____. A PATHFINDER IN THE SOUTHWEST: THE
ITINERARY OF LT. A. W. WHIPPLE DURING HIS EXPLORA-
TIONS FOR A RAILWAY ROUTE FROM FORT SMITH TO LOS
ANGELES IN THE YEARS 1853 AND 1854. American Exploration
and Travel Series. Norman: Univ. of Oklahoma Press, 1941. CAL(Ft.
Smith)-MARCY-BEALE. I. 1853.

_____. "Survey of a Wagon Road from Fort Smith to the Colorado
River." CHRONICLES OF OKLAHOMA 12(Mar 1934): 74-96.
MARCY-Genl.

FOREST, Mary R. "Yuma, Gateway to California, 1846-1877." MA
thesis, Univ. of California-Berkeley, 1946. Geog. GILA-Genl.

FORMAN, George. "Across the Plains in 1864...." Ed. T. A. Larson.
ANNALS OF WYOMING 40(Apr, Oct 1968): 5-22, 267-82. CAL(St.
Jo)-LANDER-BOZE. IV. 1864. Freight caravan.

FORREST, Earle R. Ed. Slagle, James M. "Forty-Niners."

FORSDICK, Stephen. "On the Oregon Trail to Zion in 1853." Ed.
Fletcher W. Birney, Jr. DENVER WESTERNERS BRAND BOOK
9(1953): 33-55. MORMON. III. Rem. 1853.

FORSTER, Dale E. OREGON EXPRESS COMPANIES. Eugene,
OR: Author, 1985. Stage. Mail. Graphics.

FORSTER, John H. Papers. Bentley Library, Univ. of Michigan, Ann
Arbor, MI. GILA(San Diego-Yuma). I. 1849. Graphics.

FORSYTH, John R. Journal. BANCROFT. CAL(Leav)-SANTA FE-RIO GRANDE-GILA. I. 1849.

"Fort Boise: From Imperial Outpost to Historic Site." IDAHO YESTERDAYS 12(Sum 1968): 28-31. Geog.

"Fort Davis Opened Trail through Bad Lands of Texas." TEX-Genl. Geog.

"Fort Hall, 1834-1856." IDAHO YESTERDAYS 12(Sum 1968): 28-31. Geog.

"Fort Kearny - Founding - History - Abandonment - Restoration." PUBLICATIONS Nebraska State Historical Society 21(1930): 211-318. Geog.

FORT RIDGELY AND SOUTH PASS WAGON ROAD. 37th Cong., 2d sess. H. Ex. Doc. 35. Serial 1129. 2-36. NOBLE-Genl.

"Fort Tejon Centennial." LOS TULARES 20(Sept 1954): 1-2. Pres.

FORTT, Inez. "From Sacramento to Portland in Seven Days." LANE COUNTY HISTORIAN 16(Spr 1971): 3-11. Stage-OR-CAL.

FORTUNE, Alexander L. Overland Route to Cariboo. Vancouver Public Library-NW Room. CANADA(Ft. Garry-Ft. Edmonton-Ft. George-Quesnel-Lytton). 1862. Not Seen.

"Forty-Niners as Easterners Saw Them." AMERICAN HERITAGE 1(Spr 1950): 40-43. Social.

FOSDICK, Lucy H. "Across the Plains in '61." NEW ENGLAND MAGAZINE 32(Mar 1905): 12-20. PIKES. IV. 1861.

FOSTER, Charles. THE GOLD PLACERS OF CALIFORNIA. Akron, OH: Canfield, 1849. Guide.

FOSTER, G. G., ed. THE GOLD REGIONS OF CALIFORNIA. NY: Dewitt & Davenport, 1848. Guide.

FOSTER, Isaac. The Foster Family. CSL. CAL(Council)-BRIDGER-SLCUT-LASSEN. II. 1849. CAL(Council)-BRIDGER-SLCUT. V. 1854.

FOSTER, Roxanna C., ed. THE FOSTER FAMILY. San Jose: N.p., n.d. CAL. Rem. 1854. Not Seen.

FOSTER, William C. "Gold Rush Journey...." Ed. Dwayne Bolling. NEBRASKA HISTORY 62(Fall 1981): 400-10. CAL(Council). IV. 1850.

"Fountain Springs." LOS TULARES 34(Mar 1958): 1-4. Geog.

FOURR, J. William. Manuscripts. AZHIST. SANTA FE-RIO GRANDE-GILA(Ends Prescott, AZ). I. Rem. 1863. Stock.

_____. "Reminiscences of William Fourr." ARIZONA HISTORICAL REVIEW 6(Oct 1935): 68-84. GILA-Genl.

FOUTS, D. Lambert. Diary. UPAC. CAL-RIO GRANDE(Begins at Santa Fe)-GILA-Ends Santa Cruz, Mexico). II. 1849.

FOUTS, William. Diary. NEWBERRY. OR(St. Jo). IV. 1850.

FOWLER, Harlan D. CAMELS TO CALIFORNIA. Palo Alto: Stanford Univ. Press, 1950. Govt. Teams.

_____. THREE CARAVANS TO YUMA. Glendale: Clark, 1980. Teams.

FOWLER, John M. Diary. WIHIST. CAL(Neb. City-Ft. Kearny only).

III. 1860.

FOWLER, Samuel. REMINISCENCES OF EARLY PIONEER DAYS IN AMERICA. Visalia, CA: Author, N.d. CAL-TRUCKEE. V. 1849.

FOWLER, William. WOMAN ON THE AMERICAN FRONTIER. Hartford, CN: S. S. Scranton, 1880. Social.

FOX, Florence C. NOTES ON THE OREGON TRAIL. U.S. Dept. of the Interior, Office of Education Bulletin No. 27. WA: GPO, 1930. Curriculum guide for the schools.

FOX, George W. "Diary." ANNALS OF WYOMING 8(Jan 1932): 580-601. CAL(Council)-BOZE. II. 1866.

FOX, Jared. Diary. ORHIST. OR(Council)-BARLOW. I. 1852. WASH. I. 1853.

FOX, Jesse W. GENERAL COURSES AND DISTANCES FROM GREAT SALT LAKE CITY TO FORT LEMHI AND GOLD DIGGINGS ON SALMON RIVER. SLC: Deseret News, 1862. MONTANA-Genl.

FOX, John A. CALIFORNIA AND WESTERN EXPRESS COVERS. N.p.: Author, 1954. Mail. Stage. Graphics.

FOX, Theron. THE MARGARET CALDWELL MYSTERY: A TRIBUTE. San Jose, CA: Harlan-Young, 1965. Indians.

FOY, Mary E. Ed. Cheesman, David W. "By Ox Team from Salt Lake to Los Angeles, 1850."

FRAKER, Fleming, Jr. Ed. Smith, Harriet A. "To Pike's Peak."

FRANCE, Charles B. Diary. MO-WHMC. PIKES. II. 1865. Indians. Military.

FRANCES, David W. Ed. Hunter, John A. "Letters of a Missourian."

FRANCIS, Samuel D. Journal. BEINECKE. OR(Council)-BRIDGER-SLCUT. II. 1852.

FRANCL, Joseph. THE OVERLAND JOURNEY OF.... SF: William P. Wreden, 1968. CAL(Council)-SLCUT. IV. Rem. 1854.

FRANDSEN, Rebecca. SEE: With Ruth Ann Olson. "Best Trader."

FRANKLIN, Homer, Jr. Ed. Franklin, William R. "Journal of...."

FRANKLIN, Homer, Sr. Ed. Franklin, William R. "Journal of...."

FRANKLIN, John B. HORRORS OF MORMONISM. London: Appold, 1858. MORMON. V. Rem. 1854.

FRANKLIN, William Buel. MARCH TO SOUTH PASS.... Ed. Frank N. Schubert. Engineer Historical Studies No. 1. WA: Historical Division, Office of Administrative Services, Office of the Chief of Engineers, 1979. CAL(Leav)-CHEROKEE(Ft. Laramie to Bent's Fort)-SANTA FE(to Leav). II. 1845.

FRANKLIN, William R. "Journal of William Riley Franklin to California...1850." Eds. Homer Franklin, Jr., and Homer Franklin, Sr. ANNALS OF WYOMING 46(Spr 1974): 47-74. CAL(Neb. City). III. 1850.

FRANKS, Kenny A., ed. "The California Overland Express through Indian Territory and Western Arkansas." ARKANSAS HISTORICAL QUARTERLY 33(Spr 1974): 70-81. Stage.

FRANTZ, Joe B. "Hoof and Horn on the Chisholm Trail." AMERICAN WEST 4(Aug 1967): 15-20, 70-71. Stock.

FRANZWA, Gregory M. SEE: With William E. Hill. "Who Lies Here?"

_____. MAPS OF THE OREGON TRAIL. Gerald, MO: Patrice, 1982. Superb maps and illustrations.

_____. THE OREGON TRAIL REVISITED. St. Louis: Patrice, 1972. Pres.

_____. "Sublette Cutoff Cartographic Expedition." OVERLAND JOURNAL 2(Fall 1984): 15-19. CAL-Genl.

FRAZER, Robert W. Ed. Mansfield, Joseph. CONDITION OF THE WESTERN FORTS. Ed. Gibson, George R. OVER THE CHIHUAHUA AND SANTA FE. Ed. McCall, George A. "Camp Yuma - 1852."

_____. FORTS AND SUPPLIES: THE ROLE OF THE ARMY IN THE ECONOMY OF THE SOUTHWEST, 1846-1893. Albuq: Univ. of New Mexico Press, 1983. Freight.

_____. FORTS OF THE WEST. Norman: Univ. of Oklahoma Press, 1965. Military.

FRAZIER, Jimmie L. "Early Stage Lines in Colorado, 1859-1865." MA thesis, Univ. of Denver, 1959. Stage.

FREAR, Harry J. Diary. In Paul and Helen Henderson Collection, UWY. CAL(Indep). II. 1852.

FREAR, Samuel T. "Jesse Applegate, An Appraisal of an Uncommon Pioneer." MA thesis, Univ. of Oregon, 1961. Biog.

FREDERICK, James V. BEN HOLLADAY: THE STAGECOACH KING. Glendale: Clark, 1940. Biog. Freight. Stage.

_____. "The Holladay Overland Mail and Express Company." PhD diss., Univ. of Oklahoma, 1937. Biog. Stage. Mail. Indians.

FREEDOM, Gary S. "Moving Men and Supplies: Military Transportation on the Northern Great Plains, 1866-1891." SOUTH DAKOTA HISTORY 14(Sum 1984): 114-30. Military. Freight. Maps.

FREEMAN, John F. Diaries. BANCROFT. CAL(Council)-TRUCKEE-BECKWOURTH. II. 1852.

FREEMAN, Olga. "Fortune Lost in a Cattle Drive." TRUE WEST 25(Jul-Aug 1978): 9-11. OR-CAL. IV. 1861.

FREEMAN, Otis W. "Early Wagon Roads in the Inland Empire." PACIFIC NORTHWEST QUARTERLY 45(Spr 1954): 125-130. Freight. Stage.

"Freighters and Freighting." In AN ENDURING LEGACY, vol. 2. SLC: Daughters of the Utah Pioneers, 1979. Freight.

"Freighting from Utah to Montana." MONHIST. Freight.

"Freighting in 1866." PROCEEDINGS AND COLLECTIONS Nebraska State Historical Society 1(1894): 44-49. Freight.

FREMONT, John C. The Fremont literature is so extensive that only trail-related items are included. For a thorough survey of Fremont materials see the bibliography to Donald Jackson and Mary Lee Spence's EXPEDITIONS.

_____. GEOGRAPHICAL MEMOIR UPON UPPER CALIFORNIA IN ILLUSTRATION OF HIS MAP OF OREGON AND CALIFORNIA. 30 Cong., 1st sess. S. Misc. Doc. 148. Govt.

_____. MEMOIRS OF MY LIFE. NY: Belford, Clarke, 1887. Biog.

_____. REPORT OF AN EXPLORING EXPEDITION TO THE ROCKY MOUNTAINS. 27th Cong., 3d sess. 1843. S. Doc. 243. CAL(Westport?)-Ends at South Pass. II+. 1842.

_____, and William H. Emory. NOTES OF TRAVEL IN CALIFORNIA. NY: Appleton, 1849. Guide.

FRENCH, Barsina R. Journal. HUNTL. CAL(Jefferson City)SANTA FE-BEALE. III. 1867.

FRENCH, C. Adelia. Memories. MONHIST. CAL(St. Jo)-BOZE. III. Rem. 1864.

FRENCH, Parker H. SEE: Baldridge, Michael. REMINISCENCE.

_____. JOURNAL OF THE SUFFERING AND HARDSHIPS.... Ed. William Miles. 1851. Reprint. Fairfield, WA: Ye Galleon, 1970. CAL-TEX(Port Lavaca)-GILA. III. 1850.

FREY, Howard C. SEE: Shumway, George, et al. CONESTOGA WAGON.

FRIEDMAN, Ralph. "Early Telegraph Days in California." WESTWAYS 49(Feb 1957): 10-11. Telegraph.

FRIESACH, Carl. "The Gold Rush on the Fraser." BEAVER, Spring 1958, 36-39. CANADA(Vancouver-Ft. Yale). V. 1858.

FRIIS, Herman R. "The Documents and Reports of the United States Congress: A Primary Source of Information on Travel in the West, 1783-1861." In TRAVELERS ON THE WESTERN FRONTIER, ed. John F. McDermott. Urbana: Univ. of Illinois Press, 1970. Bib.

FRINK, Margaret A. JOURNAL OF THE ADVENTURES.... Oakland: Author, 1897. CAL(Neb. City)-HALL. III. Rem. 1850.

FRISBIE, Elizabeth C. "Recollections." (In) "Pioneer Gordon Family," ed. Olive Gordon Miller. BANCROFT. CAL(Missouri). Rem. 1852.

FRISWOLD, Carroll. SEE: With Paul Hedren. THE MASSACRE OF LT. GRATTAN.

FRITZ, Henry E., ed. "The Cattlemen's Frontier in the Trans-Mississippi West: An Annotated Bibliography." ARIZONA & THE WEST 14(Spr, Sum 1972): 45-70, 169-90. Bib.

FRIZZELL, Alexander L. Diary. NBHIST. PIKES. V. 1860.

FRIZZELL, John and Mildred. "Autobiography of the 'Old Overland'." WESTERN HORSEMAN 35(Jul 1970): 58, 126-28. Stage-Eqpt.

_____. "The Celerity and the Mud Wagon." FRONTIER TIMES 49(Feb-Mar 1975): 24-28. Stage-Eqpt.

_____. "The Mud Wagon." WESTERN HORSEMAN 41(May 1976): 52, 140-44. Stage-Eqpt.

_____. "The Oklahoma Historical Society Stagecoach." CHRONICLES OF OKLAHOMA 41(Spr 1963): 3-8. Stage-Eqpt.

_____. "Search for the Old Overland." FRONTIER TIMES 44(Oct-Nov 1970): 20-23, 56-57. Stage-Eqpt.

_____. "A Stagecoach Reunion." OLD WEST 11(Fall 1974): 25, 62. Stage-Eqpt.

FRIZZELL, Lodisa. ACROSS THE PLAINS.... Ed. Victor H. Paltsits. NY: New York Public Library, 1915. CAL(St. Jo)-Ends Pacific Springs. III. 1852.

FRIZZEL, Mildred. "Anatomy of American Stagecoaches." PERSIMMON HILL 11, no. 1(1981): 8-21. Stage-Eqpt. Graphics.

FROEBEL, Julius. SEVEN YEARS TRAVEL IN CENTRAL AMERICA, NORTHERN MEXICO AND THE FAR WEST OF THE UNITED STATES. London: Richard Bentley, 1859. CAL(Indep)-SANTA FE. II+. 1852. RIO GRANDE-TEX. II+. 1853. GILA. II+. 1854.

"From California." NILES NATIONAL REGISTER 72, 24 July 1847, 330. CAL-1847-Genl.

"From Lake Erie to the Pacific." HUNTL. OR(Council)-BRIDGER-SLCUT-BARLOW. IV. Rem. 1851.

"From Texas to the Gold Mines." In SOUTHERN TRAILS TO CALIFORNIA IN 1849, ed. Ralph P. Bieber. Glendale: Clark, 1937. CAL-TEX-MEX-GILA. IV. 1849.

FROMAN, Robert. "The Red Ghost." AMERICAN HERITAGE 12(Apr 1961): 50-53, 74-77. Teams.

FRONCEK, Thomas. "Winterkill, 1846: The Tragic Journey of the Donner Party." AMERICAN HERITAGE 28(Dec 1976): 28-41. CAL-1846-Genl.

FROST, Donald M. NOTES ON GENERAL ASHLEY, THE OVERLAND TRAIL AND SOUTH PASS. Barre, MA: Gazette, 1960. Overland-Genl.

FROST, John. PICTORIAL HISTORY OF CALIFORNIA. Auburn, NY: Derby & Miller, 1850. Guide.

FROST, Lafayette. Letters. BYU. Not Seen.

FROST, Mary P. "Experience of a Pioneer." WASHINGTON HISTORICAL QUARTERLY 7(1916): 123-25. Rem. 1854 Indian attack, Idaho.

FRUSH, Charles W. "Trip from The Dalles, Oregon, to Bitter Root Valley, Montana, in 1858...." CONTRIBUTIONS Historical Society of Montana (1896): 337-42. MONTANA. III. Rem. 1858.

FRUSH, William H. Diary. ORU. OR(St. Jo)-BARLOW. II. 1850.

FRY, Ed. A. "Mormons on the Niobrara." NEBRASKA HISTORY 5(Jan-Mar 1922): 4-6. Geog.

FRY, Frederich. FRY'S TRAVELER'S GUIDE.... Cincinatti: Author, 1865. Guide.

FRY, J. O. Across the Plains. ORHIST. OR(Council). II. Rem. 1851.

FRYBERGER, Wilson. "To California by Covered Wagon." Ed. Jesse Fishburn. Iowa State Historical Society Archives, Iowa City, IA. CAL(Council)-BRIDGER-SIMPSON. III. 1864.

FRYER, Judith. "The Anti-Mythical Journey: Westering Women's Diaries and Letters." OLD NORTHWEST 9(Spr 1983): 77-90. Analysis of women's attitudes as perceived from diaries. Social.

_____. "Recovering the Garden: Women's Fantasies and Experiences of the Western Frontier." OLD NORTHWEST 10(Fall 1984): 339-61. Social.

FRYER, Roy M. "Butterfield Stage Route from Chino to El Monte." POMONA VALLEY HISTORIAN 1(Jul 1965): 105-14. Stage.

_____. "The Butterfield Stage Route, and other Historic Routes Eastward from Los Angeles." PUBLICATIONS Historical Society of Southern California 17(Mar 1935): 15-22. Stage.

_____. "When the Americans Came to Pomona Valley." SOUTHERN CALIFORNIA HISTORICAL QUARTERLY 23(Sept-Dec 1941): 156-76. Geog.

FULKERTH, Abbey E. "Aunt Abbey's Diary." Ed. I. N. Brotherton. STOCKTON WESTERNERS VALLEY TRAILS. N.p., 16-23. CAL(Neb. City)-BRIDGER-SIMPSON. III+. 1863.

FULKERTH, William L. Ed. Fulkerth, William L. "Aunt Abbey's Diary."

FULLER, A. E. "The Operation and Rigging of Shinn's Ferry." NEBRASKA HISTORY 20(Jul-Sept 1939): 181. Geog.

FULLER, Andrew. Diary. Attributed to NBHIST, but not found in catalog.

FULLER, Arthur E. "Pony Express Route and Stations in Nebraska." NBHIST. Fourteen maps drawn c.1937. Pony.

FULLER, Emeline L. LEFT BY THE INDIANS. 1892. Reprint. The Garland Library of Narratives of North American Indian Captivities, vol. 96. NY: Garland, 1978. OR. V. Rem. 1860. 1860 Indian attack near Ft. Boise.

FULLER, Randall. Randall Fuller's Book. NBHIST. CAL(Council). II. 1849.

FULSTONE, Robert. Letters. NVHIST. CAL(Begins SLC)-SLCUT. IV. Rem. 1858.

FULTON, Arabella. TALES OF THE TRAIL. Comp. B. C. Payette. Montreal: Private, 1965. OR(Neb City)-Ends Ft. Boise. II. Rem. 1864. Social.

FULTON, James F. Diary. Washington State Historical Society Library, Tacoma, WA. OR(St. Jo)-Ends Chimney Rock. III. 1847. Train Govt-"Duties of the Captain."

FULTON, William. "Freighting and Staging in Early Days." PROCEEDINGS AND COLLECTIONS Nebraska State Historical Society 5(1902): 261-64. Freight. Stage.

FURLONG, Mary. When I Crossed the Plains. CAHIST. OR(St. Jo). V-. Rem. 1843.

FURNISS, Kate M. From Prairie to Pacific. Ed. Mai Luman Hill. CSL. CAL(Council)-TRUCKEE. II+. Rem. 1853. Social.

FUSSELL, W. Rupert. "The South in the Gold Rush of 1849." BA thesis, Howard College, 1937. CAL-1849-Genl. Not Seen.

GABBEY, Roberts. Crossing the Plains. MONHIST. Stage: Council-Bridger Cutoff-Montana. III. Rem. 1864.

GABRIEL, Ralph H. Ed. Royce, Sarah. FRONTIER LADY.

GAGE, Stephen T. Diary. CSL. CAL(St. Jo). III+. 1852.

GAINES, R. Ed. Bruff, J. Goldsborough. GOLD RUSH.

GALBREATH, C. B. "Ezra Meeker: Ohio's Illustrious Pioneer." OHIO ARCHAEOLOGICAL AND HISTORICAL QUARTERLY

36(Jan 1927): 3-47. Biog.

GALDIN, Martin A. Diary. BARKER. OKLAHOMA(Georgetown, MO)-TEX(Austin). III. 1845.

GALENSON, David. "Origins of the Long Drive." JOURNAL OF THE WEST 14(Jul 1975): 3-14. Stock.

_____. "The Profitability of the Long Drive." AGRICULTURAL HISTORY 51(Oct 1977): 737-58. Stock.

GALLAHER, William H. "Ho! For the Gold Mines of Montana...." Ed. James E. Moss. MISSOURI HISTORICAL REVIEW 57(Jan, Apr 1963): 156-83, 261-84. MONTANA(Ft. Benton-Virginia City). III. 1865.

GALLATIN, E. L. "Reminiscences of...." NEW YORK POSSE BRAND BOOK 7, no. 3(1960): 52-54, 67-68. Freight:Denver-Ft. Bridger-Virginia City, MT-SLC-Denver. III. Rem. 1864.

"A Gallery of Abbot-Downing Vehicles." HISTORICAL NEW HAMPSHIRE 20(Aut 1965): 26-38. Stage-Graphics.

GALLOWAY, Andrew. "First Mormon Handcart Trip across Iowa." ANNALS OF IOWA 20(Oct 1936): 444-49. Iowa-Only. III. 1856.

GALLOWAY, James. Diary. BANCROFT. CAL(Council)-BRIDGER-SLCUT-Ends Humboldt Sink. IV. 1853.

GALLUCCI, Mary M., and Alfred D. JAMES E. BIRCH. SF: Sacramento County Historical Society, 1958. Biog. Stage.

GALVIN, John. Ed. Abert, James W. THROUGH THE COUNTRY OF THE COMANCHE.

GAMBEL, William. Life. BANCROFT. CAL(Indep)-SANTA FE-GILA? V. Rem. 1841. CAL(Indep). V. Rem. 1849.

GAMBLE, James. "Early Reminiscences of the Telegraph on the Pacific Coast." CALIFORNIAN 3(Apr 1881): 321-26. Telegraph.

_____. "Wiring a Continent." CALIFORNIA MAGAZINE 3(1881): 556-63. Telegraph.

GANNON, William L. "Carriage, Coach and Wagon: The Design and Decoration of American Horse-Drawn Vehicles." PhD diss., Univ. of Iowa, 1960. Eqpt.

GARAVAGLIA, Louis A., and Charles G. Worman. FIREARMS OF THE AMERICAN WEST, 1803-1865. Albuquerque: Univ. of New Mexico Press, 1984. Eqpt.

GARAVENTA, Frank L. "The Applegate Trail." NVHIST. Pres. APPLE-Genl.

GARBER, Vie W. "The Bozeman Trail." MA thesis, Univ. of Wyoming, 1911. BOZE-Genl.

GARD, Wayne, et al. ALONG THE EARLY TRAILS OF THE SOUTHWEST. Austin: Pemberton, 1969. Overland-Genl.

_____. "The Impact of the Cattle Trails." SOUTHWESTERN HISTORICAL QUARTERLY 71(Jul 1967): 1-6. Stock.

_____. "Up the Chisholm Trail." THE HUMBLE WAY, Spring 1967, 1-5. Stock.

GARDINER, Dorothy. Ed. Smith, Mary. "Miss Smith Crosses the Plains in 1866."

_____. WEST OF THE RIVER. NY: Crowell, 1941. Overland-Genl.

GARDINER, James F. INDIAN TRIBES AND TRAPPER TRAILS. Manhattan Beach, CA: Author, c.1949. Indians. Map.

GARDINER, R. W. Life of the late W. B. Cameron. Provincial Archives of British Columbia, Victoria, B.C. CANADA. Not Seen.

GARDNER, Alexander. SEE: Babbitt, James E. "Surveyors along the 35th Parallel."

GARDNER, D. B. Diary. Library of Congress-Ms., Washington, D.C. CAL(St. Jo)-BRIDGER-SLCUT-Ends Silver Spring, NV. II. 1850.

GARDNER, Frances T. JOHN TOWNSEND - THE PERIPATETIC PIONEER. Reprint. 1939. SF: N.p., 1939. CAL-1844-Genl. Biog.

GARDNER, Hamilton. Ed. Cooke, Philip. MARCH OF THE SECOND DRAGOONS.

_____. "Captain Philip St. George Cooke and the March of the 1st Dragoons to the Rocky Mountains in 1845." COLORADO MAGAZINE 30(Oct 1953): 246-68. CAL(Leav)-Ends South Pass. II. 1845.

GARDNER, Mercedes P. THE STORY OF MARY ELIZABETH COOLEY HARRIS. N.p.: Author, 1977. OR(St. Jo?). V-. 1853.

GARDNER, Nathan Hale. Ed. Hale, Alma H. ALMA HELAMON HALE.

GARLAND, Hamlin. "Prairie Route to the Golden River." INDEPENDENT 51(N.d.): 245. CAL-Genl. Not Seen.

_____. "Vanishing Trails." UNIVERSITY RECORD 10(Oct 1905): 53-61. Pres.

GARLICK, C. P. GARLICK FAMILY HISTORY.... Ed. Norman L. Garlick. N.p., 1970? CAL(Westport)-Ends Goose Creek. I. 1850.

GARLICK, Norman L. Ed. Garlick, C. P. GARLICK FAMILY HISTORY.

GARRISON, A. E. LIFE AND LABOURS.... 1887. Reprint. N.p.: Garrison Clan, 1943. OR(Council)-APPLE. IV. Rem. 1846.

GARRISON, Abraham H. Recollections. ORHIST. OR(Iowa Point)-APPLEGATE. Rem. 1846. Not Seen.

GARRISON, Martha E. Reminiscences. ORHIST. OR(St. Jo). IV. Rem. 1845.

GARVER, Frank H. "Early Emigrant Roads and Trails into Montana." MONHIST. MONTANA-Genl.

GARWOOD, Zimri L. Journal. CSL. CAL(St. Jo)-TRUCKEE. III+. 1849.

GASS, A. M. "From Texas to Pike's Peak." In OVERLAND ROUTES TO THE GOLD FIELDS, 1859, ed. LeRoy R. Hafen. Southwest Historical Series, No. 11. Glendale: Clark, 1942. PIKES-TEX-OK-LAHOMA-CHEROKEE. III. 1859.

GATES, Henry. Letters. MONHIST. DAKOTAS(St. Paul)-MONTANA. IV. 1866.

"A Gathering of Stagecoaches." AMERICAN HISTORY ILLUSTRATED 20(May 1985): 22-31. Stage-Graphics.

GAULDIN, Martin A. Journal. MO-WHMC. OKLAHOMA(Ft. Smith)-TEX-Ends Austin. III. 1845.

GAY, James W. "Trail Diary of James Woods Gay and Sunset Trail - Reminiscences of Martha Gay Masterson." LANE COUNTY HISTORIAN 24(Spr 1979): 3-13. OR(Indep?)-BARLOW. IV. Rem. 1851.

GAY, Martha Ann. SEE: Gay, James W. "Trail Diary."

GAY, William. Reminiscences. MONHIST. Freight: Atchison-Ft. Laramie and return. IV. Rem. 1864.

GAYLORD, Orange. "Diary." TRANSACTIONS Oregon Pioneer Association 1917 (1920): 427-36. CAL(St. Jo). IV. 1850. OR(St. Jo)-BARLOW. IV. 1853.

GEE, Perry. Journal. BEINECKE. CAL(Indep). II+. 1852.

GEER, Calvin. "My Trip to Oregon as I Remember It." ORHIST. OR(St. Jo)-BARLOW. IV. Rem. 1847.

GEER, Elizabeth D. "Diary." TRANSACTIONS 35th Annual Reunion Oregon Pioneer Association (1908): 153-79. OR(St. Jo). III. 1847.

GEER, Ralph C. "Occasional Address." TRANSACTIONS 7th Annual Reunion Oregon Pioneer Association (1881): 32-42. OR-1847-Genl.

GEHLING, Richard and Mary Ann. "Pike's Peak or Bust." OVERLAND JOURNAL 5(Win 1987): 4-15. PIKES-1859-Genl.

_____. "Platte River Itinerary, 1860." OVERLAND JOURNAL 5(Sum 1987): 14-24. PIKES-1860-Genl.

GEIGER, Vincent. SEE: Potter, David M. TRAIL TO CALIFORNIA.

GELATT, Richard. "A Simple Sketch of My Simple Life." CSL. CAL(Council)-SIMPSON. Stage(Nevada portion of SIMPSON). IV. Rem. 1861.

GELWICKS, Daniel W. Diary. Illinois State Historical Library, Springfield, IL. CAL(St. Jo)-Ends Pacific Springs. II+. 1849.

GENDLER, Carol. "Territorial Omaha as a Staging and Freighting Center." NEBRASKA HISTORY 49(Sum 1968): 103-21. Geog. Stage. Freight.

GENTRY, Leland H. "The Mormon Way Stations: Garden Grove and Mount Pisgah." BRIGHAM YOUNG UNIVERSITY STUDIES 21(Fall 1981): 445-61. Geog. MORMON-Genl.

GENTRY, Mrs. M. A. "A Child's Experiences in '49." Ed. Jennie E. Ross. OVERLAND MONTHLY 63(Mar 1914): 300-5. CAL(St. Jo). IV. Rem. 1849.

GENTRY, North T. "Asses in Missouri." MO-WHMC. Teams.

Georgetown - Central City Stage Company. Passenger Ledger, 1867 - 1870. COHIST. Stage.

Georgian, A. THE LIFE OF THE EMIGRANT. Milledgeville, GA: Author, 1854. MORMON. IV. 1850.

GHENT, William J. Ed. With LeRoy R. Hafen. BROKEN HAND.

_____. THE ROAD TO OREGON. 1929. Reprint. NY: AMS, 1970. Overland-Genl.

GHERMAN, Dawn L. "From Parlor to Tepee: The White Squaw on the American Frontier." PhD diss., Univ. of Massachusetts, 1975. Social. Not Seen.

GIANELLA, Vincent P. "Site of Williams Station, NV." NEVADA HISTORICAL SOCIETY QUARTERLY 3(Oct 1960): 3-12. Geog.

GIBBES, C. D. "C. D. Gibbes' Journal of the Thomas Gilbert Party, 1849." WESTX 19(Oct 1943): 153-66. CAL-TEX(Dallas)-Ends El Paso. III. 1849.

GIBBONS, Boyd. "The Itch to Move West: Life and Death on the Oregon Trail." NATIONAL GEOGRAPHIC 170(Aug 1986): 147-77. Overland-Genl.

GIBBS, George. SEE: Bushnell, David I. DRAWINGS OF GEORGE GIBBS.

_____. "The Diary of George Gibbs." In MARCH OF THE MOUNTED RIFLEMEN, ed. Osborne Cross. WA: Alexander, 1851. OR(Leav)-Ends Ft. Laramie. II+. 1849.

GIBBS, George T. Account. HUNTL. CAL(Neb. City)-BRIDGER-SLCUT. V. Rem. 1859.

GIBBS, Mifflin W. SHADOW AND LIGHT. WA: N.p., 1902. CAL. 1850.

GIBSON, Arrell M. SEE: With Ed Bearss. FORT SMITH.

GIBSON, George R. OVER THE CHIHUAHUA AND SANTA FE TRAILS, 1847-1848. Ed. Robert W. Frazer. Albuquerque: Univ. of New Mexico Press, 1981. RIO GRANDE. II. 1847. SANTA FE. II. 1848.

GIBSON, J. W. "Watt." RECOLLECTIONS OF A PIONEER. St. Joseph, MO: Nelson-Hanne, 1912. CAL(St. Jo). IV. Rem. 1849. CAL(East to St. Jo). V-. Rem. 1851. CAL(St. Jo). IV. Rem. 1852. CAL(St. Jo). IV. Rem. 1854. OR-BRIDGER-Ends Idaho. IV. Rem. 1865.

GIBSON, James. "From Missouri to Oregon in 1847." ORHIST. OR. V. 1847.

GIBSON, John M. Journal. In W. W. Morrison Collection, UWY. CAL(Plattsmouth-BRIDGER. I. 1859.

GIDDINGS, Emily C., and Emmie W. Mahon. "The Jackass Trail." PASSWORD 2(Aug 1957): 91-96. Stage.

GIDDINGS, George H. CASE OF CONDUCTOR OF THE OVERLAND MAIL ROUTE FROM SAN ANTONIO, TEXAS, TO SAN DIEGO, CALIFORNIA. WA: Polkinhorn, 1860. Stage.

GIFFEN, Helen S. Ed. Decker, Peter. DIARIES.

_____. TRAIL-BLAZING PIONEER, COL. JOSEPH BALLINGER CHILES. SF: Howell, 1969. CAL(Indep)-HALL(to Ft. Boise)-MEEK variant to Sutter's. III. 1843. Biog.

_____, and Arthur Woodward. THE STORY OF EL TEJON. LA: Dawson's, 1942. Geog.

"The Gila Trail." ARIZONA HIGHWAYS 60(Nov 1984): 16-29. GILA-Genl. Graphics.

GILBERT, Bil. THE TRAILBLAZERS. Time-Life - The Old West Series. NY: Time, 1973. Overland-Genl. Graphics.

_____. WESTERING MAN: THE LIFE OF JOSEPH WALKER. NY: Atheneum, 1983. Biog.

GILBERT, Edmund W. "South Pass: A Study in the Historical Geog-

raphy of the United States." SCOTTISH GEOGRAPHICAL MAGAZINE 45(1929): 144-54. Geog.

_____. THE EXPLORATION OF WESTERN AMERICA, 1800 - 1850. Cambridge: Cambridge Univ. Press, 1933. Overland-Genl.

GILBERT, John. "John Gilbert's Account of the Little Blue Tragedy." PUBLICATIONS Nebraska State Historical Society 19(1919): 17-28. Stage. Indians.

GILBERT, William W. Journal. MNHIST. CAL(Council)-SLCUT. II+. 1853.

GILCHRIST, Leonard W. Papers and Diaries. NBHIST. Pony.

GILDMEISTER, Jerry. SEE: Steber, Rick et al. TRACES.

GILES, Daniel. Biography. ORU. OR(Council). V. Rem. 1852.

GILES, John D. "Hike of 1917 - Pioneer Trail." IMPROVEMENT ERA 20(Sept 1917): 987-95. Pres: Henefer to SLC.

_____. "The M. I. A. Preserves History." IMPROVEMENT ERA 38(Feb 1935): 82-87. Pres.

_____. Papers. UTHIST. Utah Trails-Genl.

GILFILLAN, Archer B. SHEEP. Boston: Little, Brown, 1929. Stock.

GILL, Harriet T. "The Overland Journey in 1853." In CALIFORNIA LETTERS OF WILLIAM GILL, ed. Eva T. Clark. NY: Downs, 1922. CAL(Indep). V. 1853.

GILL, Nelson G. SEE: With Stephen W. Eastman. "Journal."

GILL, Thomas. "Across the Plains." Modesto, CA STANISLAUS WEEKLY NEWS, 14 Aug 1903. CAL. 1853. Not Seen.

GILL, William. CALIFORNIA LETTERS.... Ed. Eva T. Clark. NY: Downs, 1922. CAL(Indep). V. 1850.

GILLESPIE, Agnes L. "On to Oregon: The Diary of...." LANE COUNTY HISTORIAN 9(Dec 1964): 47-54. OR(Indep?)-Ends Baker, OR. III. 1852.

GILLESPIE, Robert. Diary. MO-WHMC. CAL(Indep?)-HALL-LASSEN. III. 1849.

GILLETTE, Martha L. OVERLAND TO OREGON AND THE INDIAN WARS OF 1853. Ashland, OR: Lewis Osborne, 1971. OR(St. Jo?). IV. Rem. 1852.

GILLETTE, P. W. Diary. ORU. OR(St. Jo?)-BARLOW. III+. Rem. 1852.

GILLIAM, Albert M. TRAVELS OVER THE TABLE LANDS AND CORDILLERAS OF MEXICO.... Philadelphia: Moore, 1846. MEX(Vera Cruz-Mexico City-Durango-Tampico). II. 1843.

GILLIAM, Washington S. "Reminiscences of...." TRANSACTIONS Oregon Pioneer Association (1904): 202-20. OR(St. Jo). IV. Rem. 1844.

GILMAN, Carolyn. SEE: With Rhoda Gilman and Deborah M. Stultz. THE RED RIVER TRAILS.

GILMAN, Harold F. "Origin and Persistence of a Transit Region: Eastern Mojave Desert of California." Phd diss., Univ. of California-Riverside, 1977. Not Seen.

GILMAN, Musetta. PUMP ON THE PRAIRIE: A CHRONICLE OF A ROAD RANCH, 1859-1868. Detroit: Author, 1975. CAL-Genl. PIKES-Genl.

GILMAN, Rhoda R., Carolyn Gilman, and Deborah M. Stultz. THE RED RIVER TRAILS: OXCART ROUTES BETWEEN ST. PAUL AND THE SELKIRK SETTLEMENT, 1820-1870. St. Paul: Minnesota Historical Society, 1979. DAKOTAS-Genl.

GILMER, John T. Statement. UTHIST. Stage.

GILMORE, Andrew H. Overland Journey. CSL. CAL(St. Jo). II. 1850.

GILPIN, William. GUIDE TO THE KANSAS GOLD MINES AT PIKE'S PEAK. Cincinnati: Mendenhall, 1859. Guide.

_____. HISTORY.... SF: N.p., 1889. OR. 1843. Not Seen.

GINN, John I. Personal Recollections. UTHIST. CAL(Indep)-BRIDGER-SLCOR. II+. Rem. 1857. Utah.

GIRL, Christian. HUMAN DEPRAVITY.... Decatur, IL: Author, 1888. CAL(Leav). IV. Rem. 1850.

GITTINS, H. Leigh. IDAHO'S GOLD ROAD. Moscow, ID: Univ. Press of Idaho, 1976. MONTANA-Genl.

GIVEN, Abraham. OVERLAND TRIP.... Frankfort, IN: N.p., c1900. CAL(St. Jo). IV. Rem. 1850.

GIVENS, Robert R. Letters. BANCROFT. CAL(St. Jo)-BRIDGER-SLCOR. V. 1849.

GLASSCOCK, C. B. LUCKY BALDWIN. NY: Burt, 1933. CAL(Council)-BRIDGER-SLCUT. IV. Rem. 1853.

GLATFELTER, Noah M. "Letters from Dakota Territory, 1865." MISSOURI HISTORICAL BULLETIN 18(Jan 1962): 104-34. Stage: Milwaukee-Crow Creek Agency. V. 1865.

GLEASON, Jasper. Diary. KSHIST. SANTA FE-Ends Las Animas. III. 1855.

GLENN, John G. Diary. ORHIST. OR(St. Jo). III. 1852.

GLOVER, William. THE MORMONS IN CALIFORNIA. LA: Dawson, 1954. CAL(Sacramento)-SLCUT. IV. 1849.

GLUEK, Alvin C., Jr. "The Minnesota Route." BEAVER, Spr 1956, 44-50. DAKOTAS-Genl.

GODDARD, George H. REPORT OF A SURVEY OF A PORTION OF THE EASTERN BOUNDARY OF CALIFORNIA, AND OF A RECONNAISSANCE OF THE OLD CARSON AND JOHNSON IMMIGRANT ROADS OVER THE SIERRA NEVADA. California Legislature, 7th sess. 1856. Appendix to Assembly Journal, Doc. 5, Annual Report of the Surveyor-General. See: Report 6 (Truckee): 191-92. CAL-1856-Genl.

GODFREY, Kenneth and Audrey Ann. "The Pioneer Woman." IMPROVEMENT ERA 72(May 1964): 34-37. Social.

GOETZINGER, William. Collection. MNHIST. DAKOTAS-Genl.

_____. "Travelers on a Red River Trail." MNHIST. DAKOTAS-Genl.

GOETZMAN, William H. ARMY EXPLORATION IN THE AMERICAN WEST, 1803-1863. New Haven: Yale Univ. Press, 1959.

Govt.

_____. EXPLORATION AND EMPIRE: THE EXPLORER AND THE SCIENTIST IN THE WINNING OF THE AMERICAN WEST. NY: Knopf, 1966. Govt.

GOFF, Lyman B. AN 1862 TRIP TO THE WEST. Pawtucket, RI: Author, N.d. DAKOTAS(St. Paul - Selkirk). III. 1862.

GOFF, William A. Ed. Raber, Charles. "Recollections."

GOHRES, Helen. "Bare-footed to the Gold-Fields." SAN DIEGO HISTORICAL SOCIETY QUARTERLY 9(Jul 1963): 34-41. MEX(Baja California). III. 1849.

THE GOLD RUSH: LETTERS FROM THE WOLVERINE RANGERS TO THE MARSHALL, MI, STATESMAN, 1849-1851. Mount Pleasant, MI: Cumming, 1974. CAL(Indep)-LASSEN. II. 1849.

GOLDBLATT, Kenneth, A. Ed. Baylor, George W. "Scout to Quitman Canyon."

GOLDER, Frank A. Ed. Standage, Henry. THE MARCH OF THE MORMON BATTALION.

GOLDSMITH, Oliver. OVERLAND IN FORTY-NINE.... Detroit: Author, 1896. CAL(Indep)-LASSEN. III. Rem. 1849.

GOLTRA, Elizabeth J. JOURNAL OF TRAVEL ACROSS THE PLAINS, 1853. Eugene, OR: Lane County Historical Society, 1970. OR(Kansas City)-BARLOW. II. 1853.

GOMER, P. P. "Freighting on the Plains in the '60's." TRAIL 3(Jul 1910): 5-8. Freight.

GOMEZ, Phillip J. "Fort Bowie National Historic Site: The Evolution of a Unique Western Park." JOURNAL OF ARIZONA HISTORY 25(Sum 1984): 171-90. Geog. Pres.

GOOD, Daniel H. Letters. Princeton Univ. Library-Western America, Princeton, NJ. OR(Indep)-APPLE. IV. 1846.

GOOD, Donnie D. "Traveling Westward." AMERICAN SCENE 9, no. 2(1968): entire issue. Stage-Graphics. Freight-Graphics.

GOODALE, Tim. Letter, 1861. CAHIST. Missing.

GOODE, William H. OUTPOSTS OF ZION. Cincinnati: Poe & Hitchcock, 1864. PIKES. V. Rem. 1859.

GOODELL, Anna M. Crossing the Plains. Univ. of Washington Library-MS, Seattle, WA. OR(Council). III-. 1854.

GOODEN, John H. "Life and Experiences of the Forty-Niners on the Southwestern Roads to California." MA thesis, Texas Western College, 1965. SANTA FE-Genl. MARCY-Genl. RIO GRANDE-Genl. GILA-Genl.

GOODHART, George W. SEE: Anderson, Abraham C. TRAILS OF EARLY IDAHO.

GOODING, Larry. "Across the Plains in 1849." FRONTIER TIMES 1(Aug 1924): 1-6. CAL(Ft. Smith)-MARCY-RIO GRANDE-TEXAS-OKLAHOMA. IV. 1849.

GOODMAN, Jessie H. Ed. Pearson, Gustavus C. OVERLAND IN 1849.

GOODMAN, John B., III. Ed. Wood, Harvey. PERSONAL RECOL-

LECTIONS.

GOODRICH, Sophia L. "Diary." In COVERED WAGON WOMEN, vol. 2, ed. Kenneth L. Holmes. Glendale: Clark, 1983. MORMON. III. 1850.

GOODRICH, William A. Diary. Illinois State Historical Library, Springfield, IL. OR(Council)-BARLOW. III+. 1852.

GOODSELL, Fred F. Ed. Service, John. JOHN SERVICE, PIONEER.

GOODWIN, Cardinal. "California's Pioneer Homeseekers." OVERLAND MONTHLY 59(Apr 1912): 304-10. CAL-1841-Genl.

_____. "Overland Immigration from 1843-1846." OVERLAND MONTHLY 59(Jun 1912): 561-70. Overland-Genl.

GOODWIN, Victor O. "Development of Emigrant Routes of Northern Nevada." NEVADA HISTORICAL SOCIETY QUARTERLY 8(Fall-Win 1965): 27-41. CAL-Genl.

_____. "Historic Land and Resource-Use Patterns in the Lake Tahoe Basin and their Effect Upon Its Present Milieu." Unpublished Study Held by Author, Carson City, NV. Geog. Stage. Freight.

_____. THE HUMBOLDT - NEVADA'S DESERT RIVER AND THOROUGHFARE OF THE AMERICAN WEST. U.S. Dept. of Agriculture - Nevada Humboldt River Basin Survey. N.p., 1965. Geog.

_____. "William C. (Hill) Beachey: Nevada - California - Idaho Stagecoach King." NEVADA HISTORICAL SOCIETY QUARTERLY 10(Spr 1967): 3-46. Stage. Biog.

GORDON, G. F. Statement, 1848, Laramie Plain...to Los Angeles. Attributed to BANCROFT but not found in catalog.

GORDON, Mary M. Ed. Reid, Bernard. OVERLAND TO CALIFORNIA.

_____. "Overland to California in 1849: A Neglected Commercial Enterprise." PACIFIC HISTORICAL REVIEW 52(Feb 1983): 17-36. CAL-1849-Genl. Stage.

GORDON, William A. Diary. UWY. CAL(Lexington, MO). 1850. Not Seen.

GORE, Ebenezer E. Reminiscences. Spencer Library, Univ. of Kansas, Lawrence, KS. OR(Council)-APPLE. IV. Rem. 1852.

GORGAS, Solomon A. Diary. HUNTL. CAL(St. Jo). II+. 1850.

GORRILL, William H. Diary on Horseback. BEINECKE. OR-CAL. II. Graphics. 1869.

GOTTFREDSON, Peter, comp. HISTORY OF INDIAN DEPREDATIONS IN UTAH. SLC: Author, 1919. Indians.

GOTTLIEB, Jean S. Ed. Crumb, Lawrence N. HISTORIC PRESERVATION.

GOUGHNOUR, E. ACROSS THE PLAINS IN '49. Libertyville, IA: N.p., 1908. CAL(Council). III. Rem. 1849.

GOULD, Albert L. [Written by Jane A. Gould]. "Diary." In WOMEN'S DIARIES, ed. Lillian Schlissel. NY: Schocken, 1982. CAL(Council). II+. 1860. First-person description of 1860 Indian attack at City of Rocks.

GOULD, Charles. SEE: Hannon, Jessie G. THE BOSTON-NEWTON

COMPANY.

GOULD, Jane H. "Iowa to California in 1862...." Ed. Philip K. Lack. ANNALS OF IOWA 37(1963-1965): 460-76, 544-59, 623-40; 38(1965-1967): 68-75. CAL(Council)-LANDER. II+. 1862.

GOULD, Janet W. "The Butterfield Stage Station at 'Laguna Grande'." Southern California Historical QUARTERLY 18(Jun 1936): 46-49. Geog. Stage.

GOULDER, William A. REMINISCENCE.... Boise, ID: Perrault, 1909. OR(St. Jo)-MEEK. IV. Rem. 1845.

GOULDING, William R. Journal. Attributed to HUNTL but not catalogued.

GOVE, Jesse A. THE UTAH EXPEDITION, 1857-1858. Ed. Otis G. Hammond. Concord, NH: New Hampshire Historical Society, 1928. MORMON-1857-Genl.

GOWANS, Fred R. "Fort Bridger and the Mormons." UTAH HISTORICAL QUARTERLY 42(Win 1974): 49-67. Geog.

_____. "A History of Brigham Young's Indian Superintendency (1851-1859) -- Problems and Accomplishments." MS thesis, BYU, 1963. Indians.

_____. "A History of Fort Bridger from 1841 - 1858." PhD diss., BYU, 1972. Geog.

_____, and Eugene E. Campbell. FORT BRIDGER: ISLAND IN THE WILDERNESS. Provo, UT: Brigham Young Univ. Press, 1975. Geog.

GOWDY, Mrs. John T. [Ann Eliza]. CROSSING THE PLAINS. Dayton, OR: Author, 1906. OR. V. Rem. 1852.

GOWEN, Bela E. "History of the Olds Emigrant Party of 1852." OR-HIST. OR(Council). II. 1852.

GOWER, Calvin W. "Aids to Prospective Prospectors: Guidebooks and Letters from Kansas Territory, 1858 - 1860." KANSAS HISTORICAL QUARTERLY 43(Spr 1977): 67-77. Guide.

_____. "Gold Fever in Kansas Territory: Migration to the Pike's Peak Gold Fields, 1858 - 1860." KANSAS HISTORICAL QUARTERLY 39(Spr 1973): 58-74. PIKES-Genl.

_____. "Kansas 'Border Town' Newspapers and the Pike's Peak Gold Rush." JOURNALISM QUARTERLY 44(Sum 1967): 281-88. PIKES-Genl.

_____. "Kansas Territory and the Pike's Peak Gold Rush." PhD diss., Univ. of Kansas-Lawrence, 1958. PIKES-Genl.

_____. KANSAS TOWNS AND TRADE FROM PIKE'S PEAK GOLD SEEKERS, 1858 - 1860. Manhattan, KS: MA/AH, 1980. PIKES-Genl.

_____. "The Pike's Peak Gold Rush and the Smoky Hill Route, 1859 - 1860." KANSAS HISTORICAL QUARTERLY 25(Sum 1959): 158-71. PIKES-Genl.

GRACE, Hybernia. "The First Trip West on the Butterfield Stage." WESTX 8(Jun 1932): 62-74. Stage.

GRACEY, David B., II. Ed. Whitworth, Robert. "An Englishman."

GRAFF, Everett D. "The Westerners Go Overland; Retread the Various Routes to California." CHICAGO WESTERNERS BRAND BOOK, 1944 1(1946): N.p. Bib.

GRAHAM, Alpheus N. "The Big Circle Back to Kansas." Ed. Wm. E. Kock. KANSAS MAGAZINE (1966): 52-57. CAL(Indep). III+. 1852.

GRAHAM, Calvin H. Journal. KSHIST. CAL(Indep). III. 1853.

GRAHAM, Henry W. Diary. Indiana State Historical Society. CAL(St. Jo). 1850. Not Seen.

GRAHAM, Richard H., and Sidney Smith. "Report of Journey to the Rocky Mountains." Ed. John E. Sunder. MISSOURI HISTORICAL SOCIETY BULLETIN 11(1945): 41-53. CAL(Westport)-South Pass and return. 1843. Not Seen.

GRAHAM, Robert M. Memoir. Washington State Historical Society, Tacoma, WA. OR(Kansas City). V. Rem. 1852.

GRANGE, Roger R., Jr. "Digging at Fort Kearny." NEBRASKA HISTORY 44(Jun 1963): 101-21. Geog.

GRANGER, Lewis. LETTERS: REPORTS OF THE JOURNEY FROM SALT LAKE TO LOS ANGELES IN 1849.... LA: Dawson, 1959. SLCOR. III. 1849. Extensive bibliography.

GRANNIS, John W. Diaries. MONHIST. Stage.

GRANT, Bruce. FAMOUS AMERICAN TRAILS. Chicago: Rand McNally, 1971. Overland-Genl.

GRANT, James. Biography. Arizona State Library-Arizona Room, Phoenix, AZ. Stage. Freight. BRADSHAW-Genl.

GRANT, Louis S. "Fort Hall on the Oregon Trail." MA thesis, Univ. of British Columbia, 1938. Geog. Not Seen.

_____. "Fort Hall under the Hudson's Bay Company." OREGON HISTORICAL QUARTERLY 41(Mar 1940): 34-39. Geog.

GRANT, Phil S. "The Songs of the Forty-Niners: A Collection and Survey." MA thesis, Univ. of California-Berkeley, 1924. Leisure.

GRANT, William S. "A Yankee in Arizona: The Misfortunes of William S. Grant." Ed. G. J. Pedersen. JOURNAL OF ARIZONA HISTORY 16(Sum 1975): 127-44. Freight.

Granville Company. Diary. BEINECKE. CAL(Indep)-LASSEN. II. 1849.

GRATIOT, Henry. Journal. Missouri Historical Society, St. Louis, MO. PIKES. 1859. Not Seen.

"The Grattan Massacre(?): As Drawn from the Indian Point of View." AMERICAN WEST 12(Nov-Dec 1985): 46-49. Indians. Graphics.

GRAUPNER, A. E. "A Storied Turnpike." SUNSET 17(Sept 1906): 269-73. Stage: Placerville to Lake Tahoe.

GRAVES, Jones S. "The Influence of the Canadian Rivers on the Development of Oklahoma, 1806 - 1866. MA thesis, Univ. of Oklahoma, 1937. Geog.

GRAVES, Pusey. Letters. In Paul and Helen Henderson Collection, UWY. CAL(Ft. Laramie to Sweetwater River). III. 1850.

GRAVES, W. H. "A True Narrative." COHIST. Rem. Freight. Mail.

GRAVES, William C. "Crossing the Plains in 1846." Healdsburg, California RUSSIAN RIVER FLAG, 26 Apr, 3 May, 10 May, 17 May 1877. CAL(Indep)-BRIDGER-HASTINGS-TRUCKEE. IV. 1846.

GRAY, A. A. "Camels in California." CALIFORNIA HISTORICAL QUARTERLY 9(Dec 1930): 299-317. Freight.

_____. "The Dollart Case." CALIFORNIA HISTORICAL QUARTERLY 9(Dec 1930): 318-31. Freight.

GRAY, A. B. SURVEY OF A ROUTE...THE A. B. GRAY REPORT. Ed. Lynn R. Bailey. Great West & Indian Series 24, Western Survey II. LA: Westernlore, 1963. CAL(Shreveport)-TEX-GILA. II. 1854.

GRAY, Charles. "Incidents of the Trip...." (In) CROSSING THE PLAINS, ed. Origin Thompson. Greenburg, IN: N.p., 1896. Rem. 1852. Not Seen.

GRAY, Charles G. OFF AT SUNRISE. Ed. Thomas D. Clark. San Marino: Huntington, 1976. CAL(Indep)-BRIDGER-SLCUT-LASSEN. II. 1849.

GRAY, Don. SEE: Steber, Rick, et al. TRACES.

GRAY, George. INDEX OF PONY EXPRESS MAP. St. Joseph, MO: Author, 1938? Pony. Map.

GRAY, George M. "Interview by William G. Paden." Not Seen.

GRAY, John S. "Blazing the Bridger and Bozeman Trails." ANNALS OF WYOMING 49(Spr 1977): 23-52. BOZE-Genl.

_____. "The Northern Overland Pony Express." MONTANA 16(Oct 1966): 58-73. Mail.

_____. "The Salt Lake Hockaday Mail." UTAH HISTORICAL QUARTERLY 56(Fall 1984): 12-20; 57(Spr 1958): 2-12. Stage. Mail.

GRAYDON, Charles K. "Trail of the First Wagons over the High Sierra." OVERLAND JOURNAL 4(Win 1986): 4-17. TRUCKEE-Genl.

_____. TRAIL OF THE FIRST WAGONS OVER THE HIGH SIERRA. Gerald, MO: Patrice, 1986. TRUCKEE-Genl. Maps.

GRAYSON, Andrew J. Account of Trip. BANCROFT. CAL(Indep)-BRIDGER-HALL-TRUCKEE. IV. 1846.

THE GREAT CENTRAL ROUTE VIA NEBRASKA CITY TO PIKE'S PEAK, UTAH, OREGON AND CALIFORNIA. Nebraska City: Power Press, 1859. Guide.

"The Great Comanche War Trail." FRONTIER TIMES 16(Jun 1939): 375-78. TEX-Genl.

GRECO, Joseph A. "History of Highway 50 from Placerville to Virginia City, 1849 - 1869." MA thesis, Sacramento State Univ., 1964. Geog. CAL-Genl.

GREELEY, Horace. AN OVERLAND JOURNEY FROM NEW YORK TO SAN FRANCISCO...1859. Ed. Charles T. Duncan. NY: Knopf, 1964. Stage: Atchison-SLC-SF. I. 1859.

GREEN, Caleb. A Visit to Great Salt Lake. Missouri Historical Society, St. Louis, MO. PIKES. 1856. Not Seen.

GREEN, Charles R. Diary. Buffalo, NY, Public Library. Not Seen.

GREEN, Dan L. My Ox Team Journey across the Plains." Held by Mrs. Elizabeth Hiller, Wilderville, OR. Not Seen.

GREEN, Duff C. "Exploring the Rio Grande: Lt. Duff C. Green's Report of 1852." Ed. Ronnie C. Tyler. ARIZONA & THE WEST 10(Spr 1968): 43-60. TEX-MEX. III. 1852.

GREEN, Edmund. Reminiscences. BANCROFT. CAL(St. Jo)-HALL. III. Rem. 1849.

GREEN, H. T., and O. M. Tennison. REPORT AND MAP OF THE SMOKY HILL EXPEDITION.... Leavenworth, KS: Times, 1861. Guide.

GREEN, James. "Incidents of the Indian Outbreak of 1864. Freighting on the Plains - Plum Creek Massacre." PUBLICATIONS Nebraska State Historical Society 19(1919): 1-6. Freight. Geog. Indians.

GREEN, Jay. DIARY OF JAY GREEN. San Joaquin Pioneer and Historical Society Publications No. 5. Stockton: Society, 1955. CAL(St. Jo). III. 1852.

GREEN, Nelson W. Ed. Smith, Mary. FIFTEEN YEARS.

GREEN, Robert B. ON THE ARKANSAS ROUTE TO CALIFORNIA IN 1849. Ed. J. Orin Oliphant. Lewisburg, PA: Bucknell Univ., 1955. CAL(Ft. Smith)-SANTA FE-RIO GRANDE-GILA. III. 1849.

GREEN, T. L. "A Forgotten Fur Trading Post in Scotts Bluff County." NEBRASKA HISTORY 15(Jan-Mar 1934): 38-46. Geog.

_____. "Scotts Bluffs, Fort John." NEBRASKA HISTORY 19(Jul-Sept 1938): 175-89. Geog.

GREENBURG, Dan W. Ed. Crockett, Edwin. "Crossing the Plains."

_____. "How Fort William, Now Fort Laramie, Was Named." ANNALS OF WYOMING 12(Jan 1940): 56-62. Geog.

GREENE, Jerome A., ed. "'We do not know What the Government intends to do...' Lt. Palmer Writes from the Bozeman Trail, 1867 - 68." MONTANA 28(Jul 1978): 16-35. BOZE-Gen. Graphics. Military. Indians.

GREENE, Lida L. "Markers for Remembrance: The Mormon Trail." ANNALS OF IOWA 40(Win 1970): 190-93. Pres.

GREENE, Max. THE KANZAS REGION.... NY: Fowler & Wells, 1856. Guide.

GREENLEY, Albert H. CAMELS IN AMERICA. NY: Bibliographical Society of America, 1952. Best camel bibliography.

GREENSLIT, George H. "A Day with the Indians." DENVER REPUBLICAN, 21 February 1884. PIKES-by Stage. Rem. 1864. Not Seen.

GREENWELL, Scott L. "A History of the U.S. Army Corps of Topographical Engineers in Utah, 1843 - 1859." MA thesis, Utah State Univ., 1972. Military.

GREENWOOD, C. L., ed. "Opening Routes to El Paso, 1849." SOUTHWESTERN HISTORICAL QUARTERLY 48(Oct 1944): 262-72. TEX(Austin-El Paso). II. 1849.

GREER, William A. A BOY ON THE PLAINS AND IN THE ROCKIES. Boston: Goreham, 1917. PIKES. III. Rem. 1860.

GREGG, Kate L. Ed. Field, Matthew. PRAIRIE AND MOUNTAIN SKETCHES.

_____, ed. "Boonslickers in the Gold Rush to California." MISSOURI HISTORICAL REVIEW 41(Jul 1947): 345-60. CAL-Genl.

_____, ed. "Missourians in the Gold Rush." MISSOURI HISTORI-

CAL REVIEW 39(Jan 1945): 137-54. Geog: Jumping-off Places.

GREGORY, Mrs. E. J. Adventuring. Norlin Library, Univ. of Colorado, Boulder, CO. PIKES. V. Rem. 1866.

GREGSON, James. Statement. BANCROFT. CAL(Indep)-HALL-TRUCKEE. V. Rem. 1845.

GRENBERG, Allise O. "Wagon Train Government during the Western Migration in the United States, 1840 - 1865." MA thesis, Sacramento State Univ., 1971. Train Govt.

GREVE, Alice. "Dr. McLoughlin's House." BEAVER, Outfit 272, Sept 1941, 32-35. Pres.

GREY, Don. "Branches of the Oregon Trail in the Upper Hams Fork Area." Unpublished Report for Utah Power and Light Co., 1976. Geog.

GRIDLEY, John T. Letters. HUNT. CAL(Council)-BRIDGER-SLCUT. 1850. Not Seen.

GRIFFIN, Eli A. Diaries. Bentley Library, Univ. of Michigan, Ann Arbor. CAL(Council?). 1853. CAL(Council)-BRIDGER-Ends SLC. 1856. PIKES. 1859. Not Seen.

GRIFFIN, John S. "A Doctor Comes to California: The Diary of John S. Griffin, Assistant Surgeon with Kearny's Dragoons, 1846-47." Ed. George W. Ames, Jr. CALIFORNIA HISTORICAL QUARTERLY 21(Sept, Dec 1942): 193-224, 333-57; 22(Mar 1943): 41-66. GILA. II. 1846.

GRIFFINHAGEN, George B., and William C. Felter. THE OREGON TRAIL OF PHARMACY. N.p.: American Institute of the History of Pharmacy, 1952. Medical.

GRIFFITH, Andrew J. "Hancock County, Illinois to California in 1850." Ed. David L. Hill. East Washington Historical Society, Spokane, WA. CAL(St. Jo)-BRIDGER-SLCUT. I. 1850.

GRIGGS, Monroe C. WHEELERS, POINTERS AND LEADERS. Fresno, CA: Academy Library, 1956. Teams. Freight.

GRINDELL, John. Overland Narrative. AZHIST. CAL(St. Jo). III. 1850.

GRINNELL, George B. Collection. Southwest Museum Library, Los Angeles, CA. Indians.

_____. THE FIGHTING CHEYENNES. Norman: Univ. of Oklahoma Press, 1956. Indians.

GRINSTEAD, William. Account Book. KSHIST. CAL-1850-Genl.

GRISWOLD, Harriet B. Papers. CAHIST. CAL(Council)-BRIDGER-SIMPSON? 1859. Not Seen.

GROESBECK, Nicholas H. Reminiscence. UTHIST. MORMON. IV. Rem. 1856.

GROH, George W. GOLD FEVER: BEING A TRUE ACCOUNT, BOTH HORRIFYING AND HILARIOUS, OF THE ART OF HEALING (SO-CALLED) DURING THE CALIFORNIA GOLD RUSH. NY: Morrow, 1966. Medical.

GROSS, Julia E. "Early Emigrations of the Oregon Trail." MA thesis, Univ. of Oregon, 1931. OR-Genl.

GROSS, Kelley & Co. "Business Records: 1763-1954." Zimmerman Library-SpCol, Univ. of New Mexico, Albuquerque, NM. Stock(Sheep).

GROUND, Edward. Letter. Attributed to BANCROFT but not catalogued. 1854.

GROUND, Eliza A. Letter. Attributed to BANCROFT but not catalogued. 1853.

GROUND, William B. Letter. Attributed to BANCROFT but not catalogued. 1853.

GROW, S. L. Journal. BEINECKE. CAL(Council)-Ends Ft. Laramie. III. 1850.

GRUELL, J. D. "Account." In JOURNALS OF FORTY-NINERS, SALT LAKE TO LOS ANGELES, ed. LeRoy and Ann W. Hafen. Glendale: Clark, 1954. SLCOR. V. Rem. 1849.

GUDDE, Erwin G. Ed. Bigler, Henry W. BIGLER'S CHRONICLES.

_____, and Elizabeth K. Gudde. Ed. & trans. Lienard, Heinrich. FROM ST. LOUIS TO SUTTER'S. Ed. & trans. Preuss, Charles. EXPLORING WITH FREMONT.

GUERIN, Mrs. E. J. MOUNTAIN CHARLEY. Norman: Univ. of Oklahoma Press, 1968. CAL(Indep)-LASSEN. III. 1855. Social.

GUIDEBOOK FOR BRITISH COLUMBIA. THE WONDERS OF THE GOLD DIGGINGS...BY A SUCCESSFUL DIGGER. London: N.p., 1862. Guide.

GUIDEBOOK OF THE PACIFIC. SF: Holdredge, 1866. Not Seen.

GUIDE TO CALIFORNIA AND OREGON. SLC?: N.p., c.1850. Guide.

"Guide to the Gold Mines - Table of Distances from Omaha to Denver." Council Bluff, Iowa DAILY TELEGRAPH 19 Apr 1861. Charles W. Martin Collection, Omaha. Guide.

GUIDE TO THE NEW GOLD REGION OF WESTERN KANSAS AND NEBRASKA. NY: John W. Oliver, 1859. Guide.

GUIDE TO THE NEWLY DISCOVERED GOLD FIELDS OF KANSAS AND NEBRASKA CONTAINING A BRIEF DESCRIPTION OF ROUTES, ETC. Omaha: E. D. Webster, 1860. Guide.

GUIDE TO THE ROUTE MAP OF THE MORMON PIONEERS FROM NAUVOO TO GREAT SALT LAKE, 1846 - 1848. SLC: Millroy & Haynes, c.1899. MORMON-1847-Genl.

Guidon Books. THE SANTA FE TRAIL - PEOPLE & PLACES: A CATALOG OF BOOKS & PAMPHLETS. Scottsdale, AZ: Author, c.1972. Bib.

GUILL, Mary J. Diary. CSL. CAL(Council)-LASSEN. II. 1860.

GUILLOD, Harry. "Harry Guillod's Journal of a Trip to Cariboo, 1862." Ed. Dorothy B. Smith. BRITISH COLUMBIA HISTORICAL QUARTERLY 19, nos. 3-4(1955): 187-232. CANADA(Victoria-Fraser Mines). IV. 1862.

GUINN, J. M. "Early Postal Service of California." PUBLICATIONS Southern California Historical Society 4(1897): 18-26. Mail.

_____. EL CAMINO REAL. LA: N.p., 1906. CAL-Genl.

_____. "The Old Highways of Los Angeles." PUBLICATIONS Southern California Historical Society 6(1905): 253-57. Geog.

_____. "The Pony Express." PUBLICATIONS Southern California

Historical Society 6(1903): 50-51. Pony.

_____. "Yuma Indian Depredations and the Glanton War." PUBLICATIONS Southern California Historical Society 6(1903): 50-51. Geog. Indians.

GUNDLACH, John H. Diary. Missouri Historical Society-St. Louis. CAL(Ft. Kearny)-HALL. 1850. Not Seen.

GUNN, Lewis C. RECORDS OF A CALIFORNIA FAMILY. Ed. Anna L. Marston. San Diego: Author, 1928. CAL-TEX(Brazos)-MEX(Matamoros-Mazatlan). II+. 1849.

GUNN, Otis B. NEW MAP AND HAND-BOOK OF KANSAS AND THE GOLD MINES.... Pittsburgh: W. S. Haven, 1859. Guide.

GUNNING, I. C. THE BUTTERFIELD OVERLAND MAIL THROUGH EASTERN OKLAHOMA. Wilburton, OK: Eastern Oklahoma Historical Society, 1971. Stage.

GUNNISON, John W. Diary. National Archives, Washington, D.C. CAL(Leav)-BRIDGER-Ends SLC. 1849. Not Seen.

_____. GUIDE TO THE KANSAS GOLD MINES AT PIKE'S PEAK.... 1859. Reprint. Pikes Peak Guidebooks, 10. Denver: Nolie Mumey, 1952. Guide.

GUSTAFSON, A. M. Ed. Spring, John. JOHN SPRING'S ARIZONA.

GUTHRIE, A. B., Jr. "Adventure with History." HOLIDAY, July 1953, 58-63, 86, 88, 90, 93. Pres.

GUYOL, P. N. "A Coach Comes to the Society." HISTORICAL NEW HAMPSHIRE 13(Dec 1957): 39-61. Eqpt. Pres.

H. J. E. NORTH PLATTE ROUTE TO THE GOLD MINES. N.p, n.d. Guide.

HAAS, Charles. Ed. Haas, John B. "John B. Haas."

HAAS, John B. "John B. Haas...Pioneer." Ed. Charles E. Haas. PONY EXPRESS COURIER, June, July, Aug, Sept, Oct, Nov, Dec 1938, 7-10, 7-10, 7-10, 7-10, 7-10, 7-10, 5-6, 11-12; Jan 1939, 7-10. CAL(St. Jo)-BRIDGER-SLCUT. IV. Rem. 1853.

HACKENSMITH, Mrs. M. S. Diary. BANCROFT. CAL-TEX(Georgetown)-GILA. III+. 1866.

HACKNEY, John S. Diary. MONHIST. CAL(Council)-BOZE. III+. 1864.

HACKNEY, Joseph. "Diary." In WAGONS WEST, ed. Elizabeth Page. NY: N.p., 1930. CAL(St. Jo)-HALL-TRUCKEE. II+. 1849.

HADDICK, M. A. "From Indiana to California in 1849." GRIZZLY BEAR 13(Feb 1913): 28-34. CAL(Westport)-LASSEN. V. 1849.

HADLEY, Amelia H. "Journal of Travails to Oregon." In COVERED WAGON WOMEN, vol. 3, ed. Kenneth L. Holmes. Glendale: Clark, 1984. OR(Council)-BARLOW. II. 1851.

HADLEY, C. B. "The Plains War in 1855." PROCEEDINGS AND COLLECTIONS Nebraska State Historical Society 5(1902): 273-78. Rem. Freight.

HADLEY, E. Amelia. Diary. ORU. OR(Council)-BARLOW. II. 1851.

HAENSZEL, Arda M. HISTORICAL CAJON PASS: A SELF-GUIDED DRIVING TOUR IN THREE PARTS. Redlands, CA:

San Bernardino County Museum Association, 1976. Geog. BEALE-Genl.

HAFEN, Ann W. Ed. With LeRoy R. Hafen. DIARIES OF WILLIAM HENRY JACKSON. HANDCARTS TO ZION. JOURNALS OF THE FORTY-NINERS. OLD SPANISH TRAIL. POWDER RIVER CAMPAIGNS. RELATIONS WITH THE INDIANS. TO THE ROCKIES AND OREGON. THE UTAH EXPEDITION.

HAFEN, LeRoy R. Ed. With Ann W. Hafen. THE DIARIES OF WILLIAM H. JACKSON. Ed. With Mrs. Frank Hall. "Seventy Years Ago." Ed. With Augustus Voorhees. "The Voorhees Diary."

_____. "Butterfield's Overland Mail." CALIFORNIA HISTORICAL QUARTERLY 2(Oct 1923): 211-22. Stage.

_____. "Cherokee Goldseekers in Colorado, 1849-50." COLORADO MAGAZINE 15(May 1938): 101-8.

_____. "Colonel Loring's Expedition across Colorado in 1858." COLORADO MAGAZINE 23(Mar 1946): 49-76. SPANISH(Fort Union-Grand Junction-Camp Floyd). II. 1858.

_____. "Early Colorado Mail Service, 1856 - 60." COLORADO MAGAZINE 2(Jan 1925): 23-32. Mail. Stage.

_____. "Hand Cart Migration across the Plains." In THE TRANS-MISSISSIPPI WEST: PAPERS READ...1929. Eds. James F. Willard and Colin B. Goodykoontz. Boulder: Univ. of Colorado, 1930. MORMON-Genl.

_____. "Handcarts to Zion, 1856-1860." UTAH HISTORICAL QUARTERLY 24(Oct 1965): 309-17. MORMON-Genl.

_____, ed. THE MOUNTAIN MEN AND THE FUR TRADE OF THE FAR WEST. 10 vols. Glendale: Clark, 1965-1972. Biog.

_____. "The Opening and Development of the First Route from the Rockies to the Pacific." In ESSAYS ON THE AMERICAN WEST, ed. Thomas G. Alexander. Charles Redd Monographs in Western History, No. 5. Provo, UT: Brigham Young Univ. Press, 1975. SPANISH-Genl.

_____. THE OVERLAND MAIL, 1849-1869. Cleveland: Clark, 1926. Stage. Mail. Pony.

_____. "The Overland Mail to the Pacific Coast, 1849-69." PhD diss., Univ. of California-Berkeley, 1923. Mail. Stage.

_____. OVERLAND ROUTES TO THE GOLD FIELDS, 1859. Southwest Historical Series, No. 11. Glendale: Clark, 1942. PIKES-Genl-1859.

_____, ed. PIKES PEAK GOLD RUSH GUIDEBOOKS OF 1859. Southwest Historical Series, No. 9. Glendale: Clark, 1941. Guide.

_____. "Raton Pass, An Historic Highway." COLORADO MAGAZINE 7(Nov 1930): 219-21. Geog.

_____. "The Story of the Immigration to Utah by Handcarts, 1856-1860." MA thesis, Univ. of Utah, 1919. MORMON-Genl.

_____, and W. J. Ghent. BROKEN HAND: THE LIFE STORY OF THOMAS FITZPATRICK. Denver: Old West, 1931. Biog.

_____, and Ann W. Hafen. THE DIARIES OF WILLIAM HENRY JACKSON, FRONTIER PHOTOGRAPHER. Far West and the Rockies Historical Series, 1820-1875, Vol. 10. Glendale: Clark, 1959. Biog.

_____. HANDCARTS TO ZION. Far West and the Rockies Historical Series, Vol. 14. Glendale: Clark, 1960. MORMON-Genl.

_____, eds. JOURNALS OF FORTY-NINERS, SALT LAKE TO LOS ANGELES. Far West and the Rockies Historical Series, 1820-1875, Vol. 2. Glendale: Clark, 1954. SLCOR-1849-Genl.

_____. THE OLD SPANISH TRAIL: SANTA FE TO LOS ANGELES. Far West and the Rockies Historical Series, 1820-1875, Vol. 1. Glendale: Clark, 1954.

_____, eds. POWDER RIVER CAMPAIGNS AND SAWYER'S EXPEDITION OF 1865. Far West and the Rockies Historical Series, 1820-1875, Vol. 12. Glendale: Clark, 1961. Military. Indians.

_____, eds. RELATIONS WITH THE INDIANS OF THE PLAINS, 1857-1861. Far West and the Rockies Historical Series, 1820-1875, Vol. 9. Glendale: Clark, 1959. Military. Indians.

_____, eds. TO THE ROCKIES AND OREGON, 1839-1842. Far West and the Rockies Historical Series, 1820-1875. Glendale: Clark, 1955. Overland-Genl.

_____, eds. THE UTAH EXPEDITION, 1857-1858. Far West and the Rockies Historical Series, 1820-1875, Vol. 8. Glendale: Clark, 1958. Utah. MORMON-1857-Genl.

HAFEN, LeRoy R., and F. M. Young. FORT LARAMIE AND THE PAGEANT OF THE WEST, 1834-1890. Glendale: Clark, 1938. Geog.

_____. "The Mormon Settlement at Pueblo, CO during the Mexican War." COLORADO MAGAZINE 9(Jul 1932): 121-36. CAL(Indep-Ft. Laramie)-CHEROKEE(Ft. Laramie-Pueblo,CO). III. 1846.

HAGAN, Barry J. "I Never Before Thought Death So Near." CAMP PERIODICAL 10(Spr 1978): 3-12. Military.

_____. "Save the Gun at all Hazzerds!" CAMP PERIODICAL 10(Win 1978-79): 35-47. Military.

HAGELSTEIN, George M. "The Hagelstein Diary." Trans. Walter V. Kaulfers and LaVern Cutler. AMERICAN GERMAN REVIEW 6(1936): N.p. CAL(St. Jo). II. Rem. 1850.

HAGEN, Olaf T. "Platte Bridge Station and Fort Caspar." Ed. Merrill J. Mattes. ANNALS OF WYOMING 27(Apr 1955): 3-17. Geog.

_____. "The Pony Express Starts from St. Joseph." MISSOURI HISTORICAL REVIEW 43(Oct 1948): 1-17. Pony.

HAGERTY, L. W. "Indian Raids along the Platte and Little Blue Rivers." NEBRASKA HISTORY 28(Jul-Sept, Oct-Dec 1947): 176-86, 239-60. Indians.

HAGOOD, J. Hurley, and Roberta Hagood. "A Thrilling Train Ride that Started the Pony Express." LA POSTA 15(Oct 1984): 39-45. Pony.

HAGUE, Harlan. "The First California Trail: The Southern Route." OVERLAND JOURNAL 5(Win 1987): 41-46. SPANISH-Genl. GILA-Genl.

_____. "Guides for the Pathfinders: The Indian Contribution to Exploration of the American West." PACIFIC HISTORIAN 26(Fall 1982): 55-63. Overland-Genl. Indians.

_____. "Road to California: The Search for a Southern Overland Route to 1849." PhD diss., Univ. of Nevada-Reno, 1974. GILA-Genl.

_____. THE ROAD TO CALIFORNIA: THE SEARCH FOR A SOUTHERN OVERLAND ROUTE, 1540-1848. American Trails Series 9. Glendale: Clark, 1978. GILA-Genl.

_____. "The Search for a Southern Overland Route to California."

CALIFORNIA HISTORICAL QUARTERLY 55(Sum 1976): 150-61. GILA-Genl.

HAHN, Mannel. "Communications with the West - A Recurrent Pattern." CHICAGO WESTERNERS BRAND BOOK 6(May 1949): 17-19, 21-24. Mail.

_____. "The Pony Express: 1860 Equivalent of Advertising Campaign." CHICAGO WESTERNERS BRAND BOOK 3(Mar 1946): 1-3, 9-12. Pony.

HAIGHT, Henry H. "We Walked to California in 1850." Iowa State Historical Society-MS, Iowa City, IA. CAL(Council)-BRIDGER-SLCUT. III. Rem. 1850.

HAIGHT, Isaac C. Biographical Sketch. UTHIST. MORMON. III. 1847. SLCOR. III. 1849. MORMON. III. 1850. MORMON. III. 1853.

HAINES, Asa. Diary. HUNTL. CAL(Council)-BRIDGER-SLCOR. IV. 1849.

HAINES, Aubrey L. HISTORIC SITES ALONG THE OREGON TRAIL. Gerald, MO: Patrice, 1981. A superb driving guide to the trail.

_____. HISTORIC SITES ALONG THE OREGON TRAIL. U.S. Dept. of the Interior - National Park Service. Unpublished report, 1973. Pres.

_____. "Oregon Trail Study Committee." ORHIST. Historic sites worksheets prepared c.1973.

HAINES, Francis D., Jr. Ed. Fletcher, Ellen G. BRIDE ON THE BOZEMAN.

_____. THE APPLEGATE TRAIL: SOUTHERN EMIGRANT ROUTE. N.p.: Am. Rev. Bicentennial Comm., 1976. APPLE-1846-Genl.

_____. THE BUFFALO. NY: Crowell, 1970. Fauna.

_____. "Francois Payette." IDAHO YESTERDAYS 8(Win 1964-1965): 12-21. Biog. Geog.

_____. "Francois Payette, Master of Fort Boise." PACIFIC NORTHWEST QUARTERLY 47(Apr 1956): 57-61. Geog. Biog.

_____. "Goldilocks on the Oregon Trail." IDAHO YESTERDAYS 9(Win 1965-66): 26-30. Social.

_____. "The Western Limits of the Buffalo Range." PACIFIC NORTHWEST QUARTERLY 31(Oct 1940): 389-98. Fauna. Geog.

_____, and Marjorie O'Harra. THE APPLEGATE TRAIL: SOUTHERN EMIGRANT ROUTE 1845. THE APPLEGATE BICENTENNIAL WAGON TRAIN TREK 1976. N.p., 1976. APPLE-Genl. Pres.

HAINES, James W. Life & Experiences. CSL. CAL(St. Jo). IV. Rem. 1849.

HAINES, Robert W. "Baker's Covered Wagon Centennial." OREGON HISTORICAL QUARTERLY 53(Sept 1952): 209-13. Pres.

HAKOLA, John W. FRONTIER OMNIBUS. Missoula: Montana State Univ., 1962. MONTANA-Genl.

HALBERT, Sherrill. Pony Express Centennial Collections. UPAC. Pony. Pres.

HALE, Alma H. ALMA HELAMON HALE, HISTORY AND GENEALOGY. 2 vols, ed. Nathan Hale Gardner. Ogden, UT: Private, 1961. MORMON. IV. 1862.

HALE, Edward E. KANZAS AND NEBRASKA.... Boston: Phillips, Sampson, 1854. Guide.

HALE, Israel F. "Diary of Trip to California in 1849." QUARTERLY Society of California Pioneers 2(1925): 61-130. CAL(St. Jo)-HALL-LASSEN. III +. 1849.

HALE, John. CALIFORNIA AS IT IS.... 1851. Reprint. SF: Private, 1954. CAL(Indep)-LASSEN. IV. 1849.

HALE, Titus. Diary. Society of California Pioneers Library, San Francisco, CA. Not Seen.

HALES, Lucinda. Over the Trail. Idaho State Historical Society Library, Boise, ID. OR(Indep). III. Rem. 1846.

HALEY, J. Evetts. FORT CONCHO AND THE TEXAS FRONTIER. San Angelo, TX: San Angelo Standard-Times, 1952. Geog. TEX-Genl. Stage.

_____. "The Great Comanche War Trail." PANHANDLE-PLAINS HISTORICAL REVIEW 23(1950): 11-21. Indians. TEX-Genl.

_____. "Pioneer Mail Man: Ben Ficklin." SHAMROCK (Oil and Gas Corp.), Spring 1959, 8-12. Biog.

_____. "A Survey of Texas Cattle Drives to the North, 1866 - 1895." MA thesis, Univ. of Texas-Austin, 1926. Stock.

HALL, Carroll D., ed. DONNER MISCELLANY: 41 DIARIES AND DOCUMENTS. SF: Book Club of California, 1947. CAL-1846-Genl.

HALL, Charles. Papers. Includes Minnie Hall Murphey's "Pike's Peak or Bust: The Colorado Pioneers of Fifty-Eight and Fifty-Nine," a fictionalized tale taken from family reminiscences. 345 pp. COHIST. PIKES. II +. 1858.

HALL, Edward H. THE GREAT WEST.... NY: Author, 1864. Guide.

HALL, Mrs. Frank. "Seventy Years Ago - Recollections of a Trip through the Colorado Mountains with the Colfax Party in 1868." Ed. LeRoy R. Hafen. COLORADO MAGAZINE 15(Sept 1938): 161-67. Stage(Cheyenne-Denver). 1868.

HALL, George T. Letters. BEINECKE. CAL(St. Jo). V. 1849.

HALL, John B. AN ACCOUNT OF CALIFORNIA AND THE WONDERFUL GOLD REGIONS. Boston: Hall, 1849. Guide.

HALL, Maggie. Crossing the Plains. BANCROFT. CAL-TEX(Grayson)-GILA. III. 1853.

HALL, O. J. Diary. CSL. CAL(Council)-BRIDGER-SLCUT. IV. 1849.

HALL, R. Franklin. "Chihuahua Trail Linked U.S. and Mexico." FRONTIER TIMES 8(Apr 1931): 312-17. MEX-Genl. TEX-Genl.

HALL, Sharlot M. FIRST CITIZEN OF PRESCOTT, PAULINE WEAVER.... Prescott, AZ: Courier, 1929. Biog.

_____. "Olive A. Oatman, Her Captivity with the Apache Indians and Her Later Life." OUT WEST, 19 Sept 1908, 216-26. Indians. Biog.

HALL, Thomas B. Ed. Lester, Thomas B. MEDICINE ON THE SANTA FE TRAIL.

HALL, Thomas W. RECOLLECTIONS OF A GRANDFATHER. N.p., n.d. CAL(Indep)-TRUCKEE. IV. Rem. 1849.

HALLOCK, Charles. "Red River Trail." HARPER'S MONTHLY 18(Apr 1859): 602-20. DAKOTAS-Genl.

HAM, Edward B. Ed. Myer, Nathaniel. "Journey into Southern Oregon."

HAMBLETON, Chalkley J. A GOLD HUNTER'S EXPERIENCE. Chicago: Private, 1898. Freight(St. Jo-Denver). IV. Rem. 1860.

HAMBLIN, Jacob. JACOB HAMBLIN.... SLC: Juvenile Instructor, 1881. Utah.

HAMELIN, Joseph P. Diary. BYU. CAL(St. Jo)-BRIDGER-SLCOR. II +. 1849.

HAMILTON, Allen Lee. SENTINEL OF THE SOUTHERN PLAINS: FORT RICHARDSON AND THE NORTHWEST TEXAS FRONTIER, 1866-1878. Chisholm Trail Series, No. 5. Ft. Worth: Texas Christian Univ. Press, 1987. Geog. TEX-Genl.

HAMILTON, Ezra M. Reminiscences. CSL. OR(Council)-BARLOW. Rem. 1853. Not Seen.

HAMILTON, Henry S. REMINISCENCES.... Concord, NH: Republican, 1897. CAL(Ft. Leav)-BRIDGER-Ends SLC. IV. Rem. No date. Military.

HAMILTON, James G. MY DEAR CORNELIA.... Ed. Katherine J. Moore. Fresno: Moore, 1950. CAL(Westport)-SANTA FE-RIO GRANDE-GILA. Stock drive. IV. 1857.

HAMILTON, Sarah J. A PIONEER OF FIFTY-THREE. Albany, OR: Herald, 1905. Not Seen.

HAMILTON, William T. "A Trading Expedition among the Indians in 1858...." CONTRIBUTIONS Historical Society of Montana 3(1900): N.p. MONTANA-1858-Genl. Rem.

HAMLIN, Herbert. Ed. Knott, Thomas. "The Knott Journals." Ed. Wixom, William W. "Dr. Wixom's Journal."

_____. "Gerald Kane, Nevada's Pony Express Man." PONY EXPRESS 16(Sept 1949): 9-10. Pony.

_____. "Reminiscences of Abner Blackburn." PONY EXPRESS 15(Jul, Aug, Sept, Nov 1948, Mar 1949): 3-6, 14, 8-9, 11, 7-10, 8, 13, 8-9. CAL(SLC)-SLCUT-TRUCKEE. IV. Rem. 1847. CAL(SLC)-East to Missouri. III. Rem. 1848. CAL(SLC)-SLCUT. III. Rem. 1849. CAL(SLC)-SLCUT. IV. 1850.

_____. "Westward Ho Goes the Telegraph in 1861." PONY EXPRESS 12(Oct 1944): 3-8. Telegraph.

HAMMA, Elizabeth. SEE: Hunter, Vickie. STAGECOACH DAYS.

HAMMER, Jacob. Journal. NBHIST. OR(Council). 1844. Not Seen.

HAMMON, C. J. Diary. Attributed to HUNTL but not in catalog.

HAMMOND, Andy. "Peter Lassen and his Trail." OVERLAND JOURNAL 4(Win 1986): 33-41. LASSEN-Genl.

HAMMOND, Francis A. "In Early Days. My Introduction to Mormonism." JUVENILE INSTRUCTOR 29(1894): 517-21. CAL(Sacramento)-SLCUT. V. Rem. 1848.

HAMMOND, George P. Ed. Coit, Daniel W. DIGGING FOR GOLD. Ed. Eccleston, Robert. OVERLAND TO CALIFORNIA.

HAMMOND, James. Story of Trip. BANCROFT. CAL(Indep)-SLCUT. V. Rem. 1852.

HAMMOND, John. IN MEMORIAL. Chicago: Pettibone, 1890. CAL(Ft. Smith)-MARCY-RIO GRANDE-GILA. V. 1849.

HAMMOND, John B. Journal. CSL. CAL(Ft. Smith)-OKLAHOMA-Ends Gainesville, TX. III. 1852.

HAMMOND, Otis G. Ed. Gove, Jesse A. THE UTAH EXPEDITION, 1857 - 1858.

HAMPTON, John J. SEE: Robertson, Fay H. "John Jacob Hampton."

HAMPTON, William H. DIARY.... Sacramento: California Dept. of Natural Resources, History Section, 1958. CAL(St. Jo). III. 1852.

HANCOCK, Samuel. THE NARRATIVE OF SAMUEL HANCOCK, 1845 - 1860. Vol. 1. The Argonaut Series, Ed. Arthur D. H. Smith. NY: Robert M. McBride, 1927. OR(Indep). III. Rem. 1845.

HANDLEY, Walter. Diary. KSHIST. TEX(Austin)-OKLAHOMA(to Ft. Smith)-Ends Chillecothe, MO. II. 1866.

HANDSAKER, Sarah J. "Coming to Oregon." In PIONEER LIFE, ed. Samuel Handsaker. Eugene, OR: Author, 1908. OR(Council). V. Rem. 1854.

HANDSAKER, Samuel. Autobiography.... HUNTL. OR(Council-BRIDGER-SLCUT-BARLOW. III+. Rem. 1853.

HANDSAKER, "Uncle Sam." PIONEER LIFE. Eugene, OR: Author, 1908. OR(Council)-BRIDGER-Ends SLC. III. 1853.

HANDY, W. J. "The First Mail Route in California." OUT WEST 25(Aug 1906): 174-77. Mail.

_____. "The First Mail Route in California and Dana's Ranch." OVERLAND MONTHLY 62(Aug 1913): 181-89. Mail.

HANLEY, Mike, and Omer Stanford. SAGE BRUSH AND AXLE GREASE. Jordan Valley, OR: Author, 1976. Freight. Graphics.

HANNA, Archibald, Jr. "Manuscript Resources in the Yale University Library for the Study of Western Travel." In TRAVELERS ON THE WESTERN FRONTIER, ed. John F. McDermott. Urbana: Univ. of Illinois Press, 1970. Bib.

_____. "Shreds from Henry Wagner's Mantle." AMERICAN WEST 1(Win 1974): 59-64. Bib.

HANNA, Esther B. CANVAS CARAVANS. Ed. Eleanor Allen. Portland: Binfords & Mort, 1946. OR(St. Jo)-BARLOW. III. 1852.

HANNA, Jennie E. Diary. ORU. OR(Council)-BARLOW. IV. 1866.

HANNA, William. Diary. ORHIST. CAL(St. Jo). III. 1850.

HANNANT, Owen. Ed. Daigh, James M. NUGGETS FROM '49.

HANNON, Jessie G., ed. THE BOSTON-NEWTON COMPANY VENTURE.... Lincoln: Univ. of Nebraska Press, 1969. CAL(Indep)-BRIDGER-SLCUT. II. 1849.

HANNUM, Anna P. Ed. Pancoast, Charles E. QUAKER FORTY-NINER.

HANSEN, Barbara J. "Wagon Train Governments." MA thesis, Univ. of Colorado, 1962. Train Govt.

HANSEN, George W. "A Tragedy of the Oregon Trail." COLLECTIONS Nebraska State Historical Society 17(1913): 110-26. Geog-Fairbury, NB.

HANSEN, H. N. "An Account of a Mormon Family's...Trip from Denmark to Utah." ANNALS OF IOWA 41(Sum, Fall 1971): 709-28, 765-79. MORMON. V. 1863.

HANSEN, Ralph. SEE: Jones, Ruth M., et al. "Utah, the Mormons, and the West."

HANSON, Charles, Jr. "Red River and other Carts." MUSEUM OF THE FUR TRADE QUARTERLY 19(Fall 1983): 1-12. Eqpt. Graphics.

HANSON, D. M. RECOLLECTIONS.... N.p., n.d. CAL. 1849. Not Seen.

HANSON, George M. "Old Time Reminiscences." Illinois State Historical Library, Springfield, IL. CAL(St. Jo)-LASSEN. V. Rem. 1849.

HANSON, J. M. THE TRAIL TO ELDORADO. N.p., n.d. MONTANA.

HANSON, N. E. Recollections. CSL. CAL(Council)-LASSEN. V. Rem. 1849.

HANSON, James A. "A Forgotten Fur Trade Trail." NEBRASKA HISTORY 68(Spr 1987): 2-9. DAKOTA(Ft. Laramie - Ft. Pierre)-Genl.

HANSON, Robert A. "The Butterfield Overland Mail Route." WESTERN EXPRESS 19(Jan 1969): 4-7. Stage. Graphics.

_____. "Notes on the Trail of the Pony Express." WESTERN EXPRESS 17(Jan 1967): 5-8. Pres. Map.

HARBERT, Joseph W. THE HARBERT DIARY. Ed. Lorraine H. Albright. N.p.: Private, 1983. OR(Council)-LANDER. III. 1859.

HARDEMAN, Nicholas P. WILDERNESS CALLING.... Knoxville: Univ. of Tennessee Press, 1977. OR-1843-Genl.

HARDEN, Absolom B. Trail Diary. ORHIST. OR(St. Jo)-BARLOW. II. 1847.

HARDESTY, Donald L. "The Archaeology of the Donner Party Tragedy." NEVADA HISTORICAL SOCIETY QUARTERLY 30(Win 1987): 246-68. CAL-1846-Genl.

_____. HISTORICAL AND ARCHEOLOGICAL INVESTIGATIONS OF THE ROCK CREEK STAGE AND TELEGRAPH STATIONS. Carson City, NV: U.S.BLM, 1978. Pres. Geog.

_____. THE PONY EXPRESS IN CENTRAL NEVADA: ARCHAEOLOGICAL AND DOCUMENTARY PERSPECTIVES. Cultural Resource Series No. 1. Reno: U.S.BLM, 1979. Pony.

HARDIN, Martin D. "Up the Missouri and Over the Mullan Road." Ed. John E. Parsons. NEW YORK WESTERNERS BRAND BOOK 5, nos. 1 & 2(1958): 1, 3-5, 17-18, 29-31, 34-38. MULLAN. II. 1860.

HARDIN, Robert S. Diary. Stanford Univ. Library-SpCol, Palo Alto, CA. CAL-TEX(Brownsville)-MEX(Monterey-Parras-Durango-Mazatlan). II+. 1849.

HARDING, Stephen S. Collection. LILLEY. SLCOR-1862-Genl.

_____. Letters. Indiana State Library-Ms, Indianapolis, IN. Stage(Atchison-SLC). IV. 1862.

HARDY, Clyde B. "The Historical Development of Wasatch Trails in Salt Lake County." MA thesis, Brigham Young Univ., 1975. Pres.

HARDY, Francis A. Journal. BEINECKE. CAL(Weston). II+. Rem. 1850.

HARDY, Wilabour. "A Historical Bibliography of Kansas." MS thesis, Hays State Univ., 1931. Not Seen.

HARDY, William H. Biography. Arizona State Library, Phoenix, AZ Freight(Hardyville-Prescott).

HARGETT, Janet. "Louis John Frederick Jaeger: Entrepreneur at Yuma Crossing." MA thesis, Univ. of Arizona, 1967. Geog.

_____. "Pioneering at Yuma Crossing: The Business Career of L. J. F. Jaeger, 1850-1887." ARIZONA & THE WEST 25(Win 1983): 329-54. Geog.

HARKER, George M. "Morgan Street to Old Dry Diggings, 1849." GLIMPSES OF THE PAST 6(Apr-Jun 1939): 35-76. CAL(Indep)-HALL. IV. 1849.

HARKNESS, James. "Diary of James Harkness, of the Firm of LaBarge, Harkness and Company." CONTRIBUTIONS Historical Society of Montana 2(1896): 343-61. MONTANA. III. 1862.

HARLAN, A. W. "Journal of...." ANNALS OF IOWA 11(Apr 1913): 32-62. CAL(Council)-HALL. II. 1850.

HARLAN, Anna L. "The Fort Smith - Santa Fe Trail." MA thesis, Univ. of Southern California, 1933. MARCY-Genl.

HARLAN, Charles T. Letters. BANCROFT. CAL(Indep). IV. 1849.

HARLAN, Edgar R., ed. "First Mormon Handcart Trip across Iowa." ANNALS OF IOWA 26(Oct 1936): 444-49. MORMON(Iowa only). III. Rem. 1856.

_____. THE LOCATION AND NAME OF THE MORMON TRAIL. Knoxville, TN: Express, 1914. MORMON(Iowa only)-Genl. Map.

HARLAN, Gilbert D. Ed. Harlan, Wilson B. "Walk with a Wagon Train."

HARLAN, Jacob W. CALIFORNIA '46 TO '88. Oakland: Author, 1896. CAL-1846-Genl.

HARLAN, Wilson B. "A Walk with a Wagon Train: A Teen-Age Civil War Veteran Strolls into the West." Ed. Wilson B. Harlan. JOURNAL OF THE WEST 3, no. 2(1964): 141-62. DAKOTAS(St. Cloud)-MONTANA. III. 1866.

HARLOW, Alvin F. OLD POST BAGS. NY: Appleton - Century, 1928. Mail.

_____. OLD WAYBILLS: THE ROMANCE OF THE EXPRESS COMPANIES. NY: Appleton - Century, 1934. Stage.

_____. OLD WIRES AND NEW WAVES.... NY: Appleton - Century, 1936. Excellent bibliography. Telegraph.

HARMON, Appleton M. APPLETON MILO HARMON GOES WEST. Ed. Maybelle H. Anderson. Berkeley: Gillick, 1946. MORMON. I. 1847. MORMON. V. 1852.

HARPER, Charles A. Diary. UTHIST. MORMON. III+. 1847.

HARPER, J. Russell. WILLIAM G. R. HIND, 1833-1889. Ottawa: National Gallery, 1976. CANADA-Graphics.

_____. "William Hind and the Overlanders." BEAVER, Outfit 302, Winter 1971, 4-15. CANADA-1861-Genl.

HARRIS, Benjamin B. THE GILA TRAIL: THE TEXAS ARGONAUTS AND THE CALIFORNIA GOLD RUSH. Ed. Richard H. Dillon. Norman: Univ. of Oklahoma Press, 1960. CAL(East Texas)-TEX-GILA. II+. 1849.

HARRIS, Charles W. "Pathway to the Southwest: Transportation and Communication along the Gila Trail." PhD diss., Oklahoma State Univ., 1973. GILA-Genl. Stage. Stock.

HARRIS, Earl R. "Courthouse and Jail Rocks...." NEBRASKA HISTORY 43(Mar 1962): 29-51. Geog.

HARRIS, Everett W. Ed. Yager, James. "Journals."

_____. "The Early Emigrant Pass between Mt. Judah and Mt. Lincoln." NEVADA HISTORICAL SOCIETY QUARTERLY 22(Spring 1979): 33-39. Geog(Donner Pass).

HARRIS, Howell. SEE: Dempsey, Hugh A. "Howell Harris."

HARRIS, Lewis B. SEE: Hunt, Aurora. "Overland by Boat."

_____. "Up from San Antonio." Ed. Wilmer B. Shields. SAN DIEGO HISTORICAL SOCIETY QUARTERLY 9(Jan 1963): 1-6. CAL-TEX(San Antonio)-GILA. IV. 1849.

HARRIS, Mary. "John Rowland and William Workman...." MA thesis, Univ. of California-Berkeley, 1932. SPANISH-1841-Genl.

HARRIS, Mary E. SEE: Gardner, Mercedes P. STORY OF.

HARRIS, Robert D., and Diane DeBlois. CONGRESS AND THE TELEGRAPH: A GUIDE TO DOCUMENTS IN THE CONGRESSIONAL SERIES PERTAINING TO THE TELEGRAPH, 1837 - 1902. Wynantskill, NY: A Gatherin', 1980? Bib.

HARRIS, Sarah H. AN UNWRITTEN CHAPTER OF SALT LAKE. NY: Private, 1901. MORMON. IV. 1851.

HARRISON, J. M. Account - 1846. ORHIST. OR(St. Jo). IV. Rem. 1846.

HARRISON, Paul D. "Toll Roads in Colorado." DENVER WESTERNERS BRAND BOOK 18(1963): 309-30. PIKES-Genl.

HARRITT, Jesse. "Diary of...." TRANSACTIONS Oregon Pioneer Association 1910 (1914): N.p. OR(Westport?). III. 1846.

HARSTAD, Peter T. "Constructing the Lander Trail." ORU. 1966. LANDER-Genl.

_____. "The Lander Trail." IDAHO YESTERDAYS 12(Fall 1968): 14-28. LANDER-Genl.

_____. "Use of the Lander Trail...." UTHIST. 1866. LANDER-Genl.

HART, Herbert M. TOUR GUIDE TO OLD WESTERN FORTS. Boulder, CO: Pruett, 1980. Good survey and bibliography.

HART, Newell. "Rescue of a Frontier Boy." UTAH HISTORICAL

QUARTERLY 33(Win 1965): 51-54. Indians.

HART, Robert. "Diary of a Journey by way of Santa Fe and the Gila to the California Gold Fields and Return, 1849-1850." Held by Mrs. H. L. Donovan. Lexington, KY. CAL-SANTA FE-RIO GRANDE-GILA. 1849. Not Seen.

HARTER, George. CROSSING THE PLAINS. Ed. Doris H. Chase. Sacramento: Private, 1957. CAL(Council)-BRIDGER-SIMPSON-TRUCKEE. III. Rem. 1864.

HARTLEY, William. MAP AND DESCRIPTION OF THE GOLD REGIONS IN WESTERN KANSAS AND NEBRASKA.... St. Louis: Author, 1859. Guide.

HARTLEY, William G. "'Down and Back' Wagon Trains: Bringing the Saints to Utah in 1861." ENSIGN 15(Sept 1985): 26-31. MORMON-1861-Genl.

HARTMAN, Amos W. "The California and Oregon Trail, 1849-1860." OREGON HISTORICAL QUARTERLY 25(Mar 1924): 1-35. Overland-Genl.
Revision of MA thesis, Univ. of Iowa, 1924.

HARTWELL, William H. "Two Years of Ranch Life on the Santa Fe Road, 1865-1867." CORRAL DUST 9(Spr 1964): 4-8. SANTA FE-Genl. Indians.

HARVEY, August F. "A New Map of the Principal Routes to the Gold Regions of Colorado Territory (1862)." NBHIST. Maps.

_____. SKETCHES OF THE EARLY DAYS OF NEBRASKA CITY...1854-1860. St. Louis: Western Insurance Review, 1871. Geog.

HARVEY, Isaac J. To California. BANCROFT. OR(St. Jo). IV. Rem. 1850.

HARVEY, R. E. "The Mormon Trek across Iowa Territory." ANNALS OF IOWA 10(July 1946): 36-60. MORMON-Genl.

HARVEY, Robert S. THE OREGON TRAIL: MONUMENTS AND MARKERS IN NEBRASKA...1917 TO 1923. Lincoln: Nebraska State Historical Society, 1940. Pres.

_____. Papers. NBHIST. Overland-Genl.

HASKELL, W. S. Pilgrimage. MONHIST. CAL(Leav)-BOZE. III+. 1864.

HASKETT, Bert. "Early History of the Cattle Industry in Arizona." ARIZONA HISTORICAL REVIEW 6(Oct 1935): 3-42. Stock.

HASSE, Adelaide, comp. REPORTS OF EXPLORATIONS PRINTED IN THE DOCUMENTS OF THE U.S. GOVERNMENT. Burt Franklin Bibliography and Reference Series 284. 1899. Reprint. NY: Burt Franklin, 1969. Bib.

HASSLER, John B. Ed. Wonderly, Pauline. REMINISCENCES.

HASTIE, Thomas P. Notes. Washington State Univ. Library-SpCol, Pullman, WA. OR(Council). V. 1850?

HASTINGS, Lansford W. THE EMIGRANT'S GUIDE TO OREGON AND CALIFORNIA.... Narratives of the Trans-Mississippi Frontier, Carl L. Cannon, Genl. Ed. Princeton: Princeton Univ. Press, 1932. OR(Indep). II. 1842. Eqpt. Guide.

_____. A NEW DESCRIPTION OF OREGON AND CALIFOR-NIA.... Cincinatti: H. M. Rulison, 1857. OR(Indep). II. 1842. Guide.

HASTINGS, Loren B. "Diary of...." TRANSACTIONS Oregon Pioneer Association (1926): N.p. OR(St. Jo). III. 1847.

HATCH, Alden. AMERICAN EXPRESS COMPANY: A CENTURY OF SERVICE. NY: Doubleday, 1950. Stage.

HAUCK, Louise P. "The Pony Express Celebration." MISSOURI HISTORICAL REVIEW 17(Jul 1923): 435-39. Pres.

HAUGEN, Einar I. Trans. Stabaek, Tosten. "An Account."

HAUN, Catherine M. "A Woman's Trip." In WOMEN'S DIARIES, ed. Lillian Schlissel. NY: Schocken, 1982. CAL(Council)-BRIDGER-SLCUT-LASSEN. II. Rem. 1849.

HAUSER, John. Reminiscence. Eastern Washington Historical Society Library, Spokane, WA. Freight(St. Jo-SLC). IV. Rem. 1854. CAL(SLC)-SLCUT. IV. Rem. 1855.

HAUSER, Samuel T. Three Letters. BEINECKE. MONTANA(Ft. Benton-Deer Lodge). III. 1862.

HAWK, Al R. "Strange Adventures." (In) TOLD BY THE PIONEERS, Vol. 1. Washington Pioneer Project, 1937. OR(Council). Rem. 1852. Not Seen.

HAWK, Sarah A. "Excerpts from a Diary of the 1845 Trek...." OR. 1845. Not Seen.

HAWKEN, Edward J. "The Military Problem on the Powder River Road, 1865-1868." MA thesis, Univ. of California-Berkeley, 1938. BOZE-Genl.

HAWKINS, Albert. "Centennial of the Covered Wagon." OREGON HISTORICAL QUARTERLY 31(Jun 1930): 115-24. Pres.

HAWKINS, C. W., and G. W. Starkey. "Old Trails across Chase County." CHASE COUNTY [Kansas] HISTORICAL SKETCHES 1(1940): 15. Pres.

HAWKINS, Ora B. "Historic Trails of Idaho." 18th BIENNIAL REPORT, IDAHO STATE HISTORICAL SOCIETY. Boise, ID: SPO?, n.d. 39-84. OR-Genl.

HAWKINS, T. S. SOME RECOLLECTIONS OF A BUSY LIFE. NY: Author, 1913. CAL(West Point)-BRIDGER-SLCUT. IV. Rem. 1860.

HAWKINS, Theodore. "History of the Hawkins Family." NVHIST. MORMON. V. Rem. 1851. CAL(SLC)-SLCUT. V. Rem. 1856.

HAWKS, Jabez D. Diary. Society of California Pioneers, San Francisco, CA. Not Seen.

HAWKS, James D. "A 'Forty-Niner' in Baja California." SAN DIEGO WESTERNERS BRAND BOOK 2(1971): 158-71. CAL-MEX(San Jose to San Diego). II. 1849.

HAWLEY, H. J. "Hawley's Diary of His Trip across the Plains in 1860." Ed. Lynn I. Perrigo. WISCONSIN MAGAZINE OF HISTORY 19(Mar 1936): 319-42. PIKES. III. 1860.

HAWLEY, Nirom. SEE: Clark, Wanda. "Nirom Hawley."

HAWTHORNE, Hildegarde. OX-TEAM MIRACLE: THE STORY OF ALEXANDER MAJORS. NY: Longmans, Green, 1942. Biog(Fictionalized).

HAYDEN, Charles W. Diary. ORU. OR(Council). IV. 1852.

HAYDEN, Jacob S. Diary. West Virginia State Archives, Charleston, WV. Also attributed to Library of Congress but not cited in catalog.

CAL(Indep)-TRUCKEE. 1852. Not Seen.

HAYDEN, Mary J. PIONEER DAYS. 1915. Reprint. Fairfield, WA: Ye Galleon, 1979. OR(Council). V. Rem. 1850.

HAYDEN, Rosa B. "Memoirs of Early California Days." SISKIYOU PIONEER 1(Aug 1948): 13-16. LASSEN(Goose Lake-Yreka). IV. Rem. 1859.

HAYES, Benjamin I. PIONEER NOTES FROM THE DIARIES OF JUDGE B. I. HAYES, 1849-1875. Ed. Marjorie T. Wolcott. LA: Private, 1929. CAL(Indep)-SANTA FE-RIO GRANDE-GILA. II. 1849.

_____. "Notes on Overland Journeys of the Gruwell Family, H. Stickney and Mr. Shearer, 1849." BANCROFT. CAL-HASTINGS-LASSEN. V. 1849. SLCOR. II. 1849.

HAYES, Charles W. Ed. Hayes, George. A MEMORIAL.

HAYES, George E. A MEMORIAL. Ed. Charles W. Hayes. Buffalo, NY: Hayes, 1882. CAL(Ft. Kearny)-LASSEN. IV. Rem. 1849.

HAYES, Susan E. Crossing the Plains. Washington State Univ. Library-SpCol, Pullman, WA. Poem.

HAYES, W. R. Diary. BANCROFT. Freight-SLCOR. III+. 1855. Good description of southern Utah.

HAYHURST, W. T. "The Camels in British Columbia." OKANAGAN [Wa] HISTORICAL SOCIETY 6th Report (1935): 244-51. Teams.

HAYNES, Asa. "Diary." In JAYHAWKERS OF DEATH VALLEY, ed. John G. Ellenbecker. Marysville, KS: Private, 1938. CAL(Council)-BRIDGER-SLCOR. V. 1849.

HAYS, Arthur H. Ed. Snow, Taylor N. "Diary."

HAYS, Grover L. Papers. DENVERPUB. Military. Contains three passes issued to wagon trains during Civil War.

HAYS, Jacob O. Lexington, MO to Sacramento, CA. UWY. CAL(Indep?)-TRUCKEE. III. 1854.

HAYS, Lorena L. "To the Land of Gold and Wickedness...." Ed. Jeanne H. Watson. BANCROFT. CAL(Kansas City)-BRIDGER-SLCUT. 1853. Not Seen.

HAYWOOD, C. Robert. TRAILS SOUTH: THE WAGON-ROAD ECONOMY IN THE DODGE CITY-PANHANDLE REGION. Norman: Univ. of Oklahoma Press, 1986. Freight.

HAYWOOD, Lucy M. "The Great Central Route to the Gold Fields commonly known as the Nebraska City Cut-off." In FOUNDERS AND PATRIOTS OF NEBRASKA. Omaha: Nebraska Chapter, Daughters of the Founders and Patriots, 1935. Geog.

HAZARD, Henry T. Across the Plains. BANCROFT. MORMON. V. Rem. 1852.

HAZEN, Eli W. "The California Column in the Civil War...." Ed. Konrad F. Schreier, Jr. JOURNAL OF SAN DIEGO HISTORY 22(Spr 1976): 31-48. GILA(San Pedro-Yuma-Tucson-Mesilla). III. 1861.

HAZLETT, William C. THE GREAT GOLD FIELDS OF CARIBOO. London: Routledge, Warne, and Routledge, 1862. Guide.

HEADLEY, Ezekiel W. Diary. BYU. CAL(St. Jo)-Ends Bear River. III. 1849.

HEADLEY, John W. SEE: With Richard E. Fike. PONY EXPRESS STATIONS OF UTAH.

HEALD, Samuel. Diary. Society of California Pioneers, San Francisco, CA. CAL. 1851. Not Seen.

HEAP, Gwinn H. CENTRAL ROUTE TO THE PACIFIC.... Philadelphia: Lippincott, Grambo, 1854. CAL(Westport)-SANTA FE-SPANISH-SLCOR. II+. 1853. A possible fake.

HEARD, J. Norman. WHITE INTO RED: A STUDY OF THE ASSIMILATION OF WHITE PERSONS CAPTURED BY INDIANS. Metuchen, NY: Scarecrow, 1973. Indians.

HEARST, George. "Grandpa Hearst Strikes it Rich." Ed. William R. Hearst, Jr. San Francisco SUNDAY EXAMINER, 28 August 1966, N.d. CAL(Indep). V-. Rem. 1850.

HEASTON, Michael D. Ed. Thomason, Jackson. FROM MISSISSIPPI TO CALIFORNIA.

_____. TRAILS OF KANSAS: A BIBLIOGRAPHY. Dodge City, KS: Cultural Heritage and Arts Center, 1969. Bib.

HEATH, Minnie B. "Nancy Kelsey - The First Pioneer Woman to Cross the Plains." GRIZZLY BEAR 40(Feb 1937): 3, 7. CAL-1841-Genl. Biog.

HEATON, P. S. "The Old Lone Tree." NEBRASKA HISTORY 31(Jun 1950): 147-52. Geog-Central City, NB.

HEBARD, Grace R. THE MARKING OF TRAILS AND HISTORIC PLACES BY THE OREGON TRAIL COMMISSION OF WYOMING. N.p.: Daughters of the American Revolution, 1920? Pres.

_____. THE PATHBREAKERS FROM RIVER TO OCEAN. Glendale: Clark, 1933. Overland-Genl.

_____. WASHAKIE: AN ACCOUNT OF INDIAN RESISTANCE.... Glendale: Clark, 1930. Indians.

_____, and E. A. Brininstool. THE BOZEMAN TRAIL. 2 vols. Cleveland: Clark, 1922. BOZE-Genl. Indians.

HECKMAN, Marlin L. OVERLAND ON THE CALIFORNIA TRAIL, 1846-1859. Glendale: Clark, 1984. Bib.

HECOX, Adna A. "Biographical Sketch of...." Clarke Library, Central Michigan University, Mt. Pleasant, MI. CAL(St. Jo)-TRUCKEE. Rem. 1846. Not Seen.

HECOX, Margaret M. CALIFORNIA CARAVAN. Ed. Richard Dillon. San Jose, CA: Harlan-Young, 1966. CAL(St. Jo)-BRIDGER-HALL-TRUCKEE. IV. Rem. 1846.

HEDGES, Cornelius. Diaries. MONHIST. CAL(Council)-BOZE. II. 1864.

HEDGES, William H. PIKE'S PEAK...OR BUSTED! Ed. Herbert O. Thayer. PIKES. IV. Rem. 1860.

HEDGPETH, Joel. A Trip Across.... UPAC. CAL(St. Jo)-SANTA FE-BEALE. III. Rem. 1858.

HEDREN, Paul L., and Carroll Friswold. THE MASSACRE OF LT. GRATTAN AND HIS COMMAND BY INDIANS. Glendale: Clark, 1983. Indians. Military. Not Seen.

HEFFERNAN, William J. EDWARD KERN: THE TRAVELS OF AN ARTIST-EXPLORER. 15th Annual Publication of the Kern County Historical Society. Bakersfield: The Society, 1953. Biog.

HEGEL, Richard. CARRIAGES FROM NEW HAVEN: NEW HAVEN'S 19TH CENTURY CARRIAGE INDUSTRY. Hamden, CN: Archon, 1974. Eqpt.

HEGER, Joseph. Portfolio...Sketches. BEINECKE. Graphics(Camp Floyd to San Luis Valley).

HEIKELL, Iris W. THE WINDBREAKER - GEORGE WASHINGTON BUSH: BLACK PIONEER OF THE NORTHWEST. NY: Private, 1980. Biog.

HEIN, Erwin. "Chico Carried the Mail." WESTWAYS 30(Aug 1938): 20-21. Mail(San Diego - Yuma).

HELFRICH, Devere. "The Applegate Trail." KLAMATH ECHOES no. 9(1971): 1-106. Fine maps. APPLE-Genl.

_____. "Trail, Road and Transportation History of Butte Valley." SISKIYOU PIONEER 2, no. 9(1957): 1-7. Geog.

_____, Helen Helfrich, and Thomas Hunt. EMIGRANT TRAILS WEST: A GUIDE TO TRAIL MARKERS PLACED BY TRAILS WEST, INC. ALONG THE CALIFORNIA, APPLEGATE, LASSEN, AND NOBLES' EMIGRANT TRAILS IN IDAHO, NEVADA, AND CALIFORNIA. Klamath Falls, OR: Trails West, 1984. The standard reference work for retracing these individual trails. Pres. Maps.

HELMAN, Abel D. Papers. ORU. OR. 1853. Not Seen.

HELMICK, Sarah. "Recollections...." OREGON HISTORICAL QUARTERLY 26(Dec 1925): 444-47. OR(Council). V-. Rem. 1845.

HELVEY, Frank. "Ranches and Stations on the Oregon Trail." In PIONEER TALES OF THE OREGON TRAIL.... Ed. Charles Dawson. Topeka: Crane, 1912. OR-Genl.

HEMBREE, Joel. SEE: Duffin, Reg P. "The Grave of Joel Hembree."

HEMEY, John B. Diary. ORHIST. CAL(Council)-BRIDGER-SIMPSON-Ends Moore's Station. IV. 1864.

HENDERSON, A. B. Journal of the Yellowstone Expedition of 1866 under Captain Jeff Standifer. BEINECKE. MONTANA-1866-Genl.

HENDERSON, Lucy A. "Young Adventure." Ed. Ronald T. Strong. NEVADA HISTORICAL SOCIETY QUARTERLY 16(Sum 1973): 67-99. OR(St. Jo)-APPLE. II. Rem. 1846.

HENDERSON, Paul C. SEE: With Merrill J. Mattes. "Map Collection." With Merrill J. Mattes. "The Pony Express."

_____. "Chimney Rock in History." NEW YORK WESTERNERS BRAND BOOK 1(Win 1954): 4-6. Geog.

_____. LANDMARKS ON THE OREGON TRAIL. NY: The Westerners, 1953. Pres.

_____. "The Story of Mud Springs." NEBRASKA HISTORY 32(Jun 1951): 108-19. Geog.

_____. "Wayfarers Find Rocky Ridge Still Wild, Rough and Lonely." NEW YORK WESTERNERS BRAND BOOK 3, no. 2(1956): 33-34, 45. Geog.

_____, and Helen Henderson. Collection. UWY. A windfall of unique materials for the trail historian. Overland-Genl.

HENDERSON, Randall. "Waterhole on the Old Bradshaw Trail."

DESERT 10(Jan 1947): 4-7. Bradshaw-Genl.

HENDRICKS, Gordon. "Roaming the West with Alfred Bierstadt." AMERICAN WEST 12(Jan 1975): 22-29. Graphics.

HENDRICKS, Robert J. BETHEL AND AURORA. NY: Press of the Pioneers, 1933. OR(St. Jo). II. 1855. Religious colony moving to Oregon.

HENNIGAN, R. C. Ed. Menefee, Arthur M. "Travels and Adventures."

HENRY, Anson G. Journal. Illinois State Historical Library, Springfield, IL. OR(Indep). III. 1852.

HENRY, David. Reminiscences. Norlin Library-SpCol, Univ. of Colorado-Boulder. OR(Council)-MEEK. V. Rem. 1853. CAL(Council)-LASSEN. V. Rem. 1859.

HENTZ, Charles. Letters. BANCROFT. CAL(St. Jo)-LASSEN. V. 1849.

HEPNER, Simon. "Hardships on the Oregon Trail." Senior Paper, Mount Angel [Oregon] Seminary College, 1975. ORHIST. OR-Genl.

HERMANN, William H. Ed. Welch, Adonijah S. "Document."

HERNDON, Paul C. "Ten Days to San Francisco! The Story of the Pony Express." OUR PUBLIC LANDS 26(Sum 1976): 12-19. Pony.

HERNDON, Sarah R. DAYS ON THE ROAD. NY: Burr, 1902. CAL(Neb. City)-HALL-MONTANA. IV. Rem. 1865.

HERR, Henry R. Extracts from Diary. ORHIST. OR(St. Jo). III. 1862.

HERREN, John. A Diary of 1845. ORHIST. OR(Begins Boise)-MEEK. III. 1845.

HERTZ, A. Jay. "Expresses of the Fraser River and other Gold Fields of British Columbia." WESTERN EXPRESS 7(Apr 1957): 9-14. Stage.

_____. "A Group of very Early California Expresses." WESTERN EXPRESS 14(Oct 1964): 20-34. Stage.

_____. "Via Placerville - and Before." AMERICAN PHILATELIST, March 1951, 449-51. Mail.

HERTZOG, Carl. SOME SOUTHWESTERN TRAILS. El Paso: Author, 1948. Overland-Genl.

HESLEP, Augustus M. "Diary." In SOUTHERN TRAILS TO CALIFORNIA IN 1849, ed. Ralph P. Bieber. Southwest Historical Series, No. 5. Glendale: Clark, 1937. CAL(Indep)-SANTA FE-RIO GRANDE-GILA. II. 1849.

HESS, John W. "John W. Hess, with the Mormon Battalion." Ed. Wanda Wood. UTAH HISTORICAL QUARTERLY 4(Apr 1931): 47-55. SANTA FE. V-. 1846. CHEROKEE(Bent's Fort - SLC). V-. 1847.

HESTER, Sallie. "Diary." In COVERED WAGON WOMEN, vol. 1, ed. Kenneth L. Holmes. Glendale: Clark, 1983. CAL(St. Jo)-TRUCKEE. IV. 1849.

HEWITT, Henry L. "Diary." WASHINGTON HISTORICAL QUARTERLY 24(1933): 135-46. CAL(St. Jo)-BRIDGER-SLCUT-Ends near Wells, NV. III. 1850.

HEWITT, James, ed. EYE-WITNESSES TO WAGON TRAINS WEST. NY: Scribner, c.1973. Overland-Genl.

HEWITT, Randall H. ACROSS THE PLAINS.... 1906. Reprint. NY: Argosy-Antiquarian, 1964. OR(Council)-MONTANA-MULLAN. II. 1862.

HEWITT, Rosetta W. "Joseph L. Meek." WASHINGTON HISTORICAL QUARTERLY 20(Jul 1929): 196-200. Biog.

HEWLETT, Edward S. "The Chilcotin Uprising of 1864." BRITISH COLUMBIA STUDIES, no. 19(Aut 1973): 50-72. 1864 indian attack on trail workmen from Bute Inlet to Fraser River.

HEYWOOD, Martha S. NOT BY BREAD ALONE: THE JOURNAL OF MARTHA SPENCE HEYWOOD. Ed. Juanita Brooks. SLC: Utah State Historical Society, 1978. MORMON. II+. 1850.

HIBBARD, Trenton. "Recollections of Crossing the Plains." MARION COUNTY HISTORY 10(1969-1971): 9-11. OR(St. Jo). V. 1847.

HIBBEN, Frank C. "The Medio Dia Massacre." SOUTHWEST REVIEW 45(Aut 1960): 318-28. 1870 Apache attack on Raton freight caravan. Told from indian point of view.

HICKMAN, Joseph. "Racing with the Indians: Experiences of a Pony Express Rider." IMPROVEMENT ERA 26(Aug 1923): 895-98. Pony.

HICKMAN, Peter L. Diary. CSL. CAL(St. Jo)-BRIDGER-SLCUT. III-. 1852.

HICKMAN, Richard O. "An Overland Journey to California in 1852." Ed. M. Catherine White. In FRONTIER OMNIBUS, ed. John W. Hakola. Missoula: Montana State Univ., 1962. CAL(Indep)-TRUCKEE. III. 1852.

HICKMAN, Russell K. SEE: With Frank A. Root. "Pikes Peak Express Companies."

HICKS, Frank L., Jr. "Birth of the West's Overland Mail." AMERICAN PHILATELIST, Apr 1983, 323-26, 76. Mail.

HICKS, John E. "James Brice, Overland Mail Driver." WESTPORT HISTORICAL QUARTERLY 8(Jun 1972): 19-26. Mail. Stage.

HIEB, David L. Ed. Sponsler, A. C. "An 1850 Gold Rush Letter."

HIGGINBOTHAM, Charles. "Reminiscence." MONHIST. A 120 pp. study of Montana stage and freight lines.

HIGGINS, Catherine B. Biography. UTHIST. SANTA FE-Ends Pueblo. V. 1846. CHEROKEE(Pueblo - SLC). V. 1847.

HILDT, George H. SEE: With D. McGowan. MAP OF THE UNITED STATES....

HILGER, David. "Overland Trail." CONTRIBUTIONS Montana State Historical Society 7(1910): 257-70. DAKOTAS(St. Paul)-MONTANA.
IV. Rem. 1867.

HILL, Mrs. Almoran. Our Trip to Oregon. ORHIST. OR(Indep). IV. Rem. 1843.

HILL, Burton S. "John Bozeman and the Bozeman Trail." ANNALS OF WYOMING 36(Spr 1964): 204-33. BOZE-Genl. Biog.

HILL, Clifford C. "Wagon Roads in Colorado, 1858 - 1876." MA thesis, Univ. of Colorado-Boulder, 1946. PIKES-Genl.

HILL, David L. Ed. Griffith, Andrew J. "Hancock County."

HILL, Elizabeth F. UNDAUNTED PIONEERS.... Comps. Mary E. Stevens and Mary M. Dunn. Eugene, OR: Private, 1929. OR(Council)-BARLOW. IV. Rem. 1852.

HILL, Emma S. A DANGEROUS CROSSING AND WHAT HAPPENED ON THE OTHER SIDE. Denver: Smith-Brooks, 1914. PIKES. III+. Rem. 1864.

HILL, Hanks N. The Lost Trail. Washington State Univ. Library-SpCol, Pullman, WA. OR(Indep?)-MEEK. IV. Rem. 1853.

HILL, Jasper S. THE LETTERS OF A YOUNG MINER. Ed. Doyce B. Nunis, Jr. SF: Howell - North, 1964. CAL(St. Joe)-Ends near Cottonwood Island. IV. 1849.

HILL, Jeremiah. "Origin of the Trouble between the Yumas and Glanton...." PUBLICATIONS Southern California Historical Society 6(1903): 57-62. Indians. Geog.

HILL, John B. Hill's Narrative.... CSL. CAL(St. Jo). III. Rem. 1850.

HILL, John Birney. "Gold, A Story of the Plains...." ANNALS OF WYOMING 9(Apr-Jan 1935): 35-42. OR(Scotts Bluff)-Ends American Falls. III. Rem. 1850.

HILL, Joseph J. "Free Trapper: The Story of Old Bill Williams." TOURING TOPICS 22(Mar 1930): 18-27. Biog.

_____. THE HISTORY OF WARNER'S RANCH AND ITS ENVIRONS. LA: Private, 1927. Geog.

_____. "Spanish Expeditions and Trade Northwest from Mexico into the Great Basin." UTAH HISTORICAL QUARTERLY 3(Jan 1930): 2-23. SPANISH-Genl.

HILL, Mai L. Ed. Furniss, Kate. "From Prairie to Pacific."

HILL, Nathaniel P. "Nathaniel P. Hill Makes Second Visit to Colorado, 1865." COLORADO MAGAZINE 34(Apr 1917): 121-34. Stage: Atchison-Denver. II. 1865.

HILL, W. R. Ed. Hudson, Richard. "To the Gold Fields."

HILL, William E. THE OREGON TRAIL: YESTERDAY AND TODAY. Caldwell, ID: Caxton, 1987. Pres.

_____, and Gregory M. Franzwa. "Who Lies Here?" OVERLAND JOURNAL 3(Fall 1985): 4-11. Geog: Emigrant Spring.

HILLABOLD, Adam. Letters. BANCROFT. CAL(St. Jo). V. 1850.

HILLER, Elizabeth, and Dorothy Darneille. FOOD FOR THE OVERLAND EMIGRANT. N.p.: Josephine County Historical Society, 1962. Social.

HILLGREN, Marcella M. "The History of The Dalles, Oregon, to 1870." MA thesis, Univ. of Oregon, 1935. Geog.

HILLMAN, John W. Reminiscences. HUNT. OR(Leav). Rem. 1849. Not Seen.

HILLS, Cornelius. SEE: Huntington, Hallie H. ALL THE WAY WEST.

HILLS, Ernest. "Stagecoach Days." LA PENINSULA 1(Oct 1941): 1-3. Stage: San Mateo County, CA.

_____. "Stagecoach History in San Mateo County." LA PENINSULA 8(May 1956): 7-16. Stage.

HILLYER, Edwin. "From Waupun to Sacramento in 1849...." Ed. John O. Holzhueter. WISCONSIN MAGAZINE OF HISTORY 49(Spr 1966): 210-49. CAL(Council)-BRIDGER-SLCUT-TRUCKEE. II. 1849.

HILTON, Lynn M. Comp. Savage, Levi, Jr. JOURNAL.

HILTON, William H. SKETCHES IN THE SOUTHWEST AND MEXICO, 1858-1877. LA: Dawson's, 1963. Graphics.

HIMES, George H. SEE: Dell, Minnie R. FROM OXCART TO AIRPLANE. Ed. John, James. "Diary of James St. John."

_____. "Annual Address: An Account of Crossing the Plains in 1853, and of the First Trip by Immigrants through the Cascade Mountains, via Natchess Pass." TRANSACTIONS Oregon Pioneer Association (1908): N.p. OR(Council)-WASH. IV. Rem. 1853.

HIMES, Harvey K. "Overland in Winter." LADIES REPOSITORY 29(Apr 1869): 297-300. Stage: Walla Walla-SLC. IV. 1868.

HINCKLEY, Ted and Caryl. Eds. Berrien, Joseph W. "Overland from St. Louis."

HIND, Henry Y. NARRATIVE OF THE CANADIAN RED RIVER EXPLORING EXPEDITION OF 1857, AND OF THE AS-SINIBOINE AND SASKATCHEWAN EXPLORING EXPEDI-TION OF 1858. 2 vols. 1860. Reprint. Edmonton: Hurtig, 1971. CANADA(Toronto-Pembina-St. Paul). I. 1857. CANADA(Ft. Garry-Ft. Ellice-Lake Winnipeg). I. 1858.

_____. NORTHWEST TERRITORY. Toronto: Lovell, 1859. CANADA-Genl.

_____. PAPERS RELATIVE TO THE EXPLORATION OF THE COUNTRY BETWEEN LAKE SUPERIOR AND THE RED RIVER SETTLEMENT. London: Eyre & Spottiswoode, 1859. CANADA-Genl.

_____. REPORT ON A TOPOGRAPHICAL AND GEOLOGI-CAL EXPLORATION OF THE CANOE ROUTE BETWEEN FORT WILLIAM, LAKE SUPERIOR, AND FORT GARRY, RED RIVER; AND ALSO OF THE VALLEY OF RED RIVER, NORTH OF THE 49TH PARALLEL, DURING THE SUMMER OF 1857. Toronto: Derbishire & Desbarats, 1858. CANADA(Ft. William-Lake Superior-Ft. Garry). III. 1857.

_____. A SKETCH OF AN OVERLAND ROUTE TO BRITISH COLUMBIA. Toronto: W. C. Chewett, 1862. CANADA-Genl.

HINDE, Edmund C. JOURNAL. Ed. Jerome Peltier. Fairfield, WA: Ye Galleon, 1983. CAL(Indep). III. 1850.

HINDING, Andrea, ed. WOMEN'S HISTORY SOURCES: A GUIDE TO ARCHIVES AND MANUSCRIPT COLLECTIONS IN THE UNITED STATES. 2 vols. NY: Bowker, 1979. Bib.

HINDLEY, Richard C. "On the Trail of Butterfield." NEW MEXICO 48(May-Jun 1970): 30-39. Stage.

HINDMAN, David R. THE WAY TO MY GOLDEN WEDDING. St. Joseph, MO: American, 1908. CAL(Old Ft. Kearny). III. Rem. 1849.

HINDS, Thomas W. "Crossing the Plains." In SANTA CRUZ. Santa Cruz, CA: Private, 1963. CAL(Council?). III. 1850.

HINE, Robert V. BARTLETT'S WEST: DRAWING THE MEXICAN BOUNDARY. New Haven: Yale Univ. Press, 1968. GILA-Genl. Graphics.

_____. EDWARD KERN AND AMERICAN EXPANSION. New Haven: Yale Univ. Press, 1962. Biog. Govt.

HINES, Celinda E. "Diary of...." TRANSACTIONS Oregon Pioneer Association (1921): 69-125. OR(Westport?). II. 1853.

HINES, Harvey K. "In an Emigrant Wagon." PACIFIC CHRISTIAN ADVOCATE, 19 Feb 1885, 2. Not Seen.

HINKLE, George and Bliss. SIERRA NEVADA LAKES. In-dianapolis: Bobbs, Merrill, 1949. Geog.

HINMAN, Charles G. A PRETTY FAIR VIEW OF THE ELIPHENT.... Chicago: Everett D. Graff, 1960. CAL(St. Jo)-SLCUT-LASSEN. III. 1849.

HINTON, Harwood. "Arizona Theses and Dissertations: A Preliminary Checklist." ARIZONA & THE WEST 7(Aut 1965): 239-64. Bib.

HINTON, Richard J. SEE: With James Redpath. HAND-BOOK TO KANSAS....

"A Historic Document: A Contract for Transportation across the Plains to California." CALIFORNIA HISTORICAL QUARTERLY 11(Mar 1932): 34. Train Govt-1852.

HISTORICAL TOUR OF THE CARSON RIVER ROUTE ON THE EMIGRANT TRAIL. Trash Guide 7. Carson River Route, Pt. III. Oakland: Trash, 1981. CAL-Genl.

HITCHCOCK, Catherine E., comp. "The Trans-Mississippi West in AMERICAN HERITAGE: An Annotated Bibliography." ARIZONA & THE WEST 12(Spr 1970): 63-94. Bib.

HITCHCOCK, Harriet. A FAMILY HISTORY OF CALIFORNIA. Ed. Catherine J. Webb. Berkeley: Private, 1975. PIKES. III. 1864.

HITE, Abraham. Diary. Ed. Mary F. Sanford. CSL. CAL(St. Jo)-TRUCKEE. IV-. Rem. 1853.

HITE, Joseph. Crossed the Plains. ORHIST. OR(Council). IV. 1853.

HITE, Mark P. "The Significance of the Lolo Trail in Early Western Travel." MA thesis, Univ. of Montana, 1948. MONTANA-Genl.

HITT, H. C., and G. E. Wellburn. "Barnard's Cariboo Express in the Colony of British Columbia, 1860-1871 and Later Expresses of F. J. Barnard." THE STAMP SPECIALIST (1945): 3-32. Mail.

HITTELL, John S. "Reminiscences of the Plains and Mines in '49 and '50." OVERLAND MONTHLY (1887): 193-208. CAL(St. Jo?)-LASSEN. V. Rem. 1849.

HITTLE, Jonas. Diary. Illinois State Historical Library, Springfield, IL. CAL(St. Jo)-LASSEN. II+. 1849. Graphics.

HIVELY, Sara. Journal. DENVERPUB. PIKES. II. 1863.

HIXON, Adrietta A. Ed. Applegate, Mary T. ON TO OREGON.

HIXON, Charlene. "The Handcart Expeditions of 1856 in Johnson County, Iowa." Term Paper. Iowa State Historical Society, Iowa City, Iowa. MORMON-1856-Genl.

HIXON, Jasper M. Diary. BANCROFT. CAL(Indep)-HALL. I. 1849.

HOAG, Amanda J. Papers. CAHIST. CAL(Indep)-CHEROKEE-SLCUT-BECKWOURTH. Not Seen.

HOBART, Emaline. An Account. UWY. OR(Council)-BARLOW. V. 1849.

HOBBS, James. WILD LIFE IN THE FAR WEST.... Hartford, CN: Wiley, Waterman & Eaton, 1872. CAL-MEX(Durango-Guaymas-Hermosillo)-GILA. IV. 1849.

HOBSON, E. John. Biographical Sketch. ORHIST. OR(Indep). V-. Rem. 1843.

HOCKENSMITH, Mrs. M. S. Papers. BANCROFT. CAL(Indep?). 1865. Attributed to BANCROFT but uncited in catalog.

HOCKERSMITH, Martha J. Reminiscence. ORHIST. MEEK. IV. Rem. 1853.

HOCKETT, W. A. Experiences. ORU. OR(Indep). IV. Rem. 1847.

HODDER, Frank H. Ed. Audubon, John W. AUDUBON'S WESTERN JOURNAL.

HODDER, Halie R. "Crossing the Plains in War Time." COLORADO MAGAZINE 10(Jul 1933): 131-36. PIKES. III-. Rem. 1865.

HODGE, George. Diary. MONHIST. OR(Spaulding Mission-Ft. Colville-Walla Walla). III. 1853.

HODGKINS, Pilsbury. "The Story...of a Mule-Mail Carrier in the Mother Lode." Society of California Pioneers QUARTERLY 2, no. 3(1925): 171-85. Mail. Stage.

HOFE, G. Douglas, Jr. "American Trails - Rediscovered." PARKS AND RECREATION 6(Mar 1971): 41-48. Pres.

HOFF, Byron. "Stage Coach Days in and around San Antonio." MA thesis, Southwest Texas State Teachers College, 1947. Stage.

HOFFMAN, Allen W. "Findings along a Segment of the California Trail of 1849." WESTX 33(Oct 1957): 105-16. TEX-1849-Genl.

HOFFMAN, Benjamin. "Diary." In "West Virginia Forty-Niners." Ed. C. H. Ambler. WEST VIRGINIA HISTORY 3(Oct 1941): 59-75. CAL(St. Jo)-HALL-TRUCKEE. III +. 1849.

HOFFMAN, H. Wilbur. SAGAS OF WESTERN TRAVEL AND TRANSPORT. San Diego: Howell-North, 1980. Overland-Genl. Graphics.

HOFFMAN, Velma R. "Lt. Beale and the Camel Caravans through Arizona." ARIZONA HIGHWAYS 33(Oct 1957): 7-13. BEALE-Genl.

HOFFMAN, William. Account. BEINECKE. CAL(St. Jo)-LASSEN. II. 1849.

_____. Journal. ORU. OR(Weston)-APPLE. II. 1853.

_____. SEE ALSO: Taylor, Arthur S., and William M. McKinney. "An Accurate Observer."

HOFSTATLER, ? Texas to California. NEWBERRY. CAL-TEX(Denton-Ft. Davis-El Paso)-GILA. II. 1850.

"Hogan Ouren in Nebraska and Colorado, 1861-1866." NEBRASKA HISTORY 58(Sum 1977): 219-49. Freight.

HOGARTH, Paul. ARTISTS ON HORSEBACK: THE OLD WEST IN ILLUSTRATED JOURNALISM, 1857 - 1900. NY: Watson - Guptill, 1972. Graphics.

HOLBROOK, J. TEN YEARS AMONG THE MAIL BAGS. Philadelphia: Cowperthwait, 1856. Mail.

HOLBROOK, Marion R. "Riverbank Massacre." TRUE WEST 29(Sept 1982): 42-45. 1857 Attack on Humbolt River at Battle Mountain.

HOLBROOK, S. H. "Concord Coach." AMERICAN MERCURY 70(Jan 1950): 104-10. Eqpt.

HOLCOMB, William F. Sketch. BANCROFT. CAL(Council). III-. Rem. 1850.

HOLDER, C. F. "Coaching in Southern California." CALIFORNIA ILLUSTRATED 1(N.d.): 327. Stage.

HOLDREDGE, Sterling M. STATE, TERRITORIAL AND OCEAN GUIDE BOOK OF THE PACIFIC. N.p., n.d. Stage. Guide.

HOLLADAY, Ben. Misc. Collections. HUNTL. Stage. Biog.

_____. TABLE OF DISTANCES OF THE OVERLAND DAILY STAGE LINE FROM ATCHISON, KANSAS, TO GREAT SALT LAKE.... NY: Slote & Jane, 1863. Stage.

_____. TESTIMONY AS TO THE CLAIM OF BEN HOLLADAY FOR LOSSES AND DAMAGES...1862, 1863, 1864, 1865, AND 1866.... 46th Cong., 2d sess. 1879. S. Misc. Doc. 19. Stage.

HOLLADAY Overland Mail and Express Company. AN ACT TO INCORPORATE THE HOLLADAY OVERLAND MAIL AND EXPRESS CO. N.p., 1866? Stage.

_____. AN ACT TO INCORPORATE THE OVERLAND CENTRAL CALIFORNIA AND PIKE'S PEAK EXPRESS COMPANY.... Lawrence, KS: Republican, 1860. Stage.

_____. CHARTER OF THE HOLLADAY OVERLAND MAIL AND EXPRESS COMPANY. GRANTED JANUARY, 1866, BY THE LEGISLATURE OF COLORADO TERRITORY. NY: Slote & Janes, 1866. Stage.

_____. PROSPECTUS OF, AND SUBSCRIPTIONS TO THE HOLLADAY OVERLAND MAIL AND EXPRESS COMPANY. N.p., 1865. Stage.

_____. Records. MONHIST. Stage.

_____. ...RULES AND REGULATIONS FOR THE GOVERNMENT OF THE OFFICERS AND EMPLOYEES OF THE CENTRAL OVERLAND CALIFORNIA AND PIKE'S PEAK EXPRESS COMPANY. St. Joseph, MO: Millan, 1861. Stage.

_____. THE UNITED STATES DAILY MAIL LINE, TO THE WESTERN STATES AND TERRITORIES. NY: Slote & Janes, 1866. Mail. Stage.

HOLLIDAY, George H. ON THE PLAINS IN '65. N.p., 1883. Rem. Military.

HOLLIDAY, Jaquelin S. "The California Gold Rush in Myth and Reality." PhD diss., Univ. of California-Berkeley, 1959. CAL-1849-Genl.

_____. "William Swain and the Wolverine Rangers: A Study of the California Gold Rush." MA thesis, Univ. of California-Berkeley, 1954. CAL(Indep)-LASSEN. I. 1849.

_____. THE WORLD RUSHED IN: THE CALIFORNIA GOLD RUSH EXPERIENCE. NY: Simon & Schuster, 1981. CAL(Indep)-LASSEN. I. 1849.

HOLLISTER, W. W. Statement. BANCROFT. Stock(Sheep): CAL-BRIDGER-SLCOR. IV. 1853.

HOLLON, W. Eugene. BEYOND THE CROSS TIMBERS: THE TRAVELS OF RANDOLPH B. MARCY, 1812 - 1887. Norman: Univ. of Oklahoma Press, 1955. Biog.

_____. "Great Days of Overland Stage." AMERICAN HERITAGE 8(Jun 1957): 26-31. Overland-Genl.

HOLMAN, Albert M. PIONEERING IN THE NORTHWEST - NIOBRARA - VIRGINIA CITY WAGON ROAD. Sioux City, IA: Deitch & Lamar, 1924. DAKOTAS-MONTANA. III. 1865.

HOLMAN, Cyrus K. Journal. Texas State Library-Archives, Austin, TX. CAL(Paris, TX)-OKLAHOMA-CHEROKEE-SIMPSON. II+. 1859. Party hanged a member for murder. Train Govt.

HOLMAN, Woodford C. TWENTY-FOUR YEARS RESIDENCE.... St. Louis: N.p., 1870. OR. 1845. Not Seen.

HOLMES, Blair R. Ed. Cantwell, James S. "Journal."

HOLMES, John. THE ADVENTURES OF JOHN HOLMES.... Springfield, VT: Wright, 1873. CAL-TEX(Port Lavaca)-GILA. III. 1850.

HOLMES, Julia A. A BLOOMER GIRL ON PIKE'S PEAK, 1858. Ed. Agnes W. Spring. Denver: DENVERPUB, 1949. SANTA FE. III. 1858.

HOLMES, Kenneth L. Ed. Mills, Rachel J. "Letters from a Quaker Woman."

_____, ed. & comp. COVERED WAGON WOMEN: DIARIES AND LETTERS FROM THE WESTERN TRAILS, 1840 - 1890. 4 vols. to date. Glendale: Clark, 1983+. Social.

HOLT, R. D. "Old Texas Wagon Trains." FRONTIER TIMES 25(Sept 1948): 269-78. TEX-Genl. Freight.

HOLT, Thomas. "Journal." In OVERLAND IN 1846..., ed. Dale L. Morgan. 2 vols. Georgetown, CA: Talisman, 1963. APPLE. II. 1846.

HOLT, W. M. "From Washington, Arkansas, to Los Angeles, California, in 1852." PULASKI COUNTY [Arkansas] HISTORICAL REVIEW 10(Mar 1962): 9-18. CAL-TEX(Bonham)-MEX-GILA. IV. 1852.

HOLTGRIEVE, Elizabeth R. "Recollections of Pioneer Days." WASHINGTON HISTORICAL QUARTERLY 19(Jul 1928): 193-98. OR(Westport). V. Rem. 1852.

HOLTON, Thomas A. "The Pony Express." STAMPS, 2 Oct 1937, 25-26. Pony.

HOLTZ, Milton E. "Old Fort Kearny - 1846-1848...." MONTANA 22(Aut 1972): 44-55. Geog.

HOLYOKE, William H. Notebook. MONHIST. DAKOTAS-MONTANA. II. 1863.

HOLZHUETER, John O. Ed. Hillyer, Edwin. "From Waupun to Sacramento."

HOMER, Michael W. "After Winter Quarters and Council Bluffs: The Mormons in Nebraska Territory, 1854 - 1867." NEBRASKA HISTORY 65(Win 1984): 467-83. MORMON-Genl.

_____. "For the Strength of the Hills We Bless Thee: Italian Mormons Come to Utah." LDS. MORMON-1854-Genl.

HOMSHER, Lola M. "Warm Springs, the Emigrants' Wash Tub." Wyoming Historical Society Library, Cheyenne, WY. Geog.

HONIG, Louis O. WESTPORT: GATEWAY TO THE EARLY WEST. North Kansas City, MO: Author, 1950. Geog.

HONNELL, W. R. "The Pony Express." KANSAS HISTORICAL QUARTERLY 5(Feb 1936): 67-71. Pony.

HOOBER, David. H., comp. "Nebraska History in Graduate Theses." NEBRASKA HISTORY 52(Win 1971): N.p. Bib.

HOOD, Mary V. SEE: With Richard Lillard. HANK MONK AND HORACE GREELEY.

HOOK, William H. Articles of Agreement to Finance and Furnish a Party Bound for California, February 19, 1850. BANCROFT. Train Govt.

HOOKER, William F. THE BULLWHACKER. Pioneer Life Series, ed. Howard R. Driggs. NY: World Book, 1924. Freight.

_____. THE PRAIRIE SCHOONER. Chicago: Saul Brothers, 1918. Freight.

HOOPER, Byrom. "Julesburg - Camp Rankin and Fort Sedgewick." DENVER WESTERNERS BRAND BOOK 19(1964): 267-300. Geog.

HOOPER, H. O. "To California in '49." OVERLAND MONTHLY 22(Sept 1893): 318-29. CAL-TEX(Shreveport)-MEX(El Paso-Guaymas). V. Rem. 1849.

HOOPER, John A. Papers. CAHIST. 1867 insurance policy for overland trip. Social.

HOOPER, Joseph and Esther. Journey. MONHIST. CAL(Council?). V. 1863.

HOOPES, Alban W. INDIAN AFFAIRS AND THEIR ADMINISTRATION, WITH SPECIAL REFERENCE TO THE FAR WEST, 1849 - 1860. Philadelphia: Univ. of Pennsylvania Press, 1932. Indians.

HOOPES, Chad L. WHAT MAKES A MAN. Fresno: Valley, 1973. Biog: John Bidwell.

HOOVER, Edwin H. "The Smoky Hill Route." COLORADO HIGHWAYS 4(Apr 1925): 7-9. PIKES: Smoky Hill.

HOOVER, Vincent A. Diaries. HUNTL. CAL(St. Jo)-BRIDGER-SLCOR. II. 1849.

HOPPE, Hugo. SEE: McPherren, Ida. IMPRINTS ON PIONEER TRAILS.

HOPPER, Charles. CHARLES HOPPER AND THE PILGRIMS OF THE PACIFIC...1841.... Ed. Franklin Beard. La Grange, CA: Southern Mines Press, 1981. CAL(Indep). IV. Rem. 1841. CAL(East via)-SPANISH-SANTA Fe. IV. Rem. 1842. CAL(Indep)-LASSEN. IV. Rem. 1847.

HOPPER, Silas L. "Diary by Silas Hopper." ANNALS OF WYOMING 3(Oct 1925): 117-26. CAL(Neb. City)-BRIDGER-SIMPSON-TRUCKEE. III. 1863.

HOPPING, Mary E. Incidents of Pioneer Life. CSL. CAL(Council)-BOZE. III+. Rem. 1864.

HORN, Hosea B. HORN'S OVERLAND GUIDE. NY: J. H. Colton, 1853. Guide.

HORN, Huston. THE PIONEERS. One of the Time-Life Old West Series. NY: Time-Life, 1974. Overland-Genl. Graphics.

HORNER, William B. THE GOLD REGIONS OF KANSAS AND NEBRASKA. Chicago: W. H. Tobey, 1859. Guide.

HORNUNG, Clarence. WHEELS ACROSS AMERICA: A PICTORIAL CAVALCADE ILLUSTRATING THE EARLY DEVELOPMENT OF VEHICULAR TRANSPORTATION. NY: Barnes, 1952. Eqpt-Graphics.

HORTON, Emily M. OUR FAMILY. N.p.: Author, 1922. CAL(Westport?)-TRUCKEE. IV. Rem. 1857.

HORTON, L. J. Biography. Arizona State Library-Arizona Room, Phoenix, AZ. CAL(Council). III. 1863.

HOSIE, John. Ed. Wade, Mark S. THE OVERLANDERS OF '62.

HOSLEY, Dexter P. Diary. Princeton Univ. Library-Western History. CAL(St. Jo)-TRUCKEE. 1852. Not Seen.

HOSMER, Charles B., Jr. PRESENCE OF THE PAST: A HISTORY OF THE PRESERVATION MOVEMENT IN THE U.S. BEFORE WILLIAMSBURG. NY: Putnam's, 1965. Pres.

HOSMER, J. Allen. TRIP TO THE STATES IN 1865. Ed. Edith M. Duncan. Sources of Northwest History, No. 17. Missoula: Montana State Univ., 1932. Stage: Virginia City, MT to Emigrant Gulch. III. 1865.

HOTH, H. Diary. BANCROFT. CAL(Kansas City)-BRIDGER-SLCOR. I. 1856. In German.

HOUGH, Emerson. THE WAY TO THE WEST. NY: Grosset & Dunlap, 1903. Overland-Genl.

HOUGH, Warren. "The 1850 Overland Diary...." ANNALS OF WYOMING 46(Fall 1974): 207-16. CAL(Council)-BRIDGER-SLCUT. III. 1850.

HOUGHTON, Eliza P. THE EXPEDITION OF THE DONNER PARTY AND ITS TRAGIC FATE. Chicago: A. C. McClurg, 1911. CAL(Indep)-BRIDGER-HASTINGS-TRUCKEE. III. 1846.

HOUSE, George C. "Overland Trails to the Pacific Coast before 1850." Senior thesis, University of Santa Clara, 1955. Overland-Genl.

HOUSER, G. O. REGISTER CLIFF OR 'SANDPOINT.' Guernsey, WY: Gazette, N.p. Geog.

HOUSTON, Henrietta. "The Techniques of the Emigrant Trail." MA thesis, Univ. of Southern California, 1934. Eqpt. Train Govt. Teams. Social.

"How the West Was Won." LIFE, 46, 20 Apr 1959, 76-89. Overland-Genl.

"How to Get to Pike's Peak Gold Mines." HARPER'S WEEKLY, 3, 2 Apr 1859, 220. Guide.

HOWARD, Addison. "Captain John Mullan." WASHINGTON HISTORICAL QUARTERLY 25(Jul 1934): 185-202. Biog. MULLAN-Genl.

HOWARD, Helen A. Ed. Rumley, Charles. "Diary."

_____. "Unique History of Fort Tejon." JOURNAL OF THE WEST 18(Jan 1979): 41-51. Geog.

HOWARD, Mary E. "After Lapse of Fifty Years." CSL. CAL(Council). Rem. 1852. Not Seen.

HOWARD, Minnie. "Old Fort Hall as Related to Peace through Destiny." Pocatello: Tribune, 1930. Pres.

HOWARD, Robert W., ed. HOOFBEATS OF DESTINY: THE STORY OF THE PONY EXPRESS. NY: Signet, 1960. Pony.

_____. THE SOUTH PASS STORY. NY: Putnam's, 1968. Geog.

HOWARD, Sarah A. Personal Reminiscences. Eastern Washington Historical Society Library, Spokane, WA. OR(Council). IV. Rem. 1862.

HOWARD, Waid. SEE: Settle, Raymond and Mary. OVERLAND DAYS TO MONTANA.

HOWAY, F. W. "The Overland Journey of the Argonauts of 1862." ROYAL SOCIETY OF CANADA PROCEEDINGS AND TRANSACTIONS 13(May 1919): 37-55. CANADA-1862-Genl.

HOWE, Maurice L. SEE: With Charles Kelly, MILES GOODYEAR.

HOWE, Octavius T. ARGONAUTS OF '49, HISTORY AND ADVENTURES OF THE EMIGRANT COMPANIES FROM MASSACHUSETTS, 1849 - 1850. Cambridge: Harvard Univ. Press, 1923. CAL-1849-Genl.

HOWELL, Elijah P. Diary. CSL. CAL(Neb. City)-LASSEN. II. Rem. 1849.

HOWELL, John E. "Diary of an Emigrant of 1845." WASHINGTON HISTORICAL QUARTERLY 1(Apr 1907): 138-58. OR(Indep)-BARLOW. III. 1845.

HOWES, Edward H. Ed. With George P. Hammond. Eccleston, Robert. OVERLAND TO CALIFORNIA.

HOWES, E. H. "Federal Exploration and Development of the 32nd Parallel Route West of the Rio Grande, 1846-1861." PhD diss., Univ. of California-Berkeley, 1955. Govt.

HOWK, Ordelle C. "Alice." "A Page of the Past." HUTCHINGS' 1, Oct 1856, 159-60, Dec 1856, 253-55, Jan 1857, 311-12, Mar 1857, 397-400, Apr 1857, 449-52, May 1857, 497-98, Jun 1857, 545-57. CAL(Council). III. Rem. 1849.

HOWLETT, W. J. Recollections and Reflections. DENVERPUB. PIKES. IV. Rem. 1865.

HOXIE, Frances A. "Connecticut's Forty-Niners." WESTERN HISTORICAL QUARTERLY 1(Jan 1974): 17-28. CAL-1849-Genl.

HOY, Jesse S. Manuscript. Univ. of Utah Library-SpCol, Salt Lake City, UT. Freight. Stage. Indians.

HOY, Wilton E. "The Fort Bowie Story." CAMP PERIODICAL 7(Win 1975-1976): 38-47. Geog. Military.

HOYT, A. W. "Over the Plains to Colorado." HARPER'S 35(Jun 1867): 1-21. Stage: Omaha - Denver. V. 1867. Graphics.

HOYT, Franklin. "The Bradshaw Road." PACIFIC HISTORICAL REVIEW 21(Aug 1952): 243-54. BRADSHAW-Genl.

_____. "Bradshaw's Road to the La Paz Diggins." DESERT 19(Feb 1956): 4-8. BRADSHAW-Genl.

_____. "A History of the Desert Region of Riverside County from

1540 to the Completion of the Railroad to Yuma in 1877." MA thesis, Univ. of Southern California, 1948. BRADSHAW-Genl.

HUBBARD, Cal. "The Devil's Highway." Ed. Thomas A Bailey. TRUE WEST 7(Nov-Dec 1959): 6-8, 42. CAL-MEX(Sonoita)-GILA. III. 1849.

HUBBARD, Chauncey B. SPARKS FROM MANY CAMP FIRES. Ed. Earle R. Hubbard. Clark, SD: Private, 1959. CAL(St. Jo)-HASTINGS. III. 1850.

HUBBARD, Earle R. Ed. Hubbard, Chauncey B. SPARKS FROM MANY CAMP FIRES.

HUBBELL, W. W. "Notes on Desert Life." MEIGS COUNTY TELEGRAPH, 1855-1856. Ohio Historical Society, Columbus, OH. CAL(St. Jo). 1850. Not Seen.

HUCKINS, Alonzo. Fort Leavenworth to Camp Floyd. Univ. of Utah Library-SpCol, Salt Lake City, UT. CAL(Ft. Leav)-BRIDGER-Ends SLC. III. 1860.

HUDGINS, John. California in 1849. MO-WHMC. CAL(Westport)-SANTA FE-RIO GRANDE-GILA. III. Rem. 1849.

HUDSON, David. Autobiography. BANCROFT. CAL(Indep)-HALL-TRUCKEE. IV. Rem. 1845.

HUDSON, Henry J. "Henry James Hudson and the Genoa Settlement." Ed. Marguerette R. Burke. NEBRASKA HISTORY 41(Sept 1960): 201-35. Geog.

HUDSON, John. A FORTY-NINER IN UTAH WITH THE STANSBURY EXPLORATION OF GREAT SALT LAKE.... Ed. Brigham D. Madsen. No. 11, Utah, the Mormons, and the West. SLC: Univ. of Utah Tanner Trust Fund, 1981. CAL(Kansas City)-SANTA FE-SPANISH-Ends SLC. V. 1849. Govt.

HUDSON, Richard. "To the Gold Fields...and Back." Ed. W. R. Hill. HIGH COUNTRY 48(Spr 1979): 42-46. CAL(Westport)-HASTINGS. V-. 1853.

HUDSON, T. "Jackass Mail." HIGH COUNTRY 27(Win 1973): 33-37. Stage(San Antonio and San Diego Mail)-Genl.

HUDSON, Tom. "With Couts to the Colorado." HIGH COUNTRY 49(Sum 1979): 19-28. GILA-1849-Genl.

HUFFORD, Kenneth. "Travelers on the Gila Trail, 1824-1850, Parts I & II: An Annotated Bibliography." JOURNAL OF ARIZONA HISTORY 7, no. 1(1966): 1-8; 8, no. 1(1967): 30-44. Bib.

HUGGINS, Dorothy H. Ed. Eastland, Thomas B. & Joseph G. "To California through Texas."

HUGHES, Francis W. THE CASE OF GEORGE CHORPENNING. WA: Stephens & Son, 1880. Mail.

HUGHES, Gilberta B. SEE: Brown, Ann B., et al. WAGON TRAILS.

HUGHES, Samuel. "The Murder at Oatman's Flat." ARIZONA GRAPHIC 1, 28 Oct 1899, 4, 7.

HUGHES, Tom. HISTORY OF BANNING AND SAN GORGONIO PASS. Banning, CA: Banning Record, 1938. Geog. BRADSHAW-Genl.

HUGHES, Willis B. "The First Dragoons on the Western Frontier, 1834 - 1846." ARIZONA & THE WEST 12(Sum 1970): 115-38. Military.

HULBERT, Archer B. Ed. Rumfield, Hiram. LETTERS OF AN OVERLAND MAIL AGENT.

_____, comp. THE CROWN COLLECTION OF AMERICAN MAPS. 6 vols. Series 4, The American Transcontinental Trails. Colorado Springs, CO: Stewart Commission, 1925-28. Maps.

_____. FORTY-NINERS. Boston: Little, Brown, 1932. CAL-1849-Genl.

_____. THE GREAT WESTERN STAGE COACH ROUTES.... Colorado Springs, Co: Stewart Commission, 1930. Stage.

_____, ed. OVERLAND TO THE PACIFIC. 6 vols. Denver: DENVERPUB, 1932-36. Not Seen. Overland-Genl.

_____. Papers. Colorado College Library-SpCol, Colorado Springs, Co. Overland-Genl.

_____. "Western Trails: Work of the Stewart Commission." FRONTIER 9(Nov 1928): 52-54. Pres.

HULBERT, Dorothy P. "The Trip to California: An Explanatory Notice of the Panorama." FRONTIER AND MIDLAND 14(Jan 1934): 160-61, 68-69. Graphics-Fremont Panorama.

HULIN, Lester. 1847 DIARY OF APPLEGATE TRAIL TO OREGON. Eugene, OR: Lane County Pioneer-Historical Society, 1959. OR(St. Jo)-APPLE. III+. 1847.

HULL, Charles. Recollections. Missouri Historical Society-St. Louis. OR(Council). Rem. 1859. Not Seen.

HULL, Cyrus. SEE: With Rufus Burrows. A LONG ROAD TO STONY CREEK.

HULL, Lewis B. "Soldiering on the High Plains...1864-1866." KANSAS HISTORICAL QUARTERLY 7(Feb 1938): 3-53. Military. Indians. Stage.

HULMSTON, John K. "Transplain Migration: The Trains in Mormon Immigration, 1861-1868." MS thesis, Utah State Univ., 1985. MORMON-Genl.

HULTGREN, Retta C. Ed. Chambers, Thomas. JUDGE THOMAS M. CHAMBERS.

HUME, James B. Papers. BANCROFT. CAL(Council)-BRIDGER-HASTINGS. III. 1850. Stage.

HUMPHREY, L. Manuscript Journal. Princeton Univ. Library-Western America, Princeton, NJ. OR(Council)-BARLOW. III. 1852.

HUMPHREYS, Alfred G. "Peg Leg Smith." IDAHO YESTERDAYS 10(Sum 1966): 28-32. Biog.

HUMPHREYS, James H. Reminiscences. BANCROFT. CAL(St. Jo)-HALL. IV. Rem. 1849.

HUMPHREYS, L. "Over Land Guide from Kanesville Iowa to Oregon City &c." BEINECKE. Guide.

HUMPHRIES, Keith. "Trail of the Pioneers." NEW MEXICO 17(Apr 1939): 10-11, 33-36. Stage.

HUNGERFORD, Edward. "The Story of Wells Fargo." THE BELLMAN 20(May 1916): 542-44. Stage.

_____. WELLS FARGO ADVANCING THE AMERICAN FRONTIER. NY: Random House, 1949. Stage.

HUNING, Ernestine F. "Diary, 1863." In Huning-Fergusson Papers. Zimmerman Library-SpCol, Univ. of New Mexico, Albuquerque, NM. SANTA FE. III+. 1863.

HUNING, Franz. TRADER ON THE SANTA FE TRAIL. Ed. Lina Fergusson Browne. Albuquerque: Univ. of New Mexico Press, 1973. Not Seen.

HUNNIFORD, John. Journal. Univ. of British Columbia Library-SpCol, Vancouver, BC. CANADA(Ft Garry-Edmonton-Ft. George-Vancouver). 1862. Not Seen.

HUNSAKER, Abraham. Journal. LDS. Not Seen.

HUNSAKER, William J. "Lansford W. Hastings, Empire Dreamer and California Pioneer." GRIZZLY BEAR, May 1930, 14-15, 68-71. Biog.

HUNT, Mrs. A. C. "Diary of Mrs. A. C. Hunt." COLORADO MAGAZINE 21(Sept 1944): 160-70. PIKES. II. 1859.

HUNT, Aurora. THE ARMY OF THE PACIFIC...1860 - 1866. Glendale: Clark, 1951. Military. Stage. Pony.

_____. "California Volunteers." Southern California Historical QUARTERLY 36(Jun 1954): 146-54. GILA. IV. 1865.

_____. "Overland by Boat to California in 1849." Southern California Historical QUARTERLY 31(Sept 1949): 212-18. CAL-TEX(San Antonio)-GILA. III. 1849.

HUNT, David C. SEE: With Paul Rossi. THE ART OF THE OLD WEST.

HUNT, Elmer M. "Abbot - Downing and the Concord Coach." HISTORICAL NEW HAMPSHIRE, Nov 1945, 1-20. Eqpt-Stage.

HUNT, Elvid. HISTORY OF FORT LEAVENWORTH, 1827 - 1927. Fort Leavenworth, KS: General Service School Press, 1926. Geog.

HUNT, G. W. A HISTORY OF THE HUNT FAMILY. Boston: McDonald, Gill, 1890. OR(Indep)-BARLOW. V. Rem. 1847.

HUNT, James E. Reminiscence. CSL. CAL(St Jo)-LASSEN. V-. Rem. 1855. Stock drive.

HUNT, Jefferson. SEE: Smith, Pauline U. CAPTAIN JEFFERSON HUNT.

HUNT, John C. "The Oregon Trail Today." AMERICAN HISTORY ILLUSTRATED 3(Aug 1968): 24-29. Pres.

HUNT, N. Jane, ed. BREVET'S NEBRASKA HISTORICAL MARKERS AND SITES. Sioux Falls, SD: Brevet, 1974. Pres.

HUNT, Nancy A. "By Ox-Team to California." OVERLAND MONTHLY 67(Apr 1916): 317-26. CAL(Council). IV. Rem. 1854.

HUNT, Rockwell D. JOHN BIDWELL, PRINCE OF CALIFORNIA PIONEERS. Caldwell, ID: Caxton, 1942. Biog. CAL-1841-Genl.

_____. "The Spirit of the Trail." Southern California Historical QUARTERLY 41(Dec 1959): 325-36. Overland-Genl.

_____, and William S. Ament. OXCART TO AIRPLANE. LA: Powell, 1929. Overland-Genl.

HUNT, Thomas B. Journal...Austin, Texas to Fort Craig, New Mexico, and Returning to San Antonio, July-December, 1869. National Archives, Washington, DC. TEX-RIO GRANDE. 1869. Not Seen.

HUNT, Thomas H. SEE: With Devere and Helen Helfrich. EMIGRANT TRAILS WEST.

_____. "The California Trail: A Personal Quest." AMERICAN WEST 11(Sept 1974): 14-25. Graphics.

_____. "The California Trail: A Survey." OVERLAND JOURNAL 1(Jul 1983): 30-35. CAL-Genl.

_____. GHOST TRAILS TO CALIFORNIA. Palo Alto: American West, 1974. CAL-Genl. Pres.

HUNTER, A. H. Statement. In Charles Kelly Collection. UTHIST. Stage. Geog(Roberts Creek Station).

HUNTER, George. REMINISCENCES OF AN OLD TIMER.... SF: H. S. Crocker, 1887. OR(Council). IV. Rem. 1852.

HUNTER, J. M. "Early Day Mail Lines in Texas." FRONTIER TIMES 13(Feb 1936): 233-35. Mail.

_____. "Old Stage Routes of Texas." FRONTIER TIMES 28(Apr 1951): 205-10. Stage.

_____. "The San Antonio - San Diego Mail Route." FRONTIER TIMES 25(Nov 1947): 54-57. Stage.

_____. "Thirty Day Mail Service to California." FRONTIER TIMES 26(Jun 1948): 219-22. Stage: San Antonio and San Diego.

HUNTER, John A. "The Letters of a Missourian...1848 - 1850." Ed. David W. Francis. MISSOURI HISTORICAL BULLETIN 19(Oct 1972): 38-53. CAL(St Jo)-Ends SLC. V-. 1849.

HUNTER, John W. "The Story of an Ill-Fated Expedition." FRONTIER TIMES 19(Sept 1942): 412-20. TEX(Camp Colorado-Ft. Concho-Eagle Pass). IV. 1867. Fine account of an indian skirmish.

HUNTER, Leslie G. "The Mojave Expedition of 1858 - 59." ARIZONA & THE WEST 21(Sum 1979): 137-56. Military. BEALE-1858-Genl.

HUNTER, Milton R. "The Mormon Corridor." PACIFIC HISTORICAL REVIEW 8(Jun 1939): 179-200. SLCOR-Genl.

_____. UTAH INDIAN STORIES. SLC: Author, 1946. Indians.

HUNTER, Robert. A TEXAN IN THE GOLD RUSH. Ed. Robert W. Stephens. Bryan, TX: Barnum & White, 1972. CAL-TEX(San Antonio)-GILA. V. 1849.

HUNTER, Thomas T. Early Days in Arizona. Southwest Museum Library, Los Angeles, CA. GILA. III. Rem. 1867. Stock drive.

HUNTER, Vickie, and Elizabeth Hamma. STAGECOACH DAYS. Menlo Park, CA: Lane, 1963. Stage.

HUNTER, William H. Diary. Univ. of Arizona Library-SpCol, Tucson, AZ. CAL(Boonesville)-SANTA FE-RIO GRANDE-GILA. I. 1849. Flora/Fauna.

HUNTINGTON, Hallie H. ALL THE WAY WEST. Eugene, OR: Private, 1984. OR(St. Jo)-APPLE. IV. Rem. 1847. OR(St. Jo?)-APPLE. IV. Rem. 1851.

HUNTINGTON, Oliver B. Diary. BYU. MORMON. III+. 1848. MORMON. III+. 1849. SIMPSON. III+. 1854. SIMPSON. III+. 1857.

_____. "Eighteen Days on the Desert." YOUNG WOMAN'S JOURNAL 2(Nov, Dec 1890; Jan, Feb, Mar 1891): 68-72, 117-20, 160-64, 203-7, 264-67. SIMPSON. II. Rem. 1857.

_____. "A Trip to Carson Valley." EVENTFUL NARRATIVES. Faith-Promoting Series, No. 13 (1887). SIMPSON. III. Rem. 1854.

Huntley Express Company. Records. MONHIST. Stage.

HUNTLEY, James L. FERRYBOATS IN IDAHO. Caldwell, ID: Caxton, 1979. OR-Genl.

HUNTON, John. OLD FORT LARAMIE. Torrington, WY: Goshen News, 1928. Geog.

HURST, Beulah. "History of Mountain Passes." Files of the Oregon Writer's Project, Portland, OR. OR-Genl. Not Seen.

HURT, R. Douglas. "The Construction and Development of Fort Wallace, Kansas, 1865 - 1882." KANSAS HISTORICAL QUARTERLY 43(Spr 1977): 44-55. Geog. PIKES-Smoky Hill Trail.

HUSBAND, Michael B. "The Backgrounds and Organization of the Great Oregon Migration of 1843." MA thesis, Univ. of Omaha, 1966. OR-1843-Genl.

_____. "To Oregon in 1843: The Background and Organization of the 'Great Migration'." PhD diss., Univ. of New Mexico, 1970. OR-1843-Genl.

_____. "To Oregon in 1843: The 'Great Migration'." KANSAS QUARTERLY 5(Spr 1973): 7-16. OR-1843-Genl.

HUSEAS, Marion H. "Thornburgh and Fort Steele." CAMP PERIODICAL 4(Win 1973): 17-24. Military.

HUSSEY, John A. Ed. Swan, John A. A TRIP TO THE GOLD MINES.

_____. "Fort Vancouver." AMERICAN WEST 14(Sept-Oct 1977): 12-19, 68-71. Geog.

_____. THE HISTORY OF FORT VANCOUVER AND ITS PHYSICAL STRUCTURE. Portland: Washington State Historical Society, 1957. Geog. Pres.

_____. "New Light upon Talbot H. Green." CALIFORNIA HISTORICAL QUARTERLY 18(Mar 1939): 32-63. CAL-1841-Genl.

HUSTON, Henry C. Autobiography. In Oregon Miscellanies. BANCROFT. OR(Council). IV. Rem. 1852.

HUTCHESON, Austin E. "Overland in 1852: The McQuirk Diary." PACIFIC HISTORICAL REVIEW 13(Dec 1944): 426-32. CAL(St. Jo). Description of diary pages and binding only. 1852.

HUTCHINGS, James M. "Packing in the Mountains of California." AMERICAN WEST 2(Sum 1965): 92-95. Freight.

_____. SEEKING THE ELEPHANT, 1849. Ed. Shirley Sargent. American Trails Series No. 12. Glendale: Clark, 1980. CAL(St. Jo)-BRIDGER-SLCUT. II+. 1849.

HUTCHINSON, Charles E. "Development and Use of Transportation Routes in the San Bernardino Valley Region, 1769 - 1900." MA thesis, Univ. of Southern California, 1933. SPANISH-Genl. SLCOR-Genl. BEALE-Genl. BRADSHAW-Genl. Freight.

HUTCHINSON, Elizabeth. Letter. Attributed to Bancroft but uncited in catalogs. 1854.

HYDE, William. Private Journal. UTHIST. CAL(Leav)-SANTA FE-RIO GRANDE-GILA. II. 1849. CAL(Sutter's)-TRUCKEE-HALL-BRIDGER. IV. 1847. SLCOR. IV. 1852.

Idaho Dept. of Highways. ROUTE OF THE OREGON TRAIL IN IDAHO. N.p.: The Dept., 1963. Maps.

Idaho Historical Society Reference Series.
50. The Oregon Trail in Idaho.
51. Goodale's Cutoff.
52. The California Trail in Idaho.
54. Snake River Ferries.
75. The Toano Route.
78. Boise - Idaho City Toll Road.
93. Goodrich Trail.
94. South Boise Wagon Road.
126. City of Rocks and Granite Pass.
182. Soda Springs.
184. Salmon Falls and Thousand Springs.
232. Almo Massacre.
234. Massacre Rocks.
235. Battle of Bear River.
285. Nez Perce Trail.
286. Lolo Trail.
287. Mullan Road in Idaho.
290. Hudspeth's Cutoff.
427. Skinner Road.
783. Emigrant Roads North of the Snake River.
790. Camas Prairie Stage Lines.
792. Grangeville - Florence Stage Lines.
793. Grangeville - Salmon River - New Meadows Stage Lines.
814. Grangeville - Lewiston - Mount Idaho Stage Line.

Idaho Souvenir Hand Book in Honor of the Fort Hall Centennial, 1834 - 1934. Pocatello, ID: N.p., 1934. Geog.

IDE, Simon. Ed. Ide, William. BIOGRAPHICAL SKETCH.

IDE, William B. SEE: Rogers, Fred B. WILLIAM BROWN IDE.

_____. BIOGRAPHICAL SKETCH.... Ed. Simon Ide. N.p.: Private, 1880. CAL(Indep)-HALL-TRUCKEE. III. Rem. 1845.

ILLINGWORTH, Gertrude P. "An Historical Study of the Establishment of Boise City and Fort Boise." MA thesis, Univ. of Southern California, 1937. Geog.

Independent California Assn. of Lewiston, IL. Proceedings, 1849, by Lewis W. Ross, Home Secy. Articles of the Assn., Signed by Emigrating Partners and by Home Partners; By-Laws; Minutes of Meetings, 10 Feb - 17 Mar 1849. Illinois State Historical Library, Springfield, IL. Train Govt.

"Indians in Ambush." HARPER'S WEEKLY 12(2 May 1868): 282. Indians.

INGALLS, Eleaser S. JOURNAL OF A TRIP TO CALIFORNIA.... 1852. Reprint. Fairfield, WA: Ye Galleon, 1979. CAL(St. Jo). II. 1850.

INGALLS, Rufus. REPORT OF THE SECRETARY OF WAR. 34th Cong., 1st sess. S. Doc. 1, Pt. 2. Serial 811. CAL(Leav)-BRIDGER-Ends SLC. II. 1854. CAL(SLC)-SLCUT. II. 1855.

INGERSOLL, Chester. OVERLAND TO CALIFORNIA IN 1847. Ed. Douglas C. McMurtrie. Chicago: Black Cat, 1937. CAL(Indep)-BRIDGER-HALL-TRUCKEE. III. 1847.

INGRAM, Patricia M. HISTORIC TRANSPORTATION ROUTES THROUGH SOUTHWESTERN MONTANA. Boulder, CO:

WICHE, 1976. MONTANA-Genl.

INGRIM, Godfrey C. Recollections. KSHIST. CAL(St. Jo)-BRIDGER-SLCUT. Rem. 1851. Not Seen.

INMAN, Henry, and William F. Cody. THE GREAT SALT LAKE TRAIL. NY: Macmillan, 1898. Overland-Genl.

INMAN, Joel C. SEE: Baker, Lois I. "Joel C. Inman."

INMAN, Loris F. "The Mystery of Sweet Springs Road." LANE COUNTY HISTORIAN 13(Sum 1968): 58-59. OR-Genl.

_____, and Creat Inman Marsh. "The Road across Lane County, Oregon, to California. Known as the Old Trail 1836 and Before the Applegate Trail 1846 Territorial Road 1854." LANE COUNTY HISTORIAN 12(Spr & Sum 1967): 3-56. Pres. APPLE-Genl. Maps.

INMAN, R. D. "Across the Plains in 1865." In FOURTEENTH ANNUAL CONCATENATED ORDER OF HOO-HOO. Portland: Union, 1905. OR(Council). IV. Rem. 1865.

INSTRUCTIONS TO AGENTS AND EMPLOYEE'S OF WELLS, FARGO & COMPANY'S OVERLAND EXPRESS. WITH TARIFF OF RATES, INC. NY: Seymour, 1868. Stage.

IRBY, Mrs. Alfred. "Pathfinders of '49." OVERLAND MONTHLY 69(Feb 1917): 171-74. CAL-TEX(San Antonio)-GILA. IV. 1849.

IRVINE, J. B. "A Steam Wagon in Minnesota and Nebraska in 1860 and 1862." SOUTH DAKOTA HISTORICAL COLLECTIONS 10(1920): 371-87. Eqpt. Freight.

IRWIN, George. Overland...1863. MONHIST. Not Seen.

IRWIN, Ray W. "The Mountain Meadows Massacre." ARKANSAS HISTORICAL QUARTERLY 9(Spr 1950): 1-32. Geog.

ISHAM, Giles S. GUIDE TO CALIFORNIA AND THE MINES. 1850. Reprint. Fairfield, WA: Ye Galleon, 1972. CAL(St. Jo)-HALL. II. 1849. Guide.

IVENS, Anthony W. "Traveling over Forgotten Trails, The Old Spanish Trail." IMPROVEMENT ERA 19(May 1916): 601-7; 26(Jul 1923): 771-84. SLCOR-Genl.

IVENS, Virginia W. PEN PICTURES OF EARLY WESTERN DAYS. Keokuk, IA: Private, 1908. CAL(Council)-BRIDGER-SLCUT-TRUCKEE-BECKWOURTH. III. Rem. 1853.

JACKMAN, Levi. Journal. UTHIST. MORMON. II. 1847.

JACKSON, Clarence S. PAGEANT OF THE PIONEERS: THE VERITABLE ART OF WILLIAM HENRY JACKSON. Denver: Harold Warp Pioneer Village, 1958. Graphics.

JACKSON, Donald, and Mary Lee Spence. THE EXPEDITIONS OF JOHN CHARLES FREMONT. 4 vols. Urbana: Univ. of Illinois Press, 1970-84. Govt. Biog.

JACKSON, Joseph H. BAD COMPANY: THE STORY OF CALIFORNIA'S LEGENDARY AND ACTUAL STAGE-ROBBERS, BANDITS, HIGHWAYMEN AND OUTLAWS FROM THE FIFTIES TO THE EIGHTIES. NY: Harcourt, 1949. Stage.

_____, ed. GOLD RUSH ALBUM. NY: Scribner's, 1949. CAL-1849-Graphics.

JACKSON, Mallet C. SEE: Kennedy, Glenn A. GO WEST.

JACKSON, Richard H. "The Overland Journey to Zion." In THE MORMON ROLE IN THE SETTLEMENT OF THE WEST. Charles Redd Monographs in Western History, No. 9. Provo: BYU Press, 1978. MORMON-Genl.

_____, and Raleigh W. Crausby. "Delimitation of the Pony Express Trail through Utah - Final Report." UTHIST. Pony.

JACKSON, W. Turrentine. "The Army Engineers as Road Surveyors and Builders in Kansas and Nebraska, 1854 - 1858." KANSAS HISTORICAL QUARTERLY 17(Feb 1949): 37-59. Govt. Military.

_____. "Banking, Mail and Express Service in British North America: The Role of Wells, Fargo on Vancouver Island and in British Columbia." PACIFIC NORTHWEST QUARTERLY 76(Oct 1985): 137-47. Stage.

_____. "Federal Road Building Grants for Early Oregon." OREGON HISTORICAL QUARTERLY 50(Mar 1949): 3-30. Freight.

_____. "The Fisk Expeditions to the Montana Gold Fields." PACIFIC NORTHWEST QUARTERLY 33(Jul 1942): 265-82. MONTANA-Genl.

_____. "Historical Survey of the Stampede Reservoir Area in the Little Truckee River Drainage District." SF: U.S. National Park Service, 1967. TRUCKEE-Genl.

_____. "A New Look at Wells Fargo, Stagecoach and the Pony Express." CALIFORNIA HISTORICAL QUARTERLY 35(Dec 1966): 291-324. Stage. Pony.

_____. "Portland: Wells Fargo's Hub for the Pacific Northwest." OREGON HISTORICAL QUARTERLY 86(Fall 1985): 229-267. Stage.

_____. "Racing from Reno to Virginia City by Wells Fargo and Pacific Union Expresses." NEVADA HISTORICAL SOCIETY QUARTERLY 20(Sum 1977): 75-92. Stage.

_____. "Salt Lake City: Wells Fargo's Transportation Depot during the Stagecoach Era." UTAH HISTORICAL QUARTERLY 53(Win 1985): 5-39. Stage.

_____. "Stages, Mails and Express in Southern California: The Role of Wells, Fargo & Company in the Pre-Railroad Period." Southern California Historical QUARTERLY 56(Fall 1974): 233-72. Stage.

_____. WAGON ROADS WEST: A STUDY OF FEDERAL ROAD SURVEYS AND CONSTRUCTION IN THE TRANS-MISSISSIPPI WEST, 1846 - 1869. Berkeley: Univ. of California Press, 1952. Overland-Genl. Govt.

_____. WELLS FARGO & COMPANY IN IDAHO TERRITORY. Boise: Idaho State Historical Society, 1984. Stage.

_____. "Wells Fargo & Company in Idaho Territory: The 1870's and Beyond." IDAHO YESTERDAYS 27(Spr 1983): 11-19. Stage.

_____. "Wells Fargo & Company in Idaho Territory: Old and New Routes, 1865." IDAHO YESTERDAYS 26(Spr 1982): 2-23. Stage.

_____. "Wells Fargo & Company in Idaho Territory: The Railroads and the Demise of Staging." IDAHO YESTERDAYS 26(Win 1983): 9-17. Stage.

_____. "Wells Fargo & Company in Idaho Territory: To the 'Grand Consolidation' of 1866." IDAHO YESTERDAYS 26(Fall 1982): 2-24. Stage.

_____. "Wells Fargo & Company in the Pacific Northwest: The Year of Greatest Activity." IDAHO YESTERDAYS 26(Fall 1982): 2-24. Stage.

_____. "Wells Fargo & Company: Into the Inland Empire and Idaho Territory." IDAHO YESTERDAYS 25(Win 1982): 2-19. Stage.

_____. WELLS FARGO IN COLORADO TERRITORY. Colorado Historical Society Monograph Series, No. 1. Denver: The Society, 1982. Stage. Excellent maps.

_____. "Wells Fargo Stagecoaching in Montana: Final Months." MONTANA 29(Oct 1979): 52-66. Stage.

_____. Wells Frago Stagecoaching in Montana: Into a New Territory." MONTANA 29(Jan 1979): 40-53. Stage.

_____. WELLS FARGO STAGECOACHING IN MONTANA TERRITORY. Helena: Montana Historical Society Press, 1979. Stage.

_____. Wells Fargo Stagecoaching in Montana: The Overland Mail Contract for 1868." MONTANA 29(Jul 1979): 56-68. Stage.

_____. "Wells Fargo Stagecoaching in Montana: Trials and Triumphs." MONTANA 29(Apr 1979): 38-53. Stage.

_____. "Wells Fargo Staging Over the Sierra." CALIFORNIA HISTORICAL QUARTERLY 49(Jun 1970): 99-133. Stage.

_____. "Wells Fargo: Symbol of the Wild West?" WESTERN HISTORICAL QUARTERLY 3(Apr 1972): 179-96. Stage.

_____. "Wells Fargo's Pony Expresses." JOURNAL OF THE WEST 11(Jul 1972): 405-36. Pony.

JACKSON, William H. SEE: Jackson, Clarence S. PAGEANT OF THE PIONEERS.

_____. "Bullwhacking across the Plains." In TOLD AT THE EXPLORERS CLUB. Ed. Frederick A. Blossom. NY: Albert and Charles Boni, 1931. Freight: Neb. City - SLC. II. 1866.

_____. THE DIARIES OF WILLIAM HENRY JACKSON, FRONTIER PHOTOGRAPHER, TO CALIFORNIA AND RETURN, 1866-1875.... Eds. LeRoy and Ann W. Hafen. The Far West and the Rockies Historical Series 1820 - 1875, vol. 10. Glendale: Clark, 1959. Freight: Neb. City - SLC. II. 1866. CAL-SLCOR(SLC-LA-SLC)-MORMON. II. 1867. Graphics.

_____. "The Most Important Nebraska Highway, Nebraska City - Fort Kearny - Denver Trail, or 'Steam Wagon Road'." NEBRASKA HISTORY 13(Jul-Sept 1932): 137-59. PIKES-Genl. CAL-Genl.

_____. "Notes from Diary of a 'Bull whacker' on an Overland Freighting Trip from Missouri River to Salt Lake City, 1866." COHIST. Freight: Neb. City - SLC. II. 1866.

JACOB, Norton. Life. UTHIST. MORMON. II+. 1847.

JACOBS, Nancy O. "Incidents...Whitman Massacre." (In) TOLD BY THE PIONEERS, Vol. 1. Washington Pioneer Project, 1937. OR(St. Jo). Rem. 1845. Not Seen.

JACOBS, Orange. MEMOIRS OF ORANGE JACOBS. Seattle: Lowman & Hanford, 1908. OR(Council). III. Rem. 1852.

JACOBS, Peter. JOURNAL OF THE REVEREND PETER JACOBS.... Toronto: Green, 1853. CANADA(Rice Lake-Ft. Garry-York Factory). II+. 1852.

JAEGER, Louis J. Account Books. Yuma, 1860-91. Univ. of Arizona Library-SpCol, Tucson, AZ. Geog.

_____. "Diary of a Ferryman and Trader at Fort Yuma, 1855 - 1857." Ed. George W. Beattie. PUBLICATIONS Historical Society of Southern California 19(1928): 89-128, 213-41. Biog.

JAEHNIG, Ernest W. Letters. WEST BEND [Wisconsin] NEWS, 7 & 8 March 1928. CAL(Council). III. 1852.

JAGER, Ronald G. "The Chisholm Trail's Mountain of Words." SOUTHWESTERN HISTORICAL QUARTERLY 71(Jul 1967): 61-68. Bib.

JAGGER, D. Diary. BANCROFT. CAL(Indep)-HALL-TRUCKEE. I. 1849. Pencil Sketches. Flora.

JAMES, Eugenia L., and Vivian K. McLarty, eds. "Three Generations in the Span of a Continent: The Zumwalt Family, Parts I and II." MISSOURI HISTORICAL REVIEW 48(Apr, Jul 1954): 249-63, 341-51. OR(St. Jo?). V. 1850. Also see Solomon Zumwalt.

JAMES, Harold L. "The World's Most Expensive Guidebook." NEW MEXICO 48(Jan-Feb 1970): 24-33. GILA-Genl.

JAMES, Harry. "Warner: The Man and the Place." DESERT 28(Nov 1965): 20-23. Geog: Warner Springs.

JAMES, Jason W. "A Trip to Utah in 1858." FRONTIER TIMES 4(Mar 1927): 1-6. CAL(Leav)-BRIDGER-Ends SLC. IV. 1858.

JAMES, John R. "Autobiography." (In) TOLD BY THE PIONEERS, Vol. 2. Washington Pioneer Project, 1938. OR(Council)-BARLOW. Rem. 1851. Not Seen.

JAMES, Numa. "Covered Wagon Correspondents Report Pike's Peak Gold Rush." DENVER WESTERNERS BRAND BOOK (1967): 303-40. PIKES-Genl.

JAMES, Samuel. Diary. ORHIST. OR(Council)-BARLOW. IV. 1850.

JAMES, Thomas L. "Development of the Overland Mail Service." COSMOPOLITAN, April 1896, 603-11. Mail.

JAMESON, Henry B. MIRACLE OF THE CHISHOLM TRAIL. N.p.: Tri-State Chisholm Trail Centennial Committee, 1967. Stock.

JAMESON, Jesse H. "Corinne: A Study of a Freight Transfer Point in the Montana Trade, 1869 to 1878." MA thesis, Univ. of Utah, 1951. Geog. Freight. MONTANA-Genl.

JAMISON, Belle, and Lizzie Jamison. "Journey from Egypt." Comp. Rea Jamison Kurtz. COHIST. PIKES. II. 1866.

JAMISON, Samuel M. "Diary of S. M. Jamison, 1850." NEVADA HISTORICAL SOCIETY QUARTERLY 10(Win 1967): 3-26. CAL(Indep)-BRIDGER-SLCUT. III. 1850.

JANTZEN, S. "Incredible Pony Express." SENIOR SCHOLASTIC, 14 Dec 1978, 20-22. Pony. Not Seen.

JAQUES, John. LIFE HISTORY AND WRITINGS OF JOHN JAQUES, INCLUDING A DIARY OF THE MARTIN HANDCART COMPANY. Ed. Stella Jaques Bell. Rexburg, ID: Ricks College Press, 1978. MORMON. III. 1856.

JARED, Israel. "A Trip across Nebraska in 1852." Ed. Dorothy J. Kallhoff. DENVERPUB. CAL(Council)-BRIDGER-SLCOR. V-. Rem. 1852.

JARVIS, Clarence E. "Alpine State Highway Preserves Historic Trail."

GRIZZLY BEAR 13(Mar 1913): 2, 4. Pres.

JASPER, James A. "Trail-Breakers and History-Makers of Julian - Bal-lena - Mesa Grande - Oak Grove - Warner Ranch - Banner - Cuyamaca in San Diego County, CA." SDHIST. Geog.

JATTA, Mary H. Journal. BANCROFT. CAL(Neb. City)-CHEROKEE(Julesburg-SLC)-SIMPSON. III. 1866.

"A Jaunt to Honey Lake Valley and Noble's Pass." HUTCHINGS' 1(Jun 1857): 529-41. NOBLE-Genl.

JEDLICK, William J. "Letters of Morris Sleight on the California Trail, 1850." MA thesis, De Paul Univ., 1953. Not Seen.

JEFFCOTT, P. R. NOOKSACK TALES AND TRAILS. Sedro-Wool-ley, WA: Courier-Times, 1949. CANADA(Whatcom Trail to Fraser Mines)-Genl. WASH-Genl.

JEFFERS, Mrs. Susie L. Reminiscence. Montana State Univ. Library-SpCol, Missoula, MT. MONTANA. 1865. Not Seen.

JEFFERSON, T. H. MAP OF THE EMIGRANT ROAD. 1849. Reprint. SF: California Historical Society, 1945. Guide.

JEFFREY, Julie R. FRONTIER WOMEN: THE TRANS-MISSISSIP-PI WEST, 1840-1880. NY: Hill & Wang, 1979. Social.

JENNE, Lora M. "Father's Life Story." Eastern Washington Historical Society Library, Spokane, WA. OR(Council?). V. Rem. 1864.

JENNINGS, Bill. "Following the Bradshaw Road." DESERT 40(Jul 1977): 20-23. BRADSHAW-Genl.

JENNINGS, James R. THE FREIGHT ROLLED. San Antonio: Naylor, 1969. Freight-Arizona.

JENNINGS, Oliver. Journal. BEINECKE. OR(Vancouver-Ft. Hall)-SLCUT(Ft. Hall-SLC). IV. 1851.

JENSEN, Christian. "The Ghost of the Overland Trail." FORD TIMES 47(Aug 1955): 27. SIMPSON-Genl.

JENSEN, Esther H. "A History of California Periodical Literature from 1891 - 1898.... MA thesis, Univ. of California-Berkeley, 1923. Bib.

JENSEN, James M. "The Development of the Central Valley Transpor-tation Route in California to 1920." PhD diss., Univ. of Southern California, 1965. Stage.

_____. "Cattle Drives from the Ranchos to the Gold Fields of Califor-nia." ARIZONA & THE WEST 2(Win 1960): 341-52. CAL-Genl.

JENSEN, Lee. THE PONY EXPRESS. NY: Grossett & Dunlap, 1955. Good graphics.

JENSEN, Richard L. Trans. Christensen, C. C. A. "By Handcart to Utah."

JENSEN, Ross L. "The Greenwood - Sublette Cutoff of the Oregon Trail." MA thesis, Univ. of Utah, 1975. CAL-Genl.

JENSON, Andrew. DAY BY DAY WITH THE UTAH PIONEERS. SLC: Deseret News, 1934. MORMON-1847-Genl.

_____. "The First Company of Utah Pioneers." UTAH GENEALOGICAL & HISTORICAL MAGAZINE 4(Apr 1913): 84-92. MORMON-1847-Genl.

_____. "History of Fort Bridger and Fort Supply." UTAH GENEALOGICAL & HISTORICAL MAGAZINE 3(Feb 1912): 32-39. Geog.

_____, ed. "History of the Las Vegas Mission." NEVADA HIS-TORICAL SOCIETY PAPERS 5(1925-26): 119-284. SLCOR. II. 1855.

_____. "Latter Day Saints' Emigration from Wyoming, Nebraska, 1864-66." NEBRASKA HISTORY 17(Apr-Jun 1936): 113-27. MOR-MON-Genl.

_____. "Utah Pioneer Companies." UTAH GENEALOGICAL & HISTORICAL MAGAZINE 8(Jan 1917): 1-6. MORMON-Genl.

JESSUP, Edgar B., M. C. Nathan, and Henry H. Clifford. EARLY CALIFORNIA MAIL BAG. SF: Book Club of California, 1960. Mail.

JEWETT, George E. Diary. BANCROFT. CAL(Council)-BRIDGER-SLCUT-LASSEN. III. 1849.

JEWETT, Mendall. Journal. DENVERPUB. CAL(St. Jo). II+. 1850.

JOHANNSEN, Robert W. "Overland Migrations West of the Mississip-pi." MA thesis, Univ. of Kansas, 1958. Overland-Genl.

JOHANSEN, Dorothy O. "A Working Hypothesis for the Study of Migrations." PACIFIC HISTORICAL REVIEW 36(Feb 1967): 1-12. Overland-Genl.

"John Day Ford at McDonald." SUNSET 143(Sept 1969): 30. Geog.

JOHN, James. "The Diary of James St. Johns [James John]." Ed. George H. Himes. St. John [Oregon] REVIEW, 16, 30 March, 6, 13, 20, 27 April 1906, n.p. OR(Westport)-Ends Cache Valley. III. 1841.

JOHNSGARD, Paul A. THE PLATTE: CHANNELS IN TIME. Lin-coln: Univ. of Nebraska Press, 1984. Geog.

JOHNSON, Alma D. TRAIL DUST: OVER THE B.O.D. THROUGH KANSAS. Detroit: Harlo, 1975. Stage: Smoky Hill Stage Route.

JOHNSON, Ann W. "The Long Journey of a Mormon Girl." Ed. Mike King. FRONTIER TIMES 49(Aug-Sept 1975): 8-14, 26. MORMON. V. 1851. SIMPSON. V-. 1864. Rare account of an apostate family fleeing Utah.

JOHNSON, Beulah. "Old Station." COVERED WAGON, 1974, 48-52. Stage: Shasta County, CA.

JOHNSON, Dale L. Ed. With Brian Cockhill. GUIDE TO MANUSCRIPTS.

JOHNSON, Dorothy M. THE BLOODY BOZEMAN. One of the American Trails Series. NY: McGraw-Hill, 1971. BOZE-Genl.

JOHNSON, George S. Reminiscence. AZHIST. GILA(LA to Yuma). II. 1850. Details on ferry.

JOHNSON, H. Parker. "Jones & Russell's Leavenworth and Pike's Peak Express Company." THE AMERICAN PHILATELIST 58(Nov 1944): 102-13. Mail-Graphics. Stage.

JOHNSON, H. Warren. "The First Bottle-Neck in California Traffic." OVERLAND MONTHLY 91(Jan 1933): 9-10, 16, 20, 24. Geog: Cahuenga Pass to Elizabeth Lake road.

JOHNSON, Hervey. SEE: Unrau, William. TENDING THE TALK-ING WIRE.

JOHNSON, Hezekiah. "Letters...1838 - 1849." Ed. J. Orin Oliphant. PACIFIC NORTHWEST QUARTERLY 37(Jan 1946): 15-30. OR(St. Jo). IV. 1845.

JOHNSON, Jeffrey O. "Utah's Negro Pioneers of 1847." LDS. Social. MORMON-1847-Genl.

JOHNSON, Joel H. Journal. UTHIST. MORMON. III+. 1857. MORMON. III+. 1861.

JOHNSON, John A. Journal. BEINECKE. CAL(Indep)-HALL-TRUCKEE. II+. 1849.

JOHNSON, John L. Diary. BEINECKE. OR(Council)-BARLOW. II. 1851.

JOHNSON, John Lawrence. Excerpts. ORU. OR(Savannah)-Ends on Sweetwater. V. 1851.

JOHNSON, Joseph E. TRAIL TO SUNDOWN.... Ed. Rufus D. Johnson. SLC: Johnson Family Committee, 1961. PIKES. III. 1859.

JOHNSON, Joseph H. Diary. HUNTL. CAL(St. Jo)-Ends Caspar, WY. III+. 1849.

JOHNSON, Judith. "Transportation and Communication in California, 1848-1860." MA thesis, Stanford Univ., 1929. CAL-Genl. Stage. Mail.

JOHNSON, LeRoy & Jean. JULIA, DEATH VALLEY'S YOUNGEST VICTIM. Roseville, MN: Authors, 1981. Geog.

JOHNSON, Luke S. Genealogy. UTHIST. MORMON. III+. 1847.

JOHNSON, M. R. Reminiscence. AZHIST. CAL-TEX-GILA. V. 1868. TEX-GILA-BEALE(Leaves at Hardyville and treks to Austin, NV). V. 1869. Stock drives.

JOHNSON, Mary M. "The San Antonio - San Diego Mail Line." MA thesis, Univ. of Southern California, 1938. Stage. Mail.

JOHNSON, Neil. Excerpts...Diary. ORHIST. OR(St. Jo)-BARLOW. V. 1851.

JOHNSON, Neill. Autobiography. Oregon State Library, Salem, OR. OR(Council). IV. Rem. 1858.

JOHNSON, Overton, and William H. Winter. "Route across the Rocky Mountains with a Description of Oregon and California." OREGON HISTORICAL QUARTERLY 7(1906): 62-104, 163-210, 291-327. OR(Indep). III. 1843. OR-CAL. III. 1844. CAL-Back to Missouri. III. 1845.

JOHNSON, Roy P. "Stagecoach Days were a Colorful Era in Valley History." RED RIVER VALLEY HISTORIAN 2(Aut 1968): 20-31. Stage.

JOHNSON, Rufus D. Ed. Johnson, Joseph E. TRAIL TO SUNDOWN.

JOHNSON, Sixtus E. Leaves from the Family Tree. BYU. SLCOR. III. 1854.

JOHNSON, Theodore T. SIGHTS IN THE GOLD REGION, AND SCENES BY THE WAY. NY: Baker & Scribner, 1849. Guide.

JOHNSON, Mrs. Virgil J., and J. W. Williams. "Some Northwest Texas Trails after Butterfield." WESTX 42(Oct 1966): 59-89. Stage.

JOHNSON, William. "Recollections of a Bullwhacker." IN HISTORY OF JOHNSON COUNTY, KANSAS. Ed. E. Blair. Lawrence: Stan-dard, 1915. Freight.

JOHNSON, William W. THE FORTY-NINERS. Time-Life Old West Series. NY: Time-Life, 1974. Fine graphics. CAL-1849-Genl.

JOHNSTON, Eliza. "The Diary of Eliza Johnston." Eds. Charles P. Roland and Richard C. Robbins. SOUTHWEST HISTORICAL QUARTERLY 60(Apr 1957): 463-500. OKLAHOMA(Neosho, MO)-TEX(Gainesville - San Antonio). II+. 1855.

JOHNSTON, Francis J. THE BRADSHAW TRAIL. Eds. John R. Brumgardt and Tom Patterson. Riverside: Riverside County Historical Commission Press, c.1976. Map. BRADSHAW-Genl.

_____. "Stagecoach Travel through San Gorgonio Pass." JOURNAL OF THE WEST 11(Oct 1972): 616-35. Stage.

JOHNSTON, John F. A Trip to the Gold Fields...1852. Ohio Historical Society Library, Columbus, OH. CAL(Savannah)-BRIDGER. IV. Rem. 1852.

JOHNSTON, Lysander. Recollections. Missouri Historical Society-St. Louis. CAL(Indep). Rem. 1852.

JOHNSTON, Philip. "Arid Outposts of Carrizo." WESTWAYS 26(Jan 1934): 10-11. Geog.

_____. "Gibraltar of the Old Frontier." WESTWAYS 26(May 1934): 20-21, 39. Geog: Camp Cady, CA.

_____. "Saga of Old Fort Tejon." TOURING TOPICS 28(Nov 1933): 10-11, 39. Geog.

JOHNSTON, Samuel M. "Agreement with Wesley A. Wilsey and T. P. Henley for Transportation to Sacramento, CA." LILLEY. Train Govt.

JOHNSTON, William C., Jr. "The Smoky Hill Trail." MA thesis, Univ. of Denver, 1927. Geog. Stage.

JOHNSTON, William G. OVERLAND IN 1849. 1892. Reprint. Oakland: Biobooks, 1948. CAL(Indep)-BRIDGER-SLCUT. I. Rem. 1849.

JOHNSTON, William H. Diary. CSL. CAL(St. Jo). III. 1852.

JOHNSTONE, William. Diary. MNHIST. DAKOTAS(Winona, MN)-MONTANA. II+. 1866.

JOLLY, William C. ACROSS THE PLAINS IN DAYS OF HOSTILE INDIANS. Tecumseh, NB: Chieftain, 1923? PIKES. III. 1864. Indians.

"Jonathan Rea I." MADERA COUNTY HISTORIAN 9(Oct 1969: 1-7. CAL(Indep). V-. 1853. Sheep drive.

JONES' GUIDE. In Andrew S. McClure Journal. ORU. Guide.

JONES, ? Journal. Univ. of Washington Library-MS, Seattle, WA. CAL(Indep)-Ends Chimney Rock. IV. 1850.

JONES, ? Reminiscence. Idaho State Historical Society Library, Boise, ID. Stage.

JONES, Brian. "Those Wild Reshaw Boys." In SIDELIGHTS OF THE SIOUX WARS. Ed. Francis B. Taunton. ENGLISH WESTERNERS SPECIAL PUBLICATION (1967): 5-46. Indians.

JONES, Carlton. Diary. MO-WHMC. CAL(SLC to Ringgold, CA). 1850. Not Seen.

JONES, Daniel. Travels across the Plains. MO-WHMC. Freight: Atchison-Soda Springs-MONTANA. V. 1865. Freight: Virginia City, MT-CHEROKEE-Atchison. V. 1866.

JONES, Daniel W. FORTY YEARS AMONG THE INDIANS. SLC: Juvenile Instructor, 1890. MORMON-1856-Genl.

JONES, David R. "Significance of the First Wagon Train." OVERLAND MONTHLY 88(Oct 1930): 292-94, 312, 316. Overland-Genl.

JONES, Evan O. Diary. BANCROFT. CAL(Indep). IV. 1852.

JONES, Eliza J. Letters. IDHIST. OR(Council). WASH. 1854. Indians(Ward Massacre). Not Seen.

JONES, Harvey H. Journal and Letters. IDHIST. OR(Council)-via Naches Pass to Washington. Rem. 1854. Indians-Ward Massacre. Not Seen.

JONES, Idwal. "Six-Horse Charley." WESTWAYS 29(Aug 1937): 16-17. Biog-Charley Parkhurst.

JONES, John D. Diary., UTHIST. Not Seen.

JONES, John N. Journal. KSHIST. CAL(Iowa Point)-Ends Humboldt Sink. IV. 1850.

JONES, John W. A Diary of a Trip in 1858 - 1859 from Minnesota to Oregon. NEWBERRY. OR-CANADA-DAKOTAS(St. Paul)-Ft. Garry-Ft. Edmonton-Vancouver. I. 1858. Unique route to Oregon.

JONES, John W. AMUSING AND THRILLING ADVENTURES.... Ed. John Dix. Boston: Private, 1854. CAL(Council). V-. 1858?

JONES, John Wesley. "Jones Pantoscope of California." CALIFORNIA HISTORICAL QUARTERLY 6(Jun, Sept 1927): 109-29, 238-53. Graphics.

JONES, Larry R. Ed. With Merle Wells. "Oregon Trail Cultural Resource Study."

_____. "Staging to the South Boise Mines." IDAHO YESTERDAYS 29(Sum 1985): 19-25. Stage.

JONES, Louis T. RED MAN'S TRAIL. San Antonio: Naylor, 1967. Overland-Genl. Indians.

JONES, Mrs. M. A. Reminiscences. CAL(St. Jo)-BRIDGER-HALL-TRUCKEE. IV. Rem. 1846.

JONES, Nathaniel V. "The Journal of...." UTAH HISTORICAL QUARTERLY 4(Jan 1931): 6-24. CAL(Leav)-SANTA FE-RIO GRANDE-GILA. III. 1846. CAL(Sutter's)-TRUCKEE-Leavenworth. III. 1847.

JONES, Newell. "The Jackass Mail Preceded the Pony Express." FRONTIER TIMES 14(1937): N.p. Stage-San Antonio to San Diego.

JONES, Richard W. Diary. UTHIST. CAL(Atchison)-BRIDGER-Ends SLC. II+. 1859.

JONES, Ruth M., and Robert N. McMillan. "Utah, the Mormons, and the West: A Bibliography." UTAH HISTORICAL QUARTERLY 23(Jan 1955): 79-98. Bib.

_____, S. Lyman Tyler, Ralph Hansen, and Chad Flake. "Utah, Mormons, and the West: A Bibliography." UTAH HISTORICAL QUARTERLY 23(Oct 1955): 279-98. Bib.

JONES, Sydney. My Trip Overland. Filson Club Library, Louisville, KY. CAL(Council)-MONTANA. 1866. Indians. Not Seen.

JOOST, Nicholas. "Reveille in the West: Western Travelers in the St. Louis WEEKLY REVEILLE, 1844-50." In TRAVELERS ON THE WESTERN FRONTIER. Ed. John F. McDermott. Urbana, IL: Univ. of Illinois Press, 1970. Bib.

JORDAN, David. Diary. CSL. CAL(Fort Smith)-SANTA FE-RIO GRANDE-GILA. I. 1849.

JORDAN, John. "Speech Honoring...Pioneers." BANCROFT. CAL-TEX(Red River)-GILA. V. 1850.

JORDAN, Rudolph. "Rudolph Jordan - An Autobiography." Society of California Pioneers QUARTERLY 4(Dec 1927): 174-201. CAL-MEX(Vera Cruz-Mexico City-San Blas-Mazatlan). II. 1848.

JORDAN, Terry G. TRAILS TO TEXAS: SOUTHERN ROOTS OF WESTERN CATTLE RANCHING. Lincoln: Univ. of Nebraska Press, 1981. TEX-Genl.

JORY, James. "Reminiscences of James Jory." Ed. H. S. Lyman. OREGON HISTORICAL QUARTERLY 3(Sept 1902): 271-86. OR(Indep). IV. Rem. 1847.

JOSSELYN, Amos P. THE OVERLAND JOURNAL OF AMOS PIATT JOSSELYN. Ed. J. William Barrett, II. Baltimore: Gateway, 1978. CAL(Indep)-BRIDGER-SLCUT-LASSEN. III. 1849.

JOSEPHY, Alvin M., Jr. "First 'Dude Ranch' Trip to the Untamed West." AMERICAN HERITAGE 7(Feb 1956):8-15. CAL(Kansas City)-Ends Green River. II. 1843.

_____. "The Lolo Trail." NEW YORK WESTERNERS BRAND BOOK 4, no. 4(1958): 82-85. Geog.

Journal. MONHIST. CAL(Marysville)-LASSEN-OR-CAL-Ends Deschutes, OR. III. 1862.

Journal of Overland Trip. Monroe, Michigan party including Delos Ashley. Attributed to BANCROFT but uncited in catalog. 1849.

"Journey from New Orleans to California." SEE: Edwardson, Tom.

JOY, Emmett P. "A Gold Rush Road: First Public Highway in Calaveras County." BANCROFT. CAL-Genl.

JUDD, B. Ira. "The Overland Mail." ARIZONA HIGHWAYS 34(Oct 1958): 8-13, 38-39. Stage.

JUDD, Mary D. Sketch. UTHIST. MORMON. IV. Rem. 1850.

JUDD, Zodak K. Autobiography. Univ. of Utah Library-SpCol, Salt Lake City, UT. CAL(Leav)-SANTA FE-RIO GRANDE-GILA. V. Rem. 1846. CAL(Sutter's)-SLCUT-Ends SLC. V. Rem. 1848.

JUDGE, Timothy. Diary. Attributed to BANCROFT but uncited in catalogs. 1849.

JUDSON, H. M. Diary. NBHIST. OR(Council)-LANDER. I. 1862.

JUDSON, Lewis. "The Emigration of 1843." MARION COUNTY HISTORY 7(Dec 1961): 17-19, 22. OR-1843-Genl.

JUDSON, Phoebe G. A PIONEER'S SEARCH FOR AN IDEAL HOME. Ed. John M. McClelland, Jr. 1925. Reprint. Tacoma: Washington State Historical Society, 1966. OR(Westport). III. Rem. 1853.

KAHLER, James O. ANTOINE OF OREGON. NY: American Book, 1912. OR-Genl.

KAHLER, William. Notes...1852. Oregon State Library, Salem, OR. OR(St. Jo)-Ends on Sweetwater. III. Rem. 1852.

KAISER, Leo M. Ed. With Rebecca Ketcham. "From Ithaca to Clatsop Plains."

KAISER, P. G. How We Made the Emigrant Road. BANCROFT. OR. IV. 1843.

KAISER, Thomas D. Statement. BANCROFT. OR. V. 1843.

KAISER, Verle G. "Straight as an Arrow: The 'Kentuck Trail'." PACIFIC NORTHWESTERNER 23(Spr 1979): 17-30. WASH-Genl. Map.

KALIHER, Michael. "The Applegate Trail, 1846 - 1853." JOURNAL OF THE SHAW HISTORICAL LIBRARY 1(Fall 1986): N.p. Not Seen.

KALLHOFF, Dorothy J. Ed. Jared, Israel. "Trip across Nebraska."

KANE, Doris E. "Sketches of the James Kane Stage Line and Pioneer NV-CAL Transportation." CSL. Stage.

KANE, Michael. Statement. BANCROFT. CAL(St. Jo)-HALL. V. 1849.

KANE, Paul. WANDERINGS OF AN ARTIST.... 1859. Reprint. Rutland, VT: Tuttle, 1968. CANADA(Toronto)-Ft. Garry-Norway House-Ft. Edmonton-Jasper's House-Vancouver. II+. 1846. CANADA(Walla Walla)-Ft. Colville-Edmonton-Ft. Garry. II+. 1847. Graphics.

KANE, Thomas L. THE MORMONS. Philadelphia: King & Beard, 1850. MORMON. II. 1847.

Kansas Department of Economic Development. FRONTIER TRAILS OF KANSAS; CONTINENTAL CROSSROADS. Topeka: N.p., 1975? Map.

"Kansas Historical Markers." KANSAS HISTORICAL QUARTERLY 10(Nov 1941): 339-68. Pres.

Kansas Park and Resources Authority. TRAILS IN KANSAS: A SPECIAL STUDY. Topeka?: The Authority, 1979. Pres.

Kansas State Historical Society. A SURVEY OF HISTORIC SITES AND STRUCTURES IN KANSAS. Topeka: The Society, 1957. Pres.

KARCHNER, Mrs. Nicholas H. Diary. CSL. CAL(Council)-BRIDGER-SIMPSON. III+. 1862.

KARN, Edwin D. "Pre-Railroad Transportation in the Upper Mississippi Valley." PhD diss., Univ. of Wisconsin-Madison, 1986. Overland-Genl.

KARTCHNER, William D. "Autobiography." In OUR PIONEER HERITAGE, vol. 6, ed. Kate Carter. SLC: Daughters of the Utah Pioneers, 1963. SANTA FE. V. 1846. CHEROKEE(Pueblo-SLC). V. 1847.

KASSLER, George W. Diary. COHIST. PIKES. III. 1860.

————. "George W. Kassler: Colorado Pioneer." Ed. Philip K. Alexander, Jr. COLORADO MAGAZINE 39(Jan 1962): 29-46. CHEROKEE(Denver-Santa Fe). IV. 1862.

KAULFERS, Walter V. Trans. Hagelstein, George. "The Hagelstein Diary."

KAUTZ, August V. "From Missouri to Oregon in 1860: The Diary of...." Ed. Martin F. Schmitt. PACIFIC NORTHWEST QUARTERLY 37(1946): 193-230. OR-MONTANA-MULLAN. II. 1860.

KAYE, Barry, and John Alwin. "The Beginnings of Wheeled Transport in Western Canada." GREAT PLAINS QUARTERLY 4(Spr 1984): n.p. CANADA-Genl.

KAYLOR, Raymond D. "The Immigration Activity of the Inland Empire Missions." MA thesis, State College of Washington, 1932. OR-Genl.

KEARNS, John T. Journal. In Paul & Helen Henderson Collection. UWY. OR(Council)-BARLOW. II. 1852.

KEARNY, Stephen W. REPORT OF A SUMMER CAMPAIGN TO THE ROCKY MOUNTAINS, &c., IN 1845. 29th Cong., 1st sess. 1845. S. Doc. 1, pp. 210-14. CAL(Leav)-Ends South Pass-CHEROKEE(Ft. Laramie-Pueblo)-SANTA FE-Ends Leavenworth. V-. 1845.

KEATON, Charles H. "Crossing the Plains in '61; Reminiscences of...." Ed. Martha G. Averill. FRONTIER AND MIDLAND 16(Win 1935): 148-53. Freight: St. Jo-Denver-Virginia City, MT.

KEAYS, Elizabeth. "Diary." In THE SAGA OF "AUNTIE" STONE AND HER CABIN. Ed. Nolie Mumey. Boulder, CO: Johnson, 1964. PIKES. III. 1866.

KECK, Joseph A. Diary. South Dakota Historical Society, Pierre, SD. CAL(Council. 1850. Not Seen.

KEEGAN, Elizabeth J. Letters. In DAR Pioneer Records. CSL. CAL. V-. 1852.

KEEL, Murter N. "Ox Wagons, Indians and Winchesters." FRONTIER TIMES 5(Jan 1928): 188-90. CAL. V-. 1850.

KEELER'S MAP OF THE U.S. TERRITORY FROM THE MISSISSIPPI RIVER TO THE PACIFIC OCEAN.... WA: GPO, 1868. Map.

KEEN, Richard. Account of a Journey. CSL. CAL(St. Jo). II+. Rem. 1852.

KEIL, William. "From Bethel, Missouri, to Aurora, Oregon...." Ed. William G. Bek. MISSOURI HISTORICAL REVIEW 48(Oct 1953, Jan 1954): 23-41, 141-53. OR(St. Jo). IV. 1855.

KEITH, Clayton. SEE: With James E. Carstarphen. MY TRIP TO CALIFORNIA.

KEITH, Fleury F. "Journal." In TWO ARGONAUTS ON THE OREGON TRAIL. Menlo Park, CA: Amargosa Memorial Library, 1961. CAL(St. Jo)-BRIDGER-SLCUT. III. 1850.

KELL, Elmer A., Jr. "Early Travel and Communication in Southern California." MA thesis, Univ. of Southern California, 1940. Mail. Freight. Stage. SLCOR-Genl. CAL-Genl.

KELLAM, John P. Diary. BARKER. CAL-SANTA FE-CHEROKEE. IV. 1847.

KELLER, George. A TRIP ACROSS THE PLAINS AND LIFE IN CALIFORNIA. 1851. Reprint. Oakland: Biobooks, 1955. CAL(St. Jo)-HALL-LASSEN. III. Rem. 1850. Guide.

KELLER, Robert H., Jr. Ed. Blanchard, Jonathan. "1864 Overland."

KELLER, Teddy. SEE: With Stanley Zamonski. THE FIFTY-NINERS.

KELLEY, Mary L. My Trip.... MONHIST. CAL(Atchison)-BOZE. III-. Rem. 1864.

KELLOG, Stan. "History on Wheels - The Mud Wagon." WESTERN HORSEMAN 39(Nov 1969): 66, 170. Stage-Eqpt.

KELLOGG, Mrs. B. F. "Tells about Trip across Plains." GRIZZLY BEAR 6(Dec 1909): 17, 19. CAL. V. Rem. 1853.

KELLOGG, David. "Across the Plains in 1858." TRAIL, Dec 1912, 5-8. PIKES. II. 1858. PIKES V. 1859.

KELLOGG, George. "George Kellogg Writes of the Days of '49...." WIHIST. CAL(Council)-LASSEN. III. 1849.

KELLOGG, Jane D. "Memories." TRANSACTIONS Oregon Pioneer Association (1916): N.p. OR(Council). IV. Rem. 1852.

KELLOGG, M. G. NOTES CONCERNING THE KELLOGG'S. Battle Creek, MI: Private, 1927. CAL(Council)-LANDER-LASSEN. III+. Rem. 1859. Social.

KELLY, Charles. Ed. Chalmers, Robert. "Journal."

_____. Collection. UTHIST. Large group of trail-related source materials.

_____. "California's First Covered Wagons." UTHIST. CAL-1844-Genl.

_____. "Emigrant Register [and related data, 1936-55]." BANCROFT. 3000 names collected along trail.

_____. "First Emigrant Train." DESERT 9(Mar 1946): 5-8. Bidwell-Bartleson route from Soda Springs to the Humboldt. SLCUT-Genl. CAL-1841-Genl. Map.

_____. "Forgotten Trail of the Old West." DESERT 13(Oct 1950): 19-22. SPANISH-Genl.

_____. "Gold Seekers on the Hastings Cutoff." UTAH HISTORICAL QUARTERLY 20(Jan 1952): 3-30. HASTINGS-Genl.

_____. "The Hastings Cutoff." UTAH HISTORICAL QUARTERLY 3(1930): 67-82. HASTINGS-Genl.

_____. "Lansford W. Hastings: Author, Emigrant Guide and Discoverer of the Hastings Cutoff, Who Aspired to be 'President of California'." SCENIC UTAH MOTORIST 4(Oct 1930): 6-7, 12. HASTINGS-Genl.

_____. OLD GREENWOOD: THE STORY OF CALEB GREENWOOD, TRAPPER, PATHFINDER AND EARLY PIONEER OF THE WEST. SLC: Author, 1936. Biog.

_____. "On Manly's Trail to Death Valley." DESERT 2(Feb 1939): 6-8, 41, 43. SLCOR. II. 1849. Route from SLCOR to Meadow Valley Wash.

_____. "The Salt Desert Trail." UTAH HISTORICAL QUARTERLY 3(Apr 1930): 35-52. CAL-1841-Genl.

_____. SALT DESERT TRAILS: A HISTORY OF THE HASTINGS CUT-OFF.... SLC: Western, 1930. Overland-Genl.

_____. "Treasure Hunt on the Salt Desert." DESERT 10(Dec 1946):

11-13. CAL-1846-Genl. HASTINGS-Genl.

_____, and Maurice L. Howe. MILES GOODYEAR: FIRST CITIZEN OF UTAH. SLC: Western, 1937. Biog.

KELLY, Fanny. NARRATIVE OF MY CAPTIVITY AMONG THE SIOUX INDIANS. Hartford, CN: Mutual, 1872. Indians-1864.

KELLY, William. ACROSS THE ROCKY MOUNTAINS FROM NEW YORK TO CALIFORNIA. London: Simms & M'Intyre, 1852. CAL(Indep)-BRIDGER-SLCUT. II. 1849.

KELSEY, Mrs. Benjamin [Nancy]. "A California Heroine." GRIZZLY BEAR 16(Feb 1915): 6-7. CAL-1841-Genl. Biog.

_____. "Reminiscences of an 1841 Arrival." Ed. Josephine Miles. GRIZZLY BEAR 15(Oct 1914): 7. CAL-1841-Genl. Biog.

KENDALL, George W. "George Wilkins Kendall, Newsman, and a Party of Pleasure Seekers on the Prairie, 1851." Ed. R. Eli Paul. NEBRASKA HISTORY 64(Spr 1983): 35-80. CAL(Westport)-To Ft. Kearny and Council Bluffs. II. 1851.

KENDALL, Henry. "Overland Travel to the Pacific Slope." HOURS AT HOME, July 1865, 283-90. Stage.

KENDALL, Reese P. PACIFIC TRAIL CAMP-FIRES. Chicago: Scroll, 1901. OR-Genl.

KENDERDINE, Thaddeus S. A CALIFORNIA TRAMP AND LATER FOOTPRINTS. Newton, PA: Globe, 1888. CAL(Leav)-BRIDGER-SLCOR. II. Rem. 1858. Graphics. Freight.

KENNEDY, G. W. THE PIONEER CAMPFIRE. Portland: Author, 1913. OR(St. Jo)-BARLOW. IV. Rem. 1853.

KENNEDY, Glenn A. Ed. McCutchan, Rebecca E. "Headed West."

_____. GO WEST. Stockton, CA: Author, 1967. Overland-Genl.

KENNEDY, Michael S. "Portfolio of Paul Dyck: Indians of the Overland Trail." MONTANA 12(Jul 1962): 56-66. Indians-Graphics.

_____. "W. H. D. Koerner: Portrayer of Pioneers." MONTANA 15(Jan 1965): 52-67. Graphics.

KENNEDY, William C. Westward Kennedys. In W. W. Morrison Collection. UWY. OR(St. Jo)-BARLOW. IV. Rem. 1852.

KENNER, Charles. "The Origins of the 'Goodnight' Trail Reconsidered." SOUTHWESTERN HISTORICAL QUARTERLY 77(Jan 1974): 390-94. Stock.

KENNERLY, William C. "My Hunting Trip to the Rockies in 1843." COLORADO MAGAZINE 22(Jan 1945): 23-37. CAL(Westport)-Ends South Pass. IV. Rem. 1843.

_____. PERSIMMON HILL: A NARRATIVE OF OLD ST. LOUIS AND THE FAR WEST. Norman: Univ. of Oklahoma Press, 1948. CAL(Westport)-Ends South Pass. IV. 1843.

KENT, Deborah G. SEE: With Horace Kent. "Reminiscence."

KENT, Horace A. and Deborah G. Reminiscence. ORHIST. OR(Council?). V. Rem. 1853.

KEPLEY, Ray R. TAILS UP. Garden City, NY: Author, 1980. Freight.

KERN, Edward M. "Journal, 1845." In James H. Simpson's REPORT OF EXPLORATIONS...CAMP FLOYD TO GENOA, IN CARSON

VALLEY, IN 1859. WA: GPO, 1876. CAL(Begins Elko, NV)-Reaches Central Valley by Owens River. III. 1845.

KERNS, John T. "Journal of Crossing the Plains to Oregon in 1852." TRANSACTIONS Oregon Pioneer Association, 1914 (1917): 148-93. OR(Council)-BARLOW. II. 1852. SEE ALSO: Kearns, John T.

KERR, John M. Letters. BANCROFT. CAL-1849-Genl. Geog-St. Joseph, MO.

KERWIN, M. W. Diary, 1860. DENVERPUB. PIKES. IV. 1860.

KESSELMAN, Amy. "Diaries and Reminiscences of Women on the Oregon Trail: A Study in Consciousness." MA thesis, Portland State Univ., 1974. Social. Not Seen.

KETCHAM, Rebecca. "From Ithaca to Clatsop Plains...." Eds. Leo M. Kaiser and Priscilla Knuth. OREGON HISTORICAL QUARTERLY 62(Sept, Dec 1961): 237-87, 337-402. OR(Indep)-Ends at Willow Creek. I. 1853.

KEYES, Elizabeth. "Across the Plains in a Prairie Schooner." COLORADO MAGAZINE 10(Mar 1933): 71-78. PIKES. III+. 1866.

KEYSER, S. Memoirs. Attributed to BANCROFT but uncited in catalogs.

KEYSON, Guy M. Journal. UTHIST. CAL(Leav)-SANTA FE-RIO GRANDE-GILA. II. 1846.

KIBBY, Leo P. "Patrick Edward Connor, First Gentile of Utah." JOURNAL OF THE WEST 2(Oct 1963): 425-34. Biog.

_____. "With Col. Carleton and the California Column." Southern California Historical QUARTERLY 41(Dec 1959): 337-44. GILA-Genl-1862. Military.

KIDD, William H. GLITTERING GOLD: OR, PENCILINGS ABOUT PIKE'S PEAK.... St. Louis: Missouri Democrat, 1860. Guide.

KIDDER, Earnest R. "Blood on the Lead Mule." SISKIYOU COUNTY HISTORICAL SOCIETY YEARBOOK - 1950 I, no. 5(1951): 27-30. Freight.

KIDDER, Leroy L. Story of a Siskiyou Argonaut. CSL. CAL(St. Jo). IV. Rem. 1850. CAL-LASSEN-SLCUT-Ends Omaha. V. Rem. 1861.

KIEFER, David M. Ed. Brown, Adam. "Journal."

KIELMAN, Chester V. SEE: With Emmie Mahon. "George H. Giddings."

KIFFIN, Elizabeth A. "Overland Emigration through Nebraska, 1840 - 1870." MA thesis, Univ. of Nebraska, 1930. Overland-Genl.

KILBOURNE, Lewis. Journal. ORHIST. CAL(St. Jo)-BRIDGER-SLCUT. 1850. Not Seen.

KILDARE, Maurice. "The Soda Springs Treasures." FRONTIER WEST 47(Aug-Sept 1973): 14-17, 52-53. Metal-detecting at trail sites. Pres.

KILGORE, William H. THE KILGORE JOURNAL...TO CALIFORNIA...1850. Ed. Joyce R. Muench. NY: Hastings House, 1949. CAL(Council)-BRIDGER-SLCUT. III. 1850.

KIMBALL, Charles P. Diary. Society of California Pioneers, SF. Not Seen.

KIMBALL, Gorham G. "Trailing Sheep from California to Idaho in 1865...." Ed. Edward N. Wentworth. AGRICULTURAL HISTORY 28(Apr 1954): 49-83. Stock.

KIMBALL, Heber C. "The Pioneer Journal of...." UTAH GENEALOGICAL & HISTORICAL MAGAZINE 30(Jan, Apr, Jul, Oct 1939): 9-19, 76-85, 140-49, 204-11; 31(Jan, Apr, Jul 1940): 18-24, 80-87, 150-58. MORMON. II+. 1847.

KIMBALL, Richard. "Overland Journey." Riley County [Kansas] Historical Society LOG CABIN DAYS (1929): 31-36. PIKES. IV. 1860.

KIMBALL, Stanley B. SEE: With Hal Knight. 111 DAYS TO ZION.

_____. "Another Road to Zion: Rediscovering the Overland Trail." ENSIGN 14(Jun 1984): 34-35. CHEROKEE-Genl. Graphics. Pres. Map.

_____. DISCOVERING MORMON TRAILS: NEW YORK TO CALIFORNIA, 1831 - 1868. SLC: Deseret News, 1979. MORMON-Genl. Maps.

_____. "Equal Rights on the Pioneer Trail." SUNSTONE 6(May-Jun 1981): 3-4. Social.

_____. "The Iowa Trek of 1846: The Brigham Young Route from Nauvoo to Winter Quarters." ENSIGN 2(Jun 1972): 36-45. MORMON-1846-Genl. Map.

_____. THE MORMON TRAIL. N.p.: U.S. Bureau of Outdoor Recreation, 1974. Pres.

_____. "The Mormon Trail Network in Iowa, 1838 - 1863: A New Look." BRIGHAM YOUNG UNIVERSITY STUDIES 21(Fall 1981): 417-30. MORMON-Genl.

KING, Alfred D. "Trip to the Gold Fields." ARKANSAS GAZETTE, 19-26 Jan; 2, 9, 16, 23 Feb; 2, 9, 16, 23, 30 Mar; 6, 13, 20, 27 Apr; 4, 11, 18, 25 May; 1, 8, 15, 22, 29 Jun 1941. CAL(Ft. Smith)-MARCY-RIO GRANDE-GILA. II+. 1849.

KING, Anna M. "Letter." In COVERED WAGON WOMEN, vol. 1, ed. Kenneth L. Holmes. Glendale: Clark, 1983. OR-MEEK. V. 1845.

KING, Chester, and Dennis G. Casebier. BACKGROUND TO HISTORIC AND PREHISTORIC RESOURCES OF THE EAST MOJAVE DESERT REGION. Riverside?: U.S. Bureau of Land Management, 1976. BEALE-Genl.

KING, Clarence. SEE: Dickason, David H. "Clarence King's First Western Journey."

KING, David S. MOUNTAIN MEADOWS MASSACRE: A SEARCH FOR PERSPECTIVE. The Great Western Series, No. 8, ed. William G. Bell. WA: Potomac Westerners, 1970. SLCOR-Genl.

KING, Evelyn. WOMEN ON THE CATTLE TRAIL AND IN THE ROUNDUP. N.p.: Brazos Corral of Westerners, 1983. Stock.

KING, Hannah T. Journal. UTHIST. MORMON. II. 1853.

KING, John N. Journal. BEINECKE. CAL(Weston). III. 1850.

KING, Mike. Ed. Johnson, Ann W. "Long Journey."

KINGERY, Solomon. Overland Travels. BEINECKE. CAL(Council)-NOBLES. III+. 1852.

KINGMAN, Henry. TRAVELS AND ADVENTURES OF HENRY

KINGMAN. Delavan, KS: Private, 1917. CAL(Neb. City)-LASSEN. V. Rem. 1859.

KINGMAN, Romanzo. "Documents: Romanzo Kingman's Pike's Peak Journal, 1859." Ed. Kenneth F. Millsap. IOWA JOURNAL OF HISTORY 48(Jan 1950): 55-85. PIKES. II. 1859.

KINGSBURY, Ilene. "Political and Economic Setting for the Pony Express in the Great Basin." UTHIST. Pony.

_____. "Salute to the Pony Express." UTAH HISTORICAL QUARTERLY 28(Apr 1960): 131-34. Pony.

KINGSBURY, J. C. Journal. LDS. MORMON. 1847. Not Seen.

KINGSBURY, Joseph. "Pike's Peak Rush." COLORADO MAGAZINE 4(Jan 1927): 1-6. PIKES-Genl.

KINGSFORD, Elizabeth H. Reminiscence. UTHIST. MORMON. IV. Rem. 1856.

KINGSTON, C. S. Ed. Lueg, Henry. "Northern Overland Route."

_____. "Introduction of Cattle into the Pacific Northwest." WASHINGTON HISTORICAL QUARTERLY 14(Jul 1923): 163-85. Stock.

KINNEY, J. F. "An Indian Surprise on the Plains in 1854." GOLDEN ERA 40(Jul, Aug 1891): 953-59, 997-1006. Indians.

KIRBY, William. MORMONISM EXPOSED.... Nashville: N.p., 1893. CAL(Kansas City)-BRIDGER-Ends SLC. 1853. Not Seen.

KIRK, Esley J. Ed. With Merrill J. Mattes. Farnham, Elijah B. FROM OHIO TO CALIFORNIA.

KIRKALDIE, Franklin L. Reminiscence. MONHIST. CAL(Council)-BOZE. III. 1864.

KIRKPATRICK, Charles A. Diary. BANCROFT. CAL(St. Jo)-HALL-TRUCKEE. II+. 1849.

KIRKPATRICK, James. "A Reminiscence of John Bozeman." Ed. Paul C. Phillips. In FRONTIER OMNIBUS, ed. John W. Hakola. Missoula: Montana State Univ., 1962. Biog.

KIRKPATRICK, Robert. "From Wisconsin to Montana and Life in the West, 1863 - 1889...." Ed. Michael G. McLatchy. MA thesis, Montana State Univ., 1961. CAL(Council)-BOZE-LANDER-MONTANA. II. Rem. 1863.

KIRKPATRICK, Thomas J. THE KIRKPATRICK STORY. Orland, CA: Orland Register, 1954. OR(Council)-BARLOW. III. Rem. 1854.

KISER, Joseph C. Diary and Letters. WIHIST. CAL(St. Jo)-BRIDGER-SLCUT. II. 1850.

KITCHELL, Edward. A Trip across the Plains. WIHIST. CAL(Council)-BRIDGER-SLCUT-TRUCKEE-BECKWOURTH. II+. 1852.

KITTREDGE, Dayell H. Diary. HUNTL. CAL(Council)-Ends Rock Springs. II. 1865.

KLASSEN, Henry C. "The Red River Settlement and the St. Paul Route, 1859-1870." MA thesis, Univ. of Manitoba, 1963. DAKOTAS-Genl.

KLAUBER, Laurence M. RATTLESNAKES; THEIR HABITS, LIFE HISTORY, AND INFLUENCE ON MANKIND. 2 vols. Berkeley: Univ. of California Press, 1956. Fauna.

KLEINSORGE, Charles. "Charles Kleinsorge: Missouri to California, 1854." Ed. Edward Bode. MISSOURI HISTORICAL REVIEW 76(Jul 1982): 421-46. CAL(St. Jo). III. 1854.

KLEISER, James. A. Autobiography. BANCROFT. CAL(St. Jo)-BRIDGER-SLCUT. III. Rem. 1849. CAL(Weston)-LASSEN. IV. Rem. 1853.

KLINE, Perry A. Reminiscences. COHIST. PIKES. II. Rem. 1859.

KLISE, Carlyle N. "The First Transcontinental Telegraph." MA thesis, Univ. of Iowa, 1938. Telegraph.

KLOSS, Gerald. "Thundering Pony Express." SCIENCE DIGEST 46(Jul 1959): 20-24. Pony.

KLUMP, Sally P. "Stein's Peak Station." NEW MEXICO 55(Mar 1977): 34-35, 47-48. Geog.

KNAPP, Cornelius. Letter, 1850. CAL(Council-Ends Ft. Laramie. Attributed to National Park Service Library, Omaha, but uncited in catalog.

KNAPP, Edward S. PONY EXPRESS. NY: Scott Stamp & Coin, 1936. Pony stamps and covers.

KNAPP, W. Augustus. "An Old Californian's Pioneer Story." OVERLAND MONTHLY 10(Oct, Nov 1887): 389-408, 499-518. CAL(Ft. Smith)-OKLAHOMA-TEX-MEX(El Paso-Chihuahua-Mazatlan). IV. 1849.

KNIGHT, Amelia S. "Diary...1853." TRANSACTIONS Oregon Pioneer Association (1933): 38-53. OR(Council)-BARLOW. II. 1853.

KNIGHT, Hal, and Stanley B. Kimball. 111 DAYS TO ZION. SLC: Deseret News, 1978. MORMON. II+. 1847. Guide. Maps.

KNIGHT, Thomas. Recollections. In "Sketches of California Pioneers." BANCROFT. CAL(Indep)-BRIDGER-HALL. IV. Rem. 1845.

KNIGHT, William H. SEE: Power, Bertha K. WILLIAM HENRY KNIGHT.

_____. "An Emigrant's Trip across the Plains in 1859." PUBLICATIONS Southern California Historical Society 12(1923): 32-41. CAL(St. Jo)-SLCUT. V. Rem. 1859.

KNOTT, Thomas. "The Knott Journals." Ed. H. Hamlin. PONY EXPRESS 13(Nov, Dec 1946; Jan 1947): 1-13, 7-9, 9-12. Geog-Carson Valley.

KNOWLAND, Joseph R. CALIFORNIA, A LANDMARK HISTORY: STORY OF THE PRESERVATION AND MARKING OF EARLY DAY SHRINES. Oakland: Tribune, 1941. Pres.

KNOWLTON, Eleanor F. Recollections. CAHIST. CAL(Missouri). Rem. 1857. Not Seen.

KNOX, Olive. "Red River Cart." BEAVER, Mar 1942, 39-43. Eqpt.

KNOX, Reuben. "Reuben Knox' Letters, 1849 - 1851." Ed. Charles W. Turner. NORTH CAROLINA HISTORICAL REVIEW 38(Jan, Apr, Jul 1960): 66-93, 243-70, 397-418. CAL(Old Ft. Kearny). III. 1850. Medical.

_____. A MEDIC FORTYNINER. Ed. Charles W. Turner. N.p.: McClure, 1974. CAL(Old Ft. Kearny). III. 1850. Medical.

KNOX, Thomas W. "To Pike's Peak and Denver." KNICKERBOCKER

50(Aug 1861): 115-28. PIKES-Genl.

KNUDSON, S. "Letter." In CALIFORNIA EMIGRANT LETTERS, ed. Walker D. Wyman. NY: Bookman, 1952. CAL. 1849.

KNUTH, Priscilla. Ed. With Rebecca Ketcham. "From Ithaca to Clatsop Plains." Ed. Piper, Alexander. "Alexander Piper's Reports."

KOCK, Felix J. "The Hand Cart Brigade." OUT WEST 6(Sept 1913): 111-14. MORMON-Genl.

KOCK, William E. Ed. Graham, Alpheus N. "The Big Circle."

KOENIG, George. Ed. Nusbaumer, Louis. LOST DEATH VALLEY '49ER JOURNAL. Ed. Nusbaumer, Louis. VALLEY OF SALT.

_____. "Betwixt the Devil and the Deep." LOS ANGELES WESTERNERS BRAND BOOK 10(1963): 51-61. SLCOR. III. 1849.

_____. BEYOND THIS PLACE THERE BE DRAGONS: THE ROUTES OF THE TRAGIC TREK OF THE DEATH VALLEY 1849ERS THROUGH NEVADA, DEATH VALLEY, AND ON TO SOUTHERN CALIFORNIA. Glendale: Clark, 1984. SLCOR-1849-Genl. Fine summary of the route. Maps.

KOEPP, Donna P., ed. EXPLORATION & MAPPING OF THE AMERICAN WEST. Selected Essays, Occasional Paper No. 1. Chicago: Speculum, 1986. Maps.

KOESTER, Susan. "The Indian Threat along the Santa Fe Trail." PACIFIC HISTORIAN 17(Win 1973): 13-28. SANTA FE-Genl. Indians.

KOHRS, Conrad. Autobiography. DENVERPUB. CAL(Council)-BRIDGER-SLCUT-MONTANA. V. Rem. 1862.

KONE, Ed. "Cattle Trail to Louisiana in 1866." FRONTIER TIMES 8(Mar 1931): 249-56, 273-77. TEX(San Marcos-New Iberia). III. 1866.

KONWISER, Harry M. "Utah Mail" AMERICAN PHILATELIST 68(Jun 1955): 631-34, 688. Mail.

_____. "Warren's Mormon Express." AMERICAN PHILATELIST 64(Jan 1951): 286. Mail.

KOPP, April. "Camel Corps, U.S.A." AMERICAN HISTORY ILLUSTRATED 16(Dec 1981): 8-17. Govt.

KORELL, F. F. "From Indiana to Oregon City." NATIONAL REPUBLIC 19(Mar 1932): 16-18. Not Seen.

_____. "Wagon Trails to the West from 1840 to 1850." NATIONAL REPUBLIC 19(Feb 1932): 5-7. Overland-Genl. Not Seen.

KORN, Bertram W. Ed. Carvalho, Solomon N. INCIDENTS OF TRAVEL.

KORNS, J. Roderick. Papers, 1941-1953. UTHIST. Large trail-related holding. Overland Genl.

_____, ed. "West from Fort Bridger: The Pioneering of the Immigrant Trails across Utah, 1846-1850, Original Diaries and Journals. UTAH HISTORICAL QUARTERLY 19(1951): 1-268. HASTINGS-Genl. SLCUT-Genl. BRIDGER-Genl.

KOWRACH, Edward J. Ed. Blanchet, A. M. JOURNAL OF A CATHOLIC BISHOP. Ed. Nicaise, Auguste. A YEAR IN THE DESERT.

KREPS, Simon P. Journal. HUNTL. CAL(Council). III. 1852.

KRILL, Abram. Diary. BEINECKE. CAL(Indep). II. 1850.

KROEBER, A. L., and Clifton B. "Olive Oatman's First Account of her Captivity among the Mohave." CALIFORNIA HISTORICAL QUARTERLY 41(Dec 1962): 309-18. GILA-Genl. Indians.

KROEBER, Clifton B. SEE: Above item.

KROENIG, William, Sr. Autobiography. DENVERPUB. SANTA FE(Indep). V-. 1849.

KROLL, Helen B. "The Books that Enlightened the Emigrants." OREGON HISTORICAL QUARTERLY 45(Jun 1944): 102-23. Guide.

KRUEGER, Elwood W., Robert W. Howard, Richard Cabeen, Don Russell, and John S. Gray. "Centennial of the Pony Express." CHICAGO WESTERNERS BRAND BOOK 17(Apr 1960): 9-11, 14-16. Pony. Pres.

KRYTHE, M. R. "The Longest Stage Route in the World." TRUE WEST 3(Jan-Feb 1956): 19, 45-46. Stage.

KRYTHE, Maymie. PORT ADMIRAL PHINEAS BANNING, 1830-1850. SF: California Historical Society, 1957. Biog. Freight.

KUBISTA, Arizona Bob. "The Butterfield Overland Stage." TRUE WEST 16(Sept-Oct 1968): 34-35, 54-57. Stage-AZ.

KUHRE, Martin P. Day Book. UTHIST. MORMON. III-. 1862.

KUNTZ, James W., Sr. Forty-Niner. HUNTL. CAL(Indep). V-. Rem. 1849.

KUNZ, George F. "The Transcontinental Trails." AMERICAN SCENIC AND HISTORICAL PRESERVATION SOCIETY ANNUAL REPORT 17(1912): 419-32. Pres.

KUPPER, Winifred. THE GOLDEN HOOF: THE STORY OF THE SHEEP OF THE SOUTHWEST. NY: Knopf, 1945. Stock.

KURTZ, Rea Jamison. Comp. Jamison, Belle and Lizzie. JOURNEY FROM EGYPT.

KURUTZ, Gary F. SEE: With Gary E. Strong. WESTERN AMERICANA.

KUYKENDAL, J. H. "Clippings and Fragments." BARKER. TEX-Genl. MEX-Genl.

KUYKENDALL, George B. HISTORY OF THE KUYKENDALL FAMILY. PORTLAND: Kilham, 1919. OR(Council). III. Rem. 1852.

KUYKENDALL, Sarah. "One Hundred Ten Mile Crossing: Stopover on the Santa Fe Trail." KSHIST. Geog.

KUYKENDALL, W. L. FRONTIER DAYS. N.p.: Private, 1917. Stage. Freight. Indians.

LACK, Philip K. Ed. Gould, Jane H. "Iowa to California."

LADD, Richard S. MAPS SHOWING EXPLORERS' ROUTES, TRAILS AND EARLY ROADS IN THE UNITED STATES; AN ANNOTATED LIST. WA: U.S. Library of Congress, Map Division - GPO, 1962. Maps. Govt.

LAING, F. W. "Some Pioneers of the Cattle Industry." BRITISH COLUMBIA HISTORICAL QUARTERLY 6, no. 4(1942): 257-75. CANADA-Genl. Stock.

LAIRD, Moses F. Journal. BEINECKE. OR(St. Jo). III. 1852.

LAKE, John D. Journal. DENVERPUB. PIKES. IV. 1860.

LAKE, Stuart N. "Birch's Overland Mail in San Diego County." SAN DIEGO HISTORICAL SOCIETY QUARTERLY 3(Apr 1957): 15-18. Stage.

LAMAR, Howard R. "Rites of Passage: Young Men and their Families in the Overland Trail Experience, 1843-69." In SOUL-BUTTER AND HOG WASH AND OTHER ESSAYS ON THE AMERICAN WEST. Charles Redd Monographs in Western History, No. 8. Provo, UT: Brigham Young University Press, 1978. Social.

LAMB, Stewart F. Ed. McKaig, Silas. "We Rolled West."

LAMBERT, Julia S. "Plain Tales of the Plains." TRAIL 8(Jan, Feb 1916): 5-11, 4-10. PIKES. II. Rem. 1860.

LAMBOURNE, Alfred. THE OLD JOURNEY. SLC: Cannon & Sons, 1897. MORMON-1847-Graphics.

_____. THE PIONEER TRAIL. SLC: Deseret News, 1913. MORMON-Genl.

LAMME, M. Jackson. (In) Bryan, Charles W. "From Marthasville to Marysville in 1850." MISSOURI HISTORICAL BULLETIN 19(Jan 1963): 115-26. CAL(Leav). 1850. Not Seen.

LAMMONS, Frank B. "Operation Camel: An Experiment in Animal Transportation in Texas, 1857 - 1860." SOUTHWESTERN HISTORICAL QUARTERLY 61(Jul 1957): 20-50. Overland-Genl.

LAMPSON, Robin. Ed. Carr, John. A VULCAN AMONG THE ARGONAUTS.

LAMPTON, William. Diary. BANCROFT. CAL(St. Jo). III +. 1850.

"Land Routes to the Pacific." MERCHANT'S MAGAZINE 22(Feb 1850): 149-54. Overland-Genl.

LANDER, Frederick West. SEE: Branch, Ed. Douglas. "Frederick West Lander." SEE: Norton, Lewis A. LIFE AND ADVENTURES.

_____. "Additional Estimate for Fort Kearney, South Pass and Honey Lake Wagon Road." 36th Cong., 2d sess. 1861. H. Ex. Doc. 63. Overland-Genl-1861. Govt.

_____. MAPS AND REPORTS OF THE FORT KEARNEY, SOUTH PASS, AND HONEY LAKE WAGON ROAD. 36th Cong., 2d sess. 1861. Ex. Doc. 64.

_____. Papers. Library of Congress, Washington, DC. Biog.

LANE, John L. Diaries. Texas State Library-Archives, Austin, TX. CAL-TEX(Lockhart)-MEX(Eagle Pass-Monclova-Mazatlan). III. 1852. CAL(Los Angeles)-GILA-TEX. III. 1858.

LANE, Joseph. BIOGRAPHY.... WA: Congressional Globe, 1852. OR. 1848. Not Seen.

LANE, Samuel A. GOLD RUSH. Ed. Jeffrey E. Smith. Akron: Summit County Historical Society, 1984. CAL(St. Jo)-HALL. II. Rem. 1850.

LANG, Walter B. THE FIRST OVERLAND MAIL: BUTTERFIELD TRAIL. 2 vols. NY: Roycrofters, c1940.

LANGDON, Lynn. "William Carter, Fort Bridger, and the Overland Mail." LA POSTA 15(Oct, Dec 1984; Feb, Apr 1985): 51-58, 29-34, 53-56, 25-29. Stage: Fort Bridger-SLC-Placerville. II +. 1864. Mail.

LANGELLIER, John P. "Desert Documentary: The William Lee Diary of the James H. Simpson Expedition, 1858-1859." ANNALS OF WYOMING 59((Fall 1987). SIMPSON-1859-Genl. Not Seen.

LANGFORD, Nathaniel P. "Account of Stagecoach Travel Between Virginia City and Helena, Montana in 1865." MONHIST. Stage.

LANGLEY, Harold D., ed. TO UTAH WITH THE DRAGOONS AND GLIMPSES OF LIFE IN UTAH, ARIZONA AND CALIFORNIA, 1858 - 1859. Vol. 11 of University of Utah Publications in the American West, Brigham D. Madsen, General Ed. SLC: University of Utah Press, 1974. CAL(Leav)-BRIDGER-SLCOR. IV. 1858.

Langton's Pioneer Express. SPECIAL AND GENERAL INSTRUCTIONS...AGENTS AND EMPLOYEES. SF: Towne & Bacon, 1860. Stage.

LANGUM, David J. "Pioneer Justice on the Overland Trails." WESTERN HISTORICAL QUARTERLY 5(Oct 1974): 421-39. Train Govt.

LANGWORTHY, Franklin. SCENERY OF THE PLAINS, MOUNTAINS AND MINES.... Ed. Paul C. Phillips. One of the Narratives of the Trans-Mississippi Frontier, Carl L. Cannon, General Ed. 1855. Reprint. Princeton: Princeton Univ. Press, 1932. CAL(Council)-BRIDGER-SLCUT. II. 1850. Utah.

LAPP, Rudolph M. BLACKS IN GOLD RUSH CALIFORNIA. New Haven: Yale Univ. Press, 1977. Social.

LARIMER, Asenath. "Journal of an Overland Trip from Athens, Ohio, to California, 1852 - 53." MS thesis, Univ. of Southern California, 1929. CAL. 1852. Missing from stacks.

LARIMER, Sarah L. MY CAPTURE AND ESCAPE; OR LIFE AMONG THE SIOUX. Philadelphia: Claxton, 1870. Indians.

LARKIN, Elijah. Journal. BYU. MORMON. 1861. Not Seen.

LARNARD, Ira P. Journal. Princeton University Library-Western America, Princeton, NJ. PIKES. I. 1859.

LARNED, William L. "The Fisk Expedition of 1864: The Diary of William L. Larned." Ed. Ray H. Mattison. NORTH DAKOTA HISTORY 36(Spr 1969): 209-74. DAKOTAS-MONTANA. III +. 1864.

LARSEN, Arthur J. "The Northwestern Express and Transportation Company." NORTH DAKOTA HISTORICAL QUARTERLY 6(Oct 1931): 42-62. Stage. Freight.

LARSON, Gustive O. MORMON HANDCART STORY. SLC: Deseret News, 1956. MORMON-1856-Genl.

LARSON, T. A. Ed. Forman, George. "Across the Plains in 1864."

LASATER, Herbert. "The Ward Massacre." TRUE WEST 13(Nov-Dec 1965): 17, 42-45. 1854 Indian attack near Almo, ID. OR-1854-Genl.

LASS, William E. FROM THE MISSOURI TO THE GREAT SALT LAKE: AN ACCOUNT OF OVERLAND FREIGHTING. Nebraska State Historical Society Publications 26. Lincoln: The Society, 1972. Recommended as an overall survey of freighting.

LASSALE, Stanislaus. "Diary." In A HISTORY OF TRAVEL IN

AMERICA, vol. 4, ed. Seymour Dunbar. Indianapolis: Bobbs-Merrill, 1915. CAL(Ft. Smith)-MARCY-RIO GRANDE-GILA. III. 1849.

Lathrop, George. MEMOIRS OF A PIONEER. Lusk, WYO: Lusk Herald, N.d. Stage.

LATHAM, William B., Jr. Diary. Society of California Pioneers Library, San Francisco, CA. Not Seen.

LATHROP, Amy. "Leavenworth - Pikes Peak Trail." KSHIST. Stage. Pres.

LATTA, Frank F. DEATH VALLEY '49ERS. Santa Cruz, CA: Bear State Books, 1979. SLCOR-1849-Genl.

_____. EL CAMINO VIEJO A LOS ANGELES. Annual Publication No. 2. Bakersfield, CA: Kern County Historical Society, 1936. CAL-Genl. Maps.

_____. JOAQUIN MURRIETA AND HIS HORSE GANGS. Santa Cruz, CA: Bear State Books, 1980. Stage.

LAUB, George. Diary. UTHIST. MORMON. II-. 1852.

LAUDEMAN, Peter M. "Historic Trails Management Plan, Rock Springs District, Rock Springs, Wyoming." Unpublished Report for U.S.BLM, 1979. Pres.

LAUT, Agnes C. THE OVERLAND TRAIL. NY: Stokes, 1929. Overland-Genl.

_____. PILGRIMS OF THE SANTA FE. NY: Stokes, 1931. SANTA FE-Genl.

LAVELY, Philipe. TRAILS BIBLIOGRAPHY. WA: U.S. Bureau of Outdoor Recreation, 1978. Pres.

LAVENDER, David. THE OVERLAND MIGRATIONS. National Park Service Handbook 105. WA: GPO, 1980. Overland-Genl. Graphics.

_____. WESTWARD VISION: THE STORY OF THE OVERLAND TRAIL. One of the American Trails Series. NY: McGraw-Hill, 1963. OR-Genl.

LAVERS, Norman. Ed. Parker, Wilbur F. "Glorious Orb of Day."

LAW, George. "Trailing the Old Butterfield Stage." TOURING TOPICS, Feb 1927, N.p. Stage.

LAWRENCE, Eleanor. "Horse Thieves on the Spanish Trail." TOURING TOPICS 23(Jan 1931): 22-25, 55. SPANISH-Genl.

_____. "Mexican Trade between Santa Fe and Los Angeles, 1830-1848." CALIFORNIA HISTORICAL QUARTERLY 16(Mar 1931): 27-39. SPANISH-Genl.

_____. "Mule Trains and Muleteers on early California Roads." TOURING TOPICS 24(Jul 1932): 16-18, 55. Freight.

_____. "The Old Spanish Trail from Santa Fe to California." MA thesis, Univ. of California-Berkeley, 1930. SPANISH-Genl.

_____. "On the Old Spanish Trail." TOURING TOPICS 22(Nov 1930): 36-39.

_____. "Peg-Leg Smith: His Story." TOURING TOPICS 24(Oct 1932): 18-21, 48. Biog.

LAWS, Robert C. Diary. Society of California Pioneers Library, San Francisco, CA. CAL(St. Jo)-BRIDGER-SLCUT. 1852. Not Seen.

LAWSON, George. Diary. HUNTL. CAL(St. Jo)-BRIDGER-HASTINGS. III-. 1850.

LAWTON, Harry W. With Philip Wilke. EXPEDITION.

LAYNE, J. Gregg. "Check List of Published Material on the Butterfield Overland Mail." Southern California Historical Society QUARTERLY 17(Sept 1935): 112-14. Bib-Stage.

_____. WESTERN WAYFARING: ROUTES OF EXPLORATION AND TRADE IN THE AMERICAN SOUTHWEST. LA: Automobile Club of Southern California, 1954. Maps. Overland-Genl.

LAYTON, Christopher. AUTOBIOGRAPHY. Ed. John Q. Cannon. SLC: Deseret News, 1911. MORMON-Genl.

LAYTON, Thomas N. "Massacre! What Massacre? An Inquiry into the Massacre of 1850." NEVADA HISTORICAL SOCIETY QUARTERLY 20(Win 1977): 241-51. LASSEN-1850-Genl. Indians.

_____. "Stalking Elephants in Nevada." WESTERN FOLKLORE 35(Oct 1976): 250-57. LASSEN-Genl. Graphics.

LAZEAR, Michael C. "Death Rides the California Trail." Ed. Peter Odens. BUTTERFIELD EXPRESS, Vols. 4, 6, and 7(1966). CAL(Neb. City). Rem. 1859. Not Seen.

LEACH, Adoniram J. EARLY DAY STORIES; THE OVERLAND TRAIL.... Norfolk, NB: Huse, c1916. OR(Council). IV. Rem. 1852.

LEACH, James. B. "Journey of the Leach Wagon Train across Texas, 1857." Ed. J. W. Williams. WESTX 29(Oct 1953): 115-77. TEX(Gainesville-Ft. Stockton-Ft. Davis-El Paso). I. 1857.

LEACH, James R. ITINERARY OF THE EL PASO AND FORT YUMA WAGON ROAD EXPEDITION.... WA: GPO, 1858. GILA. 1858. Not Seen.

LEACH, Joseph. "Stage Coach through the Pass - The Butterfield Overland Mail Comes to El Paso." PASSWORD 3(Oct 1958): 130-37. Stage.

LEACH, Richard E. Ed. Clark, George T. "Journal."

LEADABRAND, Russ. "Across Historic Carson Pass." WESTWAYS 53(Jun 1961): 19-21. Geog.

_____. "Across the Colorful Sonora Pass Country." WESTWAYS 53(Aug 1961): 19-21. Geog.

_____. "Along the Butterfield Trail." WESTWAYS 53(Apr 1961): 4-6. Stage: Warner Spring - Vallecito.

_____. "The Butterfield Spread." WESTWAYS 66(Dec 1974): 57-59. Stage: Temecula - Warner Springs.

_____. "Over Picturesque Ebbetts Pass." WESTWAYS 53(Jul 1961): 20-22. Geog.

LEADINGHAM, Grace. "Juliet Wells Brier: Heroine of Death Valley." PACIFIC HISTORIAN 8(Nov 1963; Feb, May, Aug 1964): 13-20, 13-20, 61-74, 121-28. SLCOR-1849-Genl.

LEBEC, Ralph. "Mercy Express to Dragoon Springs." TRUE WEST 17(Jul-Aug 1970): 8-13, 60-63. Stage. Geog.

LECOMPTE, Janet. "The Manco Burro Pass Massacre." NEW MEXICO HISTORICAL REVIEW 41(Oct 1966): 305-18. 1848 Indian attack on freight wagons near Raton, NM.

LEDBETTER, William G. "Military History of the Oregon Country, 1804 - 1859." MA thesis, Univ. of Oregon, 1935. Military.

LEDUC, Joanne. Ed. McMicking, Thomas. OVERLAND FROM CANADA.

LEDYARD, Edgar M. Ed. Loomis, Leander V. JOURNAL.

_____. "Tell 'Em and Sell 'Em: Utah's Location, Roads, Scenery, Service and History." SCENIC UTAH MOTORIST 5(Feb 1931): 9-12. Pres.

LEE, Anna G. [Mrs. Philander]. Letters. ORHIST. OR(St. Jo). IV. Rem. 1847.

LEE, Arthur T. FORT DAVIS AND THE TEXAS FRONTIER. College Station, TX: Texas A&M Univ. Press, 1976. Geog.

LEE, C. M. Journals. MONHIST. DAKOTAS(Niobrara Route)-MONTANA. II +. 1865.

LEE, Clinton H. "The Bridgeport Covered Bridge: Nevada County's Century Old Historical Treasure." Nevada County Historical Society BULLETIN 24(Apr 1970): 1-10. Freight. Pres.

LEE, John D. "Diary of the Mormon Battalion Mission." Ed. Juanita Brooks. NEW MEXICO HISTORICAL REVIEW 42(Jul, Oct 1967): 165-209, 281-93. CAL(Council)-SANTA FE-Ends Santa Fe. II. 1846.

LEE, L. W. Autobiography. BYU. CAL(Indep?). V. Rem. 1850. CAL(Indep). V. Rem. 1852. CAL(Indep?). V. Rem. 1857.

LEE, Wayne C. "Julesburg, the Wandering Town." TRUE WEST 30(Mar 1983): 18-21. Geog.

_____, and Howard C. Raynesford. TRAILS OF THE SMOKY HILL.... Caldwell, ID: Caxton, 1980. PIKES. Stage. Maps. Graphics.

LEE, William. Notes. BANCROFT. CAL(Leav)-BRIDGER-To SLC. III. 1858. CAL(Camp Floyd, UT)-SIMPSON. III. 1859.

LEEBRICK, Beryl. Ed. Ellis, Henrietta C. DIARY.

LEECH, A. P. Diary. Univ. of Iowa Library-SpCol, Iowa City, IA. CAL(Council)-By Stage to Denver-By Wagon from Denver-CHEROKEE-SLCUT. II. 1865.

LEEPER, David R. THE ARGONAUTS OF 'FORTY-NINE.... 1894. Reprint. Columbus, OH: Long's, 1950. CAL(St. Jo)-LASSEN. III. Rem. 1849.

LEITHOFF, Heather M. "A Comparative Study of Emigrants' Guidebooks Published during the 1840's." MA thesis, Univ. of Idaho, 1969. Guide. Not Seen.

LELAND, Alonzo. NEW MAP OF THE MINING REGIONS OF OREGON AND WASHINGTON TERRITORY. SF: A. Roman, 1863. Guide.

LEMERT, Bula. "Peppard's Folly." FRONTIER TIMES 37(Jun-Jul 1963): 49, 55-56. Eqpt-Wind Wagon.

LEMKE, W. J., and Ted R. Worley. THE BUTTERFIELD OVERLAND MAIL IN ARKANSAS. Little Rock: Arkansas History Commission, 1957. Stage. Maps.

LEMPFRIT, Honore-Timothee. HIS OREGON TRAIL JOURNAL AND LETTERS FROM THE PACIFIC NORTHWEST, 1848 - 1853. Ed. & trans. Patricia Meyer, and Catou Levesque. Fairfield, WA: Ye Galleon, 1985. OR(St. Jo). I. 1848.

LENOIR, Slater E. Letters. MO-WHMC. CAL(St. Jo). 1850. Not Seen.

LENOX, Edward H. OVERLAND TO OREGON IN THE TRACK OF LEWIS AND CLARKE. Ed. Robert Whitaker. Oakland: Private, 1904. OR(Westport). IV. Rem. 1843.

LEONARD, H. L. W. OREGON TERRITORY.... Cleveland: Younglove, 1846. Guide.

LEONARD, Joseph L. and Mary P. "Crossing the Plains...1853." Ed. Gertrude J. Morley. State Historical Society of Missouri Library, Springfield, MO. OR(St. Jo)-MEEK. IV. Rem. 1853.

LEONARD, Zenas. ADVENTURES OF A FUR TRADER. Ed. John C. Evers. Norman: Univ. of Oklahoma Press, 1959. Overland-Genl.

LEPPO, David T. THE FAMILY OF DAVID T. LEPPO.... Ed. Harrison M. Leppo. SF: Author, 1977. CAL(Council)-BRIDGER-SLCUT-TRUCKEE-BECK. II. 1864.

LEPPO, Harrison M. Ed. Leppo, David T. FAMILY.

LERCH, Harold A. "Pioneer Expressions of Sport and Leisure on the Oregon Trail, 1842 - 1860." ORHIST. Leisure.

LESLEY, Lewis B. Ed. Stacey, May. UNCLE SAM'S CAMELS.

_____. "The International Boundary Survey from San Diego to the Gila River, 1849 - 50." CALIFORNIA HISTORICAL QUARTERLY 9(Mar 1930): 3-15. GILA-Genl.

LESTER, Gurdon P. "A Round Trip to the Montana Mines...." Ed. Charles W. Martin. NEBRASKA HISTORY 46(Dec 1965): 273-314. Stage. II +. 1866. Unusually detailed account of stage trip from Council Bluffs to Montana.

LESTER, Lisle. "A Tour, through Northern California and Oregon." PACIFIC MONTHLY 11(Nov 1864): 830-38. Stage: Sacramento to Shasta, CA. 1864.

LESTER, Thomas B. MEDICINE ON THE SANTA FE TRAIL. Ed. Thomas B. Hall. Dayton: Morningside, 1971. SANTA FE(Leav). III +. 1847. Medical.

"Letter from an Overland Californian." HARTFORD [CN] DAILY COURANT, 24 May 1849, N.p. Social.

LETTER FROM THE POSTMASTER GENERAL. 40th Cong., 3d sess. 1868. H. Ex. Doc. 14. Wells Fargo contract.

_____. 37th Cong., 2d sess. 1862. H. Ex. Doc. 55. Serial 1131. Discontinue Ex Paso - San Diego service.

_____. 36th Cong., 2d sess. 1861. H. Ex. Doc. 73. Serial 1101. Abstract of mail contract solicitations.

_____. 36th Cong., 1st sess. H. Ex. Doc 86. Serial 1057. San Antonio - San Diego route.

_____. 40th Cong., 2d sess. 1868. H. Ex. Doc. 201. Contracts with Benjamin Holladay.

_____. 35th Cong., 2d sess. 1860. S. Ex. Doc. 26. Serial 1031. Butterfield contract of February 2, 1860.

_____. 46th Cong., 2d sess. 1880. S. Ex. Doc. 211. Copies of Holladay contracts.

LETTER FROM THE SECRETARY OF WAR...RELATIVE TO THE RAISING OF VOLUNTEER TROOPS TO GUARD OVERLAND AND OTHER MAILS FROM 1861 TO 1866. 50th Cong., 2d sess. 1889. S. Ex. Doc. 70. Stage. Mail. Military.

"Letter." In NOTES OF THE EARLY HISTORY OF THE NEBRASKA COUNTRY, ed. Albert Watkins. Publications of the Nebraska State Historical Society, Vol. 20. Lincoln: The Society, 1922.

LETTER OF THE SECRETARY OF WAR. 37 Cong., 3d sess. 1863. S. Ex. Doc 17. OR(Council). III. 1862.

LEVITIN, Sonia. "First Historic Trek across the Wild Land to California." SMITHSONIAN 2(Nov 1971): 68-73. CAL-1841-Genl.

LEVY, JoAnn. "Nevada's Fort Churchill." OVERLAND JOURNAL 4(Spr 1986): 16-19. Geog.

_____. "Crossing the 40-Mile Desert: Sorrowful Recollections of Women Emigrants." CALIFORNIANS 5(Sept/Oct 1987). CAL-Genl. Geog. Not Seen.

LEWELLING, Seth. Diary. ORU. CAL(St. Jo). III. 1850.

LEWIS, Anna. "Trading Post at the Crossing of the Chickasaw Trails." CHRONICLES OF OKLAHOMA 12(Dec 1934): 447-53. Geog. Stage.

LEWIS, B. P. Diary. CSL. CAL(Council)-CHEROKEE(Julesburg-SLC)-Simpson. II. 1863.

LEWIS, David R. "Argonauts and the Overland Trail Experience: Method and Theory." WESTERN HISTORICAL QUARTERLY 16(Jul 1985): 285-305. Overland-Genl.

LEWIS, Edward J. "Diary of a Pike's Peak Gold Seeker in 1861." Ed. Harry E. Pratt. COLORADO MAGAZINE 14(Nov 1937): 201-19. PIKES. III+. 1860.

LEWIS, Edward M. Journal. CAHIST. MORMON. 1865. Not Seen.

LEWIS, Elisha B. Overland Trip. BANCROFT. CAL(St. Jo)-TRUCKEE. II+. 1849.

LEWIS, Ella R. Ed. Ricker, John J. "Iowa to Ventura County."

LEWIS, G. W. LEWIS' MAP OF FRASER RIVER.... NY: Lewis, 1858. CANADA-1858-Map.

LEWIS, Jane D. Biography. UTHIST. MORMON. V. 1856.

LEWIS, John F. Diary. BEINECKE. CAL(St. Jo)-BRIDGER-SLCUT-TRUCKEE. II+. 1849.

LEWIS, John I. MY GARDEN OF ROSES. Berkeley: Author?, c1907. CAL-SLCUT. V-. Rem. 1853.

LEWIS, John N. Diary. BANCROFT. OR(St. Jo?). II. Rem. 1852.

LEWIS, Oscar. SUTTER'S FORT: GATEWAY TO THE GOLD FIELDS. Englewood, NJ: Prentice-Hall, 1966. Geog.

_____. THE TOWN THAT DIED LAUGHING. Boston: Little, Brown, 1955. Geog: Austin, NV.

LEVY, JoAnn. "Crossing the 40-Mile Desert: Sorrowful Recollections of Women Emigrants." CALIFORNIANS 5(Sept/Oct, 1987). CAL-Genl. Not Seen.

LEWIS, Thomas. Papers. Attributed to MO-WHMC but uncatalogued. Not Seen. Diary supposedly was a West-to-East crossing from California in 1851.

LEWIS, Thomas C. Memorandum. BEINECKE. CAL(St. Jo). III. 1852.

LIENHARD, Heinrich. FROM ST. LOUIS TO SUTTER'S FORT, 1846. Eds. & trans. Erwin G. & Elizabeth K. Gudde. Norman: Univ. of Oklahoma Press, 1961. CAL(Indep)-BRIDGER-HASTINGS-TRUCKEE. II. 1846.

LIGHTNER, Mary E. "Mary Elizabeth Rollins Lightner." UTAH GENEALOGICAL AND HISTORICAL MAGAZINE 17(July, Oct 1926): 193-205, 250-60. MORMON. III. 1863.

LIKES, Robert C. "Along the Butterfield Trail." DESERT 33(Oct 1970): 22-26. Map: Butterfield route in southern California.

LILLARD, Richard G., and Mary V. Hood. HANK MONK AND HORACE GREELEY; AN ENDURING EPISODE IN WESTERN HISTORY. Georgetown, CA: Wilmac, 1973. Stage.

"The Lincoln Massacre at Fort Yuma Ferry in 1850." Arizona State Library-Ms, Phoenix, AZ. Geog. Indians.

LINDELL, Leland E. "The Crossing of the Little River." KSHIST. Geog: Little Arkansas River.

LINDSEY, David. Ed. Salisbury, Wm. "Journal."

LINDSEY, Tipton. Diary. BANCROFT. CAL(St. Jo)-HALL. II+. 1849.

LINFORD, James H. AN AUTOBIOGRAPHY.... N.p.: Author, 1919. MORMON. 1856. Not Seen.

LINVILLE, Leslie. THE SMOKY HILL VALLEY AND BUTTERFIELD TRAIL. Colby, KS: LeRoy's, 1974. Accurately places and describes stage stations. Pres. Stage-1865-Genl.

_____. VISITING HISTORICAL SITES ON THE CENTRAL HIPLAINS. Osborne, KS: Osborne County Farmer, 1979. Pres. Overland-Genl-Kansas.

LIST, Howard M. and Edith M. Ed. Shively, John. "Memoir."

"Lists of Theses on Utah, Mormons and the West at the University of Utah, Brigham Young University and Utah State University." UTAH HISTORICAL QUARTERLY 23(Jan, Jul 1955): 79-85, 279-84. Utah. Bib.

LITTLE, Feramorz. "Mail Service across the Plains." Univ. of Utah Library-SpCol, Salt Lake City, UT. Mail. Stage.

LITTLE, James A. FROM KIRTLAND TO SALT LAKE CITY. SLC: Author, 1890. MORMON-Genl.

LITTLE, Moses F. Overland Narrative. BEINECKE. CAL(Boonville)-LASSEN. I. 1849.

LITTLETON, James. Diary. CSL. CAL(Indep)-BRIDGER-SLCUT-TRUCKEE. I. 1850.

LITTLETON, Micajah. Diary. CSL. CAL(Indep)-BRIDGER-SLCUT-TRUCKEE. II. 1850.

LIVESEY, Donald W. "Mountain Meadows Massacre: An Interpretation." MS thesis, Florida State Univ., 1967. Geog. SLCOR-1857-Genl.

LIVINGSTON, Robert D. "Felix Tracy and the Salt Lake City Express, 1854." WESTERN EXPRESS 32(Apr 1983): 21-27. SLCOR. III. 1854.

LIVINGSTON, Robert R. "Orders Concerning the Management of Escort Commands." BEINECKE. Military.

LOBA, Jean Frederick. Reminiscences. KSHIST. CAL(Leav)-BRIDGER. V-. Rem. 1854. CAL(SLC)-BRIDGER-Ends Ft. Leavenworth. V-. Rem. 1858. Rare account of an apostate, anti-Mormon family.

LOBENSTINE, William C. EXTRACTS FROM THE DIARY.... NY: Private, 1920. CAL(St. Jo)-BRIDGER-SLCUT. III. 1852.

LOCKE, Dean J. Diary. CAHIST. CAL(Indep)-BRIDGER-SLCUT. 1849. Not Seen.

LOCKETT, H. C. ALONG THE BEALE TRAIL: A PHOTOGRAPHIC ACCOUNT OF WASTED RANGE LAND. Ed. Willard W. Beatty. Lawrence, KS: Education Div., U.S. Office of Indian Affairs, 1939. BEALE-Genl-Graphics.

LOCKEY, Richard. Diary. MONHIST. CAL(Council)-BOZE. III. 1866.

LOCKHART, Andrew J. "The Williams Massacre." OVERLAND MONTHLY 12(Oct 1888): 398-404. OR-CAL-1851-Genl. Indians.

LOCKLEY, Fred. Ed. Bonney, B. F. "Recollections." Ed. Packwood, William H. "Reminiscences." Ed. Rector, W. H. "Biography."

_____. CAPTAIN SOLOMON TETHEROW, WAGON TRAIN MASTER. Portland: Author, c1925. OR(St. Jo)-MEEK. V. 1845. Train Govt.

_____. "The McNemees and Tetherows in the Migration of 1845." OREGON HISTORICAL QUARTERLY 25(Dec 1924): 353-77. OR(St. Jo)-MEEK. III. Rem. 1845.

_____. "Oregon Immigrants of 1844." WASHINGTON HISTORICAL QUARTERLY 18(Apr 1927): 93-102. OR-1844-Genl.

LOCKWOOD, C. B. MY TRIP TO CALIFORNIA IN 1850. Dayton, FL: Halifax, 1910. CAL-TEX(Port Lavaca)-MEX(El Paso-Chihuahua-Durango-Mazatlan). III. 1850.

LOCKWOOD, Frank C. "Arizona Pioneers: Francis Xavier Aubrey." ARIZONA HISTORICAL REVIEW 5(Jan 1933): 327-32. Biog.

_____. "He Rode the Wilderness Trail." DESERT 9(Mar 1946): 28-30. Biog: F. X. Aubrey.

LOEB, Julius. "The Pony Express." AMERICAN PHILATELIST 44(Nov 1930): 118-19. Pony. Graphics.

LOFINCK, Sewell "Pop." "From Coso to Carricart." LOS ANGELES WESTERNERS BRAND BOOK 12(1966): 113-26. CAL-Genl.

LOGAN, Martha. Logan Family Papers. MO-WHMC. MORMON-SIMPSON? 1864. Not Seen.

LOGSDON, Paul. "Traces of the Santa Fe Trail." NEW MEXICO 60(Feb 1982): 46-48. Pres.

LOHSE, Charles S. Diary. Society of California Pioneers Library, San Francisco, CA. Not Seen.

LOMAS, Thomas J. RECOLLECTIONS OF A BUSY LIFE. Cresco, IA?: M. D. Lomas, 1923. CAL(Council)-BRIDGER-SIMPSON-BECKWOURTH. IV. Rem. 1864.

LONG, Charles L'H. Diary. BEINECKE. CAL(Indep)-HALL-TRUCKEE. II+. 1849.

LONG, Christian L. Diary. DENVERPUB. PIKES. III. 1859.

LONG, M. M. Journal of Fort Kearney, South Pass, and Honey Lake Wagon Road Company." National Archives. CAL(Indep)-to Ft. Laramie. 1857. Not Seen.

LONG, Margaret. AUTOMOBILE LOGS OF THE SMOKY HILL AND OTHER PIONEER TRAILS IN COLORADO, OKLAHOMA AND NEW MEXICO. Denver: Private, 1943. Very complete auto guidebook. No maps.

_____. THE OREGON TRAIL: FOLLOWING THE OLD HISTORIC TRAILS ON MODERN HIGHWAYS. Denver: Private, 1954. Covers section from St. Jo to South Pass. Pres. Overland-Genl.

_____. Papers. Norlin Library-Western History, Univ. of Colorado, Boulder, CO. Materials on trail preservation in the 1930's and 1940's. Pres.

_____. "The Route of the Leavenworth and Pike's Peak Express." COLORADO MAGAZINE 12(Sept 1935): 186-94. Stage.

_____. THE SHADOW OF THE ARROW. Caldwell, ID: Caxton, 1941. SLCOR-1849-Genl.

_____. "The Smoky Hill Trail." COLORADO MAGAZINE 9(Nov 1932): 218-31. PIKES-Genl. Stage.

_____. THE SMOKY HILL TRAIL. Denver: Private, 1953. Excellent auto guidebook. Pres. Stage. Freight. Maps.

_____. "The Smoky Hill Trails in Colorado." COLORADO MAGAZINE 11(Mar 1934): 70-78. PIKES-Genl. Stage.

LONG, Mary J. CROSSING THE PLAINS IN THE YEAR OF 1852 WITH OX TEAMS. McMinnville, OR: Author, 1915. OR(Council). IV. Rem. 1852.

LONGACRE, Myrtle. A Trek West. Norlin Library-Western History, Univ. of Colorado, Boulder, CO. CAL(Atchison)-BRIDGER-Ends SLC. V-. 1865. SIMPSON(SLC to California). V-. 1866.

LONGMIRE, David. "First Immigrants to Cross the Cascades." WASHINGTON HISTORICAL QUARTERLY 8(1917): 22-28. WASH. III. Rem. 1853.

LONGMIRE, James. SEE: Bidwell, John, et al. FIRST THREE WAGON TRAINS.

_____. "Narrative of a Pioneer." WASHINGTON HISTORICAL QUARTERLY 23(Jan, Apr 1932): 47-60, 138-50. OR(Council)-WASH. IV. Rem. 1853.

LONGSTREET, Stephen. A CENTURY ON WHEELS - THE STORY OF STUDEBAKER: A HISTORY, 1852-1952. NY: Private, 1952. Eqpt.

LONGWORTH, Basil N. "Memorandum...1853." Eugene, OR: Lane County Pioneer-Historical Society, 1959. OR(St. Jo). II. 1853.

LOOMIS, Charles O. Diary. Southwest Museum Library, Los Angeles,

CA. Library closed - Not Seen.

LOOMIS, Leander V. A JOURNAL OF THE BIRMINGHAM EMIGRATING COMPANY. Ed. Edgar M. Ledyard. SLC: Legal Printing, 1928. MORMON. III. 1850.

LOOMIS, Noel M. Ed. Woods, I. C. "Journal."

_____. "Early Cattle Trails in Southern Arizona." ARIZONIANA 3(Win 1962): 18-24. TEX-Genl. GILA-Genl. Stock.

_____. WELLS FARGO: AN ILLUSTRATED HISTORY. NY: Clarkson N. Potter, 1968. Stage. Graphics.

LOOMIS, Orrin S. Life Story. Eds. Rose L. Cooper and Robert M. Loomis. ORU. CAL(Council). V. 1854.

LOOMIS, Robert M. Ed. Loomis, Orrin S. Life Story.

LOOMIS, Thaddeus L. SEE: Anderson, Niles. "Grandfather Was a Forty-Niner."

LOONEY, Jesse. "Letter." (In) TOLD BY THE PIONEERS, Vol. 1. Washington Pioneer Project, 1937. OR(Indep). 1843. Not Seen.

LOONEY, Mrs. M. A. A TRIP ACROSS THE PLAINS IN 1853. Albany, OR: Albany Printing, 1912. OR(Council). V. 1853.

LOOSBROCK, Richard J. "Joining Clio and Icarus: Historical Research from the Air." RENDEZVOUS 18(Spr 1983): 61-66. Tracing trails by air reconnaisance. Pres.

LORCH, Fred W. "Iowa and the California Gold Rush of 1849." IOWA JOURNAL OF HISTORY AND POLITICS 30(Jul 1932): 307-76. CAL-1849-Genl. Social.

LORD, Mrs. Elizabeth. REMINISCENCES OF EASTERN OREGON. Portland: Irwin-Hodson, 1903. OR(St. Jo?). IV. Rem. 1850.

LORD, Israel S. Journal. HUNTL. CAL(St. Jo)-LASSEN. I. 1849.

LORENZEN, Blanche C. "California's First Organized Stage Robbery." PACIFIC HISTORIAN 6(Feb 1962): 45-51. Stage.

LORENZO, Anthony J. "Scurvy in the Gold Rush." JOURNAL OF THE HISTORY OF MEDICINE.... 12(Oct 1957): 473-510. Medical.

LORTIE, Frank. "Sutter's Fort: Reconstruction of a Feudal Community." AMERICAN WEST 17(May-Jun 1980): 12-15, 60. Geog.

LORTON, William B. OVER THE SALT LAKE TRAIL IN THE FALL OF '49. LA: Private, 1957. SLCOR. IV. 1849.

Los Angeles STAR, 19 Dec 1857, N.p. SLCOR. 1855. Not Seen.

LOTT, Charles F. "As It Was in '49." OVERLAND MONTHLY 36(Sept 1900): 225-30. Geog: Sacramento Valley.

LOTTS, Charles F. Diary. CSL. CAL(St. Jo)-LASSEN. III. 1849.

LOUGHARY, Mrs. W. A. Diary. ORU. OR(Council)-LANDER. II. 1864.

LOVE, Alexander. Diary. BEINECKE. CAL(Indep)-HALL-TRUCKEE. II. 1849.

LOVE, Clara M. "History of the Cattle Industry in the Southwest." MA thesis, Univ. of California-Berkeley, 1914. Stock.

LOVE, Frank. "Butterfield's Backbreakers." FRONTIER TIMES 37(Jun-Jul 1963): 38-39, 46. Stage.

LOVE, Helen Marnie (Stewart). SEE: Stewart, Helen M. DIARY 1853.

LOVE, Louise. "The Dedication of Texas Trail Monuments in Wyoming." ANNALS OF WYOMING 21(Jan 1949): 93-99. Pres.

LOVEJOY, Asa L. "Asa Lovejoy's Pioneer Narrative, 1842-60." Ed. Henry E. Reed. OREGON HISTORICAL QUARTERLY 31(Sept 1930): 237-60. OR(Indep). III. Rem. 1842.

_____. Letter. ORHIST. OR(Wiilatpu)-Fort Hall-Taos-St. Louis. III. Rem. 1842.

LOVELAND, Cyrus C. CALIFORNIA TRAIL HERD.... Ed. Richard H. Dillon. Los Gatos, CA: Talisman, 1961. CAL(Indep)-HALL-TRUCKEE. II. 1850. Cattle Drive.

LOVELL, Edith. "History Buffs Explore Idaho Lander Cut-off." SNAKE RIVER ECHOES 7, no. 4(1978): 88-91. Pres.

LOVELL, Merton N. Joseph R. Walker, Mountain Man and Guide of the Far West." MS thesis, BYU, 1959.

LOVING, Mabel. THE PONY EXPRESS RIDES ON! St. Joseph, MO: Robidoux, 1961. Pony. Pres.

LOWE, Percival G. FIVE YEARS A DRAGOON. Ed. Don Russell. 1906. Reprint. Norman: Univ. of Oklahoma Press, 1965. CAL(Leav)-Ends SLC. I. Rem. 1851.

LOWELL, Daniel W. MAP OF THE NEZ PERCES AND SALMON RIVER GOLD MINES. SF: Whitton, Waters, 1862. Guide.

LOWELL, Nancy C. "Across the Plains in '57." Ed. Ruth Peterson. CSL. Route Uncertain. V. Rem. 1857.

LOWRY, James L. Diary. Washington State Historical Society Library, Tacoma, WA. CAL(Neb. City)-LASSEN. II+. 1860.

LOY, John W. Diary. Honnold Library-SpCol, Claremont Colleges, Claremont, CA. CAL(Council). II. 1852.

LUARK, Michael. Diary. University of Washington Library-Ms, Seattle, WA. OR(Council)-LANDER. II+. 1853.

LUCE, Willard. "Silent City of Rocks." IMPROVEMENT ERA 60(Oct 1957): 718-19, 766-67. Almo Massacre, 1861. Geog.

LUCHETTI, Cathy, and Carol Olwell. WOMEN OF THE WEST. St. George, UT: Authors, 1982. Social.

LUCIA, Ellis. THE SAGA OF BEN HOLLIDAY: GIANT OF THE WEST. NY: Hastings House, 1959. Biog. Freight. Stage.

_____. "Sam Barlow's Astounding Road." WESTWAYS 51(Nov 1959): 26-27. BARLOW-Genl. Maps.

_____. "Tracking the Overland Stage." WESTWAYS 52(May 1960): 19-21. Stage.

LUCKE, Thomas W. "The Establishment of Fort Larned National Historic Site: A Legislative Synopsis." PRAIRIE SCOUT 3(1975): 105-16. Geog. Pres.

LUDLOW, Fitz Hugh. THE HEART OF THE CONTINENT.... NY: Hurd & Houghton, 1870. Stage: Atchison to Denver. II. 1863. Utah.

_____. "On Horseback into Oregon." ATLANTIC MONTHLY 14(Feb 1864): 75-68. OR-CA. II. 1863.

LUEG, Henry. "The Northern Overland Route in 1867...." Ed. C. S. Kingston. PACIFIC NORTHWEST QUARTERLY 41(Oct 1950): 234-53. OR(St. Cloud)-DAKOTAS-MONTANA-MULLAN. II. 1867.

LUMMIS, Charles F. "Pioneer Transportation in America." MCCLURE'S 25(Oct 1905): 561-73; 26(Nov 1905): 81-94. Freight.

LUPER, John. Diary. In Paul & Helen Henderson Collection, UWY. OR(Council)-BARLOW. IV. 1853.

LUPTON, David W. "Fort Bernard on the Oregon Trail." NEBRASKA HISTORY 60(Spr 1979): 21-35. Geog.

_____. "Fort Platte, Wyoming, 1841-1845: Rival of Fort Laramie." ANNALS OF WYOMING 49(Spr 1977): 83-108. Geog.

LUSTER, Mary R. AUTOBIOGRAPHY. Springfield, MO: Private, 1935. CAL-Ends in Idaho. Rem. 1864. Not Seen.

LYMAN, Albert R. AMASA MASON LYMAN: TRAILBLAZER AND PIONEER.... Delta, UT: Melvin A. Lyman, 1957. Biog.

_____. Journal. UTHIST. MORMON. I. 1847. SLCOR. II. 1858.

LYMAN, Esther and Joseph. LETTERS. Eugene, OR: Lane County Pioneer - Historical Society, 1960. OR(Council)-MEEK. III. 1853.

LYMAN, George D. JOHN MARSH, PIONEER. NY: Scribner's, 1931. Biog.

LYMAN, George Dunlap. Papers. CAHIST. Pony.

LYMAN, H. S. Ed. Case, William M. "Recollections." Ed. Cone, Anson S. "Reminiscences." Ed. Cosgrove, Hugh. "Reminiscences." Ed. Jory, James. "Reminiscences." Ed. Mattthieu, Francis X. "Reminiscences."

LYMAN, Vincent P. Diary. In Paul & Helen Henderson Collection, UWY. CAL(Ash Hollow)-BRIDGER-Ends Echo Canyon. II. 1860.

LYNCH, Alice K. Society of California Pioneers, San Francisco, CA. Not Seen.

LYNE, James. Letters. BEINECKE. CAL(Indep)-Ends near Ft. Bridger. II. 1849.

LYON, Bessie L. Ed. Willis, James M. "Jasons of 1860."

LYON, Herman R. "Freighting in the '60's." PROCEEDINGS AND COLLECTIONS Nebraska State Historical Society 5(1902): 265-72. Rem. Freight.

LYON, W. Parker, and Ernest Wiltsee. "Early California Oval and Straight Line Cancellations." COLLECTOR'S CLUB PHILATELIST 8(Oct 1929): 1-8. Stage. Mail.

"M. M." "Letters." In CALIFORNIA EMIGRANT LETTERS, ed. Walker D. Wyman. NY: Bookman, 1952. Eqpt.

"M.M.G." "Letter." In CALIFORNIA EMIGRANT LETTERS, ed. Walker D. Wyman. NY: Bookman, 1952.

"M.N.O." "Marking Western Trails." INDEPENDENT 61(Jul 1906): 52-53. Pres: Santa Fe Trail.

McADAMS, Henry E. "Early History of the San Gorgonio Pass, Gateway to California." MA thesis, Univ. of Southern California, 1955. Not Seen.

McALISTER, Nehemiah S. Diary. ORHIST. OR(Council). I. 1852.

McALLISTER, John. "Diary." TRANSACTIONS Oregon Pioneer Association 1922 (1925): 471-89. OR(Council). II. 1852.

McALLISTER, John D. Journal. BYU. MORMON. 1851. Not Seen.

McARTHUR, Lewis A. "Early Scenes in Harney Valley...." OREGON HISTORICAL QUARTERLY 32(Jun 1931): 125-29. OR-MEEK. V. Rem. 1853.

McAULEY, Eliza A. "The McAuley Diary." STOCKTON WESTERNERS VALLEY TRAILS (1966): 67-78. CAL(Council)-TRUCKEE. III +. 1852.

McBRIDE, Heber R. Journal. BYU. MORMON. V. Rem. 1856. Freight: SLC-Virginia City, MT. V. Rem. 1864. MORMON. III. Rem. 1865.

McBRIDE, J. C. Diary. COHIST. Not Seen.

McBRIDE, John H. Letters. NBHIST. CAL(Council)-BRIDGER. II. 1850.

McBRIDE, John R. Overland, 1846. Oregon State Library, Salem, OR. OR(St. Jo)-BARLOW. II. Rem. 1846.

_____. "The Route By Which the Mormons Entered Salt Lake Valley in 1847." BANCROFT. MORMON-1847-Genl: Echo Canyon to SLC.

McBRIDE, Ralph L. "Utah Mail Service before the Coming of the Railroad, 1869." MA thesis, BYU, 1957. Pony. Stage. Mail-Utah.

McBRIDE, W. S. Journal. HUNTL. CAL(St. Jo)-BRIDGER-Ends SLC. II +. 1850.

McCAIN, G. S. "A Trip from Atchison, Kansas, to Laurette, Colorado." COLORADO MAGAZINE 27(Apr 1950): 95-102. PIKES. V. 1864?

McCALL, Ansel J. THE GREAT CALIFORNIA TRAIL IN 1849.... Bath, NY: Steuben Courier, 1882. CAL(St. Jo)-BRIDGER-SLCUT-TRUCKEE. II +. 1849.

McCALL, George A. "Camp Yuma - 1852." Ed. Robert W. Frazer. Southern California Historical QUARTERLY 52(Jun 1970): 170-81. Geog.

McCALL, John M. "The First Oregon Cavalry and the Oregon Central Military Road Survey of 1865." Ed. L. C. Merriam, Jr. OREGON HISTORICAL QUARTERLY 60(Mar 1959): 85-124. Freight.

McCANN, Lloyd E. "The Grattan Massacre." NEBRASKA HISTORY 37(Mar 1956): 1-25. Military.

McCANNE, Hugh. Diary. MO-WHMC. CAL(Indep). III. 1850.

McCARTHY, Max R. "Patrick Edward Connor and the Military District of Utah: Civil War Military Operations in Utah and Nevada." MS thesis, Utah State Univ., 1976. Military.

McCARVER, D. M. MCCARVER AND TACOMA. Seattle: Lowman & Hanford, 1906. OR. 1843. Not Seen.

McCAULEY, A. L. A Trip Across. ORHIST. OR(Council). III. Rem. 1865.

McCLANE, John B. The First Wagon Train. BANCROFT. OR(Indep). IV. 1843.

McCLAIN, Martha A. Reminiscence. ORHIST. IV. Rem. 1853.

McCLELLAND, John M., Jr. Ed. Judson, Phoebe. PIONEER'S SEARCH.

McCLERNAN, John B. SLADE'S WELLS FARGO COLT (HISTORICAL NOTES). Hicksville, NY: Exposition, 1977. Stage.

McCLINTOCK, Margaretta F. My Trip. ORHIST. MORMON. V. Rem. 1866.

McCLUNG, James S. Diary. ORHIST. OR(Council)-LANDER. I. 1862.

McCLUNG, Zarah. TRAVELS ACROSS THE PLAINS IN 1852. St. Louis: Chambers & Knapp, 1854. CAL(Council). III. 1852.

McCLURE, Alexander K. THREE THOUSAND MILES THROUGH THE ROCKY MOUNTAINS. Philadelphia: Lippincott, 1869. Stage: Omaha-Denver-SLC-Virginia City, MT-Helena. III. 1867. Indians.

McCLURE, Andrew S. Journal. ORU. OR(Kansas)-MEEK. II+. 1853.

McCLURE, James. Diary. ORHIST. OR(Malheur)-East to Idaho. IV. 1853. Stock.

McCLURE, John H. HOW WE CAME TO OREGON (Narrative Poem). Eugene, OR: Lane County Pioneer - Historical Society, 1967. OR(Weston)-MEEK. IV. 1853.

McCOMAS, Evans S. A JOURNAL OF TRAVEL. Portland: Champoeg, 1954. OR(Council). III. 1862.

MACOMB, J. N. REPORT OF THE EXPLORING EXPEDITION FROM SANTA FE, NEW MEXICO, TO THE JUNCTION OF THE GRAND AND GREEN RIVERS OF THE GREAT COLORADO OF THE WEST, IN 1859. N.p.: Engineer Bureau, 1876. SPANISH. 1859. Not Seen.

McCONAHAY, A. P. INCIDENTS AS I REMEMBER THEM CLOSING 1865. Van Wert, OH: Author, 1927. Stage: Nevada City, CA to Fort Leavenworth. 1864.

McCORKLE, Eugene. "Roads, Bridges and the Cars that Crossed Them." COWLITZ HISTORICAL QUARTERLY 26(Spr 1984): 3-54. WASH-Cowlitz County.

McCORMICK, Henry. ACROSS THE CONTINENT IN 1865. Harrisburg, PA: Private, 1937. Stage: Atchison-SLC-Boise-Portland-SF-Virginia City, NV. III. 1865.

McCORMICK, Margaret H. "The Personal Journal and Arizona Letters of...." Ed. Norm Tessman. JOURNAL OF ARIZONA HISTORY 26(Spr 1985): 41-52. BEALE(Los Angeles-Prescott). V. 1865.

McCOWEN, George. A Trip Across.... CSL. CAL(Council)-LASSEN. II+. 1854.

McCOY, Alexander W., John McCoy, Samuel McCoy, and John A. Johnson. PIONEERING ON THE PLAINS.... Kaukauna, WI: N.p., 1924. CAL(Indep)-LASSEN. III+. 1849.

McCOY, John. Unpublished Reminiscences.... ORHIST. OR(Council). IV. Rem. 1845.

McCOY, Joseph G. HISTORIC SKETCHES OF THE CATTLE TRADE OF THE WEST AND SOUTHWEST. Ed. Ralph P. Bieber. 1874. Reprint. Columbus, OH: Long's, 1951. Stock.

McCUBBIN, John C. "The Stockton - Los Angeles Stage Road." CSL. Stage. Very complete study and on-site survey of trail.

McCUE, James S. TWENTY-ONE YEARS IN CALIFORNIA: INCIDENTS IN THE LIFE OF A STAGE DRIVER. SF: Francis & Valentine, 187? Stage.

McCULLOCH, Henry E. Papers. BARKER. TEX-Genl.

McCULLOUGH, Samuel. Papers. HUNTL. CANADA-British Columbia-1858-Genl.

McCUNE, George H. "Extension of the Telegraph in the Northwest, 1850-1880." PhD diss., Univ. of Minnesota, 1943. Not Seen.

McCUTCHAN, James B. SEE: Kennedy, Glenn A. GO WEST.

McCUTCHAN, Rebecca E. Headed West. Ed. Glenn A. Kennedy. UPAC. CAL(Council)-BRIDGER-SIMPSON. III. 1863.

McDANNALD, David W. "A Story of Crossing the Plains in 1865." Univ. of Washington-Ms, Seattle, WA. OR(Plattsmouth). III. 1865. Fictionalized diary, with details from actual crossing.

McDERMOTT, John Francis. Ed. Field, Matthew C. PRAIRIE AND MOUNTAIN SKETCHES. Ed. Wilkins, James S. ARTIST ON THE OVERLAND TRAIL.

_____. "De Smet's Illustrator: Father Nicholas Point." NEBRASKA HISTORY 33(Mar 1952): 35-40. Biog. Graphics.

_____. "Gold Rush Movies." CALIFORNIA HISTORICAL QUARTERLY 33(Mar 1954): 29-38. CAL-1849-Genl. Graphics.

_____. "Lost Manuscripts of Western Travel." ARIZONA & THE WEST 11(Win 1969): 315-26. Bib.

_____, ed. TRAVELERS ON THE WESTERN FRONTIER. Urbana: Univ. of Illinois Press, 1970. Bib.

_____. "Up the Wide Missouri: Travelers and Their Diaries, 1794 - 1861." In TRAVELERS ON THE WESTERN FRONTIER, ed. John F. McDermott. Urbana: Univ. of Illinois Press, 1970. Bib.

McDIARMID, Finley. Letters. BANCROFT. CAL(St. Jo)-BRIDGER-HASTINGS. II+. 1850.

McDONALD, Archie P. "The Texas Road." RED RIVER VALLEY HISTORICAL REVIEW 6(Sum 1981): 57-67. OKLAHOMA(Joplin, MO-Ft. Gibson-Eufala-Red River)-Genl.

MacDONALD, Craig. COCKEYED CHARLEY PARKHURST.... Palmer Lake, CO: Filter, 1973. Biog.

McDONALD, Frank V. NOTES PREPARATORY TO A BIOGRAPHY OF RICHARD HAYES MCDONALD.... Cambridge: University Press, 1881. CAL(St. Jo?)-TRUCKEE. V. Rem. 1849.

MacDONALD, James. THE TREK OF JAMES MACDONALD...1850. Schenectady, NY: Edwin M. Stanton, 1951. CAL(St. Jo). IV. 1850.

McDONALD, James R. AUTOBIOGRAPHY OF.... Ed. Paul McDonald. N.p., n.d. Presentation copy. UPAC. CAL(St. Jo). IV. 1850.

McDONALD, Paul. Ed. McDonald, James R. AUTOBIOGRAPHY.

McDONALD, Richard Hayes. SEE: McDonald, Frank V. NOTES PREPARATORY.

McDONALD, William J. NOTES BY A PIONEER. N.p., n. d. CANADA. Not Seen.

MacDONALD, William R. "The Impact of the California Gold Rush on the Mormons in the Great Basin, 1847 - 1857." MA thesis, Colorado College, 1967. CAL-Genl. UTAH.

McDOUGALL, John. FOREST, LAKE, AND PRAIRIE.... Toronto: Rynerson, 1895? CANADA-Genl.

_____. SADDLE, SLED AND SNOWSHOE. Toronto: Briggs, 1896. CANADA-Genl.

M'DUFFEE, John. THE OREGON CRISIS.... Salem, OH: Hinchman, 1848. Guide.

McELHINNEY, Alice E. "Old Immigrant Trails into the Oregon Country." Univ. of Washington Library-MS, Seattle, WA. OR-Genl.

MacEWAN, John G. BLAZING THE OLD CATTLE TRAIL. Saskatoon, Canada: Western Producer Prairie, 1975. CANADA-Cattle Trails.

McFARLAND, G. "A Legacy Left Behind." AMERICAN HISTORY ILLUSTRATED 19(Mar 1984): 20-25. Biog: John Brown. CAL-Genl.

McFARLANE, Andrew. "Letter of a Gold Rusher of 1850." Ed. A. R. Mortensen. UTAH HISTORICAL QUARTERLY 22(Jan 1954): 57-61. CAL(Indep)-BRIDGER-Ends SLC. V. 1850.

McFARLING, Lloyd, ed. EXPLORING OUR NORTHERN PLAINS, 1804-1876. Caldwell, ID: Caxton, 1955. Overland-Genl.

McGAFFEY, Joseph W. "Across Mexico in the Days of '49." TOURING TOPICS 21(May, Jun 1929): 18-21, 48-49; 36-39, 50. CAL-TEX(Corpus Christi-Laredo)-MEX(Durango-Mazatlan). II. 1849.

McGEE, Joseph H. STORY OF THE GRAND RIVER COUNTRY, 1821-1905. Gallatin, MO: North Missourian Press, 1909. CAL(Indep). IV. Rem. 1850.

McGEE, W. J. THE OLD YUMA TRAIL. Reprinted from NATIONAL GEOGRAPHIC, March-April, 1901. WA: Judd & Detweiler, 1901. GILA-Genl.

McGEEHEE, Micajah. "Rough Times in Rough Places: A Personal Narrative of Fremont's Fourth Expedition." Ed. C. G. McGeehee. CENTURY 41(Feb 1891): 771-80. SPANISH. V. 1848-49.

McGIE, Joseph F. "Society Summer Tour over Portions of the Beckwourth Trail." DIGGINS 3(Sum 1959): 15-21. Route from Bidwell Bar to Oroville. BECK-Genl. Pres.

McGINTY, Brian. "Keep Your Seat, Horace." AMERICAN WEST 20(Nov-Dec 1983): 67. Stage. Biog.

McGLASHAN, C. F. HISTORY OF THE DONNER PARTY: A TRAGEDY OF THE SIERRA. SF: Carlisle, 1918. CAL(Indep)-BRIDGER-HASTINGS-TRUCKEE. II. 1846.

_____. Papers. BANCROFT. CAL-1846-Genl.

_____. "Why the Donner Party History Was Written." GRIZZLY BEAR 23(Jun 1918): 11.

McGLASHEN, John M. Overland Journal. UWY. CAL(Ft. Kearney)-BRIDGER-SLCUT-Ends Ragtown. II+. 1850.

McGOWAN, D., and George H. Hildt. MAP OF THE U.S. WEST...SHOWING THE ROUTES TO PIKE'S PEAK, OVERLAND MAIL ROUTE TO CALIFORNIA, AND PACIFIC RAILROAD SURVEYS. St. Louis: Gast, 1859. Guide.

McGOWAN, Edward. THE STRANGE EVENTFUL HISTORY OF PARKER H. FRENCH.... Ed. Kenneth M. Johnson. LA: Dawson, 1958. CAL-TEX(Lavaca-El Paso)-MEX(Chihuahua-Durango-Mazatlan). V. 1850. Biog.

McGOWAN, Joseph A. "Freighting to the Mines in California, 1849 - 1859." PhD diss., Univ. of California-Berkeley, 1949. Freight.

McGREGOR, Alexander C. "The Economic Impact of the Mullan Road on Walla Walla, 1860 - 1883." PACIFIC NORTHWEST QUARTERLY 65(Jul 1974): 118-29. MULLAN-Genl. Freight.

MacGREGOR, J. G. OVERLAND BY THE YELLOWHEAD. Saskatoon, Canada: Western Producer, 1974. Geog: Yellowhead Pass.

McHENRY, Maud. "Transportation Across the Great Plains." MA thesis, Univ. of Oklahoma, 1926. Overland-Genl.

McILHANY, Edward W. RECOLLECTIONS OF A '49ER...IN THE FAR WEST. Kansas City: Hailman, 1908. CAL(St. Jo)-TRUCKEE. IV. Rem. 1849.

McINTOSH, Clarence F. "The Chico and Red Bluff Route: Stage Lines from Southern Idaho to the Sacramento Valley, 1865 - 1867." IDAHO YESTERDAYS 6(Fall 1962): 12-15, 18-19. Stage. Maps.

_____. "Stage Lines from Southern Idaho to the Sacramento Valley, 1865 - 1867." DIGGIN'S 9(Spr 1965): 3-9. Stage. Maps.

McINTOSH, Walter H. ALLEN AND RACHEL: AN OVERLAND HONEYMOON IN 1853. Caldwell, ID: Caxton, 1938. OR(St. Jo)-MEEK. III. 1853.

McKAIG, Silas. "We Rolled West." Ed. Stewart F. Lamb. ORHIST. CAL(Council). II+. 1852.

MacKAY, Corday. "The Collins Overland Telegraph." BRITISH COLUMBIA HISTORICAL QUARTERLY 10, no. 3(1946): 187-215. Telegraph.

McKEAN, Samuel T. Reminiscences. ORHIST. OR. V-. Rem. 1847.

McKEE, Irving, ed. ALONZO DELANO'S CALIFORNIA CORRESPONDENCE...1849 - 1852. Pub. No. 5, Sacramento Book Collectors Club. Sacramento: Book Club, 1952. Refer to Delano, Alonzo. LIFE ON THE PLAINS.

McKEEBY, Lemuel C. "The Memoirs of...." CALIFORNIA HISTORICAL QUARTERLY 3(Apr, Jul 1924): 45-72, 126-70. CAL(Council)-BRIDGER-SLCUT. III. 1850.

MacKELLAR, Christiana. "The History of Death Valley, 1849 - 1933." MA thesis, Univ. of California-Berkeley, 1941. Geog.

McKELVEY, Susan D. BOTANICAL EXPLORATION OF THE TRANS-MISSISSIPPI WEST. Jamaica Plain, MA: Arboretum, 1955. Flora.

McKIERAN, John S. Journal. HUNTL. OR(Old Ft. Kearny)-BARLOW. II+. 1852. Social: Trial for murder.

McKINNEY, J. Wilson. "Gold Builds a Road." DESERT 1(Dec 1937): 8-9, 24. BRADSHAW-Genl. Maps.

McKINNEY, William N. SEE: With Arthur Taylor. "An Accurate Observer."

MacKINNON, William P. "The Buchanan Spoils System and the Utah Expedition: Careers of W. M. F. Magraw and John M. Hockaday." UTAH HISTORICAL QUARTERLY 31(Spr 1963): 127-50. Mail. Stage. Biog.

McKINSTRY, Bruce L. Ed. McKINSTRY, Byron. CALIFORNIA GOLD RUSH OVERLAND.

_____. "A Grandfather's Journal of the Oregon Trail." CHICAGO WESTERNERS BRAND BOOK 16(Mar 1959): 1-3, 7-8. OR-1850-Genl.

McKINSTRY, Byron N. THE CALIFORNIA GOLD RUSH OVERLAND DIARY OF...1850 - 1852. Ed. Bruce L. McKinstry. American Trails Series, No. 10. Glendale: Clark, 1975. CAL(Council)-HALL. I. 1850. Pres.

McKINSTRY, George, Jr. "Diary." In OVERLAND IN 1846, ed. Dale L. Morgan. Georgetown, CA: Talisman, 1963. CAL(Indep)-Ends near Ft. Laramie. III. 1846.

_____. "Remarkable Story of the...Donner Party." GRIZZLY BEAR 2(Jan 1908): 12-13. TRUCKEE-1846-Genl.

_____. "Thrilling and Tragic Journal." ST. LOUIS REVEILLE, undated issues in 1847. TRUCKEE-1846-Genl.

_____. Trip Across the Plains. Sharlot Hall Museum Library, Prescott, AZ. CAL(Indep)-Ends near Ft. Laramie. III. 1846.

McKNIGHT, George S. CALIFORNIA 49ER.... Toledo, OH: Andrews, 1903. CAL-TEX(Indianola-San Antonio)-MEX(Chihuahua-Durango-Mazatlan). IV. Rem. 1849.

McLANE, Allen. "Leaves from a Pencil'd Journal...." In GOLD RUSH (Joseph G. Bruff). NY: Columbia Univ. Press, 1949. LASSEN(Mud Lake to Sierra crest). II. 1849.

McLARTY, Vivian K. Ed. With Eugenia James. "Three Generations."

McLATCHY, Michael G. Ed. Kirkpatrick, Robert. "From Wisconsin to Montana."

McLAUGHLIN, Daniel. SKETCH OF A TRIP FROM OMAHA TO SALMON RIVER. 1954. Reprint. Fairfield, WA: Ye Galleon, 1976. OR(Council)-LANDER. III. Rem. 1862.

McLAUGHLIN, David H. Reminiscences. NBHIST. Pony.

McLEAN, Agnes M. "McKenzie Pass - "John Tom's Road" - Building of the Road." LANE COUNTY HISTORIAN 8(Mar 1963): 3-4, 17-19. OR-Genl.

MacLEAN, John. "A Tribute to the Red River Cart." ALBERTA HISTORY 31(Win 1983): N.p. Not Seen.

McLELLAN, William. Reminiscence. UPAC. CAL(Indep)-BRIDGER-HASTINGS. II. Rem. 1850.

McLEMORE, Clyde. Ed. Ficklin, Benjamin F. "Ficklin's Expedition."

McMICKING, Robert B. Diary, 1863. Provincial Archives of British Columbia, Victoria, BC. Not Seen.

McMICKING, Thomas. OVERLAND FROM CANADA TO BRITISH COLUMBIA. Ed. Joanne Leduc. Vancouver: Univ. of British Columbia Press, 1981. CANADA(Ft. Garry-Ft. Edmonton-Yellowhead Pass-Kamloops-New Westminster). II. 1862.

_____. "The Overlanders in Alberta, 1862." Ed. Hugh Dempsey. ALBERTA HISTORICAL REVIEW 4(Sum 1966): N.p. Not Seen.

McMILLAN, Marcus. Pioneer of 1852. Univ. of Washington Library-Ms, Seattle, WA. OR(Council). III. Rem. 1852.

McMILLAN, Robert N. SEE: With Ruth M. Jones. "Utah, the Mormons, and the West." SEE: With Ruth M. Jones, et al. "Utah, the Mormons and the West."

McMILLAN, Kathryn S. "A Descriptive Bibliography on the San Antonio - San Diego Mail Line." SOUTHWESTERN HISTORICAL QUARTERLY 59(Oct 1955): 206-14. Very complete list. Bib.

_____. "The San Antonio - San Diego Mail Line, 1857 - 1861." MA thesis, Univ. of Texas-Austin, 1960. Stage.

McMORRIS, Lewis. Papers, 1863 - 1907. Washington State Historical Society Library, Tacoma, WA. Stage-Walla Walla.

MACKMULL, Gulden. "An Aerial Liner for the Forty-Niner." TRUE WEST 17(Nov-Dec, 1969): 33, 42. Eqpt-1849.

McMULLEN, Leon. "Two Gateways to Southern California: San Carlos Pass and Cajon Pass, 1772 - 1883." MA thesis, Univ. of California-Berkeley, 1932. Geog.

MacMURPHY, John A. "Thirty-three Years Ago." TRANSACTIONS AND REPORTS Nebraska State Historical Society 3(1892): 270-78. CAL(Council)-Ends on Platte River. III. 1853.

McMURTRIE, Douglas C. Ed. Ingersoll, Chester. OVERLAND TO CALIFORNIA IN 1849.

McNARY, Lawrence A. "Route of the Meek Cutoff, 1845." OREGON HISTORICAL QUARTERLY 35(Mar 1934): 1-9. MEEK-1845-Genl.

McNAUGHTON, Margaret. OVERLAND TO CARIBOO. Toronto: Briggs, 1896. CANADA-DAKOTAS(St. Paul)-Ft. Garry-Ft. Edmonton-Yellowhead Pass-Ft. George-Victoria-Kamloops. III+. 1862.

McNEIL, Samuel. MCNEIL'S TRAVEL IN 1849.... 1850. Reprint. New Haven: Yale Univ. Press, 1958. CAL-TEX(Brazos)-MEX(Monterey-Parras-Durango-Mazatlan). III. 1849.

McNEMEE, Jack. Personal Narrative. UWY. MEEK-1845-Genl. IV. 1845.

McOMBER, Winston I. "The Indian Problem of Southern Idaho, 1855 - 1878." MA thesis, Univ. of Utah, 1951. Indians.

MacPHAIL, Elizabeth C. "Wells Fargo in San Diego." JOURNAL OF SAN DIEGO HISTORY 28(Fall 1982): 213-31. Stage.

McPHERREN, Ida. IMPRINTS ON PIONEER TRAILS. Boston: Christopher, 1950. CAL(Indep)-BRIDGER-Ends at Bear River. II. Rem. 1851.

McPHERSON, John C. "Extracts from Diary." CSL. CAL(Ft. Laramie to Devil's Gate). V-. 1848?

McPHERSON, Murdoch M. "The Reminiscences of...." PACIFIC NORTHWEST QUARTERLY 27(Jul, Oct 1936): 243-60, 369-90. PIKES(Atchison to Denver)-CHEROKEE(Denver-Ft. Bridger)-HALL. II. Rem. 1863. Freight.

McPHERSON, William. Ed. Couts, Cave J. FROM SAN DIEGO TO THE COLORADO. Ed. Pleasants, Joseph E. "Joseph Edward Pleasants, 49er."

McPHERSON, William G. "Journal of Overland Travel...." ORANGE [CA] NEWS, 6 - 12 August 1937, N.p. CAL(Council)-LANDER-LASSEN. III +. 1859.

McPIKE, Daniel M., and David C. Hunt. "Santa Fe Trade." AMERICAN SCENE 4, no. 4(1965): N.p. Graphics-Santa Fe Trail.

McQUEEN, Angus. Diary, 1852. Stanford Univ. Library-SpCol, Palo Alto, CA. CAL(St. Jo)-Ends Nimeha River in Kansas. III. 1852.

McQUOWN, Madeline R. Papers. Univ. of Utah Library-SpCol, Salt Lake City, UT. Contains significant trail material from Dale L. Morgan. Fine Register. Overland-Genl.

McWILLIAMS, John. RECOLLECTIONS OF JOHN MCWILLIAMS. Princeton: Princeton Univ. Press, N.d. OR(St. Jo)-BARLOW. III. Rem. 1849.

THE MACY CENTENNIAL, 1850 - 1950. (Mimeo family history) BANCROFT. CAL-1850-Genl.

MACY, Ralph W. "Stricker's Store." OVERLAND JOURNAL 4(Spr 1986): 25-35. Geog: Hansen, ID.

MADDOCK, Sallie H. "The Diary of a Pioneer Girl." ARGONAUT 97, 12 Sept 1925, 3-4. CAL(St Jo)-TRUCKEE (Extracts only). V. 1849.

MADSEN, Brigham D. Ed. Hudson, John. FORTY-NINER IN UTAH.

_____. "The Colony Guard: To California in '49." UTAH HISTORICAL QUARTERLY 51(Win 1983): 5-29. CAL(Indep)-Ends near Ft. Laramie. II. 1849. Train Govt.

_____. GOLD RUSH SOJOURNERS IN GREAT SALT LAKE CITY 1849 AND 1850. University of Utah Publications in the American West, S. Lyman Tyler, ed., Vol. 18. SLC: Univ. of Utah Press, 1985. Utah. Geog: Salt Lake City.

_____. THE SHOSHONI FRONTIER AND THE BEAR RIVER MASSACRE. Vol. 1, Utah Centennial Series. SLC: Univ. of Utah Press, 1985. Indians.

_____. "Shoshone-Bannock Marauders on the Oregon Trail, 1859 - 1863." UTAH HISTORICAL QUARTERLY 35(Win 1967): 3-30. Indians. Military.

_____ and Betty M. Madsen. "Corrine, the Fair: Gateway to Montana Mines." UTAH HISTORICAL QUARTERLY 37(Win 1969): 102-23. Freight. Geog: Corrine, UT.

_____. "The Diamond R Rolls Out." MONTANA 21(Spr 1971): 2-17. Freight-Montana.

_____. NORTH TO MONTANA! JEHUS, BULLWHACKERS, AND MULESKINNERS ON THE MONTANA TRAIL. SLC: Univ. of Utah Press, 1980. Freight: Montana to Utah.

MADSEN, Wilhelmina K. History. UTHIST. MORMON. IV. 1856.

MAGEE, Thomas. "A Run Overland." OVERLAND MONTHLY 1(Dec 1868): 507-16. Stage: Laramie, WY to Virginia City, NV. V. 1868.

MAGEE, William "Pap." MAGEE STATION AND THE CHURCHILL CHRONICLES. Ed. Roberta Childers. Reno: Jamison Station Press, 1985. SIMPSON-Genl. SIMPSON. II. 1863.

MAGLEY, Marsha C., comp. LEAVENWORTH & PIKE'S PEAK COMMEMORATIVE ISSUE. Littleton, CO: Prints Valiant, 1984. Stage. Pres.

_____. "Leavenworth & Pike's Peak Express." LA POSTA 16(Nov 1985): 23-31. Map and directions to sites along Smoky Hill stage route. Stage. Pres.

MAGLIN, Michael. WELLS FARGO: STAGECOACH HOLDUPS - ROBBERIES - BURGLARIES. Reno?: Author, 1974. Reprint of Jason B. Hume and John N. Thacker. REPORT. SF: Crocker, 1885. Stage.

MAGNUSSON, Elsa C. "Natches Pass." WASHINGTON HISTORICAL QUARTERLY 25(Jul 1934): 171-81. Geog.

MAHAN, Garland. Diary. MO-WHMC. CAL(Council)-LANDER-MONTANA. II +. 1864.

MAHLBERT, Blanche B. Ed. Allen, Edward J. "Edward J. Allen."

MAHON, Emmie W. SEE: With Emily C. Giddings. "The Jackass Trail."

_____, and Chester V. Kielman. "George H. Giddings and the San Antonio - San Diego Mail Line." SOUTHWESTERN HISTORICAL QUARTERLY 41(Oct 1957): 220-59. Stage.

MAHONEY, William F. Diary. COHIST. PIKES(Neb. City to Ft. Kearney). II +. 1860.

MAILLET, Louis R. Account. MONHIST. CAL(St. Jo)-HALL-MONTANA. V. Rem. 1861.

MAIN, Mildred M. "Reveries of an Old Oregon Trail Pioneer. Remembrances of Joseph Meeker's Efforts to Mark and Commemorate the Route of the Overland Trail to Oregon." ORHIST. Pres.

MAJOR-Fregeau, Madeline. Ed. Warre, H. J. OVERLAND TO OREGON IN 1845.

MAJORS, Alexander. SEVENTY YEARS ON THE FRONTIER. Chicago: Rand, McNally, 1893. Pony. Telegraph. Freight.

_____, and William H. Russell. A BRIEF STATEMENT OF THE CLAIM OF MAJORS & RUSSELL AND THE EVIDENCE UPON WHICH IT RESTS. N.p., n.d. HUNTL. Stage.

MAJORS, Harry M. Ed. Pringle, Catherine. "Seven Orphans on the Oregon Trail."

MAJORS, John. COMMON SENSE: OR THOUGHTS OF A PLAIN MAN. N.p., 1878. CAL(Indep?)-LASSEN. V. Rem. 1849.

MALBEN, Ben. Reminiscence. MONHIST. DAKOTAS(St. Cloud)-MONTANA. V. Rem. 1866.

MALIN, James C. "Indian Policy and Westward Expansion." UNIVERSITY OF KANSAS HUMANISTIC STUDIES 2(1921). Indians.

MALLORY, Samuel. "Overland to Pike's Peak with a Gold Mill." COLORADO MAGAZINE 8(May 1931): 108-14. PIKES. IV. 1860.

_____. Papers. Norlin Library-Western History, Univ. of Colorado-Boulder, CO. CHEROKEE(Denver-SLC)-HALL-MONTANA. IV. 1864.

_____. "Samuel Mallory." Ed. Agnes W. Spring. MONTANA 15(Apr 1965 and July 1965): 24-37, 68-79. PIKES. V. 1860. CHEROKEE(Denver-SLC)-HALL-MONT. II. 1864.

MALLOY, William D. "Carson Valley, 1852 - 1860." MA thesis, Univ.

of California-Berkeley, 1931. Geog.

MALONEY, Alice B. "A Botanist on the Road to Yerba Buena." CALIFORNIA HISTORICAL QUARTERLY 24(Dec 1945): 321-25. OR-CAL. IV. 1841.

_____. "Some Oatman Documents." CALIFORNIA HISTORICAL QUARTERLY 21(Jun 1942): 107-12. GILA-Genl. Indians.

MALTBY, John R. Papers. NBHIST. Geog: Spring Ranch Station.

MANLOVE, John N. Overland Trip. Illinois State Historical Library, Springfield, IL. CAL(St. Jo)-BRIDGER-SLCUT-TRUCKEE. IV. Rem. 1849.

MANLY, William L. DEATH VALLEY IN '49. 1894. Reprint. NY: Wallace Hebberd, 1929. CAL(St. Jo)-SPANISH variant-SLCOR. III. Rem. 1849.

_____. THE JAYHAWKERS' OATH AND OTHER SKETCHES. Ed. Arthur Woodward. LA: Warren F. Lewis, 1949. SLCOR-1849-Genl.

MANN, H. R. Diary. CSL. CAL(Mormon Ferry)-HALL-TRUCKEE. II+. 1849.

MANNING, James W. "Literacy on the Oregon Trail: Books across the Plains." OREGON HISTORICAL QUARTERLY 41(Jun 1940): 189-94. Social.

MANNING, Malvina V. Diary. BANCROFT. CAL(Ft. Smith)-CHEROKEE(to Ft. Riley)-BRIDGER-SLCUT. III. 1861.

MANRING, B. F. Comp. Stockman, Lawson. "Recollections of a Pioneer."

MANSFIELD, Philip. PRELIMINARY MAP OF THE OREGON TRAIL AND THE PRINCIPAL PIONEER ROUTES TO CALIFORNIA. WA: Public Roads Administration - Federal Works Agency, 1940. Maps.

MANTOR, Lyle E. "Fort Kearney and the Westward Movement." NEBRASKA HISTORY 29(Sept 1948): 175-207. Geog.

_____. "Stage Coach and Freighting Days at Fort Kearney." NEBRASKA HISTORY 29(Dec 1948): 324-38. Stage. Freight. Geog.

MANVILLE, George. Story of My Life. Washington State Historical Society Library, Tacoma, WA. OR(Council)-LANDER. III. Rem. 1862.

MANWARING, Joshua. "Journal of a Fifty-Niner." Ed. Robert M. Warner. COLORADO MAGAZINE 36(Jul 1959): 161-73. PIKES. III. 1859.

MAPEL, Eli B. Experiences. BANCROFT. OR(Council?). V. Rem. 1852.

MAPES, Charles B. "The Nebraska City - Fort Kearny Cutoff as a Factor in the Early Development of Nebraska and the West." MS thesis, Univ. of Nebraska, 1931. Geog.

MARBLE, Manton. "The Red River Trail." HARPERS 21(Aug 1860): 289-311. DAKOTAS(St. Paul-Ft. Abercrombie-Pembina). I. 1860. Graphics.

_____. "To Red River and Beyond." HARPERS 21(Oct 1860): 581-606. CANADA(Pembina-Mouse River). I. 1860. Graphics.

MARCH, David D. "Cheyenne and Sioux Indian Relations along the Oregon Trail, 1841 - 1858." MA thesis, Univ. of Missouri, 1941. Indians.

MARCY, Randolph B. SEE: Foreman, Grant. ADVENTURE ON RED RIVER. SEE: Foreman, Grant. MARCY AND THE GOLD SEEKERS. SEE: Hollon, W. Eugene. BEYOND THE CROSS TIMBERS.

_____. THE PRAIRIE TRAVELER: A HANDBOOK FOR OVERLAND EXPEDITIONS. 1859. Reprint. Williamstown, MA: Corner House, 1968. Guide. An excellent example of the genre.

MARIAGER, Dagmar. "Nomadic Experiences of a Frontierswoman." OVERLAND MONTHLY 10(Sept 1887): 316-26. Social.

_____. "A Voyage by Land." OVERLAND MONTHLY 13(Jun 1889): 630-39. CHEROKEE(Promontory, UT-Denver)-PIKES(Smoky Hill route)-Ends Sheridan, KS. III. 1869.

MARICLE, Abraham. Diary. MONHIST. DAKOTAS(St. Cloud)-MONTANA. III-. 1867.

MARKLE, John A. "Diary." GRIZZLY BEAR 55(Dec 1934): 7, 9, 14. TRUCKEE. III. 1849.

MARKS, Paula M. "What the Pioneers Read." OLD WEST 21(Sum 1985): 47-49. Social.

MARSH, Creat I. SEE: With Loris F. Inman. "The Road across Lane County."

MARSH, David. "Cheyenne and Sioux Indian Relations along the Oregon Trail, 1841 - 1858." MA thesis, Univ. of Missouri, 1941. Indians. Military.

MARSH, Edson. "Edson Marsh on the Oregon Trail." In THE NORTHWEST, ed. B. C. Payette. N.p.: Payette, 1964. OR(Council). V. Rem. 1852.

MARSHALL, Donald W. "The Mississippi Saints and Sick Detachments of the Mormon Battalion, Winter 1846 - 47." THETIAN 2(1968): 33-41. CHEROKEE-1846-Genl.

MARSHALL, Ellen. "Some Phases of the Establishment and Development of Roads in Texas, 1716 - 1845." MA thesis, Univ. of Texas-Austin, 1934. TEX-Genl.

MARSHALL, Henry. Statement. BANCROFT. CAL(Indep?)-HALL. V-. 1845.

MARSHALL, Philip C. "The Newark Overland Company." PROCEEDINGS New Jersey Historical Society 70(Jul 1952): 173-87. CAL(Indep)-BRIDGER-SLCUT-LASSEN. IV. 1849.

MARSHALL, Robert. Diary. Society of California Pioneers, San Francisco, CA. Not Seen.

MARSHALL, Thomas M. Ed. Price, Joseph. "The Road to California."

_____. "The Platte Valley Ranchers of '63 and '64." TRAIL 9(May 1919): 5-11. Geog: Stations, Ft. Kearney to Denver.

MARSTON, Anna L. Ed. Gunn, Lewis C. RECORDS OF A CALIFORNIA FAMILY.

MARTIN, Charles W. Ed. Arnold, Joseph W. "Joseph Warren Arnold's Journal." Ed. Lester, Gurdon P. "A Round Trip to the Montana Mines." Ed. Woodhams, William H. "The Diary of William H. Woodhams."

_____. "The Alcove Spring." OVERLAND JOURNAL 2(Win

1984): 4-6. Geog.

MARTIN, Charles W., Jr. "Geology and the Emigrant." OVERLAND JOURNAL 3(Win, Spr, Sum 1985): 4-8, 17-21, 28-32. Geog.

_____. "Lighter Side of the Trail Experience." OVERLAND JOURNAL 5(Sum 1987): 7-13. Social-Humor.

MARTIN, Clinton S. BOY SCOUTS AND THE OREGON TRAIL. NY: Putnam's Sons, 1930. Pres.

MARTIN, Douglas D. "Battle at Cooke's Canyon." TRUE WEST 10(Sept-Oct 1962): 16-17. Stage-1861.

_____. YUMA CROSSING. Albuquerque: Univ. of New Mexico Press, 1954. Geog.

MARTIN, Gene and Mary. TRAIL DUST: A QUICK PICTURE HISTORY OF THE SANTA FE TRAIL. Denver: Golden Bell, 1972. SANTA FE-Genl.

MARTIN, J. C., and Robert S. Martin. MAPS OF TEXAS AND THE SOUTHWEST, 1513-1900. Albuquerque: Univ. of New Mexico Press, 1984. Maps.

MARTIN, Jane S. Life and Times. UTHIST. MORMON. IV. Rem. 1856.

MARTIN, Mabelle E. Ed. Cox, C. C. "From Texas to California."

_____. "California Emigrant Roads through Texas." SOUTHWESTERN HISTORICAL QUARTERLY 28(Apr 1925): 287-301. TEX-1849-Genl.

MARTIN, Oscar F. "The Old Lassen Trail." OVERLAND MONTHLY 2(Jul 1883): 74-82. LASSEN-Genl.

MARTIN, Robert S. SEE: With J. C. Martin. MAPS.

MARTIN, Thomas S. WITH FREMONT TO CALIFORNIA AND THE SOUTHWEST, 1845 - 1849. Ed. Ferol Egan. Ashland, OR: Lewis Osborne, 1975. CAL(Indep)-SANTA FE-SPANISH-TRUCKEE. III. 1845. CAL(Sutter's to Ft. Leavenworth). III. 1847. CAL(Westport)-SANTA FE-RIO GRANDE- GILA. III. 1848.

MARTIN, William T. "Texas to California in 1853." POMONA VALLEY HISTORIAN 2(Apr 1966): 84-86. CAL-TEX(Denton)-GILA. V-. 1853.

MARTINEAU, James H. "A Tragedy of the Desert." IMPROVEMENT ERA 31(Jul 1928): 771-72. SLCOR-1849-Genl. SLCOR(White Mountain Expedition)-1857-Genl.

MARVIN, George P. "Bullwhacking Days." PROCEEDINGS AND COLLECTIONS Nebraska State Historical Society 5(1902): 226-30. Freight.

"Mary Catherine Crossing the Plains." In A HUNDRED YEARS OF RIP AND ROARIN' ROUGH AND READY: THE TOWN THAT WON'T GHOST. Ed. Andy Rogers. N.p.: Editor, 1952. CAL(Council. V-. 1854.

MASON, Dorothy. THE PONY EXPRESS IN NEVADA. Reno: A. Carlisle, 1976. Pony.

MASON, Glenn. "A PIECE OF THE OLD TENT:" BEING A CATALOG OF ITEMS IN THE LANE COUNTRY PIONEER MUSEUM THAT WERE BROUGHT ACROSS THE PLAINS IN THE 1840'S AND 1850'S. Eugene, OR: Lane County Pioneer Museum, 1976. Pres.

MASON, James. "The Diary of...1850." Ed. James C. Olson. NEBRASKA HISTORY 33(Jun 1952): 103-21. CAL(Westport)-BRIDGER-SLCUT. III. 1850.

MASON, Margaret, comp. "They Had a Dream: Feather River Highway - 1866 to 1941." Plumas County Historical Society PUBLICATIONS 37(Jul 1972): 7-56. CAL-Genl.

MASTERS, Joseph G. "Oregon Trail Memorial Association Centenary Celebration." DENVERPUB. Pres.

_____. Papers. DENVERPUB.

_____. Papers. NBHIST.

_____. Papers. KSHIST.

_____. "Tenting on Old Trails." NEBRASKA EDUCATIONAL JOURNAL 8(Feb 1928): 63-65. Pres.

_____, Harry L. Williams, Paul Henderson, and Donald E. Prather. "Pony Express Stations in Nebraska." NBHIST. Attributed to NBHIST but uncatalogued.

MASTERSON, Alfred. "The Ward Massacre." Lane County Historical Society, Eugene, OR. OR(Missouri). V. Rem. 1854. Indians.

MASTERSON, Martha G. SEE: Gay, James W. "Trail Diary."

MATHERS, James. "Journal of Travels...." In OVERLAND IN 1846, ed. Dale L. Morgan. Georgetown, CA: Talisman, 1963. CAL(Middle Crossing of Platte)-BRIDGER-HASTINGS. III. 1846.

MATHESON, Frank T. HISTORIC TRANSPORTATION. SLC: Pioneer Trail State Park, 1979. Eqpt-Stage.

MATHEWS, C. F. THE JIMMY CAMP TRAIL.... Colorado Springs, CO: Author, 1946. PIKES-Genl.

MATHEWS, Edward J. CROSSING THE PLAINS...'59. N.p., 1930. CAL(Council)-BRIDGER-SIMPSON. II. 1859.

MATTES, Merrill J. Ed. Byers, William N. "The Oregon Odyssey." Ed. Easton, L. C. "Captain L. C. Easton's Report." Ed. Farnham, Elijah B. "From Ohio to California in 1849." Ed. Hagen, Olaf T. "Platte Bridge Station and Fort Caspar." Ed. Ramsay, Alexander. "Alexander Ramsay's Diary of 1849." Ed. Rhodes, Joseph. "Joseph Rhodes and the California Gold Rush."

_____. "Chimney Rock on the Oregon Trail." NEBRASKA HISTORY 35(Mar 1955): 1-26. Geog. Graphics.

_____. "The Council Bluffs Road: A New Perspective on the Northern Branch of the Great Platte River Road." NEBRASKA HISTORY 65(Sum 1984): 179-94. Geog. MORMON-Genl.

_____. "The Council Bluffs Road: Northern Branch of the Great Platte River Road." OVERLAND JOURNAL 3(Fall 1985): 30-42. MORMON-Genl.

_____. "The Crusade to Save Fort Laramie." ANNALS OF WYOMING 50(Spr 1978): 5-58. Pres. Geog.

_____. FORT LARAMIE AND THE FORTY NINERS. Estes Park, CO: Rocky Mountain Nature Association, 1949. Geog.

_____. "Fort Laramie Centennial: 1849 - 1949." CHICAGO WESTERNERS BRAND BOOK 6(Apr 1949): 9-11, 13-16. Pres. Geog.

_____. "Fort Laramie, Guardian of the Oregon Trail: A Commemorative Essay." ANNALS OF WYOMING 17(Jan 1945): 3-20. Geog.

_____. "Fort Mitchell, Scotts Bluff, Nebraska Territory." NEBRASKA HISTORY 33(Mar 1952): 1-34. Geog.

_____. "The Gold Rush Mania: Victims and Survivors." NEBRASKA MEDICAL JOURNAL 6(1977): N.p. Not Seen.

_____. THE GREAT PLATTE RIVER ROAD: THE COVERED WAGON MAINLINE VIA FORT KEARNY TO FORT LARAMIE. Vol. 25 of Nebraska State Historical Society PUBLICATIONS. Lincoln: The Society, 1969. Superb recent analysis-bibliography of the Platte River trail network.

_____. "Hiram Scott, Fur Trader." NEBRASKA HISTORY 26(Jul-Sept 1945): 127-62. Geog.

_____. "A History of Old Fort Mitchell." NEBRASKA HISTORY 24(Apr-Jun 1943): 71-83. Geog.

_____. INDIANS, INFANTS AND INFANTRY: ANDREW AND ELIZABETH BURT ON THE FRONTIER. Denver: Fred A. Rosenstock, 1960. Military.

_____. "The Jumping-Off Places on the Overland Trail." In THE FRONTIER RE-EXAMINED, ed. John F. McDermott. Urbana: Univ. of Illinois Press, 1967. Overland-Genl.

_____. "New Horizons on Old Trails: A Review Essay." NEW MEXICO HISTORICAL REVIEW 55(Apr 1980): 157-64. Overland-Genl.

_____. "New Horizons on the Old Oregon Trail." In PEOPLE OF THE PLAINS AND MOUNTAINS..., ed. Ray A. Billington. Westport, CN: Greenwood, 1973. Overland-Genl.

_____. "Roubidoux's Trading Post at 'Scott's Bluffs' and the California Gold Rush." NEBRASKA HISTORY 30(Jun 1949): 95-138. Geog. Maps.

_____. "Scott's Bluff, Giant Landmark of the the Oregon - California Trails." OVERLAND JOURNAL 3(Sum 1985): 4-21. Geog.

_____. SCOTT'S BLUFF NATIONAL MONUMENT, NEBRASKA. Historical Handbook Series #28. WA: National Park Service, 1958. Geog. Maps.

_____. "A Tribute to Paul C. Henderson." OVERLAND JOURNAL 2(Spr 1984): 9-14. Biog.

_____. "A Tribute to the Emigrant Graves at Roubedeaux Pass." PONY EXPRESS 16(Nov 1949): 8-9, 13. GGeog.

_____. "A Tribute to the Oregon Trail Memorial Association." OVERLAND JOURNAL 2(Win 1984): 29-34. Pres.

_____, and Paul C. Henderson. Map Collection. NBHIST. Maps.

_____. "The Pony Express: Across Nebraska from St. Joseph to Fort Laramie." NEBRASKA HISTORY 41(Jun 1960): 83-122. Excellent bibliography and site descriptions. Pony.

MATTHEWS, Amanda M. A Journal of Traveling. NVHIST. CAL(Council)-BRIDGER-SLCUT. II. 1852.

MATTHEWS, Henry. "Mail Service in Idaho." SNAKE RIVER ECHOES 10, no. 4(1981): 85-90. Mail-Idaho.

MATTHEWS, L. C. Journal. BYU. CAL-MEX(Vera Cruz-Mexico City-Acapulco). III. 1851.

MATTHEWS, Leonard. A LONG LIFE IN REVIEW. St. Louis: Private, 1928. CAL(Neb. City). V. Rem. 1849.

MATTHEWS, William. AMERICAN DIARIES, AN ANNOTATED BIBLIOGRAPHY OF AMERICAN DIARIES WRITTEN PRIOR TO THE YEAR 1861. Berkeley: Univ. of California Press, 1945. Bib.

_____. AMERICAN DIARIES IN MANUSCRIPT, 1580-1954; A DESCRIPTIVE BIBLIOGRAPHY. Athens, GA: Univ. of Georgia Press, 1974. Bib.

MATTHIEU, F. X. "Reminiscences." Ed. H. S. Lyman. OREGON HISTORICAL QUARTERLY 1(Mar 1900): 73-104. OR(Begins Ft. Laramie)-BARLOW variant. IV. Rem. 1842.

MATTISON, Ray H. Ed. Larned, William L. "The Fisk Expedition of 1864." Ed. Todd, John B. "The Harney Expedition...Todd."

MATTSON, E. Neil. RED RIVER CARTS TREK; HISTORIC PEMBINA TRAIL. N.p., n.d. Eqpt. DAKOTAS-Genl.

MAUCK, Genevieve P. "The Council Bluffs Story." PALIMPSEST 42(Sept 1961): 385-448. Geog.

MAUGHAN, Mary A. Journal. UTHIST. MORMON. II. 1850.

MAWDSLEY, Dean. "The Butterfield Overland Mail." LA PENINSULA 22(Jan 1985): N.p. Stage(San Mateo County only).

MAXWELL, Ben. "Overland Staging in the 1860's." MARION COUNTY HISTORY 8(1962-1964): 15-19. OR-CAL Stage Lines.

MAXWELL, William A. CROSSING THE PLAINS - DAYS OF 1857. SF: Author, 1915. CAL(Neb. City)-TRUCKEE. IV. Rem. Indians(Holloway Massacre).

MAY, John. Correspondence. University of Arkansas Library-SpCol, Fayetteville, AK. CAL(Ft. Smith)-MARCY-RIO GRANDE-GILA. 1849. Not Seen.

MAY, Richard M. Sketch.... BANCROFT. CAL(Indep)-HALL. II+. 1848.

MAY, Sam. Sketch. In W. W. Morrison Collection, UWY. CAL(Indep)-HALL. II+. 1848. May be identical to above "Sketch."

MAYBEE, Cher. "Riding the Oregon - California Trail." OVERLAND JOURNAL 4(Sum 1986): 40-45. Pres.

MAYNADIER, Henry E. MEMOIR OF THE COUNTRY.... WA: Gibson Bros., 1864. MONTANA-Genl. Not Seen.

MAYNARD, David S. "Diary...Plains in 1850." WASHINGTON HISTORICAL QUARTERLY 1(Oct 1906): 5-62. OR(St. Jo)-WASH. III. 1850.

MAYNARD, David S. and Catherine T. DAVID S. MAYNARD AND CATHERINE T. MAYNARD...IMMIGRANTS OF 1850. Ed. Thomas W. Prosch. Seattle: Lowman & Hanford, N.d. OR(St. Jo). III. 1850.

MAYNARD, E. A. Letters. Wyoming State Archives, Cheyenne, WY. BOZE-Genl. Not Seen.

MAYS, Carleton. "Tragedy of the Pony Express." REAL WEST 3(Nov 1960): 8-12, 44-46. Pony.

MEACHAM, Walter E. APPLEGATE TRAIL. Portland: Author,

1947. APPLE-Genl.

_____. BARLOW ROAD. Portland?: Oregon Council, American Pioneer Trails, 1947. BARLOW-Genl. Maps.

_____. OLD OREGON TRAIL: ROADWAY OF AMERICAN HOME BUILDERS. Manchester, NH: Author, 1948. OR-Genl.

_____. Papers. ORU. Pres.

MEADOWS, Don, ed. THE CATTLE DRIVES OF JOSEPH E. PLEASANTS FROM BAJA CALIFORNIA IN 1867 AND 1868. LA: Dawson's, 1965. Stock.

MEAMBER, Fred J., Jr. "Augustus Meamber, Master Packer." Siskiyou County Historical Society YEARBOOK - 1950 1, no. 5(1950?): 13-19. Freight.

MEANY, Edmond S. "Ezra Meeker, the Pioneer." WASHINGTON HISTORICAL QUARTERLY 20(Apr 1929): 124-28. Biog.

MECARTNEY, Amos. Letter. Held by John M. Mecartney, Bluffton, OH. 1852. Not Seen.

MECHAM, Everett H. "The History of the Sheep Industry in Utah." MA thesis, Univ. of Utah, 1925. Stock.

MEEK, Joseph L. SEE: Tobie, Harvey E. NO MAN LIKE JOE.

MEEK, Stephen H. THE AUTOBIOGRAPHY OF A MOUNTAIN MAN, 1808 - 1889. Ed. Arthur Woodward. Pasadena: Dawson, 1948. Biog.

MEEKER, Ezra. SEE: Driggs, Howard, et al. COVERED WAGON CENTENNIAL.

_____. THE BUSY LIFE OF EIGHTY-FIVE YEARS. Seattle: Author, 1916. OR(Council). V. Rem. 1852.

_____. Correspondence. ORHIST. Pres.

_____. ORIGINAL EXPERIENCES ON THE OREGON TRAIL SIXTY YEARS AGO. Seattle: Author, 1912. OR(Council). V. Rem. 1852. Pres.

_____. THE OX TEAM OR THE OLD OREGON TRAIL, 1852 - 1906. NY: Author, 1906. OR(Council). V. Rem. 1852. Pres.

_____. Papers. Washington State Historical Society Library, Tacoma, WA. Pres.

_____. STORY OF THE LOST TRAIL TO OREGON. Seattle: Author, 1915. Pres.

_____. VENTURES AND ADVENTURES OF EZRA MEEKER.... Seattle: Author, 1908. OR(Council). V. Rem. 1853. Pres.

_____, and Howard Driggs. COVERED WAGON CENTENNIAL AND OX TEAM DAYS.... NY: Oregon Trail Memorial Association, 1931. Pres. Graphics.

_____. OX-TEAM DAYS ON THE OREGON TRAIL. Pioneer Life Series. Yonkers, NY: World, 1932. OR(Council). V. Rem. 1853. Pres.

MEIGS, Mary S. "An Old Turnpike Road of California." OUT WEST 21(Nov 1904): 403-16. Stage(Placerville to Lake Tahoe).

MEISTER, John. Diary [in German]. CSL. 1851.

MELGARD, Helen W. "The Mullan Road: The Northern Highway of the Pacific Northwest to 1917." MA thesis, Univ. of California-Berkeley, 1936. MULLAn-Genl.

MELINE, James F. TWO THOUSAND MILES ON HORSEBACK: SANTA FE AND BACK. NY: Hurd & Houghton, 1867. SANTA FE(Ft. Leav.). II. 1866.

MELTON, Florence. Reminiscences. Washington State Historical Society Library, Tacoma, WA. OR(Council)-BARLOW. III. Rem. 1868.

MEMORIAL OF CITIZENS OF THE UNITED STATES RESIDING IN THE VALLEY OF THE MISSISSIPPI. 30th Cong., 2d sess. 1849. S. Misc. Doc. 52. Military.

MEMORIAL OF OVERLAND MAIL COMPANY. BUTTERFIELD & CO. WA: Gideon, 1860. Copy of contract with Post Office Dept.

MENEFEE, Arthur M. "Arthur M. Menefee's Travels across the Plains, 1857." Ed. R. C. Hennigan. NEVADA HISTORICAL SOCIETY QUARTERLY 9(Spr 1966): 5-28. CAL(St. Jo)-TRUCKEE. III. 1857.

MENEFEE, Leah C. "Across the Plains to Oregon - Pioneer Diaries." LANE COUNTY HISTORIAN 5(Mar 1960): 15-16. OR-Genl.

_____, comp. IMMIGRATION ROSTERS OF THE ELLIOTT CUTOFF: 1853 & 1854.... Albany, OR: Early Pioneer, 1984. MEEK-Genl. Maps.

_____. "The Lost Wagon Train." LANE COUNTY HISTORIAN 3(Nov 1958): 33-37. OR-1853-Genl.

_____, and Lowell Tiller. "Cutoff Fever." OREGON HISTORICAL QUARTERLY 77(Dec 1976): 309-40; 78(May, Jun, Sept, Dec 1977): 41-72, 121-57, 207-50, 293-331; 79(Spr 1978): 5-50. Detailed analysis of the Meek Cutoff variants. Excellent maps.

MENGARINI, Gregory. SEE: Partoll, Albert J. "Mengarini's Narrative."

MEREDITH, Emily R. Experiences...1863. MONHIST. CHEROKEE(Denver-Ft. Bridger)-HALL-MONTANA. III. 1862. MONTANA. III. 1863. Freight.

MERRIAM, L. C., Jr. Ed. McCall, John M. "First Oregon Cavalry."

MERRILL, D. D. "Minnesota Route the Shortest and Best to the Idaho Gold Mines." St. Paul: Merrill, 1864? Guide.

MERRILL, H. Diary. Held by J. S. Holliday, San Francisco, CA. 1849. Not Seen.

MERRILL, Joseph H. Diary. MO-WHMC. CAL(St. Jo)-HALL-TRUCKEE. II+. 1849.

MERRILL, Julius C. Diary. MO-WHMC. OR(St. Jo)-LANDER-Ends Boise. II+. 1864.

MERRYMAN, Gertrude E. Ed. Camper, Henry W. "Why I Crossed the Plains."

MERRYWEATHER, F. LIFE AMONG THE MORMONS AND INDIANS. Sacramento: Wilson, 1868. CAL(Council)-MORMON-Stage: SLC-Virginia City, NV. III. 1859.

MERSMAN, Joseph I. Journal. Missouri Historical Society, St. Louis, MO. Not Seen.

METLIN, George R. "The Trails and Travelled Ways Used by the Pioneers...1862---in Beaverhead County in 1880." MONHIST. Not Seen.

MEYER, Bette E. "The Pend Oreille Routes to Montana, 1866 - 1870." PACIFIC NORTHWEST QUARTERLY 72(Apr 1981): 76-83. MONTANA-Genl. Freight.

MEYER, Edward S. "A Description of the Route from San Antonio to El Paso...." Ed. Escal F. Duke. WESTX 49(1973): 128-41. TEX. III. 1867.

MEYER, George. AUTOBIOGRAPHY OF GEORGE MEYER.... Shenandoah, IA: Open Door, 1908. CAL(Iowa Point)-HALL. IV. Rem. 1849.

MEYER, Henry W. MEMORIES OF THE BUGGY DAYS. Cincinnati: Author, 1965. Eqpt.

MEYER, Richard E. Ed. Denver, James M. "The Denver Diary."

MEYERS, E. L. "Roy." BARLOW TOLL ROAD, 1846 - 1919.... Portland: Genealogical Forum, 1972. BARLOW-Genl.

MEYERS, Leonard. "The BX: Stageline through the Caribou." OLD WEST 22(Spr 1986): 56-58. Stage.

_____. "Via the Fraser Canyon." BEAVER, Winter 1965, 26-31. Stage.

MEYERS, Richard E. Ed. Denver, James W. "Diary Overland, 1850."

MICHAEL, Howard. "Reminiscences." ANNALS OF WYOMING 5(Oct 1927): 79-89. Freight.

MICHELSON, Charles. "Stage Robbers of the West." MUNSEY'S MAGAZINE, July 1901, 448-50. Stage. Graphics.

MICHIE, Peter S. THE LIFE AND LETTERS OF EMORY UPTON. NY: D. Appleton, 1885. PIKES. V. 1865.

MICHLER, Nathaniel H. ROUTES FROM...TO SANTA FE AND THE VALLEY OF THE RIO GRANDE. 31 Cong., 1st sess. H. Ex. Doc. 67. Serial 577. OKLAHOMA(Ft. Washita)-TEX(Red River-Horsehead Crossing-San Antonio). II. 1849.

MIDDLETON, Joseph. Diary. BEINECKE. CAL(Indep)-LASSEN. I. 1849.

MIER, Richard. "Pony Express Rides Again...." CSL. Pony.

MIGHELS, Ella S. Ed. Clark, Sterling B. HOW MANY MILES FROM ST. JOE.

MILES, Bob. "Early Roads to El Paso." PASSWORD 31(Sum 1986): 75-83, 92. Geog: El Paso. TEX-Genl. RIO GRANDE-Genl.

MILES, Ines M. "The Trails of the Red River of the North." MA thesis, State Univ. of Iowa, 1923. DAKOTAS-Genl.

MILES, Josephine. Ed. Kelsey, Mrs. Ben. "Reminiscences of an 1841 Arrival."

MILES, Stephen B. Correspondence.... NBHIST. Stage.

MILES, Susan, and Mary B. Spence. "Major Ben Ficklin." WESTX 27(Oct 1951): 58-77. Pony. Biog. Stage.

MILES, Thomas C. Reminiscence. MONHIST. CAL(St. Jo)-BOZE. III-. Rem. 1866.

MILES, William. Ed. French, Parker H. JOURNAL.

MILGRIM, James W. "Estill & Company Express." UTAH HISTORICAL QUARTERLY 29(Oct 1961): 326-30. Stage.

MILITARY POSTS - COUNCIL BLUFFS TO THE PACIFIC OCEAN. 27th Cong., 3d sess. 1843. H. Rpt. 31. Military.

MILLARD, C. M. "Hugh Kirkendall's Wagon Train on the Bozeman Trail, 1866...." Ed. Lonnie J. White. ANNALS OF WYOMING 47(Spr 1975): 45-58. CAL(Ft. Leav.)-BOZE. IV. 1866.

MILLBROOK, Minnie D. "An Old Trail Plowed Under - Hays to Dodge." KANSAS HISTORICAL QUARTERLY 43(Aut 1977): 264-81. Military.

MILLER, Broncho Charlie. BRONCHO CHARLIE: A SAGA OF THE SADDLE. London: Darrap, 1935. Pony.

MILLER, Charles E. Diary. Society of California Pioneers, San Francisco, CA. Not Seen.

MILLER, Darlis A. ACROSS THE PLAINS...SAMUEL C. STAPLES. Manhattan, KS: MA/AH Publishing, 1980. SANTA FE(Ft. Leav)-RIO GRANDE-GILA-Ends Ft. Bowie. II. 1864.

_____. "Historian for the California Column: George H. Pettis of New Mexico and Rhode Island." RED RIVER VALLEY HISTORICAL REVIEW 5(Win 1980): 74-92. GILA(Los Angeles-Mesilla, NM). IV. 1862.

MILLER, David E. Collection. UTHIST. Overland-Genl.

_____. "The Donner Road through the Great Salt Lake Desert." PACIFIC HISTORICAL REVIEW 27(Feb 1958): 39-44. HASTINGS-Genl.

_____. "The First Wagon Train to Cross Utah, 1841." UTAH HISTORICAL QUARTERLY 30(Win 1962): 44-59. CAL(Bidwell-Bartleson)-1841-Genl.

_____. "The Parting of the Ways on the Oregon Trail: The East Terminal of the Sublette Cutoff." ANNALS OF WYOMING 45(Spr 1973): 47-52.

MILLER, David H. "A Prussian on the Plains: Balduin Mollhausen's Impressions." GREAT PLAINS JOURNAL 12(Spr 1973): 174-93. Graphics.

_____. "Touring the Oregon Trail in 1851 with Duke von Wuttemberg and Balduin Mollhausen." In WESTERN AMERICAN HISTORY IN THE SEVENTIES. Ed. Daniel Tyler. Fort Collins, CO: Educational Media and Information Systems, 1973. OR-1851-Genl.

MILLER, George. "A Trip to Death Valley [1869]." PUBLICATIONS Southern California Historical Society 11(1919): 56-64. Geog.

MILLER, Greenberry. Diary. BANCROFT. CAL(St. Jo)-TRUCKEE. II. 1849.

MILLER, Henry W. Journal. UTHIST. MORMON. IV. 1855.

MILLER, Jacob. JOURNAL. Eds. Joseph and Elna Miller. N.p., 1967. MORMON. 1848. Not Seen.

MILLER, James B. The Wild Plains. LDS. CAL(Indep)-BRIDGER-SLCUT. III. 1849.

MILLER, James D. "Early Oregon Scenes: A Pioneer Narrative."

OREGON HISTORICAL QUARTERLY 31(Mar 1930): 55-68. OR(St. Jo). III. Rem. 1848.

MILLER, James K. THE ROAD TO VIRGINIA CITY.... Ed. Andrew F. Rolle. Norman: Univ. of Oklahoma Press, 1960. CAL(St. Jo)-Stage: Ft. Halleck to SLC. IV. 1864. SLCUT-HALL-MONTANA. III. 1865.

MILLER, Joaquin. OVERLAND IN A COVERED WAGON: AN AUTOBIOGRAPHY. Ed. Sidney G. Firman. NY: Appleton, 1930. OR(St. Jo). V. Rem. 1852.

MILLER, Joel. Journal. BANCROFT. CAL(Indep?)-TRUCKEE. II-. 1853.

MILLER, Neal E. Letter. Attributed to National Park Service Library, Omaha, but uncatalogued.

MILLER, Nina H. "Jack Morrow - Road Rancher." TRUE WEST 13(Jul -Aug 1966): 18-19, 44-46. Biog.

MILLER, Olive G. Ed. Frisbie, Elizabeth C. "Recollections."

MILLER, Paul E. Papers. COHIST. PIKES-Genl.

MILLER, Reuben. Journal. HUNTL. MORMON. III +. 1849.

MILLER, Silas V. Letter. BANCROFT. OR(Council). III-. 1853.

MILLER, William T. THE OREGON AND CALIFORNIA TRAILS: NARRATIVE TO ACCOMPANY THE COLOR FILMSTRIPS. Chadron, NB: Learning through Seeing, c1959.

MILLIKEN, Ralph L. Ed. Stockton, William. PLAINS OVER. Ed. Watkins, Francis M. "Story of the Crow Emigrant."

_____. "Overland Road." LOS BANOS [CA] ENTERPRISE, 30 Jun 1966, pp. 1, 4-6. 1860 Stage Trip: Springfield, MO - San Jose, CA.

MILLIKEN, Samuel. Letters. LILLEY. CAL(St. Jo)-HASTINGS. III. 1850.

MILLINGTON, Ada. "Journal...1862." Ed. Charles G. Clarke. SOUTHERN CALIFORNIA QUARTERLY 59(Spr, Sum, Fall 1977): 13-48, 139-84, 251-70. CAL(Neb. City)-BRIDGER-SIMPSON. II+. 1862.

MILLINGTON, D. A. Journal. CSL. CAL(St. Jo). II +. 1850.

MILLROY and Hayes. GUIDE...MORMON PIONEERS FROM NAUVOO TO GREAT SALT LAKE, 1846 - 1847. SLC: Authors, N.d. MORMON. II +. 1847.

MILLS, Harlow, B. Ed. Burgess, Joseph H. "Grandfather Burgess Was a '49er."

MILLS, James. "Journalistic Remarks on the Los Angeles and Tucson Mails." SAN DIEGO HISTORICAL SOCIETY QUARTERLY 3(Jul 1957): 33-35. Mail.

MILLS, Nellie I. Ed. Marsh, Edson. "Edson Marsh on the Oregon Trail."

MILLS, Rachel J. "Letters from a Quaker Woman...." Ed. Kenneth L. Holmes. AMERICAN WEST 20(Nov-Dec 1983): 41-44. OR. IV. 1847.

MILLSAP, Kenneth F. Ed. Kingman, Romanzo. "Journal."

MILNE, Francis W. "Dust, Stickers and Mud." OVERLAND JOURNAL 3(Win 1985): 16-21. OR-1847-Genl.

MILTON, William F. AN EXPEDITION ACROSS THE ROCKY MOUNTAINS INTO BRITISH COLUMBIA, BY THE YELLOW HEAD OR LEATHER PASS. London: Petter & Galpin, 1865. CANADA. II. 1983. Graphics.

MINER, William D. "Jesse Applegate: Oregon Pioneer." MA thesis, Univ. of Oregon, 1948. Biog.

MING, Daniel. Reminiscence. AZHIST. Freight.

MINGES, Abram. Diary. Bentley Library, Univ. of Michigan - Ann Arbor. CAL(St. Jo)-BRIDGER-SLCUT-LASSEN. II. 1849.

MINTO, John. Ed. Morrison, Robert W. "Recollections."

_____. "The Occasional Address." TRANSACTIONS Oregon Pioneer Association 1876 (1877): 35-50. OR-1844-Genl.

MINTO, Mrs. Martha A. "Female Pioneering in Oregon." BANCROFT. OR. IV. 1844.

MINTZ, Lannon W. THE TRAIL: A BIBLIOGRAPHY OF THE TRAVELERS ON THE OVERLAND TRAIL TO CALIFORNIA, OREGON, SALT LAKE CITY, AND MONTANA DURING THE YEARS 1841-1864. Albuquerque: Univ. of New Mexico Press, 1987. Bib.

"Miscellaneous Clippings...Trail Markings along the Santa Fe Trail between Cimorron and Dodge City, KS." Spencer Library, Univ. of Kansas, Lawrence, KS. Pres.

"Miscellaneous Publications about Council Grove, Kansas, and the Santa Fe Trail." Spencer Library, Univ. of Kansas, Lawrence, KS.

MITCHEL, Charlotte. "William Stoops - Emigrant Boy." LANE COUNTY HISTORIAN 7(Sept 1962): 54-67. OR(Council?). IV. 1853.

MITCHELL. "Silent City of Rocks." NORTHWEST EDITION 2(Feb 1985): N.p. Geog.

MITCHELL, Annie R. JIM SAVAGE AND THE TULARENO INDIANS. Great West and Indian Series 8. LA: Westernlore, 1957. CAL(Indep)-BRIDGER-HASTINGS-TRUCKEE. V. 1846.

MITCHELL, Clara B. Diary: Austin to Orizaba. BARKER. TEX(Austin)-MEX. II. 1865.

MITCHELL, Eleanor L. A STUDY OF AN HISTORICAL TRAIL THROUGH TIJERAS CANYON. Albuquerque: Bernalillo County Planning Dept., 1978. Geog. Pres. RIO GRANDE-Genl.

MITCHELL, Lyman. Journal. BANCROFT. CAL(Council-LASSEN. III +. 1849.

MITCHELL, Samuel A. ACCOMPANIMENT TO MITCHELL'S NEW MAP OF TEXAS, OREGON, AND CALIFORNIA.... Philadelphia: Author, 1846. Guide.

_____. DESCRIPTION OF OREGON AND CALIFORNIA.... Philadelphia: Cowperthwait, 1849. Guide.

_____. TEXAS, OREGON AND CALIFORNIA. 1846. Reprint. Tacoma, WA: North Pacific Bank Note, 1925. Guide.

MITCHELL, Stewart. "A Forgotten Exploration in Search of a Route across the Sierra Nevada for the Pacific Railroad." CALIFORNIA HISTORICAL QUARTERLY 34(Sept 1955): 209-28. Geog: Sierra Passes.

_____. Trans-Sierra Routes. CSL. Geog: Sierra Passes.

MITCHELL, William C. SEE: With James H. Carleton. SPECIAL REPORT OF THE MASSACRE.

MOBERLY, Walter. SEE: "Walter Moberly's Report on the Roads."

MOBLEY, C. C. Diary. HUNTL. MEX(Acapulco-Mexico City-Jalapa). III. 1850.

MOEHLMAN, Arthur H. Ed. Bond, J. Harman. "Journey."

MOELLER, Bill and Jan. THE OREGON TRAIL: A PHOTOGRAPHIC JOURNEY. Wilsonville, OR: Beautiful America, 1985. Graphics.
Or-Genl.

MOFFAT, Gwen. HARD ROAD WEST: ALONE ON THE CALIFORNIA TRAIL. NY: Viking, 1981. Pres.

MOHLER, George. A Trip...1860. NBHIST. PIKES. II. 1860.

"Mojave Saga." In SAN BERNARDINO COUNTY GUIDE.... Writer's Project 12090. N.p.: 1942. Not Seen. BEALE-Genl.

MOKLER, Alfred J. FORT CASPAR [Platte Bridge Station]. Caspar, WY: Author, 1939. Geog. Indians. Military.

MOLDENHAUR, Roger. Ed. Doederlein. "The Doederlein Diary."

MOLEN, Simpson M. Diary. LDS. SLCOR. III+. 1854.

MOLLHAUSEN, Heinrich B. DIARY...FROM THE MISSISSIPPI TO THE COASTS OF THE PACIFIC.... 2 vols. Ed. Mrs. Percy Sinnett. London: Longman, et al., 1858. CAL(Fort Smith)-MARCY-BEALE. I. 1858.

MONAGHAN, Jay. "Handcarts on the Overland Trail." NEBRASKA HISTORY 30(Mar 1949): 3-18. Eqpt.

_____. THE OVERLAND TRAIL. One of the American Trails Series. Indianapolis: Bobbs, Merrill, 1947. Overland-Genl.

MONAHAN, Doris. DESTINATION: DENVER CITY - THE SOUTH PLATTE TRAIL. Athens, OH: Swallow/University of Ohio Press, 1985. Overland-Genl. Stage: Atchison to Denver.

MONTAIGNES, Francois des [Isaac Cooper, pseud.]. THE PLAINS. Eds. Nancy A. Mower and Don Russell. Norman: Univ. of Oklahoma Press, 1972. SANTA FE(Santa Fe to Ft. Gibson). II. 1845.

MONTESANA, Phil. "A Black Pioneer's Trip to California." PACIFIC HISTORIAN 13(Win 1969): 58-62. CAL(St. Jo)-BRIDGER-HALL-LASSEN. IV. 1849. Social.

MONTGOMERY, Mrs. Frank. "Fort Wallace and its Relation to the Frontier." KANSAS HISTORICAL COLLECTIONS 17(1926-1928): 189-283. PIKES(Smoky Hill Route)-Genl.

MONTGOMERY, Wayne. "Half-Million Dollar Stagecoach Robbery." TRUE WEST 17(Nov-Dec 1969): 22-23, 75-77. Stage-Oregon.

MONTGOMERY, William. A Journey to California. HUNTL. CAL(Old Ft. Kearney). III. 1850.

MOODY, Dan W. THE LIFE OF A ROVER, 1865 to 1926. N.p., n.d. Freight. Rem.

MOODY, Frederick W. Reminiscences. KSHIST. Freight. Rem.

MOODY, Joseph L. "An 1849 Letter from California." CALIFORNIA HISTORICAL QUARTERLY 13(Mar 1934): 84-85.

MOODY, Ralph. THE OLD TRAILS WEST. NY: Crowell, 1963. Overland-Genl.

_____. STAGECOACH WEST. NY: Promontory, 1967. Overland-Genl.

MOONEY, Thomas W., II. "The Oregon Trail, 1841 - 1846." MA thesis, Washington University - St. Louis, 1949. OR-Genl.

MOORE, A. C. "Journal of an Overland Trip to California." DUBUQUE MINER'S EXPRESS, 10 April - 13 November 1850. CAL(Council). 1850. Not Seen.

MOORE, Alexander. "Statement." In CHARLES HOPPER AND THE PILGRIMS OF THE PACIFIC, ed. Franklin Beard. La Grange, CA: Southern Mines Press, 1981. CAL(Indep)-HALL-APPLE. V. 1847.

MOORE, Arlene M. "A Study of the Impact of the Gold Rush on the Mormon Community in Salt Lake City, 1849 - 1851." MA thesis, American University, 1966. Utah.

MOORE, Bonnie C. "The Northern Drives of Texas Cattle after 1866." MA thesis, Univ. of Oklahoma, 1934. Stock.

MOORE, Helen L. "California in Communication...Before the Railroads." PUBLICATIONS Southern California Historical Society 13(1924): 69-91. Overland-Genl.

MOORE, Jonathan L. "Jonathan L. Moore Book." LANE COUNTY HISTORIAN 11(Sum 1966): 23=34. OR(Council). III. 1855.

MOORE, Katherine J. Ed. Hamilton, James G. "My Dear Cornelia."

MOORE, M. Anne. "The Economic Influence of Transportation to Colorado, 1858 - 1869." Norlin Library-Western History, Univ. of Colorado-Boulder. PIKES-Genl.

MOORE, Martha M. Journal. Missouri Historical Society-St. Louis. CAL(Missouri)-LANDER-LASSEN. 1859. Not Seen.

MOORE, Mary L. "New Mexico These and Dissertations in History: A Preliminary Checklist." ARIZONA & THE WEST 12(Aut 1970): 355-86. Bib.

MOORE, Meredith T. Papers. Univ. of Kansas City, Kansas City, MO. Not Seen.

MOORE, Miles C. Recollections. DENVERPUB. CAL(Council)-LANDER-HALL-MONTANA(Bannock). Rem. 1863. Not Seen.

MOORE, Narcissa C. Captain Dunbar's Company 1846 The Applegate Route from Fort Hall. ORU. APPLE. V. Rem. 1846.

MOORHEAD, Max L. NEW MEXICO'S ROYAL ROAD: TRADE AND TRAVEL ON THE CHIHUAHUA TRAIL. Norman: Univ. of Oklahoma Press, 1958. SANTA FE-Genl. RIO GRANDE-Genl.

MOORMAN, Madison B. THE JOURNAL OF MADISON BERRYMAN MOORMAN, 1850 - 1851. Ed. Irene D. Paden. SF: California Historical Society, 1948. CAL(Indep)-BRIDGER-HASTINGS. III. 1850.

MOOSO, Josiah. LIFE AND TRAVELS. Winfield, KS: Author, 1888. Overland-Genl.

MOREHOUSE, George P. "The Location of the Old Santa Fe Trail in Morris County [KS]." KSHIST. Pres.

MORELAND, Jesse. Diary, 1852. ORHIST. OR(Indep?)-BARLOW. III. Rem. 1852.

MORFITT, William. Memories...Forty-Seven. ORHIST. APPLE. V-. Rem. 1847.

MORGAN, Dale L. Ed. Empey, William A. "The Mormon Ferry on the North Platte." Ed. Platt, D. L., and N. M. Slater. TRAVELERS' GUIDE. Ed. Pritchard, James. OVERLAND DIARY. Ed. Rhodes, Joseph. "Joseph Rhodes and the California Gold Rush." SEE: With Charles Kelly. OLD GREENWOOD. SEE: McQuown, Madeline R. Papers.

_____. "The Administration of Indian Affairs in Utah, 1851 - 1858." PACIFIC HISTORICAL REVIEW 17(Nov 1948): 383-409. Indians.

_____. "The Ferries of the Forty-Niners." ANNALS OF WYOMING 31(Apr, Oct 1959): 5-31, 145-89; 32(Apr, Oct 1960): 51-69, 167-203. Wyoming only.

_____. THE GREAT SALT LAKE. The American Lakes Series, ed. Milo M. Quaife. Indianapolis: Bobbs-Merrill, 1947. HASTINGS-Genl. SLCUT-Genl. Utah.

_____. THE HUMBOLDT: HIGHROAD OF THE WEST. The Rivers of America Series, eds. Stephen V. Benet and Carl Carmer. NY: Farrar & Rinehart, 1943. Geog.

_____. "Letters by Forty-Niners Written from Great Salt Lake City in 1849." WESTERN HUMANITIES REVIEW 3(Apr 1949): 98-116. CAL-1849-Genl.

_____. "Miles Goodyear and the Founding of Ogden." UTAH HISTORICAL QUARTERLY 21(Jul, Oct 1953): 195-218, 307-29. Biog.

_____, ed. OVERLAND IN 1846: DIARIES AND LETTERS OF THE CALIFORNIA-OREGON TRAIL. 2 vols. Georgetown, CA: Talisman, 1963. CAL-1846-Genl. OR-1846-Genl.

_____. Papers. BANCROFT and UTHIST.

_____. "The Significance and Value of the Overland Journal." In PROBING THE AMERICAN WEST: PAPERS FROM THE SANTA FE CONFERENCE, eds. K. Ross Toole, et al. Santa Fe: Museum of New Mexico Press, 1962.

_____. UTAH'S HISTORIC TRAILS. SLC: Utah Tourist and Publicity Council, 1960. Maps.

_____, ed. "Washakie and the Shoshoni: A Selection of Documents from the Records of the Utah Superintendency of Indian Affairs, 1849 - 1862." ANNALS OF WYOMING 25(Jul 1953): 141-89; 26(Jan, Jul 1954): 65-80, 141-90; 27(Apr, Oct 1955): 61-68, 198-220. Indians.

_____. "Western Travels and Travelers in the Bancroft Library." In TRAVELERS ON THE WESTERN FRONTIER, ed. John F. Mc-Dermott. Urbana: Univ. of Illinois Press, 1970. Bib.

MORGAN, Gene. WESTWARD THE COURSE OF EMPIRE.... Chicago: Lakeside, 1945. Pony.

MORGAN, Gertrude. GERTRUDE MORGAN: OR, LIFE AND ADVENTURES AMONG THE INDIANS OF THE FAR WEST. Philadelphia: Barclay, 1866. 1855 Indian Captivity, Little Blue River.

MORGAN, Jesse. SEE: Morgan, Martha M. A TRIP ACROSS THE PLAINS.

MORGAN, Martha M. A TRIP ACROSS THE PLAINS.... 1864. Reprint. Fairfield, WA: Ye Galleon, 1983. CAL(St. Jo)-BRIDGER-

Ends SLC. III. 1849. CAL(SLC)-SLCUT. III. 1850.

MORGAN, Nicholas G. MAP OF GREAT SALT LAKE CITY AND PART OF SALT LAKE COUNTY - UTAH SHOWING THE ROUTE TAKEN BY THE FIRST GROUP OF EMIGRANT PIONEER WAGONS. SLC: Morgan, N.d. Maps.

MORIARITY, James R. "Immigrants on the Gila and Baja California Routes to San Diego in 1849." JOURNAL OF SAN DIEGO HISTORY 17(Win 1971): 22-28. GILA-1849-Genl.

MORLEY, Gertrude J. Ed. Leonard, Joseph L. and Mary P. "Crossing the Plains."

MORLEY, James H. Diary. MONHIST. MONTANA. 1862. Not Seen.

MORLEY, Thomas. "The Independence Road to Fort Laramie: By Aerial Photograph." PLAINS ANTHROPOLOGIST 6(1961): 242-51. Pres.

Mormon Battalion Files and Documents. LDS. Gila-1846-Genl.

MORMON BATTALION TRAIL SCENIC TRAILS STUDY. 94th Cong., 1st sess. 1975. H. Doc. 94. Pres.

MORMON PIONEER NATIONAL HISTORIC TRAIL. Denver?: Rocky Mountain Region, National Park Service, 1981. Maps. Pres. MORMON-Genl.

THE MORMON TRAIL: A STUDY REPORT. WA: GPO, 1978. MORMON-Genl. Pres.

MORRILL, Rosa N. MARY JANE, PIONEER. Venice, CA: Author, 1942. Mimeo. CAL(Council)-BRIDGER-SLCOR. IV. Rem. 1864.

MORRIS, Maurice O. RAMBLES IN THE ROCKY MOUNTAINS. London: Smith, Elder, 1864. PIKES. II+. 1863?

MORRIS, Thomas. Journal. UTHIST. CAL(Leav)-SANTA FE-RIO GRANDE-GILA. III+. 1846. SLCOR. IV. 1849.

MORRISON, John D. Ed. Spain, David F. "Diary of David F. Spain."

MORRISON, Robert W. "Recollections." Ed. John Minto. TRANSACTIONS Oregon Pioneer Association (1894): 53-62. OR(St. Jo). Rem. 1844. Not Seen.

MORRISON, Samuel, C. Letter. NVHIST. CAL(St. Jo)-BRIDGER-HASTINGS. V. 1850.

MORRISON, W. W. Collections. UWY. Large holding of assorted trail material.

MORROW, H. W. "Child Pioneer; Story of John Sager." READERS DIGEST 37(Dec 1940): 6-10. OR. III. 1844. Biog.

MORSE, Eva S. Papers. BYU. CAL(Illinois). 1859. Not Seen.

MORSE, H. D. L. Diary. Colorado College Library-SpCol, Colorado Springs, CO. PIKES. III. 1861.

MORSE, Horatio. Overland to California. BANCROFT. CAL. V-. 1850.

MORSMAN, Edgar M. MEMOIR OF EDGAR MARTIN MORSMAN, SR. Omaha: Omaha Printing, 1942? Stage.

MORTENSON, A. R. Ed. McFarlane, Andrew. "Letter of a Gold Rusher."

MORTON, Cyrus. AUTOBIOGRAPHY OF CYRUS MORTON. Omaha: Douglas, 1895. Freight. Rem.

MORTON, J. Sterling. "From Nebraska City to Salt Creek in 1855." TRANSCRIPTIONS AND REPORTS Nebraska State Historical Society 4(1892): 11-18. CAL(Neb. City)-Ends Salt Creek. III. Rem. 1855.

MORTON, Nancy J. Memoirs: 1860-1868. NBHIST. Freight.

MOSES, A. C. Letter. Held by Floyd E. Risvold, Minneapolis, MN. 1849. Not Seen.

MOSS, James E. Ed. Gallaher, William C. "Ho! For the Gold Mines of Montana."

MOSS, William C. "Overland to California in the Early Sixties." PONY EXPRESS, Dec 1938, Jan 1939; 14-16; 6, 12-13. CAL(Council)-BRIDGER-SIMPSON. III+. 1861.

MOSSMAN, Isaac V. A PONY EXPRESSMAN'S RECOLLECTIONS. Portland?: Champoeg, 1955. OR(Council)-BARLOW. V. Rem. 1853. Stage.

MOTT, Phyllis. Ed. Edwards, Edward H. "The Edwards Letters."

MOULTON, Emeline M. Letters. WIHIST. Social. Hardships of Gold Rush families left behind.

MOUSELY, Sarah M. Journal. UTHIST. MORMON. II-. 1856.

MOWER, Nancy A. Ed. Montaignes, Francois. THE PLAINS.

MOWRY, Sylvester. "Letter...to the U.S. Mail Contractors upon the Overland Mail Route to California. Arizona State Library-Arizona Room, Phoenix, AZ. GILA-1857-Genl.

_____. "Lt. Sylvester Mowry's Report on his March in 1855 from Salt Lake City to Fort Tejon." ARIZONA & THE WEST 7(Win 1965): 329-346. SLCOR. III. 1855.

MOXLEY, Charles G. Letters. BEINECKE. CAL(Old Ft. Kearney). V. 1849.

MOYNIHAN, Ruth B. "Children and Young People on the Overland Trail." WESTERN HISTORICAL QUARTERLY 6(Jul 1975): 279-94. Social.

MUENCH, Joyce R. Ed. Kilgore, William H. THE KILGORE JOURNAL.

MUIR, Emma M. "The Grave by the Road." NEW MEXICO 29(Apr 1951): 23, 40-41. Geog: Lordsburg, NM.

_____. "The Stage to Skakespeare." NEW MEXICO 26(Jul 1948): 25-27, 52, 59. Geog.

MULFORD, Charles W. SEE: Comstock, David A. GOLD DIGGERS AND CAMP FOLLOWERS.

MULFORD, Thomas W. Diary. Society of California Pioneers, San Francisco, CA. Not Seen.

MULLAN, John. "Journal from Fort Dalles, O. T., to Fort Wallah Wallah, W. T. (July 1851)." Ed. Pal Clark. IN FRONTIER OMNIBUS, ed. John W. Hakola. Missoula: Montana State University, 1962. OR(Dalles to Walla Walla). II. 1851.

_____. MINERS AND TRAVELER'S GUIDE TO OREGON,

WASHINGTON, IDAHO, MONTANA, WYOMING, AND COLORADO. NY: Author, 1865. Guide-Mullan Road.

_____. REPORT ON THE CONSTRUCTION OF A MILITARY ROAD FROM FORT WALLA-WALLA TO FORT BENTON. 37th Cong., 3d sess. S. Doc. 43. MULLAN-Genl.

_____. "Route of the Covered Wagon, 1865: Itinerary of the Mullan Road from the Missouri to the Columbia." MONTANA 1(Apr 1951): 13-20. Guide. MULLAN-Genl.

MULLIGAN, Raymond A. "Apache Pass and Old Fort Bowie." TUCSON WESTERNERS SMOKE SIGNAL 11(Spr 1965): 1-24. Geog.

_____. "Down the Old Butterfield Trail." ARIZONA & THE WEST 1(Win 1959): 358-67. Stage-Arizona.

_____. "Sixteen Days in Apache Pass." KIVA 24(Dec 1958): 1-13. Stage. Geog.

MULLIN, Robert N. STAGECOACH PIONEERS OF THE SOUTHWEST. Southwestern Studies Monograph No. 71. El Paso: Texas Western Press, c1983. Stage-Southwest.

MUMEY, Nolie. Ed. Barker, Anselm H. DIARY OF 1858. Ed. Keays, Elizabeth. "Diary." Ed. Rankin, Alexander. ALEXANDER RANKIN. Ed. Steck, Amos. AMOS STECK. Ed. Steele, Edward D. EDWARD D. STEELE.

_____. HISTORY OF THE EARLY SETTLEMENT OF DENVER. Glendale: Clark, 1942. Geog.

_____. HOOFS TO WINGS, THE PONY EXPRESS.... Boulder: Johnson, 1960. Pony. Graphics.

_____. JAMES PIERSON BECKWOURTH, 1856-1866. Denver: Old West, 1957. Biog.

_____. JOHN WILLIAMS GUNNISON.... Denver: Author, 1955. Biog.

_____. WYOMING BULLWHACKER: EPISODES IN THE LIFE OF JAMES MILTON SHERROD FROM HIS REMINISCENCES (1815-1919). Denver: Range, 1976. Wyoming Freighting.

MUNGER, Charles N., Jr. "Overland Trails to California." Senior thesis, Univ. of Santa Clara, 1954. CAL-Genl.

MUNKRES, Robert L. "Ash Hollow: Gateway to the Great Plains." ANNALS OF WYOMING 42(Apr 1970): 5-43. Geog.

_____. "Fort Laramie, 1834-1984...." JOURNAL OF THE WEST 23(Apr 1984): 88-90. Geog.

_____. "Independence Rock and Devil's Gate." ANNALS OF WYOMING 40(Apr 1986): 23-40. Geog.

_____. "Indian-White Contact before 1870: Cultural Factors in Conflict." JOURNAL OF THE WEST 10(Jul 1971): 439-73. Indians.

_____. "Pioneer in Petticoats." TOMBSTONE [AZ] Epitah 11(Sept, Oct 1984): 1, 10-13; 5-8. Social.

_____. "The Plains Indian Threat on the Overland Trail before 1860." ANNALS OF WYOMING 40(Oct 1968): 193-221. Indians.

_____. "The Road West: Ash Hollow to Fort Bridger." CHICAGO WESTERNERS BRAND BOOK 27(Feb 1971): 89-96. BRIDGER-Genl.

_____. SALERATUS AND SAGEBRUSH: THE OREGON TRAIL THROUGH WYOMING. Cheyenne: Wyoming State Archives and History Dept. and State Historical Society, 1974. Overland-Genl-Wyoming.

_____. "Soda Springs: Curiosity of the Trail." ANNALS OF WYOMING 43(Fall 1971): 215-35. Geog.

_____. "Wives, Mothers, Daughters: Women's Life in the Roads West." ANNALS OF WYOMING 42(Oct 1970): 191-224. Social.

MUNSON, L. E. Address. MONHIST. MULLAN-Genl.

MUNSON, Lyman E. PIONEER LIFE ON THE AMERICAN FRONTIER. Hartford, CN: Author, 1907. MONTANA. V-. 1865.

MURBARGER, Nell. "High Rock Canyon." TRUE WEST, May-Jun 1963, 22-24, 72. Geog.

_____. "Old Fort Schellbourne of Pony Express Days." DESERT 17(Dec 1954): 9-12. Geog.

_____. "Pete Lassen: The Venerable Voyager." FRONTIER TIMES 37(Feb-Mar 1963): 14-15, 40. Biog.

_____. "Pony Express." DESERT 22(Dec 1959): 8-10. Pony: SLC to Sacramento.

MURPHY, Andrew L. Diary. Spencer Library, Univ. of Kansas-Lawrence. CAL(Indep?)-LASSEN. II +. 1849.

MURPHY, Cecilia M. "The Stevens-Murphy Overland Party of 1844." MA thesis, Univ. of California-Berkeley, 1941. CAL-1844-Genl.

MURPHY, John E. Letters. Attributed to BANCROFT but uncatalogued.

MURPHY, Joseph. SEE: Bott, Emily A. JOSEPH MURPHY'S CONTRIBUTION.

MURPHY, Martin, Jr. SEE: Sullivan, Gabrielle. MARTIN MURPHY, SR.

_____. The Murphy Family. BANCROFT. CAL(Council)-HALL-TRUCKEE. IV. Rem. 1844.

MURPHY, Minnie H. "Pike's Peak or Bust: The Colorado Pioneers of Fifty-Eight and Fifty-Nine." SEE: Hall, Charles. Papers.

MURPHY, Patrick H. Diary. CSL. CAL(St. Jo). III. 1854.

MURPHY, Patrick W. Biography. BANCROFT. CAL-1844-Genl.

MURPHY, Virginia R. "Across the Plains in the Donner Party...." CENTURY 42(Jul 1891): 409-26. CAL-1846-Genl. Graphics.

_____. "A Girl with the Donner Party." AMERICAN HISTORY ILLUSTRATED 21(Oct 1986): N.p. Not Seen.

_____. Letters. UTHIST. CAL-1846-Genl.

MURRAY, Bob. "Race with Death on the Bozeman Trail." OLD WEST 20(Win 1983): n.p. BOZE-Genl. Not Seen.

MURRAY, John. Journal...1853. Washington State Historical Society Library, Tacoma, WA. OR(Council). I. 1853.

MURRAY, Keith A. "Building a Wagon Road through the Northern Cascade Mountains." PACIFIC NORTHWEST QUARTERLY 56(Apr 1965): 49-56. Freight.

MURRAY, Richard Y. "Apache Pass: Most Formidable of Gorges." CORRAL DUST 6(Jun 1961): 17-19, 24. Geog.

_____. "The History of Fort Bowie." MA thesis, Univ. of Arizona, 1951. Geog.

MURRAY, Robert A. THE ARMY MOVES WEST. Fort Collins, CO: Old Army, 1981. Freight.

_____. THE BOZEMAN TRAIL: HIGHWAY OF HISTORY. Boulder, CO: Pruett, 198? Not Seen.

_____. FORT LARAMIE: VISIONS OF A GRAND OLD POST. Fort Collins, CO: Old Army, 1974. Geog.

_____. MILITARY POSTS OF WYOMING. Fort Collins, CO: Old Army, 1974. Military.

_____. "Trading Posts, Forts, and Bridges of the Caspar Area: Unraveling the Tangle on the Upper Platte." ANNALS OF WYOMING 47(Spr 1975): 5-30. Geog.

_____. "Wagons on the Plains." BY VALOR & ARMS 2, no. 4(1976): 37-40. Freight.

MURRELL, George M. Letters. HUNTL. CAL-Ends Fort Kearney. III. 1849.

MUSCOTT, John M., and William N. Steuben. Letters. CSL. CAL(St. Jo)-HALL-TRUCKEE. IV. 1849.

MUZZAL, Thomas A. "Across the Plains in 1866." NEW MEXICO HISTORICAL REVIEW 32(Jul 1957): 246-58. SANTA FE(Ft. Smith). III. 1866.

MYER, Nathaniel. "Journey into Southern Oregon: Diary of a Pennsylvania Dutchman." Ed. Edward B. Ham. OREGON HISTORICAL QUARTERLY 60(Sept 1959): 375-407. OR(Council)-APPLE. III. 1853.

MYERS, Alice V. "The Sioux City, Iowa, Expeditions to the Montana Gold Fields, 1865 and 1866 in Relationship to the Minnesota Expeditions." MA thesis, Drake University, 1940. DAKOTAS(Niobrara River route)-MONTANA(Sawyer-Tingley route).

_____. "Wagon Roads West: The Sawyer Expeditions of 1865, 1866." ANNALS OF IOWA 23(Jan 1942): 213-37. DAKOTAS(Niobrara route)-MONTANA. IV. 1865. DAKOTAS (Niobrara route)-MONTANA. IV. 1866.

MYERS, Christine B. NEW MEXICO LOCAL AND COUNTY HISTORIES: A BIBLIOGRAPHY. Albuquerque: New Mexico Library Assn., 1983. Bib.

MYERS, E. L. "Wagon Trains: Migration and Emigration, 1832 - 1853." Genealogical Forum of Portland BULLETIN 9(May, June 1960): 71, 79. Overland-Genl.

MYERS, Joan, and Marc Simmons. ALONG THE SANTA FE TRAIL. Albuquerque: Univ. of New Mexico Press, 1986. SANTA FE-Genl. Graphics.

MYERS, Lee. "The Elusive Fort Webster." CAMP PERIODICAL 5(Win 1973): 2-4. Geog.

_____. "Pope's Wells." NEW MEXICO HISTORICAL REVIEW 38(Oct 1963): 273-99. TEX(El Paso-Denison). IV. 1853.

MYERS, S. Carl. Reminiscences. UTHIST. CAL(Indep). IV. 1849.

MYRES, Sandra L., ed. HO FOR CALIFORNIA: WOMEN'S

DIARIES FROM THE HUNTINGTON LIBRARY. San Marino: Huntington, 1980. Social.

_____. "I Too Have Seen the Elephant: Women on the Overland Trails." OVERLAND JOURNAL 4(Fall 1986): 25-33. Social.

_____. WESTERING WOMEN AND THE FRONTIER EXPERIENCE, 1800-1915. Histories of the American Frontier, Ray A. Billington, Genl. Ed. Albuquerque: Univ. of New Mexico Press, 1982. Social.

MYRICK, Elizabeth T. Diary. BANCROFT. CAL(Council)-Ends Goose Creek. II. 1854.

MYRICK, Thomas S. THE GOLD RUSH...1849 - 1855. Mount Pleasant, MI: Cumming, 1971. CAL-BRIDGER-SLCUT-LASSEN. V. 1849.

NADEAU, Remi. FORT LARAMIE AND THE SIOUX INDIANS. Englewood Cliffs, NJ: Prentice-Hall, 1967. Geog.

_____. "How They Wired the Union." WESTWAYS 53(Nov 1961): 24-5. Telegraph.

_____. "King of the Desert Freighters." LOS ANGELES WESTERNERS BRAND BOOK 11(1964): 143-68. Freight.

_____. "The Saga of Nadeau's Teams." WESTWAYS 49(Jul 1957): 10-11. Teams.

_____. "Trail of the Jackass Mail." WESTWAYS 50(Sept 1958): 20-21. Stage.

NADEN, Kim L. "The Making of a Follower of the Oregon-California Trail." OVERLAND JOURNAL 3(Win 1985): 24-29. CAL-Nebraska Only-Genl.

NANCE, Roy C. "The Major Overland Trails of the Trans-Mississippi West." MA thesis, Univ. of Texas-Austin, 1955. Overland-Genl.

NASH, Marie. Diary. CSL. CAL(St. Jo). V. 1861.

NATHAN, M. C. SEE: Jessup, Edgar. EARLY CALIFORNIA MAIL BAG.

_____. FRANKS OF WESTERN EXPRESSES. Chicago: Collectors Club, 1973. Mail.

_____, and W. S. Boggs. THE PONY EXPRESS. NY: Collectors Club, c1962.

National Pony Express Centennial Association. "Bibliography of the Pony Express." KSHIST. Bib-Pony.

National Road to California. Public Meeting in Victoria. Victoria, TX: N.p., 1847. Govt.

NATIONWIDE SYSTEM OF TRAILS: HEARINGS BEFORE THE COMMITTEE ON INTERIOR AND INSULAR AFFAIRS. 90th Cong., 1st sess. 1967. WA: GPO, 1967. Govt.

Native Sons and Daughters of Nebraska. Papers, 1924 - 1971. NBHIST. Pony.

NAUMAN, Dean S., ed. THE VANISHING TRAILS EXPEDITION 16 YEARS. Wall, SD: Vanishing Trails Committee, 1976. DAKOTAS-Genl.

NEEDHAM, Henry C., and Victor M. Berthold. HAND-STAMPED FRANKS USED AS CANCELLATIONS ON PONY EXPRESS LETTERS, 1860 AND 1861, AND THE PONY EXPRESS STAMPS AND THEIR USE. NY: N.p., 1927. Pony. Graphics.

NEFF, Andrew L. "The Mormon Migration to Utah, 1830 - 1847." PhD diss., Univ. of California-Berkeley, 1918. MORMON-1847-Genl.

NEGLEY, Felix C. Diary. Marshall Gold Discovery Area, Coloma, CA. CAL(St. Jo)-HALL. 1849. Not Seen.

NEIGHBOURS, Kenneth F. Ed. Williams, Jesse W. OLD TEXAS TRAILS.

_____. "The Expedition of Major Robert S. Neighbors to El Paso in 1849." SOUTHWESTERN HISTORICAL QUARTERLY 58(Jul 1954): 36-59. TEX-1849-Genl.

_____. "The Marcy - Neighbours Exploration of the Headwaters of the Brazos and Wichita Rivers in 1854." PANHANDLE-PLAINS HISTORICAL REVIEW 27(1954): 27-46. MARCY-Genl.

NEILSEN, Peter, Journal. UTHIST. MORMON. III. 1861.

NEIMAN, Peter. Diary. Iowa State Historical Society Archives, Iowa City, IA. CAL(Council). III. 1864.

NEISWANGER, Lilian H. "The Old St. Jo Road." KSHIST. Geog-St. Jo to Independence.

NELSON, Gaylord. "Trails across America." NATIONAL WILDLIFE, Jun-Jul 1969, 21-27. Pres.

NELSON, John. Letters. Attributed to NBHIST but uncatalogued.

NELSON, John B. "Nelson Family History." (In) TOLD BY THE PIONEERS, Vol. 1. Washington Pioneer Projects, 1937. OR(Liberty, MO). Rem. 1843. Not Seen.

NELSON, John Y. FIFTY YEARS ON THE TRAIL.... NY: Warne, 1889. MORMON-Genl.

NESMITH, James W. "Diary of the Emigration of 1843." OREGON HISTORICAL QUARTERLY 7(Dec 1906): 329-59. OR(Indep). III. Rem. 1843.

_____. "The Occasional Address." TRANSACTIONS Oregon Pioneer Association (1876): 42-62. OR. III. Rem. 1843.

NESS, Richard. Journal. BEINECKE. CAL-TRUCKEE. V. 1849.

NETTELS, Curtis. "The Overland Mail Issue during the Fifties." MISSOURI HISTORICAL REVIEW 18(Jul 1924): 521-34. Mail.

NETTLETON, Lucy. Letters. KSHIST. CAL(St. Jo?)-BRIDGER-SLCUT-TRUCKEE. II. 1863.

NEUHAUS, Carla E. "Transportation to Colorado; 1849 - 1869." MA thesis, Univ. of Colorado, 1928. PIKES-Genl. Freight. Stage.

Nevada Emigrant Trail Marking Committee. THE OVERLAND EMIGRANT TRAIL TO CALIFORNIA: A GUIDE TO TRAIL MARKERS PLACED IN WESTERN NEVADA AND THE SIERRA NEVADA MOUNTAINS IN CALIFORNIA. Reno: Nevada Historical Society, 1975. Pres.

NEVER, John W. "The Smoky Hill Trail in Western Kansas." MS thesis, Fort Hays State College, 1950. PIKES-Genl.

NEVIN, David. THE EXPRESSMEN. Time-Life's Old West Series. NY: Time-Life, 1975.

NEVIN, Julius M. Diary - 1849. CSL. CAL(St. Jo)-LASSEN. III. 1849.

NEW HELVETIA DIARY. A RECORD OF EVENTS KEPT BY JOHN A. SUTTER AND HIS CLERKS.... SF: Society of California Pioneers, 1939. Geog-Sutter's Fort.

New York Committee of Pacific Emigration. CALIFORNIA: HOW TO GO, AND WHAT TO DO THERE. NY: Nesbitt, 1856? Guide.

NEWBY, William T. "Diary of the Emigration." Ed. Harry N. Winton. OREGON HISTORICAL QUARTERLY 40(Sept 1939): 219-42. OR(Indep). III. 1843.

NEWCOMB, Alphonso B. Across the Plains. Iowa State Historical Society-Archives, Iowa City, IA. CAL(Council)-BRIDGER-HASTINGS? IV. Rem. 1850.

NEWCOMB, Silas. Journal. BEINECKE. CAL(Council)-BRIDGER-SLCUT. II+. 1850.

NEWKIRK, Coleman S. Brief History.... BANCROFT. CAL(Indep)-CHEROKEE(Cheyenne-SLC)-SIMPSON? V. 1862.

"A Newly Discovered Map of the Butterfield Overland Stage Route." Southern California Historical QUARTERLY 18(Jun 1936): 39. Stage-Maps.

NEWMAN, J. A. THE AUTOBIOGRAPHY OF AN OLD FASHIONED BOY. N.p., 1923. PIKES. V-. Rem. 1860.

NEWMAN, Orson N. Memoranda. BEINECKE. MONTANA(Virginia City)-HALL-SIMPSON-Ends San Diego, CA. III. 1969.

NEWMARK, Marco R. "Phineas Banning: Intrepid Pioneer." QUARTERLY Historical Society of Southern California 35(Sept 1953): 265-74. Biog.

NEWS FROM THE MINES. Omaha: Nebraskian and Times, 1859. Guide-PIKES.

NEWSPAPER COMENTARY - NEBRASKA AREA - 1809 TO 1850. Publications of the Nebraska State Historical Society 20. Lincoln: The Society, 1922. Overland-Genl.

"Newspaper Transcripts [Salt Lake City DESERET NEWS, 1854 - 1862] on Postal Service." UTHIST. Mail.

NEWSPAPERS ALONG AMERICAN'S GREAT TRAILS. Cleveland: Bell & Howell, 1969. Overland-Genl.

NEWTON, Dwight B. "Techniques of Overland Freighting in the Trans-Missouri West." MA thesis, Univ. of Kansas City, 1942. Freight.

NEWTON, John M. MEMOIRS OF JOHN MARSHALL NEWTON. Cambridge, NY: Washington County Post, 1913. CAL(Indep). V. Rem. 1850.

NEWTON, Jotham. Diary. BANCROFT. CAL(Ft. Kearney)-BRIDGER-SLCUT. III+. 1853.

NEYER, John W. "The Smoky Hill Trail in Western Kansas, 1859 - 1869." MA thesis, Fort Hays [Kansas] State College, 1950. PIKES-Genl.

NIBLER, Preston. EXODUS TO GREATNESS; THE STORY OF MORMON MIGRATION. SLC: Deseret News, 1947. MORMON-1847-Genl.

NIBLEY, Charles W. REMINISCENCES. SLC: N.p., 1934. MORMON. 1860. Not Seen.

NICAISE, Auguste. A YEAR IN THE DESERT. Ed. & trans. Edward J. Kowrach. Fairfield, WA: Ye Galleon, 1980. OR(Indep)-BRIDGER-SLCUT. III. 1858.

NICHOLAS, Cora S. "The History of Yuma Valley and Mesa with Special Emphasis on the City of Yuma, AZ." MA thesis, Univ. of Southern California, 1947. Geog. Missing from stacks.

NICHOLS, B. F. "Across the Plains...." MO-WHMC. OR(St. Jo). IV. Rem. 1844.

NICHOLS, Claude W., Jr. "The South Road: Its Development and Significance." MA thesis, Univ. of Oregon, 1953. APPLE-Genl.

NICHOLS, Henry K. Journal. BEINECKE. CAL(Indep)-BRIDGER-Ends near Ft. Bridger. II+. 1857.

NICHOLS, Robert A. Letters. Washington State Historical Society Library, Tacoma, WA. OR(Council)-LANDER. V. 1862.

NIEBUR, Jay E. "Fort Sedgewick and Julesburg, Colorado." Norlin Library-Western History, Univ. of Colorado-Boulder. Geog.

NIELSEN, Beatrice. "The Saga of a Trail." COVERED WAGON (1968): 5-45; (1969): 8-45. CAL(Shasta County)-Genl.

NIELSEN, Christian. Diary. UTHIST. MORMON. II. 1853.

NIELSEN, Lawrence E. "Juniper Stumps on the Yreka Trail of 1862-1864." OREGON HISTORICAL QUARTERLY 88(Spr 1987): 49-51. OR-CA-Genl.

NIELSEN, Newman and McCart. PIONEER ROADS IN CENTRAL OREGON. Bend, OR: Maverick, 1985. Not Seen.

NIELSON, P. Raymond. "Edward Creighton and the Pacific Telegraph." MID-AMERICA 24(1942): 61-74. Biog. Telegraph.

"The 1974 Discovery of Old Inscriptions on Courthouse Rock." OVERLAND JOURNAL 3(Spr 1985): 24-29. Geog.

NIXON, Alexander B. Diary. CSL. CAL(Indep)-HALL. II. 1849.

NIXON, O. B. Letters. BEINECKE. CAL(Leav). 1850. Not Seen. Same as O. W. Nixon?

NIXON, O. W. The Overland Journal of the Ringwood Rover Company, Wilmington, OH, 1850 - 51. BEINECKE. CAL(Platte City). IV. 1850.

NIXON, Orville A. Book Second.... KSHIST. CAL(Ft. Laramie to Westport). III. 1854. SANTA FE. III. 1855.

NOBLE, Bruce J., Jr. "Marking Wyoming's Oregon Trail." OVERLAND JOURNAL 4(Sum 1986): 19-31. Pres.

NOBLE, Robert W. Diary. In Parkman Family Papers, BANCROFT. CAL-MEX(Begins Chihuahua)-GILA. II. 1849.

NOBLE, William M. Events...1856. Attributed to BANCROFT but uncataloged.

NOBLES, William H. SPEECH...RELATIVE TO AN EMIGRANT ROUTE TO CALIFORNIA AND OREGON, THROUGH MINNESOTA TERRITORY. St. Paul: Olmsted & Brown, 1954. MONTANA-Genl.

NOEL, Thomas J. "W. Wilberforce A Ramsey, Esq., and the California Gold Rush." BANCROFT. CAL-SANTA FE-GILA. IV. 1849.

NOREN, Evelyn. "John Reese: Nevada's Man of Many Firsts." TRUE WEST 32(Sept 1985): 24-28. Biog.

NORRUNG, Helge. Trans. Vogel-Jorgensen, T. PETER LASSEN OF CALIFORNIA.

NORTH, Arthur W. "The Cut-Off." SUNSET, Dec 1915, 1095-1104. HASTINGS-1846-Genl.

_____. "Overland Route to California: Kelly's Excursion." COLBURN 92(Jul 1851): 345-54. CAL-Genl.

NORTH, Diane M. SAMUEL PETER HEINTZELMAN AND THE SONORA EXPLORING AND MINING COMPANY. Tucson: Univ. of Arizona Press, 1980. Biog. Stage.

NORTH, Frank. On the Plains.... MONHIST. CAL(Atchison)-BRIDGER-SIMPSON-Ends Pine Valley, NV. III. Rem. 1858.

NORTH, Luther H. Papers. NBHIST. Pony.

Northern Pacific Railway Company. Records - Engineering Department. Chief Engineer - Old Vault Files. Cascade Mountain Surveys, 1867 +. Washington State Historical Society Library, Tacoma, WA. WASH-Genl.

THE NORTHERN ROUTE TO IDAHO AND THE PACIFIC OCEAN. St. Paul, MN: Merrill, 1864. Guide.

Northwestern Express, Stage and Transportation Company. Records, 1868-1886. MNHIST. Stage-Dakotas.

NORTON, Mrs. Charles. "The Old Oregon Trail." AMERICAN MONTHLY MAGAZINE 39(Nov 1911): 254-59. OR-Genl.

NORTON, Lewis Adelbert. LIFE AND ADVENTURES OF COLONEL LEWIS ADELBERT NORTON. Oakland: Author, 1887. CAL. V. Rem. 1852.

NORTON, Maria J. Diary. BANCROFT. CAL(Council)-TRUCKEE-Ends at Truckee Hot Springs. II +. 1859.

Notes of a Trip from the Town of Abiquiu, New Mexico, to Timpanogue Lake Valley. DAILY MISSOURI REPUBLICAN, 2 Sept 1852, p. 1. CAL(Santa Fe)-SPANISH-SLCOR. III. 1850.

"Notes on the History of MOUNTAIN STATION and J. L. Denton, Ranchman." CHRONICLES OF OKLAHOMA 36(Win 1958-1959): 476-78. Geog.

"Notes of Travel by the Overland Mail, San Francisco to Fort Yuma." Southern California Historical QUARTERLY 17(Sept 1935): 96-103. Stage.

NOTT, Manford? A. ACROSS THE PLAINS IN '54. N.p., n.d. CAL(Council). III +. Rem. 1854.

NOTTAGE, James H. "The Battles of Mud Springs Station and Rush Creek." PRAIRIE SCOUT 4(1981): 97-109. Indians. Military. Geog.

NUNIS, Doyce B., Jr. Ed. Belden, Josiah. JOSIAH BELDEN. Ed. Hill, Jasper S. LETTERS OF A YOUNG MINER. Ed. Reinhart, Herman F. GOLDEN FRONTIER.

_____. ANDREW SUBLETTE: ROCKY MOUNTAIN PRINCE, 1813 - 1853. LA: Dawson, 1960. Biog.

_____. "The Enigma of the Sublette Overland Party, 1845." PACIFIC HISTORICAL REVIEW 28(Fall 1959): 331-49. CAL-1845-Genl.

_____, ed. JOSIAH BELDEN, 1841 CALIFORNIA OVERLAND PIONEER.... Georgetown, CA: Talisman, 1962. CAL(Westport). IV. 1841.

NUSBAUMER, Louis. THE LOST DEATH VALLEY '49ER JOURNAL OF LOUIS NUSBAUMER. Ed. George Koenig. Bishop: Death Valley '49ers, 1974. SLCOR-1849-Genl.

_____. VALLEY OF SALT, MEMORIES OF WINE: A JOURNAL OF DEATH VALLEY, 1849. Ed. George Koenig. Keepsakes No. 15. Berkeley: Friends of the Bancroft Library, 1967. CAL(Indep)-BRIDGER-SLCOR. III. 1849.

NUTE, Grace L. "New Light on Red River Valley History." MINNESOTA HISTORICAL BULLETIN 5(Nov 1924): 561-72. DAKOTAS-Genl.

_____. "The Red River Tails." MINNESOTA HISTORY 6(Sept 1925): 279. DAKOTAS-Genl.

NYE-STARR, Kate. A SELF-SUSTAINING WOMAN.... Chicago: Illinois Printing & Binding, 1888. CAL(Council)-BRIDGER-SIMPSON. V. Rem. 1862.

OAKES, D. C. "The Man Who Wrote the Guide Book." TRAIL 2(Dec 1909): 7-15. Guide.

OAKLEY, Edward. Diaries. KSHIST. PIKES(Smoky Hill route). III. 1859.

OAKLEY, Francile B. "Arkansas' Golden Army of '49." ARKANSAS HISTORICAL QUARTERLY 6(Spr 1947): 1-85. CAL-1849-Genl. Train Govt.

OAKLEY, Obadiah. EXPEDITION TO OREGON. NY: Author, 1914. SANTA FE(Indep)-Brown's Hole & return. 1842-45.

OATES, Stephen B. "Blazing the Trail to El Paso." TRUE WEST 12(Sept-Oct 1964): 30-31, 59-62. TEX-1849-Genl.

OBERG, Pearl M. "Old Fort Hall." TRUE WEST 30(Jul 1983): 52-54. Geog.

O'BRIEN, Jack M., Jr. "The McLoughlin Massacre." PACIFIC NORTHWESTERNER 12(Spr, Sum 1968): 29-32, 45-47. CANADA(Trail to Fraser River)-1858-Genl.

O'BRYAN, Frank J. OVERLAND CHRONICLE: EMIGRANT DIARIES IN WESTERN NEVADA LIBRARIES. Reno: Nevada Historical Society, c1978. Bib.

OCHS, E. D. "The Opening of the New Southern Route into Oregon." MA thesis, Univ. of Oregon, 1916. APPLE-Genl.

O'CONNELL, Mary-Margaret. "The Legends of Vallecito." SDHIST. Geog. Stage(San Diego County, CA).

ODELL, Elizabeth F. Ed. Thurston, Samuel R. "Biography."

ODEN, Peter. Ed. Lazear, Michael C. "Death Rides."

ODENS, Peter R. ALONG THE BUTTERFIELD TRAIL. N.p.: Author, 1982. Stage: Yuma to San Diego.

O'FALLON, John, et al. "Overland Mail to California. Report of Committee...." WESTERN JOURNAL AND CIVILIAN. (1854). 245-53. Mail.

OFFEN, Karen M. Ed. Cornell, William. "William Cornell's 1852 Journal."

OFFICER, James E. "Yanqui Forty-Niners in Hispanic Arizona: Inter-ethnic Relations on the Sonoran Frontier." JOURNAL OF ARIZONA HISTORY 28(Sum 1987). CAL-1849-Genl. GILA-1849-Genl. MEX-1849-Genl. Not Seen.

OFFIELD, James W. Offield Family History. Washington State Univ. Library-SpCol, Pullman, WA. OR. V. 1850.

OGLE, William B. Diary. Indiana Historical Society, Indianapolis, IN. CAL(St. Jo)-HALL. II+. 1850.

OGLESBY, Richard J. "Richard J. Oglesby: Forty-Niner, His Own Narrative." Ed. Mildred Eversole. PAPERS IN ILLINOIS HISTORY 1938 (1939): 158-71. CAL(St. Jo)-HALL. IV. 1849.

O'Harra, Marjorie. "The Exploration and Establishment of the Applegate Trail: Excerpts from the Diary of Lindsay Applegate." In THE APPLEGATE TRAIL, ed. Francis D. Haines. N.p.: American Revolution Bicentennial Committee of Oregon, 1976. APPLE-1846-Genl.

OKLERKING, Damon. SEE: With Steve Brower. A CORRIDOR TRAIL NETWORK.

OLCH, Peter D. "Treading the Elephant's Tail: Medical Problems on the Overland Trails." BULLETIN OF MEDICAL HISTORY 59(1985): 196-212. Medical.

THE OLD OREGON TRAIL: HEARINGS BEFORE THE COMMITTEE ON ROADS. 68th Cong., 2d sess. 1925. WA: GPO, 1925. Pres.

OLDS, THE HISTORICAL DIARY AND THE LANDSCAPE OF A PORTION OF THE APPLEGATE TRAIL. Association of Oregon Geographers Writer's Project Series, No. 5. N.p.: The Association, N.d. Pres: Humboldt River to Goose Lake.

OLIPHANT, J. Orin. Ed. Burgunder, Ben. "Recollections." Ed. Green, Robert B. ON THE ARKANSAS ROUTE. Ed. Ide, Lucy. "In a Prairie Schooner." Ed. Johnson, Hezekiah. "Letters." Ed. Stoughton, John. "Passing of an Immigrant."

_____. "The Cattle Trade from the Far Northwest to Montana." AGRICULTURAL HISTORY 6(Apr 1932): 69-83. Stock.

_____. "The Cattle Trade through the Snoqualmie Pass." PACIFIC NORTHWEST QUARTERLY 38(Jul 1947): 193-214. Stock.

_____. ON THE CATTLE RANGES OF THE OREGON COUNTRY. Seattle: Univ. of Washington Press, 1968. Stock.

OLIVA, Leo E. "The Aubry Route of the Santa Fe Trail." KANSAS QUARTERLY 5(Spr 1973): 18-29. SANTA FE-1851-Genl.

_____. "Fort Atkinson on the Santa Fe Trail, 1850 - 1854." KANSAS HISTORICAL QUARTERLY 40(Sum 1974): 212-33. SANTA FE-Genl. Geog.

_____. "Fort Hays: Kansas Outpost.: CAMP PERIODICAL 6(Spr 1974): 2-9. Geog. Military.

_____. "Soldiers on the Santa Fe Trail, 1829 - 1880." PhD diss., Univ. of Denver, 1964. SANTA FE-Genl. Military.

OLMSTEAD, Samuel R. THE GOLD MINES OF KANSAS AND NEBRASKA. NY: N.p., 1858. Guide.

OLMSTED, Duncan, "When the Pony Express Came to Petaluma." SONOMA COUNTY (CAL) JOURNAL, Extra Edition, 22 Jun 1861, p. 1. Pony.

OLSON, Bert H. "The Emigrants' Forty Mile Desert Trail through Nevada." LOS ANGELES WESTERNERS BRAND BOOK 5(1953): 28-37. Geog. Maps.

_____. "Valley of the Two Stumps." LOS ANGELES WESTERNERS BRAND BOOK 12(1966): 127-38. Geog: Donner Lake. Maps.

OLSON, James C. Ed. Creigh, Thomas A. "From Nebraska City to Montana." Ed. Mason, James. "Diary."

_____. "The 'Lasting Peace' of Fort Laramie." AMERICAN WEST 2(Win 1965): 46-53. Military.

_____, and Irene D. Paden. "Facts about the Blazing of the Gold Trail, Including a Few Never Before Published." PACIFIC HISTORICAL REVIEW 18(Feb 1949): 3-13. CAL-1841-Genl.

OLSON, Jonas W. Journal. In "Historical Notes." JOURNAL ILLINOIS STATE HISTORICAL SOCIETY 48(Win 1955): 466-69. CAL(Council?)-BRIDGER-SLCUT? V-. 1850.

OLSON, Ruth A., and Rebecca Frandsen. "Best Trader on the Emigrant Road." TRUE WEST 27(Jul-Aug 1980): 48-51. Geog: Lava Hot Springs, ID.

OLTMAN, Marlo D. "The Smoky Hill Route: From the Missouri River to Ellsworth." MA thesis, Univ. of Kansas-Lawrence, 1968. PIKES-Genl.

OLWELL, Carol. SEE: With Cathy Luchetti. WOMEN OF THE WEST.

O'MEARA, James. "Captain F. X. Aubrey." CALIFORNIAN V(Jan 1882): 5-11. Biog.

On the Overland Trail, 1865. Norlin Library-Western History, Univ. of Colorado-Boulder. PIKES. IV. Rem. 1865.

ONEAL, Ben G. Collection. Texas State Library-Archives, Austin, TX. Pres: Butterfield Centennial, 1958.

O'NEIL, Elizabeth E. Reminiscence. MONHIST. CAL(Council?)-MONTANA. V. Rem. 1863.

O'NEIL, Emily A. "Joseph Murphy's Contribution to Development of the Great American West." MA thesis, St. Louis Univ., 1947. Eqpt.

O'NEILL, Eliza. Reminiscences. MONHIST. CAL(St. Jo)-HALL-MONTANA. V. Rem. 1864.

O'NEILL, O. H. Journal of Fort Kearney, South Pass, and Honey Lake Wagon Road Company. National Archives. LANDER. 1857. Not Seen.

OPENSHAW, Samuel. "Two Important Journals." In AN ENDURING LEGACY. SLC: Daughters of the Utah Pioneers, 1981. MORMON. IV. 1856.

ORDWAY, Edward. "Reminiscences." ANNALS OF WYOMING 5(Jun 1929): 149-60; 6(Jul-Oct 1929): 169-88. Freight.

"Oregon Material Taken from a File of an Independence (MO) and Weston (MO) Paper for 1844 and 1845." OREGON HISTORICAL QUARTERLY 4(Sept 1903): 278-90. OR-1843-Genl. Train Govt.

Oregon Stage Company. Records, 1866-7. ORU. Stage.

Oregon State Highway Dept. ROUTE OF THE OREGON TRAIL FORT BOISE, IDAHO TO THE DALLES, OREGON. N.p., 1959. Maps.

THE OREGON TRAIL: A POTENTIAL ADDITION TO THE NATIONAL TRAILS SYSTEM. Seattle: U.S. Bureau of Outdoor Recreation, 1974. Pres. Maps.

Oregon Trail Memorial Association. AMERICA'S HISTORICAL OPPORTUNITY. NY: The Association, 1937. Pres.

Oregon Trail Memorial Commission. Papers. NBHIST. Pres.

"Oregon Trail Monuments Erected by the Daughters of the American Revolution." OREGON HISTORICAL QUARTERLY 18(Sept 1917): 225-27. Pres.

O'REILLY, Harrington. FIFTY YEARS ON THE TRAIL. London: Chatto & Windus, 1889. Graphics.

ORGAN, W. J. "A Pioneer in the Land of the Setting Sun." GRIZZLY BEAR 6(Jan-Dec, 1910; Jan-May 1911). CAL(St. Jo)-BRIDGER-LASSEN. III. Rem. 1849.

THE ORGANIZATIONAL JOURNAL OF AN EMIGRANT TRAIN OF 1845 CAPTAINED BY SOLOMON TETHEROW. Eugene, OR: Lane County Pioneer-Historical Society, 1960. OR(St. Jo)-MEEK. III. 1845. Train Govt.

O'REILLY, Henry. "Memorial of Henry O'Reilly concerning Military Highways or 'Stockade Routes' for Protecting Travelers and Settlers...." 35th Cong., 1st sess. 1858. S. Misc. Doc. 134. Serial 935.

_____. Telegraph Material: Letters, Documents, Pamphlets, Circulars, etc., 1845 - 1860. New York Historical Society, New York City, NY. Telegraph.

ORMSBY, Augusta. Diary of an Emigrant Train Trip to California, 1868. NVHIST. CAL(Arkansas)-CHEROKEE-SANTA FE-RIO GRANDE-GILA-Ends on Mimbres River. IV. 1868.

ORMSBY, Waterman L. THE BUTTERFIELD OVERLAND MAIL, eds. L. H. Wright and J. M. Bynum. San Marino: Huntington, 1942. Stage: Missouri-California, 1858. II.

ORR, Mary M. "Guttard Station on the St. Joe Road." NEBRASKA HISTORY 66(Sum 1985): 185-91. Geog.

ORVIS, Andrew M. Letters and Diary. WIHIST. CAL(Council)-SLCUT-TRUCKEE. III-. 1849.

OSBORNE, Kelsie R. "Tragedy on Sinker Creek, 1860." PRAIRIE SCHOONER 26, No. 4(N.d): 400-08. Indians.

OSTEEN, Ike. "Old Trails across Baca County." TRUE WEST 29(Jan 1982): 18-21. SANTA FE-Genl.

_____. "Point of Rocks." TRUE WEST 15(May-Jun 1968): 32-33, 48. SANTA FE-Cimarron Cutoff. Geog.

OSTERHOUDT, Solomon. "Ox Train Diary." TOMBSTONE EPITAPH 4(Mar 1977):1, 14-20. CAL(Council)-HALL-TRUCKEE. III+. 1850.

OSTRANDER, Alson B. THE BOZEMAN TRAIL FORTS UNDER GENERAL PHILIP ST. GEORGE COOKE IN 1866. Seattle: Author, 1932. BOZE-Genl. Military.

OSWALD, Delmont. "James Pierson Beckwourth, 1798 - 1866." MA thesis, BYU, 1967. Biog. BECK-Genl.

OTTINGER, George M. Journal. Marriott Library-Univ. of Utah. MORMON. 1861. Not Seen.

OTTO, Olive H. "A Mormon Bride in the Great Migration." Ed. Orval F. Baldwin, II. NEBRASKA HISTORY 58(Spr 1977): 53-72. MORMON-1852-Genl.

OUREN, Hogan. SEE: "Hogan Ouren in Nebraska and Colorado."

OUTLAND, Charles F. STAGECOACHING ON EL CAMINE REAL: LOS ANGELES TO SAN FRANCISCO, 1861 - 1901. American Trails Series, No. 9. Glendale: Clark, 1973. Mail. Stage-CAL.

AN OUTLINE HISTORY OF AN EXPEDITION TO CALIFORNIA CONTAINING THE FATE OF THE 'GET ALL YOU CAN' MINING ASSOCIATION. NY: N.p., 1849. Cartoons.

"Outline of the Butterfield Route." SOUTHERN CALIFORNIA HISTORICAL QUARTERLY 17(Sept 1935): 104-07. Stage.

OVENHOLT, Sara. Ed. Buss, Amelia. AUNT AMELIA'S DIARY.

"Over the Plains to Colorado." HARPER'S 35(Jun 1867): 1-21. PIKES. V. 1867.

Overland Camel Company. PROSPECTUS. NY: The Company, 1865. Freight.

"The Overland Emigrant Road in Nevada County." NEVADA COUNTY HISTORICAL SOCIETY BULLETIN 33(Oct 1979): 32-34. Pres.

"Overland from Cincinnati to Santa Fe in 1865." RECORDS OF THE AMERICAN CATHOLIC HISTORICAL SOCIETY 44(Dec 1933): 375-84. SANTA FE(Leav). V. 1865.

Overland Journey to Colorado, 1863. DENVERPUB. PIKES. II. 1863.

"Overland Mail Adventure." FRASER'S MAGAZINE 54, n.d., p. 111. Not Seen.

Overland Mail Company. ARTICLES OF ASSOCIATION OF THE OVERLAND MAIL COMPANY, 1857. NY: Root, Anthony, 1860. Stage.

_____. Correspondence and Papers, 1850 - 1898. HUNTL. Overland-Genl.

_____. THROUGH TIME SCHEDULE BETWEEN ST. LOUIS, MO., MEMPHIS, TENN., AND SAN FRANCISCO, CAL. (1858). HUNTL. Stage.

_____. THROUGH THE SCHEDULE (NO. 2, JAN. 1859) BETWEEN ST. LOUIS, MO., MEMPHIS, TENN. AND SAN FRANCISCO, CALIFORNIA...WITH SPECIAL INSTRUCTIONS TO EMPLOYEES. NY: Hellier, 1859. Stage.

"The Overland Mail Line." FRONTIER TIMES, 8 Feb 1931, pp. 227-33. Stage.

Overland Stage Line. Receipts for Express Shipments in Denver. COHIST. Stage.

_____. Records, 1862 - 1870. Univ. of Utah Library-SpCol, Salt Lake City, UT. Stage.

"Overland Trail to California, Panorama Notice, 1850." ST. LOUIS DAILY MISSOURI REPUBLICAN, 14 Oct 1850. Graphics: Stage presentation of "immense moving mirror."

OVIATT, Alton B. "The Movement for a Northern Trail; The Mullan Road." PhD diss., Univ. of California-Berkeley, 1947. MULLAN-Genl. MONTANA-Genl. Freight.

OWEN, Abraham. "Reminiscence." In TRAILS DIVIDED, ed. Theodore Ressler. Williamsburg, Iowa: Ressler, 1964. CAL(Council)-BRIDGER-SLCUT. Rem. 1849. Not Seen.

OWEN, Benjamin F. MY TRIP ACROSS THE PLAINS. Eugene, OR: Lane County Pioneer-Historical Society, 1959. OR(Westport?)-MEEK(Good account). II. Rem. 1853.

OWEN, Charley. Ed. Owen, Abraham. "Reminiscence."

OWEN, East S. Journal. BEINECKE. CAL(Council)-TRUCKEE-BECK. III+. 1852.

OWEN, Isaac. "Isaac Owen - Overland to California." Ed. John R. Purdy, Jr. METHODIST HISTORY 11(Jul 1973): 46-54. CAL. 1849. Not Seen.

OWEN, John. THE JOURNALS AND LETTERS OF MAJOR JOHN OWEN.... Ed. Seymour Dunbar. 2 vols. Helena: Montana Historical Society, 1927. MONTANA-Genl.

OWEN, Richard. Diary of Travels. MONHIST. CAL(Council)-BOZE. II+. 1864.

OWENS-ADAIR, Bethenia A. SOME OF HER EXPERIENCES. Portland: Mann & Beach, 1906. OR? 1843. Not Seen.

OXCART TRAILS IN MINNESOTA AND NORTH DAKOTA IN THE 1850'S. MNHIST. Map.

PACE, James. Journal. HUNTL. CAL(Leav)-SANTA FE-RIO GRANDE-GILA. III+. 1846. CAL(Sutter's)-TRUCKEE-HALL-SLCUT-Ends SLC. III+. 1847.

PACE, William B. Autobiography. LDS. MORMON. Rem. 1847. Not Seen.

PACIFIC RAILROAD OF MISSOURI, THE OLD ESTABLISHED AND MOST RELIABLE ROUTE TO KANSAS, NEBRASKA.... N.p., n.d. Reprint. Denver, c1963. Guide.

"The Pacific Telegraph." MERCHANTS' MAGAZINE 46(Feb 1862): 157-58. Telegraph.

PACK, John. Biography. Ed. Gwen Pack Benson. UTHIST. MORMON. V-. 1847. MORMON. V-. 1848.

PACK, Mary. "The Romance of the Pony Express." UNION PACIFIC MAGAZINE, August, 1923, n.p. Pony.

PACKARD, Wellman. EARLY EMIGRATION TO CALIFORNIA, 1849 - 1850. 1850. Reprint. Fairfield, WA: Ye Galleon, 1971. CAL(St. Jo)-BRIDGER-SLCUT. V. Rem. 1850.

PACKER, Harry B. Letters. BANCROFT. CAL(Council)-BRIDGER. IV. 1850.

"Packing in the Mountains of California." HUTCHINGS' 1(Dec 1856): 241-49. Freight.

PACKWOOD, William H. "Reminiscences of William H. Packwood." Ed. Fred Lockley. OREGON HISTORICAL QUARTERLY 16(Mar 1915): 33-54. CAL(Ft. Kearny)-BRIDGER-SLCUT. IV. Rem. 1849.

PADEN, Irene D. Ed. Moorman, Madison B. JOURNAL. Ed. Willis, Ira J. "Guide." SEE: With James C. Olson. "Facts about the Blazing of the Gold Trail."

_____. Collection. UPAC. Biog. Overland-Genl.

_____. PIONEER TRAILS OF THE WEST. SF: Traveler, 1962. Overland-Genl. Not Seen.

_____. PRAIRIE SCHOONER DETOURS. NY: MacMillan, 1949. HASTINGS-Genl. LASSEN-Genl. Recommended.

_____. THE WAKE OF THE PRAIRIE SCHOONER. NY: Macmillan, 1943. Overland-Genl. Recommended.

_____, and James C. Olson. "Facts about the Blazing of the Gold Trail." PACIFIC HISTORICAL REVIEW 18(Feb 1949): 3-13. CAL-1841-Genl.

_____, and Margaret E. Schlichtmann. THE BIG OAK FLAT ROAD: AN ACCOUNT OF FREIGHTING FROM STOCKTON TO YOSEMITE VALLEY. SF: Emil Schlichtmann, 1955. Freight.

PADEN, William G. "Bidwell's Route of the Sierras, A Field Study." MA thesis, Univ. of California-Berkeley, 1940. CAL-1841-Genl.

PAGE, Albert R. "Orson Hyde and the Carson Valley Mission, 1855 - 1857." MA thesis, BYU, 1970. Geog. Recommended.

PAGE, Elizabeth. WAGONS WEST: A STORY OF THE OREGON TRAIL. NY: Farrar & Rinehart, 1930. Letters and journal of HENRY PAGE and JOSEPH HACKNEY. CAL(St. Jo)-HALL-TRUCKEE. I. 1849.

PAGE, Henry. Letters. SEE: Page, Elizabeth. WAGONS WEST.

PAHER, Stanley W., ed. FORT CHURCHILL, NEVADA MILITARY OUTPOST OF THE 1860'S. Las Vegas: Nevada Natural History Assn., 1981. Geog. Military.

PALLISER, John. EXPLORATION - BRITISH NORTH AMERICA. London: Eyre & Spottiswoode, 1859. CANADA-Genl.

PALMER, Belle. "The Sojourn of the Mormons at Kanesville, Pottawattomie County, Iowa, 1846 - 1852." MA thesis, Colorado State University, 1936. Geog. MORMON-Genl.

PALMER, Edward. Diary. Univ. of California-Los Angeles-Archives. GILA(Yuma to Gulf of CA). 1869. Not Seen.

_____. SEE: Underhill, Lonnie E. "Dr. Palmer's Experience."

PALMER, Harriet S. CROSSING OVER THE GREAT PLAINS BY OX-WAGONS. N.p.: Author, c1931. OR(St. Jo)-BARLOW. V. Rem. 1852.

PALMER, Henry S. REPORT OF A JOURNEY OF SURVEY, FROM VICTORIA TO FORT ALEXANDER, VIA NORTH BENTINCK ARM. New Westminster, BC: Royal Engineer Press, 1863. CANADA(North Bentinck Arm - Fort Alexander). II. 1862.

PALMER, Joel. JOURNAL OF TRAVELS OVER THE ROCKY MOUNTAINS. Cincinnati: James, 1847. OR(Indep)-BARLOW. I. 1845.

PALMER, William R. "Early Day Trading with the Nevada Mining Camps." UTAH HISTORICAL QUARTERLY 26(Oct 1958): 353-68. Freight.

_____. "Latter-Day Saint Pioneers and the Old Spanish Trail." IMPROVEMENT ERA 52(Feb 1949): 88-89, 113-15. SLCOR-Genl.

Palmer's Journal, 1845 - 1846. In Charles Kelly Collection. UTHIST. OR(Indep). V. 1845. OR(East to Midwest). V. 1846.

PALTSITS, Victor H. Ed. Frizzell, Lodisa. ACROSS THE PLAINS.

PANCOAST, Charles E. A QUAKER FORTY-NINER. Ed. Anna P. Hannum. Philadelphia: Univ. of Pennsylvania Press, 1930. CAL(Weston)-SANTA FE-RIO GRANDE-GILA. II. Rem. 1849.

PANKEY, H. S. "From Texas to California in 1869." ORANGE COUNTY HISTORY SERIES 3(1939): 56-70. CAL-TEX-GILA. V. 1869.

PAREDES, Raymund A. "The Mexican Image in American Travel Literature, 1831 - 1869." NEW MEXICO HISTORICAL REVIEW 52(Jan 1977): 5-30. MEX-Genl.

PARISH, G. Diary. Clarke Library-Central Michigan Univ., Mt. Pleasant, MI. CAL(Council). 1852. Not Seen.

PARK, Mortimer and Susan. Trip to Montana. MONHIST. CAL(St. Jo)-BOZE. IV. Rem. 1863.

PARKE, Charles R. Diary. HUNTL. CAL(St. Jo)-TRUCKEE. II+. 1849. Graphics.

PARKE, John G. REPORT OF EXPLORATIONS FOR THAT PORTION OF A RAILWAY ROUTE, NEAR THE THIRTY-SECOND PARALLEL OF LATITUDE LYING BETWEEN DONA ANA, ON THE RIO GRANDE, AND PIMAS VILLAGES, ON THE GILA. 33d Cong., 1st sess. 1854. H. Ex. Doc. 129. GILA(San Diego to Mesilla). II+. 1854. Govt.

PARKER, Basil G. THE LIFE AND ADVENTURES OF BASIL G. PARKER. Plano, CA: F. W. Reed, 1902. CAL(Ft. Smith)-OKLA-TEX-GILA. IV. Rem. 1853. CAL(Ft. Smith)-CHEROKEE-SLCUT. V. Rem. 1857.

PARKER, Mrs. C. F. "Old Julesburg and Fort Sedgewick." COLORADO MAGAZINE 7(Jul 1930): 139-46. Geog.

PARKER, Ellen. Along the Immigrant Trail from Tennessee to California, 1847 - 1859. San Joaquin Pioneer and Historical Society, Stockton, CA. CAL-Genl. Not Seen.

PARKER, Horace. "A Historian's Search for Sackett's Lost Wells." Ed. Russ Ledabrand. In LOS ANGELES WESTERNERS BRAND BOOK 11(1964): 77-92. Stage.

PARKER, Inez E. "Early Recollections of Oregon Pioneer Life." TRANSACTIONS Oregon Pioneer Association 1928 (1933): N.p. OR(Council). V. Rem. 1848.

PARKER, L. Mayland. "Economic Geography of Utah's Sheep Industry." MS thesis, Univ. of Utah, 1951. Stock.

PARKER, Nathan H., and D. H. Huyett. THE ILLUSTRATED MINERS' HAND-BOOK AND GUIDE TO PIKE'S PEAK.... St. Louis: Parker & Huyett, 1859. Guide.

PARKER, Nellie B. "The Early Oregon Pioneers." OVERLAND MONTHLY 83(Jun 1925): 238-39. Pres-1923 Reinactment.

PARKER, Samuel. Diary, 1845. ORHIST. OR(St. Jo). IV. 1845.

PARKER, W. B. NOTES TAKEN DURING THE EXPEDITION COMMANDED BY CAPT. R. B. MARCY, U.S.A., THROUGH UNEXPLORED TEXAS, IN THE SUMMER AND FALL OF 1854. Philadelphia: Hayes & Zell, 1856. OKLA(Ft. Smith to Ft. Belknap). II+. 1854.

PARKER, Watson. "Wading to California: The Influence of the Forty-Niners on the Notion of a Great American Desert." GREAT PLAINS JOURNAL 3(Spr 1964): 35-43. CAL-1849-Genl.

PARKER, Wilbur F. "The Glorious Orb of Day Has Rose: A Diary of the Smoky Hill Route to Pike's Peak, 1858." Ed. Norman Lavers. MONTANA 36(Spr 1986): 50-61. PIKES. II. 1858.

PARKER, William T. Notes By the Way. HUNTL. CAL(St. Jo). II+. 1850. Flora.

PARKHILL, Forbes. "Decline and Fall of the Stagecoach Empire." DENVER WESTERNERS BRANDBOOK 7(1951): 71-93. Stage.

PARKINS, Katherine L. "A Study of the Letislative History of the Early Roads, Bridges, and Ferries in the Territory of Washington." MA thesis, Univ. of Washington, 1941. WASH-Genl.

PARKINSON, John B. "California and Her Golden Fleece." WIHIST. CAL(Council)-NOBLES. IV. Rem. 1852.

_____. "Memories of Early Wisconsin and the Gold Mines." WISCONSIN MAGAZINE OF HISTORY 5(Dec 1921): 1-25. CAL(Council)-LASSEN. IV. Rem. 1852.

PARKMAN, Francis. THE OREGON TRAIL. NY: Heritage Press, 1943. CAL(Indep)-Ends Medicine Bow Mountains. V. 1846. Graphics.

PARMAN, Henry H. "Beyond the Horizon." Ed. Ralph G. Parman. Univ. of Nevada Library-SpCol, Reno, NV. CAL(Indep)-LASSEN. IV. 1857.

PARMAN, Ralph G. Ed. Parman, Henry H. "Beyond the Horizon."

PARRISH, Edward E. "Crossing the Plains in 1844." TRANSACTIONS Oregon Pioneer Association, 1888." (1889): 82-122. OR(Indep). II. 1844.

PARRISH, Philip H. "The Great Migration - 1843." In WAGONS WEST. Portland: Old Oregon Trail Centennial Committee, 1943. OR-1843-Genl.

PARRISH, Susan. Westward in 1850. HUNTL. CAL(Indep)-SANTA FE-RIO GRANDE-GILA. IV. Rem. 1850. Indians-Oatman Massacre.

PARSONS, J. R. Diary. North Dakota Historical Society, Bismarck, ND. Not Seen.

PARSONS, John E. Ed. Hardin, Martin D. "Up the Missouri and over the Mullan Road."

PARSONS, Lucena P. "Journal." In COVERED WAGON WOMEN, ed. Kenneth L. Holmes. Vol. 2. Glendale: Clark, 1984. CAL(Council)-BRIDGER-Ends SLC. II. 1850. CAL(SLC)-SLCUT. II. 1851.

PARSONS, Mary C. Reminiscence. OR(Council). V-. Rem. 1852.

PARSONS, Phyllis R. "The Trans-Mississippi West in Selected Popular Magazine Literature, 1820 - 1870. An Annotated Bibliography." MA thesis, Univ. of Wyoming, 1950. Bib.

PARSONS, William B. THE GOLD MINES OF WESTERN KANSAS. Lawrence, KS: Republican, 1858. Guide.

_____. THE NEW GOLD MINES OF WESTERN KANSAS.... Cincinnati: G. S. Blanchard, 1859. Guide.

_____. "Pike's Peak Fourteen Years Ago." KANSAS MAGAZINE 1(Jun 1872): 552-61. PIKES. IV. Rem. 1858.

PARTOLL, Albert J., ed. "Mengarini's Narrative to the Rockies." In FRONTIER OMNIBUS, ed. John W. Hakola. Missoula: Montana State Univ., 1962. OR(Westport). V. 1841.

PASCHAL, Albert G. Overland Trip. Iowa State Historical Society, Iowa City, IA. CAL(Council)-HALL. II+. 1850. Train Govt.

PATE, R. E. "The Colorado Gold Rush of '59." Senior thesis, Princeton Univ., 1942. PIKES-1859-Genl.

PATRICK, Elizabeth N. SEE: Warren, Elizabeth, et al. CULTURAL RESOURCES OF THE CALIFORNIA DESERT.

PATRICK, Henry H. Extracts from a Journal. Iowa State Historical Society, Iowa City, IA. CAL(Council)-SLCUT. V. 1850.

PATRICK, William. Trip to Pike's Peak. Western History Library, Univ. of Oklahoma-Norman. PIKES. II. 1859.

PATTEN, F. E. W. Journal of Travels. MONHIST. CHEROKEE(Denver-Ft. Bridger-MONTANA-HALL. I. 1863.

PATTERSON, A. H., Emigrating Company. Journal. LDS. MORMON. III. 1863.

PATTERSON, Edwin H. "Chalk Marks of Overland Travel Pike's Peakward." Oquawka (Illinois) SPECTATOR, 19 Apr 1860 to 19 Sept 1860. Norlin Library-Western History, Univ. of Colorado-Boulder. PIKES. II. 1859.

PATTERSON, George W. Across Mexico to California. CAL-TEX(Port Lavaca-Eagle Pass)-MEX-Ends Durango. IV. 1849.

PATTERSON, Ida. "The Wagon Train of 1843." LANE COUNTY HISTORIAN 24(Spr 1979): 14-18. OR-1843-Genl.

PATTERSON, Martin. Trip to Pike's Peak. Held by Merrill J. Mattes, Denver, CO. Not Seen.

PATTERSON, Tom. Ed. Johnston, Francis J. THE BRADSHAW TRAIL.

PATTISON, John J. "With the U.S. Army along the Oregon Trail, 1863-66." NEBRASKA HISTORY 15(Apr-Jun 1934): 79-93. Military.

PATTISON, Nathan. Letter. In Paul & Helen Henderson Collection, UWY. CAL(St. Jo?)-Ends Ft. Hall. V-. 1849.

PATTISON, William. Diary. ORHIST. OR(St. Jo). IV. 1849.

PATTON, A. C. GREEN ROCKS. Boulder, CO: Author, 1904. Fictional account of child indian captive. Indians-1852.

PATTON, Annaleone D. CALIFORNIA MORMONS BY SAIL AND TRAIL. SLC: Deseret News, 1961. Utah and the Mormons.

PATTON, Thomas M. Diaries. Oregon State Library, Salem, OR. 1851. Not Seen.

PATZMAN, Stephen N. "Louis John Frederick Jaeger: Entrepreneur of the Colorado River." ARIZONIANA 4(Spr 1963): 31-36. Geog. Biog.

PAUL, R. Eli. Ed. Dudley, N.A. "Battle of Ash Hollow." Ed. Kendall, George W. "George Wilkins Kendall."

PAUL, Virginia. THIS IS SHEEP RANCHING: YESTERDAY AND TODAY. Seattle: Superior, 1976. Stock-Graphics.

PAUP, Harrison. ACROSS THE PLAINS IN 1861. Ed. Louise Escher. Hollywood, CA: Private, 1922. CAL(Council). IV. 1861.

PAXSON, Frederick L. Ed. Turnbull, Thomas. "Travels."

PAXTON, Matthew. "When Freight Was Hauled by Oxen." FRONTIER TIMES 24(Sept 1947): 540-42. Freight.

PAYETTE, B. C. Comp. Fulton, Arabella. TALES OF THE TRAIL. SEE: Coleman, Louis C., et al. CAPTAIN JOHN MULLAN.

PAYNE, James A. Journal. NBHIST. CAL(Indep). 1850. Not Seen.

PEABODY, Frances C. "Across the Plains Deluxe in 1865." COLORADO MAGAZINE 18(1941): 71-76. PIKES. IV. 1865. Freight trip.

PEACOCK, William. THE PEACOCK LETTERS.... Stockton: San Joaquin Pioneer & Historical Society, 1950. CAL(St. Jo). IV. 1850.

PEALE, Titian R. DIARY, OREGON TO CALIFORNIA...1841. Ed. Clifford M. Drury. Early California Travels Series 36. LA: Dawson's, 1957. OR-CAL. II. 1841.

PEARCE, Basil C. "The Jackass Mail - San Antonio and San Diego Mail Line." JOURNAL OF SAN DIEGO HISTORY 15(Spr 1969): 15-20. Stage. Mail.

PEARCE, Jean R. Diary. MORMON. II+. 1851.

PEARMAN, John W. "Early Annals of Nebraska City." PROCEEDINGS AND COLLECTIONS NEBRASKA STATE HISTORICAL SOCIETY 15(1907): 133-42. Geog.

PEARSON, Gustavus C. OVERLAND IN 1849. Ed. Jessie H. Goodman. LA: Private, 1961. MORMON(St. Jo). III-. Rem. 1849.

PEASE, David E. Diary. ORHIST. OR(St. Jo)-BARLOW. II. 1849.

PEASE, Edwin R. "Diary." In OVERLAND ROUTES TO THE GOLD FIELDS, 1859, ed. Leroy R. Hafen. Southwest Historical Series, No. 11. Glendale: Clark, 1942. CAL(St. Jo)-Ends Ft. Kearny. II. 1859.

PEASE and COLE, COMPLETE GUIDE TO THE GOLD DISTRICTS OF KANSAS 7 NEBRASKA.... Chicago: W. H. Rand, 1859. Guide.

PEATTIE, Donald C. "There Goes the Pony Express." READERS DIGEST 76(Apr 1960): 240-46. Pony.

PEAVY, Linda, and Ursula Smith. "Women in Waiting in the Westward Movement." MONTANA 35(Spr 1985): 2-17. Social.

PECK, S. L. HISTORY OF IRA, VERMONT. Rutland, VT: Tuttle, 1926. DAKOTAS(St. Paul)-MONTANA. V. 1866.

PEDERSON, G. J. Ed. Grant, William S. "A Yankee in Arizona."

PEIRCE, Eli H. Diary. UTHIST. MORMON. III+. 1857. MORMON. III-. 1858.

PEIRSON, Erma. THE MOHAVE RIVER AND ITS VALLEY. Western Lands and Waters Series IX. Glendale: Clark, 1970. Geog. BEALE-Genl. SPANISH-Genl.

PELTIER, Jerome. Ed. Hinde, Edmund C. JOURNAL.

_____. ANTOINE PLANTE, MOUNTAIN MAN, RANCHER, MINER, GUIDE, HOSTLER AND FERRYMAN. Fairfield, WA: Ye Galleon, 1983. WASH-Genl.

_____. "Romeo and Juliet on the Oregon Trail." PACIFIC NORTHWESTERNER 28(Sum 1984): 33-37. Social.

_____. "The Ward Massacre." PACIFIC NORTHWESTERNER 9(Win 1965): 12-16. Indians-1854 attack near Boise.

PELZER, Louis. "A Decade of Ox-Team Freighting on the Plains." THE TRANS-MISSISSIPPI WEST, eds. James F. Willard and Colin B. Goodykoontz. Boulder: Univ. of Colorado, 1930. Freight.

_____. "Trails of the Trans-Mississippi Cattle Frontier." In THE TRANS-MISSISSIPPI WEST, eds. James F. Willard and Colin B. Goodykoontz. Boulder: Univ. of Colorado, 1930. Stock.

PEMBERTON, J. Despard. FACTS AND FIGURES RELATING TO VANCOUVER ISLAND AND BRITISH COLUMBIA SHOWING WHAT TO EXPECT AND HOW TO GET THERE. N.p., n.d. Maps. Guide. Excellent.

PENCE, Anna. "Pioneer Hardships." Newspaper articles from Payette, ID, 1900. OR(Brownsville, Neb.). V. Rem. 1862.

PENGRA, B. J. REPORT OF THE RECENT SURVEYS AND PROGRESS OF CONSTRUCTION OF THE OREGON CENTRAL MILITARY ROAD COMPANY. Eugene City, OR: Oregon Central Company, 1865. OR-Genl.

PENGRA, Charlotte E. DIARY, 1853. Eugene, OR: Lane County Historical Society, 1966. OR(Council). II. 1853.

PENNEBAKER, W. G. "Westward from Wayne County by Wagon Train." HAWKEYE HERITAGE 14(Win 1979): 13-18. CAL(Neb. City)-CHEROKEE(Cheyenne-SLC)-SIMPSON. III. 1868.

PENNELL, William D. Letters. State Historical Society of Missouri, Columbia, MO. CAL(Indep)-SANTA FE-RIO GRANDE-GILA. V. 1849.

PENNOCK, Jake. "Diary of Jake Pennock." ANNALS OF WYOMING 23(Jul 1951): 4-29. Indian attacks on Overland stations in Wyoming, 1865. Excellent.

PENROSE, S. B. "The Wagon Train of 1843 - Its Dual Significance." OREGON HISTORICAL QUARTERLY 44(Dec 1943): 361-69. OR-1843-Genl.

PENTER, Samuel. "Recollections of Crossing the Plains with the Oregon Migration of '43." OREGON HISTORICAL QUARTERLY 7(Mar 1906): 56-61. OR(Missouri). IV. Rem. 1843.

PEOPLES, John H. GENERAL SMITH'S CORRESPONDENCE, CALIFORNIA. (Relief Report from Lassen's Cutoff, 1849). 31st Cong., 1st sess. 1852. S. Ex. Doc 52. CAL-1849-Genl. LASSEN-1849-Genl.

PERKINS, E. A. Diary. UWY. CAL(Courthouse Rock to Green River). IV 1847.

PERKINS, Elisha D. GOLD RUSH DIARY. Ed. Thomas D. Clark. Lexington: Univ. of Kentucky Press, 1967. CAL(St. Jo)-TRUCKEE. I. 1849.

PERKINS, George E. PIONEERS OF THE WESTERN DESERT. LA: Wetzel, 1947. SLCOR-Genl.

PERKINS, William. THREE YEARS IN CALIFORNIA. Berkeley: Univ. of California Press, 1964. CAL-TEX(Port Isabel)-MEX(Monterey-Parras-Mazatlan). V. 1849.

PERKO, Richard. "A Forgotten Passage to Puget Sound: The Fort Steilacoom - Walla Walla Road." MONTANA 35(Win 1985): 38-51. WASH-1853-Genl.

PERRIE, George W. BUCKSKIN MOSE. NY: Worthington, c1911.

CAL(St. Jo)-NOBLES. III. Rem. 1855.

PERRIGO, Lynn I. Ed. Hawley, H. J. "Hawley's Diary of his Trip."

PERRY, J. A. THRILLING ADVENTURES OF A NEW ENGLANDER. Boston: Redding, 1853. CAL-MEX(Vera Cruz-Puebla-Guadalajara-San Blas). II+. 1849.

PERRY, Samuel M. Diary. Ed. Virginia P. Culbert. CSL. OR-CAL-MULLAN. II. 1862.

PERSINGER, James B. A Chapter from the Diary of the late Judge James B. Persinger. State Historical Society of Missouri, Columbia, MO. CAL(Westport)-Ends on Platte. II. 1850.

PETERS, Mary E. "Texas Trails." MISSISSIPPI VALLEY HISTORICAL ASSOCIATION PROCEEDINGS 7(1913-14): 55-66. TEX-Genl.

PETERSEN, Bryan L. "A Geographic Study of the Mormon Migration from Nauvoo, Illinois, to the Great Salt Lake Valley (1846 - 1847)." MA thesis, Univ. of California-LA, 1941. Missing.

PETERSEN, Edward. "Pierson B. Reading on the Road to California." COVERED WAGON (1983): 5-14. Pres.

PETERSEN, William J. "The Handcart Expedition: 1856." PALIMPSEST 47(Sept 1956): 368-84. MORMON-1856-Genl.

_____. "The Mormon Trail of 1846." PALIMPSEST 47(Sept 1966): 353-67. MORMON-1846-Genl.

PETERSON, Charles S., et al. MORMON BATTALION TRAIL GUIDE. Western Trail Guide Series No. 1. SLC?: Utah State Historical Society, 1972. CAL-1846-Genl. Maps.

PETERSON, Guy L. FOUR FORTS OF THE SOUTH PLATTE. Fort Myers, VA: Council on America's Military Past, 1982. PIKES-Genl. Not Seen.

PETERSON, H. C. "Dare-Devils of the Pony Express." PONY EXPRESS COURIER, October, 1934, 4-5. Pony.

_____. "Notorious Characters of the Pony Express." PONY EXPRESS COURIER, August, 1934, 6-7.

PETERSON, Harold L. AMERICAN KNIVES: THE FIRST HISTORY AND COLLECTORS GUIDE. NY: Scribner's, 1958. Eqpt.

PETERSON, Peta. OUR WAGON TRAIN IS LOST. Eugene, OR: New American Gothic, 1975. OR-1853-Genl. MEEK-1853-Genl.

PETERSON, Ruth. Comp. Lowell, Nancy. "Across the Plains."

PETERSON, Stacy. "Silas Skinner's Owyhee Toll Road." IDAHO YESTERDAYS 10(Spr 1966): 12-21. Stage.

PETERSON, Susan, "The Butterfield Overland Mail in Indian Territory, 1858 - 1861." RED RIVER VALLEY HISTORICAL REVIEW 6(Sum 1981): 77-86. Stage-Oklahoma Only.

PETERSON, Thomas H., Jr. "The Buckley House: Tucson Station for the Butterfield Overland Mail." JOURNAL ARIZONA HISTORY 7(1966): 153-67. Stage.

_____. "Cash Up or No Go: The Stagecoach Era in Arizona." JOURNAL ARIZONA HISTORY 14(Aut 1973): 205-22. Stage.

PETTID, Edward. "Olive Ann Oatman's Lecture Notes and the Oatman Bibliography." SAN BERNARDINO COUNTY MUSEUM AS-

SOCIATION QUARTERLY 16(Win 1968): 1-39. Biog.

PETTIGREW, David. Autobiography. UTHIST. CAL(Leav)-SANTA FE-RIO GRANDE-GILA. III-. 1846.

PETTIJOHN, Isaac. Diary. BANCROFT. OR(St. Jo)-BARLOW. II. 1847. OR(East via)-APPLE. III. 1848.

PETTIS, George H. THE CALIFORNIA COLUMN. Historical Society of New Mexico No. 11. Santa Fe: New Mexican, 1908. GILA. III. 1862.

_____. Letters. BEINECKE. GILA. III. 1862.

_____. PERSONAL NARRATIVES OF EVENTS IN THE WAR OF THE REBELLION, FRONTIER SERVICE...OR A HISTORY OF COMPANY K, FIRST INFANTRY, CALIFORNIA VOLUNTEERS. Providence, RI: Soldiers' and Sailors' Historical Society, 1885. GILA. III. 1862.

PHELPS, Edwin. SEE: With Seeley, John V. Diary.

PHELPS, John W. "Diary." In THE UTAH EXPEDITION, eds. LeRoy R. and Ann W. Hafen. Far West and the Rockies Historical Series 1820 - 1875, Vol. 8. Glendale: Clark, 1958. CAL(Leav)-BRIDGER. II. 1857.

PHELPS, Mary. Ed. Seeley, John V., and Edwin Phelps. Diary.

PHELPS, Netta S. THE VALIANT SEVEN. Caldwell, ID: Caxton, 1941. Biog. Indians-Whitman Massacre, 1847.

PHILLIPS, Cyrus E. Journal. BYU. CAL(St. Jo)-BRIDGER-SLCUT-Ends Lovelock. II. 1852.

PHILLIPS, Marcia B. Five Stevenson Men Who Went to California in 1849. CAHIST. CAL(Ft. Smith)-SANTA FE-RIO GRANDE-GILA. III. 1849.

PHILLIPS, Paul C. Ed. Kirkpatrick, James. "A Reminiscence." Ed. Langworthy, Franklin. SCENERY OF THE PLAINS. Ed. Stuart, Granville. FORTY YEARS. Ed. Stuart, Granville. PROSPECTING FOR GOLD.

PHILLIPS, William W. "San Diego Miner and Lumberman." Province of British Columbia Archives, Victoria. CANADA-Cariboo. Rem. 1862. Not Seen.

PICARD, Madge E., and R. Carlyle Buley. THE MIDWEST PIONEER: HIS ILLS, CURES, AND DOCTORS. NY: Schuman, 1946. Medical.

PICKERING, Charles. "Pickering's Journey to Fort Colville in 1841." WASHINGTON HISTORICAL QUARTERLY 20(Jan 1929): 54-63. WASH-Genl.

PICKERING, Loring. Dictation. BANCROFT. CAL(St. Jo)-LASSEN. V. Rem. 1849.

PIERCE, E. D. THE PIERCE CHRONICLE: AS TRANSCRIBED BY LOU A. LARRICK. Eds. J. Gary Williams and Ronald W. Stark. Moscow, ID: Idaho Research Foundation, 1975. CAL(St. Jo)-LASSEN. III+. Rem. 1849. Stage: Susanville to Boise. IV. Rem. 1865.

PIERCE, Gerald S. "The Military Road Expeditions of 1840-41." TEXAS MILITARY HISTORY 6(Sum 1967): 115-35. TEX-Genl.

PIERCE, Lois A. LOST IMMIGRANTS OF 1845 AND THE BLUE BUCKET GOLD. Shelton, WA: Author, 1962. OR-1845-Genl.

PIERCY, Frederick H. ROUTE FROM LIVERPOOL TO GREAT SALT LAKE VALLEY. Ed. Fawn M. Brodie. Cambridge: Belknap Press of Harvard Univ. Press, 1962. MORMON. II. 1853.

"Pierre D. Papin Gravesite Rediscovered." OVERLAND JOURNAL 1(Fall 1983): 36-37. Geog-Scotts Bluff.

PIERSON, James R. THE PONY EXPRESS TRAIL, 1860 - 1861. St. Joseph, MO: Pony Express Productions, 1960. Pony.

PIGMAN, Walter G. THE JOURNAL OF WALTER GRIFFITH PIGMAN. Ed. Ulla S. Fawkes. Mexico, MO: Staley, 1942. CAL(St. Jo). IV. 1850.

PIGNEY, Joseph. FOR FEAR WE SHALL PERISH; THE STORY OF THE DONNER PARTY DISASTER. NY: Dutton, 1961. Fiction.

PIKALE, Henele. "Recollections of the Past." JUVENILE INSTRUCTOR 21(1886): 111-12, 119-20, 144-45, 153-55, 166-67, 189-90, 231-32, 255-56, 265-66, 300-01, 315-16, 343-44, 365-66, 371-72. CAL(Leav)-SANTA FE-RIO GRANDE-GILA. III. 1846. CAL-SLCUT-Ends SLC. III. 1848.

PIKE'S PEAK. GREAT THROUGH LINE BETWEEN THE EAST AND WEST. Cincinnati: N.p., 1859. Guide.

Pike's Peak or Bust Collection. COHIST. PIKES-1859-Genl.

"Pilsbury Hodgkins, Pony Rider." QUARTERLY CALIFORNIA PIONEERS SOCIETY 2(Sept 1925): 171-85. Stage.

PINE, George. BEYOND THE WEST. N.p., 1870. PIKES. Not Seen.

PINNEY, Marie. "Charles Becker, Pony Express Rider and Oregon Pioneer." OREGON HISTORICAL QUARTERLY 67(Sept 1966): 212-56. Pony.

Pioneer Ladies Club of Pendleton, Oregon. REMINISCENCES OF OREGON PIONEERS. Pendleton: Pioneer Club, 1937. OR-Genl.

Pioneers' Reminiscences. MONHIST. MONTANA-Genl.

PIPER, Alexander. "Alexander Piper's Reports and Journal." Ed. Priscilla Knuth. OREGON HISTORICAL QUARTERLY 69(Sept 1968): 223-68. APPLE(Fort Umpqua to Klamath Lake). III. 1860.

PISNEY, Raymond F. HISTORICAL MARKERS: A BIBLIOGRAPHY. Verona, VT: McClure, 1977.

PITZER, Henry L. THREE FRONTIERS. Ed. Robert C. Pitzer. Muscatine, IA: Prairie, 1938. PIKES. V-. Rem. 1860.

PITZER, Robert C. Ed. Pitzer, Henry L. THREE FRONTIERS.

PIZER, Irwin H. "Medical Aspects of the Westward Migrations, 1830-60." BULLETIN MEDICAL LIBRARY ASSOCIATION 53(Jan 1965): 1-14. Medical.

PLACERVILLE, OLD HANGTOWN OF '49. Placerville: Mountain Democrat, 1930. Geog.

PLANTE, Antoine. SEE: Peltier, Jerome. ANTOINE PLANTE.

PLATT, D. L., and N. M. Slater. THE TRAVELERS' GUIDE ACROSS THE PLAINS UPON THE OVERLAND TRAIL. Ed. Dale L. Morgan. 1852. Reprint. SF: John Howell, 1963. CAL(St. Jo). III. 1851.

PLEASANTS, Joseph E. SEE: Meadows, Don. THE CATTLE DRIVES OF JOSEPH E. PLEASANTS.

_____. "Joseph Edward Pleasants '49er." Ed. William McPherson.

ORANGE COUNTY HISTORY SERIES 2(1932): 5-11. CAL(Indep?)-LASSEN. IV. 1849.

_____. "Ranging on the Mojave River in 1864." TOURING TOPICS 22(Mar 1930): 42-43. BEALE-1864-Genl.

_____. "The Rout of the Horse Thieves." TOURING TOPICS 22(Apr 1930): 40-41, 54. BEALE-1861-Genl.

PLEASANTS, William J. TWICE ACROSS THE PLAIN, 1849...1856. 1906. Reprint. Fairfield, WA: Ye Galleon, 1981. CAL(Kansas)-LASSEN. IV. Rem. 1849. CAL(Indep). V-. Rem. 1856.

PLUMMER, Samuel C. Letters. MO-WHMC. CAL(Council). V. 1850.

POE, Andrew J. Diary. Held by Fred Rosenstock, Denver, CO. OR(St. Jo). 1847. Not Seen.

POE, F. "Wagon Road in California." DE BOW'S 21(N.d): 58. Not Seen.

POINT, Nicholas. "Historical Notes." [In] WILDERNESS KINGDOM, Joseph P. Donnelly, ed. NY: N.p., 1967. OR(Westport)-HALL-MONTANA. 1841. Indians. Not Seen.

POLLINGER, Elijah M. Letter. MONHIST. Stage-Montana.

POMEROY, H. B. Diary. BANCROFT. CAL(East from Bear River to St. Jo). III+. 1850.

POMEROY, Henry M. Journal. CSL. CAL(Council). II+. 1859. CAL(East via)-GILA-TEX(El Paso-San Antonio). II+. 1860.

POND, Ananias R. Diary. HUNTL. LASSEN. II+. 1849.

POND, Henry. Diary. MONHIST. MONTANA. III. 1862.

"The Pony Express." HUTCHINGS' 5(Jul 1860): 1-7. Pony.

"The Pony Express." QUARTERLY SOCIETY CALIFORNIA PIONEERS 2(Sept 1925): 155-70. Pony.

"Pony Express Centennial 1960." COHIST. Pony. Pres.

Pony Express Centennial Association Records. UPAC. Pony. Pres.

"Pony Express Issue." NEVADA HISTORICAL SOCIETY QUARTERLY 3(Spr 1960): 3-45. 1960 Rerun in Nevada.

"Pony Express Jubilee." NEWSWEEK 15(8 Apr 1940): 20. Pony.

"The Pony Express Lives!" NEWSWEEK 101(2 May 1983): 37. Pony.

"Pony Express Returns." LIFE 23(20 Oct 1947): 40-41. Pony.

"The Pony Express Riders." OUTING 44(Apr 1904): 45-49. Pony-Graphics.

"The Pony Express Rides Again." KANSAS HISTORICAL QUARTERLY 25 (Win 1959): 369-85. Pony-Kansas. Map-Kansas.

POOLE, William F. AN INDEX TO PERIODICAL LITERATURE. 6 vols. Boston: Osgood, 1882-1908. Bib.

POPE, George L. Incidents of Traveling. BEINECKE. PIKES. III+. 1859.

POPE, John. REPORT OF AN EXPLORATION OF THE TERRITORY OF MINNESOTA. 31st Cong., 1st sess. S. Doc. 42. Serial 558. DAKOTAS(St. Paul)-CANADA(to Pembina and return). II. 1849.

_____. REPORT OF EXPLORATION OF A ROUTE FOR THE PACIFIC RAILROAD, NEAR THE THIRTY-SECOND PARALLEL OF LATITUDE, FROM THE RED RIVER TO THE RIO GRANDE. 33d Cong., 1st sess. 1854. H. Ex. Doc. 129. RIO GRANDE(Dona Ana)-TEX(Hueco Tanks-Pecos River-Sand Hills-Gainesville)-OKLA(Ends Ft. Washita). II+. 1854.

PORATH, Joseph H. "Early Mail Service in Utah and Other Western Points." AMERICAN PHILATELIST 77(Apr 1964): 495-500. Mail-Utah.

PORTER, Charles F. "News from Fort Kearny, Nebraska Territory." OMAHA NEBRASKAN, 17 August 1864, n.p. PIKES-Denver to Omaha by stage. 1864. Not Seen.

PORTER, Elizabeth L. Crossing the Plains, A Diary. ORHIST. CAL(Council)-LANDER. III. 1864.

PORTER, Eugene O. "Across Northern Mexico with Wislizenus." PASSWORD 19(Sum, Fall 1974): 82-88, 133-46; 20(Spr 1975): 24-37. MEX(Chichuhua-Parras Saltillo-Monterey-Brownsville). I. 1847.

_____. "Down the Chihuahua Trail with Wislizenus." PASSWORD 18(Spr, Sum, Fall 1973, Win 1974): 21-32, 66-74, 114-18, 169-80. RIO GRANDE(Santa Fe-El Paso-Chihuahua). I. 1846.

PORTER, Henry M. "Freighting and Merchandising in Early Denver." COLORADO MAGAZINE 6(Sept 1929): 171-73. Freight.

_____. PENCILINGS OF AN EARLY WESTERN PIONEER. Denver: Author, 1929. Telegraph.

PORTER, James R. Reminiscences. NBHIST. Freight.

PORTER, Lavinia H. BY OX TEAM TO CALIFORNIA. Oakland: Enquirer, 1910. CAL(St. Jo)-CHEROKEE(Denver-Ft. Laramie)-BRIDGER-SIMPSON. II. Rem. 1860.

PORTER, Nathan S. Diary. Washington State Historical Society Library, Tacoma, WA. CAL(St. Jo?)-BRIDGER-SLCUT. V. 1853.

PORTER, William. Diary. Illinois State Historical Library, Springfield, IL. OR(St. Jo)-BARLOW. III. 1848.

POST, Charles C. "The Arkansas Route." In OVERLAND ROUTES TO THE GOLD FIELDS, 1859, ed. LeRoy R. Hafen. Southwest Historical Series, No. 11. Glendale: Clark, 1942. PIKES. II. 1859.

POST, Lauren C. "Red River Carts." SAN DIEGO WESTERNERS BRAND BOOK 1(1968): 75-82. Eqpt.

"Postmaster General's Order Relating to Route of the Overland Mail Company, March 12, 1861." Paul & Helen Henderson Collection, UWY. Mail.

"Postmen of a Century." QUARTERLY SOCIETY CALIFORNIA PIONEERS 2(Sept 1925): 135-53. Mail.

POTTER, David M., ed. TRAIL TO CALIFORNIA: THE OVERLAND JOURNAL OF VINCENT GEIGER AND WAKEMAN BRYARLY. Yale Historical Publications, Manuscripts and Edited Texts, XX. New Haven: Yale Univ. Press, 1945. CAL(St. Jo)-HALL-TRUCKEE. I. 1849.

POTTER, Jack M. CATTLE TRAILS OF THE OLD WEST. Clayton, NM: Krehbie, 1939. Stock.

POTTER, Theodore E. THE AUTOBIOGRAPHY OF THEODORE

EDGAR POTTER. Concord, NH: Private, 1913. CAL(St. Jo)-TRUCKEE-BECK. II+. Rem. 1852.

POURADE, Richard F. THE COLORFUL BUTTERFIELD OVERLAND STAGE. Palm Desert, CA: Best-West, 1966. Stage-Graphics.

POWELL, A. Kent. SEE: Peterson, Charles. MORMON BATTALION TRAIL GUIDE.

POWELL, Donald M. Ed. Browne, J. Ross. ADVENTURES.

POWELL, H. M. THE SANTA FE TRAIL TO CALIFORNIA, 1849 - 1852. Ed. Douglas S. Watson. SF: Book Club, 1931. CAL(Indep)SANTA FE-RIO GRANDE-GILA. I. 1849. Graphics.

POWELL, J. A. Diary. ORU. OR(Ft. Hall to John Day River). V. 1851.

POWELL, John W. Diary. BANCROFT. CAL(Plattsmouth)-BRIDGER-SLCUT. III+. 1859.

POWELL, Kate P., ed. "Our Covered Wagons." Oregon State Library, Salem, OR. OR. V. 1851.

POWELL, Kent. "Western Overland Trail Guides, 1842 - 1865." In David E. Miller Papers, UTHIST. Guide.

POWELL, M. "Overland Journey to California." In GOLD! GOLD!, ed. Lowell Klappholz. NY: McBride, 1959. CAL(St. Jo to Ft. Kearny). III. 1849.

POWELL, Philander. History of Philander Powell's Trip across the Plains from Arkansas to California. ORU. CAL(Fayetteville)-SANTA FE-CHEROKEE(Pueblo-SLC)-SIMPSON. II+. 1860.

POWER, Bertha K. WILLIAM HENRY KNIGHT. N.p.: Private, 1932. CAL(St. Jo)-BRIDGER-SLCUT. V. 1859.

POWERS, Alfred, ed. POEMS OF THE COVERED WAGONS. Portland: Pacific, 1947. Social.

POWERS, Laura B. "The California Historical Landmark League." OVERLAND 40(Nov 1902): 472-73. Pres.

POWERS, Mary R. A WOMAN'S OVERLAND JOURNAL TO CALIFORNIA. Ed. W. B. Thorsen. Reprint. Fairfield, WA: Ye Galleon, 1985. CAL(Council)-LASSEN. I. 1856. Rare, insightful story of a woman on the trail under protest. UTAH. TRAIN GOVT.

POWERS, Otero, Lowe & Co. Letters. KSHIST. Freight.

POWERS, Ramon, and Gene Younger. "Cholera on the Overland Trails, 1832 - 1869." KANSAS QUARTERLY 5(Spr 1973): 32-49. Medical.

_____. "Cholera on the Plains: The Epidemic of 1867." KANSAS HISTORICAL QUARTERLY 37 (Win 1971): 351-93. Medical.

POWERS, Stephen. AFOOT AND ALONE. Hartford, CN: Columbian, 1872. CAL-MEX-GILA. II. 1868.

POWERS, Thomas C. Papers. MONHIST. Freight.

POWERS, W. P. SOME ANNALS OF THE POWERS FAMILY.... LA: N.p., 1924. CAL. 1856. Not Seen.

POWNALL, Joseph. "From Louisiana to Mariposa." In RUSHING FOR GOLD, ed. John W. Caughey. Berkeley: Univ. of California Press, 1949. CAL-TEX-MEX(El Paso-Chihuahua-Santa Cruz)-GILA. IV. 1849.

PRATELLES, V. M. "Sufferings of the Overland Emigrants in 1849."

OVERLAND MONTHLY 62(Oct 1913): 345-49. 1849-Genl.

PRATT, Addison. "Diaries." In JOURNALS OF THE FORTY-NINERS, eds. Leroy and Ann W. Hafen. Far West and the Rockies Historical Series 1820 - 1875, vol. 2. Glendale: Clark, 1954. SLCOR. II. 1849.

PRATT, Harry E. Ed. Lewis, Edward. "Diary of a Pike's Peak Gold Seeker."

PRATT, John J. and Hunt. A GUIDE TO THE GOLD MINES OF KANSAS. Chicago: C. Scott, 1859. Guide.

PRATT, Orson. THE ORSON PRATT JOURNALS. Ed. Elden J. Watson. SLC: Watson, 1975. MORMON. II. 1849.

PRATT, Orville C. "Diary." In OLD SPANISH TRAIL, eds. LeRoy and Ann W. Hafen. Far West and the Rockies Historical Series, vol. 1. Glendale: Clark, 1954. SPANISH. II. 1848.

PRATT, Parley P. AUTOBIOGRAPHY OF PARLEY PARKER PRATT. Ed. Parley P. Pratt, II. SLC: Deseret News, 1950. SLCOR. II. 1851.

PRATT, Sarah. Jottings. CSL. CAL(Council)-SLCOR. III. 1852.

PREAMBLE AND CONSTITUTION OF THE COLONY GUARD. In John Hudson. A FORTY-NINER IN UTAH, ed. Brigham D. Madsen. No. 11, Utah, the Mormons, and the West. SLC: Univ. of Utah Tanner Trust Fund, 1981. TRAIN GOVT.

PRENTICE, Eliza and Margaret. SEE: "Eliza and Margaret Prentice's Trip."

PRENTISS, William. Letters. BANCROFT. CAL(St. Jo). V. 1850.

PRESTON, Leander A. Items of Travel. CSL. SIMPSON. III. 1861.

_____. "Journal of Leander A. Preston - 1860-61." PONY EXPRESS 14(Mar 1948): 4-5, 13. CAL(Council)-Ends SLC. IV. 1860. CAL-SIMPSON. IV. 1861.

PRESTON, R. N., comp. EARLY WASHINGTON: OVERLAND STAGE ROUTES. OLD MILITARY ROADS. INDIAN BATTLE GROUNDS. OLD FORTS. OLD GOLD MINES. Corvallis, OR: Western Guide, 1974. Maps.

_____. HISTORICAL OREGON. Portland: Author, 1972. Excellent map series from territorial period to present.

_____. EARLY IDAHO ATLAS. Portland: Binford & Mort, 1978. Maps.

_____. MAPS OF EARLY IDAHO. Corvallis, OR: Western Guide, 1972. Maps.

PRESTON, Richard A. Ed. Thomson, James. FOR FRIENDS AT HOME.

PREUSS, Charles. EXPLORING WITH FREMONT. Eds. E. G. & E. K Gudde. Norman: Univ. of Oklahoma Press, 1958. Govt.

_____. TOPOGRAPHICAL MAP OF THE ROAD FROM MISSOURI TO OREGON.... Baltimore: E. Weber, 1846. Guide.

PRICE, Glenn. Ed. Brady, Charles C. "From Hannibal to the GOld Fields."

PRICE, Hugh M. and Franklin. Diary. Jackson County Historical Library, Independence, MO. CAL(Indep)-HALL. 1849. Not Seen.

PRICE, Joseph. "The Road to California: Letters of Joseph Price." Ed. Thomas M. Marshall. MISSISSIPPI VALLEY HISTORICAL REVIEW 11(Sept 1924): 237-57. CAL(St. Jo)-Ends Pacific Springs. II. 1850.

PRICE, Ralph B., Jr. "The Federal Government and Emigrant Roads through Northern Territories to the Far West, 1856 - 1866." MA thesis, Univ. of Colorado-Boulder, 1939. Govt.

PRICKETT, Jacob P. "In Quest of Gold." Newspaper clippings. DENVERPUB. CAL(St. Jo). 1853. Not Seen.

PRICHET, John. Diary. BANCROFT. CAL(Indep)-TRUCKEE. II. 1849.

PRIES, Nancy. SEE: With Laura Arksey and Marcia Reed. AMERICAN DIARIES.

PRIMES, Ed. M. Journal. Society of California Pioneers, SF. CAL(Council)-BRIDGER-HASTINGS-TRUCKEE. 1850. Not Seen.

PRINGLE, Catherine S. "Seven Orphans on the Oregon Trail, 1844." Ed. Harry M. Majors. NORTHWEST DISCOVERY 1(Dec 1980): 314-60. OR(St. Jo). IV. Rem. 1844.

PRINGLE, Virgil. "Diary." In OVERLAND IN 1846, ed. Dale L. Morgan. Georgetown, CAL: Talisman, 1963. OR(Indep)-APPLE. III. 1846.

PRITCHARD, J. A. "Diary of a Journey from Kentucky to California, 1849." MISSOURI HISTORICAL REVIEW 18(Jul 1924): 535-45. CAL(Indep to St. Jo road). III. 1849.

PRITCHARD, James A. THE OVERLAND DIARY OF JAMES A. PRITCHARD FROM KENTUCKY TO CALIFORNIA IN 1849. Ed. Dale L. Morgan. Denver: Old West, 1959. CAL(Indep)-HALL. I. 1849.

PRITCHARD, J. L. Comp. Cathey, Andrew. "The Cathey Wagon Train." TRAIL 4(Sept, Oct 1911): 5-16, 5-11. PIKES. III. Rem. 1859.

PROCTOR, Arthur W. SEE: Driggs, Howard, et al. COVEREDWAGON CENTENNIAL.

PROPST, Nell B. FORGOTTEN PEOPLE: A HISTORY OF THE SOUTH PLATTE TRAIL. Boulder, CO: Pruett, 1979. PIKES-Genl. Maps.

PROSCH, Thomas W. Ed. McCarver, D. M. MCCARVER AND TACOMA.
Ed. Maynard, David and Catherine. BIOGRAPHIES.

_____. "Efforts to Save the Historic McLoughlin House." WASHINGTON HISTORICAL QUARTERLY 1(Jan 1907): 36-42. Pres.

_____. "The Military Roads of Washington Territory." WASHINGTON HISTORICAL QUARTERLY 2(Jan 1908): 118-26. Military.

_____. "The United States Army in Washington Territory." WASHINGTON HISTORICAL QUARTERLY 2(Oct 1907): 28-32. Military.

_____. "Washington Mail Routes in 1857." WASHINGTON HISTORICAL QUARTERLY 6(Apr 1915): 107-08. Mail.

"Protection Afforded Volunteers of Oregon and Washington Territories to Overland Immigrants in 1854." 35th Cong., 2d sess. H. Misc. Doc. 47. Govt. Military. Indians.

PRUCHA, Francis P. A BIBLIOGRAPHICAL GUIDE TO THE HISTORY OF INDIAN-WHITE RELATIONS IN THE UNITED STATES. Chicago: Univ. of Chicago Press, 1977. Bib.

_____. INDIAN-WHITE RELATIONS IN THE UNITED STATES: A BIBLIOGRAPHY OF WORKS PUBLISHED 1975 - 1980. Lincoln: Univ. of Nebraska Press, 1982. Bib.

PUCKETT, Henry. Diary. In Paul & Helen Henderson Collection, UWY. CAL(Ash Hollow to Upper Platte). V-. 1850.

PUGH, Byron G. "History of Utah-California Wagon Freighting." MA thesis, Univ. of California-Berkeley, 1943. MORMON-Genl. Freight. CAL-Genl.

PULLING, Hazel A. "A History of California's Range-Cattle Industry, 1770 - 1912." PhD diss., Univ. of Southern California, 1944. Stock.

PULSIPHER, John. Diary. BYU. MORMON. IV. 1850. MORMON. III. 1852.

PUMPELLY, Raphael. ACROSS AMERICA AND ASIA. NY: Leypoldt & Holt, 1871. Stage-St. Louis to Santa Rita. III. 1860. Stage-Santa Rita to SF. III. 1861.

PURCELL, Polly J. AUTOBIOGRAPHY AND REMINISCENCES OF A PIONEER. Freewater, OR?: Author, 1922. OR(St. Jo). V. Rem. 1846.

PURDY, John R., Jr. Ed. Owen, Isaac. "Overland."

_____. "A Manuscript Map of an Overland Journey from Salt Lake City to Sacramento City." WESTERN HISTORICAL QUARTERLY 6(Jan 1975): 47-62. Guide.

PURVIANCE, M. C. Journal. BEINECKE. CAL(Council)-CHEROKEE(Denver-SLC)-SLCUT-TRUCKEE-Crosses Sierra via Carson Pass. II. 1863.

PUTNAM, Joseph P. "Letters to the HARTFORD (CN) EVENING PRESS, 1863 - 1866." BANCROFT? CAL(Leav-SANTA FE-BEALE-Ends Navajo Springs. II. 1863. CAL-BEALE(Little Colorado River)-GILA. II. 1864. GILA(Yuma-La Paz). II. 1865. BRADSHAW(La Paz-LA)-OR-CAL(LA-Portland). II. 1866. Stage-SF to SLC. II. 1866.

PUTNAM, Royal P. THE JOURNAL OF ROYAL PORTER PUTNAM, SEPT, 1857 - JULY, 1860. Porterville, CA: Farm Tribune, 1961. CAL-TEX(San Antonio-El Paso)-GILA. II. 1858. Stock drive.

PYEATT, J. Rankin. "Some Pyeatt Letters." Washington County [AR] Historical Society FLASHBACK 23(May 1973): 9-36. CAL(Fayetteville)-CHEROKEE(to SLC). III. 1849.

QUAIFE, Milo M. Ed. Bidwell, John. ECHOES OF THE PAST. Ed. Shaw, Reuben. ACROSS THE PLAINS.

QUAIL. "Journal of an Overland Trip to Oregon." In Paul & Helen Henderson Collection, UWY. OR(Council)-BRIDGER-SLCUT-HALL. II. 1853.

QUESENBURY, William. "William Quesenbury's Diary." Ed. Pat Donat. Washington County [AR] County Historical Society FLASHBACK 29(Feb, May, Aug, Nov 1979): 11-15, 18-24; 11-19, 38-40; 15-17, 30-40; 1-4, 21-27. CAL(Grand Saline, OK)-CHEROKEE(to SLC)-SLCUT. II+. 1850.

RABER, Charles. "Recollections." Ed. William A. Goff. WESTPORT

HISTORICAL QUARTERLY 7(Dec, 1971; Mar, 1972): 7-23, 3-20. Freight.

_____. "Personal Recollections of Life on the Plains from 1866 to 1868." KANSAS HISTORICAL COLLECTIONS 16(1923-1925): 316-41. Freight.

RABBISON, A. B. Growth of Towns. BANCROFT. OR(Indep). IV. 1846.

RAGEN, Mary E. Recounts Her Parents' Trip from Omaha to Virginia City, 1864. MONHIST. 1864. Not Seen.

RAHM, Louise M. Diary. Washington State Historical Society Library, Tacoma, WA. OR(Council). III. 1862.

RAHT, Charles G. "The Chihuahua Trail." FRONTIER TIMES 26(Mar 1949): 119-23. RIO GRANDE-Genl.

RAILLEY, Egbert. Journal. Weston Public Library, Weston, MO. Freight.

RAINEY, Mary C. "The Development of Transportation in the Red River Valley." MNHIST. DAKOTAS-Genl.

RAMAGE, Helen. "The Wilkes Exploring Expedition on the Pacific Slope, 1841." MA thesis, Univ. of California-Berkeley, 1916. CAL-1841-Genl. OR-1841-Genl.

RAMBO, Ralph. TRAILING THE CALIFORNIA BANDIT TIBUR-CIO VASQUEZ, 1835 - 1875. Pioneer Series No. 3. San Jose: Author, 1968. Stage.

RAMEY, Earl. "The Beginnings of Marysville - Part I." CALIFORNIA HISTORICAL QUARTERLY 14(Sept, Dec 1935): 195-229, 375-407; 15(Mar 1936): 21-57. Geog.

RAMIREZ, J. P. to J. M. Edmunds, Los Angeles, CA. February 28, 1863. Record Group 49, Letter Copy Book, April 1853 - July 1880, Vol. 1. Ninth Regional Office, National Archives, Laguna Miguel, CA. CAL-Genl(Southern CA roads).

RAMSAY, Alexander. "Alexander Ramsay's Gold Rush Diary of 1849." Ed. Merrill J. Mattes. PACIFIC HISTORICAL REVIEW 43(Nov 1949): 437-68. CAL(St. Jo)-HALL-LASSEN. III. 1849.

RAMSEY, Bobby G. "Scientific Exploration and Discovery in the Great Basin from 1831 - 1891." PhD diss., BYU, 1972. Govt.

RAMSEY, Helen G. "The Historical Background of the Santa Fe Trail." MA thesis, Univ. of California-Berkeley, 1941. SANTA FE-Genl.

RAMSEY, James G. Papers. Univ. of Tennessee Library-SpCol, Knox-ville, TN. CAL(St. Jo)-SANTA FE-RIO GRANDE-GILA. III. 1849.

RAMSEY, Jerry B. "Fort Hays: An Analysis of the Federal Government's Military Activities on the Kansas Plains." MA thesis, Fort Hays [Kansas] State College, 1972. Military.

RAMSEY, W. Wilberforce. SEE: Noel, Thomas A. "W. Wilberforce A. Ramsey."

RAMSTED, David A. Ed: Byars, William H. "Carrying the Mail in Southern Oregon."

RANAHAN, Thomas. OVERLAND STAGE AND PONY EXPRESS. N.p.: Private, 1927. Pony. Stage.

RANDALL, Andrew. Diary. CSL. SANTA FE(Westport). II+. 1849.

RANDALL, Benjamin. Across the United States - 1862. Held by R. S. Weeks, Glen Ellyn, IL. Not Seen.

RANDALL, J. D. Diary. NBHIST. CAL(Westport)-LANDER-NOBLE. 1852. Not Seen.

RANDALL, P. K. TRAVELLER'S COMPANION AND GUIDE WESTWARD. Boston: Randall, 1860. Guide.

RANDOLPH, W. C. Statement. BANCROFT. CAL(Indep)-SANTA FE-CHEROKEE(Pueblo-SLC)-SLCOR. V. 1849.

RANKIN, Alexander T. ALEXANDER TAYLOR RANKIN, 1803 - 1885, HIS DIARY AND LETTERS. Ed. Nolie Mumey. Boulder, CO: Johnson, 1966. Stage-St. Jo to Denver. III. 1860.

RANSDELL, Shelton. Wagon Train Journal of the Oregon Trail. Ed. John D. Ellingsen. MONHIST. OR(Kansas City). III. 1850.

RASMUSSEN, Louise. "Artists of the Explorations Overland, 1840 - 1860." OREGON HISTORICAL QUARTERLY 43(Mar 1942): 56-62. Graphics.

RATH, Charles. THE RATH TRAIL: NON-FICTION BIOGRAPHY OF CHARLES RATH. Ed. Ida E. Rath. Wichita, KS: McCormick-Armstrong, 1961. SANTA FE-Genl. Stock-Genl.

RATH, Ida E. Ed. Rath, Charles. THE RATH TRAIL.

RATLIFF, Cecelia B. "Early-Day Transportation." HUMBOLDT HIS-TORIAN 3(Fall 1980): 19-23. Freight.

RAULSTON, Marion C. Ed. Churchill, Willoughby. MEMORIES.

RAVOUX, Augustin V. REMINISCENCES, MEMOIRS AND LEC-TURES. St. Paul: Brown, Treacy, 1890. DAKOTA-Genl.

RAWLING, Gerald. "The Oregon Trail." HISTORY TODAY 11(Nov 1961): 743-52. OR-Genl.

RAY, Asa. Letters. MNHIST. CAL(Council)-BOZE. II. 1864.

RAYMOND, A. E. Diary. COHIST. PIKES. 1859. Not Seen.

RAYMOND, Sarah. SEE: Settle, Raymond & Mary. OVERLAND DAYS.

RAYNER, James O. Journal. Princeton Univ. Library-Western History, Princeton, NJ. OR(Council). III+. 1847.

RAYNESFORD, Howard C. SEE: Lee, Wayne and Howard C. Raynes-ford. TRAILS OF THE SMOKY HILL.

RAYNOR, James. Journal of a Tour from Iowa to Oregon, April 1847. ORHIST. OR. III. 1847.

REA, J. "Seeing the Elephant." WESTERN FOLKLORE 28(Jan 1969): 21-26. Social-Explains term.

REA, Jonathan, I. SEE: "Jonathan Rea I."

REA, Ralph R. "The Mountain Meadows Massacre and its Completion as a Historic Episode." ARIZONA HISTORICAL QUARTERLY 16(Win 1957): 28-45. SLCOR-1857-Genl. Geog.

READ, B. M. "Ben Ficklin 1849 and the Pony Express." VIRGINIA MILITARY INSTITUTE ALUMNI REVIEW 49(1972): 13. Pony. Biog.

READ, Donald E. "The Development of a Northern Route to the Pacific." MA thesis, Univ. of Minnesota, 1931. Overland-Genl.

READ, George W. A PIONEER OF 1850. Boston: Little, Brown, 1927. CAL(Indep). III. 1850.

READ, Georgia W. Ed. Bruff, Joseph G. GOLD RUSH. Ed. Read, George W. A PIONEER OF 1850.

_____. "Bruff's Route in Eastern California." CALIFORNIA HISTORICAL QUARTERLY 39(Sept 1960): 263-66. LASSEN. III. 1850.

_____. "Diseases, Drugs and Doctors on the Oregon-California Trail in the Gold-Rush Years." MISSOURI HISTORICAL REVIEW 38(Jan 1944): 260-74. Medical.
_____. "Women and Children on the Oregon-California Trail in the Gold-Rush Years." MISSOURI HISTORICAL REVIEW 39(Oct 1944): 1-23. Social.

_____, and R. Gaines. Eds. Bruff, Joseph G. GOLD RUSH.

READ, Martha S. "History." In COVERED WAGON WOMEN, vol. 5. Eds. Kenneth L. Holmes and David C. Duniway. Glendale: Clark, 1986. OR(Council). III+. 1852.

READING, Pierson B. "Journal of Pierson Barton Reading." Ed. Philip B. Bekeart. QUARTERLY SOCIETY CALIFORNIA PIONEERS 7(Sept 1930): 148-98. CAL(Westport)-BRIDGER-HALL. II. 1843.

REAGAN, Albert B. "Forts Robidoux and Kit Carson in Northeastern Utah." NEW MEXICO HISTORICAL REVIEW 10(Jan 1935): 121-32. Geog.

REASONER, Henry A. Account of Trip across the Plains in 1852. ORHIST. OR(Council). IV. Rem. 1852.

REBBING, Virginia L. "Some Aspects of the Southern Overland Mail, 1857-1861." MISSOURI HISTORICAL REVIEW 40(Jul 1946): 481-502. Stage.

_____. "The Southern Overland Mail, 1857 - 1861." MA thesis, Washington Univ., 1943. Stage(Butterfield). Mail.

REBER, Bruce. THE UNITED STATES ARMY AND THE INDIAN WARS IN THE TRANS-MISSISSIPPI WEST, 1866 - 1898. Special Bibliography 17. Carlisle Barracks, PA: U.S. Army Military History Institute, 1978. Bib.

REBER, Thomas. "The Journal of Thomas Reber." Ed. Albert M. Tewksbury. MA thesis, Claremont Colleges, 1935. CAL(St. Jo). II+. 1854. Stock drive.

"Recollections of Sarah Francis Zumwalt Hammitt." LANE COUNTY HISTORIAN 16(Fall 1971): 53-56. CAL(Indep)-Ends SLC. V-. 1850. OR(SLC to Ft. Hall). V-. 1851.

RECONNAISSANCES OF ROUTES FROM SAN ANTONIO TO EL PASO. 31st Cong., 1st sess. S. Ex. Doc. 64. TEX-Genl.

"A Record Trip from California to Missouri." MISSOURI HISTORICAL REVIEW 24(Jul 1930): 608. Eqpt.

RECTOR, William H. "Biography of William H. Rector." Eds. Fred Lockley and J. Neilson Barry. OREGON HISTORICAL QUARTERLY 30(Mar 1929): 63-69. OR(Indep). IV. 1845.

REDDEMANN, Ahle. THE HENDERSON TO FORT RIDGELEY TRAIL. N.p.: Sibley County Historical Society, 1976. DAKOTAS-Genl.

REDFIELD, Francis M. REMINISCENCES. Pocatello, ID: N.p., 1949. OR. 1862. Not Seen.

REDGRAVE, Stephen. Journal. Province of British Columbia Archives, Victoria, BC. CANADA-Overland. 1859. Not Seen.

REDINGTON, Edward S. Diary. MNHIST. CAL(Council). III. 1850.

_____. Letters. MNHIST. CAL(Council)-SLCUT. V. 1853.

REDMAN, J. T. Reminiscences. NEWBERRY. CAL(St. Jo)-SIMPSON. IV. Rem. 1863.

REDPATH, James, and Richard J. Hinton. HAND-BOOK TO KANSAS TERRITORY AND THE ROCKY MOUNTAINS' GOLD REGION. NY: J. H. Colton, 1859. First-rate guide.

REED, F. S. Diary. BYU. CAL(St. Jo). II-. 1850.

REED, Henry E. Ed. Lovejoy, Asa. "Asa Lovejoy's."

REED, Jacob W. MAP OF AND GUIDE TO THE KANSAS GOLD REGION. NY: J. H. Colton, 1859. Excellent map. Guide.

REED, James F. Correspondence. BANCROFT. CAL-1846-Genl.

_____. "Diary." In DONNER MISCELLANY, ed. Carroll D. Hall. SF: Book Club, 1947. CAL(Indep)-BRIDGER-HASTINGS-Ends Battle Mountain, NV. III-. 1846. TRUCKEE. II. 1847.

_____. "Narrative of the Sufferings of a Company of Emigrants." ILLINOIS JOURNAL, 9 Dec 1847, n.p. CAL-1846-Genl.

_____. "The Snow-Bound Starved Emigrants of 1846." PACIFIC RURAL PRESS, March 25 - April 1, 1871, pp. 195-96. CAL-1846-Genl.

REED, Lester. OLD TIME CATTLEMEN AND OTHER PIONEERS OF THE ANZA-BORREGO AREA. Palm Desert, CA: Author, 1963. Stock.

REED, Marcia. SEE: With Laura Arksey and Nancy Pries. AMERICAN DIARIES.

REED, Marjorie. THE BUTTERFIELD OVERLAND STAGE ACROSS ARIZONA. N.p.: Reed, 1979. Stage-Graphics.

_____. THE BUTTERFIELD OVERLAND STAGE IN OKLAHOMA, ARKANSAS AND MISSOURI. Tombstone, AZ?: Reed, c1982. Stage-Graphics.

_____. THE BUTTERFIELD OVERLAND STAGE THROUGH NEW MEXICO AND TEXAS. Bozeman, MT: Reed, 1980. Stage-Graphics.

_____. THE COLORFUL BUTTERFIELD OVERLAND STAGE. San Diego: Union-Tribune, 1971. Stage-Graphics.

REED, T. S. Diary. BYU. CAL(St. Jo). 1850. Not Seen.

REED, Virginia E. A HAPPY ISSUE; THE HITHERTO UNPUBLISHED LETTER OF A CHILD...SURVIVOR OF THE DONNER-REED PARTY. Palo Alto, CA: De Wolf, 1935. CAL-1846-Genl.

REED, William. "From San Diego to Tucson: A Glimpse of Stage Stations, People, Trails and Transportation." SAN DIEGO WESTERNERS BRANDBOOK 1(1968): 126-36. GILA-Genl.

REEDER, Ray M. "The Mormon Trail: A History of the Salt Lake to

Los Angeles Route to 1869." PhD diss., BYU, 1966. SLCOR-Genl. Freight. SPANISH-Genl. Mail. Telegraph. Military.

REES, Decatur S. Reminiscences. KSHIST. Freight-Eqpt.

REEVE, Clayton and Rebecca. "From Tennessee to California in 1849: Letters of the Reeve Family of Medford, New Jersey." Ed. O. O. Winter. JOURNAL OF THE RUTGERS UNIVERSITY LIBRARY 2(Jun 1948): 33-84. CAL(Indep)-LASSEN. III. 1849.

REEVE, Frank D. Ed. Driver, William. "London to Salt Lake City."

REEVES, Elijah. Reminiscence. BANCROFT. Attributed to BANCROFT but uncataloged.

REEVES, Robert N. "Famous Pony Express Riders." OVERLAND MONTHLY 68(Dec 1916): 525-27. Pony.

REHLWINKEL, Frederick. Autobiography. BEINECKE. OR(Council)-BRIDGER-SLCUT-BARLOW. III. Rem. 1866. Military.

REID, Alfred D., Jr. Ed. Reid, Bernard J. "A California Gold Rush Letter."

REID, Bernard J. "A California Gold Rush Letter from Bernard J. Reid." Eds. James D. Van Trump and Alfred D. Reid, Jr. WESTERN PENNSYLVANIA HISTORICAL MAGAZINE 44(Sept 1961): 217-35. CAL(Indep). III. 1849.

_____. OVERLAND TO CALIFORNIA WITH THE PIONEER LINE. Ed. Mary M. Gordon. Stanford: Stanford Univ. Press, 1983. CAL(Indep). II. 1849. Maps.

REID, H. Lorenzo. BRIGHAM YOUNG'S DIXIE OF THE DESERT EXPLORATION AND SETTLEMENT. SLC: Zion Natural History Asson., 1964. SLCOR-Genl.

REID, James D. THE TELEGRAPH IN AMERICA. NY: Derby Bros., 1879. Telegraph.

REID, John C. REID'S TRAMP.... Selma, AL: Author, 1858. CAL-TEX(Galveston-El Paso)-GILA. II+. 1857.

REID, John P. "Binding the Elephant: Contracts and Legal Obligations on the Overland Trail." AMERICAN JOURNAL OF LEGAL HISTORY 21(1977): 285-315. Train Govt.

_____. "Dividing the Elephant: The Separation of Mess and Joint Stock Propety on the Overland Trail." HASTINGS LAW REVIEW 28(Sept 1976): 79-92. Train Govt.

_____. "Governance of the Elephant: Constitutional Theory on the Overland Trail." HASTINGS CONSTITUTIONAL LAW QUARTERLY 5(1978): 421-43. Train Govt.

_____. "Knowing the Elephant: Distinguishing Property Rights on the Overland Trail." CREIGHTON LAW REVIEW 10(1977): 640-54. Social.

_____. LAW FOR THE ELEPHANT: PROPERTY AND SOCIAL BEHAVIOR ON THE OVERLAND TRAIL. San Marino: Huntington, 1980. Train Govt.

_____. "Paying for the Elephant: Property Rights and Civil Order on the Overland Trail." HUNTINGTON LIBRARY QUARTERLY 41(Nov 1977): 37-64. Train Govt.

_____. "Replenishing the Elephant: Property and Survival on the Overland Trail." OREGON HISTORICAL QUARTERLY 79(1978): 65-90. Social.

_____. "Sharing the Elephant: Partnership and Concurrent Property on the Overland Trail." UNIVERSITY OF MISSOURI-KANSAS CITY LAW REVIEW 45(1976): 207-22. Social.

_____. "Tied to the Elephant: Organization and Obligation on the Overland Trail." UNIVERSITY OF PUGENT SOUND LAW REVIEW 1(1977): 139-59. Train Govt.

REID, Lawson P. Diary. Ohio Historical Society Library, Columbus, OH. CAL(Council)-LASSEN. IV. 1854.

REID, Robie L. "British Columbia: A Bibliographical Sketch." PAPERS OF THE BIBLIOGRAPHICAL SOCIETY OF AMERICA 3(1929): 20-44. Bib.

_____. "The Whatcom Trails to the Fraser River Mines in 1858." WASHINGTON HISTORICAL QUARTERLY 18(Jul, Oct 1927): 199-206, 271-76. WASH-Genl.

REINFELD, Fred. PONY EXPRESS. Lincoln: Univ. of Nebraska Press, 1973. Pony.

REINHART, Herman F. THE GOLDEN FRONTIER. Ed. Doyce B. Nunis, Jr. One of the Personal Narratives of the West. Austin: Univ. of Texas Press, 1962. CAL(Council)-LASSEN. III. Rem. 1851. Freight-Idaho, Montana.

REINHARTZ, Dennis, and Charles C. Colley. THE MAPPING OF THE AMERICAN SOUTHWEST. College Station: Texas A&M Press, 1986. Map.

"Re-Making Western Trails." MAGAZINE OF HISTORY 3(N.d.): 239. Pres. Not Seen.

REMARKS OF HON. JOHN CESSNA...IN EXPLANATION OF HIS OWN ACTION IN THE CASE OF GEORGE CHORPENNING. WA: Congressional Globe Office, c1879. Mail.

"Reminder of the Days of the Pony Express." LITERARY DIGEST 77, 14 Apr 1923, 60-62. Pony.

"Reminiscences of an Overland Trip." FRASER'S MAGAZINE 40(N.d.): 82. Overland-Genl. Not Seen.

REMSBURG, George J. "Bull Wagon Bosses." PONY EXPRESS COURIER, Jul 1936, pp. 8, 12. Freight.

_____. "General Bela M. Hughes, Attorney for 'The Overland'." PONY EXPRESS COURIER, May 1937, pp. 6-7.

_____. "Pony Express Riders I Have Known." PONY EXPRESS, Sept, Oct, Nov, Dec 1934, 8, 6, 6, 13; Jan, Feb, Mar 1935, 19, 11, 5-8. Pony.

_____. "The Wind Wagon." PONY EXPRESS COURIER 3(Oct 1936): 19-20. Eqpt.

REMY, Jules, and Julius Brenchley. A JOURNEY TO GREAT-SALT-LAKE CITY. 2 vols. London: W. Jeffs, 1861. CAL(East from Sacramento)-HASTINGS-End SLC. I. 1855. Possibly part-fiction or hoax.

"Renewal of Interest in the Pony Express." REVIEW OF REVIEWS 68(Oct 1923): 433-34. Pres.

RENNER, Pamela. "La Paz - Gateway to Territorial Arizona." JOURNAL ARIZONA HISTORY 24(Sum 1983): 119-44. Geog. BRADSHAW-Genl.

RENSCH, Hero E. "Lassator's in Green Valley." SAN DIEGO HISTORICAL QUARTERLY 3(Apr 1957): 18-24. Geog.

_____. "Woods' Shorter Mountain Trail to San Diego." CALIFOR-NIA HISTORICAL SOCIETY 36(Jun 1957): 117-32. Stage.

RENSHAW, Robert H. Diary. ORHIST. OR(St. Jo?). III. 1851.

REPORT OF CAPTAIN R. B. MARCY'S ROUTE FROM FORT SMITH TO SANTA FE. 31st Cong., 1st sess. S. Ex. Doc. 64. Govt.

REPORT OF THE AGENTS OF CALIFORNIA RELIEF EXPEDI-TION. CA. State S. Doc. No. 8. Session of 1853. Sacramento: State Printer, 1853. CAL-1853-Genl.

REPORT OF THE POSTMASTER GENERAL. (1 Dec 1857). 35th Cong., 1st sess. S. Ex. Doc. 11. Serial 921, pp. 965, 986-1011. Govt.

_____. (3 Mar 1859). 35th Cong., 2d sess. S. Ex. Doc. 48. Serial 984, pp. 1-12. Butterfield contract, Route 12578.

"Report on Memorial of George H. Giddings." 36th Cong., 2d sess. S. Misc. Doc. 15. Serial 1089, pp. 1-9.

"Reports of Indian Trouble. Compiled from Early Utah Newspapers in the FIles of the Salt Lake City Library, 1859 - 1864." UTHIST. In-dians.

REPORTS OF THE SECRETARY OF WAR. "Report of Captain R. B. Marcy." 31st Cong., 1st sess. S. Ex. Doc. 64. Serial 562. MARCY. II. 1849.

_____. 31st Cong., 1st sess. S. Ex. Doc. 64. Serial 562. TEX(San An-tonio-El Paso). II. 1849.

RESOLUTION OF THE TEXAS LEGISLATURE, 9 FEB 1860. 36th Cong., 1st sess. S. Misc. Docs. 40. Serial 1038. Mail.

RESSLER, John J. "John Jacob Ressler's Trip to California in 1849." Ed. Cora R. Smith. In TRAILS DIVIDED, ed. Theodore Ressler. Wil-liamsburg, IA: Editor, 1964. CAL(Council)-LASSEN. V. Rem. 1849.

RESSLER, Theodore C., ed. PARTNERS IN THE GOLD RUSH: PARALLEL ACCOUNTS OF TWO FORTY-NINERS, ABRAHAM OWEN AND JOHN JACOB RESSLER. Williamsburg, IA: N.p., 1962. See following.

_____. TRAILS DIVIDED. Williamsburg, IA: Ressler, 1964. Over-land-1849-Genl. LASSEN-1849-Genl. SLCOR-1849-General.

REYNOLDS, Charles D. Reminiscences. BANCROFT. CAL(Indep)-HALL-TRUCKEE. IV. Rem. 1849.

REYNOLDS, Edgar. Journal. NBHIST. CAL(Council). II. 1852.

REYNOLDS, G. A. "From Iowa to Scott Valley - 1861." SISKIYOU PIONEER 2(1956): 37-38. CAL(Council)-NOBLES. V. 1861.

REYNOLDS, Henrietta. PIONEERS OF SAND - PLAINS IN SAN JOAQUIN COUNTY, CALIFORNIA. N.p.: N.p., 1953. CAL(Coun-cil). V. Rem. 1853.

REYNOLDS, James. A Trip across the Plains. CSL. CAL(Neb City?)-BRIDGER-SLCUT. III. 1853.

RHINEHART, J. B. "A Story of the Oregon Trail." OVERLAND MONTHLY 23(Feb 1894): 176-78. 1851 Indian attack along Snake River.

RHOADES, Daniel. Letters. BANCROFT. CAL-TRUCKEE. IV. 1846.

RHOADES, Earl. "Maps of Emigrant Trail, Verdi, Nevada to Summit Valley, California, as Marked and Traced by P. M. Weddell of San Jose, 1920 - 1952." Held by Dan Rhoads, Monterey, CA. Not Seen.

RHODES, Joseph. "Joseph Rhodes and the California Gold Rush of 1850." ANNALS OF WYOMING 23(Jan 1951): 52-71. CAL(Indep). III 1850

RICE, Josiah M. A CANNONEER IN NAVAJO COUNTRY...1851. Ed. Richard H. Dillon. Denver: Old West, 1970. SANTA FE-BEALE. III +. 1851.

RICE, Lee M., and Glenn R. Vernam. THEY SADDLED THE WEST. Cambridge, MD: Cornell Maritime Press, 1975. Graphics. Eqpt.

RICE, William B. "The Captivity of Olive Oatman - A Newspaper Ac-count." CALIFORNIA HISTORICAL QUARTERLY 21(Jun 1942): 97-102. GILA-Genl. Indians.

_____, ed. "Early Freighting on the Salt Lake - San Bernardino Trail." PACIFIC HISTORICAL REVIEW 11(Mar 1942): 73-80. SLCOR. III. 1854. Freight.

RICH, Charles C. "Diary." In JOURNALS OF THE FORTY-NINERS, eds. LeRoy and Ann W. Hafen. Glendale: Clark, 1954. SLCOR. III. 1849.

RICH, Margaret B. Ed. Bensell, Dr. "Reminiscence."

RICH, Sarah D. Journal. BYU. MORMON. IV. 1847.

RICHARD, John C. My Diary. LILLEY. CAL(Weston)-BRIDGER-SLCUT-Ends Deep Creek, UT. II. 1853.

RICHARDS, Silas. Diary. LDS. MORMON. 1849. Not Seen.

RICHARDSON, Albert D. "Albert D. Richardson's Letters on the Pike's Peak Gold Region." KANSAS HISTORICAL QUARTERLY 12(Feb 1943): 14-57. Stage: Atchison to Denver. II. 1860.

_____. BEYOND THE MISSISSIPPI.... Hartford, CN: American Publishing, 1867. Graphics.

RICHARDSON, Albert T. Ed. With H. M. Chittenden. LIFE, LET-TERS, AND TRAVELS.

RICHARDSON, Alpheus. Diary. UPAC. CAL(St. Jo)-TRUCKEE-BECK. II. 1852. Good Wadsworth-Reno description.

RICHARDSON, Augustus G. Letters. HUNTL. Stage.

RICHARDSON, Caroline L. Journal. BANCROFT. CAL(St. Jo)-SLCUT. II +. 1852.

RICHARDSON, Earle. THE RICHARDSON FAMILY: PIONEERS OF OREGON AND UTAH. Dallas, OR: Itemizer-Observer, 1940. OR. V-. 1847.

RICHARDSON, Mary E. STORY. Dalla, OR: N.p., 1929. OR. 1847. Not Seen.

RICHARDSON, Rupert N. ALONG TEXAS OLD FORTS TRAIL. Abilene, TX: Fry, c1972. TEX-Genl.

_____. "Some Details of the Southern Overland Mail." SOUTH-WESTERN HISTORICAL QUARTERLY 29(Jul 1925): 1-18. Stage.

_____. "The Southern Overland Mail, Conveyor of News, 1857 - 1861." WESTX 34(Oct 1958): 25-37. Stage.

RICHARDSON, William H. "The Argonauts of Jersey City." PROCEEDINGS New Jersey Historical Society 11(Apr, Jul, Oct 1926): 170-86, 369-77, 525-31. 1849-Genl.

RICHEY, James H. A TRIP ACROSS THE PLAINS IN 1854. Richey, CA: N.p., 1908. CAL(Plattsmouth)-TRUCKEE-BECK. IV. Rem. 1854. Stock.

RICHMOND, Robert W. "Developments along the Overland Trail from the Missouri River to Fort Laramie, before 1854." NEBRASKA HISTORY 33(Sept, Dec 1952): 154-79, 237-47. Fine description of trail, fords and campsites. Overland-Genl.

RICKARD, Ruth L. "The Gold Rush to California: 1848 - 1850." MA thesis, Univ. of California-Berkeley, 1926. CAL-Genl.

RICKARD, T. A. "The Fraser River Gold Rush." BEAVER, Sept 1924, 32-35. CANADA-Genl. Maps.

RICKER, J. G. Reminiscences. CSL. OR(Council)-BOZE(Into Montana and back to Snake River). IV. Rem. 1866.

RICKER, John J. "Iowa to Ventura County by Covered Wagon." Ed. Ella Ricker Lewis. VENTURA COUNTY HISTORICAL SOCIETY QUARTERLY 2(Feb 1957): 2-9. OR(Council)-BOZE(Into Montana and back to Snake River). V. 1866.

RICKETTS, Norma B. TRAGEDY SPRING AND THE POUCH OF GOLD. Sacramento: Ricketts, 1983. Geog: Carson Pass, 1848.

RICKEY, Thomas B. Diary. NVHIST. CAL(Council)-BRIDGER-SLCUT. V. 1852.

RICKS, Casper S. Diary. BANCROFT. CAL(Begins Albuquerque, NM)-RIO GRANDE-GILA. I. 1849.

RIDDLE, George W. EARLY DAYS IN OREGON. Myrtle Creek, OR: Riddle PTA, 1953. OR(Council)-APPLE. III. Rem. 1851.

RIDDLEMOSER, Francis M. "The Organization of Groups of Overland Emigrants to California, 1849 - 1850." MA thesis, Colorado College, 1964. Train Govt. Social.

RIDEING, William H. THE OVERLAND EXPRESS. Ashland, OR: Lewis Osborne, 1970. Graphics. Stage.

RIDGE, John R. "John Rollin Ridge Goes to California." Ed. Pat Donat. FLASHBACK Washington County [ARK] Historical Society 28(Feb, Aug 1978): 1-11, 11-14. CAL-CHEROKEE(Fayetteville to SLC)-SLCUT. IV. 1850.

RIDGEWAY, Arthur. "The Mission of Colorado Toll Roads." COLORADO MAGAZINE 9(Sept 1932): 161-69. PIKES-Genl.

RIEMAN, Leo. SEE: With Louis C. Coleman and B. C. Payette. CAPTAIN JOHN MULLAN.

RIESENBERG, Felix, Jr. THE GOLDEN ROAD: THE STORY OF CALIFORNIA'S MISSION TRAIL. NY: McGraw-Hill, 1962. CAL-Genl.

RIGGS, John L. "William H. Hardy: Merchant of the Upper Colorado." JOURNAL OF ARIZONA HISTORY 6(Win 1985): 177-87. Freight.

RIKER, John F. JOURNAL OF A TRIP TO CALIFORNIA.... Urbana, OH: N.p., 1855. CAL(Leav)-SLCUT. II. 1852.

RILEY, Glenda. "The Frontier in Process: Iowa's Trail Women as a Paradigm." ANNALS OF IOWA 46(Win 1982): 167-97. Social.

_____. "Frontierswomen's Changing Views of Indians in the Trans-Mississippi West." MONTANA 34(Win 1984): 20-35. Social. Indians.

_____. "The Spectre of a Savage: Rumors and Alarmism on the Overland Trail." WESTERN HISTORICAL QUARTERLY 15(Oct 1984): 427-44. Indians.

_____. WOMEN AND INDIANS ON THE FRONTIER, 1825 - 1915. Albuquerque: Univ. of New Mexico Press, c1984. Social. Indians.

_____. WOMEN ON THE AMERICAN FRONTIER: THE FORUM SERIES. St. Louis: Forum, 1977. Social.

RILEY, Harvey. THE MULE: A TREATISE ON THE BREEDING, TRAINING AND USES TO WHICH HE MAY BE PUT. Philadelphia: N.p., 1869. Teams.

RILEY, James F. RECOLLECTIONS. Independence, MO: Private, 1959. Freight: Indep. to SLC. III. Rem. 1859.

RINEY, Pamela L. "Overland to California and Oregon, 1849 - 1853: A Communal Venture." MA thesis, Colorado College, 1985. Social. Train Govt.

RINEY, W. A. "Retracing the Butterfield Trail." WESTX 9(Oct 1933): 97-100. Jones County, TX area.

RINGO, Mary. THE JOURNAL OF MRS. MARY RINGO. Santa Ana: Private, 1956. CAL(Leav)-BRIDGER-SIMPSON-Ends Austin, NV. II. 1864.

RIPLEY, Vernette S. "The San Fernando Pass and the Pioneer Traffic that Went over It." Southern California Historical QUARTERLY 29(Mar, Sept-Dec 1947): 9-48, 137-43; 30(Mar, Jun 1948): 42-64, 111-60. Geog.

RITTENHOUSE, Jack D. AMERICAN HORSE-DRAWN VEHICLES. NY: Bonanza, 1948. Eqpt.

_____. CARRIAGE HUNDRED: A BIBLIOGRAPHY ON HORSE-DRAWN TRANSPORTATION. Houston: Stagecoach, 1961. Bib.

_____. THE SANTA FE TRAIL: A HISTORICAL BIBLIOGRAPHY. Albuquerque: Univ. of New Mexico Press, 1971. Bib.

"Roads, Highways and Trails." SDHIST. Overland-Genl.

ROADS, OLD TRAILS, TRACES AND HISTORICAL PLACES OF ARKANSAS. Little Rock: Univ. of Arkansas, 198? Maps.

ROBARDS, John L. Journal. MO-WHMC. CAL(Leav)-SANTA FE-RIO GRANDE-GILA-Ends Yuma. II+. 1849.

ROBB, Thomas H. "Routes to Southwestern Idaho, 1855 - 1884." MA thesis, Univ. of Idaho, 1971. OR-Genl.

ROBBINS, Eloise F. "The Original Military Post Road between Fort Leavenworth and Fort Scott." KANSAS HISTORY 1(Sum 1978): 90-100. Military.

ROBBINS, Richard C. Ed. Johnston, Eliza. "Diary."

ROBE, Robert. "Diary While Crossing the Plains in 1851." WASHINGTON HISTORICAL QUARTERLY 19(Jan 1928): 52-63. OR(St. Jo). III. 1851.

ROBERSON, Joseph S. "History of Wells, Fargo & Co. and the Pony

Express." NVHIST. Stage.

ROBERT, Henry W. ITINERARIES OF ROUTES IN ARIZONA AND SOUTHERN CALIFORNIA. SF: Engineer Office, Headquarters, Military Division of the Pacific, 1869. Guide. GILA-Genl.

_____. Journal. Arizona State Univ. Library-SpCol, Tempe, AZ. BEALE. II. 1867.

ROBERTS, B. H. Life Story. UTHIST. MORMON. II. Rem. 1866.

ROBERTS, Dan E. Blood Gates. UTHIST. Pony. Military. 1859 alleged attack of troops at Pleasant Valley, UT.

ROBERTS, James. Notes. Princeton Univ. Library-Western History, Princeton, NJ. CAL(Council)-BOZE-Ends Wood Creek. II+. 1864.

ROBERTS, Sidney. TO EMIGRANTS TO THE GOLD REGION. New Haven, CN: N.p., 1849. Guide.

ROBERTSON, Dale. WELLS FARGO - THE LEGEND. Millbrae, CA: Celestial Arts, 1975. Stage.

ROBERTSON, Fay H. "John Jacob Hampton, An Oregon Pioneer of 1845." ORU. MEEK. IV. 1845.

ROBERTSON, Frank C. FORT HALL: GATEWAY TO OREGON COUNTRY. NY: Hastings House, 1963. Geog.

ROBERTSON, Frank D. "A History of Yuma, AZ." MA thesis, Univ. of Arizona, 1942. Geog.

ROBERTSON, Theodore H. "Diary." In Letters and Diaries, ed. Dean L. Robertson. NBHIST. PIKES. III. 1861.

ROBERTSON, Wyndham, Jr. OREGON, OUR RIGHT AND TITLE.... WA: J. & G. S. Gideon, 1846. Guide.

ROBIDOUX, Orral M. MEMORIAL TO THE ROBIDOUX BROTHERS. Kansas City: Smith, Grieves, 1924. Biog.

ROBIE, S. "Stage - Driver's Story." OUTING 25(N.d.): 81. Stage. Not Seen.

ROBIE, Wendell. "Description of the Donner Lake to Johnson's Ranch Section of the Overland Emigrant Road." Nevada County Historical Society BULLETIN 19(Mar 1965): 1-4. TRUCKEE-Genl. Pres.

ROBINSON, A. P., and Edward Warner. OVERLAND TRACTION ENGINE COMPANY: TRANSPORTATION BY STEAM FROM THE MISSOURI RIVER TO THE ROCKY MOUNTAINS. Boston: Wright & Potter, 1865. Eqpt.

ROBINSON, Benjamin F. Diary. NBHIST. OR(Council)-BARLOW. 1852. Not Seen.

ROBINSON, Charles. "Charles Robinson - Yankee '49er...." Ed. Louise Barry. KANSAS HISTORICAL QUARTERLY 34(Sum 1968): 179-88. CAL(Kansas City). V-. Rem. 1849.

ROBINSON, Edwin "Scribitus." "Story of a Pioneer." CSL. CAL(Ft. Smith)-MARCY-CHEROKEE(Pueblo to SLC)-SLCUT. V. 1849.

ROBINSON, Fayette. CALIFORNIA AND ITS GOLD REGIONS.... NY: Stringer & Townsend, 1849. A fake.

ROBINSON, Henry. Journal. LDS. MORMON. 1852. Not Seen.

ROBINSON, Lavinia J. Ed. Constant, Isaac. "A Brief Review."

ROBINSON, R. B. Diary. Long Beach Public Library, Long Beach, CA. Not Seen.

ROBINSON, W. W. "Retracing the Immigrant Trails." OVERLAND MONTHLY 89(Jul 1931): 4, 22, 29. CAL-1843-Genl. Chile-Walker Party.

ROBINSON, Zirkle D. THE ROBINSON - ROSENBERGER JOURNEY TO THE GOLD FIELDS OF CALIFORNIA, 1849 - 1850.... Ed. Francis C. Rosenberger. Iowa City, IA: Private, 1966. CAL(St. Jo)-HALL. IV. 1849.

ROBROCK, David P. "The Eleventh Ohio Volunteer Cavalry on the Central Plains, 1862 - 1866." ARIZONA & THE WEST 25(Spr 1983): 23-48. Military.

ROBSON, Inez A. Reminiscence. MONHIST. CAL(Council)-BOZE. V. 1866.

"Rockwell's Station." UTHIST. Pony.

ROCKWOOD, Albert P. Journal. BYU. MORMON. II+. 1847.

ROCKWOOD, E. Ruth. Ed. Stevens, Charles. "Letters."

RODGERS, Andrew F. Reminiscences. CSL. CAL(Ft. Kearney). V-. Rem. 1849.

RODGERS Family. Records. NEWBERRY. CAL. IV. N.d.

RODMAN, Mary. Ed. Gay, James W. "Trail Diary."

ROE, Frank G. THE NORTH AMERICAN BUFFALO. Toronto: Univ. of Toronto Press, 1951. Bib.

ROE, Martha A. A Trip to Idaho. Washington State Univ. Library-SpCol, Pullman, WA. CAL(Council)-LANDER-MONTANA. II+. 1864.

ROEDER, Elizabeth A. Diary. Univ. of Washington Library-Ms, Seattle, WA. OR(Council)-WASH. III. 1854.

ROEDER, Henry. Diary. Univ. of Washington Library-Ms, Seattle, WA. OR(St. Jo)-Ends Sweetwater River. III. 1850.

ROGERS, Edmund B. Ed. Brewer, William H. ROCKY MOUNTAIN LETTERS.

ROGERS, Fred B. SOLDIERS OF THE OVERLAND. SF: Grabhorn, 1938. Military. Telegraph. Stage.

_____. WILLIAM BROWN IDE: BEAR FLAGGER. SF: John Howell, 1962. CAL(Indep)-TRUCKEE. Biog.

ROGERS, Samuel H. Journal. BYU. Not Seen.

ROLAND, Charles P. Ed. Johnson, Eliza. "Diary."

ROLFE, DeForest P. "Overland Freighting from Nebraska City." PROCEEDINGS AND COLLECTIONS Nebraska State Historical Society 5(1902): 279-93. Freight.

ROLFE, Frank. "Early Day Los Angeles: A Great Wagon Train Center." Southern California Historical QUARTERLY 35(Dec 1935):305-18. Freight. Geog.

_____. "The Location of the Butterfield Stage Station in the Temescal Valley, Riverside County." Southern California Historical QUARTERLY 17(Sept 1935): 108-11. Geog.

ROLLE, Andrew F. Ed. Miller, James K. ROAD TO VIRGINIA CITY.

ROLLINS, James H. "Recollection." In JOURNALS OF THE FORTY-NINERS, eds. LeRoy and Ann W. Hafen. Glendale: Clark, 1954. SLCOR. IV. Rem. 1849.

THE ROMANCE OF THE PONY EXPRESS. Omaha: Acorn, 1924. Pony.

ROMANI, Margaret W. "Unluckiest of the Forty-Niners." TRUE WEST 29(Apr 1982): 22-29. Social(Children).

ROMNEY, Miles P. LIFE STORY.... Ed. Romney, Thomas C. SLC: N.p., 1948. MORMON. 1856. Not Seen.

RONAGHAN, Neil E. "The Pioneer Telegraph in Western Canada." MA thesis, Univ. of Saskatchewan - Saskatoon, 1976.

RONAN, Margaret. "Memoirs of a Frontiersman, Mary C. Ronan." MA thesis, State University of Montana, 1932. CHEROKEE(Denver to Ft. Bridger)-MONTANA. III. 1863.

RONAN, Mary C. SEE: Ronan, Margaret. "Memoirs."

RONSTADT, Edward F. SEE: With James E. Sherman. "Wagon Making in Southern Arizona."

ROOT, Frank A., and William E. Connelley. THE OVERLAND STAGE TO CALIFORNIA. 1901. Reprint. Rio Grande Classic Series No. 67. Glorieta, NM: Rio Grande Press, 1970. A classic study of staging with fine graphics and maps. Stage. Freight. Telegraph. Indians.

ROOT, George A. Collections. KSHIST. Stage. Freight. Pres.

_____. "Ferries in Kansas...." KANSAS HISTORICAL QUARTERLY 2(Feb, May, Aug, Nov 1933): 3-28, 115-38, 251-93, 343-76; 3(Feb, May 1934): 15-42, 115-44; 6(Feb 1937): 14-20. Geog.

_____. "A Paper on Trails in Kansas Read at a Meeting of the American Pioneer Trails Association." KSHIST. Pres.

_____, and Russell K. Hickman. "Pike's Peak Express Companies." KANSAS HISTORICAL QUARTERLY 13(Aug, Nov 1945): 163-95, 211-42, 485-526; 14(Feb 1946): 36-92. Stage. PIKES-Genl.

ROOT, Orville. Orville's Trip...1864. In Paul & Helen Henderson Collection. UWY. CAL(St. Jo)-BOZE. V. Rem. 1864.

ROOT, Riley. JOURNAL OF TRAVELS FROM ST. JOSEPHS TO OREGON.... Ed. Edward Eberstadt. 1850. Reprint. California Relations No. 41. Oakland: Biobooks, 1955. A description of the diary and its contents appeared as "The Journal of Riley Root." CALIFORNIA HISTORICAL QUARTERLY 10(Dec 1931): 396-405. OR(St. Jo)-BARLOW. III. 1848. Guide.

ROOT, Virginia V. FOLLOWING THE POT OF GOLD...1850. Ed. Leonore Rowland. Downey, CA: Quinn, 1960. CAL(Indep)-SANTA FE-RIO GRANDE-GILA. IV. Rem. 1850. 1850 Oatman Massacre on Gila River.

ROSE, Albert C. HISTORIC AMERICAN ROADS: FROM FRONTIER TRAILS TO SUPERHIGHWAYS. NY: Crown, 1976. Overland-Genl.

ROSE, F. P. "Butterfield Overland Mail Company." ARKANSAS HISTORICAL QUARTERLY 15(Spr 1956): 62-75. Stage-ARK.

ROSE, Leonard J., Jr. L. J. ROSE OF SUNNY SLOPE, 1827 - 1899. San Marino: Huntington Library, 1959. CAL(Westport)-SANTA FE-BEALE-Ends at Colorado River after Mohave attack. II. Rem. 1858.

CAL(Albuquerque)-BEALE. II. Rem. 1859.

ROSE, Rachel C. Diary. CSL. CAL(Council)-BRIDGER-SLCUT. III-. 1852.

ROSEBOOM, Eugene H. Ed. Tinker, Charles. "Charles Tinker's Journal."

ROSEBUSH, Waldo E. AMERICAN FIREARMS AND THE CHANGING FRONTIER. Spokane: Eastern Washington Historical Society, 1962. Eqpt.

_____. FRONTIER STEEL: THE MEN AND THEIR WEAPONS. Appleton, WA: Eastern Washington Historical Society, 1958. Eqpt.

ROSENBERG, C. G. Ed. Perrie, George W. BUCKSKIN MOSE.

ROSENBERG, Daniel. MARY BROWN: FROM HARPERS FERRY TO CALIFORNIA. Occasional Paper No. 17. NY: American Institute for Marxist Studies, 1975. CAL(Council)-LASSEN. V. 1864.

ROSENBERG, Robert G. "The Dempsey - Hockaday Trail - An Experience in History." ANNALS OF WYOMING 54(Spr 1982): 58-62. Geog.

ROSENBERGER, Francis C. Ed. Robinson, Zirkle D. "The Rosenberger - Robinson Journey."

ROSKE, Ralph J. SEE: Warren, Elizabeth et al. CULTURAL RESOURCES OF THE CALIFORNIA DESERT.

_____. "The World Impact of the California Gold RUsh, 1849 - 1857." ARIZONA & THE WEST 5(Aut 1963): 187-232. CAL-Genl.

ROSS, Edith C. "The Old Shawnee Mission." COLLECTIONS Kansas State Historical Society 17(1926 - 1928): 417-35. Geog.

ROSS, Jennie. Ed. Gentry, Mrs. M. A. "A Child's Experiences in '49."

ROSS, John E. Narrative of an Indian Fighter. BANCROFT. OR(Indep). IV. Rem. 1847.

ROSS, Marvin C. THE WEST OF ALFRED JACOB MILLER. Norman: Univ. of Oklahoma Press, 1965. Graphics.

ROSS, Nancy W. "Aprons to their Eyes; Women's Role in Westward Migrations." SCHOLASTIC, 23 Apr 1945, 13-14. Social.

_____. WESTWARD THE WOMEN. NY: Knopf, 1944. Social.

ROSSI, Paul A., and David C. Hunt. THE ART OF THE OLD WEST: FROM THE COLLECTION OF THE GILCREASE INSTITUTE. NY: Knopf, 1971. Superb color printwork. Graphics.

ROTHWELL, William R. Journal. BEINECKE. CAL(St. Jo). II+. 1850.

ROTTER, Andrew J. "Matilda for Gods Sake Write: Women and Families on the Argonaut Mind." CALIFORNIA HISTORY 58(Sum 1979): 128-41. Social.

ROUNDTREE, Patrick H. AUTOBIOGRAPHY. N.p.: Private, n.d. OR(Council). IV. Rem. 1859.

ROUSSEAU, Mrs. J. A. "Rousseau Diary across the Desert to California...in 1864." San Bernardino County Museum QUARTERLY 6(Win 1958): 1-17. SLCOR. II+. 1864.

ROUSSEAU, Mrs. James (probably same as above item). Papers. Iowa State Historical Department, Des Moines, IA. CAL(Council)-

BRIDGER-SLCOR. 1864. Not Seen.

"Route from Denver to Fort Bridger, via Cherokee Trail." ROCKY MOUNTAIN NEWS, 16 May 1860, p. 1. CHEROKEE-1860-Genl.

"The Route to California." AMERICAN REVIEW 2(Aug 1848): 204-12. Review of Edwin Bryant's, WHAT I SAW IN CALIFORNIA.

ROW, A. Tracy. SEE: With Bob Cunningham. "Journal of Arizona History."

ROW, Albert M. "Dogged Courage of Originator All that Saved Pony Express." LOS ANGELES TIMES, 9 Sept 1923, n.p. Pony.

ROWE, William R. Ho for California...in company with 'Lucky' Baldwin. HUNTL. CAL(Council)-BRIDGER-SLCUT. IV. Rem. 1853.

ROWLAND, Leonore. Ed. Root, Virginia V. FOLLOWING THE POT OF GOLD.

_____. "The First Covered Wagon Train to Southern California." POMONA VALLEY HISTORIAN 1(Oct 1965): 137-49. CAL-1841-Genl.

ROWNDY, Shadrach. Journal. LDS. MORMON. 1850. Not Seen.

ROWSE, Edward. CONCORD'S WAGGON MEN. Concord, NH: Author, 1976. Stage-Eqpt.

ROYAl Family. Reminiscences. ORHIST. OR(Council). V-. Rem. 1853.

ROYAL, James H. Journal...1853. ORU. OR(Council)-APPLE. III. 1853.

ROYAL, Thomas F. SEE: Royal Family. "Reminiscences."

ROYCE, Charles C., comp. ADDRESSES, REMINISCENCES, ETC., OF GENERAL JOHN BIDWELL. Chico, CA: Bidwell, 1907. Biog.

_____. JOHN BIDWELL: PIONEER, STATESMAN, PHILANTHROPIST. Chico, CA: Private, 1906. Biog.

ROYCE, Sarah B. A FRONTIER LADY. Ed. Ralph H. Gabriel. New Haven: Yale Univ. Press, 1932. CAL(Council)-BRIDGER-HASTINGS. III. Rem. 1849.

ROYCE, Sarah E., III. "From Salt Lake to the Sierras in '49." YALE REVIEW 20(Jun 1931): 754-66. CAL(SLC)-HASTINGS. III. 1849.

RUCKER, Maude A. THE OREGON TRAIL AND SOME OF ITS BLAZERS. NY: Walter Neale, 1930. OR-Genl.

RUDD, Lydia. "Diary." In WOMEN'S DIARIES OF THE WESTWARD JOURNEY, ed. Lillian Schlissel. NY: Schocken, 1982. OR(St. Jo). III+. 1852.

RUDDELL, W. H. Reminiscence. ORHIST. OR(Council). V. Rem. 1851.

RUDKIN, Charles N., comp. EARLY CALIFORNIA TRAVEL SERIES: A CHRONOLOGICAL SUMMARY, INDEX AND DESCRIPTIVE LIST. LA: Dawson, 1961. Bib.

RUDY, Manilus S. SEE: With Daniel Burgert. "The Rough Road West."

RUE, Norman L. "Pesh-Bi-Yalti Speaks: White Man's Talking Wire in Arizona." JOURNAL OF ARIZONA HISTORY 12(Win 1971): 229-62. Telegraph.

RUEGER, John. Journal. BENICIA [CA] HERALD, 1-8-15 June 1923, n.p. Copy at BANCROFT. CAL(St. Jo)-LASSEN. IV. 1849.

RUFF, Charles and Annie. Correspondence. Held by Charles W. Martin, Omaha, NB. OR(Ft. Kearney). II. 1848.

RUGELEY, Helen J. Ed. Whitworth, Robert W. "From the Mississippi to the Pacific."

RUGGLES, Daniel. "Freighting from Sauk County, WI, to Denver, Colorado Territory." WIHIST. Freight. PIKES-Genl.

RUHLEN, George. "Kearney's Route from the Rio Grande to the Gila River." NEW MEXICO HISTORICAL REVIEW 32(Jul 1957): 213-30. GILA-Genl.

RUMBLE, Josephine R. HISTORY OLD GOVERNMENT ROAD ACROSS THE MOJAVE DESERT TO THE COLORADO RIVER. WPA Project No. 3428. N.p., n.d. BEALE-Genl.

RUMFIELD, Hiram. LETTERS OF AN OVERLAND MAIL AGENT. Ed. Archer B. Hulbert. Worcester, MA: American Antiquarian Society, 1929. Stage.

RUMLEY, Charles. "Diary...." Ed. Helen A. Howard. In FRONTIER OMNIBUS, ed. John W. Hakola. Missoula: Montana State Univ., 1962. MULLAN. III. 1862.

RUNYON, I. Diary. Clarke Library-Central Michigan Univ., Mt. Pleasant, MI. CAL(St. Jo). 1852. Not Seen.

RUSH, David H. "Singing Wires in the Wilderness." CHICAGO WESTERNERS BRAND BOOK 15(May 1958): 17-19, 24. Telegraph.

"Rush to the Rockies [Centennial 1959]." COHIST. PIKES-Genl.

"Rush to the Rockies Articles, Bibliography: Published in THE COLORADO MAGAZINE." COLORADO MAGAZINE 36(Jun 1959): 126-29. Bib.

RUSLING, James F. ACROSS AMERICA. NY: Sheldon, 1877. Stage: Atchison - Denver - SLC - Boise - Umatilla - Los Angeles - Tucson - SF - Atchison. III. Rem. 1867.

RUSSELL, Charles. BACK TRAILING ON THE OLD FRONTIER. Great Falls, MT: Cheely Rahan, 1922. Graphics.

RUSSELL, Don. Ed. Lowe, Percival G. FIVE YEARS. Ed. Montaignes, Francois. THE PLAINS.

_____. "How Many Indians Were Killed? White Man Versus Red Man: The Facts and the Legend." AMERICAN WEST 10(Jul 1973): 42-47, 61-63. Indians. Military.

RUSSELL, Isaac. A Sketch.... BANCROFT. MORMON. V-. 1848. CAL(SLC)-SLCUT. V-. 1850. Apostate family leaves Utah.

RUSSELL, Marion S. LAND OF ENCHANTMENT. Ed. Marc Simmons. Albuquerque: Univ. of New Mexico Press, 1981. SANTA FE. V. 1852. SANTA FE. V. 1856. SANTA FE. V. 1852.

RUSSELL, Ralph C. THE CARLTON TRAIL: THE BROAD HIGHWAY INTO THE SASKATCHEWAN COUNTRY FROM THE RED RIVER SETTLEMENT, 1840 - 1880. Saskatoon: Prairie Books, 1971. Canada-Genl.

RUSSELL, Robert T. IMPROVEMENT OF COMMUNICATION WITH THE PACIFIC COAST AS AN ISSUE IN AMERICAN POLITICS, 1783 - 1864. 1948. Reprint. NY: Arno, 1981. Overland-

Genl.

Russell, Majors & Waddell. Correspondence and Papers, 1839 - 1868. HUNTL. Pony. Stage. Freight.

_____. RULES AND REGULATIONS FOR THE GOVERNING OF RUSSELL, MAJORS & WADDELL'S OUTFIT. Nebraska City: N.p., 1859. Freight.

RYAN, Benjamin W. "The Bozeman Trail to Virginia City, Montana in 1864." ANNALS OF WYOMING 19(Jul 1947): 77-105. CAL(Council)-BOZE. III. 1864. A rare Indian attack on circled wagons.

RYAN, Garry D. "Camp Walbach, Nebraska Territory, 1858 - 1859: The Military Post at Cheyenne Pass." ANNALS OF WYOMING 35(Apr 1963): 5-20. Geog.

RYAN, John. "Sonora Trail and Sonora Pass of 1853." PONY EXPRESS 22(Jan, Feb 1956): 11-12, 10-12. Geog.

RYBOLT, Robert R. "The Lost Wagon Train." TRUE WEST 30(Oct 1983): 45-46. Social.

RYKER, Lois. "A Wagon Train through Crow Country." FRONTIER TIMES 37(Jun-Jul 1963): 42-43, 57. BOZE-Genl.

RYUS, W. H. THE SECOND WILLIAM PENN: A TRUE ACCOUNT OF THE INCIDENTS THAT HAPPENED ALONG THE OLD SANTA FE TRAIL IN THE SIXTIES. Kansas City: N.p., 1913. Stage.

SABAN, Vera. "The Cottonwood: Tree of the West." PERSIMMON HILL 9(Sum 1979): 8-21. Flora.

SACKS, B. "New Evidence on the Bascom Affair." ARIZONA & THE WEST 4(Aut 1962): 261-78. Geog. Military.

SAFFORD, A. P. Narrative. BANCROFT. CAL(Council). IV. Rem. 1850.

SAGE, Rufus B. ROCKY MOUNTAIN LIFE. Boston: Thayer & Eldridge, 1859. CAL(Indep)-to Ft. Laramie and back. IV. 1856?

SAGER, John. SEE: Morrow, H. W. "Child Pioneer."

ST. CLAIR, H. C. Journal. BEINECKE. CAL(St. Jo)-LASSEN. 1849. Not Seen.

ST. JOHN, Silas. "The Establishment of the Trans-Continental Mail Service Upon the Overland Stage Route." Arizona State Library-Arizona Room, Phoenix, AZ. Mail. Stage.

_____. "Tragedies of the Old Stage Days." FRONTIER TIMES 28(Jan 1951): 102-08. Stage.

ST. JOHNS, James. "Diary." In CHARLES HOPPER AND THE PILGRIMS OF THE PACIFIC, ed. Franklin Beard. La Grange, CA: Southern Mines Press, 1981. CA(Westport)-Ends on Bear River. V. 1841.

SALISBURY, Albert and Jane. HERE ROLLED THE COVERED WAGONS. Seattle: Private, 1948. OR-Genl. Photo history.

SALISBURY, William. "The Journal of an 1859 Pike's Peak Gold Seeker." Ed. David Lindsey. KANSAS HISTORICAL QUARTERLY 22(Win 1956): 321-41. PIKES. III +. 1859.

SAMPSON, Charles B. "The Sampson Trails." Idaho State Historical Society Library, Boise, ID. Pres.

San Antonio and San Diego Mail Line. "Overland to the Pacific."

BANCROFT. Graphics.

_____. Property Lists - San Diego County, CA. SDHIST. Stage.

SANDERLIN, Walter S. Ed. Erskine, M. H. "A Cattle Drive from Texas to California."

SANDERS, Harriet P. Reminiscences. MONHIST. CAL(Council)-HALL-MONTANA. II. Rem. 1863.

SANDERS, Joseph B. Diary. Whitman College-Northwest Collection, Walla Walla, WA. OR(Council). 1865. Not Seen.

SANDERS, Thomas D. Excerpts. NVHIST. CAL(Ogden). V. Rem. 1861.

SANDERSON, George H. Diary. Society of California Pioneers, San Francisco, CA. Not Seen.

SANDERSON, Winslow F. Letters. BEINECKE. CAL(Leav)-Ends Ft. Laramie. 1849. Military. Not Seen.

SANDS, Frank. A PASTORAL PRINCE.... Santa Barbara, CA: Author, 1893. CAL. V. 1851. CAL-SANTA FE-RIO GRANDE-GILA. V. 1858. Stock.

SANFORD, Albert B. "The Cherokee Trail and the First Discovery of Gold on Cherry Creek." COLORADO MAGAZINE 8(Jan 1931): 30-33. CHEROKEE-1859-Genl. PIKES-1859-Genl.

_____. "Denver to Cheyenne by Stage Coach in the Late Sixties." SONS OF COLORADO BULLETIN 20, no. 4, 3-7. Stage.

_____. "Mountain Staging in Colorado." COLORADO MAGAZINE 9(Mar 1932): 66-71. PIKES-Genl.

_____. "The Story of Bob Spottswood." COHIST. Not Seen.

SANFORD, Daisy. Ed. D'Arcy, Marianne H. "Reminiscences."

SANFORD, Mary F. Ed. Hite, Abraham. "Diary."

SANFORD, Mollie D. THE JOURNAL OF MOLLIE DORSEY SANFORD...1857-66. Lincoln: Univ. of Nebraska Press, 1976. PIKES. II. 1860.

SANTA FE AND THE FAR WEST: REPRINTED FROM NILES' NATIONAL REGISTER, VOL. LXI, P. 209, DECEMBER 4, 1841. LA: Dawson, 1949. SANTA FE. IV. 1841.

SANTLEBEN, August. A TEXAS PIONEER: EARLY STAGING AND OVERLAND FREIGHTING DAYS ON THE FRONTIERS OF TEXAS AND MEXICO. 1910. Reprint. Waco, TX: Morrison, 1967. Freight.

SARGENT, Charles. Overland Journey. Colorado College Library-SpCol, Colorado Springs, CO. CAL(St. Jo)-TRUCKEE. IV. 1849.

SARGENT, Shirley. Ed. Hutchings, James M. SEEKING THE ELEPHANT.

SAUNDERS, Mary. "The Whitman Massacre." BANCROFT. OR(St. Jo). IV. Rem. 1847. Indians.

SAVAGE, Jim. SEE: Mitchell, Annie R. JIM SAVAGE.

SAVAGE, Levi, Jr. LEVI SAVAGE, JR. JOURNAL. Comp. Lynn M. Hilton. SLC: Savage Family Assn., 1966. SLCOR. V. 1852. MORMON. II. 1856.

SAVAGE, W. Sherman. "The Negro in the Westward Movement." JOURNAL OF NEGRO HISTORY 25(Oct 1940): 531-39. Social.

Savannah Oregon Emigrating Company. THE ORGANIZATIONAL JOURNAL OF AN EMIGRANT TRAIN OF 1845 CAPTAINED BY SOLOMON TETHEROW. Eugene, OR: Lane County Pioneer-Historical Society, 1960. Train Govt.

SAWADSKY, Joanne M. "True Wayfaring Christians: Form and Meaning in the Overlander Narratives." MA thesis, Univ. of British Columbia - Vancouver, 1976. Not Seen.

SAWYER, Byrd W. NEVADA NOMADS: A STORY OF THE SHEEP INDUSTRY. San Jose, CA: Harlan - Young, 1971. Stock.

SAWYER, Eugene. THE LIFE AND CAREER OF TIBURCIO VASQUEZ, THE CALIFORNIA STAGE ROBBER. Oakland: Biobooks, 1944. Stage. Biog.

SAWYER, Mrs. Francis H. "Kentucky to California by Carriage and Feather Bed." (In) COVERED WAGON WOMEN, Vol. 4, ed. Kenneth L. Holmes. Glendale: Clark, 1985. CAL(St. Jo). II+. 1852.

SAWYER, Lorenzo. WAY SKETCHES. Ed. Edward Eberstadt. NY: Eberstadt, 1926. CAL(St. Jo). II. 1850.

SAWYERS, James A. "Niobrara - Virginia City Wagon Road." SOUTH DAKOTA HISTORICAL REVIEW 2(Oct 1936): 3-48. DAKOTAS(Niobrara)-BOZE. II+. 1865.

SAYRE, Thomas. Diary...1849. BANCROFT. CAL-MEX(Tampico-Tepec-Mazatlan). III. 1849.

SAYWARD, William T. Pioneer Reminiscences. BANCROFT. CAL-TEX(Brownsville)-MEX(Monterey-Saltillo-Durango-Mazatlan). V. 1849.

SCALF, Henry P. THE OVERLAND LETTER: BIOGRAPHY OF ELIAS BARNETT. Prestonsburg, KY: N.p., 1963. CAL-1841-Genl.

"Scalping a Woman on the Plains, Her Extraordinary Fortitude." SF DAILY EVENING BULLETIN, 19 Sept 1857, n.p. Indians.

SCAMEHORN, Howard L., ed. THE BUCKEYE ROVERS IN THE GOLD RUSH. Athens, OH: Ohio Univ. Press, 1965. CAL(St. Jo)-TRUCKEE. II. 1849.

SCANNELL, Jack C. "A Survey of the Stagecoach Mail in the Trans-Pecos, 1850 - 1861." WESTX 47(Oct 1971): 115-26. Stage.

SCARBOROUGH, A. DIARY OF A MEMBER OF THE FIRST MULE PACK TRAIN TO LEAVE FORT SMITH FOR CALIFORNIA IN 1849. Ed. Bessie L. Wright. Canyon, TX: Palo Duro, 1969. CAL(Ft. Smith)-MARCY-CHEROKEE-Ends in northern Colorado. II+. 1849.

SCARBROUGH, Richard A. Diary. CSL. CAL(Council)-BRIDGER-SLCOR. II. 1852.

SCARCE, William. Journal. UTHIST. MORMON-Ends Sweetwater River. III. 1847.

SCHAEDEL, Grace L. Papers. UWY. Collection of newspaper articles on trail topics.

SCHAEFER, Jacob. Diary. MNHIST. CAL(St. Jo). III. 1849.

SCHAEFER, Joseph. Ed. Applegate, Jesse A. A DAY WITH THE COW COLUMN. Ed. Burnett, Peter H. "Letters." Ed. Fairchild, Lucius. CALIFORNIA LETTERS OF. Ed. Steele, John. ACROSS THE PLAINS. Ed. Tuttle, Charles. "California Diary." Ed. Woodward, Thomas. "Diary."

_____. "Jesse Applegate: Pioneer, Statesman and Philosopher." WASHINGTON HISTORICAL QUARTERLY 1(Jul 1907): 217-33. Biog.

_____. "Trailing a Trail Artist in 1849." WISCONSIN MAGAZINE OF HISTORY 12(Sept 1928): 97-108. Graphics.

SCHAFFER, John G. "The Early History of the Wells Fargo Express." MA thesis, Univ. of California-Berkeley, 1922. Stage.

SCHAFFER, Mary T. OLD INDIAN TRAILS OF THE CANADIAN ROCKIES. NY: Putnam's, 1911. Indians.

SCHALLENBERGER, Moses. THE OPENING OF THE CALIFORNIA TRAIL. Ed. George R. Stewart. Berkeley: Univ. of California Press, 1953. CAL(Council)-HALL-TRUCKEE. III. Rem. 1844.

SCHARF, Thomas L. Ed. Whipple, Amiel W. "Amiel W. Whipple and the Boundary Survey."

_____. "Amiel Weeks Whipple: Boundary and Railroad Surveys in the Southwest, 1849 - 1854." MA thesis, Univ. of San Diego, 1973. Biog. Not Seen.

SCHARMANN, Herman B. SCHARMANN'S OVERLAND JOURNEY TO CALIFORNIA. 1918. Reprint. Freeport, NY: Books for Libraries Press, 1969. CAL(Indep)-LASSEN. IV. Rem. 1849.

SCHELL, H. S. Memoranda: Forts Laramie and Kearney [1842 - 1876]. Attributed to BANCROFT but uncatalogued.

SCHELLENS, Richard N. Papers. CAHIST. Stage.

SCHELLER, John J. Autobiography. CSL. CAL(St. Jo)-BRIDGER-SLCUT. IV. Rem. 1849.

SCHETTER, Adrienne E. "The Indians on the Oregon Trail, 1845 - 1849, with Emphasis on the Kansas, Pawnees, and Sioux, especially in 1846." MA thesis, Univ. of California-Berkeley, 1932. OR-Genl. Indians.

SCHICK, Robert. "Wagons to Chihuahua." AMERICAN WEST 3(Sum 1966): 72-79. TEX-Genl. MEX-Genl.

SCHIEL, Jacob H. THE LAND BETWEEN; DR. JAMES SCHIEL'S ACCOUNT OF THE GUNNISON - BECKWITH EXPEDITION INTO THE WEST, 1853 -1854. Eds. & trans. Frederick W. Bachmann and William S. Wallas. Great West and Indian Series 9. LA: Westernlore, 1957. CAL(Westport)-SANTA FE-SPANISH-SLCOR. II+. 1853. CAL(SLC)-HASTINGS-NOBLES. II+. 1854. Part of company massacred by Indians in southern Utah.

SCHINDLER, Harold. "B. Y. Express: The Company that Helped Start a War." WESTERN EXPRESS, Jan 1962, 10-15. Mail.

_____. "Utah's First Post oFfice and Postmaster." UTAH HISTORICAL QUARTERLY 30(Fall 1962): 347-51. Mail.

SCHLICHTMANN, Margaret E. SEE: With Irene D. Paden. THE BIG OAK FLAT ROAD.

SCHLISSEL, Lillian. "Diaries of Frontier Women: On Learning to Read the Obscured Patterns." In WOMAN'S BEING, WOMAN'S PLACE: FEMALE IDENTITY AND VOCATION, ed. Mary Kelley. NY: G. K. Hall, 1979. Social.

_____. "Mothers and Daughters on the Western Frontier." FRONTIERS 3(Sum 1978): 29-33. Social.

_____. WOMEN'S DIARIES OF THE WESTWARD JOURNEY.

NY: Schocken Books, 1982. Social.

_____. "Women's Diaries on the Western Frontier." AMERICAN STUDIES 18(Spr 1977): 87-100. Social.

SCHMIDT, Earl F. TRAIL GUIDE FOR THE HENNESS - ZUM-WALT PASS.... N.p., 1982? Geog.

SCHMIDT, Johann H. Across the Plains. UTHIST. SIMPSON(Virginia City, NV)-CHEROKEE(SLC to Denver)-Platte River to Atchison. I. 1866.

SCHMIDT, William T. "Follow the Oregon Trail." TRUE WEST 30(Jul 1983): 36-40. Pres.

SCHMITT, Martin F. Ed. Kautz, August. "From Missouri to California in 1860."

SCHMOLDER, B. THE EMIGRANT'S GUIDE TO CALIFORNIA.... London: Pelham Richardson, 1849. Guide.

SCHNACKENBERG, Walter C. "The Southern Route into Oregon." MA thesis, Gonzaga Univ., 1947. APPLE-Genl.

SCHNEIDER, Charles G. Diary. WIHIST. CAL(Council)-BRIDGER-SLCUT-TRUCKEE. III. 1852.

SCHOLL, Louis. Sketchbook. ORHIST. Graphics.

SCHOONOVER, T. J. THE LIFE AND TIMES OF GENERAL JOHN A. SUTTER. Sacramento: Bullock - Carpenter, 1907. Biog.

SCHRADER, Eleanor. "Historical Landmarks within my Vicinity." NVHIST. Undated Indian massacre in Emigrant Canyon, NV. Indians. Geog.

SCHRADER, George. "Dedication of Plaque in Strawberry Valley." Siskiyou County Historical Society YEARBOOK, 1947 1, no. 2. 29-31. Strawberry Valley stage station. Geog. Pres.

SCHREIBER, Harry N. "Coach, Wagon, and Motor-Truck Manufacture, 1813 - 1928: The Abbot - Downing Company of Concord." HISTORICAL NEW HAMPSHIRE 20(Aut 1965): 3-25. Stage-Eqpt.

SCHRIER, Konrad F., Jr. Ed. Hazen, Eli W. "California Column."

_____. "But First Came the Carts." TRUE WEST 30(May 1983): 42-44. Eqpt.

SCHUBERT, Frank N. Ed. Franklin, William B. MARCH TO SOUTH PASS.

SCHUESSLER, Raymond. "Stagecoach - The Bus of the West." TRUE WEST 30(May 1983): 34-35. Stage-Eqpt.

SCHULTZ, J. C. "The Old Crow Wing Trail." TRANSACTIONS AND PROCEEDINGS Historical and Scientific Society of Manitoba 1895, N. 45. Not Seen.

SCHUTT, H. R. Journal. Clarke Library-Central Michigan Univ., Mt. Pleasant, MI. OR(Council). 1850. MORMON. 1854. Not Seen.

SCHWEITZER, Cora. "Routes Los Angeles to Ventura and Los Angeles to Kern County." MA thesis, Univ. of Southern California, 1929. Freight. Mail. Stage.

SCHWENK, Sarah F. "In the Beginning - Independence." OVERLAND JOURNAL 1(July 1983): 36-37. Geog.

SCHWEIDER, Dorothy. "Historic Sites in Council Bluffs." ANNALS

OF IOWA 41(Win 1973): n.p. Geog.

SCHWIMMER, Jerome. "Los Angeles Covers: Overland via Los Angeles, 1857-1861." WESTERN EXPRESS 30(Apr, Jul 1980): 7-12, 11-16. Mail. Graphics.

SCOBEE, Barry. OLD FORT DAVIS. San Antonio: Naylor, 1947. Stage. Geog.

SCOFIELD, Joseph S. Diary. Univ. of Utah Library-SpCol, Salt Lake City, UT. MORMON-Ends Ft. Laramie. III. 1847.

SCOTT, Abigail J. "Diary...Oregon." In HISTORY OF THE OREGON COUNTRY, vol. 3. Ed. Harvey W. Scott. Cambridge: Riverside, 1924. OR(St. Jo)-BARLOW. II. 1852.

SCOTT, Charles. "The Nevada Indian Uprisings of 1860 as Seen by Private Charles A. Scott." Eds. John M. Ellis and Robert E. Slowers. ARIZONA & THE WEST 3(Win 1961): 355-76. SIMPSON. II. 1860.

SCOTT, Charlton. Diary. ORHIST. OR(St. Paul)-DAKOTAS-MONTANA. II. 1862.

SCOTT, Edwin. CALIFORNIA TO OREGON BY TRAIL, STEAMBOAT, STAGECOACH, AND TRAIN 1850 - 1887. Pasadena: Printing Students Class Project, Pasadena City College, 1976. Freight. Stage.

SCOTT, Franklin D. "Peter Lassen: Danish Pioneer of California." Southern California Historical QUARTERLY 53(Sum 1981): 113-36. Biog.

SCOTT, H. T. "Memorandum of the Trip to California." HUNTL. CAL(Leav). III. 1852.

SCOTT, Hamilton. A TRIP ACROSS THE PLAINS IN 1862, WITH NOTES BY ALVIN ZARING. American Falls, ID: Private, 1959. OR(Council). III. 1862. Indians.

SCOTT, John T. "Ox Team Journey...1852." In HISTORY OF THE OREGON COUNTRY, vol. 3. Ed. Harvey W. Scott. Cambridge: Riverside, 1924. OR(St. Jo?)-BARLOW. V. 1852.

SCOTT, Lalla. KARNEE: A PAIUTE NARRATIVE. Reno: Univ. of Nevada Press, 1966. Indian perspective on conflicts along Humbolt River section of emigrant trail. Indians.

SCOTT, Leslie M., comp. "Diary...Oregon." In HISTORY OF THE OREGON COUNTRY, ed. Harvey W. Scott. Cambridge: Riverside, 1924. OR(St. Jo)-BARLOW. II+. 1852.

SCOTT, Louisiana. "Report of Emigrants and Emigrant Routes to California before 1850 Compiked from the Pioneer Dictations in the Bancroft Library." MA thesis, Univ. of California-Berkeley, 1908. CAL-Genl.

SCOTT, Lynn. THE COVERED WAGON AND OTHER ADVENTURES. Lincoln: Univ. of Nebraska Press, 1987. Overland-Genl. Not Seen.

SCOTT, Mary H. "Missing Link of Old Oregon Trail Resurrected." ORHIST. OR-Genl.

_____. THE OREGON TRAIL THROUGH WYOMING. Aurora, CO: Powder River, 1958. Overland-Wyoming-Genl.

_____. "Wyoming's Oregon Trail West of South Pass." ANNALS OF WYOMING 22(Jul 1950): 47-63. Pres.

SCOTT, Robert C. Trip...1862. Idaho State Historical Society Library,

Boise, ID. OR(Council). III. 1862.

SCOVILLE, Adaline, B. LIFE.... Bingham Canyon, UT: N.p., 1906. MORMON. 1863. Not Seen.

SCROGGS, William L. "To the Gold Fields: Personal Recollections." DENVER WESTERNERS BRAND BOOK 11(1956): n.p. OR(Kansas City)-BARLOW. V. Rem. 1850.

SEABRIGHT, J. M. "The Pony Express Will Ride Again." OUTLOOK, 22 Aug 1923, 633-35. Pres.

SEARLE, Walt. "Packing." HOOF AND HORN 46(Oct-Nov 1976): 14-19. Teams. Good summary of packtrain elementals. Graphics.

SEARLS, Niles. SEE: Comstock, David A. GOLD DIGGERS.

_____. THE DIARY OF A PIONEER AND OTHER PAPERS. Ed. Robert M. Searls. SF: Private, 1940. CAL(Indep). III+. 1849.

SEARLES, Robert M. Ed. Searls, Niles. DIARY OF A PIONEER.

SEATON, James A. Diary. Indiana State Library-Ms, Indianapolis, IN. CAL(St. Jo)-BRIDGER-SLCUT. III. 1850.

SEDGLEY, Joseph. OVERLAND TO CALIFORNIA IN 1849. Oakland: Butler & Bowman, 1877. CAL(Indep)-LASSEN. III. 1849.

SEELEY, John V., and Edwin Phelps. Diary. Ed. Mary Phelps. Clarke Library, Central Michigan Univ. Mt. Pleasant, MI. CAL(St. Jo). 1850. Not Seen.

SELECT COMMITTEE ON OVERLAND ROUTE TO BRITISH OREGON. St. Paul: State Printer, 1858. DAKOTAS-Genl.

SELLAR, John M. Overland...1862. Univ. of British Columbia Library, Vancouver, BC. CANADA(Quebec)-Ft. Garry-Ft. George-Cariboo. 1862. Not Seen.

SELOVER, Esther M. SEE: Sengstacken, Agnes R. DESTINATION WEST!

SENGSTACKEN, Agnes R. DESTINATION WEST! A PIONEER WOMAN ON THE OREGON TRAIL. Portland: Binfords & Mort, 1942. OR(Council)-BARLOW. III. Rem. 1851.

SENTER, W. Riley. CROSSING THE CONTINENT TO THE CALIFORNIA GOLD FIELDS. Exeter, CA: Private, 1938. CAL(Council)-BRIDGER-SLCOR. III. 1849.

SERVEN, James E. "The Ill-Fated '49er Wagon Train." Southern California Historical QUARTERLY 42(Mar 1960): 29-40. SLCOR-1849-Genl.

_____. "The Pony Express...." SMOKE SIGNAL 17(Spr 1968): 160-68. Pony.

_____. "Wagons of the West." ARIZONA HIGHWAYS 52(Apr 1976): 34-43. Eqpt. Graphics.

_____. "Weapons of Early Arizona." ARIZONA HIGHWAYS 52(Nov 1976): 32-41.

SERVICE, John. JOHN SERVICE, PIONEER. Ed. Fred F. Goodsell. Waban, WA: Private, 1945. CAL(Council)-BRIDGER-SLCUT. IV. Rem. 1859. Freight.

SESSIONS, John. Diary. Society of California Pioneers, San Francisco, CA. Not Seen.

SESSIONS, Patty. "A Pioneer Mormon Diary." In COVERED WAGON WOMEN, vol. 1. Ed. Kenneth L. Holmes. Glendale: Clark, 1983. CAL(Council)-SLCOR. III. 1847.

SESSIONS, Peregrine, Emigrating Company. Journal. LDS. SLCUT(Wells, NV-SLC). III. 1857.

SETTLE, Mary Lund. SEE: With Raymond W. Settle. EMPIRE ON WHEELS. SEE: With Raymond W. Settle. "Origin of the Pony Express." SEE: With Raymond W. Settle. OVERLAND DAYS TO MONTANA. SEE: WIth Rayomnd W. Settle. SADDLES AND SPURS. SEE: With Raymond W. Settle. WAR DRUMS AND WAGON WHEELS.

SETTLE, Raymond W. Ed. Cross, Osborne. MARCH OF THE MOUNTED RIFLEMEN.

_____. "The Pony Express: Heroic Effort - Tragic End." UTAH HISTORICAL QUARTERLY 27(Apr 1959): 102-26. Pony.

_____. "The Role of Russell, Majors & Waddell in Western Overland Transportation." In THE AMERICAN WEST: AN APPRAISAL, ed. Robert G. Ferris. Santa Fe: N.p., 1963. Biog. Freight.

_____ and Mary L. "Blood on the Pony Express Trail." TRUE WEST 10(Sept-Oct 1962): 32-33, 65-68. Pony.

_____. "The Early Careers of William Bradford Waddell and William Hepburn Russell: Frontier Capitalists." KANSAS HISTORICAL QUARTERLY 26(Win 1960): 355-82. Biog.

_____. EMPIRE ON WHEELS. Palo Alto: Stanford Univ. Press, 1949. Freight. Biog.

_____. "Napoleon of the West." ANNALS OF WYOMING 32(Apr 1960): 5-47. Biog-William H. Russell.

_____. "Origin of the Pony Express." MISSOURI HISTORICAL BULLETIN 16(Apr 1960): 199-212. Pony.

_____. OVERLAND DAYS TO MONTANA IN 1865: THE DIARY OF SARAH RAYMOND AND JOURNAL OF DR. WAID HOWARD. American Trail Series 8. Glendale: Clark, 1971. CAL-MONTANA. IV. 1865.

_____. SADDLES AND SPURS: THE PONY EXPRESS SAGA. Lincoln: Univ. of Nebraska Press, 1955. The best of modern Pony Express studies.

_____. WAR DRUMS AND WAGON WHEELS: THE STORY OF RUSSELL, MAJORS AND WADDELL. Lincoln: Univ. of Nebraska Press, 1966. Freight. PIKES-Genl. Pony. Excellent.

SEVERSON, Thor. SACRAMENTO, AN ILLUSTRATED HISTORY: 1839 TO 1874. N.p.: California Historical Society, 1973. Geog.

SEVILLE, William P. NARRATIVE OF THE MARCH OF CO. A, ENGINEERS, FORT LEAVENWORTH TO FORT BRIDGER AND RETURN. Occasional Papers, U.S. Army Engineer School, No. 48. WA: Press of the Engineer School, 1912. CAL(Leav)-Ends Ft. Bridger. II+. 1858.

SEXTON, Lucy A. THE FOSTER FAMILY: CALIFORNIA PIONEERS (1849-1852). Santa Barbara: Schauer, 1925. CAL(St. Jo)-TRUCKEE-BECK. II. 1852. CAL(Council). V. 1854.

SEYD, Ernest. CALIFORNIA AND ITS RESOURCES. London: Trubner & Co., 1858. Guide.

SEYMOUR, E. Sanford. EMIGRANTS' GUIDE TO THE GOLD

MINES. Chicago: R. L. Wilson, 1850. Guide.

SEYMOUR, Edmund. Papers. UWY. Oregon Trail Memorial Association items. Pres.

SEYMOUR, Edward. Diary. COHIST. PIKES. III. 1861.

SEYMOUR, Ephraim S. EMIGRANT'S GUIDE TO THE GOLD MINES OF UPPER CALIFORNIA. Chicago: R. L. Wilson, 1849. Guide.

SHAKLEFORD, Ruth. TO CALIFORNIA IN [the] YEAR 1865. N.p., n.d. CAL(Council)-BRIDGER-SLCOR. II. 1865. CAL(San Bernardino)-GILA-TEX(El Paso-Sherman). II. 1868.

SHAFER, Gladys. "Eastward Ho! Ezra Meeker Memorializes the Oregon Trail, 1905-1910." AMERICAN WEST 5(Nov 1968): 41-49. Pres.

_____. "Trail Tragedy." TRUE WEST 25(May-Apr 1978): 31, 38-39. Grave at Casper, WY.

SHAFFER, Leslie D. "The Management of Organized Wagon Trains on the Overland Trail." MISSOURI HISTORICAL REVIEW 55(Jul 1961): 355-65. Train Govt.

SHANE, Carlos W. "Being an Account of a Journey to the Territory of Oregon...." PRESBYTERIAN HISTORICAL SOCIETY JOURNAL 21(1943): 1-33. OR(Indep). III. 1846.

SHANNON, Betty. "The New Old Mormon - Emigrant Trail." DESERT 39(Dec 1976): 24-27. CAL-1848-Genl. Carson Pass-Geog.

SHANNON, Thomas. "Journey of Peril." SAN JOSE DAILY MERCURY 16 Nov 1903, p. 1. SLCOR. V. 1849.

SHANNON, William. "The Great Gold Excitement of 1858 on the Fraser River." Province of British Columbia Archives, Victoria, BC. Not Seen.

SHARP, Cornelia A. "Diary...." TRANSACTIONS Oregon Pioneer Association 1903 (1904): 171-88. OR(Indep)-BARLOW. III. 1852.

SHARP, Cyrus. "An Adventure in an Overland Stage Coach." GOLDEN ERA 40(May 1891): 865-76. Stage.

SHARP, James M. EARLY RECOLLECTIONS. N.p., 1931. OR(Indep)-BARLOW. IV. Rem. 1852.

SHARP, James P. "The Pony Express Stations." IMPROVEMENT ERA 48(Feb, Mar 1945): 76-77, 108-09, 130-31, 155-58. Sites: SLC to Egan Canyon.

SHARP, Jay W. "Journada del Muerto." NEW MEXICO MAGAZINE 63(Jan 1985): 18-20. Geog. RIO GRANDE-Genl.

SHARP, John. Brief Pencilled Notes...1850. CSL. CAL. V-. 1850.

SHARP, Joe H. "Recollections." TRANSACTIONS Oregon Pioneer Association (1895): 91-95. OR(Blue Springs, MO)-BARLOW. Rem. 1852. Not Seen.

SHARP, Paul F. WHOOP-UP COUNTRY: THE CANADIAN - AMERICAN WEST, 1865 - 1885. Minneapolis: Univ. of Minnesota Press, 1955. Freight.

_____. "Whoop-Up Trail: International Highway on the Great Plains." PACIFIC HISTORICAL REVIEW 21(Jun 1952): 129-44. Freight.

SHARP, Robert Lee. SEE: Sharp, William H. LIFE AND DIARY.

SHARP, William H. LIFE AND DIARY OF ROBERT LEE SHARP. N.p.: Author, 1938. CAL(Kansas City). II. 1852.

SHAW, D. A. EL DORADO: OR CALIFORNIA...1850 - 1900. LA: Baumgardt, 1900. CAL(Council)-BRIDGER-HASTINGS. III. 1850.

SHAW, Dorothy R. "Jimmy's Camp on the Cherokee Trail." COLORADO MAGAZINE 27(Jan 1950): 63-72. CHEROKEE-Genl.

SHAW, Reuben C. ACROSS THE PLAINS IN FORTY-NINE. Ed. Milo M. Quaife. One of the Lakeside Classics. 1896. Reprint. Chicago: R. R. Donnelley, 1948. CAL(Indep). II. Rem. 1849.

SHAW, William. Narrative and Life. BANCROFT. OR(Indep?). IV. Rem. 1844.

SHEFRIN, Jack A. "The Chisholm Trail." MA thesis, Univ. of Kansas City, 1940. Not Seen.

SHELLENBERGER, Robert. "Missus McLellan and the Ragtown Rustlers: An Incident on the California Trail in 1850." FAR-WESTERNER 20(Apr 1979): 3-12. Geog. Stock.

SHELLER, Roscoe. "Wagontrain Bride." FRONTIER WEST 36(Win 1961): 30-31, 40. Social. Emigrant courtship.

SHELLEY, Edward. "The Western Journal of Edward Shelley." CHICAGO WESTERNERS BRAND BOOK 13(Jan 1957): 81-83. CAL(Kansas City)-CHEROKEE(Denver-Ft. Bridger?)-MONTANA. IV. 1862.

SHEPHERD, J. S. JOURNAL...AND GUIDE TO THE FUTURE EMIGRANT. Racine, WI: Rebecca Shepher, 1851. CAL(St. Jo). II. 1850. A rare diary that improves during western half of trip.

SHEPPARD, Craig. LANDMARKS ON THE EMIGRANT TRAIL: A PORTFOLIO OF NEVADA WATERCOLORS. Reno: Univ. of Nevada Press, 1971. Graphics.

SHEPPERSON, Wilbur S., ed. "Sir Charles Wentworth Dilke: A Republican Baronet in Nevada." NEVADA HISTORICAL SOCIETY QUARTERLY 3(Oct 1960): 13-29. SIMPSON. III. 1866.

SHERIFF, Matthew. Diary. COHIST. PIKES. III+. 1860.

SHERMAN, James E., and Edward F. Ronstadt. "Wagon Making in Southern Arizona." SMOKE SIGNAL 31(Spr 1975): 2-20. Eqpt. Graphics.

SHERROD, James M. "Sketches from the Life of...." ANNALS OF WYOMING 4(Jan, Apr 1928): 325-53, 389-96. Freight.

SHERWELL, Samuel. OLD RECOLLECTIONS OF AN OLD BOY. NY: Knickerbocker, 1923. PIKES. III. Rem. 1863.

SHERWOOD, J. Ely. THE POCKET GUIDE TO CALIFORNIA. NY: Author, 1849. Guide.

SHIELDS, F. R. "Crossing the Plains." SACRAMENTO DAILY RECORD-UNION, 22 May & 19 June 1886, pp. 8, 4. CAL(Council). IV. Rem. 1852.

SHIELDS, James G. California Trip. BEINECKE. CAL(St. Jo)-BRIDGER-SLCUT. I. 1850.

SHIELDS, Kathleen. "Joan Myers and the Santa Fe Trail." NEW MEXICO MAGAZINE 63(Nov 1985): 64-70, 73. Pres.

SHIELDS, Wilmer B. Ed. Harris, Lewis B. "Up from San Antonio."

SHINN, John R. Journal. UTHIST. CAL(Council)-BRIDGER-HASTINGS-TRUCKEE. III. 1850.

SHINN, Jonathan. THE MEMOIRS OF CAPTAIN JONATHAN SHINN. Greeley, CO: Weld County Democrat, 1890. Geog: Ferries in the Council Bluffs area.

SHINN, Silas. THE TRAIL OF A PIONEER. N.p., n.d. CAL(Ft. Smith)-SANTA FE-RIO GRANDE-GILA. IV. Rem. 1849.

SHIPEE, Lester B. "The Fisk Expeditions to the Gold Country." MNHIST. Biog-James Fisk.

SHIPLEY, Mrs. H. R. "Diary...New York to Oregon in 1853." PORTLAND TELEGRAM, 17 Mar & 18 Apr 1930. SEE: Hines, Celinda.

SHIPP, Ellis R. THE EARLY AUTOBIOGRAPHY.... Ed. Ellis S. Musser. N.p., 1962. MORMON. 1852. Not Seen.

SHIRES, William. Journal. In Paul & Helen Henderson Collection, UWY. CAL(Council)-Ends Upper Platte Crossing. III. 1862.

SHIRK, George H. SEE: With Muriel H. Wright. "Journal of Lt. A. W. Whipple."

SHIVELY, J. M. ROUTE AND DESTANCES TO OREGON AND CALIFORNIA.... WA: William Greer, 1846. Guide.

SHIVELY, John M. "John M. Shively's Memoir." Eds. Howard M. & Edith M. List. OREGON HISTORICAL QUARTERLY 81(Spr, Sum 1980): 5-30, 181-95. OR(Indep). IV. Rem. 1843. OR(East to Missouri). IV. Rem. 1845.

SHOBER, John H. Papers. MONHIST. DAKOTAS-MONTANA. V. 1864.

SHOCKLEY, Charlene P. Gold Rush Letters. HUNTL. SEE: PENNELL, William E.

SHOEMAKER. "The Shoemaker Diary of 1850." In TWO ARGONAUTS ON THE OREGON TRAIL. Menlo Park, CA: Amargosa Memorial Library, 1961. CAL(Council)-BRIDGER-SLCUT. II. 1850.

SHOEMAKER, Edward C. "Fort Towson: An Early Communications Route to Oklahoma." RED RIVER VALLEY HISTORICAL REVIEW 7(Sum 1982): n.p. Not Seen.

SHOEMAKER, Floyd C. "Historical Articles in Missouri Newspapers." MISSOURI HISTORICAL REVIEW 9(1914-15): 248-62, 10(1915-16): 37-44, 120-26, 288-300, 11(1916-17): 68-79, 201-13, 348-65, 12(1917-18): 44-58, 111-23, 13(1918-19): 424-57, 14(1919-20): 172-96, 15(1920-21): 58-91, 743-49, 16(1921-22): 176-86, 17(1922-23): 239-55, 405-16, 18(1923-24): 117-25, 476-501, 19(1924-25): 158-87, 508-54, 20(1925-26): 163-97, 21(1926-27): 296-330. Bib.

_____. "Missouri's New Program for Highway Historic Marking...." MISSOURI HISTORICAL REVIEW 49(Jan, Apr, Jul 1955): 105-22, 249-63, 342-56. Pres.

_____. "The Pony Express - Commemoration, Stables, and Museum." MISSOURI HISTORICAL REVIEW 44(Jul 1950): 343-63. Pres.

SHOMBRE, Henry. Diary. BANCROFT. CAL(Indep)-Ends Ft. Laramie. II+. 1849.

SHORT, George W. Diary. WIHIST. CAL(St. Jo). III. 1852.

SHOTTENKIRK, D. G. "Diary." In SCENERY OF THE PLAINS..., ed. Franklin Langworthy. Princeton: Princeton Univ. Press, 1932. Sweetwater River section only. II. 1850.

SHOUSE, Sarah N. Ed. Boyles, John R. "None Dream But of Success."

SHROCK, Thomas P. Letter. BYU. CAL(Indep)-BRIDGER-SLCUT. III-. 1849.

SHULL, Teri. "Tabitha Moffat Brown...." AMERICAN HISTORY ILLUSTRATED 20(Apr 1985): 48-49. Biog. Social.

SHUMWAY, Ernest W. "History of Winter Quarters, Nebraska, 1846 - 1848." MA thesis, Brigham Young Univ., 1953. Geog.

_____. "Winter Quarters, 1846 - 1848." NEBRASKA HISTORY 35(Jun 1954): 115-26; 36(Mar 1955): 43-54. Geog.

SHUMWAY, George, Edward Durrell, and Howard C. Frey. CONESTOGA WAGON 1750 - 1850. York, PA: Private, 1966. Eqpt. Graphics.

SHUPE, Verna I. THE ARGONAUTS AND PIONEERS. Pocatello, ID: Author, 1931. CAL(Old Ft. Kearney). IV. 1849.

SHURLY, Edmond R. "Skirmish at Goose Creek: Edmond R. P. Shurly's Bozeman Trail Reminiscence." MONTANA 33(Spr 1983): 60-63. Indians. Military. BOZE-Genl.

SHURTLEFF, Charles A. "The Late John Craddock: Stage Driver of the Fifties." Society of California Pioneers QUARTERLY 7(Jun 1930): 123-26. Stage.

SHUTTERLY, Lewis. DIARY.... Ed. Robert C. Black. Saratoga, WY: N.p., 1981. CAL(Indep). 1849. Not Seen.

SILLIMAN, Bert J. Papers. UTHIST. SPANISH-Genl.

SIMMONS, Joseph R. Diary. MO-WHMC. CAL(Westport)-SANTA FE-RIO GRANDE-GILA. I. 1849.

SIMMONS, Marc. Ed. Russell, Marian S. LAND OF ENCHANTMENT.

_____. "Arrieria: The Art of Mexican Muleteering." SOUTHWEST HERITAGE 7(Spr 1977): 2-5. Freight.

_____. FOLLOWING THE SANTA FE TRAIL: A GUIDE FOR MODERN TRAVELERS. Santa Fe: Author, 1984. SANTA FE-Genl. Guide.

_____. MURDER ON THE SANTA FE TRAIL...1843. El Paso: Texas Western Press, 1987. SANTA FE-1843-Genl.

_____. "The Old Trail to Santa Fe." OVERLAND JOURNAL 4(Spr, Sum, Fall 1986): 4-15, 61-69, 65-77. SANTA Fe-Genl.

_____. "Women on the Santa Fe Trail: Journals, Memoirs. An Annotated Bibliography." NEW MEXICO HISTORICAL REVIEW 61(Jul 1986): 233-44. Social. Bib.

SIMMONS, Ora. "Life Sketch of Howard Egan." LDS. Important study of this active, but ignored, figure.

SIMONIN, Louis L. THE ROCKY MOUNTAIN WEST IN 1867. Trans. Wilson O. Clough. Lincoln: Univ. of Nebraska Press, 1966. Stage: Julesburg to Denver. II. 1867.

SIMONS, Fanny F. "Journal." In AN ENDURING LEGACY, vol. 6.

SLC: Daughters of the Utah Pioneers, 1983. MORMON. IV. 1859.

SIMONS, George. "Diary." In THIRTIETH ANNIVERSARY BULLETIN. Omaha: Joslyn Art Museum, 1961. Graphics.

SIMPSON, Sir George. AN OVERLAND JOURNEY ROUND THE WORLD.... Philadelphia: Lea & Blanchard, 1847. OR(Walla Walla to Vancouver). V. 1841.

SIMPSON, Henry I. THE EMIGRANT'S GUIDE TO THE GOLD MINES. 1848. Reprint. MAGAZINE OF HISTORY, Extra No. 176. 1932. Guide.

SIMPSON, James H. REPORT AND MAP OF THE ROUTE FROM FORT SMITH, ARK., TO SANTA FE, NEW MEXICO, 1849. 31st Cong., 1st sess. S. Ex. Doc. 12. Govt. MARCY. I. 1849.

_____. REPORT BY CAPTAIN JAMES HERVEY SIMPSON...OF RECONNAISSANCES, &c., IN THE TERRITORY OF UTAH.... 35th Cong., 2d sess. 1859. S. Ex. Doc. 40. SIMPSON-1858-Genl. Govt.

_____. REPORT OF EXPLORATIONS ACROSS THE GREAT BASIN OF THE TERRITORY OF UTAH FOR A DIRECT WAGON-ROUTE FROM CAMP FLOYD TO GENOA, IN CARSON VALLEY, IN 1859. WA: GPO, 1876. SIMPSON. I. 1859.

_____. THE SHORTEST ROUTE TO CALIFORNIA.... Philadelphia: J. B. Lippincott, 1869. Guide.

SIMS, Edward E. Journal. Norlin Library-Western History, Univ. of Colorado-Boulder. PIKES. III. 1859.

SINCLAIR, James. "The Career of James Sinclair." Ed. Jesse S. Copely. BEINECKE. OR-CANADA(Red River-Edmonton-Kootenay)-Ends Walla Walla. V. 1854.

SINCLAIR, John. "Diary." In JOURNAL OF A TRIP TO CALIFORNIA.... Ed. John F. Riker. Urbana, OH: N.p.: 1855. TRUCKEE. II. 1846.

SINNETT, Mrs. Percy. Trans. Heinrich B. Mollhausen. DIARY OF A JOURNEY.

"Site of Plum Creek Massacre." NEBRASKA HISTORY 5(Jul-Sept 1922): 47-48. Geog.

SITGREAVES, Lorenzo. "Map of Posts along the Platte and Little Blue Rivers." National Archives, Washington, DC. Maps.

_____. REPORT OF AN EXPEDITION DOWN THE ZUNI AND COLORADO RIVERS.... 32nd Cong., 2d sess. 1853. S. Ex. Doc. 59. BEALE(Santa Fe-Mohave Villages-Yuma). IV. 1852.

SKAGGS, Jimmy M. SEE: With Seymour V. Connor. BROADCLOTH AND BRITCHES.

_____. "Between Supply and Demand: A History of the Cattle-Trailing Industry, 1866 - 1890." PhD diss., Texas Technological Univ., 1970. Stock.

_____. THE CATTLE-TRAILING INDUSTRY: BETWEEN SUPPLY AND DEMAND, 1866 - 1890. Lawrence: Univ. of Kansas Press, 1973. Stock.

_____. "The Economic Impact of Trailing: One Aspect." WESTX 43(Oct 1967): 18-30. Stock.

_____. "The Route of the Great Western (Dodge City0 Cattle Trail." WESTX 41(Oct 1965): 131-43. Stock.

SKELTON, Charles L. RIDING WEST ON THE PONY EXPRESS. NY: Macmillan, 1937. A novel, but contains elaborate and accurate detail. Pony.

SKINNER, Francis. THE CALIFORNIA WAY-BILL.... St. Louis: Hill & M'Kee, 1852. Guide.

SKINNER, Hugh A. Diary. Spencer Library, Univ. of Kansas-Lawrence. CAL(Indep)-BRIDGER-HASTINGS. II. 1850.

SLAGLE, James M. "Forty Niners from Washington County, PA." Ed. Earle R. Forrest. PONY EXPRESS 12(Sept 1945): 6-8. CAL(Council)-Ends Ft. Laramie. III. 1850.

SLATER, John L. Reminiscence. ORHIST. OR(Indep)-MEEK. IV. Rem. 1853.

SLATER, N. FRUITS OF MORMONISM. Coloma, CA: Harmon & Springer, 1851. Utah. A perceptive analysis of pioneer Mormon life.

SLATER, Nellie. Reminiscence. Washington State Univ. Library-SpCol, Pullman, WA. OR(Council). IV. Rem. 1862.

SLATER, O. B. Travels.... Washington State Univ. Library-SpCol, Pullman, WA. OR(Plattsmouth). III+. Rem. 1862. Probably written by Nellie Slater.

SLEIGHT, Morris. SEE: Jedlick, William J. "Letters."

SLOAN, William K. "The Autobiography of William K. Sloan...." ANNALS OF WYOMING 4(Jul 1926): 235-64. Rem. Freight.

SLOANE, Eleanor. THE BUTTERFIELD OVERLAND MAIL ACROSS ARIZONA. Tucson: Arizona Silhouettes, 1958. Stage.

SLOWERS, Robert E. Ed. Scott, Charles. "The Nevada Indian Uprisings of 1860."

SMART, William B. EXPLORING THE PIONEER TRAIL. SLC: Young Men's Mutual Improvement Assn., 1958. MORMON-Wasatch Crossing, Henefer, UT to SLC-Genl. Map.

SMEDLEY, William. ACROSS THE PLAINS IN '62. Denver: Author, 1916. OR(Council)-BARLOW. III+. Rem. 1862.

SMITH, Addison T. THE OLD OREGON TRAIL - THE WORLD'S MOST HISTORICAL HIGHWAY. WA: Oregon Trail Memorial Assn., 1925. Pres.

SMITH, Azariah. Journal. UTHIST. CAL(Leav)-SANTA FE-RIO GRANDE-GILA. II. 1846. CAL(Sutter's-Carson Pass)-TRUCKEE(Wadsworth-Humboldt Sink)-SLCUT. II+. 1846.

SMITH, Bathsheba W. Diary. UTHIST. MORMON. III. 1849.

SMITH, C. F. Journal.... KSHIST. PIKES. II. 1859.

SMITH, Charles. Diary. In Paul & Helen Henderson Collection. UWY. MORMON. III. 1855.

SMITH, Charles L. "The History of the United States Overland Mail to 1869." MA thesis, Ohio State Univ., 1930. Mail. Stage.

SMITH, Charles W. JOURNEY OF A TRIP TO CALIFORNIA...1850. Ed. R. W. G. Vail. NY: Cadmus, 1920. CAL(Weston). III. 1850.

SMITH, Chester. "Chester Smith's Journal 1852." COLORADO GENEALOGIST 37(Fall-Win 1976): 107-15; 38(Spr, Sum, Fall, Win 1977): 20-25, 42-47, 86-91, 122-29. CAL(St. Jo)-BRIDGER-SLCUT-TRUCKEE-BECK. II. 1852.

SMITH, Cora R. Ed. Ressler, John J. "Trip."

SMITH, Darling. "Pioneer of 1842." Ed. Gertrude Smith. ORHIST. OR(Indep). V. 1842.

SMITH, Delazon. Letters to the OREGON WEEKLY TIMES. ORHIST. Guide.

SMITH, Dorothy. Ed. Guillod, Harry. "Journal to Cariboo."

SMITH, Duane A. Ed. Bowen, E. A. "Pike's Peak Fifty-Niner."

_____. "The Army and Western Transportation, 1824-1851." DENVER WESTERNERS BRAND BOOK 1959 (1960): 279-308. Military.

SMITH, Dwight L. Ed. Young, John D. JOHN D. YOUNG.

_____. THE AMERICAN AND CANADIAN WEST: A BIBLIOGRAPHY. Clio Bibliography Series No. 6. Eric H. Boehm, ed. Santa Barbara: American Bibliographical Center, 1979. Bib.

_____. "The Westward Traveler: Unexploited Manuscript Resources of the Newberry Library." In TRAVELERS ON THE WESTERN FRONTIER, ed. John F. McDermott. Urbana: Univ. of Illinois Press, 1970. Bib.

SMITH, Edward L. Journal...1848. BANCROFT. CAL(Indep)-Ends in Kansas. III. 1848.

SMITH, Elizabeth Dixon. "Diary...1847." In COVERED WAGON WOMEN, vol. 1. Ed. Kenneth L. Holmes. Glendale: Clark, 1983. OR(St. Jo). IV. Rem. 1847.

SMITH, Elizabeth Drusilla. Account. CAHIST. CAL. V-. Rem. 1849.

SMITH, G. A. Journal. BANCROFT. CAL(St. Jo). III. 1852.

SMITH, George A. History. UTHIST. MORMON. II+. 1847.

SMITH, George G. "Parson's Progress to California: Narrative of an Overland Stage Journey from San Antonio, TX to San Francisco, in the Spring of 1859." Southern California Historical QUARTERLY 21(Jun-Sept 1939): 45-78. Stage: San Antonio-SF. II. 1859.

SMITH, George W. Account. Widener Library-Harvard Univ., Cambridge, MA. CAL. Rem. 1850. Not Seen.

SMITH, Gerald A., and Clifford J. Walker. INDIAN SLAVE TRADE ALONG THE MOJAVE TRAIL. San Bernardino, CA: County Museum, 1965. BEALE-Genl.

SMITH, Gerald G. "The Feather River Highway, 1851 - 1937." MA thesis, Univ. of California-Berkeley, 1947. BECK-Genl.

SMITH, Gertrude. Ed. Smith, Darling. "Pioneer of 1842."

SMITH, Hank. "Mining and Indian Fighting in Arizona and New Mexico, 1858 - 1861." Ed. Hattie M. Anderson. PANHANDLE-PLAINS HISTORICAL REVIEW 1(1928): 67-115; 2(1929): 65-97. Stage.

SMITH, Harriet A. My Trip. CSL. CAL-LASSEN. IV. Rem. 1849.

_____. "To Pike's Peak by Ox-Wagon, the Harriet A. Smith Day-Book." Ed. Fleming Fraker, Jr. ANNALS OF IOWA 35(1959-61): 113-48. PIKES. II+. 1863.

SMITH, Helen K., ed. WITH HER OWN WINGS: HISTORICAL SKETCHES, REMINISCENCES AND ANECDOTES OF PIONEER WOMEN. Portland: Author, 1948. OR-Genl. Social.

SMITH, Hugh I. THE OREGON MCNARY FAMILY GENEALOGY AND HISTORICAL SKETCHES. Atlanta: Author, 1938. OR(Indep?)-MEEK. V. 1845.

SMITH, I. M. A Trip. CSL. CAL(Council?). V-. Rem. 1859. Indian attack in Raft River area. Indians.

SMITH, J. A. "Big Trees - Carson Valley Road." LAS CALAVERAS 7(Apr 1959): 1-5. CAL-Genl.

_____. "Calaveras County Bridges - Ferries." LAS CALAVERAS 2(Jul 1954): 1-4. CAL-Genl.

_____. "The Ebbets Pass or Big Tree Road." LAS CALAVERAS 2(Jan 1954): 1-3. CAL-Genl.

SMITH, J. Lyman. Ed. Standage, Henry. THE MARCH OF THE MORMON BATTALION.

SMITH, Jack. SEE: With Eldon G. Bowman. BEALE'S ROAD THROUGH ARIZONA.

SMITH, Jeffrey E. Ed. Lane, Samuel A. GOLD RUSH.

SMITH, John. Diary. LDS. MORMON. III. 1847.

SMITH, John. Diary. ORHIST. OR(Council)-BARLOW. III. 1853.

SMITH, John E. "The Applegate Trail in Lane County." LANE COUNTY HISTORIAN 8(Nov 1963): 49-51. APPLE-Genl. Map.

SMITH, John Eugene. SEE: Bozeman Trail Manuscripts.

SMITH, Mary. "Miss Smith Crosses the Plains in 1866." Ed. Dorothy Gardiner. NEW YORK WESTERNERS BRAND BOOK 5, no. 4(1959): 77-82. Stage: Kansas City-Ft. Lyon by Smoky Hill Route. III. 1866.

SMITH, Mary Ettie V. FIFTEEN YEARS AMONG THE MORMONS. Ed. Nelson W. Green. NY: Scribner, 1858. MORMON? 1847. Not Seen.

SMITH, Melvin T. "The Colorado River: Its History in the Lower Canyons Area." PhD diss., Brigham Young Univ., 1972. SLCOR-Genl. BEALE-Genl.

SMITH, Moses I. Memoirs. In W. W. Morrison Collection. UWY. OR(Indep)-BARLOW. IV. Rem. 1845.

SMITH, Napoleon B. Biographical Sketch. BANCROFT. CAL(Indep)-BRIDGER-HALL-TRUCKEE. V. Rem. 1845.

SMITH, Olive F. "A History of California Periodical Literature from 1899 to 1906; together with a Descriptive Catalogue of Materials for Western History in the Most Important Magazines of the Period." MA thesis, Univ. of California-Berkeley, 1923. Bib.

SMITH, Pauline U. CAPTAIN JEFFERSON HUNT OF THE MORMON BATTALION. SLC: Morgan Foundation, 1958. MORMON. V-. 1847. SLCOR. V-. 1848. SLCOR. V-. 1850. Biog.

SMITH, Philip D., Jr. "The Sagebrush Soldiers: Nevada's Volunteers in the Civil War." NEVADA HISTORICAL SOCIETY QUARTERLY 5(Fall-Win 1962): 1-87. Military.

SMITH, Ralph A. "The Comanche Bridge between Oklahoma and Mexico, 1843 - 1844." CHRONICLES OF OKLAHOMA 39(Spr 1961): 54-69. Indians. TEX-Genl. MEX-Genl.

SMITH, Reuben. "The Fort Kearney, South Pass, and Honey Lake Wagon Road." MA thesis, Univ. of California-Berkeley, 1952. LANDER-Genl. Missing from Stacks.

SMITH, Sara. Diary. Held by Charles W. Martin, Omaha, NB. CAL(Council)-TRUCKEE. III. Rem. 1854.

SMITH, Sarah A. PIONEER EPIC. Boulder: Johnson, 1951. PIKES. V. 1864.

SMITH, Seth M. AUTOBIOGRAPHY OF 'YOUR UNCLE FULLER.' Elliott, IA: Graphic, 1905. CAL(Council). V. 1852.

SMITH, Sherry L. "The Bozeman - Trail to Death and Glory." ANNALS OF WYOMING 55(Spr 1983): 32-50. BOZE-Genl.

SMITH, Ursula. SEE: With Linda Peavy. "Women in Waiting."

SMITH, Victor B. "Oregon Stage Company." WESTERN STAMP COLLECTOR 18(Nov 1943): 13. Stage.

SMITH, W. C. A JOURNEY TO CALIFORNIA IN 1849. N.p.: Author, 1925. CAL-MEX(Vera Cruz-Mexico City-San Blas...Baja California to San Diego). III. 1849.

SMITH, Waddell F. "The Boom Days of Staging." TRUE WEST 13(Jul-Aug 1966): 22-24, 50-53. Stage.

_____. Collection. UPAC. Large Pony Express and Russell, Majors & Waddell holding.

_____. "On the Pony Express." CHICAGO WESTERNERS BRAND BOOK 22(Jan 1966): 81-83, 87-88. Pony.

_____. "The Pony Express and the Overland Mail...What Connection." SMOKE SIGNAL 17(Spr 1968): 146-59. Pony. Stage. Mail.

_____. "Pony Express Mail." FAR-WESTERNER 7(Jul 1966): 10-14. Pony.

_____. PONY EXPRESS VERSUS WELLS FARGO EXPRESS: OR HOOF PRINTS THAT CAN NOT BE ERODED BY TIME. San Rafael: Pony Express History and Art Gallery, 1966. Stage. Pony.

_____. "Stage Lines and Express Companies in California." FAR-WESTERNER 6(Jan 1965): 1-12. Stage.

_____. STAGE LINES AND EXPRESS COMPANIES IN CALIFORNIA. San Rafael: Pony Express History and Art Gallery, 1965. Stage.

_____, ed. THE STORY OF THE PONY EXPRESS. San Rafael: Pony Express History and Art Gallery, 1960. Reprint, with extensive additions, of Glenn D. Bradley's STORY OF THE PONY EXPRESS (1914).

SMITH, William. Reminiscence. ORHIST. OR(Indep)-APPLE. IV. Rem. 1846.

SMITH, William E. "The Grave of Sarah Keyes on the Oregon Trail." KANSAS HISTORICAL QUARTERLY 5(May 1936): 208-12. Geog-Alcove Springs, Marshall County, KS.

_____. "The Oregon Trail through Pottawatomie County." COLLECTIONS Kansas State Historical Society 1926-1928 17(1928): 435-64. OR-Genl. Pres.

Smith-Gilman Papers. "Early Days in San Gorgonio Pass." Held by Mrs. Harry Hunt, Banning, CA. BRADSHAW-Genl. Geog. Not Seen.

SMYTH, David. "The Yellowhead Pass and the Fur Trade." BRITISH COLUMBIA STUDIES (Winter 1984-85). Geog. Not Seen.

SNEDAKER, Morris J. "The Diary of Morris Jackson Snedaker." Ed. Norman B. Ferris. SOUTHWESTERN HISTORICAL QUARTERLY 66(Apr 1963): 516-46. MORMON. IV. 1855.

SNODGRASS, R. H. Journal. BEINECKE. CAL(Weston)-BRIDGER-SLCUT. II. 1852.

SNOW, Bernard. Diary. UTHIST. MORMON. III. 1856.

SNOW, Edwina J. "William Chandless: British Overlander, Mormon Observer, Amazon Explorer." UTAH HISTORICAL QUARTERLY 54(Spr 1986): 116-36. Biog.

SNOW, Eliza R. "Pioneer, 1847." In OUR PIONEER HERITAGE, vol. 17. SLC: Daughters of the Utah Pioneers. 1974. MORMON. III. 1847.

SNOW, Erastus. "Journey to Zion: From the Journal of Erastus Snow." UTAH HUMANITIES REVIEW 2(Apr, Jul 1948): 107-28, 264-84. MORMON. II+. 1847.

SNOW, Taylor N. "Diary of Taylor N. Snow, Hoosier Fifty-Niner." Ed. Arthur H. Hays. INDIANA MAGAZINE OF HISTORY 28(Sept 1932): 193-208. CAL(Council)-Ends Winnemucca, NV. II. 1859.

SNOW, William. Across the Plains. BYU. MORMON. IV. 1850.

SNOW, William J. "Exploration and Development of the Great Basin before the Coming of the Mormons." MA thesis, Univ. of California-Berkeley, 1922. PhD diss., same institution, 1923. Overland-Genl.

SNYDER, Jacob R. "The Diary of Jacob R. Snyder." Society of California Pioneers QUARTERLY 8(Dec 1931): 224-60. CAL(Indep)-BRIDGER-HALL-TRUCKEE. III+. 1845.

SNYDER, John F. Diary. Illinois State Historical Library, Springfield, IL. CAL(Indep). I. 1850.

SNYDER, Monroe. Letters and Diary. DENVERPUB. PIKES. V. 1859.

SOCOLOFSKY, Homer E., comp. KANSAS HISTORY IN GRADUATE STUDY: A BIBLIOGRAPHY OF THESES AND DISSERTATIONS. Topeka: Kansas State Historical Society, 1970. Not Seen.

SOLOMON, Margaret. "A Bloomer Girl Conquers Pikes Peak." AMERICAN HISTORY ILLUSTRATED 18(Jan 1984): 40-47. Social.

_____. "A Study of Feminism as a Motif in 'A Journey to Pike;s Peak and New Mexico'." In WOMEN AND WESTERN LITERATURE, eds. Helen W. Stauffer and Susan J. Rosowski. Troy, NY: Whitson, 1982. Social.

SOMERS, Belle R. "Crossing the Plains...." San Francisco ARGONAUT, 25 April & 2 May 1925, 3, 3-4. CAL(Council). IV. Rem. 1849.

SOMMER, Jane H. "Outfitting for the West, 1849." MISSOURI HISTORICAL BULLETIN 24(Jul 1968): 340-47. Eqpt.

SONNICHSEN, Charles L. PASS OF THE NORTH: FOUR CENTURIES ON THE RIO GRANDE. El Paso: Texas Western Press, 1968. Geog.

_____. TUCSON: THE LIFE AND TIMES OF AN AMERICAN

CITY. Norman: Univ. of Oklahoma Press, 1982. Geog.

SORENSEN, Cloyd. "The Oatman Massacre Site." TRUE WEST 31(Mar 1984): 40-42. Indians. Geog.

SORENSON, Alfred R. EARLY HISTORY OF OMAHA.... Omaha: Daily Bee, 1876. Geog.

SORTORE, Abram. BIOGRAPHY AND EARLY LIFE SKETCH OF.... N.p.: Jennie Thomas, 1909. CAL(Council)-SLCUT. IV. Rem. 1850.

Sotheby Parke Bernet, Inc. WESTERN EXPRESSES POSTAL HISTORY. N.p.: Sotheby, 1977. Color mail covers.

SOULE, Andrew. "Memories of the Plains." SISKIYOU PIONEER 2(Fall 1954): 8-15. CAL(Council)-LASSEN. III. Rem. 1854.

SOULE, Frank. Statement. BANCROFT. CAL-TEX(Corpus Christi)-MEX(Matamoros-Monclova-Santa Cruz)-GILA. V. Rem. 1849.

SOUTHESK, Earl of. SASKATCHEWAN AND THE ROCKY MOUNTAINS. Edmonton: Hurtig, 1969. CANADA(Ft. Garry to Rockies). 1859. Not Seen.

SOUTHWORTH, John S. "Help from an Ancient Carving." FRONTIER TIMES 51(Oct-Nov 1977): 36-40. SLCOR-1849-Genl.

SOWERS, John H. Diary. LILLEY. CAL(Leav)-CHEROKEE(Denver-SLC)-SIMPSON(Used Chorpenning mail route to Gravelly Ford)-TRUCKEE. III. 1859.

SPACE, Ralph S. THE LOLO TRAIL. Lewiston, ID: Printcraft, 1970. MULLAN-Genl.

SPAETH, Reuben L. "Heinrich Lienhard in California, 1846 - 1850." MA thesis, Univ. of California-Berkeley, 1933. SEE: Lienhard, H. FROM ST. LOUIS TO SUTTER'S FORT, 1846.

SPAIN, David F. "The Diary of...." Ed. John D. Morrison. COLORADO MAGAZINE 35(Jan, Apr 1958): 11-34, 81-112. PIKES. III. 1859.

SPARKS, Elmer. "A New Mystery on the Donner Trail." FRONTIER TIMES 35(Win 1960): 27, 41-42. Pres-Salt Desert portion of Donner Party route.

SPARKS, J. H. "Account of Trip to California." JOURNAL Fort Smith Historical Society 2(Oct 1978): 60-63. CAL(Ft. Smith). 1854. Not Seen.

SPEAR, Elsa, ed. BOZEMAN TRAIL SCRAPBOOK. Sheridan, WY: Author, 1967. BOZE-Genl.

SPENCE, Clark C. "Canines to Canaan: The Story of Some Forgotten Four-Footed Pioneers." AMERICAN HERITAGE 32(Feb-Mar 1981): 58-64. Social.

_____. "Pioneers with Wagging Tails: Dogs on the Trail to Oregon." IDAHO YESTERDAYS 25(Sum 1981): n.p. Social.

SPENCE, Mary B. SEE: With Susan Miles. "Major Ben Ficklin."

SPENCE, Mary Lee. SEE: With Donald Jackson. THE EXPEDITIONS OF JOHN C. FREMONT.

SPENCER, Almon. Diary. Montana State Univ. Library, Missoula, MT. CAL(Sacramento east to Snake River)-MONTANA. 1865. Not Seen.

SPENCER, D. S. "Utah and Telegraphy." UTAH GENEALOGICAL AND HISTORICAL MAGAZINE 1(1910): 167-73. Telegraph.

SPENCER, Elma D. GOLD COUNTRY, 1828 - 1858. San Antonio: Author, 1958. PIKES-Genl. CHEROKEE-Genl.

_____. GREEN RUSSELL AND GOLD. Austin: Univ. of Texas Press, 1966. PIKES-Genl.

SPENCER, G. K. "Hell Trail of the Forty-Niners: Butterfield Trail." TRAVEL 64(Nov 1934): 25, 44. Stage.

SPENCER, John. Daily Journal. ORHIST. OR(St. Jo). III. 1852.

SPENCER, Lafayette. "Journal of the Oregon Trail." ANNALS OF IOWA 8(Oct 1908): 304-10. OR(Council). III. 1852.

SPENCER, Omar C. Oregon Trail Centennial Association Correspondence, 1940-1951. ORHIST. Pres.

SPENCER, W. A. A THOUSAND MILES IN A CANOE...DENVER, CO. TO LEAVENWORTH, KS.... Bushnell, IL: Peoria, 1880. PIKES. II. 1867.

SPENCER, William V. Spencer Family Papers. ORHIST. OR. 1852. Not Seen.

SPINDT, H. A. "The Butterfield Stage Route from Los Angeles to Porterville." Southern California Historical QUARTERLY 18(Jun 1936): 41-45. Stage. Maps.

SPIVEY, Towana. A HISTORICAL GUIDE TO WAGON HARDWARE & BLACKSMITH SUPPLIES. Contributions of the Museum of the Great Plains, No. 9. Lawton, OK: The Museum, 1981. Eqpt.

SPLAWN, Margaret L. Papers. ORHIST. OR-Genl. Not Seen.

SPONSLER, A. C. "An 1850 Gold Rush Letter...." Ed. David L. Hieb. NEBRASKA HISTORY 32(Jun 1951): 130-39. CAL(Ft. Kearney)-Ends Ft. Laramie. III. 1850.

SPOONER, E. A. Diary. BANCROFT. CAL(Indep)-SLCUT. IV. 1849.

SPOONER, Sarah E. SEE: Williams Family Papers.

SPRAGUE, Marshall. THE GREAT GATES: THE STORY OF THE ROCKY MOUNTAIN PASSES. Boston: Little, Brown, 1964. Geog.

SPRAGUE, Royal T. Diary. Held by Frances E. Luby, Port Washington, NY. 1849. Not Seen.

SPRING, Agnes W. Ed. Collins, Catherine W. "An Army Wife." Ed. Holmes, Julia A. A BLOOMER GIRL ON PIKE'S PEAK. Ed. Mallory, Samuel. "Samuel Mallory."

_____. CASPAR COLLINS: THE LIFE AND EXPLOITS OF AN INDIAN FIGHTER OF THE SIXTIES. NY: Columbia Univ. Press, 1927. Military.

_____. "Rush to the Rockies, 1859: Colorado's Gold Rush of 1859." COLORADO MAGAZINE 36(Apr 1959): 82-120. PIKES-1859-Genl.

_____. "Samuel Mallory." MONTANA 15(Apr, Jul 1965): 24-37, 68-79. PIKES-1860-Genl.

SPRING, John. JOHN SPRING'S ARIZONA. Ed. A. M. Gustafson. Tucson: Univ. of Arizona Press, 1966. GILA. III. 1866.

_____. "A March to Arizona from California in 1866." ARIZONIANA 3(Fall 1962): 1-6. GILA. III. 1866.

SPRINGER, E. C. Daybook. BANCROFT. CAL(St. Jo)-Ends Sweetwater River. II. 1850.

SPRY, Irene M. THE PALLISER EXPEDITION: AN ACCOUNT OF JOHN PALLISER'S BRITISH NORTH AMERICA EXPEDITION, 1857 - 1860. Toronto: Macmillan, 1963. CANADA-Genl.

_____. "Routes through the Rockies." BEAVER, Autumn 1963, 26-39. CANADA-Genl. Maps.

SQUIRES, Monas N. "The Butterfield Overland Mail in Missouri." MISSOURI HISTORICAL REVIEW 26(Jul 1932): 331-41. Stage.

STAAB, Rodney. "The Smoky Hill Route and Fort Fletcher." MA thesis, Fort Hays [Kansas] State Univ., 1985. PIKES-Genl.

STAATS, Stephen. "The Occasional Address." TRANSACTIONS Oregon Pioneer Association 1877 (1878): 46-59. OR-1845-Genl.

STABAEK, Tosten K. "An Account of a Journey to California in 1851." Trans. Einar I. Haugen. NORWEGIAN-AMERICAN HISTORICAL ASSOCIATION STUDIES AND RECORDS 4(1929): 99-124. CAL(Council)-LASSEN. IV. Rem. 1852.

STACEY, May H. UNCLE SAM'S CAMELS, THE JOURNAL OF MAY HUMPHREYS STACEY, SUPPLEMENTED BY THE REPORT OF EDWARD FITZGERALD BEALE. Cambridge: Harvard Univ. Press, 1929. Freight.

STACKHOUSE, Charles. The Days of '49. NBHIST. CAL(St. Jo)-LASSEN. IV. Rem. 1849.

STACKPOLE, William T. Journal. BEINECKE. CAL(St. Jo)-Ends Green River. 1849. Not Seen.

STAFFORD, Mallie. THE MARCH OF EMPIRE. SF: George Spaulding, 1884. CAL. V. Rem. 1864.

"A Stage Ride to Colorado." HARPER'S 35(1867): 137-50. Stage: Atchison to Denver via Smoky Hill. II+. 1865. Graphics.

THE STAGECOACH IN UTAH HISTORY. 12 Parts. SLC: Dixon Paper Company, 1962. Stage. Graphics.

STAHL, Ez M. Diary. DENVERPUB. PIKES. 1860. Not Seen.

STAHL, Francis M. Diary. KSHIST. SANTA FE. II. 1865.

STAINES, William C. Account. LDS. MORMON. III+. 1847.

STANDAGE, Henry. THE MARCH OF THE MORMON BATTALION...TAKEN FROM THE JOURNAL OF HENRY STANDAGE. Eds. Frank A. Golder, Thomas A. Bailey, and J. Lyman Smith. NY: Century, 1928. CAL(Leav)-SANTA FE-RIO GRANDE-GILA. III+. 1846.

STANDIFER, Jeff. SEE: Henderson, A. B. "Journal of the Yellowstone Expedition."

STANDING, A. R. SEE: With L. A. Fleming. "The Road to Fortune."

_____. "A Friendly House by a Historic Road: The Hampton - Bigler Home." UTAH HISTORICAL QUARTERLY 36(Sum 1968): n.p. Geog: Bear River Crossing.

_____. "Through the Uintahs: History of the Carter Road." UTAH

HISTORICAL QUARTERLY 35(Sum 1967): 256-67. Utah: Ft. Bridger to Vernal. Freight.

STANDISH, John K. "A Pioneer Freighter." AMERICAN CATTLE PRODUCER 29(Mar 1948): 11-12, 30-31. Freight. Not Seen.

STANFIELD, Howard S. DIARY OF HOWARD STILLWELL STANFIELD. Ed. Jack J. Detzler. Bloomington: Indiana Univ. Press, 1969. CAL(Council)-BOZE. Stage: Virginia City, MT-SLC-Sacramento. II. 1864.

STANFORD, Omer. SEE: With Mike Hanley. SAGE BRUSH AND AXLE GREASE.

STANGER, Frank M. "The Butterfield Stages." LA PENINSULA 9(Feb 1958): 3-6. Stage: San Mateo County.

_____. "The Stagecoach Era in San Mateo County." LA PENINSULA 15(Oct 1970): 3-8, 10-12. Stage.

STANLEY, Arthur J., Jr. "Fort Leavenworth: Dowager Queen of Frontier Posts." KANSAS HISTORICAL QUARTERLY 42(Spr 1976): 1-23. Geog.

STANLEY, David S. Diary...Fort Smith, Arkansas to San Diego, California. American Antiquarian Society, Worcester, MA. CAL(Ft. Smith)-MARCY-BEALE-SLCOR. II+. 1853.

STANLEY, Gerald. "Impact of the Overland Mails on San Diego." SDHIST. Stage.

STANLEY, Reva H., and Charles L. Camp. "A Mormon Mission to California in 1851." CALIFORNIA HISTORICAL QUARTERLY 14(Mar 1935): 59-73. SLCOR. III. 1851.

STANSBURY, Howard. EXPLORATION AND SURVEY OF THE GREAT SALT LAKE OF UTAH, INCLUDING A RECONNAISANCE OF A NEW ROUTE THROUGH THE ROCKY MOUNTAINS, 1849. 32nd Cong., Sp. sess. 1853. S. Ex. Doc. 3. CAL(Leav)-BRIDGER-Ends SLC. II+. 1849. CAL(SLC)-BRIDGER-East to Ft. Leavenworth. II+. 1850.

STANSELL, Christine. SEE: With Johnny Faragher. "Women and their Families."

STANTON, George. Reminiscence. MONHIST. CAL(Council)-BOZE. III. 1863.

STAPLES, David J. "The Journal of...." Ed. Harold F. Taggart. CALIFORNIA HISTORICAL QUARTERLY 22(Jun 1943): 119-50. CAL(Indep)-BRIDGER-SLCUT-Ends on Humboldt River. II. 1849.

STARBUCK, Edith. CROSSING THE PLAINS. Nashville: Southern, 1927. OR(Council)-BARLOW. IV. Rem. 1852.

STARNES, Lee. "The Pony Express Mystery." MUSEUM GRAPHIC 3(Win 1951): 4, 10-11. Pony.

STARR, Franklin. Diary. BANCROFT. CAL(St. Jo)-TRUCKEE-Ends Hot Springs. II. 1849.

STARR, Henry W. Diary. Indiana State Library-Ms, Indianapolis, IN. CAL(St. Jo)-BRIDGER-SLCUT. II+. 1850.

STARR, J. R. Diary. ORHIST. CAL(Council)-BRIDGER-SLCUT-Ends Imlay, NV. II. 1850.

STARR, Raymond. Ed. Couts, Cave J. "Emigrants and Indians."

STAUDER, John A. Diary. MO-WHMC. CAL(Weston)-BRIDGER-

SLCUT. II. 1850.

STEARNS, Orson A. "Appendix." TRANSACTIONS Oregon Pioneer Association 1919 (1922): 227-40. APPLE-Clear Lake to Rogue River. III. 1853.

STEBER, Rick, Don Gray, and Jerry Gildmeister. TRACES. Union, OR: Bear Wallow, 1980. Graphics.

STECK, Amos. AMOS STECK (1822 - 1908) FORTY-NINER. Ed. Nolie Mumey. Denver: Range, 1981. CAL(Indep). II. 1849.

STECKEL, Samuel. Diary. Oregon State Library, Salem, OR. OR-APPLE. Not Seen.

STEED, Jack and Richard. "The Rediscovery of Johnson's Ranch." OVERLAND JOURNAL 4(Win 1986): 18-32. Geog.

STEELE, A. Diary. Illinois State Historical Library-Ms, Springfield, IL. CAL-TEX(Port Lavaca-El Paso)-GILA. II +. 1850.

STEELE, Andrew. Diary. BANCROFT. CAL-TEX(Port Lavaca-El Paso)-MEX(Chihuahua-Durango-Mazatlan). IV. 1850.

STEELE, Clara B. SEE: With Kate B. Carter. MORMON BATTALION.

STEELE, Edward D. EDWARD DUNSHA STEELE 1829 - 1865. Ed. Nolie Mumey. Boulder, CO: Mumey, 1960. PIKES. II. 1859. Superb printwork.

STEELE, Harriet. "Gold Rush Letters." PACIFIC HISTORIAN 8(Feb 1964): 43-52. CAL-BRIDGER-Ends SLC. V. 1852. CAL(SLC)-West to California. V. 1853.

STEELE, John. ACROSS THE PLAINS IN 1850. Ed. Joseph Schafer. Chicago: Caxton, 1930. CAL(Council)-TRUCKEE. III. Rem. 1850.

_____. THE TRAVELER'S COMPANION THROUGH THE GREAT INTERIOR. Galena, IL: Houghton, 1854. Guide.

STEELE, Olga S. "Geography of the Mormon Trail across Nebraska." MA thesis, Univ. of Nebraska, 1933. MORMON-Nebraska porton-Genl.

STEELE, Oliver G. STEELE'S WESTERN GUIDE BOOK AND EMIGRANT'S DIRECTORY. Buffalo: Author, c1849. Guide.

STEEN, Enoch R. Diary. Indiana State Library-MS, Indianapolis, IN. CAL(Neb. City)-CHEROKEE(Denver-Ft. Bridger)-HALL-MONTANA. III +. 1865.

"A Steeple Chase on the Prairies." THE PIONEER 4(Aug 1855): 87-92. 1849 Indian skirmish on Little Blue River.

STEFFEN, Randy. "Stagecoach! The Abbot - Downing Story." WESTERN HORSEMAN, Jun, Jul, Aug 1962, 12-13, 83; 14-15, 66-67; 12-13, 72-75. Stage-Eqpt. Graphics.

STEGNER, Wallace. THE GATHERING OF ZION: THE STORY OF THE MORMON TRAIL. NY: McGraw-Hill, 1964. MORMON-Genl.

STEIN, Gary C. Ed. Duval, Isaac. "Overland to California."

STEINER, Stan. "Love in a Covered Wagon." TRUE WEST 31(Apr 1984): 21-23. Social.

STEMMONS, John. JOURNAL.... St. Louis: Fisher & Bennett, 1850. CAL. 1849. Not Seen.

STENHOUSE, T. B. CENTRAL ROUTE: THE EMIGRANT'S GUIDE FROM GREAT SALT LAKE CITY, UTAH TO CARSON CITY, NEVADA. SLC: Deseret News, 1861. Guide.

STEPHENS, B. A. "A Biographical Sketch of L. J. F. IAEGER." ANNUAL Southern California Historical Society 1, no. 4(1888-89): 36-40. Biog.

STEPHENS, Lorenzo D. LIFE SKETCHES OF A JAYHAWKER OF '49. San Jose, CA: Nolta, 1916. CAL(Council)-BRIDGER-SLCOR. IV. Rem. 1849.

STEPHENS, Robert W. Ed. Hunter, Robert. A TEXAN IN THE GOLD RUSH.

STEPHENSON, Terry E. CAMINOS VIEJOS. Santa Ana, CA: Press of Santa Ana High School and Jr. College, 1930. Stage-CA.

STEPTOE, Edward J. Report. BANCROFT. CAL(Begins SLC)-SLCUT-LASSEN. II +. 1855.

STEUBEN, William N. SEE: With John M. Muscott. "Letters."

_____. Diary. CSL. CAL(St. Jo)-HALL-TRUCKEE. II. 1849.

STEVENS, Charles. "Letters of Charles Stevens." Ed. E. Ruth Rockwood. OREGON HISTORICAL QUARTERLY 37(Jun, Sept, Dec 1936): 137-59, 241-61, 334-53; 38(Mar, Jun, Dec 1937): 63-91, 164-92, 328-54. OR(Council). IV. 1852.

STEVENS, Isaac I. A CIRCULAR LETTER TO EMIGRANTS DESIROUS OF LOCATING IN WASHINGTON TERRITORY. WA: Gideon, 1858. Guide.

STEVENS, Mary E. Comp. Hill, Elizabeth F. UNDAUNTED PIONEERS.

STEVENS, Nancy J. Account. Iowa State Historical Deparment-Ms, Des Moines, IA. PIKES. Rem. 1864. Not Seen.

STEVENS, W. H. FIELD NOTES...ATCHISON, KS, TO DENVER. Philadelphia: J. B. Chandler, 1865. PIKES. V. 1865.

STEVENS, Zenas. Diaries. NBHIST. Freight.

STEWART, Agnes. DIARY, 1853. Ed. Claire W. Churchill. Eugene, OR: Lane County Historical Society, 1959. OR(St. Jo)-MEEK? IV. 1853.

STEWART, George R., Jr. Ed. Brown, James Berry. JOURNAL OF A JOURNEY. Ed. Schallenberger, Moses. OPENING.

_____. THE CALIFORNIA TRAIL: AN EPIC WITH MANY HEROES. NY: McGraw-Hill, 1962. Cal-Genl.

_____. "A Child's Tale of the Donner Tragedy." WESTWAYS 26(Dec 1934): 22-23, 30. CAL-1846-Genl.

_____. DONNER PASS AND THOSE WHO CROSSED IT. Menlo Park, CA: Lane, 1964. Geog.

_____. ORDEAL BY HUNGER. Boston: Houghton Mifflin, 1936. CAL-1846-Genl. The classic Donner Party study.

_____. "The Prairie Schooner Got Them There." AMERICAN HERITAGE 13(Feb 1962): 4-17, 98-102. Eqpt. Graphics.

_____. "Travelers by 'Overland': Stagecoaching on the Central Route, 1859 - 1865." AMERICAN WEST 5, no. 4(1968): 4-12, 61.

Stage.

STEWART, Helen M. DIARY, 1853. Eugene, OR: Lane County Historical Society, 1961. OR(St. Jo)-Ends Bear River. III. 1853.

STEWART, J. M. "Overland Trip to California in 1850." PUBLICATIONS Historical Society of Southern California 5(1901): 176-85. CAL(Council)-via SLC. IV. Rem. 1850.

STILLMAN, Jay. Recollections, 1852. Washington State Historical Society Library, Tacoma, WA. OR(Council)-BARLOW. III. 1852.

STIMSON, Alexander L. HISTORY OF THE EXPRESS BUSINESS. NY: Baker & Goodwin, 1881. Stage.

STIMSON, Fancher. Letter, 19 March 1851. NVHIST. CAL(Council). III. 1850.

_____. "Overland Journey to California by the Platte River Route and South Pass in 1850." ANNALS OF IOWA 13(Oct 1922): 403-40. CAL(Council). II+. 1850.

STINE, Henry A. Letters & Journal. CSL. CAL(Indep)-BRIDGER-SLCUT-TRUCKEE. III. 1850.

STITES, Thomas J. Journal of Travels. ORHIST. OR(Council)-LANDER. III. 1862.

STITZEL, Jacob. Overland Diary. BANCROFT. CAL(St. Jo). II+. 1849.

STOBIE, Charles S. "Crossing the Plains to Colorado in 1865." COLORADO MAGAZINE 10(Nov 1933): 201-12. PIKES. II. Rem. 1865. Freight.

STOCKING, Hobart E. THE ROAD TO SANTA FE. NY: Hastings House, 1971. SANTA FE-Genl. Graphics. Pres: Fine guide to trail via highways.

STOCKMAN, Lawson. "Recollections of a Pioneer of 1859...." Ed. B. F. Manring. OREGON HISTORICAL QUARTERLY 11(Jun 1910): 162-76. OR(Council). V-. Rem. 1859.

STOCKPOLE, William T. Journal. BEINECKE. CAL(St. Jo)-Ends Green River. II. 1849.

STOCKTON, N. H. Journal. BANCROFT. CAL(Ft. Smith)-OKLAHOMA-TEX-GILA. Missing section across Texas to San Pedro River, AZ. III+. 1850.

STOCKTON, William J. THE PLAINS OVER. Ed. Ralph L. Milliken. Los Banos, CA: Enterprise, 1939. CAL(St. Jo)-TRUCKEE. V. Rem. 1859.

STODDARD, Francis R. "Amiel Weeks Whipple." CHRONICLES OF OKLAHOMA 28(Fall 1950): 226-30. Biog.

STODDARD, Joseph H. Overland...1852. Oregon State Library, Salem, OR. OR(Council). IV. Rem. 1852.

STODDARD, Sheldon. "Sketch." In JOURNALS OF THE 49ERS, eds. LeRoy and Ann W. Hafen. Glendale: Clark, 1954. SLCOR. V. 1849.

STODDARD, William C. Diary. Society of California Pioneers. CAL(Council)-BRIDGER-SLCUT. 1852. Not Seen.

STOKER, Kevin. "Trek along Original Trail Gives Taste of Pioneer Trail." CHURCH NEWS 55, 21 Jul 1985, 8-10. MORMON: Hike, Henefer, UT to "This is the Place" Monument.

STOKES, George W. "Echoes of the Old West." UNION PACIFIC MAGAZINE 2(Oct, Nov 1923): 6-7, 6-7. Rem. Stage. Freight.

STOKESBURY, James L. "Francis Parkman on the Oregon Trail." AMERICAN HISTORY ILLUSTRATED 8(Dec 1973): 5-9, 44-48. Biog. OR-1846-Genl.

STONE, Arthur L. FOLLOWING OLD TRAILS. Missoula, MT: Elrod, 1913. MONTANA-Genl.

STONE, Buena C. "The Route of the Barlow Trail." MA thesis, Univ. of Oregon, 1944. BARLOW-Genl.

_____. "Southern Route into Oregon: Notes and a New Map." OREGON HISTORICAL QUARTERLY 47(Jun 1946): 135-54. APPLE-Genl.

STONE, June. "Pony Express: 1960 Pony Express Reride." NORTHEASTERN NEVADA HISTORICAL SOCIETY QUARTERLY, Summer 1985, 83-91. Pres.

STONE, Mrs. Leland M. "The Old Stage Road - Yreka to Pit River." SISKIYOU PIONEER 5, no. 7(1984): 102-05. Stage.

STONE, Lyle M. YUMA CROSSING AND ASSOCIATED SITES NATIONAL HISTORIC LANDMARK: AN ARCHEOLOGICAL PERSPECTIVE. Tempe: Archeological Research Services, 1983. Pres.

STONE, Mary A. "The Cambridge - California Companies." THE Cambridge, Ohio JEFFERSONIAN, Dec 1921 - Feb 1922. CAL(Indep)-TRUCKEE. IV. 1849.

STONE, Rose F. "Diary of a Trip from Grass Valley to Donner Lake, Lake Tahoe and Independence Lake, August 3-16, 1864." Nevada County Historical Society BULLETIN 40(Jul 1986): 23-25. TRUCKEE. IV. 1864.

STONE, Sophronia H. Diary. Colorado College Library-SpCol, Colorado Springs, CO. CAL(Council)-LASSEN. II. 1852.

STOOKEY, Walter M. FATAL DECISION: THE TRAGIC STORY OF THE DONNER PARTY. SLC: Deseret News, 1950. CAL-1846-Genl.

STORM, Colton. Ed. Hinman, Charles. A PRETTY FAIR VIEW OF THE ELIPHENT.

_____. A CATALOG OF THE EVERETT D. GRAFF COLLECTION OF WESTERN AMERICANA. Chicago: Univ. of Chicago Press, 1968. Bib.

STORRS Family. Diary. Spencer Library, Univ. of Kansas-Lawrence. CAL(Council)-BRIDGER-SIMPSON. III+. 1865.

STOTT, Clifford L. SEARCH FOR SANCTUARY: BRIGHAM YOUNG AND THE WHITE MOUNTAIN EXPEDITION. SLC: Univ. of Utah Press, 1984. SLCOR-1858-Genl.

STOTT, Edwin. "Journal." UTAH HISTORICAL QUARTERLY 9(Jul-Oct 1941): 185-89. MORMON. V-. Rem. 1852.

STOTT, Kenhelm W. "Fifty Years of Stagecoaching in Southern California." SAN DIEGO WESTERNERS BRAND BOOK 1(1968): n.p. Stage.

_____. "Stagecoach Operation in San Diego and Imperial Counties, 1857 - 1874." BA thesis, San Diego State College, 1950. Stage.

STOUGHTON, John A. "Passing of an Immigrant of 1843." Ed. J. Orin Oliphant. WASHINGTON HISTORICAL QUARTERLY 15(Jul

1924): 205-10. OR(Indep). IV. Rem. 1843.

STOUT, Ephraim. Crossing the Plains. Ed. Lewis Stout. ORHIST. OR(Council). III. 1852.

STOUT, Hosea. ON THE MORMON FRONTIER; THE DIARY OF.... 2 vols. Ed. Juanita Brooks. SLC: Univ. of Utah Press, 1964. MORMON. III. 1848. SLCOR. III. 1852. SLCOR. III. 1853.

STOUT, Joseph A., ed. FRONTIER ADVENTURERS: AMERICAN EXPLORATION IN OKLAHOMA. Vol. 4, Oklahoma Series. Oklahoma City: Oklahoma Historical Society, 1976. OKLAHOMA-Genl. Not Seen.

_____. "The Santa Fe Trail." RED RIVER VALLEY HISTORICAL REVIEW 6(Sum 1981): 48-56. SANTA FE-Genl.

STOUT, Lewis. Ed. Stout, Ephraim. "Crossing the Plains."

_____, and Rebecca Stout. CROSSING THE PLAINS TO OREGON IN 1852. N.p., n.d. ORHIST. OR(Council). III. 1852.

STOUT, Ray Lewis. Oregon Trail Material. ORHIST. Key to strip map of Oregon Trail and list of markers.

STOUT, Samuel. Diary. Washington State Univ. Library-SpCol, Pullman, WA. OR(Indep)-BARLOW. III. 1851.

STOVALL, Margaret. "Disappearing River of Destiny." WESTWAYS 54(Apr 1962): 22-24. Geog: Humboldt River.

STOVER, Jacob Y. "The Jacob Y. Stover Narrative." Ed. John W. Caughey. PACIFIC HISTORICAL REVIEW 6(Jun 1937): 165-81. CAL(Council)-BRIDGER-SLCOR. V. Rem. 1849.

STOVER, John F. TRANSPORTATION IN AMERICAN HISTORY. American Historical Assn. Pub. No. 75. WA: The Association, 1970. Overland-Genl.

STOVER, Samuel M. DIARY OF...1849. Elizabethton, TN: Folson, 1939. CAL(Indep)-LASSEN. II. 1849.

STOWELL, George. Reminiscence. ORHIST. CAL(Westport?)-LASSEN. IV. Rem. 1856.

STRACHAN, John. BLAZING THE MULLAN TRAIL. N.p.: Edward Eberstadt, 1952. MULLAN-Genl.

STRAHORN, Carrie A. FIFTEEN THOUSAND MILES BY STAGE. NY: Putnam's, 1911. Stage. Graphics.

STRANGE, Muriel. "Grandma was a Lady!" CHICAGO WESTERNERS BRAND BOOK 10(Jan 1954): 81-83, 87-88. CAL(Council). V. Rem. 1855.

STRATELER, L. B. Diary, 1864. DENVERPUB. CAL-CHEROKEE(Denver-Bear River)-HALL-MONTANA. II. 1864.

STRATTON, James. Diary. Society of California Pioneers. Not Seen.

STRATTON, Julius A. Reminiscences. ORU. OR(St. Jo). III. Rem. 1854.

STRATTON, R. B. CAPTIVITY OF THE OATMAN GIRLS. SF: Whitton, Towne, 1857. CAL(Indep)-SANTA FE-RIO GRANDE-GILA. IV. 1850. Indians.

STRAUS, R. CARRIAGES AND COACHES: THEIR HISTORY AND EVOLUTION. Philadelphia: Lippincott, 1912. Eqpt.

STREBEL, George. "Pioneer Art Tour." BYU. Tour of Mormon Trail about 1925. Graphics.

STREBEL, George L. "Freighting between the Missouri River and Utah, 1847 - 1869." MS thesis, Brigham Young Univ., 1954. Freight.

STREET, Franklin. CALIFORNIA IN 1850.... 1851. Reprint. NY: Arno, 1973. CAL(St. Jo)-BRIDGER-SLCUT. II. 1849. Guide.

STREET, James. Letter to Brigham Young, 28 Dec 1865. BYU. Telegraph.

STRENTZEL, John T. Autobiography. BANCROFT. CAL-TEX(Denton?-El Paso)-GILA. IV. 1849.

STRINGHAM, Guy E. "The Pioneer Roadometer." UTAH HISTORICAL QUARTERLY 42(Sum 1974): 258-72. Eqpt.

STROBRIDGE, Idah M. "Staging in the Sierras." LAND OF SUNSHINE 12(Feb 1900): 169-72. Stage: Placerville-Virginia City, NV.

STRONG, Gary E., and Gary F. Kurutz. WESTERN AMERICANA IN THE CALIFORNIA STATE LIBRARY. Sacramento: California State Library Foundation, 1985. Bib.

STRONG, Mary F. "Trailing the 'Pony' across Nevada." DESERT 40(Jul, Aug 1977): 8-11, 38.

STRONG, Ronald T. Ed. Henderson, Lucy Ann. "Young Adventure."

STROTHER, George B. Ed. Tappan, Henry. "Diary of Henry Tappan."

STRUDWICK, June. "Wagons West - The Conestoga." SAN DIEGO HISTORICAL SOCIETY QUARTERLY 4(Jul 1958): 33-35. Eqpt.

STUART, Charles V. Trip...1849. BANCROFT. CAL(Indep)-SANTA FE-CHEROKEE(Pueblo to SLC)-SLCOR. V. 1849.

STUART, Grace D. Ed. West, Calvin B. "Calvin B. West of the Umpqua." SEE: With Reginald Stuart. CALVIN B. WEST OF THE UMPQUA.

STUART, Granville. DIARY AND SKETCHBOOK OF A JOURNEY TO 'AMERICA' IN 1866.... LA: Dawson's, 1963. Stage: Virginia City, MT-SLC-Denver-Atchison. IV. 1866. Graphics.

_____. FORTY YEARS ON THE FRONTIER.... 2 vols. Ed. Paul C. Phillips. Early Western Journals No. 2. Cleveland: Clark, 1925. CAL(Council)-BRIDGER-SLCUT-TRUCKEE-BECK. IV. Rem. 1852. CAL(Yreka)-LASSEN-East to Malad River. IV. Rem. 1857.

_____. MONTANA AS IT IS. NY: Westcott, 1865. Guide.

_____. PROSPECTING FOR GOLD FROM DOGTOWN TO VIRGINIA CITY, 1852 - 1864. Ed. Paul C. Phillips. Lincoln: Univ. of Nebraska Press, 1977. Same trail data as FORTY YEARS ON THE FRONTIER.

STUART, J. E. B. "Journal of the March of Companies F, G, H, and K...1860." N.p., n.d. KSHIST. SANTA FE. II. 1860.

STUART, James. Diary. MONHIST. CAL-LASSEN-East to Malad River. V. 1857.

STUART, Joseph A. MY ROVING LIFE. 2 vols. AUBURN, CA: Author, 1896. CAL(Indep)-LASSEN. II+. Rem. 1849.

STUART, Reginald R. Ed. West, Calvin B. "Calvin B. West of the Umpqua."

_____, and Grace D. Stuart. CALVIN B. WEST OF THE UMPQUA. SF: California History Foundation, 1961. OR(St. Jo)-BARLOW. III. 1853.

STUART-Wortley, Lady E. TRAVELS IN THE UNITED STATES. NY: Harper, 1851. MEX(Vera Cruz-Mexico City-Vera Cruz). II. 1850.

STUCKI, John S. FAMILY HISTORY.... SLC: N.p., 1932. MORMON. 1860. Not Seen.

STUDLEY, Hiram W. "Letter Describing a Mrach...1859." ANNALS OF IOWA, April 1923, 611-18. CAL(Leav)-CHEROKEE(Ft. Laramie-SLC)-Ends Camp Floyd. IV. 1859.

STULTZ, Deborah M. SEE: With Rhoda Gilman and Carolyn Gilman. THE RED RIVER TRAILS.

SUBLETTE, William L. "A Fragmentary Journal of...." Ed. Harrison C. Dale. MISSISSIPPI VALLEY HISTORICAL REVIEW 6(Jun 1919): 99-110. OR(Indep)-Ends Little Sandy, NB. III. 1843.

SUCKLEY, George. "The 1859 Overland Journal of Naturalist George Suckley." Ed. Richard G. Beidleman. ANNALS OF WYOMING 28(Mar 1956): 68-79. CAL(Leav)-BRIDGER-Ends SLC. V. 1859. Fauna.

SUDWEEKS, Leslie. "Exploration and Settlement in Southern Idaho, 1807 - 80." MA thesis, Univ. of Utah, 1935. OR-Genl.

_____. "The Raft River in Idaho History." PACIFIC NORTHWEST QUARTERLY 32(Jul 1941): 289-305. Geog. Indians.

SULLIVAN, Gabrielle. MARTIN MURPHY, JR. CALIFORNIA PIONEER, 1844 - 1884. Pacific Center for Western Historical Studies Monograph No. 4. Stockton: UPAC, 1974. CAL-1844-Genl.

SULLIVAN, W. W. Crossing...1862. BEINECKE. PIKES. IV. Rem. 1862.

SUMMERS, Camilla G. GO TO THE COWLITZ, PETER CRAW-FORD. Longview, WA: Speedy - Litho, 1978. OR(Elizabethton, NB). III. 1847.

SUMMERS, Jospeh. Letter. BEINECKE. CAL(Ft. Kearney)-SLCUT. III. 1850.

SUNDER, John E. Ed. Delany, John O. "Up the Missouri." Ed. Graham, Richard H., and Sidney Smith. "Report."

_____. BILL SUBLETTE, MOUNTAIN MAN. Norman: Univ. of Oklahoma Press, 1959. Biog.

_____. "Solomon Perry Sublette: Mountain Man of the Forties." NEW MEXICO HISTORICAL REVIEW 36(Jan 1961): 49-61. Biog.

_____. "Telegraph Beginnings in Kansas." KANSAS HISTORICAL QUARTERLY 25(Spr 1959): 32-38. Telegraph.

SUNSERI, Alvin R. "The Hazards of the Trail." EL PALACIO 81(Fall 1975): 29-37. SANTA FE-Genl.

SUTHERLAND, James. ATCHISON CITY DIRECTORY.... Indianapolis: Author, 1860. Guide. Freight.

SUTTON, Sarah. Diary. ORU. OR(St. Jo). III+. 1851.

SWAIN, Ben. Letter - Journal. AZHIST. CAL-TEX(San Antonio-El Paso)-GILA. IV. 1854. Stock.

SWAIN, William. SEE: Holliday, Jaquelin S. "William Swain and the Wolverine Rangers." SEE: Holliday, Jaquelin S. THE WORLD RUSHED IN.

SWAN, Chauncey. "Letters of a Forty-Niner." Ed. Mildred Throne. IOWA JOURNAL OF HISTORY 47(Jan 1949): 63-77. CAL(Council)-MORMON-SLCOR. IV. 1849.

SWANNELL, Frank C. "Lieutenant Palmer Makes a Survey." BEAVER, Autumn 1961, 33-38. CANADA(Bella Coola-Ft. Alexandria)-1862-Genl.

SWANSON, Merwin. SEE: With Richard W. Etulain. IDAHO HISTORY.

SWANTZ, Alexander. "Keeping Alive on the Trail." PACIFIC NORTHWESTERNER 3(Fall 1959): 49-55. Social.

SWARTZLOW, Mrs. Carl. "The Noble Trail." COVERED WAGON (1957): 20-22. NOBLE-Genl.

SWARTZLOW, Ruby J. "Peter Lassen, Northern California's Trail-Blazer." CALIFORNIA HISTORICAL QUARTERLY 18(Dec 1939): 291-314. LASSEN-Genl. Biog.

SWASEY, William F. Statement. BANCROFT. CAL(Indep). V. Rem. 1845.

SWEENEY, J. Gray. "The Artist - Explorers of the American West: 1860 - 1880." PhD diss., Indiana Univ., 1975. Graphics.

SWEENEY, James. "Narrative of James Sweeney." WASHINGTON HISTORICAL QUARTERLY 12(1921): 202-10. MORMON-1857-Genl.

SWEENY, Thomas W. JOURNAL OF LT. THOMAS W. SWEENY. Ed. Arthur Woodward. LA: Westernlore, 1956. GILA-Genl.

SWEET, Frank H. "On the Oregon Trail: An Early Settler's Story." OVERLAND MONTHLY 50(Oct 1907): 367-70. Indian attack on Snake River.

SWEET, J. H. "Old Fort Kearny." NEBRASKA HISTORY 27(Oct-Dec 1946): 233-43. Geog.

SWEETLAND, Louisa M. Reminiscences. CSL. CAL(Council)-BRIDGER-SLCUT. Rem. 1863. Not Seen.

"The Sweetwater Stage Company - 1869." ANNALS OF WYOMING 15(Apr 1943): 177-80. Stage.

SWINGLEY, Upton. "A Brief Chronicle of my Life." Illinois Historical Society JOURNAL 42(Dec 1949): 457-62. CAL(Council). V-. Rem. 1850.

SWISHER, James. HOW I KNOW.... Cincinnati: N.p., 1880. CAL. Not Seen.

SWITZER, David. "The Switzer Log." In TRAILS DIVIDED, ed. Theodore C. Ressler. Williamsburg, IA: Private, 1964. SLCOR(Utah Lake to Enterprise, UT). II. 1849.

SWITZER, Malphus A. Reminiscence. MONHIST. CAL(Council?)-HALL-MONTANA. IV. Rem. 1865.

SWOR, W. John. Letters. Univ. of Arkansas Library-SpCol, Fayetteville, AR. CAL. 1859. Not Seen.

SYDENHAM, Moses H. "Freighting across the Plains in 1856." PROCEEDINGS AND COLLECTIONS Nebraska State Historical Society 1(1894-95): 164-84. CAL(Leav)-Ends Ft. Laramie. IV. Rem.

1856.

SYLVESTER, Frank. Diary. Province of British Columbia Archives, Victoria, BC. Not Seen.

SYPOLT, Charles M. "Keepers of the Rocky Mountain Flocks: A History of the Sheep Industry in Colorado, New Mexico, Utah and Wyoming to 1900." MA thesis, Univ. of Wyoming, 1974. Stock.

T[homas], Dr. Diary. BANCROFT. CAL(Ft. Kearney)-Ends Green River. III. 1849.

TADLOCK, Nancy. "The Migrating Orchard." OVERLAND JOURNAL 3(Sum 1986): 22-27. OR-Genl.

TAFT, Mrs. Walter. "Across the Plains in the Early Sixties." TRAIL 3(Jul 1910): 16-17. Stage.

TAGGART, Frederick J. Ed. Breen, Patrick. "Diary."

TAGGART, Harold F. Ed. Staples, David. "Journal."

TAGGART, Mary L. MODERN DAY TREK OF THE MORMON BATTALION. Sugar House, UT: Mormon Battalion, Inc., 1955. Pres: 1950 reinactment.

TALBOT, Joseph C. Diary, 1863. DENVERPUB. PIKES. III. 1863.

"Tales of the Old Santa Fe and Salt Lake Trail to California." SANTA FE 8(Mar 1914): 23-30. Not Seen.

TALBOT, Theodore. JOURNAL. N.p., n.d. OR(Westport)-BRIDGER-HALL-Ends Boise. II+. 1843.

TALKINGTON, Henry L. "Mullan Road." WASHINGTON HISTORICAL QUARTERLY 7(Oct 1916): 301-06. MULLAN-Genl.

TALLACK, William. THE CALIFORNIA OVERLAND EXPRESS, THE LONGEST STAGE-RIDE IN THE WORLD. Special Pub. No. 1. LA: Historical Society of Southern California, 1935. Stage: SF-St. Louis. II. 1860.

TAMONY, Peter. "To See the Elephant." PACIFIC HISTORIAN 12(Win 1968): 23-29. Defines origins of term.

TAPPAN, Henry. "Diary of Henry Tappan." Eds. Everett and George B. Strother. ANNALS OF WYOMING 25(Jul 1953): 113-39. CAL(St. Jo)-HALL-TRUCKEE. IV. 1849.

TAPSCOTT'S EMIGRANTS' GUIDE TO THE UNITED STATES, CANADA AND CALIFORNIA. Liverpool: Tapscott, 1851. Guide.

TARBELL, J. THE EMIGRANT'S GUIDE TO CALIFORNIA.... Keokuk, IA: Whig Book, 1853. Guide.

TATE, J. W. "Across the Plains." OVERLAND MONTHLY 22(Sept 1893): 300-02. Emigrants attack Indians.

TATE, James. Diary. BANCROFT. CAL(St. Jo)-HALL-TRUCKEE. III+. 1849. An edited verison of this item was published as Williamson, Hugh P. "One Who Went West." MISSOURI HISTORICAL REVIEW 57(Jul 1963): 369-78.

TATE, Michael. "Randolph B. Marcy: First Explorer of the Wichitas." GREAT PLAINS JOURNAL 15(Spr 1976): 80-113. Biog. Govt. OKLAHOMA.

TAUSSIG, Hugo A. RETRACING THE PIONEERS: FROM WEST TO EAST IN AN AUTOMOBILE. SF: Private, 1910. Pres.

TAYLOR, Arthur S., and William M. McKinney. "An Accurate Observer: William Hoffman's View of Idaho in 1853." IDAHO YESTERDAYS 8(Sum 1964): 20-25. CAL-Genl. Sublette and Hudspeth Cutoffs.

TAYLOR, Bayard. COLORADO: A SUMMER TRIP. NY: G. P. Putnam, 1867. Stage: Topeka to Denver return Omaha. II+. 1866.

TAYLOR, Calvin. "Overland to the Gold Fields of California in 1850...." Ed. Burton Williams. NEBRASKA HISTORY 50 (Sum 1969): 125-50. CAL(St. Jo)-Ends Ft. Laramie. II+. 1850.

_____. "Overland to the Gold Fields of California in 1850...." Ed. Burton Williams. UTAH HISTORICAL QUARTERLY 38(Fall 1970): 312-49. CAL(Ft. Laramie). II+. 1850.

TAYLOR, David G. "Boom Town Leavenworth: The Failure of the Dream." KANSAS HISTORICAL QUARTERLY 38(Win 1972): 389-415. Geog.

TAYLOR, Emerson G. GOUVERNOUR KEMBLE WARREN...1830-1882. Boston: Houghton-Mifflin, 1932. Biog.

TAYLOR, Fenton. "So They Built Fort Bowie...." DESERT 14(Aug 1951): 4-7. Geog.

_____. "The West's Bloodiest Pass." TRUE WEST 7(Mar-Apr 1960): 6-10, 38-41. Geog: Apache Pass.

TAYLOR, George N. Diary. ORHIST. OR(St. Jo)-BARLOW. III+. 1853.

TAYLOR, James. Papers. ORHIST. OR(Indep). V. Rem. 1845.

TAYLOR, John. "Comanche County, Texas, to California in 1864." In OLD TIME CATTLEMEN AND OTHER PIONEERS OF THE ANZA-BORREGO AREA, ed. Lester Reed. Palm Desert, CA: Author, 1963. CAL-TEX(Concho-El Paso)-GILA. III. 1864. Party composed of Confederate Army deserters.

TAYLOR, John S. California Journal. ORHIST. CAL(Westport)-LASSEN. III+. 1854.

TAYLOR, Joseph. A JOURNAL OF THE ROUTE FROM FORT SMITH ARKANSAS, TO CALIFORNIA IN THE YEAR 1849. Bowling Green, MO: Job Office, 1850. CAL(Ft. Smith)-MARCY-RIO GRANDE-GILA. III. 1849.

TAYLOR, L. J. LIFE HISTORY.... N.p., 1930. CAL. 1847. Not Seen.

TAYLOR, Morris F. FIRST MAIL WEST: STAGECOACH LINES ON THE SANTA FE TRAIL. Albuquerque: Univ. of New Mexico Press, 1971. Mail. Stage. SANTA FE-Genl.

_____. "The Mail Station and the Military at Camp on Pawnee Fork, 1859-1860." KANSAS HISTORICAL QUARTERLY 36(Spr 1970): 27-42. Geog. Mail.

TAYLOR, Osian H. Diary, 1851. Univ. of Montana Library-SpCol, Missoula, MT. MORMON. 1851. Not Seen.

TAYLOR, Philip A. "Emigrants' Problems in Crossing the West, 1830-1870." University of Birmingham HISTORICAL JOURNAL 5, no. 1(1955): 83-102. Train Govt.

_____. "The Mormon Crossing of the United States, 1840-1870." UTAH HISTORICAL QUARTERLY 25(Oct 1957): 319-58. MORMON-Genl. Extensive references to MILLENIAL STAR.

TAYLOR, Rachel. "Overland Trip...1853." ORU. OR(Council)-APPLE. III. 1853.

TAYLOR, Ruth M. "Across the Plains to Taylorsville." Plumas County Historical Society PUBLICATION 4(Apr 1961): 20-25. CAL(Council)-BRIDGER-SLCUT-NOBLE. III. 1861. Extensive editing.

TAYLOR, Ruth W. "A Letter Home - 1861." HUMBOLDT HISTORIAN 4(Fall 1981): 2-4. CAL(Council)-BRIDGER-SLCUT-LASSEN. IV. 1861.

TAYLOR, S. H. "Oregon Bound Correspondence of...." OREGON HISTORICAL QUARTERLY 22(Jun 1921): 117-60. OR(Council). III. 1853.

TAYLOR, T. U. "Anglo-Saxon Trails across Texas." FRONTIER TIMES 15(Mar 1938): 255-63. TEX-Genl.

TAYLOR, Ted M. "They Thought They Knew Charley." WESTWAYS 67(Jan 1975): 39-41. Biog: Charley Parkhurst.

TAYLOR, W. B. "Pioneer Reminiscences." CLOVERDALE [CA] WEEKLY REVEILLE 7, 14, 21, 28 March, 11, 18, 26 April 1896. N.p. CAL(Indep)-SANTA FE-CHEROKEE-SLCOR. IV. 1849.

TAYLOR, Waldo. Ed. Applegate, Mary E. ON TO OREGON!

TAYLOR, William. Reminiscence. BANCROFT. CAL. V. Rem. 1852.

TAYLOR, William E. Diary. CSL. CAL(St. Jo)-BRIDGER-HALL-TRUCKEE. III. 1846.

TEAL, John W. "Soldier in the California Column...." Ed. Henry P. Walker. ARIZONA & THE WEST 13(Spr 1971): 33-82. GILA(San Pedro, CA to Mesilla, NM). III. 1862.

TEETER, Charles N. "Four Years of my Life...." 13th BIENNIAL REPORT State Historical Society of Idaho (1932): n.p. Freight.

TEICHERT, Minerva K. A ROMANCE OF OLD FORT HALL. Portland: Metropolitan, 1932. Geog.

_____. SELECTED SKETCHES OF THE MORMON MARCH. San Bernardino?: Author, c1967. Graphics.

TEISER, Ruth, and Catherine Harroun. ORIGIN OF WELLS, FARGO & COMPANY, 1841 - 1852. N.p., c1948. Stage.

TELFER, William B. "Early Transportation Arteries of San Diego County." MA thesis, San Diego State Univ., 1951. Geog. Stage.

TELLER, Woolsey. Letters. BEINECKE. CAL(Ft. Smith)-MARCY-Ends Galisteo, NM. IV. 1849.

TEMPLE, Wayne C. "The Pikes Peak Gold Rush." JOURNAL Illinois State Historical Society 44(Sum 1951): 147-59. PIKES-1859-Genl.

TEMPLETON, Sardis W. THE LAME CAPTAIN: THE LIFE AND ADVENTURES OF PEGLEG SMITH. LA: Westernlore, 1965. Biog.

TENNISON, O. M. SEE: With H. T. Green. REPORT AND MAP.

TERRELL, Joseph C. REMINISCENCES OF THE EARLY DAYS IN FORT WORTH. Fort Worth: Texas Printing, 1906. CAL(St. Jo). IV. Rem. 1852.

TERRY, Chloe A. Diary. Univ. of Washington Library-Ms, Seattle, WA. OR(Council). II. 1852.

TERWILLIGER, Phoebe H. "The Diary of Mrs. P. S. (Phoebe Hogeboom) Terwilliger." SISKIYOU PIONEER 4, no. 6(1973): 1-32. CAL(Council)-LASSEN. II +. 1854. Graphics.

TESSMAN, Norm. Ed. McCormick, Margaret. "Personal Journal."

TESTIMONY AS TO THE CLAIM OF BEN HOLLIDAY FOR LOSSES AND DAMAGES SUSTAINED...1862, 1863, 1864, 1865, AND 1866.... 46th Cong., 2d sess. S. Misc. Doc. 19. Stage.

TETHEROW, Solomon. SEE: ORGANIZATIONAL JOURNAL.

TEWKSBURY, Albert M. Ed. Reber, Thomas. "Journal."

"Texas Overland Transportation Company Miscellany, 1866." BARKER. TEX-Genl.

Texas Parks and Wildlife Department. TEXAS TRAILWAYS: A FEASIBILITY REPORT ON A SYSTEM OF TRAILS IN TEXAS. Austin: The Department, 1975. Pres.

THAYER, Herbert O. Ed. Hedges, William H. PIKE'S PEAK...OR BUSTED!

THEOBALD, John and Lillian. WELLS FARGO IN ARIZONA TERRITORY. Ed. Bert M. Fireman. Tempe, AZ: Arizona Historical Foundation, 1978. Stage.

THIBODO, Augustus J. "Diary of Doctor Augustus J. Thibodo." Ed. H. S. Brode. PACIFIC NORTHWEST QUARTERLY DAKOTAS(St. Paul)-CANADA-WASH. II. 1859.

"Thirty-Three Years Ago: Through Nebraska before Settlement." TRANSACTIONS AND REPORTS Nebraska State Historical Society 3(1892): 270-78. CAL(Council)-Ends Ft. Laramie. V. 1853.

THISSELL, G. W. CROSSING THE PLAINS IN '49. Oakland: Author, 1903. CAL(Council)-BRIDGER-SLCUT. II. Rem. 1850.

THOMAS, Chauncey. "Frontier Firearms." COLORADO MAGAZINE 7(May 1930): 102-08. Eqpt.

THOMAS, Daniel S. DANIEL STILLWELL THOMAS FAMILY HISTORY. SLC: N.p., 1927. MORMON. 1849. Rem. Not Seen.

THOMAS, David H. "The Colonization of Monitor Valley, Nevada." NEVADA HISTORICAL SOCIETY QUARTERLY 25(Spr 1982): 2-27. Pony.

THOMAS, J. J. "Recollections of the Mormon War." TRAIL 2(Nov 1909): 5-11. CAL(Leav)-Ends Ft. Bridger. V. 1857.

THOMAS, Julia. Reminiscences. ORU. OR(Council?). IV. Rem. 1852.

THOMAS, Lewis H. "The Hind and Dawson Expeditions, 1857 - 58." BEAVER, Winter 1958, 39-45. CANADA-Genl.

THOMAS, Martha P. DANIEL STILLWELL THOMAS FAMILY HISTORY. SLC: N.p., 1927. MORMON? Not Seen.

THOMAS, Melvin R. "The Buckeye Argonauts." OHIO STATE ARCHEOLOGICAL AND HISTORICAL QUARTERLY 59(Jul 1960): 256-69. CAL-Genl.

_____. "The Impact of the California Gold Rush on Ohio and Ohioans." MA thesis, Ohio State Univ., 1949. CAL-Genl.

THOMAS, W. Stephen. FORT DAVIS AND THE TEXAS FRONTIER PAINTINGS BY CAPTAIN ARTHUR T. LEE, EIGHTH U.S. INFANTRY. College Station, TX: Texas A & M Univ. Press,

1976. Geog. Graphics.

THOMAS, William K. Diary. MONHIST. CAL(Atchison)-BOZE-Ends Yellowstone River. III. 1864. Full entries for BOZE section only.

THOMAS, William L. Diary. Location unknown. CAL(Indep). 1849. Not Seen.

THOMASES, Jerome. "Fort Bridger, A Western Community." JOURNAL American Military Institute 5(Fall 1941): 177-88. Geog.

THOMASON, Jackson. FROM MISSISSIPPI TO CALIFORNIA.... Ed. Michael D. Heaston. Austin: Jenkins, 1978. CAL(Indep)-BRIDGER-SLCUT. II. 1849.

THOMASSON, A. H. Diary. CSL. CAL(St. Jo). II. 1850.

THOMPSON, Clark W. Letters. CAL(Weston)-BRIDGER-SLCUT. I. 1850.

THOMPSON, Enid T. "Bibliography on Bent's Old Fort, 1829 - 1849." DENVER WESTERNERS BRAND BOOK 30(1977): n.p. Not Seen. Bib. Geog.

_____. "The Ladies of Bent's Fort." DENVER WESTERNERS BRAND BOOK 30(1977): 49-70. Geog. Social.

THOMPSON, Francis M. "Reminiscences of Four-Score Years." MASSACHUSETTS MAGAZINE 5(Supplement 1912): 123-67; 6(Jan, Apr, Jul, Oct 1913): 28-39, 63-81, 99-124, 159-90; 7(Jan, Apr, Jul 1914): 11-31, 85-94, 129-36. MONTANA(Ft. Benton)-MULLAN. II+. 1862.

THOMPSON, Francis McGee. THOMPSON'S GUIDE TO THE NEW GOLD REGIONS OF UPPER MISSOURI, DEER LODGE, BEAVER HEAD, NEZ PERCES, SALMON RIVER, BOISE RIVER.... St. Louis: Studley, 1863. Guide.

THOMPSON, G. A. HAND BOOK TO THE PACIFIC AND CALIFORNIA. London: Simpkin & Marshall, 1849. Guide.

THOMPSON, Gerald. EDWARD F. BEALE AND THE AMERICAN WEST. Albuquerque: Univ. of New Mexico Press, 1983. Biog.

_____. "Edward Fitzgerald Beale and the California Gold RUsh, 1848 - 1850." SOUTHERN CALIFORNIA QUARTERLY 63(Fall 1981): 198-225. Biog.

_____, comp. "New Mexico History in New Mexico Magazine." ARIZONA & THE WEST 17(Aut, Win 1975): 245-78, 339-74. Bib.

_____. "The Public Career of Edward Fitzgerald Beale, 1845 - 1893." PhD diss., Univ. of Arizona, 1978. Biog. BEALE-Genl.

THOMPSON, H. W. "The 'Olden, Golden Days' of the Pony Express." OVERLAND MONTHLY 81(Sept 1923): 5-10. Pres.

THOMPSON, Harlow C. Across the Continent by Foot.... CSL. CAL(Leav)-TRUCKEE-CARSON PASS. IV. Rem. 1859.

THOMPSON, James B. "Crossing the Plains in 1864." SONS OF COLORADO 2(Mar 1908): 3-9. PIKES. V-. 1864. Superior account of Indian attack.

THOMPSON, Jesse C. Diary. CSL. CAL(St. Jo)-HALL. III. 1850.

THOMPSON, Jesse E. "The Overland Staging on the Thirty-Second Parallel Route in the Fifties." OVERLAND MONTHLY 12(Aug, Sept 1888): 177-90, 289-301. Stage.

THOMPSON, John P. "Snoqualmie Wagon Road, 1868." WASH.

THOMPSON, Margaret A. "Overland Travel and the Central Sierra Nevada, 1827 - 1849." MA thesis, Univ. of California, 1932. CAL-Genl.

THOMPSON, Origin. Ed. Gray, Charles. "Incidents."

THOMPSON, Robert L. WIRING A CONTINENT: THE HISTORY OF THE TELEGRAPH INDUSTRY IN THE U.S., 1832 - 1866. Princeton: Princeton Univ., 1947. Excellent bib.

THOMPSON, W. G. Diary. Malheur County Historical Society, Vale, OR. OR. 1853. Not Seen.

THOMPSON, W. H. "Transportation in Iowa, 1846 - 1980." Iowa State Univ., Ames, IA. Bib.

THOMPSON, W. Sherman. Childhood Memories...1869. ORHIST. OR(Council)-BRIDGER-SLCUT. IV. Rem. 1869.

THOMPSON, William. REMINISCENCES OF A PIONEER. SF: Private, 1912. OR. IV. Rem. 1852.

THOMPSON, William P. Diary. BEINECKE. CAL(St. Jo)-HALL-TRUCKEE. III. 1850.

THOMSOM, James. FOR FRIENDS AT HOME. Ed. Richard A. Preston. Montreal: McGill - Queen's Univ. Press, 1974. CANADA(Victoria-Quesnelle City). III. 1862. Map.

THOMSON, Frank. "We Watched Them Die." TRUE WEST 8(Mar-Apr 1961): 10-11, 56-58. 1863 Indian attack on freighters at Cottonwood Island, Platte River.

THOMSON, Jeremiah B. Early Days in Oregon. ORU. OR(Arkansas)-CHEROKEE(to Forks of Laramie River)-BARLOW. III. Rem. 1851.

THOMSON, John P. "Snoqualmie Wagon Road: Frist to Breach Cascade Range, in 1868." PACIFIC NORTHWESTERNER 21(Sum 1977): 33-42. WASH-1868-Genl.

THOMSON, Origen. CROSSING THE PLAINS...1852. 1896. Reprint. Fairfield, WA: Ye Galleon, 1983. OR(St. Jo). III. 1852.

THONHOFF, Robert H. SAN ANTONIO STAGE LINES, 1847 - 1881. Southwestern Studies Monograph No. 29. El Paso: Texas Western Press, 1971. Stage.

THORNBROUGH, Gayle. Ed. White, Thomas. TO OREGON IN 1852.

THORNILEY, John C. Diary. CSL. CAL(St. Jo)-TRUCKEE-BECK. I. 1852.

THORNTON, J. Quinn. THE CALIFORNIA TRAGEDY. 1855. Reprint. California Centennial Edition No. 4. Oakland: Joseph A. Sullivan, 1945. CAL-1846-Genl.

_____. "Occasional Address." TRANSACTIONS Oregon Pioneer Association 1878 (1879): 29-71. OR-1846-Genl.

_____. OREGON AND CALIFORNIA IN 1848. 2 vols. 1855. Reprint. NY: Arno, 1973. OR(Indep)-APPLE. II. 1846.

THOROUGHMAN, Robert P. A Trip...1865. MONHIST. PIKES. IV. Rem. 1862. CHEROKEE(Denver to SLC)-SLCUT-HALL-MONTANA. IV. Rem. 1865.

THORP, Raymond W. "The Overland Mail." TARGET, 28 Feb 1929, n.p. Mail.

THORSEN, W. B. Ed. Powers, Mary R. A WOMAN'S OVERLAND JOURNAL.

"Thousand Springs and Salmon Falls." IDAHO YESTERDAYS 18(Fall 1974): 14-23. Geog.

THRAPP, Dan L. "South Pass - Gateway to Empire." WESTWAYS 50(Oct 1958): 32-33. Geog.

THROCKMORTON, Arthur L. OREGON ARGONAUTS: MERCHANT ADVENTURERS ON THE WESTERN FRONTIER. Portland: Oregon Historical Society, 1961. Freight.

THRONE, Mildred. Ed. Swan, Chauncey. "Letters."

THURBER, Albert K. Biographical Sketch. UTHIST. CAL(Westport)-BRIDGER-SLCOR. V. 1849.

THURMAN, Melburn D. "Lone Elm, Kansas: The History of a Trail Campground." OVERLAND JOURNAL 4(Fall 1986): 42-53. Geog.

THURMAN, Sue B. PIONEERS OF NEGRO ORIGIN IN CALIFORNIA. SF: Acme, 1949. Social.

THURSTON, Samuel R. Biography. Ed. Elizabeth F. Odell. BANCROFT. OR. 1847. Not Seen.

THURSTON, William. "Guide to the Gold Regions 1849." In Templeton - Crocker Collection. CAHIST. Guide.

TICE, Peter. Diary. BYU. CAL(Plattesville)-BRIDGER-SLCUT. II. 1850.

TIDWELL, John. A Journal...1852. BYU. MORMON. I. 1852.

TIERNEY, Luke D. HISTORY OF THE GOLD DISCOVERIES ON THE SOUTH PLATTE RIVER. Pacific City, IA: Herald, 1859. Guide.

TIFFANY, P. C. Diary. BEINECKE. CAL(St. Jo)-HALL. I. 1849.

TILLER, Lowell. SEE: With Keith Clark. TERRIBLE TRAIL. SEE: With Leah C. Menefee. "Cutoff Fever."

TIMS, Melinda. "Pioneer Women on the Move." LANE COUNTY HISTORIAN 30(Spr 1985): 11-13. Social.

TINKER, Charles. "Charles Tinker's Journal...1849." Ed. Eugene H. Roseboom. OHIO STATE ARCHEOLOGICAL AND HISTORICAL QUARTERLY 61(Jan 1952): 64-85. CAL(St. Jo)-HALL-TRUCKEE. III. 1849.

TINKER, Horace. "Round Trip to the Gold Fields." AMERICAN HISTORY ILLUSTRATED 11(Apr 1976): 4-9, 42-50. CAL(Council). V. Rem. 1849.

TINKEY, David. Statement. BANCROFT? CAL-BRIDGER-HALL-TRUCKEE. V-. 1845.

TINNEY, William T. Overland Trip. MONHIST. CAL(Council)-HALL-MONTANA. III. 1864.

TIPPETS, John H. History and Account. UTHIST? CAL(Leav)-SANTA FE-Back to Pueblo, CO). III. Rem. 1846. CHEROKEE(Pueblo-Ft. Laramie-Winter Quarters-Ft. Laramie). III. Rem. 1847.

TOBIE, Harvey E. "From the Missouri to the Columbia, 1841." OREGON HISTORICAL QUARTERLY 40(Sept 1939): 314-26. OR-1841-Genl.

_____. "Joseph L. Meek, A Conspicuous Personality." OREGON HISTORICAL QUARTERLY 39(Jun, Sept, Dec 1938): 123-46, 286-306, 410-24; 40(Mar, Sept 1939): 19-39, 243-64; 41(Mar 1940): 74-90. Biog.

_____. NO MAN LIKE JOE: THE LIFE AND TIMES OF JOSEPH L. MEEK. Portland: Oregon Historical Society, 1949. Biog.

TOBIN, Mary. "A History of California Periodical Literature from 1907 to 1914; Together with a Descriptive Catalogue of Materials for Western History in the Most Important Magazines of the Period." MA thesis, Univ. of California-Berkeley, 1923. Bib.

TODD, Abbott L. Sketch. ORU. OR(Kansas)-BARLOW. V. Rem. 1852.

TODD, Edgeley W. Ed. Wayman, John. A DOCTOR ON THE CALIFORNIA TRAIL.

TODD, John B. "The Harney Expedition against the Sioux: The Journal of Captain John B. S. Todd." Ed. Ray H. Mattison. NEBRASKA HISTORY 43(Jun 1962): 89-130. CAL(Leav)-DAKOTAS(Ft. Laramie to Ft. Pierre). II. 1855. Military. Geog: Ash Hollow.

TODD, John R. "Across the Plains in '52." TRAIL 3(Jun 1910): 11-13. CAL(Council)-CHEROKEE(Laramie to Ft. Bridger). V. Rem. 1852.

_____. "An Escape from the Mormons." TRAIL 2(Oct 1909): 5-14. Account of apostate girls leaving Utah. OR(Salem to SLC and return). IV. 1855.

TODD, Mary E. ON TO OREGON! Ed. Adrietta Applegate Hixon. 1947. Reprint. Fairfield, WA: Ye Galleon, 1977. OR(Indep)-BARLOW. III. Rem. 1852.

TODD, Stanley W. "When the Express Service was Young." FRONTIER TIMES 12(Feb 1935): 191-96. Stage.

TOLD BY THE PIONEERS. TALES OF FRONTIER LIFE AS TOLD BY THOSE WHO REMEMBER THE DAYS OF THE TERRITORY AND EARLY STATEHOOD OF WASHINGTON. U.S. Works Progress Administration Project 5841. Olympia?: N.p., 1937-39. Collection of old-timer interviews during the 1930's. WASH-Genl.

TOLL, David W. "Other Roads to California." NEVADA HIGHWAYS AND PARKS 29(Fall 1969): 24-36, 46-47, 49. Geog: Sierra Nevada passes.

TOLL, Nicholas B. Reminiscence. ORHIST. CAL(Kansas City)-BRIDGER-SLCUT. IV. 1863.

TOLLES, James S. TRAILS AND TRIALS OF '49. Ed. Doris Beard. Marysville, CA: Appeal-Democrat, 1930. II. CAL(St. Jo)-BRIDGER-SLCUT-LASSEN. II. 1849.

TOMLINSON, John J. Log. Iowa State Historical Society, Iowa City, IA. CAL(Council)-BOZE-MONTANA. III+. 1864.

TOMPKINS, Edward A. Diary. HUNTL. CAL(Indep)-BRIDGER-SLCUT. II. 1850.

TOMPKINS, Mrs. F. O. Ed. Butterfield, James T. "Interesting Account."

TOMPKINS, G. C. A COMPENDIUM OF THE OVERLAND MAIL COMPANY ON THE SOUTH ROUTE, 1858 - 1861, AND THE PERIOD SURROUNDING IT. El Paso: Author, 1985. Stage(Butterfield).

TOMPKINS, Walker A. STAGECOACH DAYS IN SANTA BARBARA COUNTY. Santa Barbara, CA: McNally & Loftin, 1982. Stage.

TOMPKINS, Walter A. "Old Fort Bowie." ARIZONA HIGHWAYS 35(Mar 1959): 28-33. Geog. Graphics.

_____. "Stagecoach Pass." WESTWAYS 46(Dec 1954): 6-7. Geog: San Marcos Pass, between Santa Barbara and Santa Ynez.

TOOMEY, Noxon. "Mountain Fever and Spotted Fever of the Rocky Mountains." ANNALS OF INTERNAL MEDICINE 3(1931): 5-17. Medical. Not Seen.

TOOTLE, Mrs. Thomas E. "The Diary of Mrs. Thomas E. Tootle." MUSEUM GRAPHIC 13(Spr 1961): 3-19. PIKES. III. 1862.

TOPHAM, Edward. "Castles in California." BANCROFT. CAL(St. Jo)-HALL. IV. Rem. 1849.

TOPONCE, Alexander. REMINISCENCES OF ALEXANDER TOPONCE, PIONEER. SLC: Katie Toponce, 1923. Freight.

TOROK, Theresa M. "The Social Aspects of Life on the Oregon Trail, 1841 - 1846." MA thesis, Indiana Univ., 1957. Social.

TORREY, Harriet F. Ed. Ford, James. JUST BETWEEN OURSELVES.
Tour to California Overland. BYU. CAL(St Jo)-Ends Ft. Kearney. I. 1849.

TOURISTS COLUMBIA HIGHWAY AND OLD OREGON TRAIL INFORMATION AND GUIDE BOOK. Baker, OR: Ryder Bros., 1921. Pres(Pocatello to Portland).

TOURTILLOT, Jane A. "Diary and Journal." In WOMEN'S DIARIES OF THE WESTWARD JOURNEY, ed. Lillian Schlissel. NY: Schocken, 1982. CAL(Council)-HALL. I. 1862.

TOWNE, Charles W., and Edward N. Wentworth. SHEPHERD'S EMPIRE. Norman: Univ. of Oklahoma Press, 1946. Stock. Fine bibliography.

TOWNLEY, John M. THE PONY EXPRESS GUIDEBOOK. Reno: Jamison Station, 1985. Nevada only.

_____. "Stalking Horse for the Pony Express: The Chorpenning Mail Contracts between California and Utah, 1851 - 1860." ARIZONA & THE WEST 24(Aut 1982): 229-52. Pony. Mail.

_____. TOUGH LITTLE TOWN ON THE TRUCKEE. Reno: Jamison Station, 1983. Geog: Truckee Meadows.

TOWNSHEND, F. Trench. TEN THOUSAND MILES OF TRAVEL, SPORT, AND ADVENTURE. London: Hurst & Blackett, 1969. Stage: Laramie-SLC-Austin-Argenta, NV(Rail connection). II. 1868.

TRACHSEL, Myrtle J. "On the Trail of the Pony Express." FRONTIER, May 1925, 119-25. Pony.

TRACY, Albert. "Journal of Captain Albert Tracy." UTAH HISTORICAL QUARTERLY 13(Jan-Oct 1945): 1-117. BRIDGER. II+. 1858. CAL(Camp Floyd)-BRIDGER-Ends Atchison. By stage. II+. 1860.

TRAFZER, Clifford E. YUMA: FRONTIER CROSSING OF THE FAR SOUTHWEST. Wichita: Yuma County Historical Society, 1980. Geog. Stage. GILA-Genl.

TRAILS WEST. WA: National Geographic Society, 1979. Overland-Genl. Graphics.

TRANSPORTATION OF MILITARY SUPPLIES FROM FORT LEAVENWORTH WESTWARD. 38th Cong., 2d sess. S. Ex. Doc. 31. Serial 1209. Freight.

"Travel Account of Journey from Indiana to Washington. MO-WHMC. OR-WASH. 1850. Not Seen.

TRAVELER'S GUIDE TO THE NEW GOLD MINES IN KANSAS AND NEBRASKA.... NY: Polhemus & De Vries, 1859. Guide.

TRAVIS, Helga A. THE NEZ PERCE TRAIL. Yakima, WA: Private, 1967. Geog: Fort Nez Perce.

TRECKEL, Paula A. "An Historiographical Essay: Women on the American Frontier." THE OLD NORTHWEST 1(Dec 1975): 391-403. Social.

TRENNERT, Robert A. "Indian Policy on the Santa Fe Road: The Fitzpatrick Controversy of 1847 - 1848." KANSAS HISTORY 1(Win 1978): 243-53. SANTA Fe-Genl. Military. Indians.

_____. "The Mormons and the Office of Indian Affairs: The Conflict over Winter Quarters, 1846 - 1848." NEBRASKA HISTORY 53(Fall 1972): 381-400. Geog.

TREXLER, Harrison A. "Missouri - Montana Highways, II - The Overland Route." MISSOURI HISTORICAL REVIEW 12(Apr 1918): 145-62. Stage. MONTANA-Genl.

_____. MISSOURI - MONTANA HIGHWAYS. Jefferson City: State Historical Society of Missouri, 1918. MONTANA-Genl. CAL-Genl. Excellent survey of routes.

TREY, Mark. "Jerk Line Jockey." TRUE WEST 5(May-June 1958): 22-23, 40-42. Freight.

"Trials and Thrills of Early Travel." FRONTIER TIMES 12(Feb 1935): 187-88. Graphics-San Antonio and San Diego Mail Line.

Trip to Oregon, 1862. Idaho State Historical Society, Boise, ID. OR(Council)-LANDER?-Ends near Ft. Hall. IV. 1862.

"A Trip to Walker's River and Carson Valley." HUTCHING'S 2(May, Jun 1858): 489-96, 529-38. CAL(Passage east from Columbia over Walker River headwaters to Carson Valley." II. 1857.

"Trip up the Columbia in 1850." KNICKERBOCKER MAGAZINE 42(n.d.): 482. Not Seen.

TRIPLETT, Richard J. "A Glimpse of Colorado's Early Overland Transportation." DENVERPUB. PIKES-Genl.

TROWBRIDGE, Mary E. Ed. With Gershom & Elizabeth Day. "Diary."

_____. PIONEER DAYS. Philadelphia: American Baptist Publication Society, 1895. CAL(St. Jo)-SLCUT. IV. 1849.

TROWBRIDGE, William P. "Diary and Sketchbook." Washington State Historical Society Library, Tacoma, WA. Graphics.

TROXEL, Kathryn. "Food of the Overland Emigrants." OREGON HISTORICAL QUARTERLY 56(Mar 1955): 12-26. Social.

TRUBODY, William Alexander. SEE: Camp, Charles L. "William

Alexander Trubody."

TRUDELL, Clyde Francis. SEE: With Carl Briggs. QUARTERDECK & SADDLEHORN.

TRUE, Charles F. COVERED WAGON PIONEERS. Ed. Sally R. True. Madison, WI: College Printing, 1966. CAL(Council)-LANDER-HALL. III. Rem. 1859.

TRUE, Sally R. Ed. True, Charles. COVERED WAGON PIONEERS.

TRULIO, Beverly. "Anglo-American Attitudes toward New Mexican Women." JOURNAL OF THE WEST 12(Apr 1973): 229-39. Social.

TRUMAN, Benjamin C. "Knights of the Lash." OVERLAND MONTHLY 31(Mar, Apr 1898): 218-26, 308-18. Stage.

_____. "The Passing of a Sierra Knight." OVERLAND MONTHLY 42(Jul 1903): 33-39. Stage.

TRUMBO, Theron M. "Waterhole at the Crossroads." DESERT 12(Jan 1949): 19-21. Geog: Ft. Cummings.

TRUTCH, Joseph W. OVERLAND COACH ROAD. New Westminster: British Columbia Lands and Works Dept., 1868. CANADA-Genl.

TUCKER, Ira. "Biographical File." CAHIST. Copy of pass issued emigrants during Civil War by military. Military.

TUCKER, Joseph C. TO THE GOLDEN GOAL AND OTHER SKETCHES. SF: Doxey, 1895. Stage: St. Louis - SF via Butterfield, 1859.

TUCKER, T. W. WAIFS FROM THE WAY-BILLS OF AN OLD EX-PRESSMAN. Boston: Lee & Shepard, 1872. Stage.

TULLER, Miriam A. "Crossing the Plains in 1845." TRANSACTIONS Oregon Pioneer Association (1895): 87-90. OR(Indep). Rem. 1845. Not Seen.

TUNIS, Joseph C. Diaries. Princeton Univ. Library-Western History, Princeton, NJ. PIKES. II. 1866.

TURNBULL, Thomas. "T. Turnbull's Travels...to California." Ed. Frederick L. Paxon. PROCEEDINGS State Historical Society of Wisconsin, 1913 (1914): 151-225. CAL(Council)-SLCOR. II. 1852.

TURNER, Allan R. "Palliser of the Triangle." BEAVER, Autumn 1957, 4-9. CANADA-Genl. Map.

TURNER, Charles. Diary. Held by Charlotte Paterson, Cleveland, OH. 1849. Not Seen.

TURNER, Charles W. Ed. Knox, Reuben. "Letters." Ed. Knox, Reuben. A MEDIC FORTYNINER.

TURNER, Ellis. "In the Trail of the Buffalo: A Descriptive Bibliography of the Oregon, California, and Texas Guidebook, 1814 - 1860." PhD diss., George Washington Univ., 1980. Bibliography of guidebooks.

TURNER, Henry S. THE ORIGINAL JOURNALS OF.... Ed. Dwight L. Clarke. Norman: Univ. of Oklahoma Press, 1966. CAL(Leav)-SANTA FE-RIO GRANDE-GILA. II. 1846. CAL(East via)-TRUCKEE-HALL. II. 1847.

TURNER, Justin G. "Men Against Mountains, Salt, and Sand." MANUSCRIPTS 12(Spr 1960): n.p. CAL-1846-Genl.

TURNER, Martha M. OUR OWN HISTORY: COLUMBUS,

NEBRASKA, 1541 - 1860. Columbus, NB: Author, 1936. Geog: Council Bluffs.

TURNER, Robert L. "Historical Markers in Texas." MS thesis, North Texas State College, 1939. Pres.

TURNER, Walter H. A Trip.... In Lawrence E. Hotchkiss Collection. Clements Library, Univ. of Michigan - Ann Arbor. OR(Weston)-BARLOW. II. 1850.

TURNER, William. Diary. WIHIST. CAL(Council)-SLCUT. III+. 1850.

_____. "Scraps of Modoc History." OVERLAND MONTHLY 11(Jul 1873): 21-25. Indian raids on Lassen Trail, 1852.

TURRILL, Miss L. M. Diary. Society of California Pioneers, San Francisco, CA. Not Seen.

TUSTIN, William I. Recollections. BANCROFT. CAL-HALL. V-. Rem. 1845.

TUTOROW, Norman E. "Mormon Battalion." In THE MEXICAN-AMERICAN WAR: AN ANNOTATED BIBLIOGRAPHY. Westport, CN: Greenwood, 198? Bib.

TUTTLE, Charles A. Letters. BANCROFT? CAL(Indep)-SLCUT. V. 1849.

TUTTLE, Charles M. "California Diary of...1859." Ed. Joseph Schafer. WISCONSIN MAGAZINE OF HISTORY 15(Sept, Dec 1931): 69-85, 219-33. CAL(Council)-BRIDGER-SIMPSON-Ends Eastgate, NV. II. 1859.

TUTTLE, Edward D. Journal and Letters. HUNTL. STAGE(San Pedro to Yuma). 1863.

TUTTLE, Hiram G. Diary. CSL. CAL(East to SLC)-SIMPSON. III. 1862. CAL(Begins SLC)-SLCUT. III. 1864.

TWAIN, Mark [Samuel Clemens]. ROUGHING IT. Hartford, CN: American, 1872. Stage: St. Jo-CHEROKEE(Laramie-SLC)-SIMPSON-Ends Carson City. I. Rem. 1861.

TWITCHELL, Jerry F. "The History of the Latter-Day Saints in Bridger Valley (Wyoming)." MA thesis, BYU, 1959. Geog.

TYLER, Daniel. A CONCISE HISTORY OF THE MORMON BAT-TALION IN THE MEXICAN WAR, 1846 - 1847. 1881. Reprint. Glorieta, NM: Rio Grande, 1964. CAL(Leav)-SANTA FE-RIO GRANDE-GILA. II. 1846.

TYLER, Ron, ed. ALFRED JACOB MILLER: ARTIST ON THE OREGON TRAIL. Ft. Worth: Amon Carter Museum of Western Art, c1982. Graphics.

TYLER, Ronnie C. Ed. Green, Duff. "Exploring the Rio Grande."

TYLER, S. Lyman. Ed. Dunlap, Catherine. MONTANA GOLD RUSH DIARY. SEE: With Ruth M. Jones, et al. "Utah, the Mormons, and the West."

_____. "Ute Indians along Civil War Communication Lines." UTAH HISTORICAL QUARTERLY 46(Sum 1978): 251-61. Indians. Military.

TYSON, T. K. "Freighting to Denver. "PROCEEDINGS AND COL-LECTIONS Nebraska State Historical Society 5(1902): 256-60. Freight.

UDALL, David. ARIZONA PIONEER MORMON. Tucson: Arizona

Silhouettes, 1959. MORMON. 1852. Not Seen.

UDELL, John. INCIDENTS OF TRAVEL TO CALIFORNIA.... Jefferson, OH: Sentinel, 1856. CAL(Council)-BRIDGER-HASTINGS. III+. 1850. CAL(Nebraska City?)-BRIDGER-SLCUT. III+. 1852. CAL(Council)-BRIDGER-SLCUT. III+. 1854.

_____. JOURNAL KEPT DURING A TRIP...1859. 1868. Reprint. California Centennial Series, vol. 3. LA: N. A. Kovach, 1946. CAL(Westport)-SANTA FE-BEALE-Returned to Albuquerque after Indian attack on Colorado River. III. Rem. 1858. CAL(Begins Albuquerque)-BEALE. III. 1859. Indian attack at Mohave villages.

ULRICH, Richard W. "The Mullan Road: Its Story and Importance to the Inland Empire." MA thesis, Willamette Univ?, 1951. Not Seen.

UNDERHILL, Lonnie E. "A History of the First Arizona Volunteer Infantry, 1865 - 1866." MA thesis, Univ. of Arizona, 1979.

_____. "Dr. Edward Palmer's Experiences with the Arizona Volunteers, 1865-1866." JOURNAL OF ARIZONA HISTORY 24(Win 1983): n.p. GILA-1865-Genl. GILA-1866-Genl. Not Seen.

UNDERHILL, W. M. "The Northern Overland Route to Montana." WASHINGTON HISTORICAL QUARTERLY 23(Jul 1932): 177-95. MONTANA-Genl. DAKOTA-Genl.

U.S. Army. Quartermaster Corps. "Consolidated Correspondence Relating to the Freighting Firm of Russell, Majors and Waddell, 1852 - 1870." KSHIST. Freight.

U.S. Bureau of Land Management. GUIDE TO THE LANDER CUT-OFF. N.p., n.d. Excellent map of trail.

U.S. Bureau of Outdoor Recreation. MORMON BATTALION TRAIL STUDY: SANTA FE TO SAN DIEGO. WA: GPO, 1975. Pres.

_____. THE NORTH COUNTRY TRAIL. WA: U.S. Department of the Interior, 1974. DAKOTA-Genl.

_____. OLD CATTLE TRAILS OF THE SOUTHWEST - SCENIC TRAILS STUDY. WA: GPO, 1975. Pres.

_____. TRAILS FOR AMERICA: REPORT ON THE NATIONWIDE TRAILS STUDY. WA: GPO, 1966. Pres.

U.S. Congress. House. SETTLERS AND EMIGRANTS BETWEEN THE MISSISSIPPI VALLEY AND THE PACIFIC OCEAN, &c. JOINT RESOLUTION OF THE LEGISLATURE OF IOWA...INCLUDING THE ESTABLISHMENT OF POSTAL AND TELEGRAPHIC CORRESPONDENCE ACROSS THE AMERICAN CONTINENT. 33rd Cong., 2d sess., 1855. H. Misc. Doc. 36. Overland-Genl.

U.S. Department of the Interior. THE OREGON TRAIL. WA: GPO, 1977. Pres.

_____. THE OREGON TRAIL...POTENTIAL ADDITION TO THE NATIONAL TRAILS SYSTEM. Seattle: Bureau of Outdoor Recreation, 1974. Pres.

_____. REPORT...PACIFIC WAGON ROADS CONSTRUCTED.... 35th Cong., 2d sess., 1858-59. S. Ex. Doc. 36 (Vol. 10 in set). Overland-Genl.

U.S. Forest Service. "Old Pioneer Wagon Road." UTHIST. Study of early roads over Wasatch Range. Geog. Mormon-Genl.

UNITED STATES LOCAL HISTORIES IN THE LIBRARY OF CONGRESS: A BIBLIOGRAPHY. Baltimore: Magna Charta, 1974. Not Seen.

U.S. National Park Service. THE NATIONAL SURVEY OF HISTORIC SITES AND BUILDINGS; REPORT ON THE SANTA FE TRAIL. N.p., c1959. Pres.

_____. SPECIAL SITE REPORT ON OREGON TRAIL RUTS AND RELATED SITES: VICINITY OF GUERNSEY, PLATTE COUNTY, WYOMING. Omaha: Midwest Regional Office of the National Park Service, 1966. Pres. Geog.

U.S. Post Office Department. OVERLAND MAIL SERVICE TO CALIFORNIA. WA: GPO?, 1869. Stage-Butterfield-1857.

U.S. Senate. AMOUNTS PAID FOR OVERLAND MAIL SERVICE, 1858 TO 1868. 46th Cong., 3d sess., 1880. S. Ex. Doc. 24. Mail.

UNRAU, William E. "Epidemic Disease and the Impact of the Santa Fe Trail on the Kansa Indians." HERITAGE OF THE GREAT PLAINS 17(Spr 1984). Medical. Not Seen.

_____. "The History of Fort Larned, Kansas: Its Relation to the Santa Fe Trail and the Plains Indians." MA thesis, Univ. of Wyoming, 1956. Geog. SANTA FE-Genl.

_____. "The Story of Fort Larned." KANSAS HISTORICAL QUARTERLY 23(Aut 1957): 257-80. Geog.

_____, ed. TENDING THE TALKING WIRE: A BUCK SOLDIER'S VIEW OF INDIAN COUNTRY, 1863-1866. SLC: Univ. of Utah Press, 1979. Detailed account of garrison duty along trail.

UNRUH, John D., Jr. "Against the Grain: West to East on the Overland Trail." KANSAS QUARTERLY 5(Spr 1973): 72-81. Review of returning Argonauts, or "Gobacks."

_____. "The Golden History of the Overland Emigrations." LOS ANGELES WESTERNERS BRAND BOOK 14(1974): 79-102. Overland-Genl.

_____. "The Plains Across: The Overland Emigrants and the Trans-Mississippi West, 1840 - 1860." PhD. diss., Univ. of Kansas, 1975. Overland-Genl.

_____. THE PLAINS ACROSS: THE OVERLAND EMIGRANTS AND THE TRANSMISSISSIPPI WEST. Urbana: Univ. of Illinois Press, 1979. Possibly the best of recent trail interpretation.

URBANEK, Mae. "1852 on the Oregon Trail." ANNALS OF WYOMING 34(Apr 1962): 52-59. CAL(Council)-Ends Ft. Laramie. IV. 1852.

_____. GHOST TRAILS OF WYOMING. Boulder, CO: Author, 1978. Maps. Graphics. CAL-Wyoming only-Genl.

Utah Pioneer Trails and Landmarks Association. CHARTING AND MARKING PIONEER TRAILS AND LANDMARKS; OUTLINE OF A CAMPAIGN, JULY 1931. SLC: The Association, c1931. Pres.

UTLEY, Beverly. "They Made the West Worth Winning." AMERICAN HISTORY ILLUSTRATED 2(Dec 1967): 26-35. Social.

UTLEY, Robert M. "Fort Bowie." AMERICAN WEST 16(Mar-Apr 1979): 14-15, 55. Geog.

_____. FORT DAVIS NATIONAL HISTORIC SITE, TEXAS. Historic Handbook Series 38. WA: National Park Service, 1965. Geog.

_____. "Fort Union and the Santa Fe Trail." NEW MEXICO HISTORICAL REVIEW 36(Jan 1961): 36-48. Military.

_____. THE INDIAN FRONTIER OF THE AMERICAN WEST, 1846-1890. One of the Histories of the American Frontier. Albuquerque: Univ. of New Mexico Press, 1983. Indian-Genl.

_____. "The Past and Future of Old Fort Bowie." ARIZONIANA 5, no. 4(1964): 55-60. Geog.

UTSEY, Glenda F. PERCEPTIONS OF THE PLAINS: VIEWED FROM THE PLATTE RIVER SECTION OF THE OREGON TRAIL. MA Graduate Project, Univ. of Oregon, 1977. Graphics.

VAIL, R. W. G. Ed. Smith, Charles W. JOURNAL OF A TRIP TO CALIFORNIA.

Vail Telegraph. Collection. Smithsonian Institution, Washington, DC. Telegraph. Not Seen.

VAN ARSDALE, De Maris O. A Pioneer Story. CSL. CAL(Council?). V. Rem. 1848.

VAN ARSDALE, Perry C. WEST-NORTHWEST, SHOWING SOME OF THE ROADS, RAILS, FORTS, TOWNS, TRAILS, 1800 AND AFTER. Tijeras, NM: Author, 1966. Maps.

VAN DORN, T. J. Diary. BEINECKE. CAL(St. Jo)-TRUCKEE. 1849. Not Seen.

VAN DYKE, Walter. "Overland to Los Angeles by the Salt Lake Route in 1849." PUBLICATIONS Historical Society of Southern California 3(1894): 76-83. CAL(Council)-BRIDGER-SLCOR. V. 1849.

VAN NOSTRAND, Jeanne S. Ed. With Jacob H. Bachman. ~ Audubon's Ill-Fated."

VAN OGLE, Mr. "Van Ogle's Memory of Pioneer Days." WASHINGTON HISTORICAL QUARTERLY 13(Oct 1922): 269-81. OR(Council)-WASH. V. Rem. 1853.

VAN ORMAN, Richard A. SEE: With Oscar O. Winther. A CLASSIFIED BIBLIOGRAPHY.

VAN SCHAICK, Holmes D. Diary. NEWBERRY. CAL(Indep). II. 1852. Train Govt.

VAN TRUMP, James D. Ed. Reid, Bernard J. "A California Gold Rush Letter."

VAN WYCK, Crittenden. Diary. Society of California Pioneers, San Francisco, CA. Not Seen.

VANBUSKIRK, William. Reminiscence. ORHIST. OR. IV. Rem. 1852.

VANCE, Laura R. Papers. NBHIST. Indians: 1864 captivity narrative.

VANCIL, Frank M. "Overland Stampede of 1849." OVERLAND MONTHLY 62(Apr 1916): 313-16. CAL(Council)-HALL-HASTINGS. V. 1849.

VANDERWALKER, George F. "The Bull-whacker or Prairie Sailor." TRAIL 1(Feb 1909): 26-28. Freight.

VARIEL, Mary A. "A Romance of the Plains." Ed. William J. Variel. GRIZZLY BEAR, July, Aug, Sept, Oct, Nov 1907, 30-32, 62-64, 74-76, 38-40, 46-48. CAL(St. Jo)-LASSEN?-NOBLE?. III. Rem. 1852.

VARIEL, William J. Ed. Variel, Mary A. "A Romance of the Plains."

VAUGHN, Alden T. NARRATIVES OF NORTH AMERICAN INDIAN CAPTIVITY: A SELECTIVE BIBLIOGRAPHY. NY: Garland, 1983. Bib.

VEEDER, Charles H. "Yuma Indian Depredations on the Colorado in 1850." PUBLICATIONS Southern California Historical Society 7(1908): 202-03. Indians. Geog.

VEER, Judy Van der. "On History's Trail to San Felipe." WESTWAYS 53(Jan 1961): 32-33. Geog.

VELAZQUEZ, Loreta J. THE WOMAN IN BATTLE.... Ed. C. J. Worthington. Hartford, CN: T. Belknap, 1876. Stage: Omaha-Cheyenne-SLC-Austin, NV. IV. 1868.

VENABLE, Austil L. Ed. Davies, John J. "Journey of a Mormon."

VERDENAL, John M. Journal...1852. BANCROFT. CAL(Jefferson City)-BRIDGER-SLCUT. III+. 1852.

VERNAM, Glenn R. SEE: With Lee M. Rice. THEY SADDLED THE WEST.

VERNEY, Edmund H. "An Overland Journey from San Francisco to New York." GOOD WORDS, 1 Jun 1866, 378-92. Stage: Sacramento-SLC-Denver-Atchison. II. 1865. An intelligent appraisal of American manners by a skeptical English naval officer.

VERNON, Mildred H. "The Daily Overland Mail to the Pacific, 1861 - 1869." MA thesis, Univ. of California-Berkeley, 1923. Mail. Stage.

VEST, Deed L. "The Chihuahua Road." TEXANA 5(Spr 1967): 1-10. TEX:Comanche Trail-Chihuahua to Staked Plains. Indians.

VESTAL, Stanley. JIM BRIDGER: MOUNTAIN MAN. NY: William Morrow, 1946. Biog.

_____. JOE MEEK, THE MERRY MOUNTAIN MAN. Caldwell, ID: Caxton, 1952. Biog.

_____. THE OLD SANTA FE TRAIL. Boston: Houghton Mifflin, 1939. SANTA FE-Genl.

_____. WARPATH AND COUNCIL FIRE: THE PLAINS INDIANS' STRUGGLE FOR SURVIVAL IN WAR AND IN DIPLOMACY, 1851 - 1891. NY: Random House, 1948. Indians.

VEVIER, Charles. "The Collins Overland Line and American Continentalism." PACIFIC HISTORICAL REVIEW 28(Aug 1959): 237-53. Telegraph.

VICTOR, Frances F. "The First Oregon Cavalry." OREGON HISTORICAL QUARTERY 3(Jun 1902): 123-63. Military.

_____. THE RIVER OF THE WEST. Hartford, CN: Columbian, 1870. Biog: Joseph L. Meek.

_____. "Trail-Making in the Oregon Mountains." OVERLAND MONTHLY 4(Mar 1870): 201-13. OR(East)-BARLOW-Return from Deschutes River southwest to Willamette River. IV. 1869.

VILLARD, Henry. THE PAST AND PRESENT OF THE PIKE'S PEAK GOLD REGIONS.... 1860. Reprint. One of the Narratives of the Trans-Mississippi Frontier. Princeton: Princeton Univ. Press, 1932. PIKES-1858-Genl. PIKES-1859-Genl. Guide.

_____. "To the Pike's Peak Country in 1859 and Cannibalism on the Smoky Hill Route." COLORADO MAGAZINE 8(Nov 1931): 225-36. Stage: Leav-Ft. Riley-Junction City-Denver. III. 1859.

VINCENT, Eliza. "The Great American Trail." In BRAY FAMILY GENEALOGY AND HISTORY, ed. T. Emery Bray. N.p., 1927? CAL(Council)-LASSEN. V. 1851.

VINTON, Stallo. Ed. Brewerton, George D. OVERLAND WITH KIT CARSON.

VIOLETTE, M. A. Diary. Princeton Univ. Library-Western History, Princeton, NJ. CAL(St. Jo)-TRUCKEE. II. 1849.

VIRDEN, Bill. THE CONCORD STAGE. N.p.: San Diego Historical Society, c1962. Graphics. Stage. Eqpt.

VISCHER, Edward. SEE: Farquhar, Francis P. "Camels."

_____. "Stage Coach Days." QUARTERLY Society of California Pioneers 7(Jun 1930): 51-53. Stage-Graphics.

VISSCHER, William L. A THRILLING AND TRUTHFUL HISTORY OF THE PONY EXPRESS.... 1908. Reprint. Olympic Valley, CA: Outbooks, 1977. Pony. Graphics.

VIVIAN, Martin. Diary. 1850 Attributed to NBHIST but uncataloged.

VIVIAN, R. Gwinn. "An Archeological Survey of the Lower Gila River, AZ." KIVA 30(Apr 1965): 95-146. Description of Mohawk and Antelope stage stations.

VOGDES, Ada. Journal. HUNTL. CAL(Ft. Sedgewick)-Ends Laramie. II. 1868.

VOGEL, Virgil J. "Indian Trails and Place Names." NAMES 33(Mar-Jun 1985): 39-50. Indians.

VOGEL-JORGENSEN, T. PETER LASSEN AF CALIFORNIA. Trans. Helge Norrung. Red Bluff, CA: Red Bluff Union High School, c1967. Biog.

VOORHEES, Augustus. "The Voorhees Diary of the Lawrence Party's Trip to Pike's Peak, 1858." Ed. LeRoy R. Hafen. COLORADO MAGAZINE 12(Mar 1935): 41-54. PIKES. III+. 1858.

VOORHEES, Luke. Manuscripts. Wyoming Historical Society Library, Cheyenne, WY. Stage-Wyoming.

WADE, Almira. "Across the Plains in 1849." Ed. Louisa Burrell. The Pioneer, 15 Dec 1894, p. 2. CAL(St. Jo)-BRIDGER-SLCOR. IV. Rem. 1849.

WADE, Mark S. THE CARIBOO ROAD. Ed. Eleanor A. Eastick. Victoria, BC: Haunted Bookshop, 1979. Canada-Genl. Not Seen.

_____. THE OVERLANDERS OF '62. Ed. John Hosie. Archives of British Columbia Memoir No. 9. Victoria, BC: Banfield, 1931. CANADA-DAKOTAS(St. Paul)-Ft. Garry-Ft. Edmonton-Fraser River-Victoria. CANADA-1862-Genl.

WADSWORTH, William. THE NATIONAL WAGON ROAD GUIDE TO CALIFORNIA. SF: Whitton, Towne & Co., 1858. Guide.

WADSWORTH'S MAP OF CARIBOO, SASKATCHEWAN, NEZ PERCES AND SALMON RIVER GOLD FIELDS.... SF: Author?, 1862. Guide.

WAGER, F. E. "Hunted End of Rainbow by Ox Team." DE PERE [WI] JOURNAL-DEMOCRAT, 10 Apr 1924, n.p. CAL(Council)-BOZE. IV. 1863.

WAGGONER, George. "Recollections." (In) STORIES OF OLD OREGON. Salem, OR: N.p., 1905. OR(Council). Rem. 1852. Not Seen.

WAGGONER, W. W. "The Donner Party and Relief Hill." CALIFORNIA HISTORICAL QUARTERLY 10(Sept 1931): 347-52. TRUCKEE-1847-Genl. Map.

WAGNER, Henry R. "The Journal of John Wood." CALIFORNIA HISTORICAL QUARTERLY 6(Dec 1927)" 360-63.

_____. SIXTY YEARS OF BOOK COLLECTING. SF: Roxburghe Club, 1951. Biog.

_____, and Charles L. Camp. THE PLAINS AND THE ROCKIES: A CRITICAL BIBLIOGRAPHY OF EXPLORATION, ADVENTURE AND TRAVEL IN THE AMERICAN WEST, 1800 - 1865. 4th ed. revised, enlarged and edited by Robert H. Becker. SF: John Howell, 1982. The standard reference tool for trail manuscripts.

WAGNER, William H. "Rough Notes of Travel of Advance Party, Fort Kearny - South Pass and Honey Lake Wagon Road." National Archives, Washington, DC. LANDER-1859-Genl.

WAGNON, Kenneth A. "Charles and Bettie O'Neal." MADERA COUNTY HISTORIAN 15(Oct 1975): 1-14. CAL-TEX(Navarro County-Ft. Belknap-El Paso)-GILA. V. 1856.

"Wagon Trains and Cattle Herds on the Trail in the 1850's." WESTX 30(Oct 1954): 141-54. TEX-Genl. Stock.

WAGON WHEELS ROLL ON TO THE OREGON COUNTRY. N.p.: Nydia Temple No. 4, Daughters of the Nile, c1971. OR-Genl.

WAHMANN, R. "Going West with Raphael Pumpelly." DESERT 39(Jan 1976): 28-31. Stage: Jefferson City, Mo to Tucson, 1860.

WAIT, Delila B. Diary. ORHIST. OR(Lawrence). II. 1866.

WAITE, Catherine V. ADVENTURES IN THE FAR WEST. Chicago: Author, 1882. CAL(St Jo)-BRIDGER(by wagon)-SIMPSON(by stage). II. 1862.

WAITE, Sidney P. "Sketch." In JOURNALS OF THE FORTY-NINERS, eds. LeRoy and Ann W. Hafen. Glendale: Clark, 1954. SLCOR. V. 1849.

WAITMAN, Leonard. "The History of Camp Cady." MA thesis, Univ. of Redlands, 1953. BEALE-Genl. Geog.

_____. "The History of Camp Cady." Historical Society of Southern California QUARTERLY 36(Mar 1954): 49-91. Geog.

_____. "The History of Fort Piute." SAN DIEGO WESTERNERS BRAND BOOK 4(1976): 29-38. Geog.

_____. "Horse Soldier Forts of the Mojave Desert." QUARTERLY San Bernardino County Museum 15(Spr 1968): n.p. BEALE-Genl. Military.

WAKEFIELD, Eliza M. THE HANDCART TRAIL. SLC?: Author, 1949. MORMON-Genl.

WALDO, Edna L. FROM TRAVOIS TO IRON TRAIL. NY: Ackerman, 1944. Overland-Genl.

WALDRON, Samuel. Daily Log. ORHIST. OR(Indep). IV. 1852.

WALES, J. H. "Field Trip on the Southern Oregon Trail." SISKIYOU COUNTY HISTORICAL SOCIETY YEARBOOK - 1949 1, no. 4(n.d.): 47-53. Pres: Trip from Merrill, OR to Lower Klamath Lake.

WALKER, Ardis M. DEATH VALLEY & MANLY: SYMBOLS OF DESTINY. Death Valley '49ers, Inc., Publication No. 8. Palm Desert, CA: Death Valley '49ers, 1962. SLCOR-1849-Genl.

_____. FREEMAN JUNCTION...THE ESCAPE ROUTE OF THE MISSISSIPPIANS AND GEORGIANS FROM DEATH VALLEY IN 1849. San Bernardino: Death Valley '49ers, 1961.

_____. THE MANLY MAP AND THE MANLY STORY. Death Valley '49ers, Inc., Publication No. 2. Palm Desert, CA: Death Valley '49ers, 1954. SLCOR-1849-Genl.

Walker Brothers, Collection. Univ. of Utah Library-SpCol, Salt Lake City, UT. UT-NV Freighting.

_____. Receipt Book, 1862-1866. UTHIST. Freight.

WALKER, Claiborne C. In Purvine - Walker Papers. State Historical Society of Missouri Archives, Columbia, MO. OR(Indep). III. 1845. OR(Begins Rock Springs). IV. 1848.

WALKER, Clifford J. SEE: With Gerald A. Smith. INDIAN SLAVE TRADE.

_____. "History of the Mojave River Trail." MA thesis, Univ. of Southern California, 1967.

_____. OPENING THE MOJAVE RIVER TRAIL. Bloomington, CA: San Bernardino County Museum Association, 1971. SPANISH-Genl. BEALE-Genl. SLCOR-Genl.

WALKER, Don D. "Longhorns Come to Utah." UTAH HISTORICAL QUARTERLY 30(Spr 1962): 135-47. Stock.

WALKER, Henry P. Ed. Teal, John. "Soldier in the California Column."

_____. "Freighting from Guaymas to Tucson, 1850 - 1880." WESTERN HISTORICAL QUARTERLY 1(Jul 1970): 291 - 304. Freight.

_____. "Pre-Railroad Transportation in the Trans-Mississippi West: Annotated Bibliography." ARIZONA & THE WEST 18(Spr 1976): 53-80. Bibliography.

_____. "The Rise and Decline of High Plains Wagon Freighting, 1822 - 1880." PhD diss., Univ. of Colorado-Boulder, 1965. Best analysis of Great Plains freighting.

_____. "Slow Freight to Denver." DENVERPUB. Freight.

_____. "Wagon Freighting in Arizona." SMOKE SIGNAL, no. 28(Fall 1973): 182-204. Freight.

_____. THE WAGONMASTERS: HIGH PLAINS FREIGHTING FROM THE EARLIEST DAYS OF THE SANTA FE TO 1880. Norman: Univ. of Oklahoma Press, 1966. An improved and expanded treatment of his dissertation.

WALKER, Joseph C. Description. MONHIST. Stage: Atchison-Denver-Ft. Bridger-Ft. Hall-Bannack. II. 1863.

WALKER, Margaret H. THE HALL FAMILY CROSSING THE PLAINS. Ed. Shirley Walker. SF: Kibbee & Son, 1952. CALTEX(Gainesville-Ft. Belknap-El Paso)-GILA. III. 1853.

WALKER, Mattie, comp. "A Brief History of the Walker Family...." CSL. CAL(Council?)-LASSEN. V. 1863.

WALKER, Shirley. Ed. Walker, Margaret H. THE HALL FAMILY CROSSING THE PLAINS.

WALKER, Zachariah. Diary. Univ. of Iowa-SpCol, Iowa City, IA. CAL(Council)-BRIDGER-SLCUT. II. 1850.

WALKUP, F. P. "The General Trends and Characteristics of Utah Pioneer Dress from 1847 - 1875." MA thesis, Univ. of Utah, 1947. Social.

WALLACE, Andrew. "Across Arizona to the Big Colorado: The Sitgreaves Expedition of 1851." ARIZONA & THE WEST 26(Win 1984): 325-65. BEALE(Begins Zuni)-to Mohave Villages area-GILA(Yuma to San Diego). I. 1851. Maps. Govt.

WALLACE, Edward P. Autobiography. Oregon State Library, Salem, OR. OR(Council)-BARLOW. IV. Rem. 1852.

WALLACE, Edward S. THE GREAT RECONNAISSANCE: SOLDIERS, ARTISTS AND SCIENTISTS ON THE FRONTIER, 1848 - 1861. Boston: Little, Brown, 1955. Overland-Genl.

WALLACE, Ernest. Ed. Williams, Clayton W. TEXAS' LAST FRONTIER.

WALLACE, Frederick T. Ed. Ferguson, Charles D. EXPERIENCES OF A FORTY-NINER.

WALLACE, Geroge B. Journal. UTHIST. MORMON. II. 1847.

WALLACE, Mr. Letters. AZHIST. Stage: SF to Tucson. III+. 1860.

WALLACE, William S. ANTOINE ROUBIDOUX, 1794 - 1860. Early California Travels Series 14. LA: Dawson, 1953. Biog.

_____, comp. "Bibliography of Published Bibliographies on the History of the Eleven Western States, 1941 - 1947: A Partial Supplement to the WRITINGS ON AMERICAN HISTORY." NEW MEXICO HISTORICAL REVIEW 29(Jul 1954): 224-33. Bib.

_____. "Short-Line Staging in New Mexico." NEW MEXICO HISTORICAL REVIEW 26(Apr 1951): 89-100. Stage.

_____. "Stagecoaching in Territorial New Mexico." NEW MEXICO HISTORICAL REVIEW 32(Apr 1957): 204-10. Stage.

_____. "Was Heap's Journal Plagiarized?" Reprint from DENVER WESTERNERS BRAND BOOK, n.d. CAL(Westport)-SANTA FE-SPANISH-SLCOR. IV. 1853.

WALLAS, William S. Ed. Schiel, Jacob H. THE LAND BETWEEN.

WALLEN, H. D. REPORT OF HIS EXPEDITION, IN 1859, FROM DALLES CITY TO GREAT SALT LAKE, AND BACK. 36th Cong., 1st sess. S. Ex. Doc. 34. OR(Dalles)-Traveled south of Snake River to Raft River-Ends Camp Floyd. Returned via Ft. Boise. III. 1859.

"Walter Moberly's Report on the Roads of British Columbia, 1863." BRITISH COLUMBIA HISTORICAL QUARTERLY 9, no. 1(1945): 37-47. CANADA-1863-Genl.

WALTER, Paul A. Ed. Davis, Sylvester. "Diary."

WALTER, William W. "Reminiscences of an Old 1845er." Washington State Univ. Library-SpCol, Pullman, WA. OR(St. Jo)-MEEK. V. Rem. 1845.

WALTERS, Archer. Journal...1856. BYU. MORMON. III. 1856.

WALTERS, Everett. Ed. Tappan, Henry. "Diary of Henry Tappan."

WALTON, Daniel. FACTS FROM THE GOLD REGIONS. Boston: N.p., 1849. Guide.

WALTON, George. SENTINEL OF THE PLAINS: FORT LEAVEN-WORTH AND THE AMERICAN WEST. Englewood Cliffs, NJ: Prentice-Hall, 1973. Geog. Military.

WARD, Artemus. THE COMPLETE WORKS OF CHARLES F. BROWNE, BETTER KNOWN AS "ARTEMUS WARD." London: Chatto & Windus, 1893. Stage: Sacramento-SLC-Atchison. III. 1864.

WARD, Dillis B. ACROSS THE PLAINS IN 1853. Seattle: Bull Bros., 1911. OR(Indep?)-SANTA FE-CHEROKEE(Pueblo to Green River). III. Rem. 1853.

_____. "From Salem, Oregon, to Seattle, Washington, in 1859." WASHINGTON HISTORICAL QUARTERLY 6(Apr 1915): 100-06. WASH-1859-Genl.

WARD, Frances E. FRANKIE'S JOURNAL. Ed. Florence S. DeWitt. LA: Editor, 1960. Social. Preparation for 1853 crossing only.

WARD, H. C. "Stage-Coach Days in California...." CALIFORNIA HISTORICAL QUARTERLY 13(Sept 1934): 255-61. Stage.

WARD, Harriet S. PRAIRIE SCHOONER LADY. Eds. Ward G. and Florence S. DeWitt. Great West and Indian Series 16. LA: Westernlore, 1959. CAL(Council)-BRIDGER-SLCUT-TRUCKEE-BECK. II. 1853.

WARD, Henry C. SEE: Bradford, James O. "Papers."

WARD, Seth. Papers. DENVERPUB. Freight.

WARDELL, M. L. "Oregon Immigration Prior to 1846." OREGON HISTORICAL QUARTERLY 27(Mar 1926): 41-64. OR-Genl.

WARE, Ellen K. Crossing...1854. In Hall-Kinney Collection. NBHIST. MORMON. I. Rem. 1854.

_____. "Nebraska City in 1858." In Hall-Kinney Collection. NBHIST. Geog.

WARE, Eugene F. "Journal." [In] THE INDIAN WAR OF 1864, ed. Clyde C. Walton. 1911. Reprint. NY: N.p., 1960. Indians. Military.

WARE, Joseph E. THE EMIGRANTS' GUIDE TO CALIFORNIA.... Ed. John Caughey. 1849. Reprint. Princeton: Princeton Univ. Press, 1932. Guide.

WARNER, Agnes S. SEE: Stewart, Agnes.

WARNER, Edward. SEE: With A. P. Robinson. OVERLAND TRACTION ENGINE COMPANY.

WARNER, Mary E. Diary. BANCROFT. CAL(Council)-SIMPSON-TRUCKEE.
II. 1864.

WARNER, Robert C. THE FORT LARAMIE OF ALFRED JACOB MILLER: A CATALOGUE OF ALL THE KNOWN ILLUSTRATIONS OF THE FIRST FORT LARAMIE. Univ. of Wyoming Publications, Vol. 43, No. 2. Laramie: Univ. of Wyoming, 1979. Geog. Graphics.

WARNER, Robert M. Ed. Manwaring, Joshua. "Journal of a Fifty-Niner."

WARNER, Ted J. SEE: With James B. Allen. "Gosiute Indians in Pioneer Utah."

WARNER, William. "Overland to California...." OHIO ARCHAEOLOGICAL AND HISTORICAL PUBLICATIONS 35(1926): 567-71. CAL. 1853. Not Seen.

WARRE, H. J. OVERLAND TO OREGON IN 1845, IMPRESSIONS OF A JOURNEY ACROSS NORTH AMERICA. Ed. Madeline Major-Fregeau. Ottawa: Public Archives of Canada, 1976. Graphics.

_____. SKETCHES IN NORTH AMERICA AND THE OREGON TERRITORY. Barre, MA: Imprint Society, 1970. Graphics.

WARREN, Daniel K. "Reminiscences of Daniel Knight Warren." OREGON HISTORICAL QUARTERLY 3(Dec 1902): 396-409. OR(Council). V. Rem. 1852.

WARREN, Elizabeth V. "Armijo's Trace Revisited: A New Interpretation of the Impact of the Antonio Armijo Route of 1829 - 1830 on the Development of the Old Spanish Trail." MA thesis, Univ. of Nevada-Las Vegas, 1974. SPANISH-Genl.

_____, Ralph J. Roske, and Elizabeth N. Patrick. CULTURAL RESOURCES OF THE CALIFORNIA DESERT, 1776 - 1980: HISTORIC TRAILS AND WAGON ROADS. Cultural Resources Publications in Anthropology - History, ed. Russell L. Kaldenberg. Riverside, CA: U.S. Bureau of Land Management, 1981. SLCOR-Genl. SPANISH-Genl. BEALE-Genl. GILA-Genl. BRADSHAW-Genl.

WARREN, Felix. On the Plains Over the Oregon Trail. Univ. of Washington Library-Ms, Seattle, WA. OR(Neb. City). IV. 1865.

WARREN, Gouverneur K. EXPLORATIONS IN NEBRASKA. 35th Cong., 2d sess., 1858. S. Doc. 1. Serial 975-6. DAKOTAS-Genl.

_____. EXPLORATIONS IN THE DACOTAH COUNTRY, IN THE YEAR 1855. 34th Cong., 1st sess., 1856. S. Ex. Doc. 76. DAKOTAS-Genl. MORMON-Genl.

_____. PRELIMINARY REPORT OF EXPLORATIONS IN NEBRASKA AND DAKOTA, IN THE YEARS 1855- '56 - '57.... WA: GPO, 1875. CAL(Ft. Kearney)-Ends Ft. Laramie. II. 1855. DAKOTAS(Council) to Black Hills and return via Niobrara River. II. 1857.

WARREN, Mrs. M. I. Diary. Society of California Pioneers, SF. Not Seen.

WARREN, Mary E. Reminiscence. ORHIST. OR. V. Rem. 1852.

WASHBURN, Catherine A. THE JOURNAL OF CATHERINE AMANDA STANSBURY WASHBURN, IOWA TO OREGON, 1853. Eugene, OR: Lane County Historical Society, 1967. OR(Council)-BARLOW. III. 1853.

WASHINGTON, George. Diary. Waukesha [WI] County Historical Society. Not Seen.

WATERHOUSE, Loyal N. Diary. Princeton Univ. Library-Western History, Princeton, NJ. CAL(Council)-BRIDGER-SLCUT. II+. 1850.

WATERS, Louisa B. "Trail Blazers of Cajon Pass." WESTWAYS 31(Jan 1939): 8-9. Geog.

WATERS, Lydia M. "Account of a Trip across the Plains in 1855." QUARTERLY Society of California Pioneers 6(Mar 1929): 59-79. CAL(Council)-TRUCKEE-BECK. III-. Rem. 1855.

WATERS, William E. LIFE AMONG THE MORMONS AND A MARCH TO THEIR ZION. NY: Moorhead, Simpson & Bond, 1868.

CAL(Leav)-Via Overland Stage Road-Cheyenne-Bridger's Pass-SLC. II. 1867. Graphics.

WATKINS, Albert. "History of Fort Kearny." PUBLICATIONS Nebraska State Historical Society 16(1911): 227-67. Geog.

_____, ed. NOTES OF THE EARLY HISTORY OF THE NEBRASKA COUNTRY. Publications of the Nebraska State Historical Society, Vol. 20. Lincoln: The Society, 1922. Overland-Genl.

WATKINS, Francis M. STORY OF THE CROW EMIGRANT TRAIN OF 1865. Ed. Ralph L. Milliken. N.p.: Author, 1935. CAL(Council)-BRIDGER-SIMPSON. III. Rem. 1865.

WATKINS, George T. "Overland Travel, 1846-1853: A Trip through a Junkyard Sewer." OVERLAND JOURNAL 5(Fall 1987): 3-7. OV-Genl.

WATROUS, R. "Notes of a Trip to California." Marshall, Michigan DEMOCRATIC EXPOUNDER, Jan-Mar, 1851. 1850 trip. Not Seen.

WATSON, Andrew. "By Wheelbarrow and by Handcart." UTHIST. MORMON. IV. 1854.

WATSON, B. A. "Letters." Springfield ILLINOIS STATE JOURNAL, May-Aug 1849. 1849. Not Seen.

WATSON, Douglas M. Ed. Powell, H. M. SANTA FE TRAIL.

WATSON, Douglas S. WEST WIND, LIFE OF JOSEPH REDDEFORD WALKER. Morongo Valley, CA: Sagebrush, 1984. Biog.

WATSON, Elden J. Comp. Pratt, Orson. THE ORSON PRATT JOURNALS.

WATSON, James T. Ed. Aram, Joseph. "Across the Continent."

WATSON, Jeanne H. Ed. Hays, Lorena L. "To the Land of Gold."

_____. "The Carson Emigrant Road." OVERLAND JOURNAL 4(Sum 1986): 4-12. CAL-Genl.

WATSON, W. W. "Early History of Jefferson County Overland Route." PROCEEDINGS AND COLLECTIONS Nebraska State Historical Society 5(1902): 217-22. Geog.

WATSON, William J. JOURNAL OF AN OVERLAND JOURNEY TO OREGON.... Jacksonville, OR; Roe, 1851. OR(St. Jo)-BARLOW. II. 1849.

WATT, James W. "Experiences of a Packer in Washington Territory Mining Camps during the Sixties." WASHINGTON HISTORICAL QUARTERLY 19(Jul, Oct 1928): 206-13, 285-93; 20(Jan 1929): 36-53. Freight.

WATT, Roberta F. FOUR WAGONS WEST: THE STORY OF SEATTLE. Portland: Metropolitan, 1931. WASH-Genl.

WATTS, Benjamin M. Diary. CAHIST. CAL(St. Jo)-HALL. II. 1849.

WATTS, John W. "Facts About and Mileage of Sublett's Cutoff as Traveled by Him in 1849, Interpolated in Diary of his Brother, John W. Watts." CAHIST. Missing.

_____. Diary. CAHIST. CAL(St. Jo)-BRIDGER-SLCUT. III. 1850. CAL(Ft. Kearney)-Ends mid-Wyoming. III. 1852. Very careful description of trail geography.

WAUGH, Lorenzo. AUTOBIOGRAPHY OF LORENZO WAUGH.

Oakland: Pacific Press, 1883. CAL. V. Rem. 1852.

WAY, Phocion R. "Overland via 'Jackass Mail' in 1858: The Diary of...." ARIZONA & THE WEST 2(Spr, Sum, Fall, Win 1960): 35-53, 147-64, 279-92, 353-70. Stage: Indianola, Texas to Tubac. II +. 1858.

WAYMAN, John H. A DOCTOR ON THE CALIFORNIA TRAIL. Ed. Edgeley W. Todd. Denver: Old West, 1971. CAL(St. Jo). II. 1852. Medical.

WAYMAN, Lydia. Life Story. Eastern Washington Historical Society Library, Spokane, WA. OR(Council). V. 1865.

"Wayside Watering Places." HUTCHINGS' 1(May 1857): 481-82. Stage.

WEARIN, Otha D. "Plattsmouth Ferry." LOS ANGELES WESTERNERS BRANDING IRON, no. 53(Jun 1960): n.p. Geog.

WEAVER, David. Pioneer Reminiscences. Ed. M. L. Wilson. MONHIST. CAL(Council)-BOZE. III +. Rem. 1864.

WEAVER, David B. Early Days in Emigrant Gulch. MONHIST. CAL(Council)-BOZE. IV. 1864.

WEAVER, Frank. "Fort Smith: Hub from which the Western Gold Seekers Went into the Wilderness." JOURNAL Fort Smith Historical Society 2(Oct 1978): 56-60. Geog. MARCY-Genl. Not Seen.

WEBB, Catherine J. Ed. Hitchcock, Harriet. A FAMILY HISTORY.

WEBB, Henry F. "Edwin Bryant's Trail through Western Utah." UTAH HISTORICAL QUARTERLY 29(Apr 1961): 129-35. HASTINGS-1846-Genl.

_____. "The First Trail across the Great Salt Desert." UTAH ENGINEERING & SCIENCE 2(Jun 1961): 8-10, 14, 16. HASTINGS-1845-Genl.

_____. "The Last Trek across the Great Salt Desert." UTAH HISTORICAL QUARTERLY 31(Win 1963): 26-33. Pres. 1962 trip from Knolls, UT to Pilot Springs. Map.

_____. "The Long Drive on the Hastings Cut-off." CALIFORNIA HISTORICAL QUARTERLY 36(Mar 1957): 57-62. HASTINGS-Genl.

WEBB, James. "The Papers of James Webb, 1841-46." Ed. Ralph P. Bieber. WASHINGTON UNIVERSITY STUDIES 11, no. 2(1924): 255-305. Not Seen.

WEBB, Lynn R. "The Contributions of the Temporary Settlements of Garden Grove, Mount Pisgah, and Kanesville, Iowa, to Mormon Emigration, 1846-1852." MA thesis, BYU, 1954. Geog.

WEBB, Todd. "Following the Gold Rush Trail Today." FRONTIER TIMES 39(Aug-Sept 1965): 26-28, 50-54. Pres.

_____. THE GOLD RUSH TRAIL AND THE ROAD TO OREGON. Garden City, NY: Doubleday, 1963. Overland-Genl. Graphics.

WEBBER, Bert. Ed. Beeson, Welborn. WELBORN BEESON.

WEBER, David J. RICHARD KERN: EXPEDITIONARY ARTIST IN THE FAR SOUTHWEST, 1848-1853. Albuquerque: Univ. of New Mexico Press, 1985. Graphics. Not Seen.

WEBER, Jean, ed. "Early Inns and Roadhouses: A History of Hospitality in San Mateo County." LA PENINSULA 18(Win 1975): 1-56. Stage: San Mateo County.

WEBSTER, Jean. "The Myth of Pioneer Hardship on the Oregon Trail." REED COLLEGE BULLETIN 24(Jan 1946): 27-46. OR-Genl.

WEBSTER, Kimball. THE GOLDSEEKERS OF '49. Manchester, NH: Standard Book, 1917. CAL(Indep)-LASSEN. II. 1849.

WEBSTER, Noah H. "Journal of Noah H. Webster...." CONTRIBU- TIONS Montana Historical Society 3(1900): 300-30. CHEROKEE(Denver-Ft. Bridger)-MONTANA. II. 1863.

WECHSELBERG, Peter. Letters. WIHIST. CAL(Council). 1850. Not Seen.

WEDDELL, P. M. "Location of Donner Camps and Marking Trail." PONY EXPRESS 15(May 1949): 3-6, 12. CAL-1846-Genl. Pres. Graphics.

_____. "Location of the Donner Family Camp." CALIFORNIA HIS- TORICAL QUARTERLY 24(Mar 1945): 73-76. CAL-1846-Genl. Geog.

WEED, L. N. Narrative. BEINECKE. CAL-TEX(Houston-Austin-El Paso)-GILA. II. 1849.

WEEKS, Carl. "Material on the Mormon Trail." Iowa State Historical Society Archives, Iowa City, IA. MORMON-Genl.

WEEKS, Lovina W. Diary. UPAC. CAL(St. Jo)-BRIDGER-SLCUT. III+. Rem. 1859.

WEIGHT, Harold O. "Desert Trails." WESTWAYS 55(Oct 1963): 6-9. GILA-Genl. CAL-Genl.

_____ and Lucille. "Forgotten Road to Gold." LOS ANGELES WESTERNERS BRAND BOOK 10(1963): 11-34. BRADSHAW- Genl. Map. Pres. Excellent summary of this little-known route.

WEINERT, Duane R. "General S. W. Kearny's New Mexico - California Expedition, 1846 - 1847." MA thesis, Univ. of Oklahoma Press, 1941. GILA-1846-Genl. RIO GRANDE-1846-Genl.

WEIR, Thomas R. "Early Trails of Burrard Peninsula." BRITISH COLUMBIA HISTORICAL QUARTERLY 9, no. 4(1945): 273-76. CANADA-Genl.

WEISEL, George F. Ed. Dodson, John F. "Dodson's Death."

WELCH, Adonijah S. SEE: With Cephas Arms. LONG ROAD TO CALIFORNIA.

_____. "Document: Three Gold Rush Letters of...." Ed. William H. Hermann. IOWA JOURNAL OF HISTORY 57(Jan 1959): 61-73. CAL-MORMON-SLCOR. V. 1849.

WELCH, Jack P. "The Butterfield Overland Mail." NEWS AND VIEWS California Division of Beaches and Parks, Jun 1963, 1-24. Pres: 1958 Centennial observances.

WELCH, John A. PERSONAL MEMOIRS. Hutchinson, KS: Author, 1920. CAL(Council). III+. Rem. 1854.

WELCH, Nancy D. "Recollections." TRANSACTIONS Oregon Pioneer Association (1897); 97-103. OR(St. Jo). Rem. 1844. Not Seen.

WELLBURN, G. E. SEE: With H. C. Hitt. "Barnard's Cariboo Ex- press."

WELLENKAMP, Henry. Diary. DENVERPUB. CAL(Weston).

III+. 1850.

WELLES, C. M. THREE YEARS' WANDERINGS OF A CONNEC- TICUT YANKEE. NY: American Subscription, 1860. CAL(Sacramento to Gold Canyon). IV. 1858?

WELLES, Thomas. "The Pony Express Museum." OVERLAND MONTHLY 91(Mar 1933): 44-45. Pony: San Marino Museum.

WELLIVER, Mrs. Andy. "The Maiden's Grave." NEVADA HISTORI- CAL SOCIETY QUARTERLY 6(Fall-Win 1963): 1-22. Geog.

WELLMAN, Paul I. "The Silent Partner Who Made History and Lost Fortunes on the Great Plains." Scrapbook. Leavenworth [KS] Public Library. Freight: Russell, Majors & Waddell.

WELLMAN, Sylvanus. Diary. COHIST. PIKES. II. 1859.

WELLS, Donald N., and Merle W. Wells. "The Oneida Toll Road Con- troversy, 1864 - 1880." OREGON HISTORICAL QUARTERLY 58(Jun 1957): 113-16. Stage.

WELLS, Epaphroditus. Letters...1850. BANCROFT. CAL(St. Jo). V. 1849.

WELLS, Eugene T. Ed. Anderson, Kirk. "Trip to Utah, 1858."

_____. "The Growth of Independence, Missouri, 1827 - 1850." MIS- SOURI HISTORICAL BULLETIN 16(Oct 1959): 33-46. Geog.

Wells, Fargo & Company. Papers, 1839 - 1911. HUNTL. Stage.

_____. CSL. Stage.

WELLS, Henry. SKETCH OF THE RISE, PROGRESS, AND PRESENT CONDITION OF THE EXPRESS SYSTEM. Albany, NY: Van Benthuysen, 1864. Stage.

WELLS, Merle W. SEE: With Donald Wells. "Oneida Toll Road Con- troversy."

_____, and Larry Jones. "Oregon Trail Cultural Resource Study: Fort Caspar, Wyoming - Fort Boise (Hudson's Bay Company), Idaho." Unpublished Report for U.S. Bureau of Land Management, 1981. Overland-Genl. Pres.

WELLS, Polk. LIFE AND ADVENTURES OF POLK WELLS. Hall, MO: G. A. Warnica, c1907. Freight: Atchison to Ft. Laramie. IV. 1864.

WELLS, William. Letters. CSL. CAL(Westport). 1849. Not Seen.

WELSH, Donald H. "The Butterfield Overland Mail, 1858 - 1861 and Its Centennial Observance in Missouri." MISSOURI HISTORICAL REVIEW 52(Apr 1958): 218-34. Stage. Pres.

_____. "The Butterfield Overland Mail Centennial in Missouri." MISSOURI HISTORICAL REVIEW 53(Jan 1959): 132-40. Pres.

_____. "Here Comes the Pony Express." Scrapbook. State Histori- cal Society of Missouri Library, Columbia, MO. Pony.

_____. "The Pony Express in Retrospect." MISSOURI HISTORI- CAL REVIEW 54(Apr 1960): 237-44. Pony.

WELSH, John P. Diaries. HUNTL. OR(Council)-APPLE. II. 1851. OR(St. Jo)-APPLE. II. 1853.

WELTON, R. W. "Map of the California State Telegraph and Overland Mail Road - Austin to Great Salt Lake City, 1866." UTHIST. Map.

WELTY, Mrs. Marion B. "Description of a Trip from Nebraska City to Colorado City in 1862." Norlin Library-Western History, Univ. of Colorado-Boulder. PIKES. V-. 1862.

WELTY, Raymond L. "Supplying the Frontier Military Posts." KANSAS HISTORICAL QUARTERLY 7(May 1938): 154-69. Freight. Military.

WENTWORTH, Edward N. Ed. Kimball, Gorham. "Trailing Sheep." SEE: With Charles Towne. SHEPHERDS' EMPIRE.

_____. AMERICA'S SHEEP TRAILS: HISTORY, PERSONALITIES. Ames, IA: Iowa State College Press, 1948. The best of sheep trail studies, with fine bibliography.

_____. "Eastward Sheep Drives from California and Oregon." MISSISSIPPI VALLEY HISTORICAL REVIEW 28(Mar 1942): 507-38. Stock.

_____. "Meat in the Diet of Westward Explorers and Emigrants." MID-AMERICA 29(Apr 1947): 75-91. Social.

_____. "The Wanderings of the 'Woolies' in the West." CHICAGO WESTERNERS BRAND BOOK 3(Jul 1946): 29-35. Stock.

WERDEN, Francis H. Journal. MONHIST. DAKOTAS(Shakopee, MN)-MONTANA. III. 1864.

WERNE, Joseph R. "Major Emory and Captain Jimenez: Running the Gadsden Line." JOURNAL OF THE SOUTHWEST 29(Sum 1987): 203-27. GOVT. MEX-Genl. GILA-1855-Genl.

WERNER, Fred H. "Mystery Graves on the Oregon Trail." TRUE WEST 28(Dec 1981): 60-61. Geog: Lingle, WY. Social.

WERNER, Morris. "The Fort Leavenworth - Fort Riley Military Road: And the Hobby of Following old Trails." KANSAS QUARTERLY 5(Spr 1973): 52-61. PIKES-Smoky Hill-Genl. Pres.

WESLEY, John. PIONEERS: A SIMULATION OF DECISION-MAKING ON A WAGON TRAIN. Lakeside, CA: Interact Company, 1974. Teaching aid for social studies classes.

WEST, Calvin B. SEE: Stuart, Reginald R. and Grace D. CALVIN B. WEST.

WEST, Daniel. Diary. State Historical Society of Missouri Library, Columbia, MO. CAL(Indep). II. 1849.

WEST, Elliott. "Splendid Misery: Stagecoach Travel in the Far West." AMERICAN WEST 18(Nov-Dec 1981): 61-64, 83-86. Stage.

WEST, G. M. "The Portion of His Memoirs...1853." BANCROFT. OR(Council)-BARLOW. IV. Rem. 1853.

WEST, George M. AN AUTOBIOGRAPHY. LA: N.p., 1937. OR. Rem. 1852. Not Seen.

WEST, Margaret E. Covered Wagon Days. ORHIST. OR(Missouri)-BARLOW. III. Rem. 1864. Includes sheet music for songs popular on trail.

WEST, S. H. THE LIFE AND TIMES OF S. H. WEST. LeRoy, IL: Author, 1908. CAL-MEX(Vera Cruz-Acapulco). V. 1852. Stage: St. Louis to SF. V. 1859.

WEST, Wells W. Autobiography. BANCROFT. CAL(Indep)-SLCUT. IV. 1853.

WEST, Willis J. "Staging and Stage Hold-ups in the Cariboo." BRITISH COLUMBIA HISTORICAL QUARTERLY 12, no. 3(1948): 185-209. Stage.

WESTERLUND, Peter. "Reminiscence...Pike's Peak Gold Craze." MNHIST. PIKES(Council to Denver)-CHEROKEE(Denver to Pueblo)-SANTA FE-RIO GRANDE-Ends El Paso. III. 1859.

WESTERMAN, Pleasant B. "How I Got to California." MENDOCINO HISTORICAL REVIEW 1(Aut 1974): 8-10. CAL-TEX(East Texas-El Paso)-GILA. V. 1869. Stock drive.

"The Western Cavalryman: Color Portfolio." AMERICAN HISTORY ILLUSTRATED 14(Oct 1979): 25-31. Graphics-Military.

WESTON, Francis F. Diary. Held by Henry Clifford, Los Angeles, CA. 1849. Not Seen.

WETZEL, Charles R. "Monument Station, Gove County [KS]." KANSAS HISTORICAL QUARTERLY 26(Aut 1960): 250-54. Geog: Station on Smoky Hill River.

WHALL, Les. THE SALT LAKE CITY POST OFFICE, 1849 - 1869. SLC: Author, 1982. Utah-Mail.

_____. "To Brownsville, Twice a Week." AMERICAN PHILATELIST 97(Sept 1983): 831-34. Utah-Mail.

WHARFIELD, H. B. FORT YUMA ON THE COLORADO RIVER. El Cajon, CA: Author, 1968. Geog.

WHARTON, Clifton. "The Expedition of Major Clifton Wharton in 1844." COLLECTIONS Kansas State Historical Society 16(1923-1925): 272-305. CAL(Ft. Leavenworth to Loup Fork). II. 1844.

WHEAT, Carl I. BOOKS OF THE CALIFORNIA GOLD RUSH. SF: Colt Press, 1949. Bib.

_____. "The Forty-Niners in Death Valley: A Tentative Census." QUARTERLY Southern California Historical Society 19(Dec 1939): 102-17. SLCOR-1849-Genl.

_____. "The Jayhawkers at the Missouri: A Remarkable Discovery." QUARTERLY Southern California Historical Society 22(Sept 1940): 103-08. SLCOR-1849-Genl.

_____. MAPPING THE AMERICAN WEST, 1540 - 1857; A PRELIMINARY STUDY. Worcester, MA: American Antiquarian Society, 1954. Maps.

_____. MAPPING THE TRANSMISSISSIPPI WEST. 6 vols. SF: Institute of Historical Cartography, 1957-63. Maps.

_____. THE MAPS OF THE CALIFORNIA GOLD REGION, 1848 - 1857. SF: Grabhorn, 1942. Maps.

_____. "Pioneer Visitors to Death Valley after the '49ers." CALIFORNIA HISTORICAL QUARTERLY 18(Sept 1939): 1-22. SLCOR-Genl.

_____. "Trailing the Forty-Niners through Death Valley." SIERRA CLUB BULLETIN 24(Jun 1939): 3-37. SLCOR-1849-Genl.

WHEELER, George N. Journal. HUNTL. CAL(Council)-TRUCKEE. II. 1850.

WHEELER, George W. Journal. HUNTL. CAL(Council)-TRUCKEE. III +. 1850.

WHEELER, Katherine D. Ed. Dean, Thaddeus. A JOURNEY TO CALIFORNIA.

WHEELER, Sessions S. THE BLACK ROCK DESERT. Caldwell, ID: Caxton, 1978. LASSEN-Genl.

_____. THE NEVADA DESERT. Caldwell, ID: Caxton, 1971. See section on Forty Mile Desert. CAL-Genl.

WHEELOCK, Charles. Letters. Iowa State Historical Society, Iowa City, IA. CAL(Council)-BRIDGER-SLCUT. 1850. Not Seen.

WHEELOCK, Harrison. GUIDE AND MAP OF REESE RIVER AND HUMBOLDT.... SF: Towne & Bacon, 1864. Guide. Maps.

WHEELOCK, Joseph A. Diary...Nobles' Expedition. MNHIST. Not Seen.

WHEELOCK, Seymour E. "The Concord Coach: A Western Legacy from the East." COLORADO HERITAGE, no. 4(1986): n.p. STAGE-Equipment-Genl.

WHEELOCK, Walt. SEE: With Pat Adler. WALKER'S RAILROAD ROUTES.

_____. "Following Fremont's Fifth Expedition." LOS ANGELES WESTERNERS BRAND BOOK 12(1966): 187-200. SLCUT-1853-Variant.

WHIPPLE, Amiel Weeks. SEE: Foreman, Grant. A PATHFINDER IN THE SOUTHWEST. SEE: Wright, Muriel H., and George H. Shirk. "The Journal."

_____. "Amiel Weeks Whipple and the Boundary Survey in Southern California." Ed. Thomas L. Scharf. JOURNAL OF SAN DIEGO HISTORY 19(Sum 1973): 18-31. GILA(San Diego-Yuma). II. 1849.

_____. REPORT OF EXPLORATIONS FOR A RAILWAY ROUTE NEAR THE THIRTY-FIFTH PARALLEL OF LATITUDE FROM THE MISSISSIPPI RIVER TO THE PACIFIC OCEAN. 33rd Cong., 1st sess., 1854. H. Ex. Doc. 129. CAL(Ft. Smith)-MARCY-BEALE. II. 1853.

_____. REPORT OF THE SECRETARY OF WAR COMMUNICATING IN ANSWER TO A RESOLUTION OF THE SENATE, THE REPORT OF LT. WHIPPLE'S EXPEDITION FROM SAN DIEGO TO THE COLORADO. 31st Cong., 2d sess., 1851. S. Ex. Doc. 19. GILA(San Diego to Yuma). II. 1849.

WHIPPLE, Charlotte L. Papers. New York Public Library-Ms & Archives, New York City, NY. OR. Not Seen.

WHIPPLE, Nelson W. History. UTHIST. MORMON. IV. Rem. 1850.

WHIPPLE-HASLAM, Mrs. Lee. EARLY DAYS IN CALIFORNIA. JAmestown, CA: Author, 1923. CAL. V-. Rem. 1852.

WHITAKER, George. Reminiscence. UTHIST. MORMON. V. 1847.

WHITAKER, Robert. Ed. Lenox, Edward H. OVERLAND TO OREGON.

WHITE, Bartholomew. LIFE AND TRAVELS WEST OF THE ROCKY MOUNTAINS. Oakland: Author, 1884. OR(Indep). V-. 1843.

WHITE, Chester L. "Surmounting the Sierras: The Campaign for a Wagon Road." CALIFORNIA HISTORICAL QUARTERLY 7(Mar 1928): 4-19. Freight. Stage.

WHITE, Daniel C. Diary. HUNTL. CAL(Council)-BRIDGER-SLCUT-TRUCKEE. III-. 1854. OR-CAL. III-. 1858.

WHITE, Douglas. THE STORY OF A TRAIL. LA: San Pedro, Los Angeles & Salt Lake Railroad, 1905. SLCOR-Genl.

WHITE, Edith. MEMORIES OF PIONEER CHILDHOOD AND YOUTH IN FRENCH CORRAL AND NORTH SAN JUAN, NEVADA COUNTY, CA. N.p.: Author, 1936. CAL. V-. 1859.

WHITE, Elijah. SEE: Allen, Miss A. J.

WHITE, Francis B. "Trip that Once Required Six Months of Hardship Now Made in Two Days." St. Joseph [MO] GAZETTE, 10 Apr 1932, pp. 1, 3. OR(St. Jo)-BARLOW. IV. 1852.

WHITE, Helen M. Ed. Bond, Samuel R. "Journal of Expedition."

_____. "Captain Fisk Goes to Washington." MINNESOTA HISTORY 38(Mar 1963): 216-30. Biog.

_____. ed. HO! FOR THE GOLD FIELDS: NORTHERN OVERLAND WAGON TRAINS OF THE 1860'S. St. Paul: Minnesota Historical Society, 1966. Finest study of the Dakota-Montana route. DAKOTAS-Genl. MONTANA-Genl.

_____. "Minnesota, Montana, and Manifest Destiny." MINNESOTA HISTORY 38(Jun 1962): 53-62. DAKOTAS-Genl. MONTANA-Genl.

WHITE, Hiram F. "The Mormon Road." WASHINGTON HISTORICAL QUARTERLY 6(Oct 1915): 243-50. MORMON-1847-Genl.

WHITE, James H. Diary. ORHIST. OR(Plattsmouth). IV. 1865.

WHITE, Lonnie J. Ed. Millard, C. M. "Hugh Kirkendall's Wagon Train."

_____. "The Santa Fe Trail in '65: The Military Defense of the Road." MILITARY HISTORY OF TEXAS AND THE SOUTHWEST 9, no. 2(1972): 107-28. SANTA Fe-1865-Genl. Military.

WHITE, M. Catherine. Ed. Hickman, Richard O. "An Overland Journey."

_____. "The North Overland Route from Minnesota to Montana." Montana State University Library, Missoula, MT. DAKOTAS-Genl. MONTANA-Genl.

WHITE, Natalie. SEE: With Helen Bouton. "How the Pioneers Moved Westward."

WHITE, Stephen. Recollections of 1850 - 1851. Held by Charles W. Martin, Omaha, NB. CAL(Council). III. Rem. 1850.

WHITE, Thomas. "To Oregon in 1852: Letter of Dr. Thomas White." Eds. Oscar O. Winther and Gayle Thornbrough. PUBLICATIONS Indiana Historical Society 23, no. 1(1964): 5-37. OR(Council). IV. 1852.

WHITE, William W. "William Wellington White - An Autobiography." QUARTERLY California Pioneer Society 4(Dec 1927): 202-16. CAL(St. Jo)-BRIDGER-SLCUT. III-. Rem. 1849.

WHITELEY, Jane K. Papers. WIHIST. Stage: Atchison to Denver. III. 1864.

WHITFORD, William C. "The Establishment of Overland Connections between the Region East of the Mississippi and Red Rivers and the Territory Lying Westward to the Rocky Mountains, with Special Reference to Dakota Territory." MA thesis, Univ. of North Dakota, 1915. DAKOTAS-Genl.

WHITING, William H. "Journal...1849." In EXPLORING SOUTH-WESTERN TRAILS, 1846 - 1854, eds. Ralph P. Bieber and A. B. Bender. Glendale: Clark, 1938. TEX(Fredericksburg to El Paso)-1849-Genl.

WHITMAN, Abial. Journal. BEINECKE. CAL(Council)-BRIDGER-SLCUT. II. 1850.

WHITMORE, Len. "Grande Ronde - Hebo Mountain - Tillamook Valley Trail." ORHIST. OR-Genl.

WHITNEY, Horace K. Journal. LDS. MORMON. II. 1847.

WHITNEY, Orson K. Journal. BYU. MORMON. III. 1854.

WHITNEY, William T. Trip...1859. CSL. CAL(Council)-SLCUT. III. Rem. 1859.

WHITTEMORE, Margaret. SKETCHBOOK OF KANSAS LANDMARKS. Topeka: College Press, 1936. Pres.

WHITWORTH, Robert W. "From the Mississippi to the Pacific: An Englishman in the Mormon Battalion." Eds. David B. Gracy, II, and Helen J. Rugeley. ARIZONA & THE WEST 7(Sum 1965): 127-60. CAL(Leav)-SANTA FE-RIO GRANDE-GILA. III. 1846.

"Why the Donner Party? Why the Donner Movement." GRIZZLY BEAR 9(Jun 1911): 15. Pres.

WICKERD, Ron and Fran. "Covered Wagon Trek - Modern Style." CAMPING GUIDE, Apr & May 1967, 22-26, 30-35. Pres: Trip from Independence to Sacramento.

WICKMAN, John E. "Hoosier Overlanders in the Gold Rush, 1849 - 1850." MA thesis, Indiana Univ., 1957. CAL-Genl.

WIDBER, J. H. Statement...1849. BANCROFT. CAL(Ft. Smith)-SANTA FE-SPANISH-SLCOR. V. 1849.

WIER, John B. "From Where the Gold Diggers Go." Hannibal MISSOURI COURIER, 7 Feb 1850, p. 1. CAL(Indep)-HALL. III. 1849.

WIGLE, Abraham J. Oregon Pioneer. Eastern Washington Historical Society Library, Spokane, WA. OR(St. Jo). II. Rem. 1852.

WILBUR, Marguerite E. JOHN SUTTER: RASCAL AND ADVENTURER. NY: Liveright, 1949. Biog.

WILCOX, Adelia A. Memoirs. UTHIST. MORMON. V. 1853.

WILCOX, WAYNE. "Thirty-Six Miles of History." UTAH HISTORICAL QUARTERLY 23(Oct 1955): 363-67. Trail over Wasatch Range into Salt Lake City. MORMON-Genl.

WILDER, Mona. "Early Trails of SHASTA COUNTY." COVERED WAGON, 1971, 55-59. Geog.

WILDMAN, Augustus and Thomas G. Correspondence. BEINECKE. PIKES. III. 1859.

WILEY, Austin. Diary. Society of California Pioneers, San Francisco, CA. Not Seen.

WILKE, Philip J., and Harry W. Lawton, eds. THE EXPEDITION OF CAPTAIN J. W. DAVIDSON FROM FORT TEJON TO THE OWENS VALLEY IN 1859. Socorro, NY: Ballena, 1976. Geog: Owens Valley.

WILKES, Charles. COLUMBIA RIVER TO THE SACRAMENTO.

Oakland: Biobooks, 1958. OR-CAL. II. 1841.

WILKES, George. THE HISTORY OF OREGON.... NY: Colyer, 1845. Guide. OR-1843-Genl.

WILKES, Homer. "Expressman Jones." FRONTIER TIMES 37(Oct-Nov 1963): 36-37, 68. GILA(Tucson-Picacho). II. Rem. 1862.

WILKES, L. C., comp. BY AN OREGON PIONEER FIRESIDE. Hillsboro, OR: Author, 1941. OR(Indep)-BARLOW. V. 1845.

WILKINS, James F. AN ARTIST ON THE OVERLAND TRAIL.... Ed. John F. McDermott. San Marino: Huntington, 1968. CAL(Weston)-BRIDGER. III. Graphics.

WILKINS, Mary B. "Samuel Kimbrough Barlow: A Pioneer Road Builder of Oregon." OREGON HISTORICAL QUARTER 26(Sept 1925): 209-24. BARLOW-Genl. Biog.

WILKINSON, Henry. Narrative. MONHIST. CAL-MONTANA. V. 1864.

WILKINSON, J. A. Across...1859. HUNTL. CAL(Neb. City). II. 1859.

WILKINSON, Joseph T. THE CARIBOO GUIDE. SF: Magee Bros., 1862. Guide.

WILKINSON, Raleigh F. Recollections. MONHIST. CAL(St. Jo)-LANDER-BOZE. Rem. 1864. Not Seen.

WILLARD, James F. "Sidelights on the Pike's Peak Gold Rush, 1858 - 59." COLORADO MAGAZINE 12(Jan 1935): 3-13. PIKES-1859-Genl.

WILLEY, Day A. "Building the Mullan Road." SUNSET 24(Jun 1910): 635-40. MULLAN-Genl.

WILLEY, Lucas. Diaries. BANCROFT. CAL(Fayetteville)-CHEROKEE(to SLC)-SLCUT-TRUCKEE. I. 1854. CAL(Fayetteville)-CHEROKEE(to SLC)-SLCUT-TRUCKEE. I. 1859. Flora and Fauna.

WILLIAMS, Burton. Ed. Taylor, Calvin. "Overland to the Gold Fields." Ed. Taylor, Calvin. "Overland to California."

WILLIAMS, Carol. "My First Indian: Interaction between Women and Indians on the Trail, 1845 - 1865." OVERLAND JOURNAL 4(Sum 1986): 13-18. Social. Indians.

WILLIAMS, Christy. SEE: Williams Family Papers.

WILLIAMS, Clayton W. Ed. Wedemeyer, George W. "Excerpts from the Diary."

_____. TEXAS' LAST FRONTIER: FORT STOCKTON AND THE TRANS-PECOS, 1861-1895. College Station: Texas A&M Univ. Press, 1982. Geog. TEX-Genl.

_____. "That Topographical Ghost - Horsehead Crossing." OLD WEST 11(Win 1974): 22-25, 50-52. Excellent. Geog.

WILLIAMS, Eleen T., ed. UTAH HISTORY OF POST OFFICES. Dutch John, UT: Utah Chapter, National Assn. of Postmasters, 1969. Utah-Mail.

WILLIAMS, Elijah. Letter...1851. Oregon State Library, Salem, OR. OR(Indep?)-BARLOW. IV. 1851.

WILLIAMS, Elizabeth. "Among the Sierras." PACIFIC MONTHLY

10(Oct 1863): 252-56. Stage: Folsom to Carson City, 1863.

Williams Family Papers. BANCROFT. CAL(Batesville, Ark)-CHEROKEE(to Ft. Bridger). III. 1853.

WILLIAMS, H. D. Diary. Attributed to BANCROFT but uncataloged.

WILLIAMS, Howard D. Diary. UTHIST. CAL(St. Jo)-BRIDGER-SLCUT-TRUCKEE(to Carson City by Carson River, then north to Truckee Meadows). II. 1859. II. 1859. Same as H. D. Williams diary?

WILLIAMS, J[esse]. W[allace]. Ed. Leach, James B. "Journey." SEE: With Mrs. Virgil Johnson. "Some Northwest Texas Trails."

_____. "The Butterfield Overland Mail Road across Texas." SOUTHWESTERN HISTORICAL QUARTERLY 61(Jul 1957): 1-19. Very complete description of Texas portion of route. Good map.

_____. "The Marcy and Butterfield Trails across North Texas." MA thesis, Hardin-Simmons Univ., 1938. TEX-Genl. Stage. MARCY-Genl.

_____. "Marcy's Road from Dona Ana." WESTX 19(Oct 1943): 128-52. MARCY-1849-Genl. Pres: Trails imposed on recent highway maps.

_____. "Military Roads of the 1850's in Central West Texas." WESTX 18(Oct 1942): 77-91. TEX-Genl.

_____. OLD TEXAS TRAILS, ed. & comp. Kenneth F. Neighbours. Burnet, TX: Eakin, 1979. TEX-Genl.

WILLIAMS, James S. and Frances H. Letters - Iowa to Oregon. NBHIST. OR(Council). V. Rem. 1852.

WILLIAMS, John B. Diary. DENVERPUB. Freight: Boise east to Ft. Hall area)-MONTANA. II. 1866.

WILLIAMS, John H. Ed. Winthrop, Theodore. THE CANOE AND THE SADDLE.

WILLIAMS, John T. "Journal of John T. Williams, 1850." INDIANA MAGAZINE OF HISTORY 32(Dec 1936): 393-409. CAL(St. Jo)-HALL. III. 1850.

WILLIAMS, Joseph. SEE: Williams Family Papers.

WILLIAMS, Joseph. NARRATIVE OF A TOUR...1841-2. 1843. Reprint. NY: Eberstadt, 1921. OR(Westport). III. 1841. OR(East from Whitman Mission)-SPANISH(South from Ft. Bridger to Taos)-SANTA FE. III. 1842.

WILLIAMS, Joseph. Diary. Held by Gregory Franzwa, St. Louis, MO. OR(Council). 1851. Not Seen.

WILLIAMS, L. White. Diary. Chester Country Historical Society, West Chester, PA. Not Seen.

WILLIAMS, Lucia L. "A Letter to Mother." In COVERED WAGON WOMEN, vol. 3. Ed. Kenneth L. Holmes. Glendale: Clark, 1985. OR-BARLOW. III. 1851.

WILLIAMS, Michael F. Ed. Anderson, William W. "Diary and Memoirs."

WILLIAMS, Moses A. Diary. Jacksonville [OR] Museum. Not Seen.

WILLIAMS, Septimus. SEE: Williams Family Papers.

WILLIAMS, V[elina] A. "Diary of a Trip across the Plains in 1853."

TRANSACTIONS Oregon Pioneer Association (1922): 178-226. OR(Council)-APPLE. II. 1853.

WILLIAMS, Wellington. THE TRAVELLER'S AND TOURIST'S GUIDE.... Philadelphia: Lippincott, Grambo, 1853. Guide.

WILLIAMSON, Hugh P. Ed. Tate, James. "One Who Went West."

WILLIAMSON, R. S. REPORT OF A RECONNAISSANCE...OF A ROUTE THROUGH THE SIERRA NEVADA.... 31st Cong., 1st sess. 1850. S. Ex. Doc. 47. CAL-1849-Genl.

WILLING, George M. "Diary of a Journey to the Pike's Peak Gold Mines in 1859." MISSISSIPPI VALLEY HISTORICAL REVIEW 14(Dec 1927): 360-78. PIKES. II. 1859.

WILLIS, Edward J. Diary. BEINECKE. CAL(Indep)-HALL-TRUCKEE. III+. 1849.

WILLIS, Ira J. "The Ira J. Willis Guide to the Gold Mines." Ed. Irene D. Paden. CALIFORNIA HISTORICAL QUARTERLY 32(Sept 1953): 193-207. Guide.

WILLIS, James M. "Jasons of 1860." Ed. Bessie L. Lyon. PALIMPSEST 17(Jul 1936): 217-34. PIKES. IV. 1860.

WILLMAN, Lilian M. "The History of Fort Kearney." PUBLICATIONS Nebraska State Historical Society 21(1930): 211-318. Geog.

WILLS, Irving. "The Jerk Line Team." NOTICIAS 5(Spr 1959): 1-13. Teams.

WILLS, John A. THE CHORPENNING CASE. WA: M'Gill & Witherow, 1873? Mail.

WILSON, Alex. "Trip across the Plains." SISKIYOU PIONEER 1, no. 3(1949): 31-34. CAL(Council)-CHEROKEE(Denver-SLC)-SLCUT? V-. 1863.

WILSON, Alfred H. Diary. Held by Charles W. Martin, Omaha, NB. CAL(Neb. City)-Ends City of Rocks. III. 1848.

WILSON, Benjamin D. "Benito Wilson - Yankee to California." Ed. Edwin H. Carpenter. DOWNEY HISTORICAL SOCIETY ANNUAL 1(1966-67): 31-43. CAL(New Mexico)-SPANISH with Workman-Rowland Party. V-. 1841.

_____. Observations on Early Days in California and New Mexico. HUNTL. CAL-SPANISH. V-. Rem. 1841.

WILSON, D. Ray. FORT KEARNY ON THE PLATTE. Dundee, IL: Crossroads Communications, n.d. Geog.

WILSON, David P. "The Mormon Battalion." MA thesis, Univ. of Utah, 1941. CAL(Leav)-SANTA FE-RIO GRANDE-GILA. II. 1846.

WILSON, Davis. Diary. NBHIST. CAL(Council)-BOZE. I. 1866.

WILSON, Elijah N. AMONG THE SHOSHONES. SLC: Skelton, 1916. Pony. SIMPSON. III. 1860. Stage: Virginia City, NV to Austin, NV. III. 1861.

WILSON, Elinor. JIM BECKWOURTH: BLACK MOUNTAIN MAN AND WAR CHIEF OF THE CROWS. Norman: Univ. of Oklahoma Press, 1972. BECK-Genl. Biog.

WILSON, Elizabeth M. Papers. UPAC-Rare Book Room. OR. 1851. Not Seen.

WILSON, Gary. "Hostage among the Comanches: The Ordeal of Jane Wilson." RED RIVER VALLEY HISTORICAL REVIEW 5(Spr

1980): 4-12. TEX. IV. 1846. Indian raid near Phantom Hill, TX.

WILSON, George D. Journal. UTHIST. CHEROKEE(Pueblo-Ft. Laramie). IV. 1846.

WILSON, Gladys M. "The Saga of Butterfield's Overland Mail." AMERICAN HISTORY ILLUSTRATED 1(Jan 1967): 14-22. Stage.

_____, and William C. Davis. "Independence: Gateway to the West." AMERICAN HISTORY ILLUSTRATED 4(Oct 1969): 36-42. Geog.

WILSON, Harold G. "Some Phases of Early Transportation in Arizona." MA thesis, Univ. of Arizona, 1923. Missing from stacks.

WILSON, James A. "West Texas Influence on the Early Cattle Industry of Arizona." SOUTHWESTERN HISTORICAL QUARTERLY 71(Jul 1967): 26-36. Stock drives from Texas to Arizona.

WILSON, James T. The Life of James T. Wilson. BYU. Not Seen.

WILSON, Jane A. "Captive among the Comanches." OLD WEST 8(Sum 1972): 36-37, 56-58. Indians. SEE ALSO: Wilson, Gary.

WILSON, John S. Diary. BEINECKE. CAL(Westport)-BRIDGER-SLCUT-NOBLES. II+. 1859.

WILSON, Lester S. Journal. Montana State Univ., Bozeman, MT. CAL(Council)-BOZE. 1866. Not Seen.

WILSON, Luzena S. LUZENA STANLEY WILSON.... Oakland: Mills College - Eucalyptus Press, 1937. CAL(Indep). V. Rem. 1849.

WILSON, M. L. Ed. Weaver, David. "Pioneer Reminiscences."

WILSON, Maud. "Federal Exploration in California from 1841 - 1855." MA thesis, Univ. of California-Berkeley, 1917. Govt.

WILSON, Milburn L. Papers. MONHIST. MONTANA-Genl. Materials gathered by trail historian.

WILSON, Neill C. TREASURE EXPRESS: EPIC DAYS OF WELLS FARGO. NY: Macmillan, 1936. Stage.

WILSON, Perkins. "An Analysis of Oregon Migration, 1842 - 1848." Senior thesis, Princeton Univ., 1951. OR-Genl.

WILSON, Robert M. Chronicle. CSL. CAL(Indep)-BRIDGER-HASTINGS. III. 1850. CAL. V-. 1858.

WILSON, Rufus R. OUT OF THE WEST: THE BEYOND THE MIS-SISSIPPI STATES IN THE MAKING. NY: Wilson-Erickson, 1936. Overland-Genl.

WILSON, Samuel H. Overland Journey, 1851. Oregon State Library, Salem, OR. OR(Council). III. 1851.

WILSON, William. Day Book. BEINECKE. CAL(Council)-BRIDGER-SLCUT. III. 1850. OR(Council). III. 1853.

WILTSEE, Ernest A. SEE: With W. Parker Lyon. "Early California Oval."

_____. THE FRANKS OF HUNTER & COMPANY'S EXPRESS. N.p.: Author, c1933. Stage. Mail.

_____. THE JOSEPH W. GREGORY EXPRESS, 1850 - 1853. American Philatelist Handbook Series No. 1. Federalsburg, MD: American Philatelist, 1937. Mail. Stage.

_____. THE PIONEER MINER AND THE PACK MULE EX-PRESS. Special Publication No. 5. SF: California Historical Society, 1931. Stage. Graphics. Map.

_____. "The Various Expresses of the Various Traceys." COLLEC-TORS CLUB PHILATELIST 14(Jul 1935): 123-38. Stage.

_____. "When the Pack Mule Express Was the United States Mail." COLLECTORS CLUB PHILATELIST 8(Apr 1929): 57-64. Mail. Stage.

_____, and W. R. Parker. "Franks of the Everts Expresses." COL-LECTORS CLUB PHILATELIST 10(Jul 1931): 1-16. Stage.

WILTSEY, Norman B. "First 'Navigator' of the Rockies." FRONTIER TIMES 33(Spr 1959): 22-23. Eqpt: Wind Wagon, 1853.

_____. "Mystery Driver of the Sierras." TRUE WEST, Dec 1954 - Jan 1955, 27, 36. Stage.

WIMMER, Peter. CALIFORNIA GOLD BOOK. Eds. W. W. Allen and R. B. Avery. SF: Donohue & Henneberry, 1893. CAL(Indep)-BRIDGER-HASTINGS-TRUCKEE. V. Rem. 1846.

WINCHELL, Elisha C. Papers. BANCROFT. CAL(St. Jo). II+. 1850.

WINKLEY, John W. "The Old Stockton - Los Angeles Stage Road.... GHOST TOWN NEWS 3(Dec 1943): 14. Stage: Stockton to Los Angeles. IV. 1865.

_____. "Shasta City - Ghost Town." GHOST TOWN NEWS 4(Dec 1944): 5-6. Geog.

WINNE, Peter. "Across the Plains in 1863: The Diary of Peter Winne." Ed. Robert G. Athearn. IOWA JOURNAL OF HISTORY AND POLITICS 49(Jul 1951): 221-40. PIKES. II. 1863.

WINSLOW, George. SEE: Bloyd, Levi. "Grave of California Gold Rush."

WINSOR, Alonzo. Journey. NEWBERRY. CAL(Weston?)-BRIDGER-SLCUT-TRUCKEE(to Wadsworth)-Across Sierra via Carson River. II+. 1849.

WINTER, William H. SEE: With Overton Johnson. "Route across the Rocky Mountains."

WINTERS, Mary A. "Reminiscence." In TREASURES OF PIONEER HISTORY, vol. 1. SLC: Daughters of the Utah Pioneers, 1952. MORMON. IV. Rem. 1853.

WINTHER, Oscar Osburn. Ed. Reeve, Clayton and Rebecca. "From Tennessee to California." Ed. Ward, H. C. "Stagecoach Days in California." Ed. White, Thomas. "To Oregon in 1852."

_____. "California Stage Company in Oregon." OREGON HIS-TORICAL QUARTERLY 35(Jun 1934): 131-38. Stage.

_____. A CLASSIFIED BIBLIOGRAPHY OF THE PERI-ODICAL LITERATURE OF THE TRANS-MISSISSIPPI WEST, 1811 - 1957. Bloomington: Indiana Univ. Press, 1961. Bib.

_____. "The Development of Transportation in Oregon, 1843 - 49." OREGON HISTORICAL QUARTERLY 40(Dec 1939): 315-26. Freight. Telegraph.

_____. "Early Commercial Importance of the Mullan Road." OREGON HISTORICAL QUARTERLY 46(Mar 1945): 22-35. MULLAN-Genl.

_____. "The Express and Stage-Coach Business in California, 1848 - 60." PhD diss., Stanford Univ., 1934. Stage.

_____. EXPRESS AND STAGECOACH DAYS IN CALIFOR- NIA: FROM THE GOLD RUSH TO THE CIVIL WAR. Palo Alto: Stanford Univ. Press, 1934. Stage.

_____. "Inland Transportation and Communication in Washington, 1844 - 1859." PACIFIC NORTHWEST QUARTERLY 30(Oct 1939): 371-77. Stage.

_____. THE OLD OREGON COUNTRY: A HISTORY OF FRONTIER TRADE, TRANSPORTATION, AND TRAVEL. In- diana University Social Science Series No. 7. Bloomington: Indiana Univ. Press, 1950. Stage. Freight. MULLAN-Genl.

_____. "Pack Animals for Transportation in the Pacific Northwest." PACIFIC NORTHWEST QUARTERLY 34(Apr 1943): 131-46. Freight.

_____. "The Persistence of Horse-Drawn Transportation in the Trans-Mississippi West, 1865 - 1900." In PROBING THE AMERICAN WEST, ed. K. Ross Toole. Santa Fe: Museum of New Mexico Press, 1962. Overland-Genl.

_____. "The Place of Transportation in the Early History of the Pacific Northwest." PACIFIC HISTORICAL REVIEW 11(Dec 1942): 383-96. Freight. Stage.

_____. "The Roads and Transportation of Territorial Oregon." OREGON HISTORICAL QUARTERLY 41(Mar 1940): 40-52. Mail. Stage.

_____. "The Southern Overland Mail and Stagecoach Line, 1857 - 1861." NEW MEXICO HISTORICAL REVIEW 32(Apr 1957): 81- 106. Stage.

_____. "Stage-Coach Service in Northern California, 1849 - 52." PACIFIC HISTORICAL REVIEW 3(Dec 1934): 386-99. Stage.

_____. THE TRANSPORTATION FRONTIER: TRANS-MISSIS- SIPPI WEST, 1865 - 1890. One of the Histories of the American Fron- tier, ed. Ray A. Billington. NY: Holt, Rinehart and Winston, 1964. Overland-Genl.

_____. VIA WESTERN EXPRESS AND STAGECOACH. Palo Alto: Stanford Univ. Press, 1945. Stage. Mail.

_____, and Richard A. Van Orman. A CLASSIFIED BIBLIOG- RAPHY OF THE PERIODICAL LITERATURE OF THE TRANS-MISSISSIPPI WEST: A SUPPLEMENT (1957 - 67). In- diana University Social Science Series No. 26. Bloomington: Indiana Univ. Press, 1970. Bib.

WINTHROP, Theodore. THE CANOE AND THE SADDLE. Ed. John H. Williams. Tacoma, WA: Private, 1913. OR(East from Dal- les to Ft. Laramie). III. 1853.

WINTON, Harry N. M. Ed. Newby, William. "Diary of the Emigration."

_____. "Overland Emigration to California, 1841 - 1848." MA thesis, Stanford Univ., 1933. CAL-Genl.

Wisconsin Blues. CONSTITUTION OF THE WISCONSIN BLUES. ORGANIZED MAY 8TH, 1850. Kanesville, IA: Frontier Guardian, 1850. Broadside. Govt.

WISE, William. MASSACRE AT MOUNTAIN MEADOWS. NY: Thomas Y. Crowell, 1976. SLCOR-1857-Genl. Utah.

WISLIZENUS, A. MEMOIR OF A TOUR TO NORTHERN MEXICO CONNECTED WITH COL. DONIPHAN'S EXPEDI- TION. 30th Cong., 1st sess., 1848. S. Misc. No. 26. SANTA FE-RIO GRANDE. I. 1846. Flora/Fauna. Maps.

WISNER, Sarah A. "The Platte River." In Paul & Helen Henderson Col- lection. UWY. CAL(Ash Hollow to Bridger's Ferry). IV. 1866.

WISTAR, Isaac J. AUTOBIOGRAPHY OF ISAAC JONES WISTAR. Philadelphia: Wistar Institute of Anatomy and Biology, 1937. CAN(Indep)-HALL-TRUCKEE. III. 1849.

WITHERS, Ethel M. Ed. Dougherty, Lewis B. "Experiences."

WITTER, CLARA V. Reminiscence. COHIST. PIKES. III. Rem. 1862.

WITTER, Daniel. Diary. COHIST. PIKES. III-. 1859.

WIXOM, W. W. Diary. In Robert A. Allen Collection. NVHIST. CAL(St. Jo). II. 1851.

_____. "Dr. Wixom's Journal of 1851." Ed. H. Hamlin. PONY EX- PRESS 18(Nov 1951): 3-7. Trip to St. Jo only.

WOJCIK, Donna M. THE BRAZEN OVERLANDERS OF 1845. Portland: Author, 1976. OR-MEEK. I. 1845.

WOLCOTT, Lucian M. Journals. HUNTL. CAL(St. Jo). II. 1850.

WOLCOTT, Marjorie T. Ed. Hayes, Benjamin I. PIONEER NOTES.

WOLF, Lambert B. Extracts from Diary...1856 - 1861. KSHIST. Military.

WOLFE, George D. "The Wonderful Concord Coach." CORRAL DUST 4(Sept 1959): 17-18, 22. Stage-Eqpt.

WOLFF, Francis. "Ambush at McLaughlin Canyon and other Adven- tures of Francis Wolff." OKANOGAN COUNTY HERITAGE 2(Jun 1964): 7-12. WASH(Dalles)-CANADA(Fraser River). V. 1857. Indian attack in northern Washington.

WOLFF, John E. ROUTE OF THE MANY PARTY OF 1849 - 50 IN LEAVING DEATH VALLEY FOR THE COAST. Pasadena?: N.p., 1931. SLCOR-1849-Genl.

WOLOSHUK, Nicholas, Jr. Comp. Borein, Edward. STAGECOACHES OF THE OLD WEST.

Woman's Kansas Day Club. "Kansas Roads to Adventure." KSHIST. Pres.

WONDERLY, Pauline. REMINISCENCES OF A PIONEER. Ed. John B. Hassler. Society Publication No. 2. Placerville, CA: El Dorado County Historical Society. 1955. CAL(Council). IV. Rem. 1852.

WOOD, Asa A. "Fort Benton's Part in the Development of the West." WASHINGTON HISTORICAL QUARTERLY 20(Jul 1929): 213- 22. Geog. MONTANA-Genl.

WOOD, Dean E. "The Westport Branch of the Oregon Trail." MO- WHMC. Geog. Pres.

WOOD, Elizabeth. "Journal of a Trip...." In COVERED WAGON WOMEN, vol. 3. Ed. Kenneth L. Holmes. Glendale: Clark, 1985. OR(Begins Ft. Laramie). III. 1851.

WOOD, Ellen L. "Samuel Green McMahan: Member of the Bidwell

Party and Owner of Bartlett Springs." CALIFORNIA HISTORICAL QUARTERLY 23(Dec 1944): 289-300. Biog.

WOOD, Harvey. PERSONAL RECOLLECTIONS OF HARVEY WOOD. Ed. John B. Goodman, III. Pasadena: Editor, 1955. CAL-TEX(Corpus to Laredo)-MEX(Monclova-Chihuahua-Santa Cruz)-GILA. III. 1849.

WOOD, Henry F. Diary. MONHIST. Freight: Atchison to Ft. Laramie(wintered 1865)-Ft. Laramie to Ft. Hall and MONTANA in 1866. III+. 1865 & 1866.

WOOD, J. C. REPORT TO HON. A. V. BROWN, POSTMASTER-GENERAL. WA: N.p., 1858. Stage: San Antonio-San Diego Stage Line.

WOOD, J. D. Reminiscence. MONHIST. Freight: Atchison-MONTANA. Rem. V. 1864.

WOOD, John. Diary (fragment). Idaho State Historical Society, Boise, ID. CAL(St. Jo)-Ft. Kearney. IV. 1850.

_____. JOURNAL OF JOHN WOOD. Columbus, OH: Nevins & Myers, 1871. CAL(St. Jo)-BRIDGER-HASTINGS. II. 1850.

WOOD, Joseph S. "The Mormon Settlement in San Bernardino, 1851-1857." Phd diss., Univ. of Utah, 1968. SLCOR. IV. 1851.

WOOD, Joseph W. Journal...1849. ORU. CAL(St. Jo)-HALL-TRUCKEE. II+. 1849. Train Govt.

WOOD, Martha M. "Early Roads in Missouri." MA thesis, Univ. of Missouri-Columbia, 1936. Overland-Genl.

WOOD, R. Coke. BIG TREE - CARSON VALLEY TURNPIKE, EBBETTS PASS AND HIGHWAY FOUR. Murphys, CA: Old Timers Museum, 1968. CAL-Genl.

WOOD, Wanda. Ed. Hess, John W. "With the Mormon Battalion."

WOODCOCK, William C. Diary. ORHIST. OR(Council)-BARLOW. III. 1853.

WOODHAMS, William H. "The Diary of William H. Woodhams, 1852-1854: The Great Deserts or Around and Across." Ed. Charles W. Martin. NEBRASKA HISTORY 61(Spr 1980): 1-101. CAL(St. Jo)-TRUCKEE-BECK. I. 1854.

WOODHOUSE, John. JOHN WOODHOUSE. SLC: Mercur, 1952. MORMON. 1852. Not Seen.

WOODMAN, David. Letters. Michigan State Univ. Library-University Archives, East Lansing, MI. CAL(St. Jo)-BRIDGER-SLCUT?-TRUCKEE? 1852. Not Seen. Described as very detailed and comprehensive.

WOODRUFF, Emma S. Sketch. Ed. Winnifred W. Daynes. UTHIST. MORMON. V-. 1850.

WOODRUFF, George H. WILL COUNTY ON THE PACIFIC SLOPES. Joliet, IL: Republic and Sun, 1885. CAL-1849-Genl. CAL-1850-Genl.

WOODRUFF, S. W. A Journal...1852. ORU. OR(Council)-BARLOW. III. 1852.

WOODRUFF, Wilford. Autobiography. LDS. MORMON. II. 1847.

WOODS, Allin W. Journal. MONHIST. CAL(St. Jo)-HALL-MONTANA. IV. 1864.

WOODS, Andrew. Diary. BEINECKE. CAL(Council). 1850. Not Seen.

WOODS, Daniel B. SIXTEEN MONTHS AT THE GOLD DIGGINGS. NY: Harper & Bros., 1851. CAL-MEX(Tampico-San Luis Potosi-Guadalajara-San Blas). II. 1849.

WOODS, Elizabeth. "Journal of a Trip to Oregon, 1851." OREGON HISTORICAL QUARTERLY 27(Mar 1926): 192-203. OR(Ft. Laramie)-Ends Grande Ronde. IV. 1851.

WOODS, I. C. "Journal of I. C. Woods on the Establishment of the San Antonio & San Diego Mail Line." Ed. Noel M. Loomis. SAN DIEGO WESTERNERS BRAND BOOK 1(1968): 84-125. CAL-TEX(San Antonio-Ft. Davis-El Paso)-GILA. I. 1857. Stage trip.

WOODS, James M. Letters. MO-WHMC. CAL(Indep). IV. 1850.

WOODS, Joseph W. Diary. Princeton Univ. Library-Western History, Princeton, NJ. CAL(St. Jo)-HALL-TRUCKEE. I. 1849.

WOODS, Ralph E. "The Saga of the Lone Grave (Susan O. Hall grave, near Kenesaw, NB)." PONY EXPRESS 18(May 1952): 3, 12. Geog.

WOODS, Robert J., ed. EARLY TRANSPORTATION IN SOUTHERN CALIFORNIA (12 parts). Pasadena: Dahlstrom, 1955. CAL-Genl.

WOODSON, Rebecca H. Sketch. BANCROFT. CAL(Council). III. Rem. 1850.

WOODWARD, Arthur. Ed. Manly, William L. THE JAYHAWKERS' OATH. Ed. Meek, Stephen H. AUTOBIOGRAPHY. Ed. Sweeny, Thomas W. JOURNAL. SEE: With Helen S. Giffen. STORY OF EL TEJON.

_____. CAMELS AND SURVEYORS IN DEATH VALLEY. Death Valley '49ers, Inc. Publication No. 7. Palm Desert, CA: Desert, 1961.
SLCOR-1861-Genl.

_____. "Gold on the Colorado." WESTWAYS 45(Mar 1953): 4-5. BRADSHAW-Genl. Map.

_____. "The Knife on the Frontier." NEW YORK WESTERNERS BRAND BOOK 2(1955): 10-14. Eqpt.

_____. "Outpost on the Colorado." DESERT 3(Nov 1939): 4-8, 34. Geog: Ft. Mohave.

_____. OX CARTS AND COVERED WAGONS. Los Angeles County Museum Leaflet Series, History, No. 10. LA: The Museum, 1951. Eqpt.

_____. STAGE COACH DAYS IN CALIFORNIA. Los Angeles County Museum Leaflet Series, History, No. 11. LA: The Museum, 1951. Stage.

_____. "When Scalp Hunters Ran the Yuma Ferryboat." DESERT 6(Apr 1943): 4-8. Geog: Yuma.

WOODWARD, Elizabeth. SEE: With George Chorpenning. REPORT OF THE COMMITTEE.

WOODWARD, Erastus. Diary, 1850. East Washington Historical Society Library, Spokane, WA. CAL-MEX(Vera Cruz-Acapulco). III. 1850.

WOODWARD, Jabez. Crossing the Plains. UTHIST. MORMON. III-. 1854.

WOODWARD, Thomas. "Diary of Thomas Woodward While Crossing the Plains to California in 1850." WISCONSIN MAGAZINE OF HISTORY 17(Mar, Jun 1934): 345-60, 433-46. CAL(St. Jo)-Ends near Elko, NV. II. 1850.

WOODWORTH, James. DIARY OF JAMES WOODWORTH. Eugene, OR: Lane County Historical Society, 1972. CAL(Westport)-BRIDGER-SLCUT-TRUCKEE-BECK. II. 1853.

WOODY, Frank H. "From Missoula to Walla Walla in 1857 on Horseback." WASHINGTON HISTORICAL QUARTERLY 3(Oct 1912): 277-86. MULLAN-Genl.

_____. "How an Early Pioneer Came to Montana and the Privations Encountered on the Journey." CONTRIBUTIONS Historical Society of Montana 7(1910): 138-64. Freight: Leavenworth to SLC-Wintered SLC in 1855. III. Rem. 1855. Freight: SLC-MONTANA. III. Rem. 1856.

WOOLLEY, Lell H. CALIFORNIA, 1849 - 1913. Oakland: DeWitt & Snelling, 1913. CAL(Indep). V. Rem. 1849.

WOOLWORTH, S. B. GUIDE TO DENVER, UTAH, CALIFORNIA, AND THE GOLD MINES OF SALMON RIVER. Omaha: Republican, 1862. Guide.

WOOSTER, David. THE GOLD RUSH...1850-1855. Mt. Pleasant, Miss.: Cumming, 1971. CAL(St. Jo)-SLCUT. IV. 1850.

WOOTON, Martha Ann. "Reminiscences...." YOLO COUNTY HISTORICAL SOCIETY BULLETIN 8(Jan 1975): 1-5. CAL(Missouri). Rem. 1857. Not Seen.

WOOTON, "Uncle Dick." SEE: Conard, Howard L. UNCLE DICK WOOTON.

WORCESTER, Don. THE CHISHOLM TRAIL: HIGH ROAD OF THE CATTLE KINGDOM. Lincoln: Amon Carter Museum, 1980. Stock.

_____, ed. PIONEER TRAILS WEST. Caldwell, ID: Caxton, 1985. Overland-Genl.

WORD, Samuel. "Diary of Col. Samuel Word." CONTRIBUTIONS Historical Society of Montana 8(1917): 37-92. CAL(St. Jo)-BRIDGER-SLCUT-MONTANA(SLC-Ft. Hall-Bannack). II. 1863.

WORKS, Lewis R. "Fremont's California...Second Exploring Expedition in the Far West, 1843 - 1844." TOURING TOPICS 22(Sept 1930): 28-31, 39. CAL(Sutter's)-South to Los Angeles-SPANISH-SANTA FE. CAL-1844-Genl.

Works Project Administration. Folklore Project Records, Indexed. Oregon State Library, Salem, OR. OR-Genl.

WORLEY, Ted R. SEE: With W. J. Lemke. BUTTERFIELD MAIL IN ARKANSAS.

WORMAN, Charles G. SEE: With Louis A. Garavaglia. FIREARMS OF THE AMERICAN WEST.

WORNELL, David C. "Diary, 1860." BARKER. PIKES-TEX(Hillsboro)-OKLA(Red River-Ft. Gibson)-CHEROKEE(Oklahoma to Denver). II. 1860.

WORTHINGTON, C. J. Ed. Valazquez, Loreta J. THE WOMAN IN BATTLE.

WOZENCRAFT, Oliver M. "Through Northern Mexico in '49." CALIFORNIAN 6(Nov 1882): 421-25. CAL-TEX(Brownsville)-MEX(Saltillo-Chihuahua-Santa Cruz)-GILA. IV. 1849.

WRIGHT, Bessie L. Ed. Scarborough, A. DIARY.

WRIGHT, Dana. "The Fort Totten - Fort Stevenson Trail, 1867 - 1872." NORTH DAKOTA HISTORY 20(Apr 1953): 67-86. DAKOTAS-Genl. Military.

_____. "Military Trails in Dakota: The Fort Totten - Abercrombie Trail." NORTH DAKOTA HISTORY 13(Jan-Apr, Jul 1946): 80-95, 103-11. Map. DAKOTAS-Genl. Military.

_____. "Military Trails in Dakota: Fort Abercrombie to Fort Ransom with Notes on the History of Fort Ransom." NORTH DAKOTA HISTORY 17(Oct 1950): 241-52. DAKOTAS-Genl. Military

_____. "Military Trails in North Dakota: Fort Abercrombie to Fort Wadsworth, 1864." NORTH DAKOTA HISTORY 18(Apr-Jun 1951): 157-70. DAKOTAS-Genl. Military.

_____. "Military Trails in North Dakota: Fort Ransom to Fort Totten." NORTH DAKOTA HISTORY 16(Oct 1949): 203-10. Map. DAKOTAS-Genl. Military.

_____. "The Sibley Trail in North Dakota." NORTH DAKOTA HISTORICAL QUARTERLY 1, nos. 3, 4(1926-1927): 30-45, 5-13; 2, no. 1(1927-1928): 120-28. DAKOTAS-Genl. Military.

WRIGHT, Dunham. Narrative. ORU. PIKES. V. 1860. OR-CHEROKEE(Begins Denver to Ft. Bridger)-Ends Florence. V. Rem. 1862.

WRIGHT, J. B. An Epic of the West. Idaho State Historical Society Library, Boise, ID. OR(Council)-LANDER-Ends Boise. IV. Rem. 1863.

WRIGHT, L. H. Ed. Ormsby, Waterman. THE BUTTERFIELD OVERLAND.

WRIGHT, Muriel H. Ed. Brown, John L. "Journal."

_____. "The Butterfield Overland Mail One Hundred Years Ago." CHRONICLES OF OKLAHOMA 35(Spr 1957): 55-71. Stage: Oklahoma portion only.

_____. "Historic Places on the Old Stage Line from Fort Smith to Red River." CHRONICLES OF OKLAHOMA 11(Jun 1933): 798-822. Map. Stage: Oklahoma portion only.

_____. "Old Boggy Depot." CHRONICLES OF OKLAHOMA 5(Mar 1927): 4-17. Geog.

_____, and George H. Shirk. "The Journal of Lt. A. W. Whipple." CHRONICLES OF OKLAHOMA 28(Fall 1950): 235-83. MARCY(Oklahoma portion only). I. 1853.

WRIGHT, Reuben G. Life History. CSL. CAL(Council)-LASSEN. V. Rem. 1849.

WRIGHT, Richard T. "The Man from Brechin." OLD West 23(Fall 1986): 38-43. CANADA-DAKOTAS(St. Paul)-Kootenay Pass-Colville Valley-Fort Victoria. V. 1858.

_____. OVERLANDERS. Saskatoon, Saskatchewan: Western Producer, 1985. Fine bibliography and appendices. CANADA-Genl.

WRIGHT, Robert C. Journal. Chicago Historical Society Library-Ms, Chicago, IL. CAL(Weston)-BRIDGER-SLCUT. II+. 1850.

WRIGHT, Robert M. "The Building of Stations in Kansas and along the Overland Road between Fort Larned and Santa Fe, for the Barlow &

Sanderson Overland Mail Company in 1864." KSHIST. Military.

WRIGHT, William L. Collection. Southwest Museum Library, Los Angeles, CA. Geog: Warner's Ranch. Stage.

_____. THE WARNER'S RANCH - BUTTERFIELD STATION PUZZLE. Reprint from LOS ANGELES WESTERNERS BRAND BOOK 9 (1961): 189-216. Geog.

WRIGHT, Williamson. Bill of Items Required for a Trip by Land to California, Two Persons to a Wagon. Indiana State Library-Ms, Indianapolis, IN. Eqpt.

WURTTEMBERG, Prince Paul W., von. "A Brief Biography of Prince Paul Wilhelm of Worttemberg." Ed. Louis C. Butscher. NEW MEXICO HISTORICAL REVIEW 17(Jul, Oct 1942): 181-225, 294-344. CAL(Westport)-Upper Platte & return. II. 1851. Biog.

WYLLY, Thomas S., III., ed. "'Westward Ho - in '49'": Memoirs of Capt. Thomas S. Wylley." PACIFIC HISTORIAN 22(Spr, Sum, Fall, Win 1978): 71-96, 120-44, 274-303, 327-52. CAL(Indep)-BRIDGER-SLCOR. III. Rem. 1849.

WYMAN, Walker D. "Atchison, A Great Frontier Depot." KANSAS HISTORICAL QUARTERLY 11(Aug 1942): 297-308. Geog.

_____. "Bullwhacking: A Prosaic Profession Peculiar to the Great Plains." NEW MEXICO HISTORICAL REVIEW 7(Oct 1932): 297-310. Freight.

_____, comp. CALIFORNIA EMIGRANT LETTERS. NY: Bookman Associates, 1952. Overland-Genl.

_____. "Council Bluffs and the Westward Movement." IOWA JOURNAL OF HISTORY AND POLITICS 47(Apr 1949): 99-118. Geog.

_____. F. X. Aubry...Explorer." NEW MEXICO HISTORICAL REVIEW 7(Jan 1932): 1-31. CAL(East from Tejon Pass)-BEALE-Ends Santa Fe. III. 1853. Same Route. III. 1854. Freight. Biog.

_____. "Freighting on the Santa Fe Trail, 1843 - 1866." MA thesis, Iowa Univ., 1931. Freight.

_____. "Kansas City, Missouri, A Famous Freighter Capital." KANSAS HISTORICAL QUARTERLY 6(Feb 1937): 3-13. Geog.

_____. "The Missouri River Towns in the Westward Movement." PhD diss., Univ. of Iowa, 1935. Missing from stacks.

_____. "Omaha: Frontier Depot and Prodigy of Council Bluffs." NEBRASKA HISTORY 17(Jul-Sept 1936): 143-44. Geog.

_____. "The Outfitting Posts." In RUSHING FOR GOLD, ed. John W. Caughey. Berkeley: Univ. of California Press, 1949. Geog.

YAGER, James P. "The Yager Journals...." Comp. Everett W. Harris. NEVADA HISTORICAL SOCIETY QUARTERLY 13(Spr, Sum, Fall, Win 1970): 5-20, 19-40, 27-48, 26-52; 14(Spr, Sum 1971): 27-54, 33-56. CAL(Neb. City)-BRIDGER-SLCUT-TRUCKEE-Turns south in Truckee Meadows to Carson River route. II. 1863.

YORK, Dorothy J. "The Early Development of the Pocatello - Fort Hall Region." MS thesis, Utah State Univ., 1955. Geog.

YOST, Nellie S. THE CALL OF THE RANGE: THE STORY OF THE NEBRASKA STOCK GROWERS ASSOCIATION. Denver: Sage, 1966. Stock.

YOUNG, Albert J. Diary. BANCROFT. CAL(Council)-BRIDGER-SIMPSON-Ends Carson City. II. 1862.

YOUNG, B. H. and J. Eager. EMIGRANT'S GUIDE...FROM GREAT SALT LAKE CITY TO SAN FRANCISCO. N.p., n.d. Guide.

YOUNG, Brigham H. Biography. UTHIST. MORMON. III-. 1847.

YOUNG, Charles E. DANGERS OF THE TRAIL IN 1865. Geneva, NY: Author, 1912. Freight: Atchison to Denver. IV. Rem. 1865.

YOUNG, Clara D. A Woman's Experiences with the Pioneer Band. UTHIST. MORMON. V. Rem. 1847.

YOUNG, F. G. "The Oregon Trail." OREGON HISTORICAL QUARTERLY 1(Dec 1900): 339-70. OR-Genl.

YOUNG, F. M. SEE: With LeRoy R. Hafen. FORT LARAMIE. SEE: With LeRoy R. Hafen. "Mormon Settlement."

YOUNG, Frank C. ACROSS THE PLAINS IN '65...GOTHAM TO PIKE'S PEAK. Denver: Author, 1905. Freight: Atchison-Julesburg-Denver. II+. 1865.

YOUNG, John. Record Book. MO-WHMC. Freight-1865.

YOUNG, John D. JOHN D. YOUNG AND THE COLORADO GOLD RUSH. Ed. Dwight L. Smith. One of the Lakeside Classics. Chicago: R. R. Donnelley, 1969. Freight: St. Jo. to Denver and return. II. 1860. Graphics.

YOUNG, John Q. Life Sketches. ORHIST. OR(Indep). IV. Rem. 1847.

YOUNG, Joseph A. Journal. Marriott Library-Univ. of Utah, SLC. MORMON. 1864. By stage. Not Seen.

YOUNG, Joseph W. Journal. UTHIST. MORMON. IV. 1847.

YOUNG, Lorenzo D. "Diary...." UTAH HISTORICAL QUARTERLY 14(Jan-Oct 1946): 133-70. MORMON. II. 1847.

YOUNG, Otis E. THE WEST OF PHILIP ST. GEORGE COOKE, 1809 - 1895. Western Frontiersman Series 5. Glendale: Clark, 1955. Biog.

YOUNG, Phineas H. Diary. LDS. MORMON. III. 1856.

YOUNG, Samuel C. "Biographical Obituary." PIONEER, 9 Nov 1878, n.p. CAL-BRIDGER-HASTINGS. V. 1846.

YOUNG, Sheldon. "Diary." In JOURNALS OF THE FORTY-NINERS, eds. LeRoy and Ann W. Hafen. Glendale: Clark, 1954. CAL)St. Jo)-BRIDGER-SLCOR. III. 1849.

YOUNG, Will H. "Journals...." ANNALS OF WYOMING 7(Oct 1930): 378-82. Freight: Nebraska City to Ft. Laramie. IV. 1865.

YOUNGER, Gene. SEE: With Ramon Powers. "Cholera on the Overland Trains."

"Youngsters and the Oregon Trail." FORD TIMES 51(Mar 1959): 40-45. Pres.

YOUNKER, Jason T. "The Early Pioneer." TRAIL 2(Jan 1910): 5-12. PIKES. V. 1858.

YURTINUS, John F. SEE: With Charles Peterson, et al. MORMON BATTALION TRAIL.

_____. "The Battle of the Bulls." MILITARY HISTORY OF TEXAS AND THE SOUTHWEST 14, no. 1(1983): 99-108. GILA-

1846-Genl.

_____. "Colorado, Mormons and the Mexican War: A History of the Mississippi Saints and Sick Detachments...." In ESSAYS AND MONOGRAPHS IN COLORADO HISTORY No. 1. Denver: Colorado Historical Society, 1983. CHEROKEE-Genl.

_____. "A Ram in the Thicket: The Mormon Battalion in the Mexican War." PhD diss., Brigham Young Univ., 1975. CAL-1846-Genl.

ZAMONSKI, Stanley. "Smoky Hill Route, Denver's Lifeline to the East in the '60's." DENVER WESTERNERS MONTHLY ROUNDUP 19(Aug 1963): 9-10, 17. PIKES-Genl.

_____, and Teddy Keller. THE FIFTY-NINERS: A DENVER DIARY. Denver: Sage, 1961. Geog.

ZEAMER, R. Jeremiah. Diary. In David E. Miller Papers. UTHIST. CAL(Council?)-BRIDGER-SIMPSON-Ends Diamond Springs. III. 1865.

ZEIBER, John S. "Diary." TRANSACTIONS Oregon Pioneer Association (1923): 301-35. OR(Council). II. 1851.

ZEILINGER, John F. "Dick Shinn's Ferry." NEBRASKA HISTORY 20(Jul-Sept 1939): 175-79. Geog.

ZENOR, B. J. "By Covered Wagon to the Promised Land." AMERICAN WEST 11(Jul 1974): 30-41. Overland-Genl.

ZERN, Frank W. "A Stage Ride in '66." TRAIL 7(Jun 1914): 24-25. Stage: Julesburg to Denver. IV. 1866.

ZIEBER, Albert. Diary. ORU. OR(Council). V. OR(St. Jo)-Ends Green River. III. 1850.

ZIEBER, Eugenia. "Journal...Oregon." In COVERED WAGON WOMEN, vol. 3. Ed. Kenneth L. Holmes. Glendale: Clark, 1985. OR(Council). V. 1851.

ZILHART, William. Diary. CSL. CAL(Indep?). IV. 1853.

ZINN, Henry, Sr. Diary. CSL. CAL(Begins Lassen Meadows)-TRUCKEE. V-. 1852.

ZOLLINGER, James P. SUTTER: THE MAN AND HIS EMPIRE. NY: Oxford, 1939. Biog. Recommended.

ZORNOW, William F. "Jeptha H. Wade in California: Beginning the Transcontinental Telegraph." CALIFORNIA HISTORICAL QUARTERLY 29(Dec 1950): 289-96. Telegraph.

ZUMWALT, Joe. JOE ZUMWALT, FORTY-NINER. Ed. Kenneth D. Zumwalt. San Diego: Trade Publishing, 1976. CAL(St. Jo)-HALL. V-. 1849. CAL(Council). V-. 1854.

ZUMWALT, Kenneth D. Ed. Zumwalt, Joe. JOE ZUMWALT.

ZUMWALT, Nancy Ann. "To California by Ox Team." PONY EXPRESS 21(Sept 1954): 3-6. CAL(Council). IV. 1854.

ZUMWALT, Solomon. THE BIOGRAPHY OF ADAM ZUMWALT. Eugene, OR: Lane County Pioneer-Historical Society, 1959. OR(St. Jo?)-Wintered 1850-51 in Utah. V. Rem. 1850. OR(SLC to Ft. Hall and Dalles). V. Rem. 1851.

ZWINK, Timothy A. "Dodging Death along the Smoky Hill River." OLD WEST 14(Sum 1978): 22-25, 51. PIKES-Genl-1865. Indians.

_____. "Theodore R. Davis: Creator of Western Images." PRAIRIE SCOUT 4(1981): 27-44. Graphics.

PART II

Readers should routinely refer to the previous section and check following internal indexes for specific annual entries. This category is intended to assist those seeking sources for an individual year or years of travel. While all diaries and reminiscences found during the research phase are included in the following index, only those secondary sources treating a particular year are shown. Secondary sources with a broader theme are indexed in the trail segment category. Quality codes permit readers to rank entries.

1841-General

Bidwell, John. Papers.

_____, et al. FIRST THREE WAGON TRAINS.

_____. "Route Travelled from Cairo." Map.

_____. "Route Travelled."

Bidwell-Bartleson Party. SEE: CAL-1841-Genl.

Brereton, George. "Overland to California in 1841."

Cleland, Robert G. "John Bidwell's Arrival."

Cody, Cora. "John Bidwell."

Collins, William. "Overland Journeys in California and Oregon."

Dillon, Richard. "Siskiyou Trail."

Goodwin, Cardinal. "California's Pioneer Homeseekers."

Harris, Mary. "John Rowland and William Workman."

Heath, Minnie B. "Nancy Kelsey."

Hunt, Rockwell D. JOHN BIDWELL.

Hussey, John A. "New Light upon Talbot H. Green."

Kelly, Charles. "First Emigrant Train."

_____. "Salt Desert Trails."

Kelsey, Mrs. Benjamin (Nancy). "A California Heroine."

_____. "Reminiscences."

Levitin, Sonia. "First Historic Trek."

Miller, David E. "First Wagon Train to Cross Utah."

Olson, James E., and Irene D. Paden. "Facts about."

Paden, William G. "Bidwell's Route of the Sierras."

Pickering, Charles. "Pickering's Journey to Fort Colville."

Pierce, Gerald S. "Military Road."

Ramage, Helen. "Wilkes Exploring Expedition."

Rowland, Leonore A. "First Covered Wagon Train to Southern California."

Scalf, Henry P. OVERLAND LETTER.

Tobie, H. E. "From the Missouri to the Columbia."

Wilkes, Charles. COLUMBIA RIVER.

1841

Allen, George T. Journal. II.

Barrows, H. D. "Don David W. Alexander." V-.

Belden, Josiah. "First Overland Emigrant Train." IV.

_____. JOSIAH BELDEN. III.

Bell, Josias F. Sketches. II.

Bernard, Sam. Recollections. Not Seen.

Bidwell, John. ECHOES OF THE PAST. II.

_____. "Emigrant Train to California." II.

_____. IN CALIFORNIA BEFORE THE GOLD RUSH. II.

_____. JOHN BIDWELL'S TRIP. II.

_____. JOURNEY TO CALIFORNIA. II.

_____. Papers. II.

Brackenridge, William D. "Journal." IV.

Chiles, Joseph B. Visit to California. V.

Dawson, Nicholas. NARRATIVE OF. III.

De Smet, Pierre J. LETTERS. II.

Farquhar, Francis P. JOHN BIDWELL'S TRIP. II.

Flett, John. "From Red River to the Columbia." V.

Gambel, William. Life. V.

Giffen, Helen S. TRAIL-BLAZING PIONEER. II.

Hopper, Charles. PILGRIMS OF THE PACIFIC. IV.

Hunt, Rockwell D. JOHN BIDWELL. III.

John, James. "Diary." III.

Maloney, Alice B. "A Botanist to Yerba Buena." IV.

Nunis, Doyce. JOSIAH BELDEN. IV.

Partoll, Albert J. "Mengarini's Narrative." V.

Peale, Titian R. DIARY. II.

Pierce, Gerald S. "Military Road Expeditions."

Point, Nicholas. "Historical Notes." Not Seen.

Sage, Rufus B. ROCKY MOUNTAIN LIFE. IV.

St. Johns, James. "Diary." V.

SANTA FE AND THE FAR WEST. IV.

Simpson, Sir George. AN OVERLAND JOURNEY. V.

Williams, Joseph. NARRATIVE. III.

Wilson, Benjamin D. "Benito Wilson." V-.

_____. Observations. V-.

1842

Allen, Miss A. J. TEN YEARS. II.

Andrews, Thomas F. "Controversial Career of Lansford W. Hastings." III.

Ballantyne, Robert M. HUDSON'S BAY. II.

Bell, Josias F. Sketches. II.

Bennett, Winston. "A Pioneer of 1843." V.

Bidwell, John, et al. FIRST THREE WAGON TRAINS. (Elijah White Diary). II.

Crawford, Medorem. JOURNAL. II.

De Smet, Pierre J. LETTERS. II.

Fremont, John C. EXPLORATION OF THE COUNTRY. II.

Giffen, Helen S. TRAIL-BLAZING PIONEER. II.

Hastings, Lansford W. EMIGRANT'S GUIDE. II.

_____. NEW DESCRIPTION. II.

Hopper, Charles. PILGRIMS OF THE PACIFIC. IV.

Hulbert, Dorothy P. "Trip to California." Graphics.

Lovejoy, Asa. "Asa Lovejoy's Pioneer Narrative." IV.

Lovejoy, Asa L. Letter. III.

Matthieu, F. X. "Reminiscences." IV.

Oakley, Obadiah. EXPEDITION. Not Evaluated.

Sage, Rufus B. ROCKY MOUNTAIN LIFE. IV.

Smith, Darling. "Pioneer of 1842." V.

Williams, Joseph. NARRATIVE. III.

1843-General

"Advice to Prospective Emigrants."

Arthur, John. "Pioneer of 1843."

"Article VI."

Bright, Verne. "Folklore and History of the 'Oregon Fever'."

Columbus, Ohio Citizens. REPORT ON THE TERRITORY.

"Documentary New Orleans Picayune."

"Documents."

"Documents."

"Emigration from Iowa to Oregon."

Hardeman, Nicholas P. WILDERNESS CALLING.

Husband, Michael B. "Backgrounds and Organization."

_____. "To Oregon in 1843."

Judson, Lewis. "Emigration of 1843."

Nesmith, James W. "Diary of the Emigration."

"Oregon Material."

Parrish, Philip H. "The Great Migration."

Patterson, Ida. "Wagon Train of 1843."

Penrose, S. B. "Wagon Train of 1843."

Robinson, W. W. "Retracing."

Simmons, Marc. MURDER ON THE SANTA FE TRAIL.

Wilkes, George. HISTORY OF OREGON.

1843

Adair, Sarah D. "Sarah Damron Adair." Not Seen.

Ankeny, Nesmith. THE WEST AS I KNEW IT. III.

Applegate, Jesse. "A Day with the Cow Column." II.

_____. RECOLLECTIONS OF MY BOYHOOD. II.

Athey, James. Narrative. V.

Atmore, Charles. Diary. V-.

Baldridge, William. Days of 1846. V.

Oakley, Francile B. "Arkansas' Golden Army of '49."

Oates, Stephen. "Blazing the Trail to El Paso."

Officer, James E. "Yanqui Forty-Niners in Hispanic Arizona."

OUTLINE HISTORY. Cartoons.

Parker, Watson. "Wading to California."

Peoples, John H. GENERAL SMITH'S CORRESPONDENCE.

Powell, H. M. SANTA FE TRAIL.

Pratelles, V. M. "Sufferings of the Overland Emigrants."

RECONNAISSANCES OF ROUTES FROM SAN ANTONIO TO EL PASO.

Ressler, John J. "John Jacob Ressler's Trip."

Ressler, Theodore C. TRAILS DIVIDED.

Reid, Bernard J. "California Gold Rush Letter."

Richardson, William H. "Argonauts of Jersey City."

Schaefer, Joseph. "Trailing a Trail Artist."

Schletter, Adrienne E. "Indians on the Oregon Trail."

Serven, James E. "Ill-Fated '49er Wagon Train."

Simpson, James H. REPORT AND MAP OF THE ROUTE.

Smith, Pauline U. CAPTAIN JEFFERSON HUNT.

Sommer, Jane H. "Outfitting."

Southworth, John S. "Help from an Ancient Carving."

Walker, Ardis M. DEATH VALLEY AND MANLY.

_____. FREEMAN JUNCTION.

_____. MANLY MAP.

Walker, Clifford J. "History of the Mojave River Trail."

Watts, John W. Facts.

Wheat, Carl I. "Forty-Niners in Death Valley."

_____. "Jayhawkers at the Missouri."

_____. "Trailing through Death Valley."

Whipple, A. W. REPORT.

Whiting, William H. "Journal."

Williams, J. W. "Marcy's Road from Dona Ana."

Williamson, R. S. REPORT OF A RECONNAISSANCE.

Wolff, John E. ROUTE MANLY PARTY.

Woodruff, George H. WILL COUNTY.

1849

Abbott, George. Recollections. V.

Abell, James S. Papers. I.

Account of a Journey. III-.

Adams, William. Recollections. Not Seen.

Aldrich, Lorenzo D. JOURNAL. III.

Anderson, Niles. "Grandfather Was a Forty-Niner." IV.

Anderson, William W. Diary. III.

Applegate, Virginia W. Recollections. V-.

Arms, Cephas, and Adonijah S. Welch. LONG ROAD. II.

Armstrong, J. E. Diary. III.

Armstrong, J. Elza. "Diary." II.

Armstrong, J. Ezra. Diary. III.

Armstrong, John. Journal. Not Seen.

Armstrong, John C. Diary. V.

Ashley, Delos R. Diary. III.

Athearn, P. A. "Diary." III+.

Audubon, John W. AUDUBON'S WESTERN JOURNAL. I.

_____. ILLUSTRATED NOTES. I.

Austin, Henry. Diary. II+.

Averett, George W. Autobiography. IV.

Babcock, Leonard. Recollections. II.

Bachman, Jacob H. "Audubon's Ill-Fated Western Journey." III.

Backus, Gurdon. Diary. II+.

Badman, Philip. Diary. III.

Baker, George H. "Records." III.

Baldwin, Lewis. Diary. Not Seen.

Banks, John E. "Diary." II.

Baudle, James. Diary. II.

Beeching, Robert. Diary. II.

Beesley, E. Maurice. Journal. III.

Benjamin, Theodosia. "The Audubon Party." III.

Benson, John E. Forty-Niner. II+.

Benson, John H. From St. Joe to Sacramento. III+.

Berrien, Joseph W. "Overland from St. Louis." I.

Bickford, William H. Diary. III.

Biddle, B. R. "Diary." Not Seen.

Bigler, Henry W. "Bigler's Journal." II.

_____. "Extracts." III.

Blackburn, Abner. Reminiscences. IV.

Blunt, Phineas U. Notes of Travel. I.

Boggs, John. Diary. III.

Boggs, William M. Reminiscences. IV.

Bolton, Curtis E. Diary. Not Seen.

Bond, Robert. Diary. IV.

Bonestell, Louis H. "Autobiography." II.

Bonine, Dr. Diary. Not Seen.

Booth, Edmund. EDMUND BOOTH. III+.

Bouldin, James E. Diary. II+.

Bowman, E. L. "Diary." V-.

Boyle, Charles E. "Diary." Not Seen.

Boyles, John R. "None Dream But of Success." V-.

Brady, Charles C. "From Hannibal to the Gold Fields." IV.

Brainard, David. Diary. II+.

Breyfogle, Joshua D. Diary. II.

Brisbane, William. Journal. I.

Brockway, H. S. ACROSS THE SOUTHERN TRAIL. IV.

Brooks, E. W. JOURNAL. III.

Brown, Harvey S. Statement. IV.

Brown, James S. LIFE. II.

Brown, John Evans. "Memoirs." II.

Brown, John Z. AUTOBIOGRAPHY. IV.

Brown, Joseph. CROSSING THE PLAINS. V.

Browne, J. Ross. "A Dangerous Journey." III.

Brownlee, Robert. AN AMERICAN ODYSSEY. II.

Bruff, Joseph G. GOLD RUSH. I.

Buffum, Joseph C. Diary. II+.

Burbank, Augustus R. Journals. I.

Burgert, Daniel, and Manilus S. Rudy. "The Rough Road West." III.

Burgess, Joseph H. "Grandfather Burgess." V.

Burrall, George P. A Trip. II.

Burris, David. Narrative. IV.

Burton, Henry W. Diary. II.

Bush, Charles W. Five Letters. V.

Caldwell, T. G. "Notes of a Journey." III.

Call, W. W. Reminiscence. IV.

Cameron, J. B. Journal. II+.

Campbell, Robert L. Journal. II.

Candee, J. G. Letter. IV.

Cannon, George Q. A TRIP TO CALIFORNIA. III.

Caperton, John. Letter. Not Seen.

Caples, Mrs. James. Overland Journey. IV.

Cardinell, Charles. "Adventures on the Plains." III.

Carnes, David. Journal. II+.

Carstarphen, James E., and Clayton Keith. MY TRIP. V.

Cassin, Francis. Statement. V-.

Castleman, P. F. Diary. II+.

Caughey, John W. "Southwest from Salt Lake." II.

Chamberlain, William E. Diary. II.

Chamberlain, William Edwin. Diary. II.

Chamberlain, William H. "From Lewisburg to California." I.

Chambers, William and Robert. "Journey from New Orleans." IV.

Chapman, W. W. Diary. III.

Chatham, J. W. Diary. I.

Chenoweth, F. A. "Occasional Address." IV.

Chick, Washington H. Reminiscences. V-.

Churchill, Stillman. Diary. II+.

Clapp, John T. JOURNAL OF TRAVELS. III+.

Clark, Bennett C. "Diary of a Journey." II.

"Notes of a Trip." III.
Offield, James W. Offield Family History. V.
Ogle, William B. Diary. II+.
Olson, Jonas W. "Journal." V-.
Osterhoudt, Solomon. "Ox Train Diary." III+.
Packard, Wellman. EARLY EMIGRATION. V.
Packer, Harry B. Letters. IV.
Paden, Irene D. JOURNAL. III.
Parker, William T. Notes. II+.
Parrish, Susan. Westward. IV.
Parsons, Lucena P. "Journal." II.
Paschal, Albert G. Overland Trip. II+.
Patrick, Henry H. Extracts. V.
Payne, James A. "St. Louis to San Francisco." I.
Peacock, William. PEACOCK LETTERS. IV.
Persinger, James B. A Chapter. II.
Pigman, Walter G. JOURNAL. IV.
Plummer, Samuel C. Letters. V.
Pomeroy, H. B. Diary. III+.
Prentiss, William. Letters. V.
Price, Joseph. "Road to California." II.
Primes, Ed. M. Journal. Not Seen.
Puckett, Henry. Diary. V-.
Pulsipher, John. Diary. IV.
Quesenbury, William. "William Quesenbury's Diary." II+.
Randall, J. D. Diary. Not Seen.
Ransdell, Shelton. Wagon Train Journal. III.
Read, George W. A PIONEER. III.
"Recollections of Sarah Hammitt." V-.
Redington, Edward S. Diary. III.
Reed, F. S. Diary. II-.
Reed, T. S. Diary. Not Seen.
Rhodes, Joseph. "Joseph Rhodes." III.
Ridge, John R. "John Rollin Ridge." IV.
Roeder, Henry. Diary. III.
Root, Virginia V. FOLLOWING. IV.
Rothwell, William R. Journal. II+.
Rowndy, Shadrach. Journal. Not Seen.
Russell, Isaac. A Sketch. V-.
Safford, A. P. K. Narrative. IV.
Sawyer, Lorenzo. WAY SKETCHES. II.
Scheller, John J. Autobiography. IV.
Schutt, H. R. Journal. Not Seen.
Scroggs, William L. "To the Gold Fields." V.
Seaton, James A. Diary. III.
Seeley, John V., and Edwin Phelps. Diary. Not Seen.
Sharp, John. Brief Pencilled Notes. V-.
Shaw, D. A. ELDORADO. III.
Shepherd, James S. JOURNAL OF TRAVEL. II.
Shields, James G. California Trip. I.
Shinn, John R. Journal. III.
Shoemaker, ? "Diary." II.
Shottenkirk, D. G. "Diary." II.
Skinner, Hugh A. Diary. II.
Slagle, James M. "Forty Niners." III.
Sleight, Morris. SEE: Jedlick, William J.
Smith, C. W. JOURNAL. III.
Smith, George W. Account. Not Seen.
Smith, Pauline R. CAPTAIN JEFFERSON HUNT. V-.
Snow, William. Across the Plains. IV.
Snyder, John F. Diary. I.
Sortore, Abram. BIOGRAPHY. IV.
Sponsler, A. C. "An 1850 Gold Rush Letter." III.
Springer, E. C. Daybook. II.
Stansbury, Howard. EXPLORATION AND SURVEY. II+.
Starr, Henry W. Diary. II+.
Starr, J. R. Diary. II.
Stauder, John A. Diary. II.

Steele, A. Diary. II+.
Steele, Andrew. Diary. IV.
Steele, John. ACROSS THE PLAINS. III.
Stewart, J. M. "Overland Trip." IV.
Stimson, Fancher. Letter. III.
_____. "Overland Journey." II+.
Stine, Henry A. Letters. III.
Stockton, N. H. Journal. III+.
Stoddard, William C. Diary. Not Seen.
Stratton, R. B. CAPTIVITY. IV.
Street, Franklin. CALIFORNIA. II.
Stuart-Wortley, Lady E. TRAVELS. II.
Summers, Joseph. Letter. III.
Swingley, Upton. "A Brief Chronicle." V-.
Taylor, Calvin. "Overland to the Gold Fields." II+.
Thissell, G. W. CROSSING THE PLAINS. II.
Thomasson, A. H. Diary. II.
Thompson, Clark W. Letters. I.
Thompson, Jesse C. Diary. III.
Thompson, William P. Diary. III.
Tice, Peter. Diary. II.
Tompkins, Edward A. Diary. II.
Travel Account of Journey from Indiana. Not Seen.
"Trip up the Columbia." Not Seen.
Turner, Walter H. A Trip. II.
Turner, William. Diary. III+.
Udell, John. INCIDENTS. III+.
Vivian, Martin. Diary. Not Seen.
Walker, Zachariah. Diary. II.
Waterhouse, Loyal N. Diary. II+.
Watrous, R. "Notes of a Trip." Not Seen.
Watts, Benjamin M. Diary. III.
Watts, John W. Diary. III.
Wechselberg, Peter. Letters. Not Seen.
Wellenkamp, Henry. Diary. III+.
Wheeler, George N. Journal. II.
Wheeler, George W. Journal. III+.
Wheelock, Charles. Letters. Not Seen.
Whipple, Nelson W. History. IV.
White, Stephen. Recollections. III.
Whitman, Abial. Journal. II.
Williams, John T. "Journal." III.
Wilson, Alfred H. Diary. III.
Wilson, Robert M. Chronicle. III.
Wilson, William. Day Book. III.
Winchell, Elisha C. Papers. II+.
Wolcott, Lucian M. Journals. II.
Wood, John. Diary. IV.
_____. JOURNAL. II.
Woodruff, Emma S. Sketch. V-.
Woods, Andrew. Diary. Not Seen.
Woods, James M. Letters. IV.
Woodson, Rebecca. Sketch. III.
Woodward, Erastus. Diary. III.
Woodward, Thomas. "Diary." II.
Wooster, David. GOLD RUSH. IV.
Wright, Robert C. Journal. II+.
Zieber, Albert. Diary. III.
Zieber, John S. Diary. III.
Zumwalt, Solomon. BIOGRAPHY. V.

1851-General
Dillon, Richard. "Tragedy at Oatman Flat."
Lockhart, Andrew J. "Williams Massacre."
Miller, David H. "Touring the Oregon Trail."
Oliva, Leo E. "Aubry Route of the Santa Fe Trail."

Alden, Wyllis. ANCESTORS. IV.
Arrington, James M. Diary. III.
Bacon, Daniel. Letters. Missing.
Baker, Jean R. "By Windjammer and Prairie Schooner." III.
Barber, T. M. Diary. Not Seen.
Bartlett, John R. PERSONAL NARRATIVE. I.
Bigelow, Daniel R. Diary. V.
Blackburn, Abner. Reminiscences. IV.
Booth, William. "Diary." Not Seen.
Bowen, James E. Diary. III.
Brandt, Charles A. TO OREGON. II.
Brooks, Quincy A. "Letter." V.
Brown, Orlando. Diary. Not Seen.
Buckingham, Harriet T. "Crossing the Plains." III.
Buckner, Simon B. Letters. Not Seen.
Carrington, Albert. "Diary." II+.
Carter, B. F. OVERLAND TO SANTA FE. IV.
Chambers, Margaret W. "Reminiscences." V.
Churchill, Willoughby. MEMORIES. IV.
Clark, Alvah. "Diary." Not Seen.
Cleminson, John. Diary. II.
Cooper, Joseph W. Statement. V.
Cranston, E. "Letters." V.
Cranston, Susan A. "An Ohio Lady." III.
Cranstone, Sarah M. Diary. III.
Crawford, Charles H. SCENES. III.
Crawford, P. V. "Journal." III.
Crooks, George. Diary. V-.
Davenport, Timothy W. Dividing the Train. III.
Denny, Arthur A. Journal. III.
From Lake Erie to the Pacific. IV.
Fry, J. O. Across the Plains. II.
Gay, James W. "Trail Diary." IV.
Gibson, J. W. RECOLLECTIONS OF A PIONEER. V-.
Hadley, Amelia H. "Journal." II.
Hadley, E. Amelia. "Diary." II.
Harris, Sarah H. AN UNWRITTEN CHAPTER. IV.
Hawkins, Theodore. History Hawkins Family. V.
Heald, Samuel. Diary. Not Seen.
Huntington, Hallie H. ALL THE WAY WEST. IV.
_____. "Cornelius Hills Crosses the Plains." IV.
Ingrim, Godfrey C. Recollections. Not Seen.
Jacobs, Orange. MEMOIRS. III.
James, John R. "Autobiography." Not Seen.
James, Samuel. Diary. IV.
Jennings, Oliver. Journal. IV.
Johnson, Ann W. "Long Journey." V.
Johnson, John L. Diary. II.
Johnson, John Lawrence. Excerpts. V.
Johnson, Neil. Excerpts. V.
Kendall, George W. "George Wilkins Kendall." II.
Lewis, Thomas. Papers. Not Seen.
Lowe, Percival G. FIVE YEARS A DRAGOON. I.
McAllister, John D. Journal. Not Seen.
McDonald, William J. NOTES. Not Seen.
McPherren, Ida. IMPRINTS. II.
Matthews, L. C. Journal. III.
Meister, John. Diary [in German]. Not Seen.
Mullan, John. "Journal." II.
Parsons, Lucena P. "Journal." II.
Patton, Thomas M. Diaries. Not Seen.
Pearce, Jean R. Diary. II+.
Platt, D. L., and N. M. Slater. TRAVELERS' GUIDE. III.
Powell, J. A. Diary. V.
Powell, Kate P. Our Covered Wagons. V.
Pratt, Parley P. AUTOBIOGRAPHY. II.
"Recollections of Sarah Hammitt." V-.
Reinhart, Herman F. GOLDEN FRONTIER. III.

Renshaw, Robert H. Diary. III.
Rice, Josiah M. A CANNONEER. III+.
Riddle, George W. EARLY DAYS. III.
Robe, Robert. "Diary." III.
Ruddell, W. H. Reminiscence. V.
Sands, Frank. A PASTORAL PRINCE. V.
Schutt, H. R. Journal. Not Seen.
Sengstacken, Agnes R. DESTINATION, WEST! III.
Stanley, Reva H., and Charles L. Camp. "A Mormon Mission." III.
Stout, Samuel. Diary. III.
Sutton, Sarah. Diary. III+.
Taylor, Osian H. Diary. Not Seen.
Thomson, Jeremiah B. Early Days. III.
Tice, Peter. Diary. V.
Vincent, Eliza. "Great American Trail." V.
Wallace, Andrew. "Across Arizona." I.
Watt, Roberta F. FOUR WAGONS WEST. V.
Welsh, John P. Diaries. II.
Williams, Elijah. Letter. IV.
Williams, Joseph. Diary. Not Seen.
Williams, Lucia L. "A Letter." III.
Wilson, Elizabeth M. Papers. Not Seen.
Wilson, Samuel H. Overland Journey. III.
Wixom, W. W. Diary. II.
_____. "Doctor Wixom's Journal." II.
Wood, Elizabeth. "Journal." III.
Wood, Joseph S. "Mormon Settlement." IV.
Wurttemberg, Paul W. "Brief Biography." II.
Zeiber, John S. "Diary." II.
Zieber, Eugenia. "Journal." V.
Zumwalt, Solomon. BIOGRAPHA. V.

1852-General
Arnold, Oren. "Slave Girl of the Mojaves."
Battey, Marion W. SCENES AND ADVENTURES. Not Seen.
Eaton, Herbert. OVERLAND TRAIL IN 1852.
Otto, Olive H. "A Mormon Bride."
Tate, Michael. "Randolph B. Marcy."

1852
Abbott, John G. "To Oregon by Ox Team." IV.
Ackley, Mary E. CROSSING THE PLAINS. IV.
Adams, Cecelia E. "Crossing the Plains." II.
Adams, David M. "Biographical Sketch." V.
Akin, James. "Journal." III.
Aldrich, Nathan. Letters. Not Seen.
Allen, Edward. Letters. I.
Allen, Edward J. "Edward J. Allen." IV.
Allred, Reddick. "Journal." III.
Anable, Henry S. Journals. II+.
Anderson, David. NET IN THE BAY. II+.
Andrews, D. B. Journal. II+.
Angell, Susan P. "Sketch." V.
Anon. "Crossing the Plains." Not Seen.
Applegate, Mary E. ON TO OREGON! III.
Ashley, Angeline J. Crossing the Plains. II.
Bagley, Clarence B. ACQUISITION. IV.
_____. "Crossing the Plains." IV.
Bailey, Mary S. "Journal." III.
Baker, Lois I. "Joel C. Inman." V.
Baker, William B. Diary. III.
Baldy, Henry T. Diary. II+.
Banks, Henry P. Diary. III.
Barry, J. Neilson. "On the Plains." V.
Bartlett, John R. PERSONAL NARRATIVE. I.
Barton, William K. COPY OF DIARY. Not Seen.
Baskerville, William. Diary. II+.
Beers, Lewis. Across the Continent. I.

Beresford, J. H. Diary. II.
Bixby-Smith, Sarah. ADOBE DAYS. IV.
Blake, Winslow. Diary. II.
Blanchard, James L. Letter. V.
Bliss, Beatrice L. MARY VOWELL ADAMS. II.
Boatman, Mary R. Biography. III.
Boatman, Willis. Story of My Life. V.
Bowering, George. Journal. I.
Bozorth, Mrs. L. A. Narrative. V.
Bradley, Henry and Nancy. Journal. II.
Bradley, N. J., and H. Journal. Not Seen.
Brooks, Elisha. PIONEER MOTHER. IV.
Brown, John. Diary. V.
_____. Diary. II.
Brown, Orlando. Diary. Not Seen.
Buchner, John S. Overland Trip. III.
Budd, Daniel H. Diary. Not Seen.
Bunch, E. J. and Thomas. Journal. II+.
Bushnell, James A. AUTOBIOGRAPHY. V.
Byers, William N. "Oregon Odyssey." II.
Callison, John J. DIARY. III.
Campbell, Newton G. Memories. Not Seen.
Caples, Margaret S. Reminiscences. IV.
Carpenter, James C. I Crossed the Plains. III.
Carter, E. S. LIFE AND ADVENTURES. V-.
Cartwright, David W. "A Tramp." III.
Cathey, Andrew. Cathey Wagon Train. V-.
Chadwick, Samuel. Diary. II.
Chandler, Knowlton H. Journal. III.
Clark, ? Diary. III.
Clark, Alvah. "Diary." Not Seen.
Clark, John. "California Guide." Illegible.
Clark, John Hawkins. "Overland to the Gold Fields." II+.
Clark, Wanda. "History of Nirom Hawley." IV.
Coburn, Catherine A. "Narrative." IV.
Cole, Gilbert L. IN THE EARLY DAYS. IV.
Collins, Martha A. "Memories." V.
Conard, Howard L. UNCLE DICK WOOTTON. IV.
Constant, Isaac. "A Brief Review." III.
Conyers, E. W. "Diary." II+.
Cook, Gertrude. Family Papers. Not Seen.
Cooke, Lucy R. CROSSING THE PLAINS. II.
Coon, Polly. "Journal." III.
Cornell, William. "William Cornell's Journal." III.
Council Point Emigration. I.
Couper, J. C. Diary. III+.
Cox, George W. Reminiscences. IV.
Crane, Addison M. Journal. I.
Cummings, Mariett F. "Diary." II.
Dalton, John E. Diary. II+.
Daughters, J. M. Journal. III.
Davis, Alvah I. "Diary." V.
Dean, Thaddeus. JOURNEY. V.
Dickinson, D. C. Journal. II+.
Dodson, John F. "Dodson's Death." III.
Draper, Elias J. AUTOBIOGRAPHY. IV.
Duffin, Reg. "The Miller-Tate Murder and the John F. Miller Grave."
Duniway, Abigail S. "Journal." II.
Dunlop, John W. "From Milwaukee." V.
Egbert, Eliza A. "Across the Plains." II.
Empey, William A. Diary. II-.
Farrar, John C. Diary. II+.
Ferris, Mrs. Benjamin. MORMONS AT HOME. II.
Ferris, Benjamin. UTAH AND THE MORMONS. II+.
Finley, Newton G. Memories. IV.
Fisher, James S. Diary. III.
Fisher, Samuel. Diary. Not Seen.
Ford, James. JUST BETWEEN OURSELVES. IV.

Foreman, Grant. ADVENTURE. II+.
Fox, Jared. Diary. I.
Francis, Samuel D. Journal. II.
Frear, Harry J. Diary. II.
Freeman, John F. Diaries. II.
Frisbie, Elizabeth C. "Recollections." Not Seen.
Frizzell, Lodisa. ACROSS THE PLAINS. III.
Froebel, Julius. SEVEN YEARS TRAVEL. II+.
Gage, Stephen T. Diary. III+.
Gee, Perry. Journal. II+.
Gibson, J. W. RECOLLECTIONS. IV.
Giles, Daniel. Biography. V.
Gillespie, Agnes L. "On to Oregon." III.
Gillette, Martha L. OVERLAND. IV.
Gillette, P. W. Diary. III+.
Glenn, John G. Diary. III.
Goodrich, William A. Diary. III+.
Gore, Ebenezer E. Reminiscences. IV.
Gowdy, Mrs. John T. CROSSING THE PLAINS. V.
Gowen, Bela E. History of the Olds Emigrant Party. II.
Graham, Alpheus N. "Big Circle." III+.
Graham, Robert M. Memoir. V.
Gray, Charles. "Incidents." Not Seen.
Green, Duff. "Exploring the Rio Grande." III.
Green, Jay. DIARY. III.
Hammond, James. Story of Trip. V.
Hammond, John B. Journal. III.
Hampton, William H. DIARY. III.
Hanna, Esther B. CANVAS CARAVANS. III.
Harmon, Appleton M. APPLETON MILO HARMON. V.
Hawk, Al R. "Strange Adventures." Not Seen.
Hayden, Charles W. Diary. IV.
Haydon, Jacob S. Diary. Not Seen.
Hazard, Henry T. Across the Plains. V.
Henry, Anson G. Journal. III.
Hickman, Peter L. Diary. III-.
Hickman, Richard O. "An Overland Journey." III.
Hill, Elizabeth F. UNDAUNTED PIONEERS. IV.
Hoag, Amanda J. Papers. Not Seen.
Hobart, Emaline. An Account. V.
Holt, W. M. "From Washington, Arkansas." IV.
Holtgrieve, Elizabeth R. "Recollections." V.
Hosley, Dexter. Diary. Not Seen.
Howard, Mary E. After Lapse. Not Seen.
Humphrey, L. Manuscript Journal. III.
Hunter, George. REMINISCENCES. IV.
Huston, Henry C. Autobiography. IV.
Hutcheson, Austin E. "Overland."
Hyde, William. Private Journal. IV.
Jacobs, Orange. MEMOIRS. III.
Jacobs, Peter. JOURNAL. II+.
Jaehnig, Ernest. "Letters." III.
Jared, Israel. "A Trip across." V-.
Johnston, John F. A Trip. IV.
Johnston, Lysander. Recollections. Not Seen.
Johnston, William H. Diary. III.
Jones, Evan O. Diary. IV.
Kahler, William. Notes. III.
Kearns, John T. Journal. II.
Keegan, Elizabeth J. Letters. V-.
Keen, Richard. Account. II+.
Kellogg, Jane D. "Memories." IV.
Kennedy, William C. Westward Kennedys. IV.
Kerns, John T. "Journal." II.
Kingerly, Solomon. Overland Travels. III+.
Kitchell, Edward. A Trip. II+.
Kreps, Simon P. Journal. III.
Kuykendall, George B. HISTORY. III.

McClure, Alexander K. THREE THOUSAND MILES. III.
Maricle, Abraham. Diary. III-.
Meyer, Edward S. "Description of the Route." III.
"Over the Plains to Colorado." V.
Robe, Henry W. Journal. II.
Robert, Henry M. Journal. II.
Rusling, James F. GREAT WEST. III.
Simonin, Louis. ROCKY MOUNTAIN WEST. II.
Spencer, W. A. THOUSAND MILES. II.
Waters, William E. LIFE AMONG THE MORMONS. II.

1868-General
Thompson, John P. "Snoqualmie Wagon Road."

1868
Baker, Sarah A. Papers. Not Seen.
Bell, William A. NEW TRACKS. II.
Blinn, Richard F. Diary. V.
Blythe, Samuel F. Diary. IV.
Bunyard, Harriet. "Diary." II.
Cook, Mary E. Diary. Stage.
Farrer, Deerin. Narrative. V.
Hall, Mrs. Frank. "Seventy Years Ago." Stage.
Himes, Harvey K. "Overland in Winter." IV.
Johnson, M. R. Reminiscence. V.
Magee, Thomas. "A Run Overland." V.
Melton, Florence. Reminiscences. III.
Ormsby, Augusta. Diary. IV.
Pennebaker, W. G. "Westward from Wayne County." III.
Powers, Stephen. AFOOT AND ALONE. II.
Shackleford, Ruth. TO CALIFORNIA. II.
Townshend, F. Trench. TEN THOUSAND MILES. II.
Velazquez, Loreta J. WOMAN IN BATTLE. IV.
Vogdes, Ada. Journal. II.

1869-General
Robert, Henry M. ITINERARIES OF ROUTES.

1869
Anon. Diary. Not Seen.
Baker, J. H. "A Trail Driver." III.
Borthwick, Alexander E. "Westering Journal." III.
Brackett, A. G. "A Trip." II.
Brewer, William H. ROCKY MOUNTAIN LETTERS. IV.
Clifford, Josephine. "Crossing Deserts." Stage.
Culver, E. S. "Crossing the Plains." V.
Gorrill, William H. Diary. II.
Hunt, Thomas B. Journal. Not Seen.
Jatta, Mary H. Journal. III.
Johnson, M. R. Reminiscence. V.
Mariager, Dagmar. "A Voyage by Land." III.
Miller, George. "Trip to Death Valley."
Newman, Orson N. Memoranda. III.
Palmer, Edward. Diary. Not Seen.
Pankey, H. S. "From Texas." V.
"Sweetwater Stage Company." Stage.
Thompson, W. Sherman. Childhood Memories. IV.
Victor, Frances. "Trail-Making." IV.
Westerman, Pleasant B. "How I Got to California." V.

There are many related topics that pertain to western trails. Carefully scan the subject list of such categories shown on the Contents page. Use the subject areas listed below to expand sources for specific trails.

BIBLIOGRAPHIES

This category comprises "general" bibliographies. For specialized bibliographies, such as those pertaining to graphics, government publications and other topics, refer to the specific subject area.

Abajian, James D. BLACKS AND THEIR CONTRIBUTIONS.
Adams, Ramon. RAMPAGING HERD.
Andrews, Thomas F. "Ho! For Oregon and California!"
Arksey, Laura, Nancy Pries, and Marcia Reed. AMERICAN DIARIES.
Austin, Judith, and Gary Bettis. "Preliminary Checklist to Idaho History."
Barry, Louise. BEGINNING OF THE WEST.
Bepler, Doris W. "Descriptive Catalog of California Periodicals."
Bleich, Pamela A. "Graduate Research in California History."
Bromberg, Erik. "Bibliography Pacific Northwest and Alaska." (to 1949).
_____. "Bibliography, 1949-1957."
_____. "Theses and Dissertations, 1958-1963."
_____. "Theses and Dissertations, 1964-70."
_____. "Further Bibliography of Pacific NW."
Canady, Nicholas, Jr. "Letters from the West."
Clark, Carter B. "Research Tools Arizona History."
Cockhill, Brian, and Dale L. Johnson. GUIDE TO MONTANA MANUSCRIPTS.
Cole, Garold L. TRAVELS IN AMERICA.
Collins, Karen L. "Guide to Diaries University of Texas Archives."
Cooper, Thomas C. "Arizona History in ARIZONA HIGHWAYS."
Crumb, Lawrence N. HISTORIC PRESERVATION IN THE PACIFIC NORTHWEST.
Cunningham, Bob, and A. Tracy Row. "The Journal of Arizona History: A Bibliography of Articles Published during the First Twenty-Five Years."
Daniels, Sherrill F. "An Index to and Bibliography of Reminiscences in the Nebraska State Historical Society Library." PhD diss., Univ. of Nebraska, 1986.
Diaz, Albert J. "Bibliography Arizona and New Mexico."
DICTIONARY CATALOG EDWARD E. AYER COLLECTION.
Edwards, Elza I. DESERT VOICES.
_____. LOST OASES ALONG THE CARRIZO.
Etulain, Richard W., and Merwin Swanson. IDAHO HISTORY.
Evans, Henry H. WESTERN BIBLIOGRAPHIES.
Friis, Herman R. "Documents and Reports U. S. Congress."
Graff, Everett D. "Westerners Go Overland."
Hanna, Archibald, Jr. "Manuscript Resources Yale University Library for Western Travel."
_____. "Shreds from Henry Wagner's Mantle."
Hardy, Wilabour. "Historical Bibliography of Kansas."
Heaston, Michael D. TRAILS OF KANSAS.
Heckman, Marlin L. OVERLAND ON THE CALIFORNIA TRAIL, 1846-1859.
Hinding, Andrea. WOMEN'S HISTORY SOURCES.
Hinton, Harwood. "Arizona Theses and Dissertations."
Hitchcock, Catherine E. "Trans-Mississippi West in AMERICAN HERITAGE."
Hoober, David H. "Nebraska History in Graduate Theses."
Hufford, Kenneth. "Travelers on the Gila Trail."
Jager, Ronald G. "Chisholm Trail's Mountain of Words."
Jensen, Esther H. "California Periodical Literature, 1891-1898."
Joost, Nicholas. "Reveille in the West."
McDermott, John F. "Lost Manuscripts of Western Travel."
_____. TRAVELERS ON THE WESTERN FRONTIER.
McMillan, Kathryn S. "Descriptive Bibliography San Antonio-San Diego Mail Line."

Mattes, Merrill J. GREAT PLATTE RIVER ROAD.
Matthews, William. AMERICAN DIARIES.
_____. AMERICAN DIARIES IN MANUSCRIPT 1580-1954.
Mintz, Lannon W. THE TRAIL.
Moore, Mary L. "New Mexico Theses and Dissertations."
Morgan, Dale L. "Western Travels and Travelers Bancroft Library."
Myers, Christine B. NEW MEXICO LOCAL AND COUNTY BIBLIOGRAPHIES.
O'Bryan, Frank. OVERLAND CHRONICLE.
Parsons, Phyllis R. "Trans-Mississippi West in Popular Magazine 1820-1870."
Poole, William F. AN INDEX TO PERIODICAL LITERATURE.
Prucha, Francis P. INDIAN-WHITE RELATIONS IN THE UNITED STATES.
Reber, Bruce. U.S. ARMY AND INDIAN WARS.
Reid, Robie L. "British Columbia."
Rittenhouse, Jack D. SANTA FE TRAIL.
Roe, Frank G. NORTH AMERICAN BUFFALO.
Rudkin, Charles N. EARLY CALIFORNIA TRAVELS.
"Rush to the Rockies Articles."
Shoemaker, Floyd C. "Historical Articles in Missouri Newspapers."
Smith, Dwight L. AMERICAN AND CANADIAN WEST.
_____. "Unexploited Manuscript Resources Newberry Library."
Smith, Olive F. "California Periodical Literature 1899-1906."
Socolofsky, Homer E. KANSAS HISTORY IN GRADUATE STUDY.
Storm, Colton. CATALOG EVERETT D. GRAFF COLLECTION.
Strong, Gary E., and Gary F. Kurutz. WESTERN AMERICANA IN THE CALIFORNIA STATE LIBRARY.
Thompson, Enid T. "Bibliography on Bent's Old Fort, 1829-1849."
Thompson, Gerald. "New Mexico History in NEW MEXICO MAGAZINE."
Thompson, W. H. "Transportation in Iowa, 1846-1980."
Tobin, Mary. "California Periodical Literature 1907 to 1914."
Turner, Ellis. "Oregon, California, and Texas Guidebook, 1814-1860."
Tutorow, Norman E. MEXICAN-AMERICAN WAR.
UNITED STATES LOCAL HISTORIES IN THE LIBRARY OF CONGRESS.
Wagner, Henry R., and Charles L. Camp. PLAINS AND THE ROCKIES.
Walker, Henry P. "Pre-Railroad Transportation."
Wallace, William S. "Bibliographies Eleven Western States, 1941-1947."
Wheat, Carl I. BOOKS OF THE CALIFORNIA GOLD RUSH.
Winther, Oscar O. CLASSIFIED BIBLIOGRAPHY PERIODICAL LITERATURE, 1811-1957.
_____, and Richard A. Van Orman. CLASSIFIED BIBLIOGRAPHY PERIODICAL LITERATURE, 1957-67.
Wright, Richard T. OVERLANDERS. (Canada)

BIOGRAPHIES

The following index is arranged alphabetically by biographee's name, not by author. For example, all entries relating to Jesse Applegate are grouped together and appear before entries for John Fremont. In general, biographee names appear in the item's title rather than as author.

Applegate Family Papers.
Blake, Charlotte. "Jesse Applegate."
Brown, Wilfred H. THIS WAS A MAN.
Frear, Samuel T. "Jesse Applegate."
Miner, William D. "Jesse Applegate."
Schafer, Joseph. "Jesse Applegate."
Bundschu, Henry A. "Francis X. Aubry."
Burr, Eugene P. "Aubrey Cutoff."
Chaput, Donald. FRANCOIS X. AUBRY.
Lockwood, Frank C. "Francis X. Aubrey."
_____. "He Rode the Wilderness Trail."
O'Meara, James. "Captain F. X. Aubrey."

EQUIPMENT AND TEAMS

Here are grouped publications relating to tools, implements, animals and weapons used on the trail. Only dray animals appear in this listing. Wildlife species are found in the following section on flora and fauna.

Faulk, Odie B. U.S. CAMEL CORPS.
Fellows, Fred. "Illustrated Study of Western Saddles."
Florin, Lambert. WESTERN WAGON WHEELS.
Fowler, Harlan D. CAMELS TO CALIFORNIA.
_____. THREE CARAVANS TO YUMA.
Frizzell, John and Mildred. "Anatomy of American Stagecoaches."
_____. "Autobiography of the 'Old Overland'."
_____. "Oklahoma Historical Society Stagecoach."
Froman, Robert. "The Red Ghost."
Gannon, William L. "Carriage, Coach and Wagon."
Garavaglia, Louis A., and Charles G. Worman. FIREARMS OF THE
    AMERICAN WEST.
Gentry, North T. "Asses in Missouri."
Griggs, Monroe C. WHEELERS, POINTERS AND LEADERS.
Guyol, P. N. "A Coach Comes to the Society."
Hanson, Charles. "Red River and other Carts."
Hastings, Lansford W. EMIGRANT'S GUIDE.
Hayhurst, W. T. "Camels in British Columbia."
Hegel, Richard. CARRIAGES FROM NEW HAVEN.
Holbrook, S. H. "Concord Coach."
Houston, Henrietta. "Techniques of the Emigrant Trail."
Irvine, J. B. "A Steam Wagon."
Knox, Olive. "Red River Cart."
Lammons, Frank B. "Operation Camel."
Lass, William E. FROM THE MISSOURI.
Lemert, Bula. "Peppard's Folly." (Wind Wagon).
Longstreet, Stephen. STORY OF STUDEBAKER.
M. M. "Letter."
Mackmull, Gulden. "An Aerial Liner."
MacLean, John. "Tribute to the Red River Cart."
Mattson, E. Neil. RED RIVER CARTS TREK.
Meyer, Henry W. MEMORIES OF THE BUGGY DAYS.
Monaghan, Jay. "Handcarts."
Nadeau, Remi. "Saga of Nadeau's Teams."
O'Neil, Emily A. "Joseph Murphy's Contribution."
Peterson, Harold L. AMERICAN KNIVES.
Post, Lauren C. "Red River Carts."
"A Record Trip."
Rees, Decatur S. "Reminiscences."
Remsburg, George J. "Wind Wagon."
Rice, Lee M., and Glenn R. Vernam. THEY SADDLED THE WEST.
Riley, Harvey. THE MULE.
Rittenhouse, Jack D. AMERICAN HORSE-DRAWN VEHICLES.
Robinson, A. P., and Edward Warner. OVERLAND TRACTION EN-
    GINE COMPANY.
Robinson, Fayette. CALIFORNIA.
Rosebush, Waldo E. AMERICAN FIREARMS.
_____. FRONTIER STEEL.
Schreier, Konrad F. "But First Came the Carts."
Searle, Walt. "Packing."
Serven, James E. "Wagons of the West."
Sherman, James, and Edward F. Ronstadt. "Wagon Making in Southern
    Arizona."
Shumway, George, Edward Durrell, and Howard C. Frey. CONES-
    TOGA WAGON.
Simmons, Marc. "Arrieria, the Art of Mexican Muleteering."
Sommer, Jane H. "Outfitting for the West, 1849."
Spivey, Towana. HISTORICAL GUIDE TO WAGON HARDWARE
    AND BLACKSMITH SUPPLIES.
Straus, R. CARRIAGES AND COACHES.
Stringham, Guy E. "Pioneer Roadometer."
Strudwick, June. "Wagons West - The Conestoga."
Thomas, Chauncey. "Frontier Firearms."
Walker, Henry P. WAGONMASTERS.
Wills, Irving. "Jerk Line Team."
Wiltsey, Norman B. "First 'Navigator' of the Prairies."
_____. "Mystery Driver of the Sierras."
Wolfe, George D. "Wonderful Concord Coach."

Woodward, Arthur. "Knife on the Frontier."
_____. OX CARTS AND COVERED WAGONS.
Wright, Williamson. Bill of Items Required, Two Persons to a Wagon.

FLORA AND FAUNA

Occasionally, a diarist would describe geography, weather conditions and
    wildlife in detail. These items, plus later studies of natural history, are
    shown below.

Baltimore, J. M. "In the Prime of the Buffalo."
Bouldin, James E. Diary. 1849. II +.
Bradway, Joseph R. 1853. II.
Brown, Dee. "The Day of the Buffalo."
Dary, David A. THE BUFFALO BOOK.
De Smet, Pierre J. LETTERS AND SKETCHES. 1843. II.
Haines, Francis D. THE BUFFALO.
_____. "Western Limits of the Buffalo Range."
Hunter, William H. Diary. I.
Jagger, D. Diary. 1849. I.
Klauber, Laurence M. RATTLESNAKES.
McKelvey, Susan D. BOTANICAL EXPLORATION OF THE
    TRANSMISSISSIPPI WEST.
Maloney, Alice B. "A Botanist on the Road to Yerba Buena." 1850. IV.
Parker, William T. Notes By the Way. 1850. II +.
Roe, Frank G. THE NORTH AMERICAN BUFFALO. Bibliography.
Saban, Vera. "The Cottonwood."
Suckley, George. "1859 Overland Journal of Naturalist." 1859. V.
Willey, Lucas. Diaries. 1854. I.
Wislizenus, A. MEMOIR OF A TOUR. 1846. I.

FREIGHT

A significant portion of trail literature derives from freighting. Often,
    authors of freighting diaries or reminiscences also participated in stag-
    ing. Readers should also refer to the staging subject category to lo-
    cate all possible items containing freight material.

Freight-Graphics
Beadle, J. H. THE UNDEVELOPED WEST.
Burnett, Hugh B. "Wagons in the Southwest."
Dines, Glen. BULL WAGON.
Good, Donnie D. "Traveling Westward."
Hanley, Mike, and Omer Stanford. SAGE BRUSH AND AXLE
    GREASE.
Hooker, William F. THE BULLWHACKER.
Jackson, William H. DIARIES.
Jensen, Lee. PONY EXPRESS.
Madsen, Brigham and Betty. "Diamond R Rolls Out."
Sherman, James E., and Edward F. Ronstadt. "Wagon Making in
    Southern Arizona."
Young, John D. JOHN D. YOUNG.

Freight-Maps
Freedom, Gary S. "Moving Men and Supplies."
Lass, William E. FROM THE MISSOURI TO THE GREAT SALT
    LAKE.

Freight-General
Allen, Sylvester. Diary.
Amundson, Carroll J. "History of the Willamette Valley and Cascade
    Road Company."
Anderson, Mardi. "Freighting in Buffalo County."
Angus, Ina M. "Toll Roads of Western Nevada."
Barnes, Cass C. THE SOD HOUSE.
Batty, Donald. "History of Early Roads and Freighting in the Eastern
    Uintah Basin, 1672-1920."

Murray, Keith A. "Building a Wagon Road through the Northern Cascade Mountains."
Murray, Robert A. THE ARMY MOVES WEST.
_____. "Wagons on the Plains."
Nadeau, Remi. "King of the Desert Freighters."
Neuhaus, Carla E. "Transportation to Colorado."
Newton, Dwight B. "Techniques of Overland Freighting in the Trans-Missouri West."
Ordway, Edward. "Reminiscences."
Overland Camel Company. PROSPECTUS.
Oviatt, Alton B. "Movement for a Northern Trail: The Mullan Road."
"Packing in the Mountains of California."
Paden, Irene D., and Margaret E. Schlichtmann. THE BIG OAK ROAD.
Palmer, William R. "Early Day Trading with the Nevada Mining Camps."
Paxton, Matthew. "When Freight Was Hauled by Oxen."
Pelzer, Louis. "A Decade of Ox-Team Freighting on the Plains."
Peterson, Stacy. "Silas Skinner's Owyhee Toll Road."
Porter, Henry M. "Freighting and Merchandising in Early Denver."
Porter, James R. Reminiscences.
Powers, Otero, Lowe & Co. Letters.
Powers, Thomas C. Papers.
Pugh, Byron G. "History of Utah-California Wagon Freighting."
Raber, Charles. "Recollections."
Railley, Egbert. Journal.
Ratliff, Cecelia B. "Early-Day Transportation."
Reeder, Ray M. "The Mormon Trail."
Rees, Decatur S. Reminiscences.
Reinhart, Herman F. GOLDEN FRONTIER.
Remsburg, George J. "Bull Wagon Bosses."
Rice, William B., ed. "Early Freighting on the Salt Lake - San Bernardino Trail."
Riggs, John L. "William H. Hardy."
Rolfe, DeForest P. "Overland Freighting from Nebraska City."
Rolfe, Frank. "Early Day Los Angeles."
Root, Frank A., and William Connelley. OVERLAND STAGE TO CALIFORNIA.
Root, George A. Collections.
Ruggles, Daniel. Freighting from Sauk County, WI.
Russell, Majors and Waddell. Correspondence and Papers, 1839-1868.
_____. RULES AND REGULATIONS.
Santleben, August. A TEXAS PIONEER.
Schweitzer, Cora. "Routes Los Angeles to Kern County."
Scott, Edwin. CALIFORNIA TO OREGON.
Settle, Raymond W. "The Role of Russell, Majors and Waddell."
_____, and Mary. EMPIRE ON WHEELS.
_____. WAR DRUMS AND WAGON WHEELS.
Sharp, Paul F. WHOOP-UP COUNTRY.
_____. "Whoop-Up Trail."
Sherrod, James M. "Sketches from the Life."
Simmons, Marc. "Arrieria: The Art of Mexican Muleteering."
Sloan, William K. "Autobiography."
Stacey, May H. UNCLE SAM'S CAMELS.
Standing, Arnold R. "Through the Uintahs."
Standish, John K. "A Pioneer Freighter."
Stevens, Zenas. Diaries.
Stokes, George W. "Echoes of the Old West."
Streble, George L. "Freighting between the Missouri River and Utah, 1847-1869."
Sutherland, James. ATCHISON CITY DIRECTORY.
Teeter, Charles N. "Four Years of My Life."
Thomson, Frank. "We Watched them Die."
Throckmorton, Arthur L. OREGON ARGONAUTS.
Toponce, Alexander. REMINISCENCES.
Torok, Theresa M. "Social Aspects of Life on the Oregon Trail, 1841-1846."
TRANSPORTATION OF MILITARY SUPPLIES FROM FORT LEAVENWORTH WESTWARD.

Trey, Mark. "Jerk Line Jockey."
Tyson, T. K. "Freighting to Denver."
U.S. Army Quartermaster Corps. Correspondence - Russell, Majors and Waddell.
Vanderwalker, George F. "The Bull-whacker or Prairie Sailor."
Walker Brothers. Collections.
Walker, Henry P. "Freighting from Guaymas to Tucson."
_____. "Rise and Decline of High Plains Freighting, 1822 - 1880."
_____. Slow Freight to Denver.
_____. "Wagon Freighting in Arizona."
_____. WAGONMASTERS.
Walker Brothers and Co. Receipt Book, 1862-1866.
Ward, Seth. Papers.
Watt, James W. "Experiences of a Packer."
Wellman, Paul I. "The Silent Partner Who Made History and Lost Fortunes on the Great Plains."
Welty, Raymond L. "Supplying the Frontier Military Posts."
White, Chester L. "Surmounting the Sierras."
Wills, Irving. "The Jerk Line Team."
Winther, O. O. "Development of Transportation in Oregon."
_____. THE OLD OREGON COUNTRY.
_____. "Pack Animals."
_____. "Place of Transportation."
Wyman, Walker D. "Bullwhacking."
_____. "F. X. Aubry."
_____. "Freighting on the Santa Fe Trail, 1843-1866."
Young, John. Record Book, 1865.

1848
Withers, Ethel M. "Experiences." II.

1851
Cheek, Larry. "Bushwhacked on the Trail."

1853
Daily, Moses Freight Co. Journal.

1854
Dougherty, Lewis B. "Experiences."
Hauser, John. Reminiscences. IV.
Rice, William B. "Early Freighting on the Salt Lake - San Bernadino Trail. III.

1855
Hadley, C. B. "Plains War in 1855."
Hayes, W. R. Diary. III+.
Woody, Frank H. "How an Early Pioneer Came to Montana."

1856
Dowell, B. F. Diary. III.
Sydenham, Moses H. "Freighting across the Plains in 1856." IV.
Woody, Frank H. "How an Early Pioneer Came to Montana."

1857
Clark, William. "A Trip across." II.

1858
Beehrer, George W. "Freighting across the Plains."
Kenderdine, Thaddeus S. A CALIFORNIA TRAMP. II.

1859
Riley, James F. RECOLLECTIONS. III.
Service, John. JOHN SERVICE. IV.

1860
Anthony, Webster D. "Journal of a Trip from Denver." III.
Berkin, William. Reminiscence.
Hambleton, Chalkley J. A GOLD HUNTER'S EXPERIENCE. IV.

Young, John D. JOHN D. YOUNG. II.

1861
Keaton, Charles H. "Crossing the Plains."
Draper, D. M. The Santa Fe Trail. IV.

1863
Gay, William. Reminiscences. IV.
McPherson, Murdoch M. Reminiscences. II.

1864
Forman, George. "Across the Plains." Genl.
Gallatin, E. L. "Reminiscences." III.
Keaton, Charles H. "Crossing the Plains."
McBride, Heber. Journal. V.
Wells, Polk. LIFE AND ADVENTURES. IV.
Wood, J. D. Reminiscence. V.

1865
Adkins, H. Frank. Reminiscence. IV.
Case, Frank. "Experiences on the Platte."
Hadley, C. B. "The Plains War in 1865."
Hodder, Halie R. "Crossing the Plains." III-.
Jones, Daniel. Travels. V.
Longacre, Myrtle. A Trek West. V-.
Leech, A. P. Diary. II.
McBride, Heber R. Journal. V.
McCall, John M. "The First Oregon Cavalry."
Peabody, Frances C. "Across the Plains." IV.
Stobie, Charles S. "Crossing the Plains." II.
Wood, Henry F. Diary. III+.
Young, Charles E. DANGERS OF THE TRAIL. IV.
Young, Frank C. ACROSS THE PLAINS.
Young, John. Record Book.
Young, Will H. "Journals." IV.

1866
Creigh, Thomas A. "From Nebraska City to Montana." III.
Fisher, Marcius C. "Recollections." III.
"Freighting in 1866." Genl.
Jackson, William H. DIARIES. II.
_____. "Notes from Diary." II.

1867
Jackson, William H. "Bullwhacking." II.
Williams, John B. Diary. II.
Wood, Henry F. Diary. III+.

1868
Beadle, J. H. THE UNDEVELOPED WEST.
Blythe, Samuel F. Diary. IV.

GEOGRAPHY

Many trail questions involve specific geographical sites. Local historians, in particular, need to reach sources limited to an individual site or segment of a larger trail network. Many sources reflecting study of detailed subdivisions of western trails exist and are represented here. This listing is arranged alphabetically by geographic location - such sites always described within the title - although the author's name is shown first as is usual in shortened references. This arrangement is identical to the BIOGRAPHICAL format.

Readers interested in broader topics, such as the Pony Express, should also check individual station placenames for additional data. The Pony Express subject category does not include all the narrower geographic items shown below. Nor do other general trail or subject listings. Also, beware that the same site might have two or more placenames, i.e., Apache Pass and Fort Bowie. Check all options.

General
Martin, Charles W. "The Alcove Spring."
Smith, William E. "The Grave of Sarah Keyes on the Oregon Trail." (Alcove Spring).
Vivian, R. Gwinn. "An Archeological Survey of the Lower Gila River." (Antelope Stage Station)
Mulligan, R. A. "Apache Pass and Old Fort Bowie."
_____, Sixteen Days in Apache Pass."
Murray, Richard Y. "Apache Pass."
Taylor, Fenton W. "The West's Bloodiest Pass." (Apache Pass)
Dudley, N. A. M. "Battle of Ash Hollow."
Munkres, Robert L. "Ash Hollow: Gateway to the High Plains."
Todd, John B. "Harney Expedition Against the Sioux." (Ash Hollow)
Anderson, George L. "Atchison."
Beckman, Peter. "Atchison's Beginnings."
Wyman, Walker D. "Atchison."
Burr, Eugene P. "Aubry Cutoff."
Lewis, Oscar. THE TOWN THAT DIED LAUGHING. (Austin, NV)
Lucia, Ellis. "Sam Barlow's Astounding Road."
California Interstate, ROMANTIC HERITAGE OF MOJAVE RIVER VALLEY. (Barstow)
Standing, A. R. "Friendly House." (Bear River Crossing)
Thompson, Enid T. "Bibliography on Bent's Old Fort, 1829 - 1849."
_____, "The Ladies of Bent's Fort."
Blair, Roger P. "Saving Our Powder." (Big Sandy, WY)
Agnew, Mrs. James D. "Idaho Pioneer of 1864." (Boise)
Bird, Annie L. OLD FORT BOISE.
Chaffee, Eugene B. "Early History of the Boise Region, 1811 - 1864."
Illingworth, Gertrude P. "An Historical Study of Boise."
Clark, Jessie L. "Boyd's Ferry on the Cache La Poudre."
Beuman, Edna L. "Story of Fort Churchill and Samuel Buckland." (Buckland's Station.)
Haines, Francis B. "Western Limits of the Buffalo Range."
Helfrich, Devere. "Trail, Road and Transportation History of Butte Valley."
Warren, H. Warren. "The First Bottle-Neck in California Traffic." (Cahuenga Pass)
Haenszel, Arda M. HISTORICAL CAJON PASS.
McMullen, Leon. "Two Gateways." (Cajon Pass)
Waters, Louisa B. "Trail Blazers of Cajon Pass."
Beldon, L. Burr. "Camp Cady."
Casebier, Dennis G. THE BATTLE AT CAMP CADY.
Johnston, Philip. "Gibraltar of the Old Frontier." (Camp Cady)
Waitman, Leonard. "The History of Camp Cady."
Alexander, Thomas G., and Leonard J. Arrington, "Camp in the Sagebrush." (Camp Floyd)
Casebier, Dennis G. CAMP ROCK SPRING.
Ryan, Garry D. "Camp Walbach."
Graves, Jones S. "Influence of the Canadian Rivers."
Edgar, William F. "Cantonment Loring."
Johnston, Philip. "Arid Outposts of Carrizo."
Greco, Joseph A. "History of Highway 50 from Placerville to Virginia City." (Carson Pass)
HISTORICAL TOUR OF THE CARSON RIVER ROUTE.
Leadabrand, Russ. "Across Historic Carson Pass."
Ricketts, Norma B. TRAGEDY SPRING. (Carson Pass, 1848)
Shannon, Betty. "New Old Mormon-Emigrant Trail."
Watson, Jeanne H. "The Carson Emigrant Road."
Dangberg, Grace. CARSON VALLEY.
Elliott, Russell R. "Nevada's First Trading Post." (Carson Valley)
Knott, Thomas. "The Knott Journals." (Carson Valley)
Malloy, William D. "Carson Valley, 1852 - 1960."
Page, Albert R. "Orson Hyde and the Carson Valley Mission."
Standing, A. R. "Through the Uintahs." (Carter Road)
Murray, Robert A. "Trading Posts, Forts, and Bridges of the Casper Area."
Shafer, Gladys P. "Trail Tragedy." (Casper, WY)

GENERAL OVERLAND SOURCES

Here are shown those "general" sources that describe the trail experience
in a larger context than individual trails or years.

GOVERNMENT

This category includes the major federal and state surveys of western states and territories, plus later studies of the surveys and participants. No attempt was made to be comprehensive in such "government" materials since there were bibliographies available for readers' use in both primary and secondary sources.

While collecting these sources, it was noticed that many authors commonly listed federal items by either author-title or appropriate congressional document number, but seldom cross-referenced the two types of citation for identical documents. This resulted in situations where readers may encounter a congressional document by number alone, i.e., S. Ex. Doc. 3. 36th Cong., 1st sess., without an explanatory author-title addendum. The omission causes undue time spent in searching for a possibly immaterial reference item. Therefore, for materials included herein, both author-title and corresponding congressional references are listed so that readers with congressional document numbers alone can quickly find the associated author-title entry.

Bibliography

Maps

General

"Memorial of Citizens." S. Misc. 52. 30th Cong., 2d sess.

MILITARY POSTS - COUNCIL BLUFFS TO THE PACIFIC OCEAN.

National Road to California. Public Meeting.

NATIONWIDE SYSTEM OF TRAILS.

O'Reilly, Henry. "Memorial."

Parke, John G. REPORT RAILWAY ROUTE.

Pope, John. REPORT PACIFIC RAILROAD.

"Postmaster General's Order Relating to Route of the Overland Mail Company, March 12, 1861."

Preuss, Charles. EXPLORING WITH FREMONT.

Price, Ralph B. "The Federal Government and Emigrant Roads through the Northern Territories to the Far West, 1856 - 1866."

"Protection to Overland Immigrants."

Ramsey, Bobby Gene. "Scientific Exploration and Discovery in the Great Basin from 1831 - 1891."

REPORT OF CAPTAIN R. B. MARCY'S ROUTE FROM FORT SMITH TO SANTA FE.

REPORT OF THE AGENTS OF THE CALIFORNIA RELIEF EXPEDITION.

REPORT OF THE POSTMASTER GENERAL. (1 Dec 1857)

_____. (3 Mar 1859)

"Report on Memorial of George H. Giddings."

REPORTS OF THE SECRETARY OF WAR.

Robert, Henry M. ITINERARIES OF ROUTES IN ARIZONA AND SOUTHERN CALIFORNIA.

S. Doc. 1. 29th Cong., 1st sess. Kearny, REPORT.

S. Doc. 1. 35th Cong., 2d sess. Warren, EXPLORATIONS IN NEBRASKA.

S. Doc. 42. 31st Cong., 1st sess. Pope, REPORT TERRITORY OF MINNESOTA.

S. Doc. 43. 37th Cong., 3d sess. Mullan, REPORT ON THE CONSTRUCTION OF A MILITARY ROAD.

S. Doc. 243. 27th Cong., 3d sess. Fremont, REPORT OF AN EXPLORING EXPEDITION TO THE ROCKY MOUNTAINS, 1842.

S. Ex. Doc. 1. 37th Cong., Sp. sess. Fergusson, REPORT TUCSON AND LOBOS BAY.

S. Ex. Doc. 2. 31st Cong., Sp. sess. Cooke, "Journal."

S. Ex. Doc. 3. 32nd Cong., Sp. sess. Stansbury, EXPLORATION AND SURVEY OF THE GREAT SALT LAKE.

S. Ex. Doc. 11. 35th Cong., 1st sess. "Report of the Postmaster General, 1 Dec 1857."

S. Ex. Doc. 12. 31st Cong., 1st sess. Simpson, ROUTE FROM FORT SMITH TO SANTA FE.

S. Ex. Doc. 17. 37th Cong., 3d sess. Train escorted by Medorem Crawford, 1862.

S. Ex. Doc. 19. 31st Cong., 2d sess. Whipple, REPORT SAN DIEGO TO THE COLORADO.

S. Ex. Doc. 24. 46th Cong., 3d sess. AMOUNTS PAID FOR OVERLAND MAIL SERVICE, 1858 TO 1868.

S. Ex. Doc. 26. 35th Cong., 1st sess. "Letter from the Postmaster General."

S. Ex. Doc. 31. 38th Cong., 2d sess. TRANSPORTATION OF MILITARY SUPPLIES FROM FORT LEAVENWORTH WESTWARD.

S. Ex. Doc. 34. 36th Cong., 1st sess. Wallen, REPORT DALLES CITY TO GREAT SALT LAKE.

S. Ex. Doc. 36. 35th Cong., 2d sess. PACIFIC WAGON ROADS.

S. Ex. Doc. 40. 35th Cong., 2d sess. REPORT BY CAPTAIN JAMES H. SIMPSON.

S. Ex. Doc. 48. 35th Cong., 2d sess. "Report of Postmaster General."

S. Ex. Doc. 52. 31st Cong., 1st sess. Peoples, GENERAL SMITH'S CORRESPONDENCE.

S. Ex. Doc. 59. 32nd Cong., 2d sess. REPORT OF AN EXPEDITION DOWN THE ZUNI AND COLORADO RIVERS BY CAPTAIN L. SITGREAVES.

S. Ex. Doc. 64. 31st Cong., 1st sess. RECONNAISSANCES OF ROUTES FROM SAN ANTONIO TO EL PASO.

S. Ex. Doc. 70. 50th Cong., 2d sess. "Letter from the Secretary of War - Volunteer Troops to Guard Overland and other Mails from 1861 to 1866."

S. Ex. Doc. 76. 34th Cong., 1st sess. Warren, EXPLORATIONS IN THE DACOTAH COUNTRY.

S. Ex. Doc. 78. 33rd Cong., 2d sess. Beckwith, REPORT OF EXPLORATIONS. (Gunnison's Route)

S. Ex. Doc. 96. 35th Cong., 1st sess. San Antonio - San Diego Mail contract, 1857 - 1861.

S. Ex. Doc. 135. 34th Cong., 1st sess. Emory, "Report on the U.S. and Mexican Boundary Survey."

S. Ex. Doc. 211. 46th Cong., 2d sess. "Copies of Contracts with Benjamin Holladay."

S. Misc. Doc. 15. 36th Cong., 2d sess. REPORT ON MEMORIAL OF GEORGE H. GIDDINGS.

S. Misc. Doc. 19. 46th Cong., 2d sess. TESTIMONY BEN HOLLADAY OVERLAND STAGE LINE.

S. Misc. Doc. 52. 30th Cong., 2d sess. "Memorial of Citizens."

S. Misc. Doc. 148. 30th Cong., 1st sess. Fremont, GEOGRAPHICAL MEMOIR.

S. Report Comm. No. 275. 36th Cong., 1st sess. COMMITTEE ON POST OFFICES, CALIFORNIA STAGE COMPANY.

SETTLERS AND EMIGRANTS BETWEEN THE MISSISSIPPI VALLEY AND THE PACIFIC OCEAN.

Simpson, James H. REPORT BY CAPTAIN JAMES H. SIMPSON, 1858.

_____. REPORT OF EXPLORATIONS CAMP FLOYD TO CARSON VALLEY, 1859.

_____. ROUTE FROM FORT SMITH TO SANTA FE.

Sitgreaves, Lorenzo. REPORT OF AN EXPEDITION DOWN THE ZUNI AND COLORADO RIVERS.

Stansbury, Howard. EXPLORATION AND SURVEY OF THE GREAT SALT LAKE.

Tate, Michael. "Randolph B. Marcy: First Explorer of the Wichitas."

TESTIMONY BEN HOLLADAY OVERLAND STAGE LINE.

U.S. Dept. of Interior. PACIFIC WAGON ROADS.

Wallace, Andrew. "Across Arizona to the Big Colorado."

Wallace, Edward S. THE GREAT RECONNAISSANCE: SOLDIERS, ARTISTS AND SCIENTISTS ON THE FRONTIER, 1848 - 1861.

Wallen, H. D. REPORT 1859 DALLES CITY TO GREAT SALT LAKE.

Warren, G. K. EXPLORATIONS IN THE DACOTAH COUNTRY, 1855.

_____. EXPLORATIONS IN NEBRASKA.

Werne, Joseph R. "Major Emory and Captain Jimenez: Running the Gadsden Line."

Wheelock, Walt. "Following Fremont's Fifth Expedition."

Whipple, A. W. SEE ALSO: Conrad, David E.

_____. REPORT RAILROAD ROUTE.

_____. REPORT SAN DIEGO TO THE COLORADO.

Wilson, Maud. "Federal Exploration in California from 1841 - 1855."

GRAPHICS

References to sources with exceptional illustrations (line drawings, photographs or color work) or items pertaining to trail artists are collected below. Readers seeking specific types of graphics, i.e., coach design or geographic sites, should also refer to such individual subject categories where graphics are shown in separate entries.

Bibliographies

Bashore, Melvin L. "Index to Art Works in LDS Church Periodicals."

Dykes, Jeff. FIFTY GREAT WESTERN ILLUSTRATORS: A BIBLIOGRAPHIC CHECKLIST.

General

Abert, James W. THROUGH THE COUNTRY. (Southern Great Plains)

Alcorn, Rowena and Gordon. PAUL KANE, FRONTIER ARTIST. (Canada, Washington)

Audubon, John W. THE DRAWINGS OF JOHN WOODHOUSE

GUIDEBOOKS

Bibliographies

General

INDIANS

Sources included below represent primary items with indian-related content or secondary sources concentrating on contact between indian and white. Purely indian studies - those of ethnographic value alone - are not shown. The volume of indian publications prevent listing any but items relating to indian-white relations on the trail. Various subject and geographic categories are introduced to assist in locating specific indian sources.

Bibliographies

Graphics

General

Jolly, William C. ACROSS THE PLAINS IN DAYS OF HOSTILE INDIANS.

Kelly, Fanny. NARRATIVE.

Ryan, Benjamin W. "The Bozeman Trail."

Thompson, James B. "Crossing the Plains."

Vance, Laura R. S. Papers.

1865-General

Davis, Theodore R. "A Stage Ride to Colorado."

Dunn, Ruth. THE BURNING OF JULESBURG.

France, Charles B. Diary.

Hartwell, William H. "Two Years."

Pennock, Jake. "Diary of Jake Pennock."

Zwink, Timothy A. "Dodging Death along the Smoky Hill River."

1866-General

Jones, Sydney. "My Trip Overland."

1867-General

Hunter, John W. "Story of an Ill-Fated Expedition."

McClure, Alexander K. THREE THOUSAND MILES.

LIVESTOCK TRAILS

Items cited in this category primarily contain trail accounts of cattle and sheep drives rather than general studies of the overall western livestock industry. Some materials included below do share trail and other data, but the intent is to list only trail-centered works. Since the various trails north from Texas originated following the Civil War, much of the primary material for this trail subject area falls after the terminal year, 1869, of this finding aid. Readers should consult the bibliographies shown below for post-1869 sources.

Bibliographies

Adams, Ramon. THE RAMPAGING HERD.

Fritz, Henry E. "The Cattlemen's Frontier in the Trans-Mississippi West."

Jager, Ronald G. "The Chisholm Trail's Mountain of Words."

Towne, Charles W., and Edward N. Wentworth. SHEDHERD'S EMPIRE.

Illustrations

Flanagan, Sue. TRAILING THE LONGHORNS.

Paul, Virginia. THIS WAS SHEEP RANCHING.

Livestock-General

Anshutz, M. W. Letters. (Cattle)

Atkinson, J. H. "Cattle Drives from Arkansas to California."

Baxter, John O. "Las Carneradas: New Mexico's Sheep Trade to Chihuahua and Durango before 1846."

Baydo, Gerald R. "Cattle Ranching in Territorial New Mexico."

Benson, Mr. and Mrs. Robert R. "Trinchera Plaza." (Cattle - Goodnight)

Brayer, Garnet M., and Herbert O. Brayer. AMERICAN CATTLE TRAILS: 1546 - 1900.

Burns, Louis F. "Old Trails across Northern Osage County." (Oklahoma)

Chrisman, Harry E. LOST TRAILS OF THE CIMARRON. (Cattle)

Clough, L. W. "Sheep Follow Advancing Golden Frontier."

Cureton, Gilbert. "The Cattle Trail to California, 1840 - 1860."

Dallam, Richard. Diary and Journal. (Cattle)

Demke, Siegried. CATTLE DRIVES OF EARLY CALIFORNIA.

Dick, Everett. "The Long Drive."

Drago, Harry S. GREAT AMERICAN CATTLE TRAILS.

Erskine, Ignatius. Journals. (Cattle)

Etulain, Richard W. "Archer B. Gilfillan: Scholarly Sheepherder of South Dakota."

Ewing, Floyd F. "James H. Baker: Cattleman and Trail-Driver."

Frantz, Joe B. "Hoof and Horn on the Chisholm Trail."

Galenson, David. "Origins of the Long Drive."

————. "The Profitability of the Long Drive."

Gard, Wayne. "The Impact of the Cattle Trails."

————. "Up the Chisholm Trail."

Gilfillan, Archer B. SHEEP.

Gross, Kelly, Business Records: 1863 - 1954. (Sheep)

Haley, J. Evetts. "A Survey of Texas Cattle Drives to the North, 1866 - 1895."

Harris, Charles W. "Pathway to the Southwest." (Cattle)

Haskett, Bert. "Early History of the Cattle Industry in Arizona."

Hollister, W. W. Statement. (Sheep)

Jameson, Henry B. MIRACLE OF THE CHISHOLM TRAIL.

Jensen, James M. "Cattle Drives from the Ranchos to the Gold Fields of California."

Jordan, Terry G. TRAILS TO TEXAS.

Kenner, Charles. "The Origins of the 'Goodnight' Trail."

King, Evelyn. WOMEN ON THE CATTLE TRAIL.

Kingston, C. S. "Introduction of Cattle into the Pacific Northwest."

Kupper, Winifred. THE GOLDEN HOOF. (Sheep)

Laing, F. W. "Some Pioneers of the Cattle Industry." (Canada)

Loomis, Noel M. "Early Cattle Trails in Southern Arizona."

Love, Clara M. "History of the Cattle Industry in the Southwest."

McCoy, Joseph G. HISTORIC SKETCHES OF THE CATTLE TRADE.

McCue, James S. TWENTY-ONE YEARS IN CALIFORNIA.

MacEwan, John G. BLAZING THE OLD CATTLE TRAIL.

Meadows, Don. THE CATTLE DRIVES OF JOSEPH E. PLEASANTS.

Mecham, Everett H. "The History of the Sheep Industry in Utah."

Moore, Bonnie C. "Northern Drives of Texas Cattle after 1866."

Oliphant, J. Orin. "Cattle through Snoqualmie Pass."

————. "Cattle Trade Northwest to Montana."

————. ON THE CATTLE RANGES OF THE OREGON COUNTRY.

Parker, L. Mayland. "Economic Geography of Utah's Sheep Industry."

Pelzer, Louis. "Trails of the Trans-Mississippi Cattle Frontier."

Potter, Jack M. CATTLE TRAILS OF THE OLD WEST.

Pulling, Hazel A. "A History of California's Range-Cattle Industry, 1770 - 1912."

Rath, Charles. THE RATH TRAIL.

Reed, Lester. OLD TIME CATTLEMEN AND THE ANZA-BORREGO AREA.

Sands, Frank. A PASTORAL PRINCE.

Sawyer, Byrd W. NEVADA NOMADS.

Shefrin, Jack A. "The Chisholm Trail."

Shellenberger, Robert. "Missus McLellan and the Ragtown Rustlers."

Skaggs, Jimmy M. "Between Supply and Demand."

————. THE CATTLE TRAILING INDUSTRY.

————. "The Economic Impact of Trailing."

————. "The Route of the Great Western (Dodge City) Cattle Trail."

Sypolt, Charles M. "Keepers of the Rocky Mountain Flocks."

Towne, Charles W., and Edward N. Wentworth. SHEPHERD'S EMPIRE.

"Wagon Trains and Cattle Herds on the Trail in the 1850's."

Walker, Don D. "Longhorns Come to Utah."

Wentworth, Edward N. AMERICA'S SHEEP TRAILS. Best sheep study. Good bibliography.

————. "Eastward Sheep Drives from California and Oregon."

————. "Wanderings of the Woolies."

Wilson, James A. "West Texas Influence on the Early Cattle Industry of Arizona."

Worcester, Don. THE CHISHOLM TRAIL.

Yost, Nellie S. THE CALL OF THE RANGE.

1849

Gibson, J. W. RECOLLECTIONS OF A PIONEER.

1850

Loveland, Cyrus. CALIFORNIA.

1851 & 1852
Gibson, J. W. RECOLLECTIONS OF A PIONEER.

1853
Bailey, Washington. TRIP TO CALIFORNIA.
Cole, James H. "James Harvey Cole's Story."
"Jonathan Rea I."
Reber, Thomas. Journal.

1854
Bell, James G. TEXAS-CALIFORNIA CATTLE TRAIL.
Erskine, M. H. "A Cattle Drive from Texas to California."
Gibson, J. W. RECOLLECTIONS OF A PIONEER.
Reber, Thomas. "The Journal of Thomas Reber."
Richey, James H. A TRIP ACROSS.
Swain, Ben. Original Manuscript.

1855
Hunt, James. Reminiscence.

1857
Aldridge, Sarnigan. Diary.
Hamilton, James G. MY DEAR CORNELIA.

1858
Putnam, Royal P. JOURNAL.

1863
Fourr, J. William. Manuscripts.

1865
Gibson, J. W. RECOLLECTIONS OF A PIONEER.
Kimball, Gorham G. "Trailing Sheep."

1866
Duffield, George C. "Driving Cattle from Texas to Iowa, 1866."

1867
Hunter, Thomas T. Early Days in Arizona.

1868
Johnson, M. R. Reminiscence.

1869
Baker, J. H. "A Trail Driver Who Kept a Diary."
Johnson, M. R. Reminiscence.
Westerman, Pleasant B. "How I Got to California."

MAIL

This subject category lists sources describing mail service in western North America during 1841 - 1869. Many of these items are also involved in staging, express services and government. Readers should also check those subjects for mail-related data. Primary materials are concentrated at the National Archives (Office of the Postmaster General) and The Library, Post Office Department, both in Washington, DC. There are several appropriate periodicals that regularly publish western mail studies, in and out of print, and readers can expect to find western mail strengths in LA POSTA and WESTERN EXPRESS. Those interested in western philatelic rather than trail interests should scan each issue of those two publications.

Illustrations (Covers and Stamps)
Beals, David T. "The Leavenworth and Pikes Peak Express Companies."
Coburn, Jesse E. LETTERS OF GOLD: CALIFORNIA POSTAL HISTORY THROUGH 1869.
Dietrich, F. J. "Early California in a Mail Bag."

Fox, John A. CALIFORNIA AND WESTERN EXPRESS COVERS.
Johnson, H. Parker. "Jones & Russell's Leavenworth and Pike's Express Company."
Nathan, Mel C., and W. S. Boggs, THE PONY EXPRESS.
Schwimmer, Jerome. "Los Angeles Covers."
Sotheby Parke. WESTERN EXPRESSES POSTAL HISTORY.

General
AMOUNTS PAID FOR OVERLAND MAIL SERVICE, 1858 TO 1868.
Barnard, Helen M. THE CHORPENNING CLAIM.
Bayard, William. MEMORIAL OF WILLIAM BAYARD.
Berthold, Victor. "Franks of the Western Express Companies."
_____. "Gregory's Expresses." Not Seen.
_____. HANDBOOK OF WELLS FARGO HANDSTAMPS.
_____. "Todd's Express Companies."
Brice, James. REMINISCENCES OF TEN YEARS EXPERIENCE.
Barker, Emerson. "Western Mail Trails."
Braatz, Ned E. "Some Aspects of Postal Extension into the West."
Case, Chester. "Development of Roads between Oregon and California."
Coburn, Jesse L. LETTERS OF GOLD: CALIFORNIA POSTAL HISTORY THROUGH 1869.
De Quille, Dan. SNOW-SHOE THOMPSON.
Deaville, A. S. THE COLONIAL POSTAL SYSTEMS AND POSTAGE STAMPS OF VANCOUVER ISLAND AND BRITISH COLUMBIA, 1849 - 1871.
Dietrich, F. J. "Early California in a Mail Bag."
Drake, J. Raman. "Howard Egan."
Durley, Jeff. Diary.
Elwell, R. F. "Story of the Overland Mail."
Fine, Harry L. "Fort Laramie and the Historic Postal Markings."
_____. "Fort Laramie: Post Office in the Old West."
_____. "Montana Postal Mark."
Fox, John A. CALIFORNIA AND WESTERN EXPRESS COVERS.
Frederick, James V. "Holliday Overland Mail."
Graves, W. H. "A True Narrative."
Gray, John S. "Northern Overland Pony Express."
Hafen, Leroy. THE OVERLAND MAIL.
_____. "Overland Mail to the Pacific Coast, 1849 - 69."
Hahn, Mannel. "Communications with the West."
Harlow, Alvin F. OLD POST BAGS.
Hertz, A. Jay. "Via Placerville."
Hicks, Frank L. "Birth of the West's Overland Mail."
Hicks, John Edward. "James Brice, Overland Mail Driver."
Hodgkins, Pilsbury. "The Story of Pilsbury Hodgkins."
Holbrook, J. TEN YEARS AMONG THE MAIL BAGS.
James, Thomas L. "Development of the Overland Mail Service."
Knapp, Edward S. PONY EXPRESS.
Langdon, Lynn. "William Carter."
Letter from the Secretary of War. "Volunteer Troops to Guard Overland and Other Mails from 1861 to 1866."
Little, Feramorz. "Mail Service across the Plains."
Mackinnon, William P. "Buchanan Spoils System."
Mills, James. "Journalistic Remarks on the Los Angeles and Tucson Mails."
Nathan, Mel C. FRANKS OF WESTERN EXPRESSES.
Needham, Henry C., and Victor M. Berthold, "Hand-Stamped Franks."
Nettels, Curtis. "The Overland Mail Issue during the Fifties."
"Newspaper Transcripts [Deseret News, 1854 - 62] on Postal Service."
O'Fallon, John, et al. "Overland Mail to California."
"Overland Mail Adventure."
"Postmaster General's Order Relating to Route of the Overland Mail Company, March 12, 1861."
"Postmen of a Century."
Reeder, Ray M. MORMON TRAIL.
Smith, Charles L. "The History of the United States Overland Mail to 1869."
Sotheby Parke. WESTERN EXPRESSES POSTAL HISTORY.
Taylor, Morris F. "The Mail Station and the Military at Camp on Pawnee Fork, 1859 - 1860."

Gray, John S. "The Salt Lake Hockaday Mail."

Konwiser, Harry M. "Utah Mail."

_____. "Warren's Mormon Express."

"Mail Routes, Utah, 1862 - 1866."

McBride, Ralph L. "Utah Mail Service."

"Newspaper Transcripts [Deseret News, 1854 - 62] on Postal Service."

McBride, Ralph L. "Utah Mail Service before 1869."

"Mail Routes, Utah, 1862-1866."

"Newspaper Transcripts [DESERET NEWS, 1854-62] on Postal Service."

Porath, Joseph H. "Early Mail Service in Utah."

Reeder, Ray M. "The Mormon Trail."

Schindler, Harold. "B. Y. Express: The Company that Helped Start a War."

_____. "Utah's First Post Office and Postmaster."

Thorp, Raymond W. "The Overland Mail."

Todd, John R. "An Escape from the Mormons."

Whall, Les. THE SALT LAKE CITY POST OFFICE, 1849 - 1869.

_____. "To Brownsville, Twice a Week."

Williams, Eleen T. UTAH HISTORY OF POST OFFICES.

Washington

Ernest, Clement S. "History in a Mail Pouch."

Prosch, Thomas W. "Washington Mail Routes in 1857."

1848

Bayley, Thomas S. "First Overland Mail Bag."

1862

Craig, James. "Letters of 1862 Reveal Indian Trouble along the Overland Mail - Route."

MAPS

Citations below indicate to the reader that the item includes maps of good to superior quality. Also check the "Map" subcategory for individual trail or subject indexes.

General

Dunlop, Richard. GREAT TRAILS OF THE WEST.

Gardiner, James F. INDIAN TRIBES AND TRAPPER TRAILS.

Hanson, Robert A. "Notes on the Trail of the Pony Express."

Hulbert, Archer B. CROWN COLLECTION OF AMERICAN MAPS.

Jackson, W. Turrentine. WAGON ROADS WEST.

KEELER'S MAP FROM THE MISSISSIPPI RIVER TO THE PACIFIC OCEAN.

Koepp, Donna P. EXPLORATION AND MAPPING OF THE AMERICAN WEST.

Ladd, Richard S. MAPS SHOWING EXPLORERS' ROUTES, TRAILS AND EARLY ROADS IN THE UNITED STATES.

Layne, J. Gregg. WESTERN WAYFARING.

Mansfield, Philip. PRELIMINARY MAP OF THE OREGON TRAIL AND THE PRINCIPAL PIONEER ROUTES TO CALIFORNIA.

Martin, J. C., and Robert S. Martin. MAPS OF TEXAS AND THE SOUTHWEST, 1513-1900.

Mattes, Merrill J. SCOTT'S BLUFF.

_____, and Paul C. Henderson. Map Collection.

Moody, Ralph. STAGECOACH WEST.

Reinhartz, Dennis, and Charles C. Colley. THE MAPPING OF THE AMERICAN SOUTHWEST.

Settle, Raymond and Mary. WAR DRUMS AND WAGON WHEELS.

Wheat, Carl I. MAPPING THE AMERICAN WEST.

_____. MAPPING THE TRANSMISSISSIPPI WEST.

Wislizenus, A. MEMOIR.

Applegate Trail

Helfrich, Devere. "The Applegate Trail."

_____, and Thomas Hunt. EMIGRANT TRAILS WEST.

Inman, Loris F., and Creat I. Marsh. "Road across Lane County, Oregon."

Smith, John E. "Applegate Trail in Lane County."

Arkansas

ROADS, OLD TRAILS, TRACES, AND HISTORICAL PLACES OF ARKANSAS.

Barlow Cutoff

Lucia, Ellis. "Sam Barlow's Astounding Road."

Meacham, Walter. BARLOW ROAD.

Bradshaw Trail

Beattie, George W. "Development of Travel between Southern Arizona and Los Angeles."

Johnston, Francis J. THE BRADSHAW TRAIL.

McKinney, J. Wilson. "Gold Builds a Road."

Weight, Harold and Lucille. "Forgotten Road to Gold."

Woodward, Arthur. "Gold on the Colorado."

Butterfield Overland Trail

Ahnert, Gerald T. RETRACING THE BUTTERFIELD OVERLAND TRAIL THROUGH ARIZONA.

"Butterfield Stage Route, Tulare County, California."

"Committee Report Butterfield Overland Map."

Leadabrand, Russ. "The Butterfield Spread." Southern CA.

_____. "Along the Butterfield Trail." Southern CA.

Lemke, W. J., and Ted R. Worley. BUTTERFIELD OVERLAND IN ARKANSAS.

Likes, Robert C. "Along the Butterfield Trail."

"A Newly Discovered Map of the Butterfield Overland Stage Route."

Spindt, H. A. "The Butterfield Stage Route from Los Angeles to Porterville."

Tuttle, Joseph. "Map of Arizona Territory."

Williams, J. W. "The Butterfield Overland Mail Road across Texas."

Wright, Muriel H. "The Butterfield Overland Mail One Hundred Years Ago." Oklahoma.

_____. "Historic Places on the Old Stage Line from Fort Smith to Red River."

California Route

Graydon, Charles K. TRAILS OF THE FIRST WAGONS OVER THE SIERRA NEVADA.

Hunt, Thomas. GHOST TRAILS TO CALIFORNIA.

Latta, Frank F. EL CAMINO VIEJO. Los Angeles to San Francisco.

Olson, Bert H. "Forty Mile Desert."

Rhoades, Earl. "Maps Verdi to Summit Valley."

Sitgreaves, Lorenzo. "Map of Posts along the Platte and Little Blue Rivers."

U.S. Bureau of Land Management. GUIDE TO THE LANDER CUTOFF.

Wheat, Carl I. THE MAPS OF THE CALIFORNIA GOLD REGION, 1848 - 1857.

Wiltsee, Ernest A. THE PIONEER MINER AND THE PACK MULE EXPRESS.

California Route-Route

Bidwell, John. JOHN BIDWELL'S TRIP TO CALIFORNIA.

_____. "Route Travelled from Cairo, Illinois to Reach California in 1841."

Kelly, Charles. "First Emigrant Train." Soda Springs to the Humboldt.

Miller, David E. "The First Wagon Train to Cross Utah, 1841."

California Route-1842

Fremont, John C. EXPLORATION OF THE COUNTRY LYING BETWEEN THE MISSOURI RIVER AND THE ROCKY MOUNTAINS.

California Route-1846

Davidson, A. F. Maps.

_____. "Hudspeth's Cutoff."
_____. "The Oregon Trail."
Dicken, Samuel N. PIONEER TRAILS OF THE OREGON COAST.
Franzwa, Gregory. MAPS OF THE OREGON TRAIL.
Mansfield, Philip. PRELIMINARY MAP OF THE OREGON TRAIL.
Menefee, Leah C., and Lowell Tiller. "Cutoff Fever." (Meek Cutoff)
Oregon State Highway Dept. ROUTE OF THE OREGON TRAIL FORT BOISE, IDAHO TO THE DALLES, OREGON.
THE OREGON TRAIL: A POTENTIAL ADDITION TO THE NATIONAL TRAILS SYSTEM.
Preston, R. N. HISTORICAL OREGON.
Stout, Ray L. "Oregon Trail Material."

Oregon-to-California
Cramer, Howard L. "California-Oregon Trail."

Overland Stage Trail
Root, Frank A., and William E. Connelley. OVERLAND STAGE.

Pacific Northwest
Van Arsdale, Perry C. WEST-NORTHWEST.

Pony Express
Denny, Arthur J. "Pony Express Trail."
Hanson, Robert A. "Notes on the Trail."
Mattes, Merrill J., and Paul C. Henderson, "The Pony Express: Across Nebraska from St. Joseph to Fort Laramie."

Red River
Belde, Walter W. "Red River Trails."
OXCART TRAILS IN MINNESOTA AND NORTH DAKOTA IN THE 1850'S.

Salt Lake Corridor
Koenig, George. BEYOND THIS PLACE THERE BE DRAGONS.

Santa Fe Trail
Brown, William E. THE SANTA FE TRAIL.
Burr, Eugene P. "Aubry Cutoff."
Stocking, Hobart E. THE ROAD TO SANTA FE.

Simpson Trail
Simpson, James H. REPORT OF EXPLORATIONS ACROSS THE GREAT BASIN.
Welton, R. W. MAP AUSTIN TO GREAT SALT LAKE CITY, 1866.
Wheelock, Harrison. GUIDE AND MAP OF REESE RIVER AND HUMBOLDT.

Smoky Hill Trail
Lee, Wayne, and Howard Raynesford. TRAILS OF THE SMOKY HILL.

Sonora Trail
Leadabrand, Russ. "Across the Colorful Sonora Pass Country."

Truckee Cutoff
Waggoner, W. W. "Donner Party and Relief Hill."

Utah
Crampton, Gregory C. "Utah's Spanish Trail."
Kimball, Stanley B. DISCOVERING MORMON TRAILS.
Knight, Hal, and Stanley B. Kimball. 111 DAYS TO ZION. (Excellent survey)
Morgan, Dale L. UTAH'S HISTORIC TRAILS.
Morgan, Nicholas G. MAP OF GREAT SALT LAKE CITY SHOWING THE ROUTE TAKEN BY THE FIRST GROUP OF EMIGRANT PIONEER WAGONS.
MORMON PIONEER NATIONAL HISTORIC TRAIL.
Smart, William B. EXPLORING THE PIONEER TRAIL. (Wasatch

Crossing)

Washington
Kaiser, Verle G. "Straight as an Arrow: The 'Kentuck Trail'."
Preston, R. N. EARLY WASHINGTON.

Wyoming
Bagley, William L. MAPS OF EMIGRANT TRAIL THROUGH WYOMING.
Kimball, Stanley B. "Another Road to Zion."
Urbanek, Mae. GHOST TRAILS OF WYOMING.

MEDICAL ASPECTS

Barrett, James T. "Cholera in Missouri."
Bauer, John E. "Health Factors in the Gold Rush Era."
_____. "The Health Seeker in the Westward Movement."
Bill, Joseph H. "Notes on Arrow Wounds."
Divett, Robert T. "Cholera Epidemics and the Mormons."
Doetsch, Raymond N. JOURNEY.
Dunlop, Richard. DOCTORS OF THE AMERICAN FRONTIER.
Griffenhagen, George B., and William C. Felter. OREGON TRAIL OF PHARMACY.
Groh, George W. GOLD FEVER.
Knox, Reuben. A MEDIC FORTYNINER.
Lester, Thomas B. MEDICINE ON THE SANTA FE TRAIL.
Lorenzo, Anthony J. "Scurvy in the Gold Rush."
Mattes, Merrill J. "The Gold Rush Mania: Victims and Survivors."
Morrell, Joseph R. "Medicine of the Pioneer Period in Utah."
Olch, Peter D. "Treading the Elephant's Tail: Medical Problems on the Overland Trails."
Pickard, Madge E., and R. Carlyle Buley. THE MIDWEST PIONEER.
Pizer, Irwin H. "Medical Aspects of the Westward Migrations, 1830-60."
Powers, Ramon, and Gene Younger. "Cholera on the Overland Trails."
_____. "Cholera on the Plains: The Epidemic of 1867."
Read, Georgia W. "Diseases, Drugs and Doctors."
Toomey, Noxon. "Mountain Fever and Spotted Fever of the Rocky Mountains."
Unrau, William E. "Epidemic Disease and the Impact of the Santa Fe Trail on the Kansa Indians."
Wayman, John H. A DOCTOR ON THE CALIFORNIA TRAIL.

MILITARY

Military references include only those documents directly involved with trails and/or emigration. Items with no immediate relation to trails, overland emigration, or staging-freighting, have been excluded. This distinction ignores most of the Indian wars literature. Also, the materials regarding military forts and other sites not located on trail networks have been excluded. There exist bibliographies that direct readers to the larger field of military history in western North America.

Bibliographies
Reber, Bruce. THE U.S. ARMY AND THE INDIAN WARS, 1860 - 1898.

Illustrations
"The Western Cavalryman: Color Portfolio."

Forts-General
Frazer, Robert W. FORTS OF THE WEST.
Hart, Herbert M. TOUR GUIDE TO OLD WESTERN FORTS. (Good survey, with extensive bibliography)

General
Avillo, Philip J. "Fort Mojave (Arizona) Territory: 1859 - 1865."

PONY EXPRESS

Bibliographies

SOCIAL, RACIAL AND FUNCTIONAL TOPICS

Bibliographies

Climate

Entertainment

Ethnicity and Race

Food

General

TOLD BY THE PIONEERS. (Oral interviews)
Torok, Theresa M. "The Social Aspects of Life on the Oregon Trail."
Walkup, F. P. "Utah Pioneer Dress, 1847 - 1875."
Ward, Frances E. FRANKIE'S JOURNAL. (Preparation for trip)
Werner, Fred. "Mystery Graves on the Oregon Trail."
McDermott, John F. "Up the Wide Missouri."

Graphics
Bennett, Debra S. "Dress of the Mormons, 1840 - 1860."
CHILDREN ON THE PLAINS.
Daniel, Janice P. "Dust On Their Petticoats."

Religious Influences
Adams, B. H. Autobiography.
"Boy's Funeral."
Fee, Art. "The Most Unique Crossing on the Oregon Trail."
Hendricks, Robert J. BETHEL AND AURORA.
Sawadsky, Joanne M. "True Wayfaring Christians."

Romance and Courtship
Peltier, Jerome. "Romeo and Juliet on the Oregon Trail."
Sheller, Roscoe. "Wagontrain Bride."
Steiner, Stan. "Love in a Covered Wagon."

Women and the Family
Allen, Martha M. TRAVELING WEST.
_____. "Women in the West."
Apostol, Jane. "Gold Rush Widow."
Armitage, Susan. "Reluctant Pioneers."
Bennett, Elmer F. "Pioneer Women in the Rush to the Rockies."
Brooks, Elisha. A PIONEER MOTHER OF CALIFORNIA
Brown, Sharon A. "Women on the Overland Trails."
Brown, Terry. "Emigrants' Guide for Women."
Carter, Kate B. "Women of the Mormon Battalion and the Mississippi Saints."
Curtis, Mary. "Amelia Bloomer's Curious Costume."
Daniel, Janice P. "Dust on their Petticoats."
Douthit, Mary O. A SOUVENIR OF WESTERN WOMEN.
Faragher, Johnny M. "Men and Women's Work on the Overland Trail."
_____. "Midwestern Families in Motion."
_____. WOMEN AND MEN ON THE OVERLAND TRAIL.
_____, and Christine Stansell. "Women and Their Families on the Overland Trail."
Faulkner, Hazel P. "Ladies on the Overland Trail."
Fischer, Christiane. LET THEM SPEAK FOR THEMSELVES.
Fowler, William. WOMAN ON THE AMERICAN FRONTIER.
Fryer, Judith. "The Anti-Mythical Journey: Westering Women's Diaries and Letters."
_____. "Recovering the Garden: Women's Fantasies and Experiences of the Western Frontier."
Furniss, Kate. From Prairie to Pacific. (Women's tasks)
Gherman, Dawn L. "From Parlor to Tepee."
Godfrey, Kenneth and Audrey. "The Pioneer Woman."
Guerin, Mrs. E. J. MOUNTAIN CHARLEY.
Haines, Francis D. "Goldilocks on the Oregon Trail."
Holmes, Kenneth L. COVERED WAGON WOMEN. Recommended.
Jeffrey. Julie R. FRONTIER WOMEN.
Kesselman, Amy. "Diaries and Reminiscences of Women."
Kimball, Stanley B. "Equal Rights on the Pioneer Trail."
King, Evelyn. WOMEN ON THE CATTLE TRAIL.
Luchetti, Cathy, and Carol Olwell. WOMEN OF THE WEST.
Mariager, Dagmar. "Nomadic Experiences of a Frontierswoman."
Moulton, Emeline M. Letters. (Troubles of a trail "widow")
Moynihan, Ruth B. "Children and Young People on the Overland Trail."
Munkres, Robert L. "Pioneers in Petticoats."
_____. "Wives, Mothers, Daughters: Women's Life in the Roads West."
Myres, Sandra. HO FOR CALIFORNIA.

_____. "I Too Have Seen the Elephant: Women on the Overland Trails."
_____. WESTERING WOMEN.
Peavy, Linda, and Ursula Smith. "Women in Waiting in the Westward Movement." (Trail "widows")
Powers, Mary R. A WOMAN'S OVERLAND JOURNAL.
Pringle, Catherine O. "Seven Orphans."
Read, Georgia W. "Women and Children on the Trail."
Riley, Glenda. "The Frontier in Process: Iowa's Trail Women as a Paradigm."
_____. "Frontierswomen's Changing Views of Indians in the Trans-Mississippi West."
_____. WOMEN AND INDIANS ON THE FRONTIER, 1825 - 1915.
_____. WOMEN ON THE AMERICAN FRONTIER.
Riney, Pamela L. "Overland to California and Oregon, 1849 - 1853."
Romani, Margaret W. "Unluckiest of the Forty-Niners." (Children)
Ross, Nancy W. "Aprons to their Eyes: Women's Role in Westward Migrations."
_____. WESTWARD THE WOMEN.
Rotter, Andrew J. "Matilda for Gods Sake Write."
Schlissel, Lillian. "Diaries of Frontier Women."
_____. "Mothers and Daughters on the Western Frontier."
_____. "Women's Diaries on the Western Frontier."
_____. WOMEN'S DIARIES OF THE WESTWARD JOURNEY.
Shull, Teri. "Tabitha Moffat Brown."
Smith, Helen K. WITH HER OWN WINGS.
Solomon, Margaret. "A Bloomer Girl Conquers Pikes Peak."
_____. "A Study of Feminism as a Motif in "A Journey to Pike's Peak and New Mexico."
Thompson, Enid T. "The Ladies of Bent's Fort."
Tims, Melinda. "Pioneer Women."
Treckel, Paula A. "An Historiographical Essay: Women on the American Frontier."
Trulio, Beverly. "Anglo-American Attitudes Toward New Mexican Women."
Utley, Beverly. "They Made the West Worth Winning."
Williams, Carol. "Interaction between Women and Indians, 1845 - 1865."

STAGING AND EXPRESS SERVICE

This category combines both staging and express service since the two functions were often provided by a single firm. Transportation historians have also combined study of these two vital businesses in their publications. Where possible, subcategories will list sources for particular companies and make a distinction between staging and express service.

Bibliographies
Adams, Ramon. SIX-GUNS AND SADDLE LEATHER. (Stage holdups)
Rittenhouse, Jack. CARRIAGE HUNDRED: A BIBLIOGRAPHY ON HORSE-DRAWN TRANSPORTATION.

Maps
Moody, Ralph. STAGECOACH WEST.

Graphics
Borein, Edward. STAGECOACHES OF THE OLD WEST.
Carter, Kathryn T. STAGECOACH INNS OF TEXAS.
Clifford, Henry H. "Western Express."
Crawford, Jeanne R. WHEELS LED THE WAY.
Dines, Glen. OVERLAND STAGE.
Florin, Lambert. WESTERN WAGON WHEELS.
Forster, Dale E. OREGON EXPRESS COMPANIES.
"Gallery of Abbot-Downing Vehicles."
"Gathering of Stagecoaches."
Good, Donnie D. "Traveling Westward."

TRAIL PRESERVATION

These sources describe trail preservation and marking efforts beginning in the late 19th century and increasing substantially to date. Included are associated preservation activities such as reinactments, annual ceremonies and programs to translate trail history into tourist attractions.

Readers seeking contemporary guidebooks to specific trails or subsections should scan the following categories and individual trail indexes.

Stage/Freight Trails

Bostwick, Norris. "Camping on the Butterfield Trail."

"Butterfield Overland Mail, 1958 in Oklahoma."

Butterfield Overland Mail Centennial. "Scrapbook."

"Butterfield Stage Route." (Tule River Stage Station, Tulare County, CA)

Carley, Maurine. "Overland Stage Trail - Trek Nos. 1 through 3."

"Committee Report Butterfield Overland Mail."

Dunning, Harold M. THE OVERLAND TRAIL NORTH. (Berthoud, Colorado to Virginia Dale Station.)

Frizzell, John and Mildred. "A Stagecoach Reunion."

Hardesty, Donald L. ROCK CREEK STAGE STATION.

Leadabrand, Russ. "Along the Butterfield Trail." (Warner Springs to Vallecito)

Oneal, Ben G. Collection. (Centennial records)

Riney, W. A. "Retracing the Butterfield Trail."

Welch, Jack P. "Butterfield Overland Mail."

Welsh, Donald P. "The Butterfield Overland Centennial Observance."

_____. "The Butterfield Overland Mail Centennial in Missouri."

Utah and the Mormon Trail

Beesley, Clarissa A. "The Mormon Pioneer Caravan of 1931."

Burton, Alma P. THE MORMON TRAIL FROM VERMONT TO UTAH.

Cannon, D. James. CENTENNIAL CARAVAN: REINACTMENT OF THE ORIGINAL MORMON TREK.

Giles, John D. "Hike of 1917." (Henefer, UT to SLC)

_____. "The M.I.A. Preserves History."

Greene, Lida L. "Markers for Remembrance: The Mormon Trail."

Hardy, Clyde B. WASATCH TRAILS.

Kimball, Stanley B. "Another Road to Zion." (Laramie to Ft. Bridger)

_____. THE MORMON TRAIL.

MORMON PIONEER NATIONAL HISTORIC TRAIL.

MORMON TRAIL.

Sparks, Elmer. "A New Mystery on the Donner Trail." (1936 Salt Desert Trip)

Stoker, Kevin. "Trek along Original Trail Gives Taste of Pioneer Trail." (Henefer, UT to SLC)

Strebel, George. "Pioneer Trail Art Tour."

Utah Pioneer Trails and Landmarks Assn. CHARTING AND MARKING PIONEER TRAILS AND LANDMARKS, 1931.

Webb, Henry J. "The Last Trek across the Great Salt Desert." (1962 Salt Desert Trip)

Wilcox, Wayne. "Thirty-Six Miles of History." Trail over Wasatch Range into Salt Lake City.

TRAIN GOVERNMENT AND ADMINISTRATION

The following items represent primary and secondary sources containing details of internal administration of groups on the trail as well as legal agreements for property and behavior.

Applegate, Jesse. A DAY WITH THE COW COLUMN.

"Articles of Agreement, 1849."

"Articles of Agreement for an Expedition to California."

Berry, William and Thomas. Contract.

Brinckerhoff, Sidney R. "Passport to Mexico."

Clark, Harrison C. "The Organization of the Oregon Emigration Company."

Conlin, Joseph R. "Eating on the Rush."

Cotton, A. R. "Constitution Adopted by a Pioneer Train of 1849."

Cranfil, Isom. Diary.

Cranmer, Tom. RULES AND REGULATIONS.

"Organization of the Oregon Emigrating Companies."

Dale, Harrison C. "Organization of the Oregon Emigrating Companies."

Dana, Joseph. Papers.

Duffin, Reg. "The Miller-Tate Murder and the John F. Miller Grave."

Eccleston, Robert. OVERLAND TO CALIFORNIA.

Fancher, J. Diary.

Fulton, James F. Diary of a Wandering Pilgrim.

Grenberg, Allise O. "Wagon Train Government, 1840 - 1865."

Hannon, Jessie G. BOSTON-NEWTON. (Pre-trip details)

Hansen, Barbara J. "Wagon Train Governments."

"A Historic Document: A Contract for Transportation across the Plains to California (1852)."

Holman, Cyrus K. Journal. Member hanged for murder.

Hook, William H. Articles of Agreement to Finance and Finance and Furnish a Party Bound for California, February 19, 1850.

Hooper, John A. Papers. (Insurance policy, 1867)

Houston, Henrietta. "The Techniques of the Emigrant Trail."

Independent California Association of Lewiston, Illinois. Proceedings, 1849.

Johnston, Samuel M. Agreement for Transportation to Sacramento, CA.

Langum, David J. "Pioneer Justice on the Overland Trails."

Lockley, Fred. CAPTAIN TETHEROW. (Train constitution)

Madsen, Brigham D. "The Colony Guard."

Oakley, Francile B. "Arkansas' Golden Army of '49."

"Oregon Material." (Train regulations)

ORGANIZATIONAL JOURNAL.

Paschal, Albert G. Overland Trip.

Powers, Mary S. A WOMAN'S OVERLAND JOURNAL.

PREAMBLE AND CONSTITUTION OF THE COLONY GUARD.

Reid, John P. "Binding the Elephant."

_____. "Dividing the Elephant."

_____. "Governance of the Elephant."

_____. "Knowing the Elephant."

_____. LAW FOR THE ELEPHANT.

_____. "Paying for the Elephant."

_____. "Replenishing the Elephant."

_____. "Sharing the Elephant."

_____. "Tied to the Elephant."

Riddlemoser, Francis M. "The Organization of Groups of Overland Emigrants to California, 1849 - 1850."

Riney, Pamela L. "Overland to California and Oregon, 1849 - 1853."

Savannah Oregon Emigrating Company. THE ORGANIZATIONAL JOURNAL.

Sawadsky, Joanne M. "True Wayfaring Christians."

Shaffer, Leslie D. "Management of Wagon Trains."

Sommer, Jane H. "Outfitting for the West, 1849."

Taylor, P. A. M. "Emigrants' Problems in Crossing the West, 1830 - 1870."

Tucker, Ira. Biographical File. (Military pass issued during Civil War)

Van Schaick, Holmes D. Diary.

Wisconsin Blues. CONSTITUTION.

Wood, Joseph W. Journal.

Woods, Joseph W. Diary. I.

Wright, Williamson. "Bill of Items Required for a Trip by Land to California, Two Persons to a Wagon."

UTAH AND THE MORMONS

This category includes topical rather than trail-oriented references to Utah. See the MORMON TRAIL, OLD SPANISH TRAIL, SALT LAKE CUTOFF, and SALT LAKE CORRIDOR sections for other Utah sources.

Bibliographies

"Bibliography of Indexes to L.D.S. Sources and Utah Periodicals."

Bitton, Davis. GUIDE TO MORMON DIARIES AND AUTOBIOGRAPHIES.

CATALOGUE OF THESES AND DISSERTATIONS MORMONISM AND UTAH, COMPLETE TO JANUARY, 1970.

Flake, Chad. A MORMON BIBLIOGRAPHY: 1830 - 1930.

Jones, Ruth M., and Robert N. McMillan. "Utah Bibliography."

"List of Theses on Utah, Mormons and the West."

Graphics
Waters, William E. LIFE AMONG THE MORMONS.

Maps
Morgan, Dale L. UTAH'S HISTORIC TRAILS.
Morgan, Nicholas G. MAP OF GREAT SALT LAKE CITY.

General
Ahmanson, John. PRESENT DAY MOHAMED.
Barber, James V. "History of Highways in Utah."
Batty, Donald M. "History of Early Roads and Freighting in the Eastern Uintah Basin, 1672 - 1920."
Birge, Julius C. THE AWAKENING OF THE DESERT.
Bowles, Samuel. ACROSS THE CONTINENT.
Brooks, Juanita. THE MOUNTAIN MEADOWS MASSACRE.
Buchanan, James. MESSAGE OF THE PRESIDENT OF THE UNITED STATES.
Burton, Richard. CITY OF THE SAINTS.
Caldemeyer, Richard H. "The Overland Mail and Stage to Salt Lake City, 1847 - 1861."
Carter, Kate B. "Communication of Early Utah."
_____. "Development of Transportation."
_____. "Mississippi Saints."
_____. "Roads of Early Utah."
_____, and Clara B. Steele. MORMON BATTALION.
Chandless, William. A VISIT TO SALT LAKE.
Clark, William. A Trip Across. (Mormon attitudes during Mormon War)
Conway, Cornelius. THE UTAH EXPEDITION.
Cooke, Lucy R. CROSSING THE PLAINS.
Creer, Leland H. THE FOUNDING OF AN EMPIRE: THE EXPLORATION AND COLONIZATION OF UTAH, 1776 - 1856.
Davies, J. Kenneth. MORMON GOLD. (Utah and the Gold Rush)
Giles, John D. Papers.
Ginn, John I. Personal Recollections. II +.
Hafen, Leroy and Ann. THE UTAH EXPEDITION.
Hamblin, Jacob. JACOB HAMLIN.
Hayes, W. R. Diary.
Johnson, Ann W. "The Long Journey of a Mormon Girl." (Apostate family)
King, David S. MOUNTAIN MEADOWS MASSACRE.
Langworthy, Franklin. SCENERY.
Lass, William E. FROM THE MISSOURI TO THE GREAT SALT LAKE.
Loba, Jean F. Reminiscences. (Apostate family)
Ludlow, Fitz H. HEART OF THE CONTINENT.
MacDonald, William R. "The Impact of the California Gold Rush on the Mormons in the Great Basin, 1847 - 1857."
Madsen, Brigham D. GOLD RUSH SOJOURNERS IN SALT LAKE CITY.
Madsen, Brigham and Betty. "Diamond R Rolls Out."
Moore, Arlene M. "A Study of the Impact of the Gold Rush on the Mormon Community in Salt Lake City, 1849 - 1851."
Morgan, Dale L. THE GREAT SALT LAKE.
Patton, Annaleone D. CALIFORNIA MORMONS BY SAIL AND TRAIL.
Powers, Mary R. A WOMAN'S OVERLAND JOURNAL.
Slater, N. FRUITS OF MORMONISM.
Standing, A. R. "Through the Uintahs."
Stegner, Wallace. GATHERING OF ZION.
Thomas, J. J. "Recollections of the Mormon War."
Todd, John B. "An Escape from the Mormons." (Apostates flee Utah)
Wallace, William S. "Was Heap's Journal Plagiarized!." (Gunnison Route)
Wise, William. MASSACRE AT MOUNTAIN MEADOWS.

1846
Carter, Kate B., and Clara B. Steele. MORMON BATTALION.
Gudde, Erwin G. BIGLER'S CHRONICLE.

1850
Langworthy, Franklin. SCENERY. II.
Slater, Nellie B. FRUITS OF MORMONISM.

1852
Cooke, Lucy. CROSSING THE PLAINS.

1853
Wallace, William S. "Was Heap's Journal Plagiarized?" IV.

1855
Chandless, William. VISIT TO SALT LAKE. II.
Hayes, W. R. Diary. III +.
Todd, John R. "An Escape from the Mormons." IV.

1856
Powers, Mary R. A WOMAN'S OVERLAND JOURNAL. I.

1857
Brooks, Juanita. MOUNTAIN MEADOWS MASSACRE. II.
Buchanan, James. MESSAGE.
Clark, William. "A Trip across." II.
Conway, Cornelius. "The Utah Expedition."
Hafen, Leroy and Ann. UTAH EXPEDITION.
King, David S. MOUNTAIN MEADOWS MASSACRE.
Lass, William E. FROM THE MISSOURI.
Thomas, J. J. "Recollections." V.
Wise, William. MASSACRE AT MOUNTAIN MEADOWS.

1858
Loba, Jean F. Reminiscences. V-.

1860
Burton, Richard. CITY OF THE SAINTS. I.

1863
Ludlow, Fitz Hugh. HEART OF THE CONTINENT. II.

1864
Johnson, Ann W. "Long Journey." V-.

1865
Todd, John R. "Escape from the Mormons." IV.

1866
Birge, Julius. AWAKENING OF THE DESERT.

For the convenience of readers, the major trails have been divided into individual segments that represent independent portions of the western American trail network. Each of these segments is arranged in general and subject categories as well as by year. This format enables individuals to reach sources for trails other than the overall California or Oregon-bound routes. Readers interested only in the Mullan road or Old Spanish Trail, for example, can subsequently find in this listing sources for those and other segments. Trails are arranged alphabetically.

Refer to the Table of Contents for a complete list of trail segments.

APPLEGATE TRAIL

General

Applegate Family Papers.
Garaventa, Frank L. "The Applegate Trail." NV only.
Haines, Francis D., and Marjorie O'Harra. APPLEGATE TRAIL.
Hammond, Andy. "Peter Lassen and his Trail."
Helfrich, Devere. "Applegate Trail." Fine maps and photos.
_____. EMIGRANT TRAILS WEST.
Inman, Loris, and Creat Marsh. "The Road across Lane County, Oregon."
Kaliher, Michael. "The Applegate Trail, 1846 - 1853."
Meacham, Walter E. APPLEGATE TRAIL.
Miner, William D. "Jesse Applegate."
Nichols, Claude W. "The South Road."
Ochs, E. D. "The Opening of the New Southern Route into Oregon."
Olds, Eric. HISTORICAL DIARY. Humboldt River to Goose Lake.
Schnackenberg, Walter C. "The Southern Route into Oregon."
Smith, John E. "Applegate Trail in Lane County."
Steckel, Samuel. Diary. Not Seen.

1846-General

Burcham, Mildred B. "Old South Road."
Haines, Aubrey D. APPLEGATE TRAIL.
Ochs, E. D. "Opening of the New Southern Route into Oregon."
O'Harra, Marjorie. "The Exploration and Establishment of the Applegate Trail."
Smith, John E. "The Applegate Trail in Lane County."

1846

Applegate, Lindsay. "Notes and Reminiscences." II.
Brown, Tabitha. "A Brimfield Heroine." IV.
Carter, Tolbert. Pioneer Days. III.
Collins, Smith. SMITH COLLINS. III.
Cornwall, Joseph. Crossing the Plains. V.
Cornwall, Josephus A. "Cornwall Trek." IV.
Deady, Lucy A. Crossing the Plains. IV.
Garrison, A. E. LIFE. IV.
Garrison, Abraham H. Recollections. Not Seen.
Good, Daniel H. Letters. IV.
Henderson, Lucy A. "Young Adventure." II.
Holt, Thomas. Journal. II.
Moore, Narcissa C. "Captain Dunbar's." V.
Pringle, Catherine S. Diary. III.
Smith, William. Reminiscence. IV.
Stone, Buena C. "Southern Route into Oregon."
Thornton, J. Quinn. OREGON AND CALIFORNIA IN 1848. II.

1847

Davidson, T. L. "By the Southern Route." IV.
Findla, James. Statement. V.
Hopper, Charles. PILGRIMS OF THE PACIFIC. IV.
Hulin, Lester. 1847 Diary. III+.
Huntington, Hallie H. ALL THE WAY WEST. IV.
_____. "Cornelius Hills crosses the Plains." IV.
Moore, Alexander. Statement. V.
Morfitt, William. Memories. V-.

1848

Pettijohn, Isaac. Diary. III.

1849

McLane, Allen. "Leaves from a Pencil'd Journal." II.

1851

Bowen, James E. Diary. III.
Huntington, Hallie H. ALL THE WAY WEST. IV.
_____, "Cornelius Hills Crosses the Plains." IV.
Riddle, George W. EARLY DAYS. III.
Welsh, John P. Diaries. II.

1852

Constant, Isaac. "A Brief Review." III.
Gore, Ebenezer E. Reminiscences. IV.

1853

Beeson, Welborn. WELBORN BEESON. II+.
Hoffman, William. Journal. II.
Myer, Nathaniel. "Journey into Southern Oregon." III.
Royal, James H. Journal. III.
Stearns, Orson A. Appendix.
Taylor, Rachel. Overland Trip. III.
Welsh, John P. Diaries. II.
Williams, Velina A. "Diary." II.

1859

Brown, Alonzo F. AUTOBIOGRAPHY. IV.
Cummings, Charles J. Diary. II+.

1860

Piper, Alexander. "Alexander Piper's Reports." III.

1861

Freeman, Olga. "Fortune Lost in Cattle Drive." IV.

BARLOW ROAD

This less-known trail enabled emigrants to reach the Willamette Valley across the Cascade Range.

General

Bailey, Walter. "The Barlow Road."
Baker, Glen, et al. "Barlow Road."
BARLOW ROAD.
Beckham, Stephen D. "The Barlow Road."
Lucia, Ellis. "Sam Barlow's Astounding Road."
Meacham, Walter. BARLOW ROAD.
Meyers, E. L. BARLOW TOLL ROAD, 1846 - 1919.
Stone, Buena C. "Route of the Barlow Road."
Wilkins, Mary B. "Samuel Kimbrough Barlow."

Maps

Lucia, Ellis. "Sam Barlow's Astounding Road."
Meacham, Walter. BARLOW ROAD.

1842

Matthieu, Francis X. "Reminiscences." IV. (Variant of later trail).

1845

Bacon, John M. Narrative. V.
Cummins, Sarah J. AUTOBIOGRAPHY. IV.
Howell, John E. Diary. III.
Palmer, Joel. JOURNAL. I.
Smith, Moses I. Memoirs. IV.

Wilkes, L. E. BY AN OREGON PIONEER FIRESIDE. V.

1846
Cox, John T. Reminiscences. V.
McBride, John R. Overland. II.

1847
Brown, Joseph H. Autobiography. III.
Cory, Benjamin. Crossing the Plains. II.
Geer, Calvin. My Trip. IV.
Harden, Absolom. Trail Diary. II.
Hunt, G. W. A HISTORY. V.
Pettijohn, Isaac. Diary. II.

1848
Anderson, William W. Diary. III.
Cleaver, Benjamin. Diary. II.
Porter, William. Diary. III.
Root, Riley. JOURNAL. III.

1849
Applegate, Virginia W. Recollections. V-.
Cross, Osborne. MARCH OF THE MOUNTED RIFLEMEN. I.
Hobart, Emaline. "An Account of the Fletchers' Crossing." V.
McWilliams, John. RECOLLECTIONS. III.
Pease, David E. Diary. II.
Watson, William J. JOURNAL OF AN OVERLAND JOURNEY. II.

1850
Frush, William H. Diary. II.
James, Samuel. Diary. IV.
Scroggs, William L. "To the Gold Fields." V.
Turner, Walter H. A Trip across the Plains. II.

1851
Alden, Wyllis. ANCESTORS AND DESCENDANTS. IV.
Brandt, Charles A. TO OREGON WITH OX TEAMS. II.
Clark, Alvah. "Diary." Not Seen.
Crawford, Charles H. SCENES. III.
Crawford, P. V. "Across the Plains." III.
From Lake Erie to the Pacific. IV.
Gay, James W. Trail Diary. IV.
Hadley, Amelia H. Journal. II.
Hadley, E. Amelia. "Diary." II.
James, John R. "Autobiography." Not Seen.
Johnson, John L. Diary. II.
Johnson, Neil. Excerpts. V.
Sengstacken, Agnes R. DESTINATION, WEST! III.
Stout, Samuel. Diary. III.
Thomson, Jeremiah B. Early Days in Oregon. III.
Williams, Elijah. Letter. IV.
Williams, Lucia L. "A Letter." III.

1852
Angell, Susan P. "Sketch." V.
Applegate, Mary. ON TO OREGON. III.
Byers, William N. "Oregon Odyssey." II.
Clark, Wanda. "History of Nirom Hawley." IV.
Coburn, Catherine. Narrative. IV.
Conyers, E. W. "Diary." II+.
Duniway, Abigail S. "Journal." II.
Fox, Jared. Diary. I.
Gillette, Martha. OVERLAND TO OREGON. IV.
Goodrich, William A. Diary. III+.
Hanna, Esther. CANVAS CARAVAN. III.
Hill, Elizabeth F. UNDAUNTED PIONEERS. IV.
Humphrey, L. Manuscript Journal. III.
Jared, Israel. "Trip across Nebraska." V-.

Kearns, John T. Journal. II.
Kennedy, William C. "Westward Kennedys." IV.
Kerns, John T. Journal. II.
McKieran, John S. Journal. II+.
Moreland, Jesse. Diary. III.
Palmer, Harriet S. CROSSING. V.
Robinson, Benjamin F. Diary. Not Seen.
Scott, Abigail J. "Diary Narrative." II.
Scott, John T. "Ox Team." V.
Sharp, Leslie M. Diary. III.
Sharp, James M. EARLY RECOLLECTIONS. IV.
Sharp, Joe H. "Recollections." Not Seen.
Starbuck, Edith. CROSSING THE PLAINS. IV.
Stillman, Jay. Recollections. III.
Todd, Abbott. Sketch. V.
Todd, Mary E. ON TO OREGON! III.
Wallace, Edward P. Autobiography. IV.
White, Francis B. "Trip." IV.
Woodruff, S. W. Journal. III.

1853
Dinwiddie, David or John. OVERLAND. III.
Dunning, Ira S. Journal. III.
Gaylord, Orange. "Diary." IV.
Goltra, Elizabeth. JOURNAL OF TRAVEL. II.
Hamilton, Ezra M. Reminiscences. Not Seen.
Handsaker, Samuel. Autobiography. III+.
Kennedy, G. W. THE PIONEER CAMPFIRE. IV.
Knight, Amelia S. "Diary." II.
Luper, John. Diary. IV.
Mossman, Isaac. PONY EXPRESSMAN'S RECOLLECTIONS. V.
Smith, John. Diary. III.
Stuart, Grace and Reginald. CALVIN B. WEST. III.
Taylor, George N. Diary. III+.
Washburn, Catherine A. JOURNAL. III.
West, G. M. Portion of his Memoirs. IV.
Woodcock, William C. Diary. III.

1854
Condit, Sylvanus. Diary. III.
Kirkpatrick, Thomas J. STORY. III.

1862
Smedley, William. ACROSS THE PLAINS. III+.

1863
Bailey, James L. Diary. III-.
Cooper, Arvazena. "Our Journey." IV.
_____. "Pioneer across the Plains." IV.

1864
Fletcher, B. F. Diary. V-.
West, Margaret E. Covered Wagon Days. III.

1865
Black, Mary L. DIARY. III.
Cauthorn, Benjamin. Trip to Montana. I.

1866
Eakin, Stewart B. A SHORT SKETCH. III.
Hanna, Jennie E. Diary. IV.
Rehlwinkel, Frederick. Autobiography. III.

1868
Melton, Florence. Reminiscences. III.

1869
Victor, Francis. "Trail-Making." IV.

BEALE ROAD

This route begins near Albuquerque, NM and heads west for the Colorado River via Flagstaff, AZ. At the Mohave villages on the Colorado, the trail joins the Government Road which ends in southern California.

General
Avillo, Philip J. "Fort Mojave."
Beldon, L. Burr. "Forgotten Army Forts of the Mojave."
_____. "Hostile Indian Attacks."
_____. "Indian Attacks Beset Mailmen, Mojave Stages."
Bieber, Ralph P., and A. B. Bender. EXPLORING SOUTHWESTERN TRAILS.
Bonsal, Stephen. BEALE.
Bowman, Eldon G. "Beale's Road."
_____, and Jack Smith. BEALE'S ROAD THROUGH ARIZONA.
Briggs, Carl, and Clyde F. Trudell. QUARTERDECK & SADDLEHORN.
Briggs, Catherine C. "Beale's Road across Northern Arizona."
Casebier, Dennis. CAMP ROCK SPRING.
_____. CARLETON'S PAH-UTE CAMPAIGN.
_____. THE MOJAVE ROAD.
_____. MOJAVE ROAD GUIDE.
_____. THE MOJAVE ROAD IN NEWSPAPERS.
Davis, Alonzo E. Pioneer Days in Arizona.
Dodge, Bertha S. THE ROAD WEST.
_____. THE STORY OF INSCRIPTION ROCK.
Floyd, William P. Journal Beale's Wagon Road Expedition.
Foreman, Grant. "Survey, Fort Smith to Colorado River."
Haenszel, Arda M. HISTORICAL CAJON PASS.
Hoffman, Velma R. "Lt. Beale and the Camel."
Howes, E. H. "Federal Exploration and Development of the 32nd Parallel Route West of the Rio Grande, 1846 - 1861."
Hutchinson, Charles E. "Development San Bernardino Valley."
King, Chester, and Dennis Casebier. BACKGROUND TO HISTORIC AND PREHISTORIC RESOURCES.
"Mojave Saga."
Pierson, Erma. THE MOJAVE RIVER.
Rumble, Josephine R. HISTORY OLD GOVERNMENT ROAD.
Smith, Gerald A., and Clifford J. Walker. INDIAN SLAVE TRADE ALONG THE MOJAVE TRAIL.
Smith, Melvin T. "The Colorado River."
Thompson, Gerald. "The Public Career of Edward F. Beale."
Waitman, Leonard. "The History of Camp Cady."
_____. "Horse Soldier Forts of the Mojave Desert."
Walker, Clifford J. "History of the Mojave River Trail."
_____. OPENING THE MOJAVE RIVER TRAIL.
Warren, Elizabeth, et al., CULTURAL RESOURCES OF THE CALIFORNIA DESERT.

Graphics
Babbitt, James E. "Surveyors along the 35th Parallel."
Casebier, Dennis. THE MOJAVE ROAD IN NEWSPAPERS.
Lockett, H. C. ALONG THE BEALE TRAIL.

1851
Rice, Josiah M. A CANNONEER IN NAVAJO COUNTRY. III+.
Wallace, Andrew. "Across Arizona." I.

1852
Sitgreaves, Lorenzo. REPORT OF AN EXPEDITION. IV.

1853
Aubrey, Francois X. "Diaries." II.
Baskerville, William. Diary. II+.
Chaput, Donald. FRANCOIS X. AUBREY. III.

Conrad, David E. "The Whipple Expedition in Arizona, 1853 - 1854." II.
_____. "The Whipple Expedition on the Great Plains." II.
Foreman, Grant. A PATHFINDER IN THE SOUTHWEST. I.
Stanley, David S. Diary. II+.
Whipple, A. W. REPORT RAILROAD ROUTE. II.
Wyman, Walker D. "F. X. Aubry." III.

1854
Aubrey, Francois X. "Diaries." II.
Wyman, Walker D. "F. X. Aubry." III.

1857
Beale, Edward. WAGON ROAD FROM FORT DEFIANCE TO THE COLORADO RIVER. II+.

1858
Allen, Sallie F. Account. III.
Beale, Edward F. Diary. II.
_____. WAGON ROAD FROM FORT SMITH TO THE COLORADO. II+.
Cheney, J. W. "Story." III.
_____. FROM A SOLDIER'S PEN. V-.
Floyd, William P. Journal. II+.
Hedgpeth, Joel. A Trip Across. III.
Hunter, Leslie G. "The Mojave Expedition of 1858-59." Genl.
Mollhausen, Baldwin. DIARY. I.
Rose, L. J. L. J. ROSE. II.
Udell, John. JOURNAL. III.

1859
Bandel, Eugene. FRONTIER LIFE IN THE ARMY. III.
Cheney, J. W. "Story." III.
Hedgpeth, Joel. A Trip Across. III.
Rose, Leonard J. L. J. ROSE. II.
Udell, John. JOURNAL. III.

1861
Pleasants, J. E. "The Rout of the Horse Thieves."

1862
Brown, John. "Diary of John Brown." III.

1863
Allyn, Joseph P. WEST BY SOUTHWEST. II+.
Carlson, Edward. "The Martial Experiences of the California Volunteers." IV.
Putnam, Joseph P. "Letters." II.

1864
Pleasants, J. E. "Ranging on the Mojave River."
Putnam, Joseph P. Letters. II.

1865
McCormick, Margaret. "Personal Journal." V.

1867
Bell, William A. NEW TRACKS IN NORTH AMERICA. II.
French, Barsina R. Journal. III.
Robert, Henry M. Journal. II.
Rusling, James F. GREAT WEST. III.

1869
Johnson, M. R. Reminiscence. V.

BECKWOURTH CUTOFF

This little-used cutoff began in Reno, NV and extended over the Sierra via Beckwourth Pass - the easiest crossing of the Sierra Nevada.

General
Bonner, Thomas D. LIFE AND ADVENTURES OF JAMES P. BE-CKWOURTH. II.
Mason, Margaret. "They Had a Dream."
McGie, Joseph F. "Summer Tour."
Oswald, Delmont. "James P. Beckwourth."
Smith, Gerald G. "The Feather River Highway, 1851 - 1937."
Wilson, Elinor. JIM BECKWOURTH. II.

1852
Andrews, D. B. Journal. II+.
Baldy, Henry T. Diary. II+.
Brooks, Elisha. PIONEER MOTHER. IV.
Chadwick, Samuel. Diary. II.
Chandler, Knowlton H. Journal. III.
Cummings, Mariett F. "Diary." II.
Dalton, John E. Diary. II+.
Ford, James. JUST BETWEEN OURSELVES. IV.
Freeman, John F. Diaries. II.
Hoag, Amanda J. Papers. Not Seen.
Kitchell, Edward. Trip. II+.
Owen, East S. Journal. III+.
Potter, Theodore E. AUTOBIOGRAPHY. II+.
Richardson, Alpheus. Diary. II.
Sexton, Lucy A. FOSTER FAMILY. II.
Smith, Chester. "Chester Smith's Journal." II.
Stuart, Granville. FORTY YEARS. IV.
Thornily, John C. Diary. I.

1853
Ivens, Virginia W. PEN PICTURES. III.
Ward, Harriet S. PRAIRIE SCHOONER LADY. II.
Woodworth, James. DIARY. II.

1854
Doyle, Simon. Diary. III.
Richey, James H. A TRIP. IV.
Woodhams, William H. "The Diary of William H. Woodhams." I.

1855
Waters, Lydia M. "Account of a Trip." III-.

1859
Favour, John. Diary. III+.

1864
Leppo, David T. FAMILY. II.
Lomas, Thomas J. RECOLLECTIONS. IV.

BOZEMAN TRAIL

This trail provided Montana-bound emigrants with a shorter route from the Fort Laramie area to Virginia City, Helena and other gold camps. Indian resistance to travel made the route both dangerous and well-known.

General
Bozeman, Estate Papers, 1866 - 1869.
Bozeman Trail Manuscripts.
Brown, Dee. FORT PHIL KEARNY.
Burlingame, Merrill C. JOHN M. BOZEMAN.
Carrington, Francis D. MY ARMY LIFE. III.
Dailey, Benjamin. Diary. Not Seen.
Edwards, E. S. TRAILING THE CAMPFIRES. Not Seen.

Garber, Vie W. "The Bozeman Trail."
Gray, John S. "Blazing the Bridger and Bozeman Trails."
Greene, Jerome A. "We Do Not Know."
Hawken, Edward J. "The Military Problem on the Powder RIver Road, 1865 - 1868."
Hebard, Grace R., and E. A. Brininstool. THE BOZEMAN TRAIL.
Hill, Burton S. "John Bozeman and the Bozeman Trail."
Johnson, Dorothy M. THE BLOODY BOZEMAN.
Maynard, E. A. Letters.
Murray, Robert A. THE BOZEMAN TRAIL. Not Seen.
_____. "Race with Death."
Ostrander, Alson B. THE BOZEMAN TRAIL FORTS.
Ryker, Lois. "A Wagon Road through Crow Country."
Shurly, Edmond R. "Skirmish at Goose Creek."
Smith, Sherry L. "The Bozeman - Trail to Death and Glory."
Spear, Elsa. BOZEMAN TRAIL SCRAPBOOK.

Graphics
Greene, Jerome A. "We Do Not Know."

1863
Brown, John G. JOHN M. JACOBS AND THE BOZEMAN TRAIL. Genl.
Card, Cicero. Diary. Not Seen.
Emery, Joseph A. Omaha to Virginia City. Not Seen.
Kirkpatrick, Robert. "From Wisconsin to Montana." II.
Park, Mortimer and Susan. Trip to Montana. IV.
Stanton, George. Reminiscence. III.
Wager, F. E. "Hunted End of Rainbow." IV.

1864
Alderson, William W. Across to Montana. Genl. Not Seen.
Atchison, William E. Diary. III.
Baker, Charles W. Westward Ho! III.
Blanchard, Jonathan. "The 1864 Overland Trail." IV.
Brundage, T. J. Diary. IV.
Captain Townsend's Battle on the Powder River. II.
Flory, A. P. Life and Memoirs. III.
Forman, George. "Across the Plains in 1864." IV.
French, C. Adelia. Memories. III.
Gabbey, Roberts. Crossing the Plains. III.
Gallatin, E. L. "Reminiscences of." III.
Hackney, John S. Diary. III+.
Haskell, W. S. Pilgrimage. III+.
Hedges, Cornelius. Diaries. II.
Hopping, Mary E. Incidents. III+.
Kelley, Mary L. My Trip. III-.
Kirkaldie, Franklin L. Reminiscence and Letters. III.
Maynard, E. A. Letters. Not Seen.
Owen, Richard. Diary of Travels. II+.
Ray, Asa. Letters. II.
Roberts, James. Notes to Idaho. II+.
Root, Orville. Orville's Trip. V.
Ryan, Benjamin W. "The Bozeman Trail." III. Rare Indian attack on circled wagons.
Stanfield, Howard S. DIARY. II.
Thomas, William K. Diary. III.
Tomlinson, John J. Log. III+.
Wager, F. E. "Hunted End of Rainbow by Ox Team." IV.
Weaver, David. Pioneer Reminiscences. III+.
Weaver, David B. Early Days. IV.
Wilkinson, Raleigh F. Recollections. Not Seen.

1865
Lee, C. M. Journals. II+.
Sawyers, James A. "Niobrara - Virginia City Wagon Road." II+.

1866

Bailey, Theodore A. Personal Narrative. Not Seen.
Blythe, Samuel F. Diary. III.
Burgess, Perry A. "From Illinois to Montana." II.
Carrington, Henry. History of Indian Operations on the Plains, 1866. Genl.
Creigh, Thomas A. "From Nebraska City to Montana." III.
Dailey, Benjamin. Diary. Not Seen.
Fisher, Marcius C. "Recollections." III.
Fletcher, Ellen G. BRIDE. II.
Fox, George W. "Diary." II.
Lockey, Richard. Diary. III.
Miles, Thomas C. Reminiscence. III-.
Millard, C. M. S. "Hugh Kirkendall's Wagon Train." IV.
Ricker, J. G. Reminiscences. IV.
Ricker, John J. "Iowa to Ventura County." V.
Robson, Inez A. Reminiscence. V.
Thomas, William K. Diary. III.
Willson, Lester S. Journal. Not Seen.
Wilson, Davis. Diary. I.

BRADSHAW TRAIL

This link between southern California and the La Paz placer district on the Colorado River provided an alternate route to the more common GILA trace. Its maximum use came during the early 1860's.

General
"Bancroft's Guide."
Beattie, George W. "Travel between Southern Arizona and Los Angeles."
Coombs, Susan B. "San Gorgonio Pass." Not Seen.
Gilman, Harold F. "Origin Eastern Mojave Desert." Not Seen.
Grant, James. Biography.
Henderson, Randall. "Waterhole on the Old Bradshaw Trail."
Hoyt, Franklin. "The Bradshaw Road."
_____. "Bradshaw's Road to the La Paz Diggin's."
_____. "A History of the Desert Region."
Hutchinson, Charles E. "Development San Bernardino Valley."
Jennings, Bill. "Following the Bradshaw Road."
Johnston, Francis J. THE BRADSHAW TRAIL.
McAdams, Henry E. "Early History of the San Gorgonio Pass." Not Seen.
McKinney, J. Wilson. "Gold Builds a Road."
Ramirez, J. P., to J. M. Edmunds. Letter.
Renner, Pamela. "La Paz."
Smith - Gilman Papers, "Early Days in San Gorgonio Pass." Not Seen.
Warren, Elizabeth, et al., CULTURAL RESOURCES OF THE CALIFORNIA DESERT.
Weight, Harold O. "Forgotten Road to Gold."
Woodward, Arthur. "Gold on the Colorado."

Maps
Beattie, George W. "Travel between Southern Arizona and Los Angeles."
McKinney, J. Wilson. "Gold Builds a Road."
Weight, Harold O. "Forgotten Road to Gold."

1862
DeGroot, Henry. "Crossing the California Sahara." IV.
Fairchild, Mahlon D. "A Trip to the Colorado Mines in 1862." III.

1866
Putnam, Joseph P. "Letters." II.

BRIDGER CUTOFF

This trail segment covers the network of pathways linking the "parting of the ways" west of South Pass with Fort Bridger and Salt Lake City. There were several variants between Fort Bridger and Salt Lake Valley and each is included here.

General
Gowans, Fred R. "Fort Bridger and the Mormons."
Korns, Roderick. "West from Fort Bridger."
Munkres, Robert. "The Road West: Ash Hollow to Fort Bridger." II.

1841
Belden, Josiah. "The First Overland Emigrant Train." IV.
_____. JOSIAH BELDEN. III.
Bernard, Sam. Recollections. Not Seen.
Bidwell, John. JOHN BIDWELL'S TRIP. II.
Chiles, Joseph B. Visit to California in 1841. V.

1842
Williams, Joseph. NARRATIVE. III.

1843
Applegate, Jesse. RECOLLECTIONS. II.
Baldridge, William. The Days of 1846. V.
Boardman, John. "Journal." II.
Giffen, Helen S. TRAILBLAZING. III.
Hobson, E. John. Biographical Sketch. V-.
Newby, William T. "Diary." III.
Reading, Pierson B. "Journal." II.
Talbot, Theodore. JOURNALS. II+.
White, Bartholomew. LIFE AND TRAVELS. V-.

1844
Bray, Edmund. Letter. V.
Camp, Charles. JAMES CLYMAN. I.
Gilliam, Washington S. "Reminiscences." IV.
Minto, John. "Reminiscences." II.
Murphy, Patrick W. Biography. V-.

1845
Findley, William C. Diary. III.
Howell, John E. "Diary." III.
Johnson, Hezekiah. "Letters." IV.
Knight, Thomas. Recollections. IV.
Palmer's Journal, 1845 - 1846. V.
Palmer, Joel. JOURNAL. I.
Smith, Napoleon B. Biographical. V.
Snyder, Jacob R. "Diary." III+.
Tinkey, David. Statement. V-.

1846
Allen, Isaac. Biography. V.
Boggs, William M. Reminiscences. IV.
Breen, John. Dictation. II.
Brown, Elam. BIOGRAPHY. IV.
Bryant, Edwin. WHAT I SAW IN CALIFORNIA. I.
Camp, Charles L. JAMES CLYMAN. I.
Carriger, Nicholas. "Diary." III-.
Clark, Thomas D. "Edwin Bryant." III.
Clark, William. "A Trip across." II. Freight.
Clark, William S. Biographical Sketch. V.
Croy, Homer. WHEELS WEST. III.
Graves, William C. "Crossing the Plains." IV.
Grayson, Andrew J. Account. IV.
Harlan, Jacob W. CALIFORNIA. III.
Harrison, J. M. Account. IV.
Harritt, Jesse. "Diary." III.
Hecox, Margaret M. CALIFORNIA CARAVAN. IV.
Houghton, Eliza P. EXPEDITION OF THE DONNER PARTY. III.

Jamison, Samuel M. "Diary of S. M. Jamison." III.
Keith, Fleury F. "Journal." III.
Kilbourne, Lewis. Journal. Not Seen.
Kilgore, William H. KILGORE JOURNAL. III.
Kiser, Joseph C. Diary and Letters. II.
Knox, Reuben. MEDIC 49ER. III.
Langworthy, Franklin. SCENERY OF. II.
Lawson, George. Diary. III-.
Littleton, James. Diary. I.
Littleton, Micajah. Diary. II.
McBride, John H. Letters. II.
McBride, W. S. Journal. II +.
McDiarmid, Finley. Letters. II +.
McFarlane, Andrew. "Letter of a Gold Rusher." V.
McGlashan, John. Overland Journal. II +.
McKeeby, Lemuel C. "Memoirs." III.
McLellan, William. Reminiscence. II.
Mason, James. "Diary." III.
Moorman, Madison B. JOURNAL. III.
Morrison, Samuel C. Letter. V.
Newcomb, Alphonso B. Across the Plains. IV.
Newcomb, Silas. Journal. II +.
Olson, Jonas W. "Journal." V-.
Packard, Wellman. EARLY EMIGRATION. V.
Packer, Harry B. Letters. IV.
Paden, Irene D. JOURNAL. III.
Parsons, Lucena P. "Journal." II.
Primes, Ed. M. Journal. Not Seen.
"Recollections of Sarah Hammitt." V-.
Ridge, John R. "John R. Ridge Goes." IV.
Seaton, James A. Diary. III.
Shaw, D. A. ELDORADO. III.
Shields, James G. California Trip. I.
Shinn, John R. Journal. III.
Shoemaker, ? "Diary." II.
Skinner, Hugh A. Diary. II.
Stansbury, Howard. EXPLORATION AND SURVEY. II +.
Starr, Henry W. Diary. II +.
Starr, J. R. Diary. II.
Stauder, J. A. Diary. II.
Stine, Henry A. Letters. III.
Stoddard, William C. Diary. Not Seen.
Street, Franklin. CALIFORNIA. II.
Taylor, Calvin. "Overland to California." II +.
Thissell, G. W. CROSSING THE PLAINS. II.
Thompson, Clark W. Letters. I.
Tice, Peter. Diary. II.
Tompkins, Edward A. Diary. II.
Udell, John. INCIDENTS. III +.
Walker, Zachariah. Diary. II.
Waterhouse, Loyal N. Diary. II +.
Watts, John W. Diary. III.
Wheelock, Charles. Letters. Not Seen.
Whitman, Abial. Journal. II.
Wilson, Robert M. Chronicle. III.
Wilson, William. Day Book. III.
Wood, John. JOURNAL. II.
Wright, Robert C. Journal. II +.
Zumwalt, Solomon. ADAM ZUMWALT. V.

1851

Buckingham, Harriet T. "Crossing the Plains." III.
Crawford, Charles H. SCENES. III.
Crawford, P. V. "Journal, 1851." III.
From Lake Erie to the Pacific. IV.
Ingrim, Godfrey C. Recollections. Not Seen.
Lowe, Percival G. FIVE YEARS. I.
McPherren, Ida. IMPRINTS ON PIONEER TRAILS. II.

1852

Anable, Henry S. Journals. II +.
Ashley, Angeline J. Crossing the Plains. II.
Baker, William. Diary. III.
Banks, Henry P. Diary. III.
Blake, Winslow. Diary. II.
Bradley, Henry and Nancy. Journal. II.
Carpenter, James C. I Crossed the Plains. III.
Clark, John Hawkins. "Overland to the Gold Fields." II +.
Constant, Isaac. "A Brief Review." III.
Cooke, Lucy R. CROSSING THE PLAINS. II.
Couper, J. S. Diary. III +.
Crane, Addison M. Journal. I.
Cummings, Mariett F. "Diary." II.
Davis, Alvah I. "Diary." V.
Dean, Thaddeus. JOURNEY. V.
Draper, Elias J. AUTOBIOGRAPHY. IV.
Ferris, Mrs. Benjamin G. THE MORMONS AT HOME. II.
Ferris, Benjamin G. UTAH AND THE MORMONS. II +.
Fisher, James Samuel. Diary. III.
Francis, Samuel D. Journal. II.
Frisbie, Elizabeth C. "Recollections." Not Seen.
Gowen, Bela E. "History of the Olds Emigrating Party." II.
Hickman, Peter L. Diary. III-.
Johnston, John F. A Trip to the Gold Fields. IV.
Kitchell, Edward. A Trip across the Plains. II +.
Laws, Robert C. Diary. Not Seen.
Lobenstine, William C. EXTRACTS. III.
Matthews, Amanda M. A Journal. OO/
Phillips, Cyrus. Journal. II.
Rickey, Thomas B. Diary. V.
Rose, Rachel C. Diary. III-.
Scarbrough. Richard A. Diary. II.
Schneider, Charles G. Diary. III.
Smith, Chester. "Chester Smith's Journal." II.
Snodgrass, R. H. P. Journal. II.
Steele, Harriet. "Gold Rush Letters." V.
Stoddard, William C. Diary. Not Seen.
Stuart, Granville. FORTY YEARS. IV.
Udell, John. INCIDENTS. III +.
Verdenal, John M. Journal. III +.
Woodman, David. Letters. Not Seen.

1853

Ayres, Irvin and Romeyn. Recollections. V-.
Beadle, Elisha. "Letter." IV.
Bradway, Joseph R. Diary. II.
Brown, William R. AN AUTHENTIC WAGON TRAIN JOURNAL. II.
Burns, James F. "James Franklin Burns." V-.
Cipriani, Count Leonetto. CALIFORNIA AND OVERLAND. III.
Cloud, Roy W. ON THE TRAILS. IV.
Compton, Henria. MARY MURDOCK COMPTON. IV.
Compton, James H. Diary. III +.
Davis, A. S. Diary. III.
Desmond, Lucille H. "Henry C. Daulton." V-.
Flint, Thomas. "Diary." III.
Forbes, Solomon. Diary. II.
Fulkerth, Abbey E. "Aunt Abbey's Diary." III +.
Galloway, James. Diary. IV.
Glasscock, C. B. LUCKY BALDWIN. IV.
Haas, Charles E. "John B. Haas." IV.
Handsaker, Samuel. Autobiography. III +.
_____. PIONEER LIFE. III.
Hays, Lorena L. "To the Land of Gold." Not Seen.
Hill, Hanks N. The Lost Train. IV.
Hollister, W. W. Statement. IV.

Ivens, Virginia W. PEN PICTURES. III.
Kirby, William. MORMONISM EXPOSED. Not Seen.
Lewis, John I. MY GARDEN OF ROSES. V-.
Newton, Jotham. Diary. III+.
Porter, Nathan. Diary. V.
Quail. Journal. II.
Reynolds, James. A Trip across the Plains. III.
Richard, John C. My Diary. II.
Rowe, William R. Ho for California. IV.
Ward, Harriet S. PRAIRIE SCHOONER LADY. II.
Williams Family Papers. III.
Winthrop, Theodore. CANOE AND SADDLE. III.
Woodworth, James. DIARY. II.

1854

Baker, John F. Personal Experiences. Not Seen.
Burrel, Mary. Diary and Letters. II.
Davies, John J. "The Journey of a Mormon." V.
Foster, Isaac. Foster Family. V.
Handsaker, Sarah J. "Coming to Oregon." V.
Ingalls, Rufus. REPORT. II.
Loba, Jean F. Reminiscences. V-.
Udell, John. INCIDENTS. III+.
White, Daniel C. Diary. III-.

1855

Chandless, William. A VISIT TO SALT LAKE. II.

1856

Brown, J. Robert. A JOURNAL OF A TRIP. I.
Griffen, Eli A. Diaries. Not Seen.
Hoth, H. Diary. I.

1857

Carter, William A. "Diary of Judge." II.
Clark, William. "A Trip across." II.
Cureton, William H. Trekking to California. II.
Ginn, John I. Personal Recollections. II+.
Hamilton, Henry S. REMINISCENCES. IV.
Nichols, Henry K. Journal. II+.
Phelps, John W. "Diary." II.
Thomas, J. J. "Recollections." V.

1858

Ackley, Richard T. "Across the Plains." III.
Anderson, Kirk. "Kirk Anderson's Trip." III.
Farmer, J. E. MY LIFE. IV.
Ficklin, Benjamin F. "Ficklin's Expedition." IV.
James, Jason W. "A Trip to Utah." IV.
Kenderdine, Thaddeus S. A CALIFORNIA TRAMP. II.
Langley, Harold D. TO UTAH. IV.
Lee, William. Notes. III.
Loba, Jean F. Reminiscences. V-.
Nicaise, Auguste. YEAR IN THE DESERT. III.
North, Frank. On the Plains. III.
Seville, William P. NARRATIVE. II+.
Tracy, Albert. "Journal." II+.

1859

Baker, Hozial H. OVERLAND JOURNEY. III.
Beehrer, George W. "Freighting." V.
Brooks, A. F. Diary. II.
Casler, Melyer. JOURNAL TO CALIFORNIA. III+.
Cramer, Thomas. Diary. II.
Day, Alphonso. Diary. III+.
Evans, Robley D. A SAILOR'S LOG. IV.
Favour, John. Diary. III+.
Gibbs, George T. Account. V.

Gibson, John M. Journal. I.
Greeley, Horace. AN OVERLAND JOURNEY.
Griswold, Harriet B. Papers. Not Seen.
Jones, Richard W. Diary. II+.
Mathews, Ed J. CROSSING THE PLAINS. II.
Merryweather, F. LIFE. III.
Powell, John W. Diary. III+.
Power, Bertha K. WILLIAM HENRY KNIGHT. V.
Service, John. JOHN SERVICE. IV.
Suckley, George. "The 1859 Overland Journal." V.
Tuttle, Charles M. "California Diary." II.
Weeks, Lovina W. Diary. III+.
Whitney, William T. Trip. III.
Williams, H. D. Diary. II.
Williams, Howard D. Diary. II.
Wilson, John S. Diary. II+.

1860

Anderson, John C. MACKINAWS. Stage.
Ayer, Edward E. Early Reminiscences. IV.
Dodge, Elvira. Diary. II.
Downes, Clara E. Journal. I.
Dyer, Ellen. Journals. III.
Eliza and Margaret Prentice's Trip. IV.
Fish, Lafayette. Across the Plains. II.
Fish, Mary C. Diary. II+.
Hawkins, T. S. SOME RECOLLECTIONS. IV.
Huckins, Alonzo. Fort Leavenworth to Camp Floyd. III.
Lyman, Vincent P. Diary. II.
Manning, Malvina V. Diary. III.
Porter, Lavinia H. BY OX TEAM TO CALIFORNIA. II.
Powell, Philander. History. II+.
Tracy, Albert. "Journal." II+.

1861

Lockhart, Edith A. Diary. III.
Moss, William C. "Overland to California." III+.
Taylor, Ruth W. "A Letter Home." IV.

1862

Anderson, Charles L. Letters. II.
Boquist, Laura B. CROSSING. III.
Burlingame, Mr. & Mrs. Journals. II.
Karchner, Mrs. Nicholas H. Diary. III+.
Kohrs, Conrad. Autobiograpphy. V.
Millington, Ada. "Journal." II+.
Nye-Starr, Kate. SELF-SUSTAINING WOMAN. V.
Redfield, Francis M. REMINISCENCES. Not Seen.
Waite, Catherine V. ADVENTURES IN THE FAR WEST. II.
Young, Albert J. Diary. II.

1863

Bender, Flora I. "Notes." III.
Briggs, Joshua and Ruth. A PIONEER MISSOURIAN. V.
Dickason, David H. "Clarence King's First." IV.
Fulkerth, Abbey E. "Aunt Abbey's Diary." III+.
Hopper, Silas L. "Diary." III.
McCutchan, Rebecca E. Headed West. III.
Nettleton, Lucy. Letters. II.
Sweetland, Louisa M. Across the Plains. IV.
Toll, Nicholas B. Reminiscence. IV.
Walker, Joseph H. Description. II.
Word, Samuel. "Diary." II.
Yager, James P. "Yager Journal." II.

1864

Allton, Hiram. Diary. III.
Alton, Hiram. Journal. II+.

Bowers, John H. Letters. IV.
Davis, William F. "Hitting the Oregon Trail." IV.
Epperson, Mrs. B. C. "Diary." Not Seen.
Fryberger, Wilson. To California. III.
Gallatin, E. L. "Reminiscences." III.
Harter, George. CROSSING. III.
Hemey, John B. Diary. IV.
Leppo, David T. FAMILY. II.
Lomas, Thomas J. RECOLLECTIONS. IV.
Morrill, Rosa N. MARY JANE.
Ringo, Mary. JOURNAL. II.
Rousseau, Mrs. James. Papers. Not Seen.
Warner, Mary E. Diary. II.

1865

Adams, Franklin E. "Overland Trail Diary." III.
Adkins, H. Frank. Reminiscence. IV.
Argyle, Archie. CUPID'S ALBUM. V-. Fiction.
Case, Frank M. "Experiences." IV.
Cauthorn, James D. Diary. III.
Chillson, Lorenzo D. Diary. III.
Dam, Frances L. Account. V-.
Ellis, James A. "Diary." III.
Gibson, J. W. RECOLLECTIONS. IV.
Longacre, Myrtle. A Trek West. V-.
Shackleford, Ruth. TO CALIFORNIA. II.
Storrs Family, Diary. III+.
Watkins, Francis M. STORY. III.
Zeamer, R. Jeremiah. Diary. III.

1866

Eakin, S. B. SKETCH. III.
Jackson, William H. "Bullwhacking across the Plains." II.
_____. DIARIES. II.
_____. "Notes from Diary." II.
Lockey, Richard. Diary. III.
McClintock, Margaretta F. My Trip. V.
Rehlwinkel, Frederick. Autobiography. III.
Ricker, J. G. Reminiscences. IV.

1867

Jackson, William H. DIARIES. II.

1869

Jatta, Mary H. Journal. III.
Thompson, W. Sherman. Childhood Memories. IV.

CALIFORNIA ROUTE

This category includes most trail accounts (diaries, reminiscences, and secondary sources) that begin on the Missouri River and move west. There are some few sources that strike east from the Pacific coast. Exceptions are those items that can be identified as OREGON (the principal omission), CANADA, DAKOTAS, MORMON, PIKES PEAK, and SANTA FE. Accordingly, accounts written by individuals ultimately arriving in Bannack, Montana via Council Bluffs, the Platte River and the Bozeman Trail in 1865 would have entries under the CALIFORNIA (1865) list below, as well as entries in the MONTANA and BOZEMAN trail segment categories. This organizational framework is chosen in order to combine most entries for the larger Midwest-Pacific Coast route along the Platte River in a few, easily referenced, formats. If a reader wishes to survey all entries for the Missouri River-South Pass pathway, he should combine entries in the CALIFORNIA, CANADA, OREGON, MONTANA, MORMON, and PIKES PEAK categories.

General
Adams, B. H. Autobiography.

Adams, Benjamin F. Correspondence.
Allen, Edward V. "Transportation in the Marysville Area.
Bailey, P. A. Southwestern Adventure and Exploration.
Barras, Judy. THE LONG ROAD TO TEHACHAPI.
Baxter, Don J. GATEWAYS TO CALIFORNIA. Sierra Passes.
Blondeau, Bernard S. Account Books. Platte River.
Breton, Thor. "Old Mariposa Road."
Bristow, John T. THE OVERLAND TRAIL. Kansas only.
Brooks, Noah. "The Plains Across."
Brown, Kenneth. "California Roads and Trails, 1825 to 1848."
California Div. Beaches and Parks, REPORT OVERLAND EMIGRANT TRAIL.
California Gold Rush Letters, 1849 - 1859.
"California Overland Express." Not Seen.
Campbell, Mrs. Paul. "Benoni Morgan Hudspeth." (Hudspeth Cutoff)
Carmer, Carl. "Here is my Home."
Carpenter, Augustine D. Diary. Not Seen.
Caughey, John W. "The Transit of the Forty-Niners."
Cleland, Robert G. "Transportation in California."
Cook, Clarice. "To California by Prairie Schooner, 1841 - 1860."
Cramer, Howard R. "Geology and Hudspeth's Cutoff."
_____. "Hudspeth's Cutoff - Southeastern Idaho."
Cross, Ralph H. EARLY INNS OF CALIFORNIA.
Darby and Miller. HISTORY OF CALIFORNIA.
Davies, J. Kenneth. MORMON GOLD.
Davis, Leonard M. THE HISTORIC SACRAMENTO-AUBURN ROAD.
Day, Sherman. REPORT ON THE IMMIGRANT WAGON ROAD EXPLORATIONS. Carson Pass.
Decker, Dean. "Variants of the Slate Creek Cutoff."
"Distances on Road between Fort Kearny, Nebraska Territory, and Junction Station, Colorado."
Dornin, May. "Emigrant Trails into California."
Dowling, E. "California - Or Bust." Not Seen.
Eaton, Edna B. "Charles Camden and the Camden Toll Road."
Eppard, Mabelle. "The Southern Emigrant Trails to California."
Epstein, Daniel M. "The California Gold Rush as Reported by the Marshall STATESMAN."
"Extracts from WABASH COURIER."
Franzwa, Gregory M. "Sublette Cutoff Cartographic Expedition."
Garland, Hamlin. "Prairie Route to the Golden River." Not Seen.
Gill, Thomas. "Across the Plains." Not Seen.
Gilman, Musetta. PUMP ON THE PRAIRIE. Ft. Kearny-Julesburg.
Goddard, George H. REPORT OF THE EASTERN BOUNDARY.
Gooden, John H. "Life and Experiences on the Southwestern Roads to California."
Goodwin, Victor O. "Development of Emigrant Routes of Northern Nevada."
_____. THE HUMBOLDT.
Greco, Joseph A. "History of Highway 50 from Placerville to Virginia City; 1849 - 1869."
Gregg, Kate L. "Boonslickers in the Gold Rush to California."
_____. "Missourians in the Gold Rush."
Green, Charles R. Diary. Not Seen.
Guinn, J. M. EL CAMINO REAL. Los Angeles to San Francisco roads.
Helfrich, Devere. EMIGRANT TRAILS WEST.
Hines, Harvey K. "In an Emigrant Wagon."
HISTORICAL TOUR OF THE CARSON RIVER ROUTE.
Hunt, Thomas H. "The California Trail." Raft River to Sacramento.
_____. GHOST TRAILS TO CALIFORNIA.
Jackson, William H. "The Most Important Nebraska Highway, Nebraska City-Fort Kearny-Denver Trail."
Jensen, James M. "Cattle Drives to the Gold Fields."
Jensen, Ross L. "The Greenwood-Sublette Cutoff of the Oregon Trail."
Johnson, Judith. "Transportation and Communication in California, 1848 - 1860."
Joy, Emmett P. "A Gold Rush Road."
Kell, Elmer A. "Early Travel and Communication in Southern California."

Latta, Frank F. EL CAMINO VIEJO. Los Angeles to San Francisco roads.

Levy, JoAnn. "Crossing the 40-Mile Desert."

Lofinck, Sewell. "From Coso to Carricart."

MacDonald, William R. "The Impact of the California Gold RUsh on the Mormons in the Great Basin, 1847 - 1857."

McFarland, G. "A Legacy Left Behind." Not Seen.

Mason, Margaret. "Feather River Highway."

Miller, David E. "Parting of the Ways on the Oregon Trail - The East Terminal of the Sublette Cutoff."

Moore, Helen L. "California in Communication with the Rest of the Continent."

Morley, Thomas. "The Independence Road to Fort Laramie: By Aerial Photograph."

Munger, Charles N. "Overland Trails to California."

Murray, Robert A. "Trading Posts, Forts and Bridges of the Casper Area."

Naden, Kim L. "The Making of a Follower of the Oregon-California Trail." Nebraska only.

Neiswanger, Lilian H. The Old St. Jo Road. St. Jo to Independence, MO.

Nielsen, Beatrice. "The Saga of a Trail." Shasta County, CA.

North, Arthur W. "Overland Route to California: Kelly's Excursion."

Parker, Ellen. Along the Immigrant Trail from Tennessee to California. Not Seen.

Poe, F. "Wagon Road in California." Not Seen.

Pugh, Byron G. "History of Utah-California Wagon Freighting."

Ramirez, J. P. to J. M. Edmunds. (Southern CA roads)

Richmond, Robert W. "Overland Trail from the Missouri River to Fort Laramie before 1854."

Rickard, Ruth L. "The Gold Rush to California, 1848 - 1850."

Riesenberg, Felix. THE GOLDEN ROAD: THE STORY OF CALIFORNIA'S SPANISH MISSION TRAIL.

Rodgers Family, Records. IV.

Rosenberg, Robert G. "The Dempsey-Hockaday Trail."

Roske, Ralph. "World Impact of the California Gold Rush."

Scott, Louisiana. "Report of Emigrants and Emigrant Routes to California."

Smith, J. A. "Big Trees - Carson Valley Road."

_____. "Calaveras County Bridges - Ferries."

_____. "The Ebbetts Pass or Big Tree Road."

Smith, William E. "The Oregon Trail through Pottawatomie County." East Kansas only.

Stewart, George R. THE CALIFORNIA TRAIL. Recommended.

Sudweeks, Leslie L. "The Raft River in Idaho History."

Thomas, Melvin R. "The Buckeye Argonauts."

_____. "The Impact of the California Gold Rush on Ohio and Ohioans."

Thompson, Margaret A. "Overland Travel and the Central Sierra Nevada, 1827 - 1849."

Trexler, Harrison A. MISSOURI-MONTANA HIGHWAYS.

Urbanek, Mae. GHOST TRAILS OF WYOMING.

Watson, Jeanne H. "The Carson Emigrant Road."

Webb, James. Papers. Not Seen.

Weight, Harold O. "Desert Trails."

Wheeler, Sessions S. THE NEVADA DESERT. Forty Mile Desert crossings.

Wickman, John E. "Hoosier Overlanders in the Gold Rush, 1849 - 1850."

Wilson, Maud. "Federal Exploration in California from 1841 - 1855."

Winton, Harry N. "Overland Emigration to California, 1841 - 1848."

Wood, R. Coke. BIG TREE-CARSON VALLEY TURNPIKE.

Woods, Robert J. EARLY TRANSPORTATION IN SOUTHERN CALIFORNIA.

Graphics
Bryant, William C. THE PLAINS AND THE SIERRAS.
THE DRAWINGS OF JOHN WOODHOUSE AUDUBON.
Hunt, Thomas. "California Trail."
"Overland Trail to California, Panorama Notice, 1850."

1841-General
Bidwell, John. Papers.

_____. "Route Travelled from Cairo." Map.

_____, et al., FIRST THREE WAGON TRAINS.

Brereton, George. "Overland to California in 1841."

Cleland, Robert G. "John Bidwell's Arrival in California." Sierra to Marsh's Ranch.

Cody, Cora. "John Bidwell."

Dillon, Richard. "When the Siskiyou Trail Came to San Carlos."

Goodwin, Cardinal. "California's Pioneer Homeseekers."

Harris, Mary. "John Rowland and William Workman."

Heath, Minnie B. "Nancy Kelsey."

Hunt, Rockwell D. JOHN BIDWELL.

Hussey, John A. "New Light upon Talbot H. Green."

Kelly, Charles. "First Emigrant Train."

_____. "Salt Desert Trails." Bidwell-Bartleson party in Utah.

Kelsey, Mrs. Benjamin A. "A California Heroine."

_____. "Reminiscences of an 1841 Arrival."

Levitin, Sonia. "First Historic Trek."

Miller, David E. "The First Wagon Train to Cross Utah, 1841."

Olson, James C., and Irene D. Paden, "Facts about."

Paden, William G. "Bidwell's Route of the Sierras."

Ramage, Helen. "Wilkes Exploring Expedition."

Rowland, Leonore A. "The First Covered Wagon Train to Southern California."

Scalf, Henry P. OVERLAND LETTER.

1841
Belden, Josiah. "The First Overland Emigrant Train." IV.

_____. JOSIAH BELDEN. III.

Bell, Josias F. Sketches. II.

Bernard, Sam. Recollections. Not Seen.

Bidwell, John. ECHOES OF THE PAST ABOUT CALIFORNIA. II.

_____. "The First Emigrant Train to California. III.

_____. IN CALIFORNIA BEFORE THE GOLD RUSH. II.

_____. A JOURNEY TO CALIFORNIA. II.

Chiles, Joseph B. Visit to California in 1841. V.

Dawson, Nicholas. NARRATIVE OF NICHOLAS 'CHEYENNE' DAWSON. III.

Gambel, William. Life. V.

Giffen, Helen S. TRAIL-BLAZING PIONEER. III.

Hopper, Charles. CHARLES HOPPER. IV.

Nunis, Doyce. JOSIAH BELDEN. IV.

Sage, Rufus B. ROCKY MOUNTAIN LIFE. IV.

St. Johns, James. "Diary." V.

Wilson, Benjamin D. "Benito Wilson." V-.

_____. Observations. V-.

1842
Fremont, John C. EXPLORATION OF THE COUNTRY. II.

Giffen, Helen S. TRAIL-BLAZING PIONEER. V.

Hopper, Charles. CHARLES HOPPER. IV.

Sage, Rufus B. ROCKY MOUNTAIN LIFE. IV.

1843
Atmore, Charles. Diary. V-.

Baldridge, William. Days of 1846. V.

Brown, John Henry. REMINISCENCES AND INCIDENTS. V.

Burnett, Peter H. AN OLD CALIFORNIA PIONEER. IV.

Field, Matthew C. PRAIRIE AND MOUNTAIN SKETCHES. I. Westport to Green River.

Giffen, Helen S. TRAIL-BLAZING PIONEER. III.

Graham, Richard H., and Sidney Smith. "Report." Westport - South Pass and back. Not Seen.

Josephy, Alvin M. "First 'Dude Ranch' Trip." II. Kansas to Green River.

Kennerly, William C. "My Hunting Trip." IV.

_____. PERSIMMON HILL. IV. Westport to Green River.

Reading, Pierson B. "Journal of Pierson Barton Reading." II.

Hecox, Adna A. "Biographical Sketch." Not Seen.
Hecox, Margaret M. CALIFORNIA CARAVAN. IV.
Henderson, Lucy A. "Young Adventure." II.
Houghton, Eliza P. EXPEDITION OF THE DONNER PARTY. III.
Hyde, William. Private Journal. II.
Jones, Mrs. M. A. Reminiscences. IV.
Jones, Nathaniel V. "Journal." III.
Judd, Zodak K. Autobiography. V.
Keyson, Guy M. Journal. II.
Lee, John D. "Diary." II.
Lienhard, Heinrich. FROM ST. LOUIS. II.
McGlashan, C. F. HISTORY OF THE DONNER PARTY. II.
McKinstry, George. "Diary." III.
_____. "Remarkable Story of the Donner Party." III.
_____. "Thrilling of Tragic Journal." III.
_____. Trip across the Plains. III.
Martin, Thomas S. WITH FREMONT TO CALIFORNIA. III.
Mathers, James. "Journal of Travels." III.
Mitchell, Annie R. JIM SAVAGE. V.
Morris, Thomas. Journal. III+.
Pace, James. "Journal." III+.
Parkman, Francis. OREGON TRAIL. V.
Pettigrew, David. Autobiography. III-.
Pikale, Henele. "Recollections." III.
Pringle, Virgil. "Diary." III.
Reed, James F. "Diary." III-.
_____. "Snow-Bound Starved Emigrants." IV.
Rhoades, Daniel. Letters. IV.
Smith, William. Reminiscence. IV.
Standage, Henry. MARCH OF THE MORMON BATTALION. III+.
Stewart, George R. ORDEAL BY HUNGER. II.
Taylor, William E. Diary. III.
Thornton, J. Quinn. OREGON AND CALIFORNIA IN 1848. II.
Tippets, John H. History and Account. III.
Turner, Henry S. ORIGINAL JOURNALS. II.
Tyler, Daniel. CONCISE HISTORY. II.
Whitworth, Robert W. "From the Mississippi to the Pacific." III.
Wilson, David P. "Mormon Battalion." II.
Wimmer, Peter. CALIFORNIA GOLD BOOK. V.
Young, Samuel C. "Biographical Obituary." V.

1847-General
Buchanan, George W. "Oregon and California."
"From California."
Shannon, Betty. "New Old Mormon-Emigrant Trail."
Waggoner, W. W. "Donner Party and Relief Hill."

1847
Bigler, Henry W. "Diary." III.
Blackburn, Abner. Reminiscences. IV.
Breen, Patrick. "Diary." III.
Camp, Charles L. "William Alexander Trubody." IV.
Craig, John. Letter. V.
Fallon, William. "Extracts." II.
Farris, William M. 1847 CROSSING. III.
Findla, James. "Statement." V.
Giffen, Helen S. TRAIL-BLAZING PIONEER. V.
Hopper, Charles. CHARLES HOPPER.
Hyde, William. Private Journal. IV.
Ingersol, Chester. OVERLAND. III.
Jones, Nathaniel V. "Journal." V.
Kellam, John P. Diary. IV.
Martin, Thomas S. WITH FREMONT. III.
Moore, Alexander. "Statement." V.
Pace, James. Journal. III+.
Perkins, E. A. Diary. IV.
Reed, James F. "Diary." II.
Shannon, Betty. "New Old Mormon-Emigrant Trail."

Taylor, L. J. LIFE HISTORY. Not Seen.
Turner, Henry S. ORIGINAL JOURNALS. II.
Tyler, Daniel. CONCISE HISTORY. IV.

1848-General
Choteau, B. "Choteau's Log."
Egan, Ferol. "Incident at Tragedy Springs."
Shannon, Betty. "New Old Mormon Trail."

1848
Allsop, I. P. C. Recollections. Not Seen.
Bayley, Thomas S. "First Overland Mail Bag." IV.
Bigler, Henry W. BIGLER'S CHRONICLE. II.
_____. "Diary." III.
_____. "Extracts." V.
Blackburn, Abner. "Reminiscences." III.
Brewerton, George D. OVERLAND. II.
Brown, James S. LIFE. II.
Burrows, Rufus G. Anecdotes. IV.
_____, and Cyrus Hull. A LONG ROAD. V.
Chamberlain, Samuel E. MY CONFESSION. IV.
Cornwall, Bruce. LIFE SKETCH. IV.
Couts, Cave J. HEPAH. I.
Dunphy, William. Statement. V.
Fifield, Allen. "First Two-Way Road." II.
_____. "Wagons East." II+.
Giffen, Helen S. TRAIL-BLAZING PIONEER. V.
Gordon, G. F. Statement. Not Seen.
Hammond, Francis A. "In Early Days." V.
Huntington, Oliver B. Diary. III+.
Jordan, Rudolph. "Rudolph Jordan." II.
Judd, Zodak K. Autobiography. V.
McPherson, John C. Extracts. V-.
Martin, Thomas S. WITH FREMONT. III.
May, Richard M. Sketch. II+.
May, Sam. Sketch. II+.
Pikale, Henele. "Recollections." III.
Pratt, Orville C. "Diary." II.
Ricketts, Norma. TRAGEDY SPRING. II.
Smith, Azariah. Journal. II.
Smith, Edward L. Journal. III.
Tappan, Henry. "Diary." IV.
Tyler, Daniel. CONCISE HISTORY. IV.
Van Arsdale, De Maris. A Pioneer Story. V.
Willis, Ira J. "Ira J. Willis Guide." III.
Withers, Ethel M. "Experiences." II.

1849-General
"Adventures on the Prairies."
Bari, Valeska. THE COURSE OF EMPIRE.
Barker, Watson. "Wading to California."
Benjamin, Theodosia. "The Audubon Party."
Bidlack, Russell E. LETTERS HOME.
Bieber, Ralph P. SOUTHERN TRAILS TO CALIFORNIA.
_____. "Southwestern Trails to California."
Billington, Ray A. "The Overland Ordeal."
Birch, Brian P. "Crossing Wyoming With the Forty-Niners."
Blouet, B. W. "Meteorological Experiences."
Breckenridge, William C. "Gold Hunters of Forty-Nine."
Brinckerhoff, Sidney B. "Passport to Mexico."
Caughey, John W. RUSHING FOR GOLD.
_____. "Transit of the Forty-Niners."
Comstock, David A. GOLD DIGGERS.
Cotton, A. R. Constitution.
Dumke, Glenn S. "Across Mexico in '49."
Ferris, A. C. "Arrival of Overland Trains in California."
Fussell, W. Rupert. "The South in the Gold Rush." Not Seen.
Gordon, Mary M. "Overland to California."

Graham, Martha M. THE POLYGAMIST'S VICTIM. Not Seen.

Holliday, Jaquelin S. "The California Gold Rush in Myth and Reality."

Howe, Octavius T. ARGONAUTS OF '49.

Hoxie, Frances A. "Connecticut's Forty-Niners."

Hulbert, Archer B. FORTY-NINERS.

Jackson, Joseph H. GOLD RUSH ALBUM.

Johnson, William W. THE FORTY-NINERS.

Knudson, S. "Letter."

Lorch, Fred W. "Iowa and the Gold Rush."

McDermott, John F. "Gold Rush Movies."

Madsen, Brigham D. GOLD RUSH SOJOURNERS IN SALT LAKE CITY.

Morgan, Dale L. "Letters by Forty-Niners written from Great Salt Lake City."

Oakley, Francile B. "Arkansas' Golden Army of '49."

Officer, James E. "Yanqui Forty-Niners in Hispanic Arizona."

OUTLINE HISTORY. Cartoons.

Parker, Watson. "Wading to California."

Peoples, John H. GENERAL SMITH'S CORRESPONDENCE.

Pratelles, V. M. "Sufferings."

Reid, Bernard J. "California Gold Rush Letter."

Ressler, Theodore C. TRAILS DIVIDED.

Richardson, William H. "The Argonauts of Jersey City."

Schaefer, Joseph. "Trailing a Trail Artist."

Sommer, Jane H. "Outfitting."

Williamson, R. S. REPORT OF A RECONNAISSANCE. Not Seen.

Woodruff, George H. WILL COUNTY ON THE PACIFIC SLOPES.

Graphics

Coit, Daniel W. DIGGING FOR GOLD. V.

⸻. DRAWINGS AND LETTERS. V.

Drury, Aubry. "Forty-Niners: As Easterners Saw Them."

Hittle, Jonas. Diary. II+.

Jackson, Joseph H. GOLD RUSH ALBUM. Best illustrated work.

Jagger, D. Sketches. I. Pencil Sketches.

Johnston, William W. THE FORTY-NINERS.

McDermott, John F. "Gold Rush Movies."

1849

Abell, James S. Papers. I.

Account of a Journey. III-.

Aldrich, Lorenzo D. JOURNAL. III.

Anderson, Niles. "Grandfather was a Forty-Niner." IV.

Arms, Cephas, and Adonijah S. Welch. LONG ROAD TO CALIFORNIA. II.

Armstrong, J. E. Diary. III.

Armstrong, J. Elza. "Diary." II.

Armstrong, J. Ezra. Diary. III.

Armstrong, John. Journal. Not Seen.

Ashley, Delos R. Diary. III.

Athearn, P. A. "Diary." III+.

Audubon, John W. AUDUBON'S. I.

⸻. "Illustrated Notes." I.

Austin, Henry. Diary. II+.

Averett, George W. Autobiography. IV.

Babcock, Leonard. Recollections. II.

Bachman, Jacob H. "Audubon's Ill-Fated Western Journey." III.

Backus, Gurdon. Diary. II+.

Badman, Philip. Diary. III.

Baker, George H. "Records of a California Journey." III.

Banks, John E. "Diary, 1849." II.

Batchelder, Amos. Journal. I.

Baudle, James. Diary. II.

Beeching, Robert. Diary. II.

Beesley, E. Maurice. Diary. III.

Benjamin, Theodosia. "The Audubon Party." III.

Benson, John E. Forty-Niner. II+.

Benson, John H. From St. Joe to Sacramento. III+.

Berrien, Joseph W. "Overland from St. Louis." I.

Bickford, William H. Diary. III.

Biddle, B. R. "Diary." Not Seen.

Bigler, Henry W. "Extracts from the Journal." III.

Blackburn, Abner. "Reminiscences." IV.

Blunt, Phineas U. Notes of Travel. I.

Boggs, John. Diary. III.

Bond, Robert. Diary. IV.

Bonestell, Louis H. "Autobiography." II.

Bonine, Dr. Diary. Not Seen.

Booth, Edmund. EDMUND BOOTH. III+.

Bouldin, James E. Diary. II+.

Bowman, E. L. "Diary." V-.

Boyle, Charles E. "Diary." Not Seen.

Boyles, John R. "None Dream But of Success." V-.

Brady, Charles C. "From Hannibal to the Gold Fields." IV.

Brainard, David. Diary. II+.

Breyfogle, Joshua D. Diary. II.

Brisbane, William. Journal. I.

Brockway, H. S. ACROSS THE SOUTHERN TRAIL. IV.

Brooks, E. W. JOURNAL. III.

Brown, Harvey S. Statement. IV.

Brown, John Evans. "Memoirs." II.

Brown, Joseph. CROSSING THE PLAINS. V.

Browne, J. Ross. "A Dangerous Journey." III.

Brownlee, Robert. AN AMERICAN ODYSSEY, II.

Bruff, Joseph Goldsborough. GOLD RUSH. I. Recommended.

Buffum, Joseph. Diary. II.

Burbank, Augustus R. Journals and Diaries. I.

Burgert, Daniel, and Manilus S. Rudy. "The Rough Road West." III.

Burgess, Joseph H. "Grandfather Burgess." V.

Burrall, George P. A Trip. II.

Burris, David. Narrative. IV.

Burton, Henry W. Diary. II.

Bush, Charles W. Five Letters. V.

Caldwell, T. G. "Notes of a Journey." III.

Call, W. W. Reminiscence. IV.

Cameron, J. B. Journal. II+.

Candee, J. G. Letter. IV.

Caples, Mrs. James. Overland Journey. IV.

Cardinell, Charles. "Adventures." III.

Carnes, David. Journal. II+.

Carstarphen, James E., and Clayton Keith. MY TRIP. V.

Cassin, Francis. Statement. V-.

Castleman, P. F. Diary. II+.

Chamberlain, William E. Diary. II.

Chamberlain, William Edwin. Diary. II.

Chamberlain, William H. "From Lewisburg to California." I.

Chambers, William and Robert. "Journey from New Orleans." IV.

Chapman, W. W. Diary. III.

Chatham, J. W. Diary. I.

Chick, Washington H. Reminiscences. V-.

Churchill, Stillman. Diary. II+.

Clark, Bennett C. "Diary of a Journey." II.

Clark, Jonathan. "Diary of Dr. Jonathan." IV.

Clark, Sterling B. HOW MANY MILES FROM ST. JOE? IV.

Clarke, Asa B. TRAVELS IN MEXICO AND CALIFORNIA. II+.

Clifton, John. "Diary." III.

Coats, Felix G. On the Golden Trail. V.

Coffey, Alvin A. "A Black Pioneer's Trip." V.

Coit, Daniel W. DIGGING FOR GOLD. V.

⸻. DRAWINGS AND LETTERS. V.

Cole, Cornelius. MEMOIRS. V.

Coleman, William T. Biographical Sketch. V.

Conger, Sarah M. "Journal of a Journey." Not Seen.

Conway, Mary. "Little Rock Girl." IV.

Cooper, Joseph W. Statement. V-.

Coquillard, Alexis. Diary. III+.

Savage, Levi. JOURNAL. V.

Sawyer, Mrs. Francis H. "Kentucky to California." II + .

Scarbrough, Richard A. Diary. II.

Schneider, Charles G. Diary. III.

Scott, H. T. Memorandum of the Trip. III.

Sexton, Lucy A. FOSTER FAMILY. II.

Sharp, William H. LIFE AND DIARY. II.

Shields, F. M. "Crossing the Plains." IV.

Short, George W. Diary. III.

Smith, Chester. "Chester Smith's Journal." II.

Smith, G. A. Journal. III.

Smith, Seth M. AUTOBIOGRAPHY. V.

Snodgrass, R. H. P. Journal. II.

Spencer, Lafayette. "Journal of the Oregon Trail." III.

Stabaek, Tosten K. JOURNAL. IV.

Steele, Harriet. "Gold Rush Letters." V.

Stoddard, William C. Diary. Not Seen.

Stone, Sophronia H. Diary. II.

Stuart, Granville. FORTY YEARS. IV.

_____. PROSPECTING FOR GOLD. IV.

Taylor, William. Reminiscence. V.

Terrell, Joseph C. EARLY DAYS IN FORT WORTH. IV.

Thornily, John C. Diary. I.

Todd, John R. "Across the Plains." V.

Turnbull, Thomas. "Thomas Turnbull's Travels." II.

Udell, John. INCIDENTS. III + .

Urbanek, Mae. "1852 on the Oregon Trail." IV.

Van Schaick, Holmes D. Diary. II.

Variel, Mary A. "A Romance of the Plains." III.

Verdenal, John M. Journal. III + .

Watts, John W. Diary. III.

Waugh, Lorenzo. AUTOBIOGRAPHY. V.

Wayman, John H. A DOCTOR ON THE CALIFORNIA TRAIL. II.

West, S. H. LIFE AND TIMES. V.

Whipple-Haslam, Mrs. Lee. EARLY DAYS IN CALIFORNIA. V-.

Wonderly, Pauline. REMINISCENCES OF A PIONEER. IV.

Woodman, David. Letters. Not Seen.

Zinn, Henry. Diary. V-.

1853-General

Conrad, David E. "Explorations and Railway Survey."

Emory, William. REPORT.

Enloe, Rachel. Papers. Not Seen.

Kirby, William. MORMONISM EXPOSED. Not Seen.

REPORT OF THE AGENTS.

Ryan, John. "Sonora Trail and Pass of 1853."

Taylor, Arthur S., and William M. McKinney. "An Accurate Observer."

Warner, William. "Overland." Not Seen.

1853

Ayres, Irvin and Romeyn. Recollections. V-.

Bailey, Washington. TRIP TO CALIFORNIA. IV.

Baskerville, William. Diary. II + .

Beadle, Elisha. "Letter." IV.

Beeson, Welborn. Diary. II + .

Blackwood, Jane. Diary. Not Seen.

Booth, John. IN MEMORIAL. Not Seen.

Bradway, Joseph R. Diary. II.

Browder, William. Diary. V.

Brown, William R. AN AUTHENTIC WAGON TRAIN JOURNAL. II.

Bryant, Isaiah W. Diary. Not Seen.

Burns, James F. "James Franklin Burns." V-.

Burwell, Lewis. Dictated Statement. V.

Butterfield, James T. "Interesting Account of a Trip." V-.

_____. Journeys. IV.

Campbell, Remembrance. Carry On. IV.

Carvalho, Solomon N. INCIDENTS. II.

Chaput, Donald. FRANCOIS X. AUBREY. III.

Cipriani, Count Leonetto. CALIFORNIA AND OVERLAND. III.

Cloud, Roy W. ON THE TRAILS. IV.

Cole, James H. "James Harvey Cole's Story." V.

Compton, James H. Diary. III + .

Compton, Mary M. MARY MURDOCK COMPTON. IV.

Comstock, Noah D. Diary. II.

Conrad, David E. "Whipple Expedition in Arizona." II.

_____. "Whipple Expedition on the Great Plains." II.

Cooke, Lucy R. CROSSING THE PLAINS. II.

Cornaby, Hannah. AUTOBIOGRAPHY. Not Seen.

Cowden, James S. Diary. II.

Creer, Leland H. "Explorations." IV.

Crockett, Edwin. Crossing the Plains. IV.

Dallam, Richard. Diary and Journal. II.

Davis, A. S. Diary. III.

Desmond, Lucille H. "Henry Clay Daulton I." V-.

Enloe, Rachel. Papers. Not Seen.

Farrar, Josia H. Farrar-Caldwell Family Papers. V.

Ferris, Mrs. Benjamin. THE MORMONS AT HOME. II.

Ferris, Benjamin. UTAH AND THE MORMONS. II + .

Fletcher, Daniel C. REMINISCENCES. Not Seen.

Flint, Thomas. "Diary." III.

Forbes, Soloman. Diary. II.

Foreman, Grant. A PATHFINDER IN THE SOUTHWEST. I.

Furniss, Kate M. From Prairie to Pacific. II + .

Galloway, James. Diary. IV.

Giffen, Helen S. TRAILBLAZING PIONEER. V.

Gilbert, William W. Journal. II + .

Gill, Harriet T. "Overland Journey in 1853." V.

Gill, Thomas. "Across the Plains." Not Seen.

Glasscock, C. B. LUCKY BALDWIN. IV.

Graham, Alpheus N. "Big Circle." III.

Graham, Calvin H. Journal. III.

Gray, Charles. "Incidents." Not Seen.

Griffin, Eli A. Diaries. Not Seen.

Ground, Eliza A. Letter. Not Seen.

Ground, William B. Letter. Not Seen.

Haas, John B. "John B. Haas." IV.

Hall, Maggie. Crossing the Plains. III.

Hays, Lorena L. "To the Land of Gold." Not Seen.

Heap, Gwinn H. CENTRAL ROUTE. II + .

Hite, Abraham. Diary. IV-.

Hollister, W. W. Statement. IV.

Hudson, Richard. "To the Gold Fields." V-.

Ivens, Virginia W. PEN PICTURES. III.

"Jonathan Rea I." V-.

Jones, John Wesley. AMUSING AND THRILLING ADVENTURES. V-.

Kellogg, Mrs. B. F. E. "Tells about Trip." V.

Kleiser, James A. Autobiography. IV.

Lewis, John I. MY GARDEN OF ROSES. V-.

MacMurphy, John A. "Thirty-Three Years Ago." III.

Martin, William T. "Texas to California." V-.

Miller, Joel. Journal. II-.

Newton, Jotham. Diary. III + .

Parker, Basil G. LIFE AND ADVENTURES. IV.

Porter, Nathan S. Diary. V.

Prickett, Jacob P. "In Quest of Gold." Not Seen.

Redington, Edward. Letters. V.

Reeves, Elijah. Reminiscence. Not Seen.

Reynolds, Henrietta. PIONEERS OF SAND. V.

Reynolds, James. A Trip across the Plains." III.

Richard, John C. My Diary. II.

Rowe, William R. Ho for California. IV.

Schiel, Jacob H. THE LAND BETWEEN. II + .

Stanley, David S. Diary. II + .

Steele, Harriet. "Gold Rush Letters." V.

Udell, John. JOURNAL. III.
Weeks, Lovina W. Diary. III+.
White, Edith. MEMORIES. V-.
Whitney, William T. Trip. III.
Wilke, Philip J., and Harry W. Lawton. EXPEDITION OF CAPTAIN
    J. N. DAVIDSON. II.
Wilkinson, J. A. Across the Plains. II.
Willey, Lucas. Diaries. I.
Williams, H. D. Diary. Not Seen.
Williams, Howard D. Diary. II.
Wilson, John S. Diary. II+.

1860
Anderson, John C. MACKINAWS DOWN THE MISSOURI. Stage.
Ayer, Edward E. Early Reminiscences. IV.
Begges, James G. Diary. Stage.
Bemis, Stephen A. RECOLLECTIONS. Not Seen.
Burton, Richard F. CITY OF THE SAINTS. I.
Crane, Ellery. "An Overland Trip." IV.
Dodge, Elvira. Diary. II.
Downes, Clara E. Journal. I.
Dyer, Ellen. Journal of Travels. III.
Eliza and Margaret Prentice's Trip. IV.
Evans, James A. Journal. III.
Fish, Lafayette. Across the Plains. II.
Fish, Mary C. Diary. II+.
Fowler, John M. Diary. III.
Gould, Albert L. "Diary." II+.
Guill, Mary J. Diary. II.
Hawkins, T. S. SOME RECOLLECTIONS. IV.
Huckins, Alonzo. Fort Leavenworth to Camp Floyd. III.
Lowry, James L. Diary. II+.
Lyman, Vincent P. Diary. II.
Mahoney, William F. Diary. II+.
Manning, Malvinia V. Diary. III.
Pomeroy, Henry M. Journal. II+.
Porter, Lavinia H. BY OX TEAM TO CALIFORNIA. II.
Powell, Philander. History. II+.
Preston, Leander A. "Journal of Leander A. Preston." IV.
Tracy, Albert. "Journal." II+.

1861-General
Lander, Frederick W. "Additional Estimate."

1861
Benjamin, Israel J. THREE YEARS IN AMERICA. II.
Bonner, John H. Daily Journal. II.
Brown, John M. "Diary." II+.
Butterfield, Ira H. "Michigan to California." III.
Cook, Peter. LIFE OF PETER COOK. IV.
Countryman, Ardell J. A PIONEER'S TRIP. IV.
Fish, Lafayette. Crossing the Plains. IV.
Gelatt, Richard. A Simple Sketch. IV.
Goodale, Tim. Letter. Not Seen.
Hazen, Eli W. "The California Column." III.
Kidder, Leroy L. Story of a Siskiyou Pioneer. V.
Lockhart, Edith A. Diary. III.
Maillet, Louis R. Account. V.
Moss, William C. "Overland to California." III+.
Nash, Marie. Diary. V.
Paup, Harrison. ACROSS THE PLAINS. IV.
Reynolds, G. A. "From Iowa to Scott Valley." V.
Sanders, Thomas D. Excerpts. V.
Taylor, Ruth M. "Across the Plains." III.
Taylor, Ruth W. "A Letter Home." IV.
Twain, Mark. ROUGHING IT. I.

1862

Anderson, Charles L. Letters. II.
Bailey, James G. "Journal." II+.
Boquist, Laura B. CROSSING THE PLAINS. III.
Brown, John. "Diary." III.
Burlingame, Mr. and Mrs. "Journals." II.
Bushnell, Daniel E. Diary. Not Seen.
Fish, Juliette W. Crossing the Plains in 1862. IV.
Ford, A. T. Life and History. V.
Gould, Jane H. "Iowa to California." II+.
Hewett, Randall H. ACROSS THE PLAINS. II.
Journal. III.
Karchner, Nicholas H. Diary. III+.
Kohrs, Conrad. Autobiography. V.
Millington, Ada. "Journal." II+.
Newkirk, Coleman S. Brief History. V.
Nye-Starr, Kate. SELF-SUSTAINING WOMAN. V.
Redfield, Francis M. REMINISCENCES. Not Seen.
Shelley, Edward. "Western Journal." IV.
Shires, William. Journal. III.
Tourtillot, Jane A. "Diary and Journal." I.
Tuttle, Hiram G. Diary. III.
Waite, Catherine V. ADVENTURES IN THE FAR WEST. II.
Young, Albert J. Diary. II.

1863
Adams, Ellen T. Manuscript Diary. II.
Aulbach, Adam. "Voice Out of the Past." V.
Briggs, Joshua E., and Ruth Flowerree. A PIONEER MISSOURIAN.
    V.
Bruffey, George A. EIGHTY-ONE YEARS. V.
Caples, Mrs. James. Overland Journey. IV.
Card, Cicero. Diary. Not Seen.
Colegrove, George L. Life Story. V.
Cutting, A. Howard. Journal. II+.
Darling, Lucia. Diary. I.
Dickason, David H. "Clarence King's First Western Journey." IV.
Edgerton, Mary. A GOVERNOR'S WIFE.... II.
Emery, Joseph A. Omaha to Virginia City. Not Seen.
Fulkerth, Abbey E. "Aunt Abbey's Diary." III+.
Gay, William. Reminiscences. IV.
Hooper, Joseph and Esther. Journey. V.
Hopper, Silas L. "Diary by Silas Hopper." III.
Horton, L. J. Biography. III.
Kirkpatrick, Robert. "From Wisconsin to Montana." II.
Lewis, B. P. Diary. II.
McCutchan, Rebecca E. Headed West. III.
Moore, Miles C. Recollections. Not Seen.
Nettleton, Lucy. Letters. II.
Park, Mortimer and Park. Trip to Montana. IV.
Purviance, M. C. Journal. II.
Redman, J. T. Reminiscences. IV.
Sanders, Harriet P. Reminiscences. II.
Stanton, George. Reminiscence. III.
Sweetland, Louisa M. Across the Plains. IV.
Toll, Nicholas B. Reminiscence. IV.
Wager, F. E. "Hunted End of Rainbow." IV.
Walker, Mattie. Brief History of the Walker Family. V.
Wilson, Alex. "Trip across the Plains." V-.
Word, Samuel. "Diary." II.
Yager, James P. "The Yager Journals." II.

1864
Allton, Hiram. Diary. III.
Alton, Hiram. Journal. II+.
Arnold, Joseph W. "Joseph Warren Arnold's Journal." III+.
Atchison, William E. Diary. III.
Baker, Charles W. Westward Ho! III.
Beall, Frank E. A Dream of an Empire. III.

Blanchard, Jonathan. "The 1864 Overland Trail." IV.

Bowers, John Henry. Letters. IV.

Briggs, Joshua E., and Ruth Flowerree. A PIONEER MISSOURIAN. V.

Broadwell, J. W. "Crossing the Plains." IV.

Brubaker, Albert. A Trip. IV.

Brundage, T. J. Diary. IV.

Bushnell, George E. Diary. Not Seen.

Chaffin, Thomas A. Traveling. IV.

Clandening, William H. "Across the Plains." V.

Collins, Catherine W. "An Army Wife Comes West." IV. By Stage.

Collins, John S. ACROSS THE PLAINS. III.

Creel, Virginia F. Diary. II.

Dalrymple, Ward. Reminiscence. V.

Dickson, Albert J. COVERED WAGON DAYS. II.

Dunham, E. Allene. FROM IOWA TO CALIFORNIA. IV.

Dunlap, Catherine. MONTANA GOLD RUSH DIARY. II.

Durfee, Joseph A. Diaries. Not Seen.

Dyer, Ellen. Journal. This trip could have been made in either 1860 or 1864.

Epperson, Mrs. B. C. "Diary." Not Seen.

Evans, James A. EXPLORATION TO GREEN RIVER. III.

———. Report. III.

Fisk, Mrs. Van. Reminiscence. V.

Flory, A. P. Life and Memoirs. III.

Forbis, Jonathan F. Reminiscence. V.

Forman, George. "Across the Plains." IV.

French, C. Adelia. Memories. III.

Fryberger, Wilson. To California by Covered Wagon. III.

Gabbey, Roberts. Crossing the Plains. III.

Hackney, John S. Diary. III+.

Harter, George. CROSSING. III.

Haskell, W. S. Pilgrimage, III+.

Hedges, Cornelius. Diaries. II.

Hemey, John B. Diary. IV.

Hopping, Mary E. Incidents of Pioneer Life. III+.

Johnson, Ann W. "Long Journey of a Mormon Girl." V-.

Kelley, Mary L. My Trip. III-.

Kirkaldie, Franklin L. Reminiscence. III.

Leppo, David T. FAMILY. II.

Logan, Martha. Logan Family Papers. Not Seen.

Lomas, Thomas J. RECOLLECTIONS. IV.

Mahan, Garland. Diary. II+.

Miller, Darlis. ACROSS THE PLAINS. II

Miller, James K. THE ROAD TO VIRGINIA CITY. IV.

Morrill, Rosa Neil. MARY JANE, PIONEER. IV.

Neiman, Peter. Diary. III.

O'Neill, Eliza. Reminiscences. V.

Owen, Richard. Diary of Travels. II+.

Porter, Elizabeth L. Crossing the Plains. III.

Putnam, Joseph P. "Letters." II.

Ray, Asa. Letters. II.

Ringo, Mary. JOURNAL. II.

Roberts, James. Notes. II+.

Roe, Martha A. Trip to Idaho. II+.

Root, Orville. Orvill's Trip. V.

Rosenberg, Daniel. MARY BROWN. V.

Rousseau, Mrs. James. Papers. Not Seen.

Ryan, Benjamin W. "The Bozeman Trail." III.

Stanfield, Howard S. DIARY. II.

Strateler, L. B. Diary. II.

Taylor, John. "Comanche County, Texas." III.

Tomlinson, John J. Log. III+.

Tuttle, Hiram G. Diary. III.

Wager, F. E. "Hunted End of Rainbow." IV.

Warner, Mary Eliza. Diary. II.

Weaver, David. Pioneer Reminiscences. III+.

Weaver, David B. Early Days. IV.

Wilkinson, Henry. Narrative. V.

Wilkinson, Raleigh F. Recollections. Not Seen.

Woods, Allin W. Journal. IV.

1865

Adams, Franklin E. "Overland Trail Diary." III.

Adkins, H. Frank. Reminiscence. IV.

Anthony, Erasmus L. Reminiscence. V-.

Argyle, Archie. CUPID'S ALBUM. V.

Bailey, David J. Diary. II+.

Barton, H. D. Diary. III-.

Bell, Lizzie. Papers. Not Seen.

Boatman, Mary L. Reminiscence. V-.

Bond, ? FOOT TRAVELS. V.

Burgess, Perry A. "From Illinois to Montana." II.

Case, Frank. "Experiences on the Platte." IV.

Cauthorn, Benjamin. Trip to Montana. I.

Colfax, Schuyler. "Honorable Schuyler Colfax's Trip." II.

Cowden, Henry. Diary. III.

Dam, Frances L. Account. V-.

David, James C. "Diary." Not Seen.

Ellis, Henrietta C. DIARY. II.

Ellis, James Addison. "Diary." III.

Gibson, J. W. RECOLLECTIONS. IV.

Herndon, Sarah. DAYS ON THE ROAD. IV.

Hockensmith, Mrs. M. S. Papers. Not Seen.

Jeffers, Susie L. Reminiscence. Not Seen.

Jones, Daniel. Travels across the Plains. V.

Kittredge, Dayelle. Diary. II.

Lee, C. M. Journals. II+.

Leech, A. P. Diary. II.

Longacre, Myrtle. A Trek West. V-.

Sawyers, James A. "Niobrara-Virginia City Wagon Road." II+.

Settle, Raymond and Mary. OVERLAND DAYS TO MONTANA. IV.

Shackleford, Ruth. TO CALIFORNIA. II.

Spencer, Almon. Diary. Not Seen.

Steen, Enoch R. Diary. III+.

Storrs Family, Diary. III+.

Switzer, Malphus A. Reminiscence. IV.

Watkins, Francis. CROW EMIGRANT TRAIN. III.

Young, Will H. "Journals." IV.

Zeamer, R. Jeremiah. Diary. III.

1866

Agatz, Cora W. "A Journey across the Plains." V.

Bailey, Theodore A. Personal Narrative. Not Seen.

Barnes, Demas. FROM THE ATLANTIC. IV.

Birge, Julius C. AWAKENING OF THE DESERT. III.

Blythe, Samuel F. Diary. III.

Boller, Henry A. "Across the Sierra Nevada." II.

Burgess, Perry A. "From Illinois to Montana." II.

Carrington, Francis D. MY ARMY LIFE. III.

Creigh, Thomas A. "From Nebraska City to Montana." III.

Fletcher, Ellen G. BRIDE. II.

Fox, George W. "Diary." II.

Hackensmith, Mrs. M. S. Diary. III+.

Jackson, William H. "Bullwhacking across the Plains." II.

———. DIARIES. II.

———. Notes from Diary of a 'Bull Whacker.' II.

Jatta, Mary H. Journal. III.

Jones, Sydney. My Trip Overland. Not Seen.

Lester, Gurdon P. "Round Trip to the Montana Mines." II+.

Lockey, Richard. Diary. III.

Longacre, Myrtle. A Trek West. V-.

McClintock, Margaretta F. My Trip across the Plains. V.

Miles, Thomas C. Reminiscence. III-.

Millard, C. M. "Hugh Kirkendall's Wagon Train." IV.

Robson, Inez A. Reminiscence. V.

Schmidt, Johann H. Across the Plains. I.
Thomas, William K. Diary. III.
Tinney, William T. Overland Trip. III.
Willson, Lester S. Journal. Not Seen.
Wilson, Davis. Diary. I.
Wisner, Sarah A. The Platte River. IV.

1867

Bell, William A. NEW TRACKS. II.
Carrington, Francis D. MY ARMY LIFE. III.
Duncan, Elizabeth. Diary. II.
Evans, C. B. ANOTHER MONTANA PIONEER. V.
French, Barsina R. Journal. III.
Jackson, William H. DIARIES. II.
Waters, William E. LIFE AMONG THE MORMONS. II.

1868

Blythe, Samuel F. Diary. IV.
Bunyard, Harriet. "Diary." II.
Johnson, M. R. Reminiscence. V.
Ormsby, Augusta. Diary. IV.
Pennebaker, W. G. "Westward from Wayne County." III.
Powers, Stephen. AFOOT AND ALONE. II.
Shackleford, Ruth. TO CALIFORNIA. II.
Vogdes, Ada. Journal. II.

1869

Anon., Diary. Not Seen.
Culver, E. S. "Crossing the Plains." V.
Mariager, Dagmar. "A Voyage by Land." III.
Newman, Orson N. Memoranda. III.
Pankey, H. S. "From Texas to California." V.
Westerman, Pleasant B. "How I Got to California." V.

CANADA

General

Akrigg, G. P., and Helen B. BRITISH COLUMBIA JOURNAL.
Alcock, Frederick. "Past and Present Routes to the Canadian Northwest."
Balf, Mary. THE OVERLANDERS AND OTHER NORTH THOMPSON TRAVELERS.
Barrett-Lennard, C. E. TRAVELS IN BRITISH COLUMBIA. Not Seen.
Begbie, Matthew B. "Journey into the Interior of British Columbia."
Belanger, Art J. CALGARY-EDMONTON, EDMONTON-CALGARY TRAIL.
Berry, Gerald. THE WHOOP-UP TRAIL.
Bradley, Theodore X. "The Cariboo Trail to Barkerville."
British Columbia. OVERLAND COACH ROAD.
Campbell, Murray. "Postal History."
CANADA AND BRITISH COLUMBIA.
Coutant, Frank R. CARIBOO HIGHWAY.
Creech, E. P. "Similkameen Trails, 1846 - 1861."
Draper, W. P. "Early Trails and Roads in the Lower Fraser Valley."
_____. "Some Early Roads and Trails in New Westminster District."
Elliott, Gordon R. BARKERVILLE CARIBOO GOLD RUSH.
Gardiner, R. W. Life of the Late W. B. Cameron. Not Seen.
Gilman, Rhoda, Carolyn Gilman, and Deborah M. Stultz. RED RIVER TRAILS.
Gluek, Alvin C. "The Minnesota Route."
Hertz, A. Jay. "Expresses of British Columbia."
Hind, Henry Y. NORTHWEST TERRITORY.
_____. PAPERS LAKE SUPERIOR AND THE RED RIVER.
_____. SKETCH OF AN OVERLAND ROUTE.
Jeffcott, P. R. NOOKSACK TALES AND TRAILS.

Kaye, Barry, and John Alwin. "The Beginnings of Wheeled Transport in Western Canada."
Laing, F. W. "Some Pioneers of the Cattle Industry."
McDonald, William J. NOTES BY A PIONEER. Not Seen.
McDougall, John. FOREST, LAKE, AND PRAIRIE.
_____. SADDLE, SELD AND SNOWSHOE.
MacEwan, John G. BLAZING THE OLD CATTLE TRAIL.
Meyers, Leonard W. "Via the Fraser Canyon."
Palliser, John. EXPLORATION BRITISH NORTH AMERICA.
Rickard, T. A. "Fraser River Gold Rush."
Russell, Ralph C. THE CARLETON TRAIL.
Schaffer, Mary T. S. OLD INDIAN TRAILS OF THE CANADIAN ROCKIES.
Schultz, J. C. "The Old Crow Wing Trail." Not Seen.
Spry, Irene M. THE PALLISER EXPEDITION.
_____. "Routes through the Rockies."
Sylvester, Frank. Diary. Not Seen.
Thomas, Lewis H. "The Hind and Dawson Expeditions, 1857-58."
Trutch, Joseph W. OVERLAND COACH ROAD.
Turner, Allan R. "Palliser of the Triangle."
Wade, Mark S. THE CARIBOO ROAD. Not Seen.
Weir, Thomas R. "Early Trails of Burrard Peninsula."
Wright, Richard T. OVERLANDERS.

Bibliographies

Reid, Robie L. "British Columbia: A Bibliographical Sketch."
Wright, Richard T. OVERLANDERS.

Maps

Spry, Irene M. "Routes through the Rockies."

Graphics

Ballantyne, Robert M. HUDSON'S BAY.
Cheadle, Walter B. CHEADLE'S JOURNAL OF TRIP ACROSS CANADA.
Harper, J. Russell. WILLIAM G. R. HIND.
Milton, William F. AN EXPEDITION ACROSS THE ROCKY MOUNTAINS.

1841

Allen, George T. "Journal of a Voyage." II
Flett, John. "From Red River to the Columbia." V.

1842

Ballantyne, Robert M. HUDSON'S BAY. II.

1846

Alcorn, Rowena L., and Gordon D. PAUL KANE. III.
De Smet, Pierre. OREGON MISSIONS, 1845-46. IV.
Kane, Paul. WANDERINGS OF AN ARTIST. II +.

1847

Alcorn, Rowena L., and Gordon D. PAUL KANE. III.
Kane, Paul. WANDERINGS OF AN ARTIST. II +.

1849

Pope, John. REPORT TERRITORY OF MINNESOTA. II.

1851

McDonald, William J. NOTES. Not Seen.

1852

Anderson, David. NET IN THE BAY. II +.
Jacobs, Peter. JOURNAL FROM RICE LAKE. II +.

1854

Campbell, John V. "The Sinclair Party." III.
Sinclair, James. Career. V.

1857

Hind, Henry Y. NARRATIVE CANADIAN RED RIVER EXPEDI-
TION. I.

_____. REPORT CANOE ROUTE BETWEEN FORT WILLIAM
AND FORT GARRY. III.

Wolff, Francis. "Ambush at McLaughlin Canyon." V.

1858-Genl

Evans, Elwood. "The Fraser River Excitement, 1858."
Lewis, G. W. LEWIS' MAP OF FRASER RIVER.
McCullough, Samuel. Papers.
O'Brien, Jack M. "The McLoughlin Massacre."

1858

Friesach, Carl. "Gold Rush on the Fraser." V.
Hind, Henry Y. NARRATIVE CANADIAN RED RIVER EXPLORA-
TION. I
Jones, John W. Diary. I.
Shannon, William. The Great Gold Excitement of 1858. Not Seen.
Wright, Richard T. "The Man from Brechin." V.

1859

Babcock, Willoughby M. "Gateway to the Northwest." II.
Damon, John F. Trip Up Fraser River. II.
Marble, Manton. "The Red River Trail." I.
Redgrave, Stephen. Journal. Not Seen.
Southesk, Earl of. SASKATCHEWAN AND THE ROCKY MOUN-
TAINS. Not Seen.
Thibodo, Augustus, J. "Diary." II.

1860

Marble, Manton. "To Red River and Beyond." I.

1861

Harper, J. Russell. "William Hind and the Overlanders." Genl.
1862-Genl
Howay, F. W. "Overland Journal."
Swannell, Frank C. "Lt. Palmer Makes a Survey."
Wade, Mark S. OVERLANDERS OF '62.

1862

Alexander, Richard H. DIARY AND NARRATIVE. II.
Champness, W. TO CARIBOO AND BACK. I.
Cheadle, Walter B. CHEADLE'S JOURNAL OF TRIP ACROSS
CANADA. I.
Fortune, Alexander L. Overland Route to Cariboo. Not Seen.
Guillod, Harry. "Harry Guillod's Journal of a Trip." IV.
Hunniford, John. Journal. Not Seen.
McMicking, Robert B. Diary. Not Seen.
_____. "Overlanders in Alberta." Not Seen.
_____. OVERLAND FROM CANADA. II.
McNaughton, Margaret. OVERLAND TO CARIBOO. III+.
Palmer, Henry S. REPORT OF A JOURNEY. II.
Phillips, William W. San Diego Miner and Lumberman. Not Seen.
Sellar, John M. Overland to Cariboo. Not Seen.
Thomson, James. FOR FRIENDS AT HOME. III.

1863

Milton, William F. AN EXPEDITION ACROSS THE ROCKY
MOUNTAINS. II.
"Walter Moberly's Report on the Roads." Genl.

1864

Hewlett, Edward S. "The Chilcotin Uprising of 1864." Genl.

CHEROKEE TRAIL

This variant incorporated parts of the SANTA FE road, was a major
feeder to Colorado, and later became the Overland Stage Company
route across Colorado, Wyoming and into Salt Lake City. Never well-
traveled, it nevertheless offered an alternative route to Gold Rush
country for emigrants from the southern states. The road started in
northwestern Arkansas, followed the Canadian River to Pueblo,
Colorado, turned north to the Cache La Poudre and Bridger Pass,
then reached Fort Bridger and, ultimately, Salt Lake City.

General

Braatz, Ned E. "An Historical Geography across the Laramie Plains."
Dott, Robert H. "Lt. Simpson's California Road."
Foreman, Grant. MARCY AND THE GOLD SEEKERS.
Kimball, Stanley B. "Another Road to Zion."
Shaw, Dorothy P. "Jimmy's Camp on the Trail."
Spencer, Elma D. GOLD COUNTRY.
Yurtinus, John F. "Colorado, Mormons and the Mexican War."

Maps

Dott, Robert H. "Lt. Simpson's California Road."
Dunning, Harold M. THE OVERLAND TRAIL NORTH.

1843

Brown, John Henry. REMINISCENCES AND INCIDENTS. V.

1844

Brown, John Henry. REMINISCENCES AND INCIDENTS. V.

1845

"Abstract of Journals." V-.
Franklin, William B. MARCH TO SOUTH PASS. II.
Kearny, Stephen W. REPORT. V-.

1846-General

Carter, Kate B. "Mississippi Saints."
_____. THE MORMON BATTALION.
Marshall, Donald W. "The Mississippi Saints and Sick Detachments."

1846

Allen, Franklin. Journal. IV.
Andrus. Manomus L. Statement. V.
Arrington, Leonard J. "Mississippi Saints." IV.
Brown, John. PIONEER JOURNEYS. V.
Brown, John Z. AUTOBIOGRAPHY. IV.
Hafen, Leroy R., and Frank M. Young. "Mormon Settlement at Pueblo,
CO." III.
Wilson, George D. Journal. IV.

1847

Allen, Franklin. Journal. IV.
Arrington, Leonard J. "Mississippi Saints." IV.
Bingham, Thomas. History. V.
Hess, John W. "John W. Hess." V-.
Higgins, Catherine B. Biography. V.
Kartchner, William D. "Autobiography." V.
Kellam, John P. Diary. IV.
Tippets, John H. History and Account. III.

1849-Genl

Bieber, Ralph P. SOUTHERN TRAILS.
Dott, Robert H. "Lt. Simpson's California Road across Oklahoma."
Hafen, Leroy R. "Cherokee Goldseekers in Colorado."

1849

Brown, Harvey S. Statement. IV.
Chamberlain, William H. "From Lewisburg to California." I.
Davis, Hiram. "Journal." III.

Eastin, Thomas D. Collected Data. IV.
Eliot, Robert. "Off to the Gold Fields."
Foreman, Grant. MARCY AND THE GOLD SEEKERS. II+.
Pyeatt, J. Rankin. "Some Pyeatt Letters." III.
Randolph, W. C. Statement. V.
Robinson, Edwin. Story of a Pioneer. V.
Scarborough, A. DIARY. II+.
Stuart, Charles V. Trip. V.
Taylor, W. B. "Pioneer Reminiscence." IV.

1850
Brown, John Lowery. "Journal En Route to California." III+.
Quesenbury, William. "William Quesenbury's Diary." II+.
Ridge, John R. "John Rollin Ridge." IV.
Stansbury, Howard. EXPLORATION AND SURVEY. II+.

1851
Thomson, Jeremiah B. Early Days in Oregon. III.

1852
Hoag, Amanda J. Papers. Not Seen.
Todd, John R. "Across the Plains." V.

1853
Ward, Dillis B. ACROSS THE PLAINS. III.
Williams Family. Papers. III.

1854
Anon., Diary. III+.
Engels, William H. "Diary of a Cattle Drive." III.
Willey, Lucas. Diaries. I.

1856
Bryan, F. T. "Report." III.

1857
Cureton, William H. Trekking to California. II.
Dunn, J. W. Diary. II+.
Parker, Basil G. LIFE AND ADVENTURES. V.

1858
Kellogg, David. "Across the Plains." II.
Parsons, William B. "Pike's Peak." IV.
Younker, Jason T. "The Early Pioneer." V.

1859
Burton, Richard F. CITY OF THE SAINTS. I.
Day, Alphonso. Diary. III+.
Faulkner, Harry. Diary. III.
Gass, A. M. "From Texas to Pike's Peak." III.
Holman, Cyrus K. Journal. II+.
Post, Charles C. "The Arkansas Route." II.
Sanford, Albert B. "The Cherokee Trail." Genl.
Sowers, John H. Diary. III.
Studley, Hiram W. "Letter." IV.
Westerlund, Peter. Reminiscence. III.
Willey, Lucas. Diaries. I.
Willing, George M. "Diary of a Journey." II.

1860
Lambert, Julia S. "Plain Tales of the Plains." II.
Manning, Malvina V. Diary. III.
Porter, Lavinia H. BY OX TEAM TO CALIFORNIA. II.
Powell, Philander. History. II+.
Preston, Leander A. "Journal." IV."
Route from Denver to Fort Bridger." Genl.
Wornell, David C. Diary. II.
Wright, Dunham. Narrative. V.

1861
Benjamin, Israel. THREE YEARS. II.
Brown, John Mason. "Diary." II+.
Fosdick, Lucy H. "Across the Plains." IV.
Manning, Malvina V. Diary. III.
Preston, Leander A. "Journal." IV.
Twain, Mark. ROUGHING IT. I.

1862
Bliss, Edward. "Denver to Salt Lake by Stage." II.
Durley, Jeff. Diary. II+.
Kassler, George W. "George W. Kassler." IV.
Meredith, Emily R. Experiences. III.
Newkirk, Coleman S. Brief History. V.
Shelley, Edward. "Western Journal." IV.
Wright, Dunham. Narrative. V.

1863
Bruffey, George A. EIGHTY-ONE YEARS. V.
Cutting, A. Howard. Journal. II+.
Ferster, James S. Sketch. V.
Lewis, B. P. Diary. II.
McPherson, Murdoch M. "Reminiscences of." II.
O'Neil, Elizabeth E. Reminiscence. V.
Patten, F. E. W. Journal of Travels. I.
Purviance, M. C. Journal. II.
Ronan, Margaret. "Memoirs." III.
Walker, Joseph C. Description. II.
Webster, Noah H. "Journal of Noah Webster." II.
Wilson, Alex. "Trip across the Plains." V-.

1864
Allton, Hiram. Diary. III.
Bushnell, George E. Diary. Not Seen.
Creel, Virginia F. Diary. II.
Evans, James A. Report. III.
Gallatin, E. L. "Reminiscences." III.
Keaton, Charles H. "Crossing the Plains." Freight.
Luster, Mary R. AUTOBIOGRAPHY. Not Seen.
Mallory, Samuel. Papers. IV.
_____. "Samuel Mallory." II.
Stafford, Mollie. MARCH OF EMPIRE. V.
Strateler, L. B. Diary. II.
Tomlinson, John J. Log. III+.

1865
Bowles, Samuel. ACROSS THE CONTINENT. II.
Cauthorn, Benjamin R. Trip to Montana. I.
Chillson, Lorenzo D. Diary. III.
Colfax, Schuyler. "Honorable Schuyler Colfax's Trip." II. Stage.
Ellis, Henrietta. DIARY. II.
Leech, A. P. Diary. II.
Steen, Enoch R. Diary. III+.
Thoroughman, Robert P. A Trip. IV.

1866
Barnes, Demas. FROM THE ATLANTIC. IV.
Birge, Julius C. AWAKENING. III.
Jatta, Mary H. Journal. III.
Jones, Daniel. Travels across the Plains. V.
Muzzal, Thomas A. "Across the Plains." III.
Schmidt, Johann H. Across the Plains. I.

1867
Duncan, Elizabeth. Diary. II.
Waters, William E. LIFE AMONG THE MORMONS. II.

Myers, Alice V. "Sioux City, Iowa, Expeditions." Genl.
_____. "Wagon Roads West." IV.
Peck, S. L. HISTORY. V.
Hilger, David. "Overland Trail." IV.
Lueg, Henry. "Northern Overland Route. II.

1867
Hilger, David. "Overland Trail." IV.
Lueg, Henry. "Northern Overland Route." II.
Maricle, Abraham. Diary. III-.

FORT HALL CUTOFF

This trail segment is normally a part of the Oregon Trail category since the customary route taken by Oregon emigrants reached the Snake River via Fort Hall. Readers seeking information on this segment should also scan those items listed under the Oregon Trail. Geographic extent of this segment begins at Soda Springs, continues to Fort Hall, but also includes the trail southwest of Fort Hall to the headwaters of the Humboldt. Most entries in this list are California-bound emigrants who visited Ft. Hall prior to establishment of Hudspeth's Cutoff in 1849, or those who later chose to take the longer Fort Hall dogleg road to City of Rocks. In the 1860's many Montana-bound parties passed Fort Hall while en route for Bannack and other camps.

1841
Belden, Josiah. "The First Overland Emigrant Train." IV.
_____. JOSIAH BELDEN. III.
Bidwell, John. JOHN BIDWELL'S TRIP. II.
Chiles, Joseph B. Visit to California in 1841." V.
Dawson, Nicholas. NARRATIVE OF. III.

1843
Brown, John Henry. REMINISCENCES AND INCIDENTS. V.
Giffen, Helen S. TRAIL-BLAZING PIONEER. III.
Reading, Pierson B. "Journal of Pierson Barton Reading." II.

1844
Bray, Edmund. Letter. V.
Brown, John Henry. REMINISCENCES AND INCIDENTS. V.
Murphy, Martin. The Murphy Family. IV.
Murphy, Patrick W. Biography. V-.
Schallenberger, Moses. OPENING. III.

1845
Gregson, James. Statement. V.
Hudson, David. Autobiography. IV.
Ide, William. BIOGRAPHICAL SKETCH. III.
Knight, Thomas. Recollections. IV.
Marshall, Henry. Statement. V-.
Smith, Napoleon B. Biographical Sketch. V.
Snyder, Jacob. "Diary of Jacob Snyder." III+.
Tinkey, David. Statement. V-.
Tustin, William I. Recollections. V-.

1846
Applegate, Lindsay. "Notes and Reminiscences." II.
Aram, Joseph. "Across the Continent." V.
Brown, Elam. BIOGRAPHY. IV.
Campbell, David. Pioneer of 1846. V.
Craig, John. Letter. V.
Dickenson, Luella. REMINISCENCES. IV.
Garrison, A. E. LIFE AND LABORS. IV.
Good, Daniel H. Letters. IV.
Grayson, Andrew J. Account. IV.
Hecox, Margaret M. CALIFORNIA CARAVAN. IV.
Jones, Mrs. M. A. Reminiscences. IV.

Pettigrew, David. Autobiography. III-.
Taylor, William E. Diary. III.
Thornton, J. Quinn. OREGON AND CALIFORNIA. II.

1847
Davidson, T. L. By the Southern Route. IV.
Findla, James. "Statement." V.
Hyde, William. Private Journal. IV.
Ingersoll, Chester. OVERLAND. III.
Moore, Alexander. "Statement." V.
Pace, James. Journal. III+.
Turner, Henry S. ORIGINAL JOURNALS. II.

1848
Bayley, Thomas S. The First Overland Mail Bag. IV.
Belknap, Kitturah P. "Commentaries." IV.
Burrows, Rufus G. Anecdotes. IV.
_____, and Cyrus Hull. A LONG ROAD TO STONY CREEK. V.
Cornwall, Bruce. LIFE SKETCH. IV.
May, Richard M. Sketch. II+.
May, Sam. Sketch. II+.
Pettijohn, Isaac. Diary. III.
Tappan, Henry. "Diary." IV.

1849
Anderson, Niles. "Grandfather Was a Forty-Niner." IV.
Averett, George W. Autobiography. IV.
Beesley, E. Maurice. Diary. III.
Berrien, Joseph W. "Overland from St. Louis." I.
Bonine, Dr. Diary. Not Seen.
Buffum, Joseph. Diary. II+.
Burton, Henry W. Diary. II.
Caldwell, T. G. "Notes of a Journey." III.
Carstarphen, James E. MY TRIP TO CALIFORNIA. V.
Chamberlain, William E. Diary. II.
Clark, Bennett C. "Diary of a Journey from Missouri." II.
Coats, Felix G. On the Golden Trail. V.
Coffey, Alvin A. "A Black Pioneer's Trip." V.
Cosad, David. Journal. III+.
Daigh, James M. NUGGETS FROM '49. IV.
Denver, A. "Letter-Journal." IV.
Drake, Joshua. Diary. II.
Gillespie, Robert. Diary. III.
Green, Edmund. Reminiscences. III.
Hackney, Joseph. "Diary." II+.
Hale, Israel F. "Diary of Trip." III+.
Harker, George M. "Morgan Street to Old Dry Diggings." IV.
Hixson, Jasper M. Diary. I.
Hoffman, Benjamin. "Diary." III+.
Humphreys, James H. Reminiscences. IV.
Isham, Giles S. GUIDE. II.
Jagger, D. Diary. I.
Johnson, John A. Journal. II+.
Kane, Michael. Statement. V.
Kirkpatrick, Charles A. Diary. II+.
Lindsey, Tipton. Diary. II+.
Long, Charles L. Diary. II+.
Love, Alexander. Diary. II.
Mann, H. R. Diary. II+.
Merrill, Joseph H. Diary. II+.
Meyer, George. AUTOBIOGRAPHY. IV.
Montesano, Phil. "A Black Pioneer's Trip." IV.
Muscott, John M., and William N. Steuben. Letters. IV.
Negley, Felix C. Diary. Not Seen.
Nixon, Alexander B. Diary. II.
Oglesby, Richard J. "Richard J. Oglesby." IV.
Page, Elizabeth. WAGONS WEST. I.
Pattison, Nathan. Letter. V-.

Patton, Thomas M. Diaries. Not Seen.
Potter, David M. TRAIL TO CALIFORNIA. I.
Price, Hugh M. and Franklin. Diary. Not Seen.
Pritchard, James A. OVERLAND DIARY. I.
Ramsey, Alexander. "Alexander Ramsey's Gold Rush Diary." III.
Reynolds, Charles D. Reminiscences. IV.
Robinson, Zirkle. ROBINSON-ROSENBERGER. IV.
Steuben, William N. Diary. II.
Tate, James. Diary. III+.
Tiffany, P. C. Diary. I.
Tinker, Charles. "Charles Tinker's Journal." III.
Topham, Edward. Castles in California. IV.
Vancil, Frank M. "Overland Stampede." V.
Watts, Benjamin M. Diary. II.
Wier, John B. "From Where the Gold Diggers Go." III.
Willis, Edward J. Diary. III+.
Wistar, Isaac J. AUTOBIOGRAPHY. III.
Wood, Harvey. PERSONAL RECOLLECTIONS. III.
Wood, J. W. Journal. II+.
Woods, Joseph W. Diary. I.
Zumwalt, Joe. FORTY-NINER. V-.

1850
Bowman, Frank. Diary. IV.
Daggy, Elias. Diary. II+.
Dowell, B. F. Crossing the Plains. III+.
Frink, Margaret A. JOURNAL. III.
Gundlach, John H. Diary. Not Seen.
Harlan, A. W. "Journal." II.
Keller, George. TRIP ACROSS. III.
Lane, Samuel A. GOLD RUSH. II.
Loomis, Leander V. JOURNAL. III.
Loveland, Cyrus C. CALIFORNIA. II.
McKinstry, Bruce L. CALIFORNIA GOLD RUSH. I.
Ogle, William B. Diary. II+.
Osterhoudt, Solomon. "Ox Train Diary." III.
Paschal, Albert G. Overland Trip. II+.
Thompson, Jesse C. Diary. III.
Thompson, William P. Diary. III.
Williams, John T. "Journal of John T. Williams." III.

1851
Jennings, Oliver. Journal. IV.

1852
Constant, Isaac. "A Brief Review." III.
Dodson, John F. "Dodson's Death." III.
True, Charles F. COVERED WAGON PIONEERS. III.

1853
Quail. Journal. II.
Winthrop, Theodore. CANOE AND THE SADDLE. III.

1858
Ficklin, Benjamin F. "Ficklin's Expedition." IV.

1859
Chillson, Lorenzo D. Diary. III.
True, Charles F. COVERED WAGON PIONEERS. III.

1861
Maillet, Louis R. Account. V. (May be an 1859 reminiscence)

1862
Bushnell, Daniel E. Diary. Not Seen.
Durley, Jeff. Diary. II+.
Meredith, Emily R. Experiences. III.
Toutillot, Jane A. "Diary and Journal." I.

1863
Aulbach, Adam. A Voice. V.
Bruffey, George. EIGHTY-ONE YEARS. V.
Darling, Lucia. Diary. I.
McPherson, Murdoch M. "Reminiscences." II.
Moore, Miles C. Recollections. Not Seen.
Patten, F. E. Journal. I.
Sanders, Harriet P. Reminiscences. II.
Word, Samuel. "Diary." II.

1864
Arnold, Joseph W. "Joseph Warren Arnold's Journal." III+.
Beall, Frank E. Dream of an Empire. III.
Brubaker, Albert. A Trip. IV.
Dalrymple, Ward. Reminiscence. V.
Fisk, Mrs. Van. Reminiscence. V.
Forbis, Jonathan F. Reminiscence. V.
Mallory, Samuel. Papers. IV.
_____. "Samuel Mallory." II.
O'Neill, Eliza. Reminiscences. V.
Strateler, L. B. Diary. II.
Woods, Allin W. Journal. IV.

1865
Cowden, Henry. Diary. III.
Flory, A. P. Life and Memoirs. III.
Gibson, J. W. RECOLLECTIONS. IV.
Herndon, Sarah R. DAYS ON THE ROAD. IV.
Miller, James K. ROAD TO VIRGINIA CITY. III.
Steen, Enoch R. Diary. III+.
Thoroughman, Robert P. A Trip. IV.

1866
Agatz, Cora W. "A Journey." V.
Tinney, William T. Overland Trip. III.
Williams, John B. Diary. II.

1867
Evans, C. B. ANOTHER MONTANA PIONEER. V.

1869
Newman, Orson N. Memoranda. III.

GILA TRAIL

General
Allyn, Joseph P. THE ARIZONA OF ALLYN.
Bieber, Ralph P., and A. B. Bender, EXPLORING SOUTHWESTERN
    TRAILS.
Bowman, Eldon G. A GUIDE TO THE GENERAL CROOK TRAIL.
Box, James. ADVENTURES AND EXPLORATIONS.
Brandes, Ray. FRONTIER MILITARY POSTS OF ARIZONA.
Bynum, Lindley. RECORD BOOK, RANCHO SANTA ANA DEL
    CHINO.
Cox, Douglas M. "America's Greatest Infantry March."
Cremony, John C. LIFE AMONG THE APACHES.
Cross, Jack L. "El Paso-Fort Yuma Wagon Road."
_____. "Pre-Road Building Period in New Mexico Territory."
Edwards, Elza I. LOST OASES ALONG THE CARRIZO.
Egan, Ferol. EL DORADO TRAIL.
Faulk, Odie B. DESTINY ROAD
_____. TOO FAR NORTH.
Forbes, Jack D. "Development of the Yuma Route."
Forest, Mary Rose. "Yuma, 1846 - 1877."
Fourr, J. William. "Reminiscences."
"The Gila Trail."

Wallace, Mr. Letters. III +.

1861
Hazen, Eli W. "California Column." III.
Pumpelly, Raphael. ACROSS AMERICA AND ASIA. III.

1862
California Volunteer. CALIFORNIA CIVIL WAR DIARY. III.
Fergusson, David. REPORT. I.
Kibby, Leo P. "With Col. Carleton and the California Column." Genl.
Miller, Darlis A. "Historian for the California Column." IV.
Pettis, George H. CALIFORNIA COLUMN. III.
_____. Letters. III.
_____. PERSONAL NARRATIVES. III.
Teal, John W. "Soldier in the California Column." III.
Wilkes, Homer. "Expressman Jones." II.

1863
Fourr, J. William. Manuscripts. I.
_____. "Reminiscences." Genl.

1864
Allyn, Joseph P. THE ARIZONA OF JOSEPH PRATT ALLYN. Genl.
Browne, J. Ross. ADVENTURES. II.
Miller, Darlis A. ACROSS THE PLAINS. II.
Putnam, Joseph P. "Letters." II.
Taylor, John. "Comanche County." III.

1865
Allyn, Joseph P. THE ARIZONA OF JOSEPH PRATT ALLYN. Genl.
Hunt, Aurora. "California Volunteers." IV.
Putnam, Joseph P. "Letters." II.
Underhill, Lonnie E. "Dr. Edward Palmer." Genl.

1866
Hackensmith, Mrs. M. S. Diary. III +.
Putnam, Joseph P. "Letters." II.
Spring, John. JOHN SPRING'S ARIZONA. III.
_____. "A March to Arizona from California." III.
Underhill, Lonnie. "Dr. Edward Palmer." Genl.

1867
Bell, William A. NEW TRACKS. II.
Hunter, Thomas T. Early Days in Arizona. III.

1868
Bunyard, Harriet. "Diary." II.
Johnson, M. R. Reminiscence. V.
Ormsby, Augusta. Diary. IV.
Powers, Stephen. AFOOT AND ALONE. II.
Shackleford, Ruth. TO CALIFORNIA. II.

1869
Johnson, M. R. Reminiscence. V.
Palmer, Edward. Diary. Not Seen.
Pankey, H. S. "From Texas to California." V.
Robert, Henry. ITINERARIES OF ROUTES IN ARIZONA. Genl.
Westerman, Pleasant B. "How I Got to California." V.

HASTINGS CUTOFF

General
Andrews, Thomas F. "Controversial Hastings Overland Guide."
_____. "Lansford W. Hastings, A Reappraisal."
Bluth, John. CONFRONTATION.
Kelly, Charles. "Gold Seekers on the Hastings Cutoff."
_____. "The Hastings Cutoff."

_____. "Lansford W. Hastings."
_____. SALT DESERT TRAILS.
_____. "Treasure Hunt on the Salt Desert."
Korns, J. Roderick. "West from Fort Bridger.
Miller, David E. "Donner Road through the Great Salt Lake Desert."
Morgan, Dale L. THE GREAT SALT LAKE.
Paden, Irene D. PRAIRIE SCHOONER DETOURS.
Webb, Henry F. "Long Drive on the Hastings Cut-off."

1845-General
Webb, Henry F. "The First Trail across the Great Salt Desert."

1846-General
Andrews, Thomas F. "Lansford W. Hastings."
Creer, Leland H. "Lansford W. Hastings."
Kelly, Charles. "Treasure Hunt on the Salt Desert."
McGlashan, C. F. HISTORY. II.
Miller, David. "The Donner Road through the Great Salt Lake Desert."
North, Arthur W. "The Cut-off."
Sparks, Elmer. "A New Mystery on the Donner Trail."
Webb, Henry F. "Edwin Bryant's Trail.

1846
Allen, Isaac. Biography. V.
Boggs, William M. Reminiscences. IV.
Breen, John. Dictation. II.
Bryant, Edwin. WHAT I SAW IN CALIFORNIA. I.
Camp, Charles L. JAMES CLYMAN. I.
Clark, William S. Biographical Sketch. V.
Croy, Homer. WHEELS WEST. III.
Graves, William C. "Crossing the Plains." IV.
Harlan, Jacob W. CALIFORNIA. III.
Houghton, Eliza P. EXPEDITION. III.
Lienhard, Heinrich. FROM ST. LOUIS. II.
McGlashan, Charles F. HISTORY OF THE DONNER PARTY. II.
Mathers, James. "Journal of Travels." III.
Mitchell, Annie R. JIM SAVAGE. V.
Reed, James F. "Diary." III-.
_____. "Snow-Bound." IV.
Wimmer, Peter. CALIFORNIA GOLD BOOK. V.
Young, Samuel C. Biographical Obituary. V.

1847
Craig, John. Letter. V.

1849
Chamberlain, William Edwin. Diary. II.
Eastin, Thomas D. Collected Data. IV.
Hayes, Benjamin I. Notes. V.
Royce, Sarah B. FRONTIER LADY. III.
_____. "From Salt Lake to the Sierras." III.
Vancil, Frank M. "Overland Stampede." V.

1850
Ayres, Samuel M. Letters. IV.
Bloom, Henry S. Diary. II.
Brown, John Lowery. "Journal of John Lowery Brown." III +.
Chalmers, Robert. "Journal of Robert Chalmers." II.
Clark, Costmor H. Journal of Costmor H. Clark. II.
Davenport, O. F. Letters. Not Seen.
Davis, A. S. Diary. III.
Denver, James W. "Denver Diary Overland." II.
Edmundson, William. "Overland Diary." II.
Hubbard, Chauncey B. SPARKS FROM MANY CAMP FIRES. III.
Hume, James B. Papers. III.
Lawson, George. Diary. III-.
McDiarmid, Finley. Letters. II +.
McLellan, William. Incidents of a Trip. II.

Milliken, Samuel. Letters. III.
Moorman, Madison B. JOURNAL. III.
Morrison, Samuel C. Letter. V.
Newcomb, Alphonso B. Across the Plains. IV.
Primes, Ed M. Journal. Not Seen.
Randall, J. D. Diary. Not Seen.
Shaw, D. A. EL DORADO. III.
Shinn, John R. Journal. III.
Skinner, Hugh A. Diary. II.
Udell, John. INCIDENTS. III+.
Wilson, Robert M. Chronicle. III.
Wood, John. JOURNAL. II.

1853
Hudson, Richard. "To the Gold Fields." V-.

1854
Schiel, Jacob H. LAND BETWEEN. II+.

1855
Remy, Jules, and Julius Brenchley. JOURNEY TO GREAT-SALT-
    LAKE CITY. II.

1857
Huntington, "Eighteen Days on the Desert." II.

LANDER ROAD

General
Boyack, Mrs. A. R. "Oregon Trail Trek No. Eight."
Harstad, Peter T. "Constructing the Lander Road."
_____. "The Lander Trail."
_____. "Use of the Lander Trail."
Lander, Papers.
Smith, "Fort Kearney, South Pass, and Honey Lake Wagon Road."

1842
Crawford, Medorem. JOURNAL. II.

1853
Luark, Michael. Diary. II+.

1857
O'Neill, O. H. Journal. Not Seen.

1859
Armstrong, William. '49 Experiences. III.
Babcock, William H. Journal. Not Seen.
Barnett, Joel. A LONG TRIP. III.
Brown, Alonzo F. Autobiography. IV.
Brown, James Berry. JOURNAL OF A JOURNEY. III.
Byrne Family. Papers. V.
Case, Hamet H. Diary. III+.
Cooper, Arvazine A. "Pioneer across the Plains." IV.
Cummings, Charles J. Diary. II+.
Harbert, Joseph W. DIARY. III.
Kellogg, M. G. NOTES CONCERNING THE KELLOGG'S. III+.
McPherson, William G. "Journal of Overland Travel." III+.
Moore, Martha M. Journal. Not Seen.
True, Charles F. COVERED WAGON PIONEERS. III.
Wagner, William H. Rough Notes. Genl.

1860
Earnshaw, William. Across the Plains. Not Seen.
Evans, James A. Journal. III.

1862

Bristol, D. Sherlock. PIONEER PREACHER. V.
Burgunder, Ben. "Recollections." V.
Bushnell, Daniel E. Diary. Not Seen.
Ford, A. T. Life and History. V.
Gould, Jane H. "Iowa to California." II+.
Judson, H. M. Diary. I.
McClung, James S. Diary. I.
McLaughlin, Daniel. SKETCH. III.
Manville, George. Story of My Life. III.
Nichols, Robert A. Letters. V.
Stites, Thomas J. Journal of Travels. III.
Trip to Oregon, 1862. IV.

1863
Bailey, James L. Diary. III-.
Card, Cicero. Diary. Not Seen.
Cooper, Arvazena A. "Pioneer across the Plains." IV.
Edgerton, Mary. A GOVERNOR'S WIFE. II.
Kirkpatrick, Robert. "From Wisconsin to Montana." II.
Moore, Miles. Recollections. Not Seen.

1864
Arnold, Joseph W. "Joseph Warren Arnold's Journal." III+.
Dickson, Albert J. COVERED WAGON DAYS. II.
Dunlap, Catherine C. MONTANA. II.
Durfee, Joseph A. Diaries. Not Seen.
Fisk, Mrs. Van. Reminiscence. V.
Forman, George. "Across the Plains." IV.
Loughary, Mrs. W. A. Diary. II.
Mahan, Garland. Diary. II+.
Merrill, Julius C. Diary. II+.
Porter, Elizabeth L. Crossing the Plains. III.
Roe, Martha A. A Trip to Idaho. II+.
Wilkinson, Raleigh F. Recollections. Not Seen.
Wright, J. B. Epic of the West. IV.

1865
Bailey, David J. Diary. II+.

LASSEN CUTOFF

General
Colby, W. Howard. A CENTURY OF TRANSPORTATION.
Cox, Evelyn. "Northern Trail to California in 1849."
Hammond, Andy. "Peter Lassen and his Trail."
Helfrich, Devere. "Applegate Trail."
_____. EMIGRANT TRAILS WEST.
Layton, Thomas N. "Stalking Elephants in Nevada."
Martin, Oscar F. "The Old Lassen Trail."
Paden, Irene D. PRAIRIE SCHOONER DETOURS. Recommended.
Swartzlow, Ruby J. "Peter Lassen."
Wheeler, Sessions S. THE BLACK ROCK DESERT.

Graphics
Layton, Thomas. "Stalking Elephants in Nevada."

Maps
Helfrich, Devere. "Applegate Trail."

1846
Garrison, A. E. LIFE AND LABORS. IV.
Henderson, Lucy A. "Young Adventure." II.

1847
Findla, James. "Statement." V.
Hopper, Charles. CHARLES HOPPER. IV.
Moore, Alexander. "Statement." V.

1856
Powers, Mary R. A WOMAN'S OVERLAND JOURNAL. I.
Stowell, George. Reminiscence. IV.

1857
Parman, Henry H. Beyond the Horizon. IV.
Stuart, Granville. FORTY YEARS. IV.
Stuart, James. Diary. V.

1859
Brown, James Berry. JOURNAL. III.
Hayden, Rosa B. "Memoirs of Early California Days." IV.
Henry, David. Reminiscences. V.
Kellogg, M. G. NOTES CONCERNING THE KELLOGG'S. III +.
Kingman, Henry. TRAVELS. V.
McPherson, William G. "Journal of Overland Travel." III +.
Moore, Martha M. Journal. Not Seen.

1860
Guill, Mary J. Diary. II.
Lowry, James L. Diary. II +.

1861
Butterfield, Ira H. "Michigan to California." III.
Freeman, "Fortune Lost in Cattle Drive." IV.
Kidder, Leory L. Story. IV.
Taylor, Ruth W. "A Letter Home." IV.

1862
Fish, Juliette. Crossing the Plains. IV.
Josephy, Alfred M. "Lolo Trail." III.
Scott, Charlton. Diary. II.

1863
Walker, Mattie. A Brief History. V.

1864
Briggs, Joshua E., and Ruth Floweree. A PIONEER MISSOURIAN. V.
Rosenberg, Daniel. MARY BROWN. V.

1865
Cowden, Henry. Diary. III.

MARCY TRAIL

This road extends west from Fort Smith, Arkansas to Santa Fe via the
   Canadian River. Never as well-traveled as other, better known routes,
   the Marcy trace had its maximum utilization in 1849.

General
Archambeau, Ernest R. "Fort Smith-Santa Fe Trail along the Canadian
   River in Texas."
Barnhill, J. Herschel. "The Way West."
Gooden, John H. "Life and Experiences of the Forty-Niners on the
   Southwestern Roads."
Harlan, Anna Louise. "The Fort Smith-Santa Fe Trail."
Neighbours, Kenneth F. "The Marcy-Neighbors Exploration of the
   Headwaters of the Brazos and Wichita Rivers in 1854."
Weaver, Frank. "Fort Smith, Hub into the Wilderness."
Williams, J. W. "Marcy and Butterfield Trails across Texas."

Graphics
Abert, James W. THROUGH THE COUNTRY. I.

Maps
Archambeau, Ernest R. "The Fort Smith-Santa Fe Trail."

1845
Abert, James W. THROUGH THE COUNTRY. I.
Montaignes, Francois des. THE PLAINS. II.

1849
Aldrich, Lorenzo D. JOURNAL. III.
Blunt, Phineas W. Notes of Travel. I.
Boyles, John R. "None But Dream of Success." V-.
Brownlee, Robert. AN AMERICAN ODYSSEY. II.
Candee, J. G. Letter. IV.
Chamberlain, William H. "From Lewisburg to California." I.
Conway, Mary. "Little Rock Girl." IV.
Counts, George. Journal. III-.
Creighton, Mary E. Reminiscences. V.
Crumpton, H. J., and W. B. ADVENTURES. Rem. IV.
Dott, Robert H. "Lt. Simpson's Road across Oklahoma." Genl.
Eliot, Robert. "Off to the Gold Field." IV.
Foreman, Grant. MARCY AND THE GOLD SEEKERS. II +.
Gooding, Larry. "Across the Plains." IV.
Green, Robert B. ON THE ARKANSAS ROUTE. III.
Hammond, John. IN MEMORIAM. V.
Jordan, David. Diary. I.
King, Alfred D. "Trip to the Gold Fields." II +.
Lasselle, Stanislaus. "Diary." III.
Marcy, R. B. "Report." II.
May, John. Correspondence. Not Seen.
Phillips, Marcia B. Five Stevenson Men. III.
REPORTS SECRETARY OF WAR. II.
Robinson, Edwin. Story of a Pioneer. V.
Scarborough, A. DIARY. II +.
Shinn, Silas. TRAIL OF A PIONEER. IV.
Simpson, James H. REPORT AND MAP OF THE ROUTE. I.
Taylor, Joseph. JOURNAL OF THE ROUTE. III.
Teller, Woolsey. Letters. IV.
Widber, J. H. Statement. V.
Williams, J. W. "Marcy's Road from Dona Ana." Genl.

1852
Cathey, Andrew. The Cathey Wagon Train. V-.
Foreman, Grant. ADVENTURE ON RED RIVER. II +.
Tate, Michael. "Randolph B. Marcy." Genl.

1853
Conrad, David E. "Whipple Expedition in Arizona." II.
_____. "Whipple Expedition on the Great Plains." II.
Foreman, Grant. PATHFINDER IN THE SOUTHWEST. I.
Stanley, David E. Diary. II +.
Whipple, A. W. REPORT RAILROAD ROUTE. II.
Wright, Muriel H., and George H. Shirk, "Journal of Lt. Whipple." I.

1854
Neighbours, Kenneth F. "Marcy-Neighbours Exploration." Genl.
Parker, W. B. NOTES TAKEN THROUGH UNEXPLORED TEXAS.
   II +.

1858
Floyd, William P. Journal. II +.
Mollhausen, Heinrich B. DIARY OF A JOURNEY. I.

1866
Handley, Walter. Diary. II.

MEEK CUTOFF

This route is an alternative approach to the Willamette Valley from the
   Snake River-Fort Boise area. It includes the Elliott route as well.

General

Clark, Keith, and Lowell Tiller, TERRIBLE TRAIL: THE MEEK CUTOFF, 1845.

McNemee, Jack. Personal Narrative. IV

Menefee, Leah C. IMMIGRATION ROSTERS.

_____, and Lowell Tiller, "Cutoff Fever."

Maps

Menefee, Leah C. IMMIGRATION ROSTERS OF THE ELLIOTT CUTOFF.

1843

Giffen, Helen S. TRAIL-BLAZING PIONEER. III.

1845

Baldwin, Alfred. Recollections. V-.

Bayley, Betsey. Letter. V.

Bennett, Lucy J. Reminiscence. V-.

Clark, Keith, and Lowell Tiller. TERRIBLE TRAIL. Genl.

Field, James. Diary. II.

Fitzgerald, Maurice. The Lost Immigrants. III.

Goulder, William A. REMINISCENCES. IV.

Herren, John. Diary. III.

King, Anna M. "Letter." V.

Lockley, Fred. CAPTAIN SOLOMON TETHEROW. V.

_____. "McNenees and Tetherows." III.

McNary, Lawrence A. "Route of the Meek Cutoff, 1845."

McNemee, Jack. Personal Narrative. IV.

ORGANIZATIONAL JOURNAL. III.

Robertson, Fay H. John Jacob Hampton. IV.

Smith, Hugh I. THE OREGON MCNARY FAMILY. V.

Walter, William W. "Reminiscences of an Old 1845'r." V.

Wojcik, Donna M. BRAZEN OVERLANDERS. I. Recommended.

1853

Bushnell, John C. NARRATIVE. V.

Drew, Susan. Crossing the Plains. V.

"Elliott Expeditionary Cutoff." III.

Henry, David. Reminiscences. V.

Hill, Hanks N. The Lost Trail. IV.

Hockersmith, Martha J. Reminiscence. IV.

Leonard, Joseph L., and Mary Purdom. Crossing the Plains. IV.

Longworth, Basil N. "Memorandum." II.

Lyman, Esther and Joseph. LETTERS. III.

McArthur, Lewis A. "Early Scenes in Harney Valley." V.

McClure, Andrew S. Journal. II+.

McClure, John H. HOW WE CAME TO OREGON. IV.

McIntosh, Walter H. ALLEN AND RACHEL. III.

Menefee, Leah C. IMMIGRATION ROSTERS OF THE ELLIOTT CUT-OFF. Genl.

Owen, Benjamin F. MY TRIP ACROSS THE PLAINS. II.

Peterson, Peter. OUR WAGON TRAIN IS MISSING. III.

Slater, John L. Reminiscence. IV.

Stewart, Agnes. DIARY. IV.

1865

Kimball, Gorham G. "Trailing Sheep from California to Idaho." Genl.

MEXICAN TRAILS

This category includes references to travel through Mexico. Trips do not necessarily begin there, but most often approach Mexico's east coast by ship and cross to major western ports, such as Mazatlan or San Blas, before resuming travel again by sea. Readers should also refer to the GILA category for journals or studies of the portion of that trail that briefly touched Mexico via the Santa Cruz Valley and Guadalupe Pass. Another trail sement with Mexican ties is RIO GRANDE. For trails linking New Mexico and Texas to northern Mexico, refer to that category.

General

Box, James. ADVENTURES AND EXPLORATIONS.

DESPATCHES, ACAPULCO.

DESPATCHES AND DIPLOMATIC INSTRUCTIONS.

DESPATCHES, CIUDAD JUAREZ.

DESPATCHES, MONTEREY.

DESPATCHES, VERA CRUZ.

Egan, Ferol. THE EL DORADO TRAIL.

_____. "Journada del Muerto."

Falconer, Arthur R. "A Historical Geography of the Transportation Routes in Baja California from 1533 to 1920."

Farnham, Thomas F. MEXICO.

Hall, R. Franklin. "Chihuahua Trail."

Kuykendal, J. H. Clippings and Fragments.

Moorhead, Max L. NEW MEXICO'S ROYAL ROAD.

Paredes, Raymund A. "The Mexican Image in American Travel Literature, 1831 - 1869."

Schick, Robert. "Wagons to Chihuahua."

Smith, Ralph A. "Comanche Bridge between Oklahoma and Mexico."

Walker, Henry P. "Freighting from Guaymas to Tucson, 1850 - 1880."

Werne, Joseph R. "Major Emory and Captain Jimenez: Running the Gadsden Line."

Bibliographies

Cole, Garold. AMERICAN TRAVELERS TO MEXICO, 1821 - 1972.

1842

Bell. Josias F. Sketches. II.

1843

Gilliam, Albert M. TRAVELS MEXICO. II.

1847

Gibson, George R. OVER THE CHIHUAHUA. II.

Porter, Eugene O. "Across Northern Mexico with Wislizenus. I.

Wislizenus, A. MEMOIR. I.

1848

Chamberlain, Samuel E. MY CONFESSION. IV.

Couts, Cave J. HEPAH. I.

Dunphy, William. Statement. V.

Jordan, Rudolph. "Rudolph Jordan." II.

1849-General

Balling, E. E. "The Mexico Trails of '49."

Bieber, Ralph P. SOUTHERN TRAILS.

Brinckerhoff, Sidney P. "Passport to Mexico."

Dumke, Glenn S. "Across Mexico in '49."

Officer, James E. "Yanqui Forty-Niners in Hispanic Arizona."

1849

Account of a Journey. III-.

Audubon, John W. AUDUBON'S WESTERN JOURNAL. I.

_____. ILLUSTRATED NOTES. I.

Bachman, Jacob H. "Audubon's Ill-Fated Western Journey." III.

Baker, George H. "Records of a California Journey." III.

Benjamin, Theodosia. "The Audubon Party." III.

Bonestell, Louis H. "Autobiography." II.

Cardinell, Charles. "Adventures on the Plains." III.

Clarke, Asa B. TRAVELS IN MEXICO AND CALIFORNIA. II+.

Coit, Daniel W. DIGGING FOR GOLD. V.

_____. DRAWINGS AND LETTERS. V.

Counts, George. Journal. III-.

Cox, C. C. "From Texas to California." II

Dawson, Nicholas. NARRATIVE. IV.

Durivage, John E. "Through Mexico to California." I.

Duval, Isaac H. "Overland to California." III.
Earl, Guy C. The Enchanted Valley. V.
Eastland, Joseph G. Letters. III.
_____, and Thomas B. Eastland, "To California through Texas and Mexico." II.
Emerson, William H. Diary. II.
Evans, George W. MEXICAN GOLD TRAIL. I.
Ferris, A. C. "To California in 1849 through Mexico." III.
"From Texas to the Gold Mines." IV.
Gohres, Helen. "Bare-footed." III.
Gunn, Lewis C. RECORDS OF A CALIFORNIA FAMILY. II+.
Hardin, Robert S. Diary. II+.
Harris, Ben. THE GILA TRAIL. II+.
Hawks, James D. "A Forty-Niner in Baja California." II.
Hobbs, James. WILD LIFE. IV.
Hooper, H. O. "To California in '49." V.
Hubbard, Cal. "The Devil's Highway." III.
Hunter, Robert. A TEXAN IN THE GOLD RUSH. V.
Knapp, W. Augustus. "An Old California's Story." IV.
McGaffey, Joseph W. "Across Mexico in the Days of '49." II.
McKnight, George S. CALIFORNIA 49ER. IV.
McNeil, Samuel. MC'NEIL'S TRAVELS. III.
Noble, Robert W. Diary of a Journey. II.
Patterson, George W. Across Mexico to California. IV.
Perkins, William. THREE YEARS IN CALIFORNIA. V.
Perry, J. A. THRILLING ADVENTURES. II+.
Phillips, Marcia B. Five Stevenson Men. III.
Powell, H. M. SANTA FE TRAIL. I.
Pownall, Joseph. "From Louisiana to Mariposa." IV.
Sayre, Thomas. Diary of a Gold-Seeker. III.
Sayward, William T. Pioneer Reminiscences. V.
Shinn, Silas. TRAIL OF A PIONEER. IV.
Smith, W. C. A JOURNEY TO CALIFORNIA. II.
Soule, Frank. Statement. V.
Wood, Harvey. PERSONAL RECOLLECTIONS. III.
Woods, Daniel B. SIXTEEN MONTHS. II.
Wozencraft, Oliver M. "Through Northern Mexico in '49." IV.

1850
Baldridge, Michael. A REMINISCENCE. II.
Forbes, ? A TRIP TO MEXICO. III.
Lockwood, C. B. MY TRIP. III.
McGowan, Edward. STRANGE EVENTFUL HISTORY. V.
Mobley, C. C. Diary. III.
Steele, Andrew. Diary. IV.
Stuart-Wortley, Lady E. TRAVELS IN THE UNITED STATES. II.
Woodward, Erastus. Diary. III.

1851
Bartlett, John R. PERSONAL NARRATIVE. I.
Matthews, L. C. Journal. III.

1852
Green, Duff. "Exploring the Rio Grande." III.
Holt, W. M. "From Washington, Arkansas." IV.
Lane, John L. Diaries. III.
West, S. H. LIFE AND TIMES. V.

1853
Schick, Robert. "Wagons to Chihuahua." Freight.

1854
Bell, James G. "Texas-California Cattle Trail." II+.
Brady, Peter R. Biography. II.
Erskine, M. H. "Cattle Drive from Texas to California." III.
Froebel, Julius. SEVEN YEAR'S TRAVEL. II+.
Swain, Ben. Original Manuscript. IV.

1861
Pumpelly, Raphael. ACROSS AMERICA AND ASIA. III.

1862
Ferguson, David. REPORT TUCSON AND LOBOS BAY. I.

1864
Browne, J. Ross. ADVENTURES. II.

1865
Mitchell, Clara B. Diary. II.

1867
Bell, William A. NEW TRACKS. II.

1868
Powers, Stephen. AFOOT AND ALONE. II.

MONTANA TRAILS

Sources which traverse Montana, usually from the east and south, are listed here. Also check the BOZEMAN, DAKOTAS and MULLAN categories.

General
Berry, Gerald. THE WHOOP-UP TRAIL.
Bradley, James H. Papers.
Burlingame, Merrill G. JOHN M. BOZEMAN.
_____. "The Influence of the Military."
Edrington, "L. Kay. A Study of Early Utah-Montana Trade."
"Expeditions of Captain James L. Fisk."
Fish, Herbert C. "Early Development of the Northern Route."
Fox, Jesse W. GENERAL COURSES.
Fox, John A. CALIFORNIA AND WESTERN EXPRESS COVERS.
Fry, F. FRY'S TRAVELER'S GUIDE.
Garver, Frank C. Early Roads and Trails into Montana.
Gilman, Carolyn, Rhoda Gilman, and Deborah M. Stultz. RED RIVER TRAILS.
Gittins, H. Leigh. IDAHO'S GOLD ROAD.
Hakola, John W. FRONTIER OMNIBUS.
Hanson, J. M. TRAIL TO ELDORADO. Not Seen.
Hite, Abraham. "Significance of the Lolo Trail."
Holman, Albert M. PIONEERING IN THE NORTHWEST.
Ingram, Patricia M. HISTORIC TRANSPORTATION ROUTES THROUGH SOUTHWESTERN MONTANA.
Jackson, W. Turrentine. "Fisk Expeditions to the Montana Gold Fields."
_____. "Wells Fargo Contract for 1868."
_____. "Wells Fargo Final Months."
_____. "Wells Fargo into a New Territory."
_____. "Wells Fargo Trials and Triumphs."
Jameson, Jesse H. "Corrine; A Study of a Freight Transfer Point."
Madsen, Brigham D., and Betty M. "Diamond R Rolls Out."
_____. NORTH TO MONTANA.
Maynadier, Henry E. MEMOIR OF THE COUNTRY. Not Seen.
Metlin, George R. Trails Used by the Pioneers. Not Seen.
Meyer, Bette E. "Pend Oreille Routes to Montana."
Myers, Alice V. "Sioux City, IA., Expeditions."
Nobles, William H. SPEECH.
Oviatt, Alton B. "Movement for a Northern Trail."
Owen, John. LETTERS AND JOURNALS.
Pioneers' Reminiscences.
Ritchey, Charles J. "Northern Overland Expeditions." Not Seen.
Sharp, Paul F. "Whoop-Up Trail."
Stone, Arthur L. FOLLOWING OLD TRAILS.
Trexler, Harrison A. "Missouri-Montana Highways."
Underhill, "Northern Overland Route to Montana."
Walker, Wyman P. WAGONMASTERS.

Roberts, James. Notes to Idaho. II +.
Roe, Martha A. A TRIP TO IDAHO. II +.
Root, Orville. Orville's Trip. V.
Shober, John H. Papers. V.
Stanfield, Howard S. DIARY. Stage. II.
Strateler, L. B. Diary. II.
Tomlinson, John J. Log. III +.
Wager, F. E. "Hunted End of Rainbow." IV.
Werden, Francis H. Journal. III.
Wilkinson, Henry. Narrative. V.
Wood, J. D. Reminiscence. V.
Woods, Allin W. Journal. IV.

1865
Adkins, H. Frank. Reminiscence. IV.
Agatz, Cora W. "A Journey." V.
Anthony, Erasmus. Reminiscence. V-.
Bailey, David J. Diary. II +.
Boatman, Mary L. Reminiscence. V-.
Cauthorn, Benjamin. Trip to Montana. I.
Cowden, Henry. Diary. III.
Edwards, Edward H. "The Edwards Letters." V.
"Expeditions of Captain James L. Fisk." Genl.
Gallaher, William H. "Ho! For the Gold Mines." III.
Glatfelter, Noah M. "Letter from Dakota Territory." V.
Herndon, Sarah. DAYS ON THE ROAD. IV.
Holman, Albert M. PIONEERING IN THE NORTHWEST. III.
Jeffers, Susie L. Reminiscence. Not Seen.
Jones, Daniel. Travels across the Plains. V.
Lee, C. M. Journals. II +.
Miller, James K. ROAD TO VIRGINIA CITY. III.
Munson, Lyman E. PIONEER LIFE. V-.
Myers, Alice V. "Sioux City Expeditions." Genl.
_____. "Wagon Roads West." IV.
Sawyers, James A. "Niobrara-Virginia City Wagon Road." II +.
Settle, Raymond and Mary. OVERLAND DAYS TO MONTANA. IV.
Spencer, Almon. Diary. Not Seen.
Steen, Enoch R. Diary. III +.
Switzer, Malphus A. Reminiscence. IV.
Thoroughman, Robert P. A Trip. IV.

1866
Agatz, Cora W. "A Journey across the Plains." V.
Blythe, Samuel F. Diary. III.
Burgess, Perry A. "From Illinois to Montana." II.
Campbell, J. A. A Trip across the Plains. V.
Creigh, Thomas A. "From Nebraska City to Montana." III.
Dexter, Wheeler O. Reminiscences. V.
"Expeditions of Captain James L. Fisk." Genl.
Fisk Family Papers, Diary. II +.
Fox, George W. "Diary." II.
Gates, Henry. Letters. IV.
Harlan, Wilson B. "A Walk with a Wagon Train." III.
Henderson, A. B. Journal. Genl.
Johnstone, William. Diary. II +.
Jones, Daniel. Travels across the Plains. V.
Jones, Sydney. My Trip Overland. Not Seen.
Lester, Gurdon P. "A Round Trip. II +.
Lockey, Richard. Diary. III.
Malben, Ben. Reminiscence. V.
Miles, Thomas C. Reminiscence. III-.
Myers, Alice V. "Sioux City Expeditions." Genl.
_____. "Wagon Roads West." IV.
Peck, S. L. HISTORY. V.
Ricker, J. G. Reminiscences. IV
Ricker, John J. "Iowa to Ventura County." V.
Tinney, William T. Overland Trip. III.
Williams, John B. Diary. II.

Wilson, Davis. Diary. I.
Wood, Henry F. Diary. III +.

1867
Evans, C. B. ANOTHER MONTANA PIONEER. V.
Hilger, Marcella M. "Overland Trail." IV.
Lueg, Henry. "Northern Overland Route." II.
Maricle, Abraham. Diary. III-.

1868
Blythe, Samuel F. Diary. IV.
Cook, Mary E. Diary. Stage.

1869
Brackett, A. G. "A Trip through the Rocky Mountains." II.
Newman, Orson N. Memoranda. III.

MORMON TRAIL

This category separates sources originating in the Midwest and ending in Utah, and which would have normally been part of the CALIFORNIA TRAIL and BRIDGER lists. All MORMON TRAIL entries begin in the Council Bluff area and follow the Platte River to the Fort Bridger turnoff, then over the Wasatch to Salt Lake Valley - with some few exceptions. Readers having an interest in the BRIDGER or Platte River sections of the trail should also consult the CALIFORNIA TRAIL and OREGON TRAIL listings.

During the research phase of the project, the LDS Church Historical Department was closed for construction of new storage and research areas. It was not possible to review all their extensive holdings. While some LDS manuscript items have been copied and are available in other Utah repositories, the LDS collection of diaries and journals is probably the largest for Utah-centered sources. Readers concentrating on Utah trails should review this facility for further entries.

General
Aitchison, Clyde B. "Mormon Settlements in the Missouri Valley."
Atwood, Harriet T. "Mormon Migration and Geographic Environment."
Bennett, Richard E. "Mormons at the Missouri."
Brown, Joseph E. THE MORMON TREK WEST.
Burton, Alma P. THE MORMON TRAIL FROM VERMONT TO UTAH.
Carter, Kate B. "The Spirit of Emigration."
Christian, Lewis C. "Mormon Westward Migration."
Davies, J. Kenneth. "Thomas Rhoads."
Driggs, Howard R. MORMON TRAIL.
Easton, Susan W. "Suffering and Death."
Egan, Howard. PIONEERING THE WEST.
Gentry, Leland H. "The Mormon Way Stations."
Hafen, Leroy and Anne. "Hand Cart Migration."
_____. "Story of the Immigration by Handcarts."
_____. Hafen, HANDCARTS TO ZION.
Harlan, Edgar R. LOCATION AND NAME OF THE MORMON TRAIL.
Harvey, R. E. "Mormon Trek across Iowa."
Homer, Michael W. "Mormons in Nebraska Territory."
Hulmston, John K. "Transplain Migration."
Jackson, Richard H. "Overland Journey to Zion."
Jenson, Andrew. "Latter Day Saints' Emigration."
_____. "Utah Pioneer Companies."
Kimball, Stanley B. DISCOVERING MORMON TRAILS.
_____. "Mormon Trail Network in Iowa."
Kock, Felix J. "The Hand Cart Brigade."
Lambourne, Alfred. THE OLD JOURNEY.
_____. THE PIONEER TRAIL.
Layton, Christopher. AUTOBIOGRAPHY.
Little, James A. FROM KIRTLAND TO SALT LAKE CITY.

McBride, John R. "Route by which the Mormons Entered Salt Lake Valley in 1847."

Mattes, Merrill J. "The Council Bluffs Road."

Monaghan, Jay. "Handcarts on the Overland Trail."

MORMON TRAIL.

Nelson, John Y. FIFTY YEARS ON THE TRAIL.

Palmer, Belle. Sojourn at Kanesville."

Pugh, Byron G. "History of Utah-California Wagon Freighting."

Smart, William B. EXPLORING THE PIONEER TRAIL.

Steele, Olga S. "Geography of the Mormon Trail across Nebraska."

Stegner, Wallace. GATHERING OF ZION. Recommended.

Stoker, Kevin. "Trek along Original Trail Gives Taste of Pioneer Trail."

Taylor, Philip A. "Mormon Crossing of the United States."

Teichert, Minerva K. SELECTED SKETCHES OF THE MORMON MARCH.

U.S. Forest Service, "Old Pioneer Wagon Road." Wasatch Passes.

Wakefield, Eliza M. THE HANDCART TRAIL.

Warren, Gouverneur K. DACOTAH COUNTRY.

Weeks, Carl. "Material On the Mormon Trail."

Wilcox, Wayne. "Thirty-Six Miles of History." Emigrant Canyon.

Graphics

Lambourne, Alfred. THE OLD JOURNEY.

Strebel, George. "Pioneer Trail Art Tour."

Teichert, Minerva K. SELECTED SKETCHES OF THE MORMON MARCH.

Maps

Smart, William B. EXPLORING THE PIONEER TRAIL. Emigrant Canyon.

1846-General

Arrington, Leonard J. "Mississippi Saints."

Durham, Reed C. "The Iowa Experience."

Kimball, Stanley B. "Iowa Trek of 1846."

Petersen, William J. "The Mormon Road of 1846."

1846

Clayton, William. WILLIAM CLAYTON'S JOURNAL. I.

Hafen, Leroy R., and Frank M. Young. "Mormon Settlement at Pueblo." III.

Higgins, Catherine B. Biography. V.

Wilson, George D. Journal. IV.

1847-General

Beecher, Maureen. "Women at Winter Quarters."

Brown, Joseph E. THE MORMON TREK WEST.

Carter, Kate B. "Here Is My Home at Last."

_____. "They Came in 1847."

Christian, Lewis C. "A Study of the Mormon Westward Migration."

Duehlmeier, Fred D. "The 1847 Mormon Migration."

GUIDE TO THE ROUTE MAP OF THE MORMON PIONEERS.

Jenson, Andrew. DAY BY DAY WITH THE UTAH PIONEERS.

_____. "First Company of Utah Pioneers."

Johnson, Jeffrey D. "Utah's Negro Pioneers of 1847."

Knight, Hal and Kimball. 111 DAYS TO ZION.

McBride, John R. "Route Salt Lake Valley in 1847."

Neff, Andrew L. "The Mormon Migration to Utah, 1830 - 1847."

Nibley, Preston. STORY OF MORMON MIGRATION.

Petersen, Bryan L. "A Geographic Study of the Mormon Migration."

White, Hiram F. "The Mormon Road."

1847

Arrington, Leonard J. "Mississippi Saints." IV.

Barney, Lewis. History. III-.

Bingham, Erastus. SKETCH. Not Seen.

Bingham, Thomas. History. V.

Brown, John Z. AUTOBIOGRAPHY. IV.

Bullock, Thomas. Diary. III.

Clayton, William. WILLIAM CLAYTON'S JOURNAL. I.

Crosby, Jesse W. "History and Journal." III.

Dowdle, John C. Journal. IV.

Empey, William A. "The Mormon Ferry on the North Platte." II.

Haight, Isaac C. Biographical Sketch. III.

Harmon, Appleton M. APPLETON MILO HARMON GOES WEST. I.

Harper, Charles A. Diary. III+.

Hess, John W. "John W. Hess." V-.

Higgins, Catherine B. Biography. V.

Jackman, Levi. Journal. II.

Jacob, Norton. Life. II+.

Johnson, Luke S. Genealogy. III+.

Kane, Thomas L. THE MORMONS. II.

Kartchner, William D. "Autobiography." V.

Kimball, Heber C. "Pioneer Journal." II+.

Kingsbury, J. C. Journal. Not Seen.

Knight, Hal, and Stanley B. Kimball. 111 DAYS TO ZION. II+.

Lyman, Amasa M. Journal. I.

Millroy and Hayes. GUIDE TO THE ROUTE MAP. II+.

Pace, William B. Autobiography. Not Seen.

Pack, John. Biography. V-.

Pratt, Orson. ORSON PRATT JOURNALS. II.

Rich, Sarah. Journal. IV.

Rockwood, Albert. Journal. II+.

Scarce, William. Journal. III.

Scofield, Joseph S. Diary. III.

Sessions, Patty. "A Pioneer Mormon Diary." III.

Smith, George A. History. II+.

Smith, John. Diary. III.

Smith, Mary E. FIFTEEN YEARS. Not Seen.

Smith, Pauline U. CAPTAIN JEFFERSON HUNT. V-.

Snow, Eliza R. "Pioneer, 1847." III.

_____. "Journey to Zion." II+.

Snow, Erastus. "Journey to Zion." II+.

Staines, William C. "Account." III+.

Taylor, L. J. LIFE HISTORY.... Not Seen.

Tippets, John H. History and Account. III.

Wallace, George B. Journal. II.

Whitaker, George. Reminiscence. V.

Whitney, Horace K. Journal. II.

Woodruff, Wilford. Autobiography. II.

Young, Brigham H. Biography. III-.

Young, Clara D. A Woman's Experiences. V.

Young, Joseph W. Journal. IV.

Young, Lorenzo D. "Diary." II.

1848

Adams, William H. Short History. V.

Ballantyre, Richard. Memorandum. III-.

Blackburn, Abner. Reminiscence. IV.

Bliss, Robert S. "Journal of Robert S. Bliss." III.

Brown, John Z. AUTOBIOGRAPHY. IV.

Carter, Kate L. "They Came in '48." Genl.

Cook, Phineas W. LIFE AND HISTORY.... Not Seen.

Huntington, Oliver. Diary. III+.

Miller, Jacob. JOURNAL.... Not Seen.

Pack, John. Biography. V-.

Russell, Isaac. A Sketch. V-.

Stout, Hosea. ON THE MORMON FRONTIER. III.

1849

Adams, William. Recollections. Not Seen.

Arms, Cephas. LONG ROAD TO CALIFORNIA. II.

Bolton, Curtis E. Diary. Not Seen.

Campbell, Robert L. Journal. II.

Clarke, Isaac. Journal. II.

Derrickson, Frankie M. Reminiscence. V.
Ellenbecker, John G. JAYHAWKERS. III.
Granger, Lewis. LETTERS. III.
Haynes, Asa. "Diary." V.
Huntington, Oliver. Diary. III+.
Jewett, George E. Diary. III.
Miller, Reuben. Journal. III+.
Myers, S. Carl. Reminiscences. IV.
Pearson, Gustavus C. OVERLAND IN 1849. III-.
Pratt, Orson. JOURNALS. II.
Richards, Silas. Diary. Not Seen.
Smith, Bathsheba. Diary. III.
Swan, Chauncey. "Letters of a Forty-Niner." IV.
Thomas, Martha P. DANIEL STILLWELL THOMAS.... Not Seen.
Welch, Adonijah S. "Document." V.

1850

Adams, Elias. ANCESTORS. Not Seen.
Buckingham, Henry. Journey. III.
Campbell, Robert. Letter. Not Seen.
Carrington, Albert. "Diary." II+.
Carter, Kate L. "They Came in '50." Genl.
Christy, Thomas. THOMAS CHRISTY'S ROAD. II.
Clark, Roger W. "Annotated and Critical Study." IV.
Cluff, Harvey. Journal. V.
Dresser, William. Dresser Family Papers. V.
Flake, Lucy H. TO THE LAST FRONTIER. Not Seen.
Georgian, A. LIFE. IV.
Goodridge, Sophia L. "Diary." III.
Haight, Isaac C. Biographical Sketch. III.
Heywood, Martha S. NOT BY BREAD ALONE. II+.
Judd, Mary D. Sketch. IV.
Loomis, Leander V. BIRMINGHAM EMIGRATING COMPANY.
    III.
McKeeby, Lemuel C. "Memoirs." III.
Maughan, Mary A. Journal. II.
Pulsipher, John. Diary. IV.
"Recollections of Sarah Hammitt." V-.
Rowndy, Shadrach. Journal. Not Seen.
Slater, N. FRUITS OF MORMONISM. Genl.
Snow, William. Across the Plains. IV.
Stimson, Fancher. Letter. III.
Whipple, Nelson W. History. IV.
Woodruff, Emma S. Sketch. V-.

1851

Baker, Jean R. "By Windjammer and Prairie Schooner." III.
Barber, T. M. Diary. Not Seen.
Booth, William. "Diary." Not Seen.
Buckingham, Harriet T. "Crossing the Plains." III.
Carrington, Albert. "Diary of Albert Carrington." II+.
Crooks, George. Diary. V-.
Hadley, Amelia H. "Journal of Travails." II.
Harris, Sarah H. UNWRITTEN CHAPTER OF SALT LAKE. IV.
Hawkins, Theadore. History of the Hawkins Family. V.
Johnson, Ann W. "Long Journey of a Mormon Girl." V.
McAllister, John D. Journal. Not Seen.
Pearce, Jean R. Diary. II+.
Riddle, George W. EARLY DAYS. III.
Taylor, Osian H. Diary, 1851. Not Seen.

1852

Ashley, Angeline J. Crossing the Plains. II.
Barton, William K. COPY OF DIARY. Not Seen.
Bixby-Smith, Sarah. ADOBE DAYS. IV.
Blake, Winslow. Diary. II.
Bowering, George. Journal. I.
Conyers, E. W. "Diary." II+.

Council Point Emigration Company Journal. I.
Dodson, John. "Dodson's Death." III.
Empey, William A. Diary. II-.
Harmon, Appleton M. HARMON GOES WEST. V.
Hazard, Henry T. Across the Plains. V.
Jared, Israel. A Trip across Nebraska. V-.
Kerns, John T. "Journal of Crossing the Plains." II.
Laub, George. Diary. II-.
Leach, Adoniram J. EARLY DAY. IV.
McAllister, John. "Diary." II.
Matthews, Amanda M. Journal of Traveling. II.
Otto, Olive H. "A Mormon Bride." Genl.
Pratt, Sarah. Jottings. III.
Pulsipher, John. Diary. IV.
Robinson, Henry. Journal. Not Seen.
Scarbrough, Richard A. Diary. II.
Shipp, Ellis R. EARLY AUTOBIOGRAPHY.... Not Seen.
Stott, Edwin. "Journal." V-.
Stout, Hosea. ON THE MORMON FRONTIER. III.
Tidwell, John. Journal Council Point. I.
Turnbull, Thomas. "Thomas Turnbull's Travels." II.
Udall, David. ARIZONA PIONEER MORMON.... V.
Woodhouse, John. JOHN WOODHOUSE.... Not Seen.

1853

Allyn, Henry. "Journal." II.
Beadle, Elisha. "Letter." IV.
Burns, James F. "James Franklin Burns." V-.
Carter, Kate B. FORSGREN COMPANY. III.
Cornaby, Hannah. AUTOBIOGRAPHY. Not Seen.
Davis, John E. MORMONISM UNVEILED. V.
Dinwiddie, David or John. OVERLAND. III.
Farmer, James. Journal. II+.
Forsdick, Stephen. "On the Oregon Trail to Zion." III.
Galloway, James. Diary. IV.
Haight, Isaac C. Biographical Sketch. III.
Handsaker, Uncle Sam. PIONEER LIFE. III.
King, Hannah T. Journal. II.
Kirby, William. MORMONISM EXPOSED.... Not Seen.
Piercy, Frederick H. ROUTE. II.
Stout, Hosea. ON THE MORMON FRONTIER. III.
Taylor, S. H. "Oregon Bound Correspondence." III.
Ward, Harriet S. PRAIRIE SCHOONER LADY. II.
Wilcox, Adelia A. Memoirs. V.
Williams, V. A. Diary. II.
Winters, Mary A. "Reminiscence." IV.

1854

Blood, Jane W. JANE WILKIE HOOPER BLOOD. Not Seen.
Burrel, Mary. Diary and Letters. II.
Davies, John J. "Journey of a Mormon." V.
Franklin, John B. HORRORS OF MORMONISM. V.
Homer, Michael W. "Italian Mormons Come to Utah."
Johnson, Sixtus E. Leaves from the Family Tree. III.
Molen, Simpson M. Diary. III+.
Schutt, H. R. Journal. Not Seen.
Ware, Ellen K. Crossing the Plains. I.
Watson, Andrew. By Wheelbarrow and by Handcart. IV.
Whitney, Orson K. Journal. III.
Woodward, Jabez. Crossing the Plains. III-.

1855

Bean, George W. "Journal." IV.
Chandless, William. VISIT TO SALT LAKE. II.
Davis, Daniel. Journal. III.
Martin, Jane S. Life and TImes. IV.
Miller, Henry W. Journal. IV.
Nielsen, Christian. Diary. II.

Smith, Charles. Diary. III.
Snedaker, Morris J. "Diary." IV.
Warren, Gouvernour K. EXPLORATIONS IN NEBRASKA. II.

1856-General

Cornwall, Rebecca, and Leonard J. Arrington. RESCUE OF THE 1856
    HANDCART COMPANIES.
Ellsworth, Edmund. "The First Hand-Cart Companies."
Edmund Ellsworth Handcart Company.
Hixon, Charlene. The Handcart Expeditions of 1856 in Johnson County,
    Iowa.
Jones, Daniel W. FORTY YEARS AMONG THE INDIANS.
Larson, Gustive O. MORMON HANDCART STORY.
Petersen, William J. "The Handcart Expedition."

1856

Ahmanson, John. PRESENT DAY MOHAMED. Not Seen.
Archer, Patience. Diary. II.
Bermingham, Twiss. "To Utah by Hand." II.
Bleak, James G. Handcart Travelog. III-.
Burton, Mary. TELL IT ALL. Not Seen.
Cantwell, James S. Journal. V.
Chislett, Mr. "Narrative." Not Seen.
Cluff, Harvey. Journal. V.
Cole, Lucy W. Story. IV.
Crook, John. "John Crook's Journal." V.
Cropper, Thomas W. FAMILY HISTORY. Not Seen.
Elder, Joseph B. Diary. IV.
Galloway, Andrew. "First Mormon Handcart Trip." III.
Green, Caleb. A Visit to Great Salt Lake. Not Seen.
Griffin, Eli A. Diaries. Not Seen.
Groesbeck, Nicholas H. Reminiscence. IV.
Harlan, Edgar R. "First Mormon Handcart Trip." III.
Jaques, John. LIFE HISTORY. III.
Kingsford, Elizabeth H. Reminiscence. IV.
Lewis, Jane D. Biography. V.
Linford, James H. AN AUTOBIOGRAPHY.... Not Seen.
McBride, Heber. Journal. V.
Madsen, Wilhelmina K. History. IV.
Martin, Jane S. Life and Times. IV.
Mousely, Sarah M. Journal. II-.
Openshaw, Samuel. "Two Important Journals." IV.
Romney, Miles P. LIFE STORY.... Not Seen.
Savage, Levi. JOURNAL. II.
Snow, Bernard. Diary. III.
Stenhouse, Thomas B. ROCKY MOUNTAIN SAINTS. II.
Walters, Archer. Journal. III.
Young, Phineas. Diary. III.

1857-Genl

Conway, Cornelius. UTAH EXPEDITION.
Gove, Jesse A. UTAH EXPEDITION.
Hafen, Leroy and Ann. UTAH EXPEDITION.
Sweeney, James. "Narrative."

1857

Christensen, C. C. "By Handcart to Utah." V.
Cummings, Elizabeth. Letters. II+.
Johnson, Joel H. Journal. III+.
Lyman, Amasa M. Journal. II.
Pierce, Eli H. Diary and Journal. III+.

1858

Beehrer, George W. "Freighting across the Plains." Genl.
Fisher, Henry W. TO UTAH. IV.
James, Jason W. "A Trip to Utah." IV.
Lyman, Amasa M. Journal. II.
Peirce, Eli H. Diary and Journal. III-.

Stenhouse, Mrs. T. B. "TELL IT ALL." II.

1859

Alexander, Sara. Little Story. IV.
Atkin, William. Handcart Experience. II+.
Cooper, Frederick A. Biography. IV.
Evans, Robley D. A SAILOR'S LOG. IV.
Merryweather, F. LIFE. III.
Simons, Fanny Fry. "Journal." IV.

1860

Brown, John Z. AUTOBIOGRAPHY. IV.
Fish, Mary C. Diary. II+.
Fjeld, Carl J. BRIEF HISTORY.... Not Seen.
Lyman, Vincent P. Diary. II.
Nibley, Charles W. REMINISCENCES. Not Seen.
Stucki, John S. FAMILY HISTORY. Not Seen.
Tracy, Albert. "Journal." II+. Stage.

1861

Archer, Patience. Diary. III.
Eldredge, Ira. Journal. III.
Hartley, William G. "Down and Back Wagon Trains." Genl.
Johnson, Joel H. Journal. III+.
Larkin, Elijah. Journal. Not Seen.
Neilsen, Peter. Journal. III.
Ottinger, George M. Journal. Not Seen.

1862

Ajax, William and Emma. Diary. I.
Boquist, Laura B. CROSSING THE PLAINS. III.
Brown, John Z. AUTOBIOGRAPHY. IV.
Burton, Robert T. Account. III.
Hale, Alma H. ALMA HELAMON HALE. IV.
Kuhre, Martin P. Day Book. III-.

1863

Archer, Patience. Diary. IV.
Hansen, H. N. "An Account of A Mormon Family's." V.
Lightner, Mary. "Mary Lightner." III.
Patterson, A. H. Journal. III.
Scoville, Adaline B. LIFE. Not Seen.

1864

Ballard, Henry. Private Journal. III.
Bowers, John H. Letters. IV.
Clark, John R. Diary. Not Seen.
Dunham, E. Allene. ACROSS THE PLAINS. V.
Dunlap, Catherine C. MONTANA. II.
Logan, Martha. Logan Family Papers. Not Seen.
Morrill, Rosa N. MARY JANE, PIONEER. IV.
Young, Joseph A. Journal. Not Seen.

1865

Adkins, H. Adkins. Reminiscence. IV.
Argyie, Archie. CUPID'S ALBUM. V.
Barton, H. D. Diary. III-.
Case, Frank M. "Experiences on the Platte." IV.
Cluff, Harvey. Journal. V.
Draper, Mabel. THOUGH LONG THE TRAIL. IV.
Lewis, Edward M. Journal. Not Seen.
McBride, Heber. Journal. III.

1866

Aveson, Robert. "Leaving Home." V.
Birge, Julius C. AWAKENING OF THE DESERT. III.
Driver, William. "London to Salt Lake City." III-.
Jackson, William H. DIARIES. II.

McClintock, Margaretta F. My Trip. V.
Roberts, B. H. Life Story. II.

1867
Jackson, William H. DIARIES. II.
Waters, William E. LIFE AMONG THE MORMONS. II.

MULLAN ROAD

This route extended from Fort Benton, MT west to Walla Walla, WA. It
    was a federal project and linked the Montana mines with the Pacific
    Northwest.

General
"Account of the Building of Mullen's Military Road."
Baily, Joe. "Mullan's Axe and Shovel Passage."
Bemis, Samuel F. "Captain John Mullan and the Engineers' Frontier."
Clarke, Helen P. "Sketch of Malcolm Clarke."
Coleman, Louis C., et al. CAPTAIN JOHN MULLAN.
Elliott, T. C. "The Mullan Road."
Erickson, Harvey. "Mullan's 1862 Interstate Road."
Fish, Herbert C. "Early Development of the Northern Route."
Howard, Addison. "Captain John Mullan."
McGregor, Alexander C. "Economic Impact of the Mullan Road."
Melgard, Helen W. "The Mullan Road."
Mullan, John. MINERS GUIDE.
_____. REPORT ON THE CONSTRUCTION OF A MILITARY
    ROAD.
_____. "Route of the Covered Wagon."
Munson, L. E. Address.
Oviatt, Alton B. "Movement for a Northern Trail."
Space, Ralph S. THE LOLO TRAIL.
Strachan, John. BLAZING THE MULLAN TRAIL.
Talkington, Henry L. "Mullan Road."
Ulrich, Richard W. "The Mullan Road."
Willey, Day A. "Building the Mullan Road."
Winther, Oscar O. "Early Commercial Importance of the Mullan Road."
_____. THE OLD OREGON COUNTRY.
Woody, Frank H. "From Missoula to Walla Walla in 1857."

1846
De Smet, Pierre J. OREGON MISSIONS. IV.

1860
Blake, George A. "Journal Fort Benton to Fort Vancouver." I.
Hardin, Martin D. "Up the Missouri and Over the Mullan Road." II.
Kautz, August V. "From Missouri to Oregon." II.
Strachan, John. BLAZING THE MULLAN TRAIL. Genl.

1861
Brown, John M. "Diary." II +.

1862
Bond, Samuel R. Journal of Expedition. I.
Delany, John O. "Up the Missouri to the Montana Mines." III +.
Dibb, William D. Diary. II.
Febes, J. H. Story of His Trip. Genl.
Fisk, James M. EXPEDITION FROM FORT ABERCROMBIE. II.
Hewett, R. H. ACROSS THE PLAINS. II.
Perry, Samuel M. Diary. II.
Rumley, Charles. "Diary." III.
Scott, Charlton. Diary. II.
Thompson, Francis M. "Reminiscences of Four-Score Years." II +.
Wright, Dunham. Narrative. V.

1865
Mullan, John. "Route of the Covered Wagon."

1867
Lueg, Henry. "Northern Overland Route in 1867." II.

NOBLE'S CUTOFF

This segment was an offshoot of the better-traveled Applegate route and
    offered the shortest and possibly best passage of the Sierra Nevada.
    Despite these advantages, there was minimal utilization by emigrants.

General
Amesbury, Robert. NOBLE'S EMIGRANT TRAIL.
Dreibelbeis, John A. "Description of the Country."
Ferguson, Charles D. EXPERIENCES OF A FORTY-NINER.
FORT RIDGELY AND SOUTH PASS WAGON ROAD.
Helfrich, Devere, et al. EMIGRANT TRAILS WEST.
"A Jaunt to Honey Lake Valley and Noble's Pass."
Kingerly, Solomon. Overland Travels. III +.
Parkinson, John B. California and Her Golden Fleece. IV.
Swartzlow, Mrs. Carl. "The Noble Trail."

1852
Parkinson, John B. "California." IV.
Randall, J. D. Journal. Not Seen.
Variel, Mary A. "Romance." III.

1853
Bradway, Joseph R. Diary. II.

1854
"A Jaunt to Honey Lake Valley and Noble's Pass." Genl.
Schiel, Jacob H. THE LAND BETWEEN. II +.

1855
Perrie, George W. BUCKSKIN MOSE. III.

1857
Ables, T. J. Letter. IV.
Bishop, Frances A. Itinerary. II +.

1859
Brown, James Berry. JOURNAL OF A JOURNEY. III.
Favour, John. Diary. III +.
Wilson, John S. Diary. II +.

1860
Earnshaw, William. Diary. Not Seen.
Evans, James A. Journal. III.
Fish, Mary C. Diary. II +.

1861
Bonner, John H. Daily Journal. II.
Reynolds, G. A. "From Iowa to Scott Valley." V.
Taylor, Ruth M. "Across the Plains." III.

1864
Broadwell, J. W. "Crossing the Plains." IV.

OKLAHOMA TRAILS

Despite the MARCY and CHEROKEE categories using Oklahoma as a
    point of origin, there was considerable additional traffic across the
    state southwest toward Texas and the Red River. This list contains
    those sources other than MARCY and CHEROKEE which cross Ok-
    lahoma as part of more extensive trips.

General

Agnew, Brad. "Military Roads in Indian Territory."
Barnhill, J. Herschel. "The Way West."
"Committee Report Butterfield Overland Mail."
Corbett, William P. "Oklahoma's Highways." Not Seen.
_____. "Rifles and Ruts: Army Road Builders in Indian Territory."
Foreman, Grant. "Early Trails through Oklahoma."
_____. "Survey of a Wagon Road from Fort Smith."
Franks, Kenny A. "The California Overland Express through Indian Territory."
Graves, Jones S. "Influence of the Canadian Rivers."
McDonald, Archie P. "The Texas Road."
Shoemaker, Edward C. "Fort Towson."
Stout, Joseph A. FRONTIER ADVENTURERS. Not Seen.
Tate, Michael. "Randolph B. Marcy."

Maps

Dott, Robert H. "Lt. Simpson's California Road."

1845

Donat, Pat. "Bill Cush's Trek to Texas." I.
Galdin (Gauldin?), Martin A. Journal. III.

1849

Aldrich, Lorenzo D. JOURNAL OF THE OVERLAND ROUTE. III.
Counts, George. Journal. III-.
Dott, Robert H. "Lt. Simpson's California Road." Genl.
Gooding, Larry. "Across the Plains." IV.
Knapp, W. Augustus. "An Old Californian's Pioneer Story." IV.
Michler, Nathaniel H. ROUTES. II.

1850

Stockton, N. H. Journal. III+.

1852

Adams, David M. "Biographical Sketch." V.
Cathey, Andrew. The Cathey Wagon Train. V-.
Hammond, John B. Journal. III.

1853

Parker, Basil G. LIFE AND ADVENTURES. IV.
Wright, Muriel H., and George H. Shirk. "Journal of Lt. A. W. Whipple." I.

1854

Parker, W. B. NOTES TAKEN. II+.
Pope, John. REPORT RED RIVER TO THE RIO GRANDE. II+.

1855

Johnston, Eliza. "Diary of Eliza Johnston." II+.

1859

Gass, A. M. "From Texas to Pike's Peak." III.
Holman, Cyrus K. Journal. II+.
Smith, George G. "Parson's Progress." II.

1860

Wornell, David C. Diary. II.

1866

Duffield, George C. "Driving Cattle from Texas." III.
Handley, Walter. Diary. II.

1869

Baker, J. H. "A Trail Driver." III.

OLD SPANISH TRAIL

Although this route began prior to 1841, there was some travel on it between 1841 and 1869. It was also incorporated into the road linking Salt Lake City and southern California.

General

Auerbach, Herbert E. "Old Trails, Old Forts."
Beattie, George W. "San Bernardino Valley."
Bolton, Herbert. PAGEANT IN THE WILDERNESS.
Choteau, B. "Choteaus's Log."
Collins, Dabney O. "Escalante's Trail."
Crampton, Gregory C. "Utah's Spanish Trail."
Cutter, Donald C. "Prelude to a Pageant in the Wilderness."
Denhardt, Robert M. "Driving Livestock East."
Hafen, Leroy. "Opening and Development of the First Route."
_____, and Mary. OLD SPANISH TRAIL. Recommended.
Hague, Harlan. "The First California Trail."
Hill, Joseph J. "Spanish Expedition."
Hutchinson, Charles E. "Development San Bernardino Valley."
Ivens, Anthony W. "Traveling over Forgotten Trails."
Kelly, Charles. "Forgotten Trail of the Old West."
Lawrence, Eleanor. "Horse Thieves on the Spanish Trail."
_____. "Mexican Trade between Santa Fe' and Los Angeles."
_____. "Old Spanish Trail."
_____. "On the Old Spanish Trail."
Peirson, Erma. MOHAVE RIVER AND ITS VALLEY.
Reeder, Ray M. "The Mormon Trail." Recommended.
Silliman, Bert J. Papers.
Walker, Clifford J. "History of the Mojave River Trail."
_____. OPENING THE MOJAVE RIVER TRAIL.
Warren, Elizabeth V. "Armijo's Trace Revisited." Recommended.
_____, et al., CULTURAL RESOURCES OF THE CALIFORNIA DESERT.

Maps

Crampton, Gregory C. "Utah's Spanish Trail."

1841

Barrows, H. D. "Don David W. Alexander." V-.
Harris, Mary. "John Rowland and William Workman." Genl.
Wilson, Benjamin D. "Benito Wilson." V-.
_____. Observations. V-.

1842

Giffen, Helen S. TRAIL-BLAZING PIONEER. V.
Hopper, Charles. PILGRIMS OF THE PACIFIC. IV.
Williams, Joseph. NARRATIVE. III.

1844

Works, Lewis R. "Fremont's California." Genl.

1845

Martin, Thomas S. WITH FREMONT. III.

1848

Brewerton, George D. OVERLAND WITH KIT CARSON. II.
Choteau, B. "Choteau's Log." Genl.
McGeehee, Micajah. "Rough Times in Rough Places." V.
Pratt, Orville C. "Diary." II.

1849

Hudson, John. A FORTY-NINER IN UTAH. V.
Manly, William L. DEATH VALLEY. III.
Widber, J. H. Statement. V.

1850

"Notes of a Trip." III.

1852

Conard, Howard L. UNCLE DICK. IV.

1853

Beckwith, E. G. REPORT PACIFIC RAILROAD. II +.

Burwell, Lewis. Dictated Statement. V.

Carvalho, Solomon N. INCIDENTS OF TRAVEL. II.

Creer, Leland H. "Explorations of Gunnison and Beckwith in Colorado and Utah." IV.

Heap, Gwinn H. CENTRAL ROUTE. II +. A fake?

Schiel, Jacob H. THE LAND BETWEEN. II +.

Wallace, William S. "Was Heap's Journal Plagiarized?" IV.

1858

Hafen, Leroy. "Col. Loring's Expedition across Colorado." II.

1859

Macomb, J. N. REPORT OF THE EXPLORING EXPEDITION. Not Seen.

OREGON-TO-CALIFORNIA TRAILS

The network of trails between Oregon and California generated considerable traffic. Such travel descriptions are located here.

General

Case, Chester. "Development of Roads between Oregon and California."

Dillon, Richard. THE SISKIYOU TRAIL. Recommended.

McIntosh, Clarence F. "The Chico and Red Bluff Route."

Maxwell, Ben. "Overland Staging."

Neilson, Lawrence E. "Juniper Stumps on the Yreka Trail of 1862-1864."

Scott, Edwin. CALIFORNIA TO OREGON BY TRAIL.

1841

Brackenridge, William D. "Journal." IV.

Collins, William. "Overland Journeys in Oregon and California of the U.S. Navy Exploring Expedition." Genl.

Dillon, Richard. "When the Siskiyou Trail came to San Carlos."

Maloney, Alice B. "A Botanist on the Road to Yerba Buena." IV.

Peale, Titian R. DIARY. II.

Ramage, Helen. "Wilkes Exploring Expedition on the Pacific Slope." Genl.

Wilkes, Charles. COLUMBIA RIVER TO THE SACRAMENTO. Genl.

1842

Hopper, Charles. CHARLES HOPPER AND THE PILGRIMS. IV.

1843

Bennett, Winston. "A Pioneer of 1843." V.

1844

Johnson, Overton and William H. Winter. "Route Across." III.

1851

Lockhart, Andrew J. "The Williams Massacre." Genl.

1853

Dallam, Richard. Diary and Journal. II.

1858

Dallam, Richard. Diary. IV.

White, Daniel C. Diary. III-.

1860

Earnshaw, William. Diary. Not Seen.

Piper, Alexander. "Alexander Piper's Reports." III.

1861

Brown, John M. "Diary." II +.

Freeman, Olga. "Fortune Lost in a Cattle Drive." IV.

1862

Journal. III.

Perry, Samuel M. Diary. II.

1863

Evans, Mrs. S. D. A Trip from Washoe. III.

Ludlow, Fitz-Hugh. "On Horseback into Oregon." II.

1865

Bowles, Samuel. ACROSS THE CONTINENT. II.

Kimball, Gorham G. "Trailing Sheep from California to Idaho." Genl.

1866

Putnam, Joseph P. "Letters." II.

1869

Gorrill, William H. Diary on Horseback. II.

OREGON TRAIL

Sources for OREGON begin on the Missouri River and generally reach the Pacific coast via the Platte River, South Pass, Fort Hall, Snake River and The Dalles. Variants included are routes through Fort Bridger. Also check the BARLOW or MEEK categories for travelers using those roads. Many WASHINGTON entries first reached Oregon before crossing north of the Columbia River.

General

Bailey, Tom. "Mystery of the Vanishing Wagons."

Baker, Abner S. "Experience, Personality and Memory."

Beard, John W. SADDLES EAST.

Beckham, Stephen D. "Oregon Trail in Oregon."

Bell, James C. OPENING A HIGHWAY.

Bennett, Robert A. A SMALL WORLD OF OUR OWN.

Bowen, William A. "Migration and Settlement, Oregon to 1850."

_____. THE WILLAMETTE VALLEY.

Bradley, Lenore, and William Crowley. TREKKIN' WEST.

Bruce, Henrietta S. "A History of the Oregon Central Military Wagon Road Company."

Burnett, Betty. "Goodale's Cutoff."

Clarke, S. A. PIONEER DAYS OF OREGON HISTORY.

Coons, Frederica B. TRAIL TO OREGON.

Cowan, John L. "The Oregon Trail."

Cramer, Howard R. "California-Oregon Trail, Thomas Fork to Fort Hall, ID."

_____. "California-Oregon Trail, Fort Fall to Goose Creek, ID."

_____. EMIGRANT TRAILS OF SOUTHEASTERN IDAHO.

_____. "Geology and Hudspeth's Cutoff."

_____. "Oregon Trail, Raft River to Salmon Falls Creek, ID."

Crow, Norma L. "Pioneer Travel Stereotypes on the Oregon Trail."

Davis, Horace. THE OREGON TRAIL.

Derby, George H. Three Reports, 1855-56.

DeVoto, Bernard. "The Great Medicine Road."

Dorris, J. T. "Federal Aid to Oregon Trail Prior to 1850."

_____. "The Oregon Trail."

Dryden, C. P. GIVE ALL TO OREGON.

Duggleby, Donald R. "Hoosiers Travel the Oregon Trail, 1841 to 1853."

Dunlop, R. "History Comes Alive along the Road to Oregon."

Ellenbecker, John G. "Graves along the Oregon Trail."

Follmer, George D. Correspondence.

Fox, Florence C. "Notes on the Oregon Trail."

Franzwa, Gregory. OREGON TRAIL REVISITED.

Ghent, Willima J. THE ROAD TO OREGON.

Gross, Julia E. "Early Emigrations on the Oregon Trail."

Haines, Aubrey L. HISTORIC SITES ALONG THE OREGON TRAIL.

Hawkins, Ora B. "Historic Trails of Idaho."

Helvey, Frank. "Ranches and Stations."

Henderson, Paul C. LANDMARKS ON THE OREGON TRAIL.

Hepner, Simon. "Hardships on the Oregon Trail."

Hill, William E. THE OREGON TRAIL: YESTERDAY AND TODAY. Not Seen.

Huntley, James L. FERRYBOATS IN IDAHO.

Hurst, Beulah. History of Mountain Passes.

Idaho Historical Society Reference Series.

Inman, Loris. "Mystery of Sweet Springs Road."

Kahler, James O. ANTOINE OF OREGON.

Kaylor, Raymond D. "Immigration Activity of the Inland Empire Missions."

Kendall, Reese P. PACIFIC TRAIL.

Korell, F. F. "From Indiana to Oregon City." Not Seen.

Lavender, David. WESTWARD VISION.

McElhinney, Alice E. "Old Immigrant Trails into the Oregon Country."

McLean, Agnes M. "McKenzie Pass."

Meacham, Walter E. OLD OREGON TRAIL.

Menefee, Leah C. "Across the Plains."

Miller, David E. "Parting of the Ways."

Moeller, Bill and Jan. OREGON TRAIL.

Mooney, Thomas W. "The Oregon Trail."

Nielsen, Newman and McCart. PIONEER ROADS IN CENTRAL OREGON. Not Seen.

Norton, Mrs. Charles. "The Old Oregon Trail."

Pengra, B. J. REPORT OREGON CENTRAL MILITARY ROAD COMPANY.

Pioneer Ladies Club, REMINISCENCES.

Prosch, Thomas W. McCARVER AND TACOMA.

Rawling, Gerald. "The Oregon Trail."

Robb, Thomas H. "Routes to Southwestern Idaho."

Rucker, Maude A. OREGON TRAIL.

Salisbury, Albert and Jane. HERE ROLLED THE COVERED WAGONS.

Schetter, Adrienne E. "Indians on the Oregon Trail, 1845 - 1849."

Scott, Mary H. Missing Link of the Old Oregon Trail."

Settle, Raymond and Mary. WAR DRUMS AND WAGON WHEELS. Recommended.

Smith, Helen K. WITH HER OWN WINGS.

Smith, William E. "THe Oregon Trail through Pottawatomie County [Kansas].

Splawn, Margaret L. Papers. Not Seen.

Steckel, Samuel. Diary. Not Seen.

Sudweeks, Leslie. "Exploration and Settlement in Southern Idaho."

Tadlock, Nancy. "The Migrating Orchard."

WAGON WHEELS ROLL ON TO THE OREGON COUNTRY.

Wardell, M. L. "Oregon Immigration Prior to 1846."

Warre, H. J. SKETCHES IN OREGON TERRITORY.

Webster, Jean. "The Myth of Pioneer Hardship on the Oregon Trail."

Whipple, Charlotte L. Papers. Not Seen.

Whitmore, Len. Grande Ronde - Hebo Mountain - Tillamook Valley Trail.

Wilson, Perkins. "An Analysis of Oregon Migration, 1842 - 1848."

Works Project Administration, Folklore Project.

Young, F. G. "The Oregon Trail."

Graphics

Eide, Ingvard H. OREGON TRAIL.

Moeller, Bill and Jan. THE OREGON TRAIL.

Warre, H. J. SKETCHES IN OREGON TERRITORY.

Maps

Franzwa, Gregory. MAPS OF THE OREGON TRAIL

Idaho Dept. of Highways. ROUTE OF THE OREGON TRAIL IN IDAHO.

Stout, Ray L. Oregon Trail Material.

1841

De Smet, Pierre J. LETTERS AND SKETCHES. II.

John, James. "Diary." III.

Partoll, Albert J. "Mengarini's Narrative." V.

Point, Nicholas. "Historical Notes." Not Seen.

Ramage, Helen. "Wilkes Exploring Expedition." Genl.

Simpson, Sir George. AN OVERLAND JOURNEY. V.

Tobie, Harvey E. "From the Missouri to the Columbia." Genl.

Williams, Joseph. NARRATIVE. III.

1842

Allen, Miss A. J. TEN YEARS IN OREGON. II.

Andrews, Thomas F. "Controversial Career of Lansford W. Hastings." Genl.

Bennett, Winston. "A Pioneer of 1843." V.

Bidwell, et al. FIRST THREE WAGON TRAINS. Genl.

Crawford, Medorem. JOURNAL. II.

De Smet, Pierre J. LETTERS AND SKETCHES. II.

Hastings, Lansford W. EMIGRANT GUIDE TO OREGON AND CALIFORNIA. II.

_____. NEW DESCRIPTION. II.

Lovejoy, Asa. Letter. III.

_____. Pioneer Narrative. IV.

Matthieu, Francis X. "Reminiscences." IV.

Smith, Darling. "Pioneer of 1842." V.

Williams, Joseph. NARRATIVE. III.

1843-General

"Advice to Prospective Emigrants."

Arthur, John. "Pioneer of 1843."

Bright, Verne. "Folklore and History of the 'Oregon Fever'."

Columbus, Ohio Citizens, REPORT ON THE TERRITORY OF OREGON.

"Documentary New Orleans PICAYUNE."

"Documents."

"Documents.

"Emigrants from Iowa to Oregon in 1843."

Hardemann, Nicholas P. WILDERNESS CALLING.

Husband, Michael. "Backgrounds and Organization of the Great Overland Oregon Migration of 1843."

_____. "To Oregon in 1843: The 'Great Migration'."

Judson, Lewis. "The Emigration of 1843."

Nesmith, James W. "Occasional Address."

"Oregon Material Taken from a File."

Parrish, Philip H. "Great Migration."

Patterson, Ida. "Wagon Train of 1843."

Penrose, S. B. L. "Wagon Train of 1843."

Wilkes, George. THE HISTORY OF OREGON.

1843

Adair, Sarah D. "Sarah Damron Adair." Not Seen.

Ankeny, Nesmith. WEST AS I KNEW IT. III.

Applegate, Jesse. A DAY WITH THE COW COLUMN. II.

_____. RECOLLECTIONS OF MY BOYHOOD. II.

Athey, James. Narrative. V.

Boardman, John. "Journal." II.

Bogart, Nancy M. Reminiscences. V.

Burnett, Peter H. AN OLD CALIFORNIA PIONEER. IV.

Ford, Nineveh. Pioneer Road Makers. IV.

Furlong, Mary. When I Crossed the Plains. V-.

Gilpin, William. HISTORY. Not Seen.

Hill, Mrs. Almoran. Our Trip to Oregon. IV.

Hobson, E. John. Biographical Sketch. V-.

Johnson, Overton, and William H. Winter, ROUTE ACROSS. III.

Kaiser, P. G. How We Made the EMigrant Road. IV.

Kaiser, Thomas D. Statement. V.

1847

Beal, Josiah. A Trip across the Plains. V-.
Blanchet, A. M. JOURNAL OF A CATHOLIC BISHOP. II.
Braly, John H. MEMORY PICTURES. III+.
Briggs, Albert. Narrative. IV.
Brown, Joseph Henry. Autobiography. III.
Brown, Milton. Diary. V.
Cory, Benjamin. Crossing the Plains. II.
Cosgrove, Hugh. "Reminiscences." V.
Cranfill, Isom. Diary. V.
Crawford, Peter W. "Peter Crawford's Cowlitz Journal." III.
Cullen, John W. Letter. IV.
Darst, Paul. Diary. IV.
Davidson, T. L. "By the Southern Route." IV.
Fulton, James F. Diary of a Wandering Pilgrim. III.
Geer, Calvin. My Trip to Oregon. IV.
Geer, Elizabeth D. "Diary." III.
Gibson, James. From Missouri to Oregon. V.
Harden, Absolom B. Trail Diary. II.
Hastings, Loren B. "Diary." III.
Hibbard, Trenton. "Recollections of Crossing." V.
Hockett, W. A. Experiences. IV.
Hulin, Lester. 1847 Diary. III+.
Hunt, G. W. A HISTORY. V.
Huntington, Hallie H. ALL THE WAY WEST. IV.
_____. "Cornelius Hills crosses the Plains." IV.
Jory, James. "Reminiscences." IV.
Lee, Anna G. Letters. V.
McKean, Samuel T. Reminiscences. V-.
Mills, Rachel J. "Letters from a Quaker Woman." IV.
Moore, Alexander. "Statement." V.
Pettijohn, Isaac. Diary. II.
Poe, Andrew J. Diary. Not Seen.
Rayner, James. Journal. III+.
Raynor, James O. Journal. III. See above.
Richardson, Earle. RICHARDSON FAMILY. V-.
Richardson, Mary E. STORY. Not Seen.
Ross, John E. Narrative of an Indian Fighter. IV.
Saunders, Mary. The Whitman Massacre. IV.
Smith, Elizabeth Dixon. "Diary." IV.
Summers, Camilla G. GO TO THE COWLITZ. III.
Thurston, Samuel R. Biography. Not Seen.
Young, John Q. Life Sketches. IV.

1848

Adams, W. L. LECTURE ON THE OREGON. Not Seen.
Anderson, William W. Diary. III.
Atkinson, G. H. "Occasional Address." Genl.
Belknap, Kitturah. History. IV.
Boone, George L. Recollections. Not Seen.
Brown, Joseph H. Trip in Winter. III.
Cleaver, Benjamin. Diary. II.
Ebbert, George W. "George Wood Ebbert." V.
Lane, Joseph. BIOGRAPHY. Not Seen.
Lempfrit, Honore-Timothee. HIS OREGON TRAIL JOURNAL. I.
Miller, James D. "Early Oregon Scenes." III.
Parker, Inez E. "Early Recollections." V.
Pettijohn, Isaac. Diary. III.
Porter, William. Diary. III.
Root, Riley. JOURNAL. III.
Ruff, Charles and Annie. Correspondence. II.
Walker, Claiborne C. Purvine-Walker Papers. IV.

1849

Abbot, George H. Recollections. V.
Anderson, William W. Diary and Memoirs. III.
Applegate, Virginia W. Recollections. V-.
Baldwin, Lewis. Diary. Not Seen.

Chenoweth, F. A. "Occasional Address." IV.
Crockett, Samuel B. "Diary." III.
Cross, Osborne. MARCH OF THE MOUNTED RIFLEMEN. I.
Delano, Alonzo. LIFE ON THE PLAINS. I.
Dougherty, Lewis B. "Experiences." Not Seen.
Gibbs, George. "Diary." II+.
Hillman, John W. Reminiscences. Not Seen.
Hobart, Emaline. An Account. V.
McWilliams, John. RECOLLECTIONS. III.
Pattison, William. Diary. IV.
Pease, David E. Diary. II.
Watson, William J. JOURNAL OF AN OVERLAND JOURNEY. II.

1850

Armytage, W. H. G. "H. J. Coke." IV.
Buckingham, Henry. Journey to the Pacific. III.
Charlton, Joseph J. Autobiography. IV.
Coke, Henry J. A RIDE. I.
Fouts, William. Diary. IV.
Frush, William H. Diary. II.
Harvey, Isaac J. To California. IV.
Hastie, Thomas P. Notes. V.
Hayden, Mary J. PIONEER DAYS. V.
Hill, John B. "Gold, A Story of the Plains." III.
James, Eugenia L., and Vivian K. McLarty. "Three Generations." V.
Jones, ? Journal. IV.
Lord, Elizabeth. REMINISCENCES. IV.
McKinstry, Bruce L. "A Grandfather's Journal." Genl.
Maynard, David S. "Diary." III.
_____., and Catherine T. BIOGRAPHIES. III.
Offield, James W. Offield Family History. V.
Ransdell, Shelton. Wagon Train Journal. III.
"Recollections of Sarah Hammitt." V-.
Roeder, Henry. Diary. III.
Schutt, H. R. Journal. Not Seen.
Scroggs, William L. "To the Gold Fields." V.
Travel Account of Journey to Washington. Not Seen.
"Trip Up the Columbia in 1850." Not Seen.
Turner, Walter H. A Trip. II.
Zieber, John S. Diary. III.
Zumwalt, Solomon. BIOGRAPHA. V.

1851

Alden, Wyllis. ANCESTORS AND DESCENDANTS. IV.
Bacon, Daniel. Letters. Missing.
Baker, Jean R. "By Windjammer and Prairie Schooner." III.
Bigelow, Daniel R. Diary. V.
Bowen, James E. Diary. III.
Brandt, Charles A. TO OREGON WITH OX TEAMS. II.
Brooks, Quincy A. "Letter." V.
Brown, Orlando. Diary. Not Seen.
Buckingham, Harriet T. "Crossing the Plains." III.
Chambers, Margaret W. "Reminiscences." V.
Churchill, Willoughby. MEMORIES. IV.
Cranston, E. "Letters." V.
Cranston, Susan A. Diary. III.
Cranstone, Sarah M. "An Ohio Lady." III.
Crawford, Charles H. SCENES. III.
Crawford, P. V. "Journal." III.
Davenport, Timothy W. Dividing the Train. III.
Denny, Arthur A. Journal. III.
From Lake Erie to the Pacific. IV.
Fry, J. O. Across the Plains. II.
Gay, James W. "Trail Diary." IV.
Hadley, Amelia H. "Diary." II.
Hadley, E. Amelia. "Journal." II.
Huntington, Hallie H. ALL THE WAY WEST. IV.
James, John R. "Autobiography." Not Seen.

Nicaise, Auguste. YEAR IN THE DESERT. III.
North, Frank. On the Plains. III.
Seville, William P. NARRATIVE OF THE MARCH. II+.

1859
Abram, Cynthia. Individual Folder. Not Seen.
Babcock, William H. Journal. Not Seen.
Barnett, Joel. LONG TRIP. III.
Brown, Alonzo F. Autobiography. IV.
Case, Hamet H. Diary. III+.
Cummings, Charles J. Diary. II+.
Harbert, Joseph W. HARBERT DIARY. III.
Hull, Charles. Recollections. Not Seen.
Roundtree, Patrick H. AUTOBIOGRAPHY. IV.
Stockman, Lawson. "Recollections." V-.
Thibodo, Augustus J. "Diary." II.
Wallen, H. D. REPORT OF HIS EXPEDITION. III.

1860
Blake, George A. "Journal." I.
Brown, Benjamin. Diary. III.
Dixon, Joseph. TOPOGRAPHICAL MEMOIR. II.
Earnshaw, William. Across the Plains. Not Seen.
Fuller, Emeline L. LEFT BY THE INDIANS. V.
Kautz, August V. "From Missouri to Oregon." II.
Piper, Alexander. "Alexander Piper's Reports." III.

1861
Beebe, Beatrice B. "Hunting for the Blue Bucket." V-.
Brown, John M. "Diary." II+.
Crawford, Leroy. Diary. II.
Robertson, Theodore H. Diary. III.

1862
Bond, Samuel R. Journal. I.
Bristol, D. Sherlock. PIONEER PREACHER. V.
Bryant, Luvina C. "Recollections." Not Seen.
Burgunder, Ben. "Recollections." V.
Fisk, James L. EXPEDITION. II.
Herr, Henry R. Extracts from Diary. III.
Hewett, Randall H. ACROSS THE PLAINS. II.
Howard, Sarah A. Personal Reminiscences. IV.
Judson, H. M. Diary. I.
Kohrs, Conrad. Autobiography. V.
LETTER FROM THE SECRETARY OF WAR. III.
McClung, James S. Diary. I.
McComas, Evans S. JOURNAL. III.
McLaughlin, Daniel. SKETCH OF A TRIP. III.
Manville, George. Story of My Life. III.
Nichols, Robert A. Letters. V.
Pence, Anna. "Pioneer Hardships." V.
Rahm, Louise M. Diary. III.
Redfield, Francis M. REMINISCENCES. Not Seen.
Scott, Charlton. Diary. II.
Scott, Hamilton, A TRIP ACROSS. III.
Scott, Robert C. Trip to Washington. III.
Slater, Nellie. Reminiscence. IV.
Slater, O. B. Travels. III.
Smedley, William. ACROSS THE PLAINS. III+.
Stites, Thomas J. Journal of Travels. III.
Trip to Oregon. IV.
Wright, Dunham. Narrative. V.

1863
Aulbach, Adam. A Voice Out of the Past. V.
Bailey, James L. Diary. III-.
Cooper, Arvazena A. "Pioneer across." IV.
Darling, Lucia. Diary. I.

Gay, William. Reminiscences. IV.
Kirkpatrick, Robert. "From Wisconsin to Montana." II.
O'Neil, Elizabeth E. Reminiscence. V.
Sanders, Harriet P. Reminiscences. II.
Scott, Hamilton. A TRIP. III.
Stanton, George. Reminiscence. III.
Walker, Joseph C. Description. II.
Wright, J. B. An Epic. IV.

1864
Babb, Mrs. E. S. Papers. Not Seen.
Baker, Charles W. Westward Ho! III.
Brubaker, Albert. A Trip. IV.
Brundage, T. J. Diary. IV.
Chaffin, Thomas A. Traveling across. IV.
Clinkinbeard, Philura V. ACROSS THE PLAINS. III.
Cramer, Ora M. Pioneer Experiences. III.
Dalrymple, Ward. Reminiscence. V.
Davis, William F. "Hitting the Oregon Trail." IV.
Drew, Charles S. OFFICIAL OWYHEE. II.
Dunlap, Catherine C. MONTANA. II.
Fisk, Mrs. Van. Reminiscence. V.
Fletcher, B. F. Diary. V-.
Flory, A. P. Life and Memoirs. III.
French, C. Adelia. Memories. III.
Fulton, Arabella. TALES. II.
Gabbey, Roberts. Crossing the Plains. III.
Hackney, John S. Diary. III+.
Haskell, W. S. Pilgrimage. III+.
Hedges, Cornelius. Diaries. II.
Jenne, Lora M. Father's Life Story. V.
Loughary, Mrs. W. A. Diary. II.
Luster, Mary R. AUTOBIOGRAPHY.... Not Seen.
Merrill, Julius C. Diary. II+.
O'Neill, Eliza. Reminiscences. V.
Owen, Richard. Diary. II+.
Porter, Elizabeth L. Diary. III.
Roe, Martha A. A Trip to Idaho. II+.
Ryan, Benjamin W. "The Bozeman Trail." III.
Stanfield, Howard S. DIARY. II.
Thomas, William K. Diary. III.
Tinney, William T. Overland Trip. III.
Weaver. David. Pioneer Reminiscences. III+.
Weaver, David B. Early Days. IV.
West, Margaret E. Covered Wagon Days. III.
Wilkinson, Henry. Narrative. V.
Wood, J. D. Reminiscence. V.
Woods, Allin W. Journal. IV.

1865
Adkins, H. Frank. Reminiscence. IV.
Anthony, Erasmus L. Reminiscence. V-.
Bailey, David J. Diary. II+.
Black, Mary L. DIARY OF OVERLAND TRIP. III.
Boatman, Mary L. Reminiscence. V-.
Bundy, R. A. Reminiscence. V-.
Cauthorn, Benjamin R. Trip to Montana. I.
Cauthorn, James D. Diary. III.
Davis, William F. "Hitting the Oregon Trail." IV.
Flory, A. P. Life and Memoirs. III.
Gibson, J. W. RECOLLECTIONS. IV.
Inman, R. D. "Across the Plains." IV.
Jeffers, Susie L. Reminiscence. Not Seen.
Kimball, Gorham G. "Trailing Sheep." Genl.
Lee, C. M. Journals. II+.
McCauley, A. L. A Trip across. III.
McDannald, David W. A Story of Crossing. III.
Pattison, John J. "With the U.S. Army along the Oregon Trail." Genl.

PIKES PEAK ROUTES

Beginning in 1859, a rush to the Rockies generated hundreds of journals and, later, a growing secondary literature related to Colorado's mining frontier. The majority of "Peakers" used the Platte River to reach Colorado, but a substantial number used the CHEROKEE, SANTA FE or Smoky Hill River routes to reach Denver. All such sources have been entered below. Also see the CHEROKEE and SANTA FE categories for supplemental data.

1849
Easton, L. C. "Captain L. C. Easton's Report." Genl.

1853
Schiel, Jacob H. THE LAND BETWEEN. II +.

1858
Barker, Amselm H. DIARY OF 1858. III +.
Burgess, Jackson. PILLAR OF CLOUD. II +.
Cobb, Frank M. "Lawrence Party of Pike's Peakers." IV.
Downs, H. D. "Letter." Not Seen.
Hafen, Leroy R. "Col. Loring's Expedition." II.
Hall, Charles. Papers. II +.
Kellogg, David. "Across the Plains in 1858." II.
Parker, Wilbur F. "Glorious Orb of Day." II.
Parsons, William B. "Pike's Peak." IV.
Villard, Henry. PAST AND PRESENT. Genl.
Voorhees, Augustus. "The Voorhees Diary." III +.
Younker, Jason T. "The Early Pioneer." V.

1859-General
Athearn, Robert G. "The Fifty-Niners."
Burkey, Elmer R. Collection.
Eberstadt, Charles. "On Colorado Guidebooks."
Gehling, Richard and Mary. "Pike's Peak or Bust."
Hafen, Leroy R. OVERLAND ROUTES TO THE GOLD FIELDS.
Oakes, D. C. "The Man Who Wrote the Guide Book."
Pate, R. E. "Colorado Gold RUsh of '59."
Pike's Peak or Bust Collection.
Rush to the Rockies.
Sanford, Albert B. "The Cherokee Trail."
Spring, Agnes W. "Rush to the Rockies, 1859."
Temple, Wayne C. "Pike's Peak Gold Rush."
Villard, Henry. PAST AND PRESENT.
Willard, James F. "Sidelights of Pike's Peak."

1859
Archibald, J. Annie. "Journey to Pike's Peak." IV.
Anderson, David. "Recollections." Not Seen.
Baird, William J. Diary. III +.
Barney, Libeus. LETTERS. Stage.
Berkeley, George C. ENGLISH SPORTSMAN. II.
Blue, Daniel. THRILLING NARRATIVE. III.
Bowen, E. A. "Pikes Peak Fifty-Niner." III.
Bradway, J. C. Journal. I.
Bruyn, Kathleen. "AUNT" CLARA BROWN. V.
Burkley, Frank J. FADED FRONTIER. V-.
Burnap, Willard A. WHAT HAPPENED. IV.
Burton, Richard F. CITY OF THE SAINTS. I.
Chapman, Darius H. Diary. II.
Clark, Calvin. TWO DIARIES. IV.
Collins, Dabney O. "First Stagecoach into Denver." Stage.
Connor, Daniel E. CONFEDERATE IN THE COLORADO GOLD
     FIELDS. I.
Dailey, John L. Diary. III.
Davis, Sylvester. "Diary." III +.
Day, Alphonso. Diary. III +.
Dunstan, Edwin. AUTOBIOGRAPHY. II.
Faulkner, Harry. Diary. III.
Gass, A. M. "From Texas to Pike's Peak." III.
Goode, William H. OUTPOSTS OF ZION. V.
Gratiot, Henry. Journal. Not Seen.
Griffin, Eli A. Diaries. Not Seen.
Hunt, Mrs. A. C. "Diary." II.
Johnson, Joseph E. TRAIL TO SUNDOWN. III.
Kellogg, David. "Across the Plains." V.
Kingman, Romanzo. "Documents." II.

Kline, Perry A. Reminiscences. II.
Larnard, Ira P. Journal. I.
Long, Christian L. Diary. III.
Manwaring, Joshua. "Journal of a Fifty-Niner." III.
Oakley, Edward. Diaries. III.
Patrick, William. Trip to Pike's Peak. II.
Patterson, Edwin H. "Chalk Marks." II.
Patterson, Martin. Trip. Not Seen.
Pope, George L. Incidents. III +.
Post, Charles C. "The Arkansas Route." II.
Pritchard, Jesse L. "To Pike's Peak in Search of Gold." III.
Raymond, A. E. Diary. Not Seen.
Salisbury, William. "Journal of 1859 Gold Seeker." III +.
Sims, Edward E. Journal. III.
Smith, C. F. Journal. II.
Snyder, Monroe. Letters and Diary. V.
Sowers, John H. Diary. III.
Spain, David F. "Diary." III.
Steele, Edward D. EDWARD DUNSHA STEELE. II.
Villard, Henry. "To the Pike's Peak Country." III.
Wellman, Sylvanus. Diary. II.
Westerlund, Peter. Reminiscence. III.
Wildman, Augustus and Thomas. Correspondence. III.
Willing, George M. "Diary of a Journal." II.
Witter, Daniel. Diary. III-.

1860
Andree, E. W. TRAVELING IN THE SUNSET TRAIL. IV.
Anthony, Webster. "Journal of a Trip." III.
Bayless, William H. Diary. III.
Cisne, Jonah G. "Across the Plains." III.
Clark, Charles M. A TRIP TO PIKE'S PEAK. I.
Clark, George F. "Across the Plains." III +.
Clark, Helen. TWO DIARIES. IV.
Conley, Washington. Diary. Not Seen.
Cozad, Justus L. Life and Times. III.
Frizzell, Alexander L. Diary. V.
Gehling, Richard and Mary Ann. "Platte River Itinerary, 1860." Genl.
Greer, William A. A BOY ON THE PLAINS. III.
Hambleton, Chalkley J. A GOLD HUNTER'S EXPERIENCE. IV.
Hawley, H. J. "Hawley's Diary." III.
Hedges, William H. PIKE'S PEAK. IV.
Kassler, George W. Diary. III.
Kerwin, M. W. Diary. IV.
Kimball, Richard. "Overland Journey." IV.
Lake, John D. Journal. IV.
Lambert, Julia S. "Plain Tales of the Plains." II.
Lewis, Edward J. "Diary of a Gold Seeker." III +.
Mahoney, William F. Diary. II +.
Mallory, Samuel. "Overland to Pike's Peak." IV.
_____. "Samuel Mallory." V.
Mohler, George. A Trip. II.
Newman, J. A. AUTOBIOGRAPHY. V-.
Pitzer, Henry L. THREE FRONTIERS. V-.
Porter, Lavinia H. BY OX TEAM TO CALIFORNIA. II.
Richardson, Albert D. "Albert D. Richardson's Letters." II.
Sanford, Mollie D. JOURNAL OF MOLLIE DORSEY SANFORD. II.
Sheriff, Matthew. Diary. III +.
Spring, Agnes W. "Samuel Mallory."
Stahl, Ez M. Diary. Not Seen.
Stuart, J. E. B. "Journal of the March." II.
Willis, James M. "Jasons of 1860." IV.
Wornell, David C. Diary. II.
Wright, Dunham. Narrative. V.
Young, John D. JOHN D. YOUNG. II.

1861
Benjamin, Israel. THREE YEARS. II.

Billingsley, Amos S. Diary. V.
Birge, Julius C. AWAKENING. III.
Cleghorn, Daniel B. Diary. V.
"Crossing the Great American Desert." IV.
Draper, D. M. Santa Fe Trail. IV.
Fosdick, Lucy H. "Across the Plains." IV.
Morse, H. D. L. Diary. III.
Robertson, Theodore H. "Diary." III.
Seymour, Edward. Diary. III.

1862

Coy, Mrs. John G. "Crossing the Plains." V.
Dodge, James H. ACROSS THE PLAINS. V.
Kassler, George W. "George W. Kassler." IV.
Meredith, Emily R. Experiences. III.
Shelley, Edward. "Western Journal." IV.
Sullivan, W. W. Crossing. IV.
Thoroughman, Robert P. A Trip. IV.
Tootle, Mrs. Thomas E. "Diary." III.
Welty, Marion B. Description of a Trip. V-.
Witter, Clara V. Reminiscence. III.

1863

Austin, H. B. Trip to Denver. IV.
Bruffey, George A. EIGHTY-ONE YEARS. V.
Downing, Finis E. Recollections. Not Seen.
Ferster, James S. Sketch. V.
Hively, Sara. Journal. II.
Lewis, B. P. Diary. II.
McPherson, Murdoch M. "Reminiscences." II.
Morris, Maurice O. RAMBLES IN THE ROCKY MOUNTAINS. II+.
Overland Journey to Colorado. II.
Patten, F. E. Journal. I.
Purviance, M. C. Journal. II.
Sherwell, Samuel. OLD RECOLLECTIONS. III.
Smith, Harriet A. "To Pike's Peak." II+.
Talbot, Joseph C. Diary. III.
Winne, Peter. "Across the Plains." II.

1864

Alton, Hiram. Journal. II+.
Edwards, Solomon. Diary. III.
Estabrook, Joseph H. "Crossing the Plains." V.
Greenslit, George H. "A Day." Not Seen. Stage.
Hill, Emma S. A DANGEROUS CROSSING. III+.
Hitchcock, Harriet. FAMILY HISTORY. III.
Jolly, William C. ACROSS THE PLAINS. III.
Keaton, Charles H. "Crossing the Plains." Freight.
McCain, G. S. "A Trip from Atchison." V.
Porter, Charles F. "News." By stage. Not Seen.
Smith, Sarah A. PIONEER EPIC. V.
Stevens, Nancy J. Account. Not Seen.
Thompson, James B. Crossing the Plains. V-. Excellent indian raid description.

1865-General

Davis, Theodore R. "Stage Ride to Colorado." I.
Dodge, Grenville M. "Diary." Not Seen.
Dodge, Nathan P. Diary. Not Seen.
Fitch, J. R. Report on the Smoky Hill.
Zwink, Timothy A. "Dodging Death."

1865-General

"A Stage Ride to Colorado." II+.

1865

Bowles, Samuel. ACROSS THE CONTINENT. II.
Byers, Frank S. "From West to East." IV.

Cauthorn, Benjamin R. Trip to Montana. I.
Colfax, Schuyler. "Honorable Schuyler Colfax's Trip." II.
Davis, Theodore R. "A Stage Ride to Colorado." I.
Ellis, Henrietta. DIARY. II.
France, Charles B. Diary. II.
Hodder, Halie R. "Crossing the Plains." III-.
Howlett, W. J. Recollections. IV.
Leech, A. P. Diary. II.
Michie, Peter S. LIFE AND LETTERS. V.
On the Overland Trail, 1865. IV.
Peabody, Frances C. "Across the Plains Deluxe." IV.
Steen, Enoch R. Diary. III+.
Stevens, W. H. FIELD NOTES. V.
Stobie, Charles S. "Crossing the Plains." II.
Young, Frank C. ACROSS THE PLAINS. II+.
Young, John D. JOHN D. YOUNG. II.

1866

Buss, Mrs. George E. AUNT AMELIA'S DIARY. III.
Gregory, Mrs. E. J. Adventuring. V.
Jamison, Belle and Lizzie. Journey from Egypt. II.
Keays, Elizabeth. "Diary." III.
Keyes, Elizabeth. "Across the Plains." III+.
Meline, James F. TWO THOUSAND MILES. II.
Schmidt, Johann H. Across the Plains. I.
Smith, Mary. "Miss Smith Crosses the Plains." III.
Taylor, Bayard. COLORADO. II.
Tunis, Joseph C. Diaries. II.
Zern, Frank W. "A Stage Ride in '66." IV.

1867

Bell, William A. NEW TRACKS. II.
Duncan, Elizabeth. Diary. II.
Hoyt, A. W. "Over the Plains to Colorado." V.
"Over the Plains to Colorado." V.
Simonin, Louis. ROCKY MOUNTAIN WEST. II.
Spencer, W. A. THOUSAND MILES. II.

1869

Brewer, William H. ROCKY MOUNTAIN LETTERS. IV.
Culver, E. S. "Crossing the Plains." V.
Mariager, Dagmar. "A Voyage by Land." III.

RIO GRANDE TRAIL

Between Taos, NM and Chihuahua, Mexico travelers followed this trail. Most emigrants took only the Santa Fe - Jornada portion and turned west for California.

General

Austerman, Wayne R. "Return to the *Journal*."
Baxter, John O. "Las Carneradas: New Mexico's Sheep Trade."
Blumenschein, Helen G. "Historic Roads and Trails to Taos."
Cross, Jack L. "Army Road-Building in New Mexico."
_____. "Wagon Roads across New Mexico."
Egan, Ferol. "Journada del Muerto."
Gooden, John H. "Life and Experiences."
Hall, R. Franklin. "Chihuahua Trail."
Miles, Bob. "Early Roads to El Paso."
Mitchell, Eleanor L. A STUDY OF TIJERAS CANYON.
Moorhead, Max L. NEW MEXICO'S ROYAL ROAD. Recommended.
Peterson, Charles S., et al. MORMON BATTALION TRAIL GUIDE.
Raht, Charles G. "The Chihuahua Trail."
Rowland, Leonore A. "First Covered Wagon Train."
Sharp, Jay W. "Journada del Muerto."

1841

Bell, Josias F. Sketches. II.

1846
Abert, J. W. WESTERN AMERICA. I.
Bigler, Henry W. BIGLER'S CHRONICLE. II.
Bliss, Robert S. "Journal of Robert S. Bliss." III.
Cooke, Philip St. G. CONQUEST OF NEW MEXICO. I.
_____. JOURNAL. I.
Elmer, Elijah. Journal. III+.
Emory, William H. LT. EMORY REPORTS. II+.
Griffin, John S. "A Doctor Comes to California." II.
Hyde, William. Private Journal. II.
Jones, Nathaniel V. "Journal." III.
Judd, Zodak K. Autobiography. V.
Keyson, Guy M. Journal. II.
Morris, Thomas. Journal. III+.
Pace, James. Journal. III+.
Peterson, Charles S., et al. MORMON BATTALION TRAIL GUIDE.
Pettigrew, David. Autobiography. III-.
Pikale, Henele. "Recollections." III.
Porter, Eugene O. "Down the Chihuahua Trail." I.
Smith, Azariah. Journal. II.
Standage, Henry. MARCH OF THE MORMON BATTALION. III+.
Turner, Henry S. ORIGINAL JOURNALS. II.
Tyler, Daniel. CONCISE HISTORY. II.
Weinert, Duane R. "Kearny's Expedition." Genl.
Whitworth, Robert W. "From the Mississippi to the Pacific." III.
Wilson, David P. "Mormon Battalion." II.
Wislizenus, A. MEMOIR. I.

1847
Gibson, George R. OVER THE CHIHUAHUA AND SANTA FE
   TRAILS. II.

1848
Martin, Thomas S. WITH FREMONT. III.

1849
Aldrich, Lorenzo D. JOURNAL. III.
Blunt, Phineas U. Notes of Travel. I.
Boyles, John R. "None Dream But of Success." V-.
Brainard, David. Diary. II+.
Brisbane, William. Journal. I.
Brownlee, Robert. AN AMERICAN ODYSSEY. II.
Candee, J. G. Letter. IV.
Chamberlain, William H. "From Lewisburg to California." I.
Conway, Mary. "Little Rock Girl." IV.
Counts, George. Journal. III-.
Creighton, Mary E. Reminiscences. V.
Crumpton, H. J., and W. B. ADVENTURES. IV.
Deaderick, David A. Diary. V.
Eliot, Robert. "Off to the Gold Fields." IV.
Foreman, Grant. JAMES COLLIER. IV.
Forsyth, John R. Journal. I.
Fouts, D. Lambert. Diary. II.
Gooding, Larry. "Across the Plains." IV.
Green, Robert B. ON THE ARKANSAS ROUTE. III.
Hammond, John. IN MEMORIAM. V.
Hart, Robert. Diary. Not Seen.
Hayes, Benjamin I. PIONEER NOTES. II.
Heslip, Augustus M. "Diary." II.
Hudgins, John. To California in 1849. III.
Hunter, William H. Diary. I.
Hyde, William. Private Journal. II.
Jordan, David. Diary. I.
King, Alfred D. "Trip to the Gold Fields." II+.
Lasselle, Stanislaus. "Diary." III.
May, John. Correspondence. Not Seen.

Noel, Thomas J. "W. Wilberforce A. Ramsey." IV.
Pancoast, Charles E. A QUAKER FORTY-NINER. II.
Pennell, William D. Letters. V.
Phillips, Marcia B. Five Stevenson Men. III.
Powell, H. M. T. SANTA FE TRAIL. I.
Ramsey, James G. Papers. III.
Ricks, Casper S. Diary. I.
RoBards, John L. Journal. II+.
Shinn, Silas. TRAIL OF A PIONEER. IV.
Simmons, Joseph R. Diary. I.
Taylor, Joseph. JOURNAL OF THE ROUTE. III.

1850
Parrish, Susan. Westward in 1850. IV.
Root, Virginia V. FOLLOWING THE POT OF GOLD. IV.
Stratton, R. B. CAPTIVITY OF THE OATMAN GIRLS. IV.

1851
Cleminson, John. Diary. II.

1852
Baskerville, William. Diary. II+.

1853
Froebel, Julius. SEVEN YEARS TRAVEL. II+.

1854
Pope, John. REPORT RED RIVER TO THE RIO GRANDE. II+.

1857
Carter, Henry W. Narrative. III+.
Hamilton, James G. MY DEAR CORNELIA. IV.

1858
Lyman, Amasa M. Journal. II.
Mollhausen, Heinrich B. DIARY OF A JOURNEY. I.
Rose, Leonard J. L. J. ROSE. II.
Sands, Frank. A PASTORAL PRINCE. V.

1859
Westerlund, Peter. Reminiscence. III.

1863
Fourr, J. William. Manuscripts. I.

1864
Miller, Darlis. ACROSS THE PLAINS. II.

1867
Bell, William A. NEW TRACKS. II.
French, Barsina R. Journal. III.

1868
Ormsby, Augusta. Diary. IV.

1869
Culver, E. S. "Crossing the Plains. V.
Hunt, Thomas B. Journal. Not Seen.

SALT LAKE CORRIDOR

This major road connected Salt Lake City and southern California. It en-
   joyed some Gold Rush traffic, but served primarily to link Utah with
   the Pacific.

General
Beldon, L. Burr. GOODBYE, DEATH VALLEY.

Bennion, Israel. "Before the Arrowhead Trail."
Corbett, Pearson H. JACOB HAMLIN.
Driggs, Howard R. MORMON TRAIL.
Gilman, Harold F. "Origin Eastern Mojave Desert." Not Seen.
Hamblin, Jacob. JACOB HAMBLIN.
Harding, Stephen S. Collection.
Hunter, Milton R. "The Mormon Corridor."
Hutchinson, Charles E. "Development and Use of Transportation."
Ivens, Anthony W. "Traveling over Forgotten Trails."
Kell, Elmer A. "Early Travel and Communication."
King, David S. MOUNTAIN MEADOWS MASSACRE.
Palmer, William R. "Latter-Day Saint Pioneers."
Perkins, George E. PIONEERS OF THE WESTERN DESERT.
Pugh, Byron G. "History of Utah-California Wagon Freighting."
Reeder, Ray M. "The Mormon Trail."
Reid, H. Lorenzo. BRIGHAM YOUNG'S.
Smith, Melvin T. "The Colorado River."
Walker, Clifford J. "History of the Mojave River Trail."
_____. OPENING THE MOJAVE RIVER TRAIL.
Warren, Elizabeth, et al. CULTURAL RESOURCES.
Wheat, Carl I. "Pioneer Visitors to Death Valley."
White, Douglas. STORY OF A TRAIL.

1848
Gordon, G. F. Statement. Not Seen.

1849-General
Beldon, L. Burr. GOODBYE DEATH VALLEY!
_____. DEATH VALLEY HEROINE.
Boyles, J. C. "He Witnessed the Death Valley Tragedy."
Brier, J. W. "Argonauts of Death Valley.
_____. "Death Valley Party."
Chalfant, W. A. DEATH VALLEY: THE FACTS.
Edwards, Elza I. "Mystery of Death Valley's."
Hafen, Leroy and Ann. JOURNALS OF FORTY-NINERS.
Johnson, LeRoy and Jean. JULIA, DEATH VALLEY'S YOUNGEST VICTIM.
Koenig, George. BEYOND THIS PLACE.
Latta, Frank F. DEATH VALLEY '49ERS.
Long, Margaret. SHADOW OF THE ARROW.
Manly, William L. JAYHAWKERS' OATH.
Martineau, James H. "A Tragedy of the Desert."
Nusbaumer, Louis. LOST DEATH VALLEY '49ER JOURNAL.
Ressler, John J. "John Jacob Ressler's Trip."
Serven, James E. "Ill-Fated '49er Wagon Train."
Smith, Pauline U. CAPTAIN JEFFERSON HUNT. V-.
Southworth, John S. "Help."
Walker, Ardis M. DEATH VALLEY AND MANLY.
_____. FREEMAN JUNCTION.
_____. MANLY MAP AND THE MANLY STORY.
Walker, Clifford J. "History of the Mojave River Trail."
Wheat, Carl I. "Forty-Niners in Death Valley."
_____. "Jayhawkers at the Missouri."
_____. "Trailing the Forty-Niners."
Wolff, John E. ROUTE OF THE MANLY PARTY.

1849
Arms, Cephas, and Adonijah S. Welch. LONG ROAD TO CALIFORNIA. II.
Armstrong, John C. Diary. V.
Babcock, Leonard. Recollections. II.
Bigler, Henry W. "Bigler's Journal." II.
_____. "Extracts from the Journal." III.
Blackburn, Abner. "Reminiscences." III.
Brown, Harvey S. Statement. IV.
Brown, James S. LIFE OF A PIONEER. II.
Brown, John Z. AUTOBIOGRAPHY. IV.
Campbell, Robert L. Journal. II.

Cannon, George Q. A TRIP TO CALIFORNIA. III.
Caughey, John W. "Southwest from Salt Lake." II.
Derr, Peter. "Account of Experiences." V.
Edwards, Elza I. VALLEY WHOSE NAME IS DEATH. II.
Ellenbecker, John G. JAYHAWKERS OF DEATH VALLEY. III.
Erkson, Alexander C. "Statement." III.
Farrer, William. "Diary." II.
Freeman, Dick. "On Manley's Trail." Not Seen.
Givens, Robert R. Letters. V.
Granger, Lewis. LETTERS. III.
Gruell, J. D. "Account." V.
Haight, Isaac C. Biographical Sketch. III.
Haines, Asa. Diary. IV.
Hamelin, Joseph P. Diary. II+.
Hayes, Benjamin I. Notes on Overland Journeys. IV.
Haynes, Asa. "Diary." V.
Hoover, Vincent A. Diaries. II.
Kelly, Charles. "On Manly's Trail." III.
Koenig, George. "Betweixt the Devil and the Deep." III.
Leadingham, Grace. "Juliet Wells Brier." III.
Locke, Dean J. Diary. Not Seen.
Long, Margaret. SHADOW OF THE ARROW. II.
Lorton, William B. OVER THE SALT LAKE TRAIL. IV.
Manly, William L. DEATH VALLEY IN '49. III.
Morris, Thomas. Journal. IV.
Nusbaumer, Louis. VALLEY OF SALT. III.
Pearson, Gustavus C. OVERLAND IN 1849. III-.
Pratt, Addison. "Diaries." II.
Randolph, W. C. Statement. V.
Rich, Charles C. "Diary." III.
Rollins, James H. "Recollection." IV.
Senter, W. Riley. CROSSING THE CONTINENT. III.
Shannon, Thomas. "Journey of Peril." V.
Stephens, Lorenzo D. LIFE SKETCHES. IV.
Stoddard, Sheldon. "Sketch." V.
Stover, Jacob Y. "The Jacob Y. Stover Narrative." V.
Stuart, Charles V. Trip. V.
Swan, Chauncey. "Letters of a Forty-Niner." IV.
Switzer, David. "The Switzer Log." II.
Taylor, W. B. "Pioneer Reminiscences." IV.
Thurber, Albert K. Biographical Sketch. V.
Van Dyke, Walter. "Overland to Los Angeles." V.
Wade, Almira. "Across the Plains." IV.
Waite, Sidney P. "Sketch." V.
Welch, Adonijah S. "Document." V.
Widber, J. H. Statement. V.
Wylly, Thomas S. "Westward Ho." III.
Young, Sheldon. "Diary." III.

1850
Blackburn, Abner. "Reminiscences." IV.
Cheesman, David W. "By Ox Team from Salt Lake." III.
Kilbourne, Lewis. Journal. Not Seen.
"Notes of a Trip." III.
Smith, Pauline U. CAPTAIN JEFFERSON HUNT. V-.
Wheelock, Charles. Letters. Not Seen.

1851
Ingrim, Godfrey C. Recollections. Not Seen.
Pratt, Parley P. AUTOBIOGRAPHY. II.
Stanley, Reva H., and Charles L. Camp. "A Mormon Mission." III.
Wood, Joseph S. "The Mormon Settlement." IV.

1852
Allred, Reddick. "Journal." III.
Bixby-Smith, Sarah. ADOBE DAYS. IV.
Hazard, Henry T. Across the Plains. V.
Hyde, William. Private Journal. IV.

Jared, Israel. "A Trip across Nebraska." V-.
Pratt, Sarah. Jottings. III.
Savage, Levi. JOURNAL. V.
Scarbrough, Richard A. Diary. II.
Stoddard, William C. Diary. Not Seen.
Stout, Hosea. ON THE MORMON FRONTIER. III.

1853
Burns, James F. "James Franklin Burns." V-.
Burwell, Lewis. Dictated Statement. V.
Carvalho, Solomon N. INCIDENTS OF TRAVEL. II.
Desmond, Lucille H. "Henry Clay Daulton." V-.
Flint, Thomas. "Diary of Dr. Thomas Flint." III.
Hays, Lorena L. "To the Land of Gold." Not Seen.
Heap, Gwinn H. CENTRAL ROUTE TO THE PACIFIC. II+.
Hollister, W. W. Statement. IV.
Myer, Nathaniel. "Journey into Southern Oregon." III.
Schiel, Jacob H. LAND BETWEEN. II+.
Stanley, David S. Diary. II+.
Stout, Hosea. ON THE MORMON FRONTIER. III.
Wallace, William S. "Was Heap's Journal Plagiarized?" IV.
Wheelock, Walt. "Following Fremont's Fifth Expedition."

1854
Bell, Eli. A History of the Travels. II.
Caine, John T. "Journal." III+.
Johnson, Sixtus. Leaves from the Family Tree. III.
Livingston, Robert D. "Felix Tracy and the Salt Lake City Express." III.
Molen, Simpson M. Diary. III+.
Rice, William B. "Early Freighting." III.
Whitney, Orson K. Journal. III.

1855
Allred, Reddick. "Journal." III.
Bean, George W. "Journal." IV.
Hayes, W. R. Diary. III+.
Jenson, Andrew. "History of the Las Vegas Mission." II.
Los Angeles STAR. Not Seen.
Miller, Henry W. Journal. IV.
Mowry, Sylvester. "Lt. Sylvester Mowry's Report." III.

1856
Chandless, William. A VISIT TO SALT LAKE. II.
Hoth, H. Diary. I.

1857-Genl
Beckwith, Frank. "Shameful Friday."
Boring, Claude T. "Mountain Meadows Massacre."
Brooks, Juanita. MOUNTAIN MEADOWS MASSACRE.
King, David S. MOUNTAIN MEADOWS MASSACRE.
Livesey, Donald W. "Mountain Meadows Massacre."
Martineau, James H. "A Tragedy of the Desert."
Rea, Ralph R. "Mountain Meadows Massacre."
Wise, William. MASSACRE AT MOUNTAIN MEADOWS.

1857
Clark, William. "A Trip across the Plains." II.
Ginn, John I. Personal Recollections. II+.
Lyman, Amasa M. Journal. I.

1858
Brooks, Juanita. "A Place of Refuge." Genl. Survey of White Mountain Expedition.
Kenderdine, Thaddeus S. A CALIFORNIA TRAMP. II.
Langley, Harold D. TO UTAH WITH THE DRAGOONS. IV.
Stott, Clifford L. SEARCH FOR SANCTUARY: BRIGHAM YOUNG AND THE WHITE MOUNTAIN EXPEDITION. Genl.

1861
Woodward, Arthur. CAMELS AND SURVEYORS IN DEATH VALLEY. Genl.

1862
Harding, Stephen S. Collection. Genl.

1863
Bender, Flora I. "Notes by the Way." III.
Sweetland, Louisa M. Across the Plains. Not Seen.

1864
Dowdle, John C. Journal. III+.
Leppo, David T. FAMILY. II.
Morrill, Rosa N. MARY JANE, PIONEER. IV.
Rousseau, Mrs. J. A. "Rousseau Diary." II+.
_____. Papers. Not Seen.

1865
Shackleford, Ruth. TO CALIFORNIA. II.

1867
Jackson, William H. DIARIES. II.

SALT LAKE CUTOFF

The majority of California-bound emigrants who visited Salt Lake City continued west by this cutoff. It began in Emigrant Park (the present location of City Hall) passed Ogden and the Bear River before joining the California Trail just south of City of Rocks.

General
Cramer, Howard R. "California Trail in Idaho."
Fleming, L. A., and A. R. Standing. "The Salt Lake Cutoff." Recommended.
Kelly, Charles. "First Emigrant Train." (Bidwell-Bartleson 1841 Route through Utah)
Korns, J. Roderick. "West from Fort Bridger."
Morgan, Dale L. GREAT SALT LAKE.
Standing, A. R. "Friendly House." Bear River Crossing.

Maps
Fleming, L. A., and A. R. Standing. "The Salt Lake Cutoff."

1847
Blackburn, Abner. "Reminiscences." IV.
Hyde, William. Private Journal. IV.
Pace, James. Journal. III+.

1848
Bigler, Henry W. BIGLER'S CHRONICLE. II.
Brown, James S. LIFE. II.
Fifield, Allen. "First Two-Way Road." II.
Hammond, Francis A. "In Early Days." V.
Judd, Zodak K. Autobiography. V.
Pikale, Henele. "Recollections." III.
Smith, Azariah. Journal. II.
Tyler, Daniel. CONCISE HISTORY. IV.
Willis, Ira J. "The Ira J. Willis Guide." III.

1849
Benson, John E. Forty-Niner. II+.
Benson, John H. From St. Joe to Sacramento. III+.
Breyfogle, Joshua D. Diary. II.
Brooks, E. W. JOURNAL OF A FORTY-NINER. III.
Bush, Charles W. Five Letters. V.
Call, W. W. Reminiscence. IV.

Clark, Sterling. HOW MANY MILES. IV.
Cole, Cornelius. MEMOIRS. V.
Darwin, Charles B. Diaries. I.
Davis, Hiram. "Journal." III.
Dewolf, David. "Diary of the Overland Trail." II.
Doyle, Simon. Diary. II+.
Dundass, Samuel R. JOURNAL. II.
Eastin, Thomas N. "Kentucky Gold Rusher." II+.
Evans, Burrell W. Diary. III.
Evershed, Thomas. "Gold Rush Journal." II.
Ferguson, Charles D. EXPERIENCES OF A 49ER. III.
Foster, Isaac. Foster Family. II.
Glover, William. THE MORMONS IN CALIFORNIA. IV.
Gray, Charles G. OFF AT SUNRISE. II.
Hall, O. J. Diary. IV.
Hannon, Jessie G. BOSTON-NEWTON COMPANY. II.
Haun, Catherine M. "A Woman's Trip." II.
Hillyer, Edwin. "From Waupun to Sacramento." II.
Hinman, Charles G. A PRETTY FAIR VIEW. III.
Hutchings, James M. SEEKING THE ELEPHANT. II+.
Jewett, George E. Diary. III.
Johnston, William G. OVERLAND IN 1849. II.
Josselyn, Amos P. OVERLAND JOURNAL. III.
Kelly, Charles. "On Manly's Trail to Death Valley." III.
Kelly, William. ACROSS THE ROCKY MOUNTAINS. II.
Kleiser, James A. Autobiography. III.
Lewis, John F. Diary. II+.
Locke, Dean J. Diary. Not Seen.
McCall, Ansel J. GREAT CALIFORNIA TRAIL. II+.
Manlove, John N. Overland Trip. IV.
Marshall, Philip C. "Newark Overland Company." IV.
Miller, James B. The Wild Plains. III.
Minges, Abram. Diary. II.
Moody, Joseph L. LETTER. Not Seen.
Myrick, Thomas S. GOLD RUSH. V.
Orvis, Andrew. Letters and Diary. III-.
Owen, Abraham. "Reminiscence." V.
Packwood, William H. "Reminiscences." IV.
Royce, Sarah E. "From Salt Lake to the Sierras." III.
Scheller, John J. Autobiography. IV.
Shrock, Thomas. Letter. III-.
Spooner, E. A. Diary. IV.
Staples, David J. "Journal." II.
Thomason, Jackson. FROM MISSISSIPPI TO CALIFORNIA. II.
Tolles, James S. TRAILS AND TRIALS. II.
Trowbridge, Mary. PIONEER DAYS. IV.
Tuttle, Charles A. Letters. V.
White, William W. "William Wellington White." III-.
Winsor, Alonzo. Journey. II+.

1850
Abbott, Carlisle S. RECOLLECTIONS. III.
Baldwin, J. F. DIARY KEPT. III.
Blood, James. Diary. III.
Booth, Caleb. Diary. III.
Brown, Adam. "Over Barren Plains." III.
Buckingham, Henry. Journey. III.
Camper, Henry W. "Why I Crossed the Plains." IV.
Carr, John. A VULCAN AMONG THE ARGONAUTS. IV.
Clark, Anson. Overland in 1850. III.
Davis, Sarah. "Diary." III.
Enos, A. A. ACROSS THE PLAINS. IV.
Fonda, Charles I. Diary. IV.
Gardner, D. B. Diary. II.
Gridley, John T. Letters. Not Seen.
Griffith, Andrew J. Hancock County, Illinois. I.
Haight, Henry H. We Walked to California. III.
Hewitt, Henry L. "Diary." III.

Hough, Warren. "1850 Overland Diary." III.
Jamison, Samuel M. "Diary." III.
Keith, Fleury F. "Journal." III.
Kidder, Leroy L. Story of a Siskiyou Argonaut. V.
Kilbourne, Lewis. Journal. Not Seen.
Kilgore, William H. KILGORE JOURNAL. III.
Kiser, Joseph C. Diary and Letters. II.
Knox, Reuben, MEDIC 49ER. III.
Langworthy, Franklin. SCENERY. II.
Littleton, James. Diary. I.
Littleton, Micajah. Diary. II.
McGlashan, John M. Overland Journal. II+.
McKeeby, Lemuel C. "Memoirs." III.
Mason, James. "Diary." III.
Morgan, Martha M. TRIP ACROSS THE PLAINS. III.
Newcomb, Silas. Journal. II+.
Olson, Jonas W. "Journal." V-.
Packard, Wellman. EARLY EMIGRATION. V.
Patrick, Henry H. Extracts. V.
Quesenbury, William. "William Quesenbury's Journal." II+.
Ridge, John R. "John Rollin Ridge." IV.
Russell, Isaac. A Sketch. V-.
Seaton, James A. Diary. III.
Shields, James G. California Trip. I.
Shoemaker, DIARY. II.
Sortore, Abram. BIOGRAPHY. IV.
Starr, Henry W. Diary. II+.
Starr, J. R. Diary. II.
Stauder, John A. Diary. II.
Stine, Henry A. Letters & Journal. III.
Street, Franklin. CALIFORNIA. II.
Summers, Joseph. Letter. III.
Taylor, Calvin. "Overland to the Gold Fields." II+.
Thissell, G. W. CROSSING THE PLAINS. II.
Thompson, Clark W. Letters. I.
Tice, Peter. Diary. II.
Tompkins, Edward A. Diary. II.
Turner, William. Diary. III+.
Walker, Zachariah. Diary. II.
Waterhouse, Loyal N. Diary. II+.
Watts, John W. Diary. III.
Wheelock, Charles. Letters. Not Seen.
Whitman, Abial. Journal. II.
Wilson, William. Day Book. III.
Wooster, David. THE GOLD RUSH. IV.
Wright, Robert C. Journal. II+.

1851
Buckingham, Harriet T. "Crossing the Plains." III.
From Lake Erie to the Pacific. IV.
Ingrim, Godfrey C. Recollections. Not Seen.
Jennings, Oliver. Journal. IV.
Parsons, Lucena P. "Journal." II.
Sands, Frank. A PASTORAL PRINCE. V.
Zumwalt, Solomon. ADAM ZUMWALT. V.

1852
Bailey, Mary S. "Journal." III.
Baker, William B. Diary. III.
Banks, Henry P. Diary. III.
Blake, Winslow. Diary. II.
Bradley, Henry and Nancy. Journal. II.
Bradley, N. J., and H. Journal. Not Seen.
Carpenter, James C. I Crossed the Plains. III.
Clark, John Hawkins. "Overland to the Gold Fields." II+.
Conard, Howard L. UNCLE DICK. IV.
Couper, J. C. Diary. III+.
Cox, George W. Reminiscences. IV.

Westerlund, Peter. Reminiscence. III.
Willing, George M. "Diary to Pike's Peak." II.

1860
Lambert, Julia S. "Plain Tales of the Plains." II.
Powell, Philander. History. II+.
Russell, Marian S. LAND OF ENCHANTMENT. V.
Stuart, J. E. B. "Journal Against the Hostile Kiowas." II.

1861
Draper, D. M. Santa Fe Trail. IV.
Fosdick, Lucy H. "Across the Plains." IV.

1863
Allyn, Joseph P. WEST BY SOUTHWEST. II+.
Fourr, J. William. Manuscripts. I.
Huning, Ernestine F. Diary. III+.
Putnam, Joseph P. "Letters." II.

1864
Miller, Darlis. ACROSS THE PLAINS. II.
Wright, Robert M. Building of Stations. Genl.

1865
"Overland from Cincinnati." V.
Stahl, Francis M. Diary. II.
White, Lonnie J. "Santa Fe Trail in '65." Genl.

1866
Meline, James F. TWO THOUSAND MILES. II.
Muzzal, Thomas A. "Across the Plains." III.

1867
Bell, William A. NEW TRACKS IN NORTH AMERICA. II.
French, Barsina R. Journal. III.

1868
Blinn, Richard F. Diary. V.
Ormsby, Augusta. Diary. IV.

1869
Culver, E. S. "Crossing the Plains." V.

SIMPSON ROUTE

This road, linking Salt Lake City and Carson Pass, was also the approximate route for the Pony Express and Overland Stage Company.

General
Alexander, Thomas, and Leonard Arrington. CAMP IN THE SAGEBRUSH.
Beeton, Barbara. "James Hervey Simpson."
Bennion, Owen C. "Good Indian Spring."
Bluth, John. "Confrontation with an Arid Land."
CENTRAL OVERLAND ROUTE AND TRANSCONTINENTAL TELEGRAPH THROUGH NEVADA.
Egan, Howard. PIONEERING THE WEST.
Fisher, William F. "Battle of Egan Canyon."
Greenwell, A HISTORY.
Jensen, Christian. "Ghost of the Overland."
Magee, William. MAGEE STATION. II.
Simpson, James H. SHORTEST ROUTE TO CALIFORNIA.
Lewis, Oscar. TOWN THAT DIED LAUGHING.
Townley, John M. "Stalking Horse for the Pony Express."

1854
Huntington, Oliver B. Diary. III+.

_____. TRIP TO CARSON VALLEY. III.
Schiel, Jacob H. THE LAND BETWEEN. II+.

1855
Bean, George W. Report. V.

1856
Huntington, Oliver B. Diary. III+.
_____. "Eighteen Days on the Desert." II.

1858
North, Frank. On the Plains. III.
Simpson, James H. REPORT OF RECONNAISSANCES. Genl.

1859-General
Langellier, John P. "Desert Documentary - James H. Simpson Expedition." Not Seen.

1859
Burton, Richard F. CITY OF THE SAINTS. I.
Douglas, Charles D. Narrative. II+.
Greeley, Horace. AN OVERLAND JOURNEY. I.
Griswold, Harriet B. Papers. Not Seen.
Holman, Cyrus K. Journal. II+.
Lee, William. Notes. III.
Mathews, Edward J. CROSSING THE PLAINS. II.
Simpson, James H. REPORT OF EXPLORATIONS. I.
Sowers, John H. Diary. III.
Tuttle, Charles M. "California Diary." II.

1860
Anderson, John C. MACKINAWS DOWN THE MISSOURI.
Ayer, Edward E. Early Reminiscences. IV.
Crane, Ellery. "An Overland Trip." IV.
Downes, Clara E. Journal. I.
"Eliza and Margaret Prentice's Trip." IV.
Porter, Lavinia H. BY OX TEAM. II.
Powell, Philander. History. II+.
Scott, Charles. "Nevada Indian Uprisings." II.
Wilson, Elijah N. AMONG THE SHOSHONES. III.

1861
Baker, E. M. "Journal of a March." III.
Benjamin, Israel J. THREE YEARS IN AMERICA. II.
Brown, John Mason. "Diary." II+.
Gelatt, Richard. A Simple Sketch. IV.
Moss, William C. "Overland to California." III+.
Preston, Leander A. Items of Travel. III.
Twain, Mark. ROUGHING IT. I.

1862
Anderson, Charles L. Letters. II.
Boquist, Laura B. CROSSING THE PLAINS. III.
Karchner, Mrs. Nicholas H. Diary. III+.
Millington, Ada. "Journal." II+.
Newkirk, Coleman S. Brief History. V.
Nye-Starr, Kate. SELF-SUSTAINING WOMAN. V.
Redfield, Francis M. REMINISCENCES.... III.
Tuttle, Hiram G. Diary. III.
Waite, Catherine V. ADVENTURES. II.
Young, Albert J. Diary. II.

1863
Bender, Flora I. "Notes by the Way." III.
Briggs, Joshua and Ruth. A PIONEER MISSOURIAN. V.
Colegrove, George L. Life Story. V.
Cutting, A. Howard. Journal. II+.
Dickason, David H. "Clarence King's First Western Journey." IV.

Egan, William M. Journal. IV.
Fulkerth, Abbey E. "Aunt Abbey's Diary." III+.
Hopper, Silas L. "Diary." III.
Lewis, B. P. Diary. II.
McCutchan, Rebecca E. Headed West. III.
Magee, William. MAGEE STATION. II.
Redman, J. T. Reminiscences. IV.
Sweetland, Louisa M. Across the Plains. IV.

1864
Bowers, John H. Letters. IV.
Bushnell, George E. Diary. Not Seen.
Dunham, E. Allene. FROM IOWA TO CALIFORNIA. IV.
Epperson, Mrs. B. C. "Diary." Not Seen.
Fryberger, Wilson. To California. III.
Harter, George. CROSSING THE PLAINS. III.
Hemey, John B. Diary. IV.
Johnson, Ann W. "The Long Journey." V-.
Logan, Martha. Logan Family Papers. Not Seen.
Lomas, Thomas J. RECOLLECTIONS. IV.
Ringo, Mary. JOURNAL. II.
Warner, Mary Eliza. Diary. II.

1865
Adams, Franklin E. "Overland Trail Diary." III.
Argyle, Archie. CIPID'S ALBUM. V.
Barton, H. D. Diary. III-.
Bond, FOOT TRAVELS. V.
Bowles, Samuel. ACROSS THE CONTINENT. II.
Chillson, Lorenzo D. Diary. III.
Colfax, Schuyler. "Honorable Schuyler Colfax's Trip." II.
Dam, Frances L. Account. V-.
Ellis, Henrietta C. DIARY. II.
Ellis, James A. "Diary." III.
Storrs Family, Diary. III+.
Watkins, Francis. CROW EMIGRANT TRAIN. III.
Zeamer, R. Jeremiah. Diary. III.

1866
Barnes, Demas. FROM THE ATLANTIC. IV.
Jatta, Mary H. Journal. III.
Longacre, Myrtle. A Trek West. V-.
Schmidt, Johann H. Across the Plains. I.
Shepperson, Wilbur S. "Sir Charles W. Dilke." III.

1867
Duncan, Elizabeth. Diary. II.

1868
Bell, William A. NEW TRACKS. II.
Pennebaker, W. G. "Westward from Wayne County." III.

1869
Newman, Orson N. Memoranda. III.

TEXAS TRAILS

All trail sources for Texas can be found here. Most items represent
California-bound parties crossing west between the Gulf Coast and El
Paso, although many reached Texas ports and thereafter traveled
south to Mexico before again heading west. There is also a significant
number of individuals following a trail between the Red River and El
Paso.

General
Ainsworth, E. M. "Old Austin and Round Rock Road."
Barrett, Lenora. "Transportation, Supplies, and Quarters."

Baylor, George W. "Scout to Quitman Canyon."
Bender, Averam B. "Opening Routes across West Texas."
_____. "The Texas Frontier, 1848 - 1861."
Browne, J. M. "Out on the Plains."
Campbell, T. N., and William T. Field. "Identification of Comanche Raid-
    ing Trails."
"Comanches and the Comanche War Trail."
Corning, Leavitt. BARONIAL FORTS OF THE BIG BEND.
Egan, Ferol. THE EL DORADO TRAIL.
Evans, Cleo F. "Transportation in Early Texas."
"Fort Davis Opened Trail."
"Great Comanche War Trail."
Haley, J. Evetts, FORT CONCHO.
_____. "Great Comanche War Trail."
Hall, R. Franklin. "Chihuahua Trail."
Hamilton, Allen L. SENTINEL OF THE SOUTHERN PLAINS:
    FORT RICHARDSON AND THE NORTHWEST TEXAS FRON-
    TIER, 1866-1878.
Holt, R. D. "Old Texas Wagon Trains."
Johnson, Mrs. Virgil, and J. W. Williams. "Some Northwest Texas Trails
    after Butterfield."
Jordan, Terry G. TRAILS TO TEXAS.
Kuykendal, J. H. Clippings and Fragments.
Loomis, Noel M. "Early Cattle Trails in Southern Arizona."
McCulloch, Henry E. Papers.
Marshall, Ellen. "Some Phases of Roads."
Miles, Bob. "Early Roads to El Paso."
Peters, Mary E. "Texas Trails."
Pierce, Gerald S. "Military Road Expeditions."
Richardson, Rupert N. ALONG TEXAS OLD FORTS TRAIL.
Riney, W. A. "Retracing the Butterfield Trail."
Schick, Robert. "Wagons to Chihuahua."
Smith, Ralph A. "Comanche Bridge between Oklahoma and Mexico,
    1843 - 1844."
Taylor, T. U. "Anglo-Saxon Trails across Texas."
Texas Overland Transportation Company.
Vest, Deed L. "The Chihuahua Road."
Wagon Trains and Cattle Herds in the 1850's.
Williams, Clayton W. TEXAS' LAST FRONTIER: FORT STOCK-
    TON AND THE TRANS-PECOS, 1861-1895.
Williams, J. W. "Butterfield Overland Mail Road across Texas."
_____. "Marcy and Butterfield Trails across North Texas."
_____. "Military Roads of the 1850's in Central West Texas."
_____. OLD TEXAS TRAILS.

Bibliographies
Cole, Garold. AMERICAN TRAVELERS TO MEXICO, 1821 - 1972.
Elliott, Claude. "A Check List of Theses and Dissertations, 1907 - 1952."
Floyd, Jennie W. "Annotated Bibliography on Texas in Periodicals
    before 1900."

Graphics
Thomas, W. Stephen. FORT DAVIS FRONTIER PAINTINGS.

1841
Pierce, Gerald S. "Military Road Expeditions." Genl.

1845
Donat, Pat. "Bill Cush's Trek." I.
Galdin (Gauldin?), Martin A. "Journal." III.

1846
Wilson, Gary. "Hostage among the Comanches." IV.

1848
Brown, John Henry. "Chihuahua - El Paso Expedition." IV.
Dunphy, William. Statement. V.

1864
Taylor, John. "Comanche County, Texas." III.

1865
Mitchell, Clara B. Diary. II.

1866
Duffield, George C. "Driving Cattle to Iowa." III.
Hackensmith, Mrs. M. S. Diary. III+.
Handley, Walter. Diary. II.
Kone, Ed. "Cattle Trail to Louisiana." III.
"Texas Overland Transportation Company." Genl.

1867
Hunter, John W. "Story." IV.
Meyer, Edward S. "A Description." III.

1868
Bunyard, Harriet. "Diary." II.
Johnson, M. R. Reminiscence. V.
Shackleford, Ruth. TO CALIFORNIA. II.

1869
Baker, J. H. "A Trail Driver." III.
Hunt, Thomas B. Journal. Not Seen.
Johnson, M. R. Reminiscence. V.
Pankey, H. S. "From Texas to California." V.
Westerman, Pleasant B. "How I Got to California." V.

TRUCKEE CUTOFF

This route is a less popular Sierra crossing used prior to the discovery of the Carson Pass route in 1848. It departs from the primary California Trail south of Humboldt Lake and reaches Sacramento via Wadsworth, NV, Truckee Meadows, and Donner Pass.

General
Graydon, Charles K. "Trail of the First Wagons."
_____. TRAIL OF THE FIRST WAGONS OVER THE SIERRA NEVADA. Recommended.
Jackson, W. Turrentine. "Stampede Reservoir Area."
Mulcahy, Walter. "Overland Trail through Reno."
Robie, Wendell. "Donner Lake to Johnson's Ranch."
Townley, John M. TOUGH LITTLE TOWN ON THE TRUCKEE.

Maps
Graydon, Charles K. TRAILS OF THE FIRST WAGONS OVER THE SIERRA NEVADA.
Rhoads, Earl. Maps of Emigrant Trail, Verdi, Nevada to Summit Valley, California.
Waggoner, W. W. "Donner Party and Relief Hill."

1841
Bernard, Sam. Recollections. Not Seen.

1843
Brown, John Henry. REMINISCENCES. V.

1844
Bray, Edmund. Letter. V.
Brown, John H. REMINISCENCES AND INCIDENTS. V.
Murphy, Martin. The Murphy Family. IV.
Murphy, Patrick W. Biography. V-.
Schallenberger, Moses. OPENING OF THE CALIFORNIA TRAIL. III.

1845
Bonney, Benjamin F. "Recollections of." IV.
Gregson, James. Statement. V.
Hudson, David. Autobiography. IV.
Ide, William. BIOGRAPHICAL SKETCH. III.
Johnson, Overton, and William H. Winter. ROUTE ACROSS THE ROCKY MOUNTAINS. III.
Martin, Thomas S. WITH FREMONT. III.
Rogers, Fred B. WILLIAM BROWN IDE. IV.
Smith, Napoleon B. Biographical Sketch. V.
Snyder, Jacob R. "The Diary of Jacob R. Snyder." III+.
Tinkey, David. Statement. V-.

1846-Genl
McGlashan, C. F. HISTORY OF THE DONNER PARTY.
McKinstry, George. "Remarkable Story of the Donner Party."
_____. "Thrilling and Tragic Journal."
Thornton, J. Quinn. CALIFORNIA TRAGEDY.

1846
Allen, Isaac. Biography. V.
Aram, Joseph. "Across the Continent." V.
Boggs, William M. Reminiscences. IV.
Breen, John. Dictation. II.
Breen, Patrick. DIARY. III.
Brown, Elam. BIOGRAPHY. IV.
Bryant, Edwin. WHAT I SAW IN CALIFORNIA. I.
Camp, Charles L. JAMES CLYMAN. I.
Campbell, David. Pioneer of 1846. V.
Carriger, Nicholas. "Diary." III-.
Clark, Thomas D. "Edward Bryant and the Opening." III.
Clark, William S. Biographical Sketch. V.
Croy, Homer. WHEELS WEST. III.
Dickinson, Luella. REMINISCENCES. IV.
Graves, William C. "Crossing the Plains." IV.
Grayson, Andrew J. Account. IV.
Harlan, Jacob W. CALIFORNIA '46 TO '88. III.
Hecox, Adna A. Biographical Sketch. Not Seen.
Hecox, Margaret M. CALIFORNIA CARAVAN. IV.
Houghton, Eliza P. EXPEDITION OF THE DONNER PARTY. III.
Jones, Mrs. M. A. Reminiscences. IV.
Jones, Nathaniel V. "Journal." III.
Lienhard, Heinrich. FROM ST. LOUIS TO SUTTER'S FORT. II.
Mitchell, Annie R. JIM SAVAGE. V.
Reed, James F. "Snow-bound Starved Emigrants of 1846." IV.
Rhoades, Daniel. Letters. IV.
Sinclair, John. "Diary." II.
Taylor, William E. Diary. III.
Wimmer, Peter. CALIFORNIA GOLD BOOK. V.

1847
Breen, Patrick. DIARY. III.
Blackburn, Abner. "Reminiscences." IV.
Fallon, William. "Extracts from a Journal." II.
Hyde, William. Private Journal. IV.
Ingersoll, Chester. OVERLAND. III.
Jones, Nathaniel V. "Journal." V.
Pace, James. Journal. III+.
Reed, James F. "Diary." II.
Turner, Henry S. ORIGINAL JOURNAL. II.
Waggoner, W. W. "Donner Party and Relief Hill." Genl.

1848
Bigler, Henry W. CHRONICLE. II.
_____. "Diary." IV.
Burrows, Rufus G. Anecdotes. IV.
_____, and Cyrus Hull. LONG ROAD TO STONY CREEK. V.
Smith, Azariah. Journal. II.

Willis, Ira J. "The Ira J. Willis Guide." III.

1849

Abell, James S. Papers. I.
Armstrong, J. E. Diary. III.
Armstrong, J. Elza. "Diary." II.
Armstrong, J. Ezra. Diary. III.
Ashley, Delos R. Diary. III.
Athearn, P. A. "Diary." III+.
Averett, George W. Autobiography. IV.
Backus, Gurdon. Diary. II+.
Banks, John E. "Diary." II.
Beesley, E. Maurice. Diary. III.
Bonine, Dr. Diary. Not Seen.
Brady, Charles C. "From Hannibal to the Gold Fields." IV.
Buffum, Joseph C. Diary. II.
Burbank, Augustus R. Journal & Diaries. I.
Burton, Henry W. Diary. II.
Caples, Mrs. James. Overland Journey. IV.
Carnes, David. Journal. II+.
Chamberlain, William E. Diary. II.
Clark, Bennett C. "Diary of a Journey." II.
Clark, Sterling B. HOW MANY MILES FROM ST. JOE. IV.
Clifton, John. "Diary." III.
Coats, Felix G. On the Golden Trail. V.
Darwin, Charles B. Diaries. I.
DeMilt, Alonzo P. LIFE, TRAVELS AND ADVENTURES. V.
Eastin, Thomas D. Collected Data. IV.
Evans, James W. "A Missouri Forty-Niner's Trip." V.
Fairchild, Lucius. "California Letters." IV.
Fowler, Samuel. REMINISCENCES. V.
Garwood, Zimri L. Journal. III+.
Hackney, Joseph. "Diary." II+.
Hall, Thomas. RECOLLECTIONS. IV.
Hester, Sallie. "Diary." IV.
Hillyer, Edwin. "From Waupun to Sacramento." II.
Hoffman, Benjamin. "Diary." III+.
Hoffman, William. Account. II.
Jagger, D. Diary. I.
Johnson, John A. Journal. II+.
Kirkpatrick, Charles A. Diary. II+.
Lewis, Elisha B. Overland Trip. II+.
Lewis, John F. Diary. II+.
Long, Charles L. Diary. II+.
Love, Alexander. Diary. II.
McCall, Ansel J. GREAT CALIFORNIA TRAIL. II+.
McDonald, Frank V. NOTES PREPARATORY. V.
McIlhany, Edward W. RECOLLECTIONS. IV.
Maddock, Sallie H. "Diary of a Pioneer Girl." V.
Manlove, John N. Overland Trip. IV.
Mann, H. R. Diary. II+.
Markle, John A. "Diary." III.
Merrill, Joseph H. Diary. II+.
Miller, Greenberry. Diary. II.
Muscott, John M., and William N. Steuben. Letters. IV.
Ness, Richard. Journal. V.
Orvis, Andrew. Letters & Diary. III-.
Page, Elizabeth. WAGONS WEST. I.
Parke, Charles R. Diary. II+.
Perkins, Elisha D. GOLD RUSH DIARY. I.
Potter, David M. TRAIL TO CALIFORNIA. I.
Prichet, John. Diary. II.
Reynolds, Charles D. Reminiscences. IV.
Sargent, Charles. Overland Journey. IV.
Scamehorn, Howard L. BUCKEYE ROVERS. II.
Starr, Franklin. Diary. II.
Steuben, William N. Diary. II.
Stone, Mary A. "Cambridge-Califoria Companies." IV.

Tappan, Henry. "Diary." IV.
Tate, James. Diary. III+.
Tinker, Charles. "Journal." III.
Van Dorn, T. J. Diary. Not Seen.
Violette, M. A. Diary. II.
Willis, Edward J. Diary. III+.
Winsor, Alonzo. Journey. II+.
Wistar, Isaac J. AUTOBIOGRAPHY. III.
Wood, Joseph W. Journal. II+.
Woods, Joseph W. Diary. I.

1850

Bowles, J. Frank. "Overland Trip." IV.
Branstetter, Peter L. Diary. II+.
Brouster, George W. Letters. IV.
Campbell, James. Diary. III-.
Curtis, Mable R. The Rowe Family. III.
Davenport, O. F. Letters. Not Seen.
Davis, A. S. Diary. III.
Davis, Sarah. "Diary." III.
Dowell, B. F. Crossing the Plains. III+.
Evans, James W. Journal. II+.
Littleton, James. Diary. I.
Littleton, Micajah. Diary. II.
Loveland, Cyrus C. CALIFORNIA TRAIL HERD. II.
Osterhoudt, Solomon. "Ox Train Diary." III+.
Primes, Ed. M. Journal. Not Seen.
Shinn, John R. Journal. III.
Steele, John. ACROSS THE PLAINS. III.
Stine, Henry A. Letters & Journal. III.
Thompson, William P. Diary. III.
Wheeler, George N. Journal. II.
Wheeler, George W. Journal. III+.

1852

Andrews, D. B. Journal. II+.
Baker, William B. Diary. III.
Baldy, Henry T. Diary. II+.
Blake, Winslow. Diary. II.
Brooks, Elisha. A PIONEER MOTHER. IV.
Chadwick, Samuel. Diary. II.
Chandler, Knowlton H. Journal. III.
Cox, George W. Reminiscences. IV.
Cummings, Mariett F. "Diary." II.
Dalton, John E. Diary. II+.
Daughters, J. M. Journal. III.
Egbert, Eliza Ann. "Across the Plains." II.
Ford, James. JUST BETWEEN OURSELVES. IV.
Freeman, John F. Diaries. II.
Haydon, Jacob S. Diary. Not Seen.
Hickman, Richard O. "An Overland Journey." III.
Hosley, Dexter P. Diary. Not Seen.
Kitchell, Edward. A Trip. II+.
McAuley, Eliza A. "McAuley Diary." III+.
Owen, East S. Journal. III+.
Potter, Theodore E. AUTOBIOGRAPHY. II+.
Richardson, Alpheus. Diary. II.
Schneider, Charles G. Diary. III.
Sexton, Lucy A. FOSTER FAMILY. II.
Smith, Chester. "Chester Smith's Journal." II.
Stuart, Granville. FORTY YEARS. IV.
Thornily, John C. Diary. I.
Zinn, Henry. Diary. V-.

1853

Blackwood, Jane. Diary. Not Seen.
Butterfield, James T. Journeys. IV.
Compton, Henria P. MARY MURDOCK COMPTON. IV.

Comstock, Noah D. "Diary." II.
Davis, A. S. Diary. III.
Furniss, Kate M. From Prairie to Pacific. II+.
Hite, Abraham. Diary. IV.
Ivens, Virginia W. PEN PICTURES. III.
Miller, Joel. Journal. II-.
Ward, Harriet S. PRAIRIE SCHOONER LADY. II.
Woodworth, James. DIARY. II.

1854
Doyle, Simon. Diary. III.
Drumheller, "Uncle Dan." UNCLE DAN. IV.
Hays, Jacob O. Lexington to Sacramento. III.
Richey, James H. A TRIP. IV.
Smith, Sara. Diary. III.
White, Daniel C. Diary. III-.
Willey, Lucas. Diaries. I.
Woodhams, William H. "Diary." I.

1855
Comstock, Loring S. JOURNAL OF TRAVELS. III+.
Waters, Lydia M. "Account of a Trip." III-.

1857
"Arthur M. Menefee's Travels." III.
Carpenter, Helen M. "Across the Plains." II.
Horton, Emily M. OUR FAMILY. IV.
Maxwell, William A. CROSSING THE PLAINS. IV.
Menefee, Arthur M. "Travels." III.

1859
Brooks, A. F. Diary. II.
Norton, Maria J. Diary. II+.
Sowers, John H. Diary. III.
Stockton, William J. PLAINS OVER. V.
Thompson, Harlow C. Across the Continent. IV.
Willey, Lucas. Diaries. I.
Williams, Howard D. Diary. II.

1861
Countryman, Ardell J. A PIONEER'S TRIP. IV.

1863
Cutting, A. Howard. Journal. II+.
Hopper, Silas L. "Diary." III.
Nettleton, Lucy. Letters. II.
Purviance, M. C. Journal. II.
Yager, James P. "Yager Journals." II.

1864
Allton, Hiram. Diary. III.
Alton, Hiram. Journal. II+.
Epperson, Mrs. B. C. "Diary." Not Seen.
Harter, George. CROSSING THE PLAINS. III.
Leppo, David T. FAMILY. II.
Love, Alexander. Diary. II.
Stone, Rose F. "Diary." IV.
Warner, Mary E. Diary. II.

WASHINGTON TRAILS

General
Alcorn, Rowena and Gordon. Across to Montana.
Brown, Arthur J. "Promotion of Emigration."
Derby, George H. Three Reports.
Jeffcot, P. R. NOOKSACK TALES AND TRAILS.
Kaiser, Verle G. "Straight as an Arrow."

McCorkle, Eugene. "Roads, Bridges and the Cars."
Magnusson, Elsa C. "Naches Pass."
Murray, Keith A. "Building a Wagon Road through the Northern Cascade Mountains."
Northern Pacific Railway Company. Records-Engineering Dept.
Parkins, Katherine L. "A Study of the Legislative History."
Peltier, Jerome. ANTOINE PLANTE.
Reid, Robie L. "Whatcom Trails."
TOLD BY THE PIONEERS.
Watt, Roberta F. FOUR WAGONS WEST.
Winther, Oscar O. "Inland Transportation."

1841
Pickering, Charles. "Pickering's Journey." Genl.

1843
Prosch, Thomas W. McCARVER AND TACOMA. V.

1844
Cantwell, James and Catherine. Jessie Cantwell Hilburger Papers. Not Seen.

1846-General
Alcorn, Rowena and Gordon. PAUL KANE.

1847
Kane, Paul. WANDERINGS OF AN ARTIST. II+.

1850
Maynard, David. "Diary." III.
Travel Account of Journey from Indiana to Washington. Not Seen.

1851
Watt, Roberta F. FOUR WAGONS WEST. V.

1853
Bidwell, John et al. FIRST THREE WAGON TRAINS. Genl.
Dee, Minnie R. FROM OXCART TO AIRPLANE. IV.
Fox, Jared. Diary. I.
Himes, George H. "Annual Address." IV.
Hodge, George. Diary. III.
Longmire, David. "First Immigrants to Cross the Cascades." III.
Longmire, James. "Narrative of a Pioneer." IV.
Perko, Richard. "Ft. Steilacoom-Walla Walla Road." Genl.
Van Ogle, Mr. "Van Ogle's Memory." V.

1854
Baydo, Gerald R. "Overland from Missouri." III.
Campbell, John V. "The Sinclair Party." III.
Jones, Eliza J. Letters. Not Seen.
Jones, Harvey H. Journal and Letters. Not Seen.
Roeder, Elizabeth A. Diary. III.
Sinclair, James. Career. V.

1857
Wolff, Francis. "Ambush at McLaughlin Canyon." V.

1858-General
Reid, R. L. "Whatcom Trails to the Fraser River."

1859
Thibodo, Augustus J. "Diary." II.
Ward, Dilles B. "From Salem to Seattle."

1860
Dixon, Joseph. TOPOGRAPHICAL MEMOIR. II.

1861

Brown, John M. "Diary." II+.

1862
Hewett, R. H. ACROSS THE PLAINS. II.

1863
Allen, Edward J. "Edward J. Allen." IV.

1865
Bowles, Samuel. ACROSS THE CONTINENT. II.

1868
Thompson, John P. "Snoqualmie Wagon Road." Genl.